the
Unofficial
Guide® to
Cruises

Also available from Macmillan Travel

The Unofficial Disney Companion: The Inside Story of Walt Disney World and the Man Behind the Mouse, by Eve Zibart

The Unofficial Guide to Atlanta, by Fred Brown and Bob Sehlinger

The Unofficial Guide to Branson, Missouri, by Bob Sehlinger and Eve Zibart

The Unofficial Guide to Chicago, by Bob Sehlinger and Joe Surkiewicz

The Unofficial Guide to Disneyland, by Bob Sehlinger

The Unofficial Guide to Disneyland Paris, by Bob Sehlinger

The Unofficial Guide to Ethnic Cuisine and Dining in America, by Eve Zibart, Muriel Stevens, and Terrell Vermont

The Unofficial Guide to the Great Smoky and Blue Ridge Mountains, by Bob Sehlinger and Joe Surkiewicz

The Unofficial Guide to Las Vegas, by Bob Sehlinger

The Unofficial Guide to Miami and the Keys, by Bob Sehlinger and Joe Surkiewicz

The Unofficial Guide to New Orleans, by Bob Sehlinger and Eve Zibart

The Unofficial Guide to Skiing in the West, by Lito-Tejada Flores, Peter Shelton, Seth Masia, and Bob Sehlinger

The Unofficial Guide to Walt Disney World, by Bob Sehlinger

The Unofficial Guide to Washington, D.C., by Bob Sehlinger and Joe Surkiewicz with Eve Zibart

The Unofficial Mini Mickey: The Pocket-Sized Guide to Walt Disney World, by Bob Sehlinger

the Unofficial Guide® to *Cruises*

1998

KAY SHOWKER

with **BOB SEHLINGER**

MACMILLAN • USA

Every effort has been made to ensure the accuracy
of information throughout this book. Bear in mind,
however, that prices, schedules, etc., are constantly
changing. Readers should always verify information
before making final plans.

Macmillan Travel
A Simon & Schuster Macmillan Company
1633 Broadway
New York, New York 10019-6785

Produced by Menasha Ridge Press
Design by Suzanne H. Holt

MACMILLAN is a registered trademark of Macmillan, Inc.

UNOFFICIAL GUIDE is a registered trademark of Simon & Schuster, Inc.

ISBN 0-02-862033-X
ISSN 1083-1460

Manufactured in the United States of America

10 9 8 7 6 5 4 3 2

1998 edition

CONTENTS

PART TWO: *Cruise Lines and Their Ships*

Best of the Best 97–98　148
The Heart of the Matter　149

PART THREE: *Cruising Alternatives*

River and Barge Cruises　724

Norwegian Coastal Cruises and Other Cruise Ferries　753

LIST OF ILLUSTRATIONS

LAURELS FOR THE LABORERS

It goes almost without saying that a book of this scope, covering more than a hundred cruise lines with upward of 300 ships sailing to destinations from the North Pole to the South Pole and around the world, is the work of many people. It required extensive research, interviews with passengers, seemingly endless discussions with specialized travel agents and other people knowledgeable about cruises, not to mention the incredible amount of follow-up due to the constantly changing nature of the cruise industry.

So many people were tireless in their effort to help that it would take another book to name them all, but we would be remiss not to mention some. Michael Brown, editor, *Cruise and Vacation Views,* helped every step of the way. Steve Gordan, publisher and managing editor of Star Service, which issues reports and evaluations on hotels and cruise ships worldwide for its travel agency subscribers, generously allowed us access and use of the publication's material.

Ron Bitting, Leaders in Travel, Great Neck, NY, and founding president of the National Association of Cruise Only Travel Agencies; Larry Fishkin and Don Lansky, The Cruise Line, Inc., Miami, FL; Lloyd Cole, Amstad Travel, NY, and Dr. Bradley Feuer, Pace Travel, Lake Worth, FL, gave us insights during our discussions and never seemed to tire of our endless questions.

We are grateful to all our public relations friends at the cruise lines who helped us check the nitty-gritty details that can drive you crazy and who have been our hosts over the years, without any obligation whatsoever. Rich Steck, Royal Caribbean Cruise Lines, and Julie Benson and Jill Biggins, Princess Cruise Lines, went far and beyond the call of duty and have our everlasting gratitude.

TEXT CONTRIBUTIONS

Time constraints in writing a book such as this make it impossible for two people to visit and revisit every ship prior to our deadlines, as we would want to do. We called on colleagues for help, particularly on writers who specialize in cruising and are as qualified as we to write this book.

Some folks contributed material written specifically for the book, others shared their knowledge from recent cruises or allowed us to use material from recent research published elsewhere, while still others reviewed or helped with the updating of information we had written.

Specifically for Part Two, sections were written by Ann Kalosh (Abercrombie & Kent International); Dave Houser (Alaska Sightseeing/ Cruise West); Betsy McNeil (Commodore Cruise Line); William Miller (Dolphin Cruise Line); Randy Mink (Premier Cruise Lines); Ted Scull (P&O Cruises); Amy Fried (Seawind Cruise Line); and Michael Brown (Sun Line Cruises); and for Part Three, Ted Scull (Norwegian Coastal Cruises and European Cruise Ferries) and Dave Houser (Freighter Cruises), who not only wrote parts of this book, but also generously contributed their insights and information to many of the cruise lines and ships profiled in Part Two.

Major input came from James Simmons (American Canadian Caribbean Line); Joan Edwards and Amy Fried (American Hawaii Cruises); Carol Scutt (Club Med); Luisa Frey-Gaynor and Randy Mink (Delta Queen Steamboat Company); Dr. Llwewllyn Toulmin (Orient Lines); and Lea Lane (World Explorer Cruises).

Many other writing colleagues shared their firsthand experience with us, too. We particularly want to thank Arlene and Sam Blecker, Ernest Blum, Jerry Brown, Lisa Chickering, Jeannie Porterfield, George Devol, Marilyn Green, Mary Ann Hemphill, Francis Kay Harris, Elizabeth Harryman, Paul Lasley, Harry Magenheim, Joan Scobey, Shirley Slater, and Harry Basch.

Many, many friends, friends of friends, travel agents, and cruise passengers along the way willingly gave us their time for interviews, helped with ship ratings, phoned and sent us letters about their latest cruise, and to them we express our heartfelt thanks.

Last but not least, we thank Mary Lou Melendez who worked tirelessly on the manuscript, researching, typing, and checking facts.

Kay Showker
Bob Sehlinger

INTRODUCTION

About This Guide

HOW COME "UNOFFICIAL"?

The material in this guide has originated with the authors and researchers and has not been reviewed, edited, or in any way approved by the cruise lines profiled. In this "unofficial" guide we have elected to represent and serve you, the consumer. If a ship serves mediocre food, has cramped cabins, or offers poor shore excursions, we say so. In the process, we hope we can make selecting a cruise efficient and economical, and your cruise experience more fun.

MAKING IT EASY

In the nearly two years it took to write this book, Kay had pinned on a wall in front of her a note that read: "This book has one purpose: To help readers select the right cruise—i.e., the cruise that's right for them." She kept it there to help us never lose sight of that goal.

Most guides to cruising approach their subject on a ship-by-ship basis, giving only the briefest attention to the cruise line and putting the stress on ships—the hardware, if you like. But people don't buy ships, they buy cruises, and those cruises—the software—have been designed by a cruise line with an objective, a philosophy, and a point of view, or in today's terms, a business plan.

Daily the cruise lines are being challenged by their competitors and all the other leisure products vying for your attention—from the latest car and computer to a vacation at Disney—to make their cruises irresistible. Yet, they are the first to tell you that while there's a cruise for everyone, not every cruise is for everyone.

As one person put it, all the hardware has certain standard features—shuffleboard, bingo, and afternoon teas. What it boils down to is you can listen to Beethoven's Ninth played by a high school band, with all due respect, or you can listen to it played by the New York Philharmonic. It's the same music, but it's going to come out differently.

This book has been designed to help you recognize the differences. With an understanding of the cruise lines and the cruise experience each offers, you will be able to recognize the different types of cruises available and identify the ones that are likely to appeal to you. Cruises on a particular line have certain features that make them different and distinctive from the others. It is these features or "style" as we call it, that is the very essence of the cruise experience.

A Carnival cruise is a Carnival cruise, for example. Each Carnival ship offers a "Fun Ship" vacation, and, except for the length of the cruise and its destinations, there is very little difference in the cruise experience, regardless of which Carnival ship you select. Carnival has designed it to be that way.

The same is true of Royal Caribbean Cruise Line, Holland America, Seabourn, and every other cruise line that has built ships of a class or style cut from the same mold. On the other hand, a Carnival cruise is as different from a Princess cruise or Holland America, Crystal, or a Seabourn cruise, as night is from day.

As cruise lines continue to standardize their operations as a way to keep costs down and to clarify and strengthen their image to distinguish themselves from their competition, it becomes more important in selecting a cruise for you (or your travel agent) to understand the cruise line and the type of cruises it offers. With that goal in mind, this guidebook was organized in three parts:

Part One: Planning Your Cruise Vacation covers the nuts and bolts information on what cruises contain, tips on finding the best values, and preparing for your cruise.

Part Two: Cruise Lines and Their Ships profiles all the major cruise lines that sell their cruises primarily to a U.S. and Canadian audience. They are what the cruise world terms as being in the mainstream. At the end of Part Two is a group of ships also in the mainstream but not necessarily on this side of the Atlantic. Most, but not all, are based in Europe and cruise on less-traveled byways, catering mainly to Europeans.

Part Three: Cruising Alternatives includes such options as river, adventure, and expedition cruises, as well as freighters, coastal ships, cruise ferries, and sailing ships.

LETTERS, COMMENTS, AND QUESTIONS
FROM READERS

Many of those who use the *Unofficial Guides* write to us asking questions, making comments, or sharing their own strategies for planning and enjoying their travel. We appreciate all such input, both positive and critical, and encourage our readers to continue writing. Readers' comments and observations are frequently incorporated into revised editions of the *Unofficial Guides* and have contributed immeasurably to their improvement. Please write to:

Kay and Bob
The Unofficial Guide to Cruises
P.O. Box 43059
Birmingham, AL 35243

When you write, be sure to put a return address on your letter as well as on the envelope; sometimes envelopes and letters get separated. We would also appreciate it if you'd include your phone number if you are available for a possible follow-up interview. And remember, our work often requires that we be out of the office for long periods of time, so forgive us if our response is a little slow.

A Reader Survey is included at the end of the book for your convenience. Please give us your impressions, clip it out, and send it in.

CRUISING:
A LOOK BACK, A LOOK AHEAD

In 1996 modern cruising marked its thirtieth anniversary. December 19, 1966, is recognized as a bench mark because it saw the launch of a series of cruises that, for the first time, had been created and packaged as a mass-market product and sold on a year-round basis.

The ship, the *Sunward* of Norwegian Caribbean Line (later to be named Norwegian Cruise Line), sailed from Miami to Nassau with 540 passengers on the first ever three- and four-day cruises to be offered year-round between Miami and the Bahamas.

No one, including the creators, could have imagined where such a small step would lead them. And indeed, many people in the steamship business of those days dismissed the move as a crazy idea, declaring there was not enough of a market to support such cruises year-round.

Cruising, of course, did not actually start in 1966; rather, it evolved through trends and events occurring over 150 years. But it's true that until the 1960s the closest most people got to a big ship was on the big screen, either in movies about glamorous people living romantic lives or in Movietone newsreels that had stargazers standing 50 deep at the piers to catch a glimpse of the Duke and Duchess of Windsor arriving on the *Queen Mary,* or to wave to F. Scott and Zelda, the Astors, the Vanderbilts, and other socialites and celebrities in the most fashionable pursuit of the time—sailing off to Europe aboard a great oceanliner whose elegance epitomized stylish travel for many generations.

From the start of the first regular transatlantic steamship service by Samuel Cunard in 1840, a voyage on a great liner became the ultimate dream shared by people around the world. In the early days, a sea voyage was more in the nature of an expedition, requiring passengers to endure hardships with few amenities on board ship or at docks on land. Passenger comfort, even in first class, was not a priority, but as competition developed and steamship travel gained in popularity, each generation of new ships brought enhancements in comfort.

Then, too, throughout the late nineteenth century and up to World War I, ships carrying passengers had other purposes. A young America was expanding and booming and needed people to build the new nation. This need fueled another dream—that of thousands of immigrants who traveled from the four corners of the globe to a new life in the New World.

To meet the demand—and reap big profits—many steamship companies were born and ships built, and except for the war years when the vessels were pressed into service to transport troops, oceanliners paraded across the Atlantic and the Pacific in an endless stream, with the world's elite in their top decks and the huddled masses below.

Then in 1921, the passage of the Immigration Act, intended to slow the torrent of new arrivals, forced the steamship companies to change course. To make up for the lost revenue from steerage, the companies created cabin, or tourist, class in the several decks below first class, and perhaps unwittingly, took the next giant step toward creating today's cruising. Although an ocean voyage remained basically a means to get from one continent to another, it was no longer a pastime only for the privileged.

Cabin class did not have the elegance and panache of first class, but it wasn't bad. It found a ready market in the GIs who had fought in Europe and wanted to return with their families, immigrants who had made good and wanted to visit relatives in their homelands, and America's growing middle class who wanted to emulate the celebrities and aristocrats in first class and get out and see the world with their newly acquired wealth.

THE GOLDEN AGE

The Roaring Twenties was the golden age for steamship travel. It was a time of new prosperity and blithe spirits—and Prohibition in America. As with the speakeasy on shore, ships developed a style and aura that made getting there half the fun. Prohibition also spawned a new type of cruise. With no prohibition against alcohol at sea, ship companies were quick to offer short party cruises that came to be known as a booze cruise.

Meanwhile, many improvements to enhance passenger comfort had been introduced on ships. The main lounge of first class had become an elegant room resembling one in a chateau, with wood, marble, and an open fireplace to make its aristocratic passengers feel at home. It was used for all passenger activities—as a smoker during the day and for entertainment, such as bingo, films, or dancing, in the evening. When it was used for dancing, the furniture would be cleared away.

Reflecting the social mores of the time as they always have, ships until the 1920s maintained separate smokers for the men and lounges for the ladies where they repaired after dinner. In the dining room, passengers sat at long tables on chairs bolted to the floor as ships did not have stabilizers. In 1910, Ritz restaurants, replicating the setting of their shoreside restaurants of round tables and carpeted floors, were introduced in first class on the ships of Hapag-Lloyd of Germany. The style soon became the standard for other ships.

Private bathrooms were available in first class on the grandest liners, but in cabin class, passengers shared bath facilities until the 1950s. Air conditioning was introduced by P&O Lines in the 1930s but did not become commonplace until the 1950s.

The first indoor swimming pool appeared in 1910 on the *Olympic* of White Star Line. (It was the first of the line's three superliners; the others were the *Titanic* and *Gigantic,* later renamed the *Britannic.*) Known as a plunge bath, it had elaborate Arabian Nights decor and a balcony where others could sit to watch the bathers. The first permanent outdoor pool was introduced in 1926 on the *Roma* of Italian Lines. The top deck, however—usually a sports deck on today's cruise ship— was still fitted with winches and other machinery and was not available for passenger use. Not until the late 1950s did the trend to use the top deck for sports and recreation take hold.

A NEW ERA

After weathering the storms of the Great Depression and another war, the oceanliners resumed their traditional role and by the 1950s were conveying hordes of students to Europe and masses of refugees to our shores. The glamour returned, too, as we watched the comings and goings of a young Liz Taylor and waved goodbye to Grace Kelly when she sailed away to her fairyland prince.

After World War II, changes such as radar and improved navigational equipment were added to passenger vessels that made them safer and more accurate with regard to their arrival times and thus enabled their operators to plan reliable itineraries. By the mid-1950s, most oceanliners had stabilizers. Radios were added in staterooms.

The tradition to separate first class and tourist class on transatlantic service continued, but in 1958, Holland America launched the *Rotterdam*, which had the flexibility to be converted to one class for cruising. It was a sign of things to come, but meanwhile dark clouds had gathered over the future of oceanliners. By the end of the decade, most of their elite passengers had taken flight—literally.

The final blow came in 1958 when the first commercial jets streaked across the Atlantic, cutting travel time from five days to slightly over five hours. Instead of dying as the pundits predicted, however, the ships changed course and became part of the revolution that took place on the sea as well as in the sky.

THE CRUISE REVOLUTION

The turnaround of the 1960s brought a host of radical changes. Brand new cruise lines, untethered to the past, exchanged formality for fun and brought a totally new atmosphere to shipboard life. Separate classes along with their barriers were removed, and the added space was used for sports, recreation, and entertainment that turned the ship into a floating resort. Getting there was no longer half the fun. It was the fun.

Gone were the passengers bundled under blankets on their deck chairs. Instead, they were bouncing around in aerobics classes, swinging at golf and tennis balls, plunging into the sea with masks and fins, soaking in hot tubs and luxuriating in shipboard spas.

Bingo survived, but now it was competing with jazzy casinos and lottos, Broadway shows and discos, wine and piano bars, comics and cabarets. New passengers as well as younger ones were being attracted by the activity and informality. Families with children, too, were finding cruises to be an ideal vacation where everyone wins.

But change came wrapped in skepticism. To take only one example, the hot news in 1968 was the new mod look of the *S.S. Independence*. With a red, orange, and yellow sunburst splashed across the length of its sides and a riot of color throughout its interiors, it was quickly dubbed the psychedelic ship. A story on the shakedown cruise in a trade magazine called it a "floating water pad for the turned on generation" and suggested that "dancing until the wee hours . . . , the informal atmosphere of the one-class ship, and ever-changing program of top-talent entertainment may prove a real drawing card."

The 1970s began with Royal Caribbean Cruise Lines making its debut with a fleet of ships built specifically for Caribbean cruising. It was followed two years later by Carnival Cruise Lines, which had created the "Fun Ship" concept aimed squarely at stripping away the elitist traditions of the oceanliners and appealing to a mass market of younger, first-time passengers from all walks of life.

As the final irony of this revolution, the spectacular growth in cruise vacations really took off in the 1970s when cruise lines discovered the benefits of joining forces with the airlines, who had almost put the steamship companies out of business. The union resulted in the creation of air/sea programs that combine air transportation and ground transfers with a cruise in one package at one price up front.

The programs not only enhanced the value of a cruise vacation, they simplified their purchase and eliminated the hassle for travelers. With them, the cruise lines all but brought their ships to people's doorsteps regardless of where they lived. Across the land, millions of Americans who might never have considered a cruise in the past were climbing aboard.

The marriage also enabled cruise lines to base their ships in warm weather ports from where they could cruise year-round and to fly passengers from far away places to begin their cruises. A sun-filled holiday with a relaxed, informal style that was available year-round became the essence of today's popular cruising. Ships were no longer merely transportation; they became a destination in themselves.

Flying passengers to their ships saved time, enabled cruise lines to offer shorter, less expensive cruises that fit well into the national trend toward shorter vacations, and greatly broadened the spectrum of people who could afford them. It also allowed cruise lines to open up new parts of the world to cruising and to create an endless variety of itineraries. No matter how many cruises a person may have taken, there were new ones to enjoy. Or so it seemed at least, until the oil crisis hit in the early 1970s and once again dark clouds hung over the future of vacations at sea.

Then in 1978, despite the oil crisis, skyrocketing fuel prices, and many saying that cruising was doomed, Carnival Cruise Lines, to the dismay of all, placed an order for a new, large, technologically advanced passenger ship. It became the forerunner of the 1980s superliners.

Two years later, Norwegian Cruise Line set the cruise world on its ear when it bought the fabulous *France* and transformed her into the *Norway*, the floating resort that set cruise trends for the decade, introducing a variety of entertainment lounges, a theatre to stage Broadway scale productions, a shopping plaza, a "sidewalk" cafe, and other innovations.

Holland America followed with *Nieuw Amsterdam* and *Noordam,* twin ships with square sterns that allowed over 20 percent more open deck space for sports and recreation, including two swimming pools. The ships also introduced computer keys to open cabin doors and many other innovations.

Princess Cruises' stylish *Royal Princess,* which debuted in 1984, set new standards of comfort with all outside cabins fitted with minibars, television, and baths with tubs in every category. About the same time, the *QE2* introduced the first Golden Door spa at sea, the first computer learning center, and the first satellite delivered newspaper.

Among the most interesting entries was the *Windstar* in 1986, a cruise ship with computerized sails. *Windstar* married the romance of sailing under canvas with the comforts of a cruise ship and the electronic age; she brought to cruising a totally new experience. In the same time period, Carnival's superliners, *Holiday, Jubilee,* and *Celebration,* were introduced. Their madcap design totally changed the interior look of cruise ships and use of public space.

Yet nothing since the *Norway* caused as much excitement as the debut in 1988 of Royal Caribbean Cruise Line's *Sovereign of the Seas.* It was the world's largest cruise ship and became the pacesetter for the 1990s. Among its many new features was the first shipboard atrium rising through five decks at the center of the ship and creating a new shipboard environment. The ship offered so many and such varied entertainment and recreation options that passengers needed several cruises to experience all of them.

As the decade closed, some old cruise lines disappeared, merger mania had taken hold, and new cruise lines were popping up from all directions. Health and fitness facilities became integrated into the cruise experience. Light food selections for health-conscious passengers were readily available. Well-equipped gyms, elaborate spas, VCRs, cable television, and worldwide direct-dial telephone were rapidly becoming standard amenities. To these can be added tennis and basketball courts, golf practice facilities and clinics, continuous movies, language classes, art classes, and lectures on topics ranging from astronomy to zoology by experts as different as a drama critic and a football player.

Small boutique cruise ships, such as Cunard's *Sea Goddess I* and *II* and Seabourn Cruise Line's ships had brought new levels of luxury to today's cruising. Special interest cruise lines were finding their niche. The interest in adventure and nature cruises was on the increase, to the extent that some traditional cruise ships have added them to their agenda. Environmental concerns have had a major impact on cruise ship technology.

The late 1960s and early 1970s saw the conversion of oceanliners to cruise ships and the early start of new ships built specifically for cruising, but it was the 1980s that became the decade of innovation. Ships, particularly those designed to sail in warm climates, came with features and facilities never before seen on board. They added greater pleasure and diversity to the cruise experience and attracted people who might never have considered taking a cruise.

TOWARD THE YEAR 2000

The cruise boom has now had a 30-year run and shows no signs of letup. In that time, the number of people taking cruises has swollen from under 500,000 annually to over 5,000,000 annually—not a bad endorsement—and the numbers are expected to reach 8,000,000 by the end of the century.

Fifteen of the 33 members of the Cruise Lines International Association (CLIA), the major cruise trade association, did not exist 15 years ago. Two new cruise lines recently made their debut, another has ordered its first two ships, and hardly a week passes without word of more.

The 1990s have already been a blockbuster decade with 36 new ships costing an estimated $9 billion in the water or on their way by 1998, adding 40 percent more capacity to the inventory. For the most part, the ships are getting bigger and bigger with more and more dazzle and many travel specialists are asking, where's the sky?

The ships over 75,000 tons and particularly over 100,000 tons represent a new generation of megaliners. Most have new design features and facilities—perhaps the most publicized being the 18-hole miniature golf course on the new *Legend of the Seas*. The innovations likely to stimulate the most curiosity are the virtual reality theatre on Carnival's *Holiday,* and the interactive computers on Celebrity's new *Century* and *Galaxy.*

Along with innovations, cruise lines are giving more attention to enhancing the cruise experience. Passengers will find larger standard cabins on most of the new ships and more verandas in the mid-price range. They will also find more dining options, as seen already on Norwegian Cruise Lines' newest fleet, more choices for entertainment, and more opportunity for sports.

In the face of intensified competition, particularly in the Caribbean, cruise lines once focused only in that region are branching out and becoming worldwide cruise lines providing greater diversity with their new itineraries. And in 1996, an unprecedented seven ships sailed on cruises around the world.

The immediate impact of the huge number of new ships will be to keep prices down and that's good news for consumers. It also accelerates the need for every cruise line to define its style, find its niche, and differentiate itself from its competition and that, too, is good news because options are greater than they have ever been. But that, too, makes it all the more difficult to make a choice. Helping you make the right choice is, in a nutshell, what this book is designed to do.

Part One

PLANNING YOUR
CRUISE VACATION

UNDERSTANDING CRUISES

THE CRUISE PACKAGE

While it's possible (and sometimes desirable) to buy the various components of a cruise vacation a la carte, most cruises are sold as complete vacation packages. The basic cruise package includes the following:

1. Your shipboard accommodations.
2. Three full-service dining room meals a day (breakfast, lunch, and dinner) plus alternative breakfast, lunch, and late-night buffets. On most ships, room service meals are offered at no extra charge. In addition to the meals and buffets, many ships offer various options such as early-bird breakfast, morning bouillon, and afternoon events, such as tea, pizza snacks, ice cream parties, wine and cheese tastings, and pool-side cookouts.
3. All shipboard entertainment options including music, dancing and shows in the lounges, discos, live bands, Las Vegas–style productions, nightclubs, karaoke, and movies.
4. All shipboard sports and recreational facilities including swimming pool, health club or exercise room, promenade or jogging track, Jacuzzi, sauna, library, game room, and child care facilities. (Spa and beauty treatments and some specialized sports equipment, such as computerized golf analyzer are extra.)
5. All shipboard activities including the casino, a variety of on-board organized games and contests, lectures, demonstrations, and on most ships, a children's program (however, babysitting is usually extra).
6. Stops at ports of call on the itinerary.
7. Round-trip airfare* to and from the port city.

8. Transfers* (ground transportation) from the airport to the ship and back from the ship to the airport.

Port charges (which approximate $120 per person on a seven-day Caribbean cruise) may or may not be included in the advertised cruise price, depending on the cruise line. If they are not, the cruise line's brochures will show the exact amount to be added for each cruise.

Taxes, optional shore excursions, alcoholic beverages and soft drinks, casino play, on-board shopping, and tips are not included in most (but not all) cases. On a few very upscale cruise lines, wine and alcoholic beverages as well as tipping are included in the price of the cruise. On some, too, tips are pooled, meaning that you are asked to contribute a suggested amount per day to be divided among all staff except officers and senior staff. We include a section on Suggested Tipping in our coverage of each major line in Part Two.

CRUISING'S UNFORTUNATE STEREOTYPES

You have probably heard it said that "cruising is not for everyone." But that's like saying travel is not for everyone. Expressed differently, if you like to travel, you will almost certainly enjoy cruising. It's that simple.

---

* The air/sea package, as the cruise package is known when the air transportation and transfers are included in one inclusive price, is becoming an endangered species. More and more cruise lines now sell their cruises as "cruise-only" and sell the air transportation separately as an "add-on." You have the choice of buying your air transportation from the cruise line or on your own.

The main reason for the change is that cruise lines are losing money on air fares. They can no longer get the great deals from the airlines that they got in the past and they are finding that often, passengers get better airfares on their own. It may seem hard to believe that cruise lines would willingly give up their most successful marketing vehicle—one-price-buys-all—but the "unbundling" of the package is definitely happening.

The price of the cruise line's air add-on is always printed in its brochure. When you buy the cruise line's air add-on, the transfers are included. When you purchase your air transportation on your own (or use your frequent flyer award), you can sometimes buy airport transfers from the cruise line; otherwise, you will need to make your own arrangements. All of this may seem a bit complicated, but a travel agent can handle all such details so that you will still be able to pay one inclusive price for a "seamless" package.

Over the years, however, cruising has run afoul of some unfortunate stereotypes which, while essentially untrue, continue to recycle.

Myth No. 1: I'll Be Bored.   Many people, particularly men and younger, active folks persist in believing that cruising is dull and for the sedentary. They picture bulk loaders running from buffet to buffet while active folks sit bored and unstimulated watching barnacles attach themselves to the hull. Sorry, not so.

Today, most, if not all, cruises offer around-the-clock activities and recreation. The ships have exercise rooms with quality equipment, jogging tracks, swimming pools, and daily aerobics and other exercise classes. Some larger ships have volleyball and basketball courts and deck tennis. At ports of call, golf, sailing, road biking, mountain biking, hiking, snorkeling, scuba diving, rafting, canoeing, and kayaking are variously offered. There are enough options to run most jocks into the ground, and certainly far more opportunities for athletic endeavor than most of us have at home. Simply put, if you go on a cruise and sit on your butt, that's your decision.

For the active but less athletically inclined, almost all ships offer swimming, shuffleboard, Ping-Pong, a shaded promenade for walking, and spa amenities, such as hot tubs, whirlpools, steam rooms, saunas, and massage. In addition, many ships schedule classes in yoga and stretching. At night, for those with any energy left, there's dancing—and that, too, comes with options: ballroom dancing, disco, line dancing, and dancing to latin, reggae, jazz, country, and a variety of other beats. You probably don't have those options at home either.

For the gregarious and fun loving, most ships provide a wide range of organized activities. On-board versions of television game shows are popular, as are more traditional events like bridge tournaments. There are crafts classes, dancing lessons, and even karaoke. For those who enjoy games of chance, most cruise ships have casinos and almost all have bingo.

If learning and edification are your goals, you will find dozens of cruises that specialize in providing an educational experience and an in-depth exploration of a region in the company of experts. Like floating graduate schools, these cruises may focus on the political and natural history encountered on the cruise itinerary or offer serious lectures on topics unrelated to the ship's destinations or both.

Finally, there is no place better than a cruise ship to relax. For many people, the favorite cruise activity is to curl up in a comfortable deck chaise with a good book. Even a big ship offering constant activity offers many quiet spots to meditate, read, or just enjoy the beauty of the sea.

Myth No. 2: Cruising Is for Rich People; I Can't Afford a Cruise.
If you take a vacation of three or more days where you stay in hotels and
eat meals in restaurants, then you can afford a cruise.

Let's compare cruising to a modest vacation: Vic and Edna's one-
week trip to Gatlinburg, Tennessee, and the Smoky Mountains. Driving
from their home near Cleveland, Ohio, Vic and Edna spent about $160
on gas for the Chevy. They averaged $65 a night plus tax for motels, or
$498 total for the week. For breakfast and lunch it was Shoney's- or
Denny's-type restaurants. They'd go a bit more upscale for dinner, and
they liked to have a little beer or wine with their meal. Total for seven
days' food: $388. In the mountains they mostly hiked and drove
around. One day, however, they played golf, and on another visited a
museum and a theme park. On the Friday before leaving for home, they
rented horses for half a day. Golf, admissions, and horses came to
approximately $190. So, to recap:

Vic and Edna's Splendid Vacation

Lodging	$	498
Gas	$	160
Meals	$	388
Admissions	$	190
TOTAL		$ 1,236

During the same time period, Royal Caribbean Cruise Lines, a
good middle-of-the-market line (i.e., not super budget or super luxury), was offering a seven-night Southern Caribbean cruise on the *Song
of America* for $699 per person, including airfare from Cleveland to and
from the home port. The cruise visited St. Croix, St. Kitts, Guadeloupe,
St. Maarten, St. John, and St. Thomas. Regal Cruises, a small line with
an old but commodious ship, offered a seven-night Caribbean cruise,
including airfare, for a remarkable $499 per person!

All of these were promotional rates with large discounts and not
the "rack" rates listed in the brochures. We'll have more to say about
these later, but for now the point is this: On the seven-night cruise, Vic
and Edna could have enjoyed all of the amenities of a full resort, dined
in grand style on white linen, danced to live music, visited six beautiful
romantic tropical islands, and soaked in a whirlpool under the
Caribbean moon for about the same amount. We are not suggesting
that Vic and Edna should give up the Smokies for the Caribbean, but
only making the point that they could afford to, if they are so inclined.

Incidently, the previous year Vic and Edna went to Walt Disney World for a week. For what they spent on that vacation, they could have taken two seven-night cruises! In fact, several cruise lines (including Disney's own) can help you both cruise and visit Walt Disney World, and it still will not cost more.

Myth No. 3: *Cruises Are Stuffy, Elitist, and Formal.* Cruises, by and large, are none of the above, though the description fits some of the people who go on them. While a few cruises resemble floating debutante balls, these are easily avoided if you are disinclined to get trussed up in a tuxedo. Cruises vary considerably and cover a broad range of dress and social protocols. The bottom line is that you can choose a cruise at whatever level of formality or casualness feels right for you. Actually, the bottom line is that cruises have become very casual and informal. Even on the nights that are "formal"—usually the captain's welcome aboard party and/or farewell party—half of the men are in a suit like the one they might wear to church (not get married in), and women are in cocktail or party dresses. You might also like to note that on the most informal ships like Carnival, where you can wear about anything short of a burlap bag, people get gussied up to the nines—and it's often the men more than the women. And they love it.

Myth No. 4: *Cruises Are Too Regimented for Me.* True, it takes a bit of orderliness to get everyone on board a cruise ship. It takes a similar modicum of regimentation to get everyone off at the end of the cruise. In between, meals are often served at a specific time at assigned tables, but many ships assign dinner only and have buffets for breakfast and lunch. Moreover, not all ships require this uniformity. At ports of call, all you have to do is get back on the ship before it sails. If the animals on the Ark could handle it, so can you.

Some folks lump cruises into the same category as escorted bus tours and whirlwind tours of Europe—eight countries in five days and that sort of thing. You might actually visit eight countries in five days on a cruise, but you will only have to check in and unpack once. That's the beauty of cruising—you can hang out on the ship and just enjoy the ride, or you can get off at each port and pursue your own agenda. Cruises offer the variety of an escorted land tour without constantly uprooting you or herding you around.

Myth No. 5: *I'm Afraid I'll Get Seasick.* Well, you might, but the vast majority of people don't, particularly on a Caribbean cruise where the water usually is as smooth as your bathtub. Even those who get queasy in the back seat of a car can usually handle a cruise. Over-the-counter antinausea medications like Bonine (doesn't make you drowsy) or Dramamine get the vast majority of folks over the acclimatization period of the first few hours at sea. Bring some along; you may never need it but having it with you is comforting. Usually, Dramamine or Bonine tablets are available from the purser's desk or your cabin steward, or you can dial room service and the medication will be delivered to your cabin.

If you are really worried, however, purchase some Sea Bands—a pair of elasticized wristbands (similar to a tennis band), each with a small plastic disk which, based on the principle of acupuncture, applies pressure to the inside wrist. They are particularly useful for people who have difficulty taking medication. Sea Bands are found in drug, toiletry, and health care stores and can be ordered from Travel Accessories, P.O. Box 391162, Solon, OH 44139; (216) 248-8432. They even make sequined covers in a dozen colors to wear like brackets over the bands for evening. If you take these precautions and get seasick anyway, not to worry: the ship's doctor will administer a more powerful medication and get you up and running.

There are two important things to remember about seasickness: Don't dwell on your fear, and if you happen to get a queasy feeling, take some medicine immediately. The worst mistake you can make is to play the hero, thinking it will go away. When you deal with the symptoms immediately, relief is fast, and you are seldom likely to be sick.

You can also minimize the probability of getting seasick by choosing a cruise itinerary that travels calmer waters. A cruise along the Inside Passage to Alaska, for example, traverses open sea for just a few hours. The rest of the time, in the Passage, the going is nice and smooth. In general, cruises in the Caribbean, the Mediterranean, and the Gulf of Mexico will be smoother than voyages on the Atlantic, Pacific, or Indian oceans or on the South China Sea.

Myth No. 6: I'm Apprehensive about Walking on a Moving Ship. Many prospective cruise passengers worry about their ability to get around a ship. If you are not exactly agile or particularly fit on land, you might be conjuring up tortuous visions of navigating narrow gangways or climbing on ladders through tiny hatches while the ship rolls and pitches on the sea. Once again, not true. Generally speaking, if you can handle a hotel, you can handle a cruise ship. Large cruise ships have wide carpeted halls and slip-resistant outside decks. Elevators serve all passenger decks so that it is not even necessary on many ships to use the stairs—but you should, if for no other reason than the exercise. In any event, for passengers, there are no tricky ladders or tiny hatches.

Modern cruise ships have stabilizers, and in bad weather and heavy seas they are amazingly stable, allowing passengers to enjoy a relatively normal day. Small ships, depending on their draft and build, may be more subject to the motion of the ocean and are a little more challenging to get around. Being smaller, however, there's less territory to cover. Most ships built in the last ten years have taken into consideration not only the concerns of healthy passengers, but also those with ambulatory disabilities. Many modern cruise ships are now built with specialized cabins and ramps to enable wheelchair users to have access to most of the vessel.

A TYPICAL DAY ON A CRUISE

Let's say we're cruising in the Caribbean. At sea you can start your morning with an early bird's breakfast or a walk or jog around the deck, or have breakfast in the dining room, ordering from the menu. If you are a late sleeper, you can order breakfast from room service (no extra charge on most ships) or catch the breakfast buffet, which stays open later than the dining room. It is usually served on the "lido" deck—a term cruise ships use to indicate a casual indoor/outdoor dining facility on the same deck as the swimming pool or the sports facilities. The lido buffet has longer and more flexible hours, thus enabling you to come and go as you like.

Days at sea are the most laid back and relaxing days of the cruise itinerary. The casino is open, as is the ship's shopping arcade, the spa, exercise room, and shore excursion desk, where you may purchase various tours and excursions for the days when the ship will be in port. Throughout the day on large ships, programs and activities for those who are interested are virtually nonstop; most folks, however, hang out by the pool or elsewhere on deck to enjoy the beauty of the sea and the relaxing movement of being under way. From time to time, the captain updates the passengers with announcements on the public address system concerning the progress of the ship toward the next port of call. The captain or cruise director may also point out interesting sights along the route.

Lunch works pretty much like breakfast: you can eat in the dining room and order a fancy lunch or sandwich from the menu, or you can keep your bathing suit on and eat burgers or pizza by the pool where there is likely to be a combo playing calypso or some other upbeat rhythms to set the holiday mood. You can join the pool games—a good way to meet people—or you can watch or simply ignore them. In the afternoon, you might work out, read, nap, try your hand at bridge, or learn the latest dance steps—another easy way to meet people. During the afternoon, recently released movies are shown in the ship's movie theatre or on the television in your cabin. There are also orientation lectures on the ship's next port of call. And then afternoon tea—some ships make a big deal of it, white gloves and all. As the cocktail hour approaches, there is usually live music by the pool, often accompanied by some special drink or appetizer, or happy hour in one of the bars.

As the dinner hour approaches, it's time to get dressed for the evening. On most ships there is a dress code that will be specified on the daily agenda slipped under your door every evening. It is also spelled out in detail in the cruise line's brochure, so that you can know what to expect and how to pack for your cruise. Usually, too, it will be given to you on the first day of your cruise so you can plan for the week. (More information on dress codes is available later in this section under Preparing for Your Cruise.)

Some folks stroll on the deck before dinner, particularly at sunset, one of the most beautiful times at sea. Others gather for a drink in one of the ship's lounges. Dinner in the dining room is a social culmination and celebration of the day's activity, relaxation, and beauty. Spirits are always high for the evening meal.

After lingering over a well-prepared meal of several courses, it's off to the ship's showroom, where live entertainment, ranging from Las Vegas–style variety shows with jugglers and magic to Broadway musicals, is offered nightly. Following the show, early risers or those who might have had a long day of touring retire to their cabins. The more nocturnal or party-minded head for the casino, the disco, or another lounge where a comedian is spilling out naughty jokes. By now, it's time for the midnight buffet. Rather than trot out acres of food (which in these days of health-conscious living, many passengers don't seem to want) many cruise ships now give their chefs the stage to be their most creative, devoting each night to a theme—all pasta, or all salads, or all desserts, or Tex-Mex barbecue, and so on. But, at least one night will be the Grand Buffet when the galley can really show off their skills. That's the night you go with your camera. Every platter on the buffet table is a work of art.

Before calling it a night, stretch out in a chaise lounge on the open deck with a glass of wine. Breathe in the balmy salt-sea air and allow yourself to be caressed by the warm wind blowing over the bow. Gaze into the Caribbean night and lose yourself for a moment in the million distant stars lighting your path across the sea.

Usually, cruise ships sail through the night and arrive at the next port of call early in the morning. If you have been smart like an old salt and gotten up in time to enjoy the early morning—the most beautiful time at sea—you can watch your ship come into port and "park." It's interesting and it's fun. You may be surprised to discover how many other passengers are there ahead of you to relish the dawn and to watch the captain and his officers and the deck hands at work docking the ship. But if you have slept in, when you awaken and peek out the window, the ship is securely moored at the dock. After breakfast, the captain announces that the ship has been cleared by local customs officials and that passengers are free to disembark. Those who have signed up for shore excursions are given last minute instructions about when and where to meet and are normally the first to get off the ship.

Although port calls range from three hours to two days (with an overnight at dock), most port calls are five to ten hours in duration, hardly enough time even to sample an island or port city. As you exit the ship, crew members remind you of tonight's sailing time and make sure you are carrying your cruise identification, which you must present to reboard. Once off the ship, some people explore the port town on foot, taking walking tours, shopping, and perhaps trying a shoreside restaurant. Others hire a cab and take a driving tour of the town and island, while still others set out on the shore excursions they have purchased on the ship.

Shore excursions take many forms. Some are as passive as a bus tour around the island, while others, featuring snorkeling, sailing, hiking, biking, or fishing, are quite active. Surprisingly, many folks, particularly those who have cruised often, stay on board the ship. The ship is quiet and seems almost deserted with most of the passengers ashore, but is, nonetheless, in full operation except for the casinos and shops. Lunch is served as always in the dining room for those on board.

At the end of the day and at least 30 minutes before sailing, you reboard the ship. Just prior to casting off you go topside to watch the crew prepare for departure. Finally, the ship edges away from the dock and slowly makes its way into the channel. Leaving port is always interesting, and the higher decks of a cruise ship offer a great viewing platform. Once at sea, the ship settles down to its normal nighttime dining and entertainment routine. You get ready to enjoy your evening.

SO MANY CRUISES TO CHOOSE FROM

To the first-time cruiser, and even to many veteran cruisers, the number of cruise lines, ships, and itineraries is staggering. Larry Fishkin, senior partner of the Cruise Line, Inc., a high-volume travel agency in Miami that sells only cruises, eases his customers into the seemingly overwhelming array of choices by comparing cruise lines with well-known hotel chains. While you can argue whether Fishkin has the right lines in the right categories, the comparison is useful.

Fishkin sees Commodore and Dolphin cruise lines, for example, as Budget or Quality Inn cruises. Carnival is the Holiday Inn of cruises. Holland America and Celebrity Cruise Line are up a notch, such as the Hyatt.

Ritz-Carlton cruises, says Fishkin, "appeal to the most discriminating cruise goers and are at the upper end of the spectrum in terms of expense and quality of service and amenities. Ships in this deluxe class would include Crystal Cruises' *Crystal Harmony* and Cunard's *Royal Viking Sun*. Boutique cruises overlap the deluxe and super-deluxe category and include the smaller all-suite ships of Radisson Seven Seas, Silversea, Seabourn, and Sea Goddess, and the cruise/sail ships of Windstar."

As an addendum to Fishkin's categorization, be aware that none of the hotel chains mentioned (except Radisson) have anything to do with cruising, and that Fishkin mentioned only a handful of the lines available.

While the foregoing may give you a sense of where you fit in the general scheme of things, you need to dig much deeper to find the perfect cruise for you.

GETTING YOUR ACT TOGETHER

In choosing a cruise, you need to ask yourself dozens of questions. Because cruises are so varied and different, you need to pinpoint your requirements and preferences as exactly as possible. Once you have settled on what you want in a cruise, matching your demands and budget with the best suited cruise line and ship is much easier.

What Is My Vacation Budget?

Unless price is no object, your budget is a good place to start your planning. How much can you afford for your cruise? What is the amount that you are willing to spend on this vacation? Take into consideration that in addition to the cruise itself, you will be assessed port charges and taxes. Also, you might take some shore excursions, will probably do some shopping, will be charged extra on board for bar drinks and dinner wine (on most ships), may gamble a little, have a massage, do some laundry, and will be leaving a fair amount in tips to various ship personnel. Once you have nailed down an amount that represents your uppermost limit for the whole shooting match, you can begin to explore what kind of cruise your money can buy.

Though we will revisit this issue and discuss discounts in the section titled How to Get the Best Deal on a Cruise, let us say here that three-day cruises start at about $280 a person, assuming two to a cabin. Seven-day cruises begin at about $550, while ten-day cruises go from about $800 and up. These prices are deeply discounted and represent the least you would expect to pay, usually for an inside cabin without windows.

How Many Days Do I Want to Cruise?

This question relates to the time you have available for your cruise vacation, and obviously, to your budget. In general, the larger your vacation budget, the more cruise days you will be able to buy. Or put another way, the longer the cruise the more money it will cost. If your budget isn't up to the number of days you've got your heart set on, you have several options. First, you can trade luxury for cruise days. In other words, consider a cruise on a less luxurious ship than might ordinarily have attracted you. The investment that funds a week on an upscale cruise ship will easily buy two weeks on a midrange ship. Be careful, however, not to veer too far away from your lifestyle or expectations or you will be disappointed with your cruise. Second, you can cruise during the off-season when prices are at their lowest. Third, you can settle for the least expensive cabin. Once on board, all passengers are accorded the same privileges, eat the same meals, enjoy the same entertainment, etc. Unless you plan to spend an extraordinary amount of time in your cabin, you probably can tolerate the less expensive accommodations. We're not talking about special suites here, just the difference between the highest deck outside cabin (with a window) and the lowest deck inside cabin (without a window). As an example, on a seven-day Celebrity Cruise Line itinerary to Bermuda, the upper deck outside cabin is more than twice the price of the lower deck inside cabin. The point is, there are lots of ways to save money and stretch your cruise time, all of which we will address in How to Get the Best Deal on a Cruise.

Most folks on a cruise are so pampered and well treated they wish they could stay aboard forever. In the Caribbean and Mexico, a seven-day cruise is about right for your first trip. Though there is extraordinary

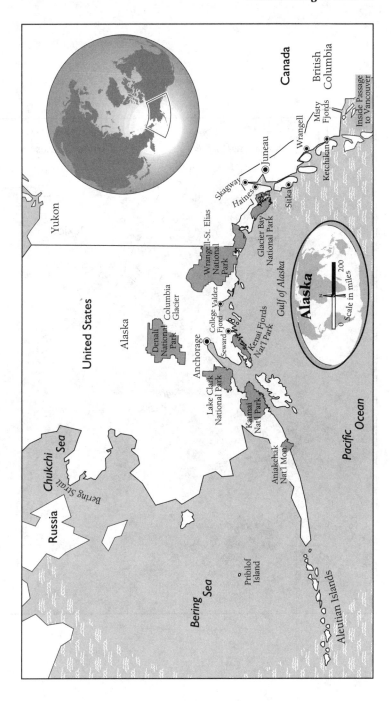

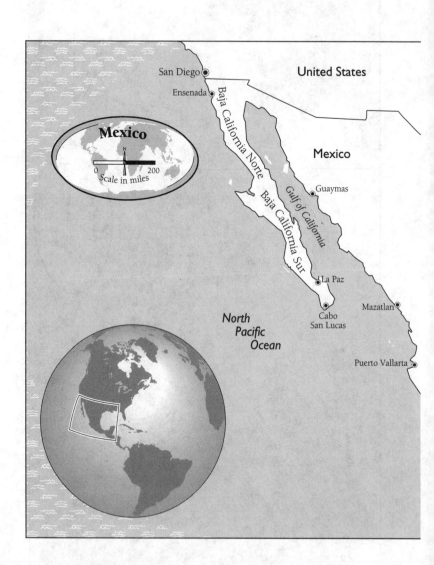

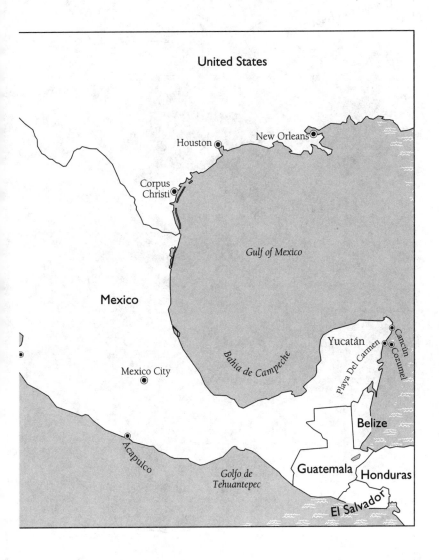

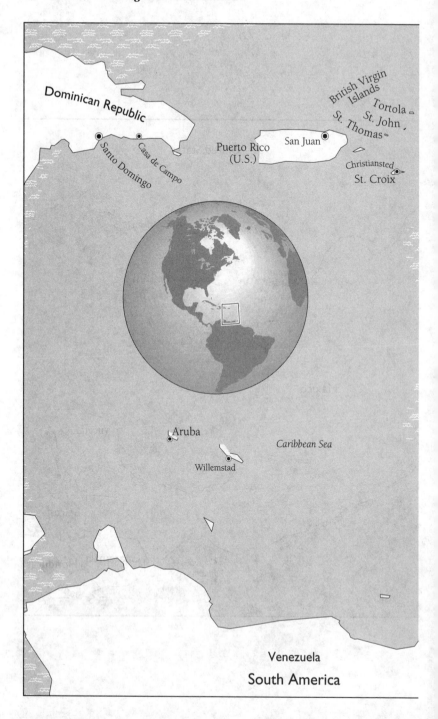

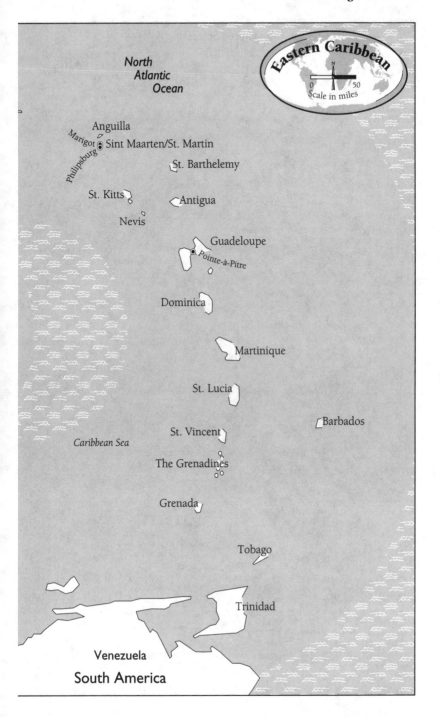

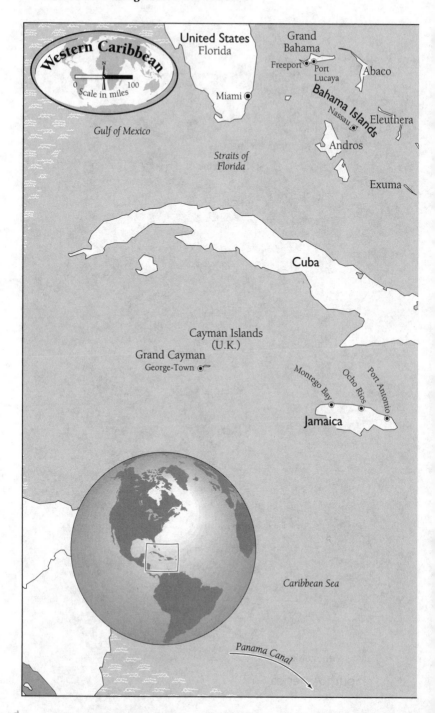

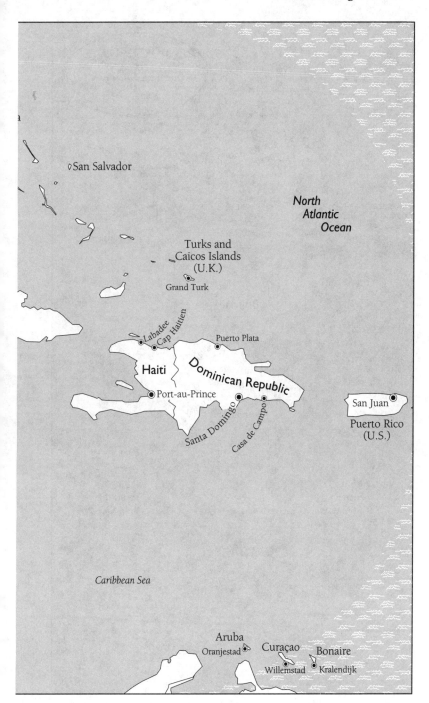

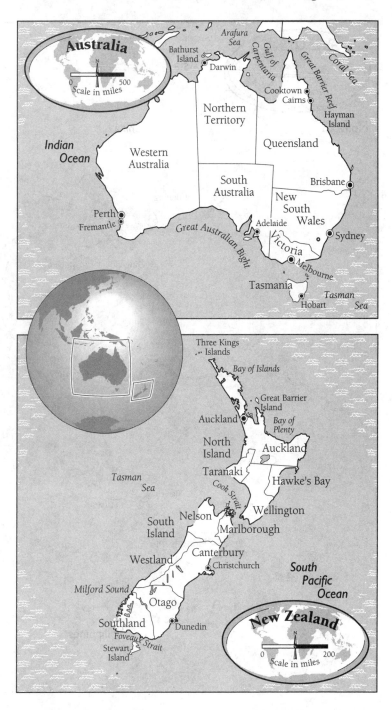

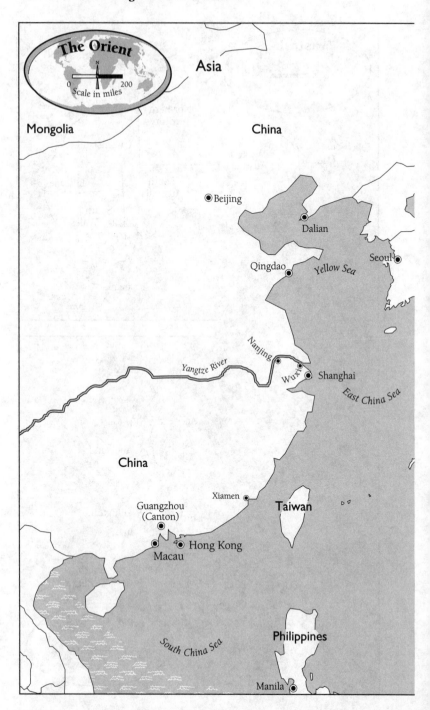

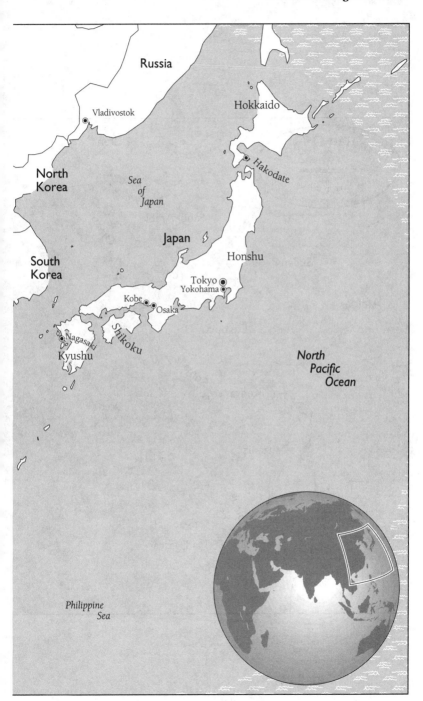

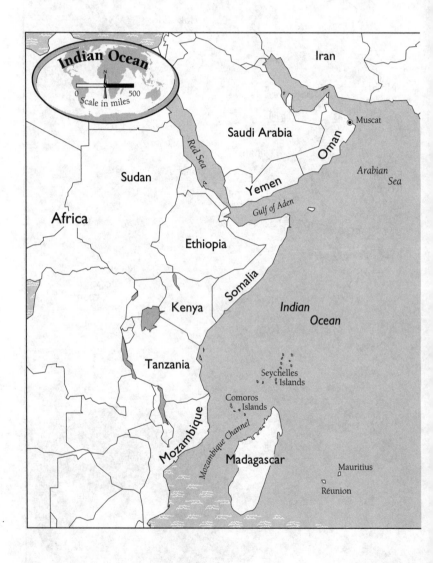

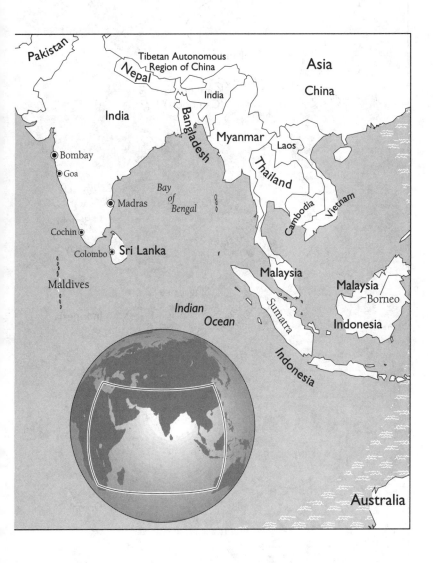

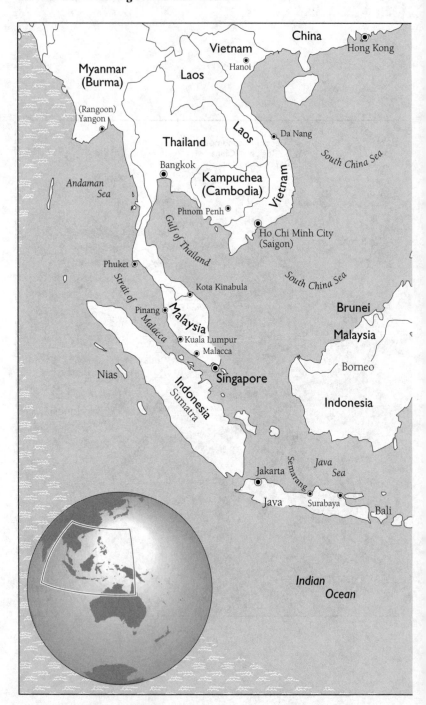

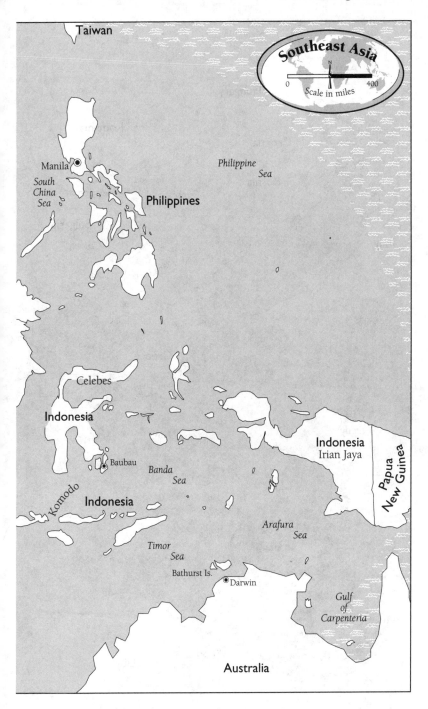

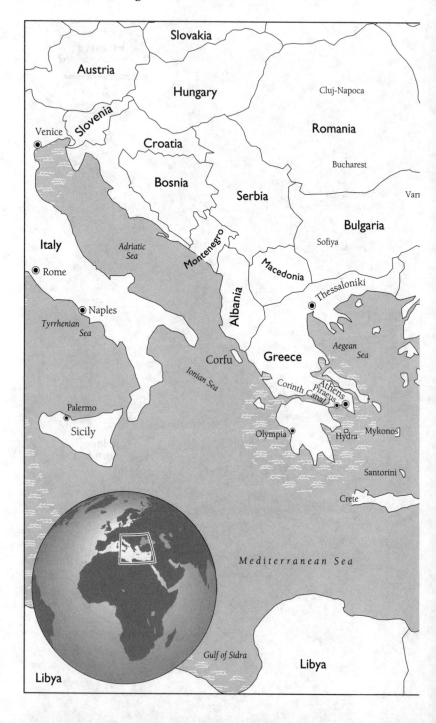

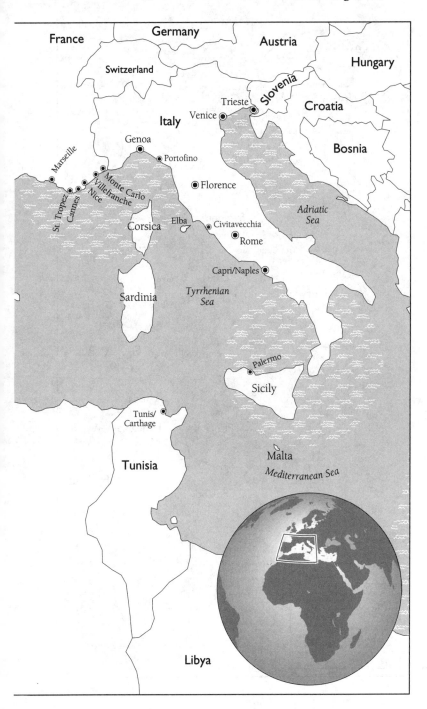

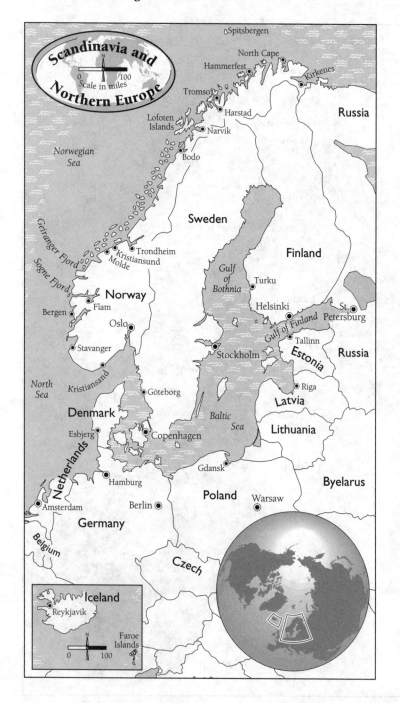

beauty in most cruising areas, there is also a certain amount of, shall we say, scenic redundancy. Sometimes less is more, until you learn if cruising is really for you.

A seven-day cruise is a better test, but if you can't afford the time or money, a three- or four-night cruise will give you a good preview in a relatively inexpensive and time-limited way to determine whether or not cruising is something you'll enjoy. Though they hardly provide enough time to really get settled in, the shorter cruises do give you a sense of life aboard a cruise ship.

Where Do I Want to Go?

Today you can cruise just about anywhere there is enough water to float a ship. This includes all of the world's oceans and seas, and many rivers. Where you want to cruise, of course, depends primarily on your own "wild goose," but also hinges on the style of cruising you enjoy and whether your enjoyment would derive primarily from the destinations or from the ship itself.

Some cruise destinations, like Alaska and Europe, are seasonal. Others, like the Caribbean and Mexico, offer cruising year-round. For almost all cruise areas around the world, the cruise product is tailored to the market and the weather. Many cruises to the Caribbean and Mexico, for example, tend to be festive and high spirited with a lot of emphasis on activity and fun. Mild temperatures allow more time outdoors, and the cruise passengers tend to be younger. By contrast, for Alaskan, Canadian, North Atlantic, Scandinavian, and Baltic Sea cruises, the beauty of the forests, islands, fjords, and glaciers make for a more laid-back, passive experience. For these northerly venues, colder temperatures and rainier weather, coupled with longer cruise durations, contribute to a more sedate cruise experience and attract families or an older clientele.

Mediterranean itineraries tend to revolve around the antiquities and port cities of southern Europe, North Africa, and the Middle East. Most ships visit a port of call each day, and sightseeing is the backbone of the cruise experience. On ships where English is spoken and Americans make up the majority of passengers, the clientele is 50+ years of age and affluent. On cruise ships where Europeans predominate, passengers are younger, and there is more emphasis on sun and fun, like in the Caribbean.

Hawaiian cruises occupy the middle of the spectrum, with an accent on both festivity and scenery, though the passengers are older on average than those sailing the Caribbean. For other North Pacific, South

Pacific, Indian Ocean, and South China Sea settings, the distance of the cruise areas and home ports from the United States ensures a somewhat older, wealthier market. Like Mediterranean cruises, sightseeing and cultural attractions are the focus.

Though a great way to see distant lands and exotic places without shuffling from hotel to hotel, cruises allow only a cursory glimpse of the countries and ports visited. Ten hours in Venice on a cruise is no substitute for visiting Italy. Ten hours, in fact, permits only a superficial exploration of Venice. Even for ports of call at small Caribbean islands, short stopovers expose only the tip of the iceberg.

Some travelers use cruising as a way to sample cities and countries to determine whether they might want to return later for a more in-depth visit. If you are interested in exploring a particular destination more, consider the add-ons that most cruise lines offer at the beginning and end of cruises. A cruise that originates in Barcelona and ends in Athens, for example, offers an opportunity for extra days in Barcelona before, and Athens after the cruise. This arrangement costs more, of course, but it provides a much enhanced opportunity to experience the cities. Almost all cruise lines offer two- or three-night packages that include a hotel and some sightseeing. They are usually well priced and can simplify your life, as the arrangements can be booked at the time you buy your cruise.

Defining the Caribbean   On a map with the arm of the compass pointing north, the islands closest to the United States are known as the Greater Antilles; they include Cuba, the Caymans, Jamaica, Haiti, the Dominican Republic, and Puerto Rico. All but Cuba are visited by cruise ships from U.S. ports and have daily, direct air service from New York, Miami, and other major U.S. cities.

The Bahamas and the British colony of the Turks and Caicos lie north of the Greater Antilles and generally southeast of Florida. They are entirely in the Atlantic Ocean, but because their tropical environment is so similar to that of the Caribbean, they are thought of as being part of the region. The Bahamas, not the Turks and Caicos, are cruise stops; both have air service from the United States.

Further along the compass to the Eastern Caribbean are the Lesser Antilles, the group starting with the Virgin Islands in the north and curving south to Grenada. The northern of these many small islands are known as the Leewards and comprise the United States and British Virgin Islands, Anguilla, St. Maarten, St. Barts, Saba, St. Eustatius, St. Kitts, Nevis, Antigua, Barbuda, Montserrat, and Guadeloupe. The south islands, called the Windwards, include Dominica, Martinique, St. Lucia, Barbados, St. Vincent and the Grenadines, and Grenada.

The Virgin Islands, St. Maarten, Antigua, Guadeloupe, Martinique, St. Lucia, Barbados, and Grenada are frequent cruise stops and have direct air service from the United States. The others can be reached by local airlines, and most are stops for small ships, particularly during the winter cruise season. In the south are Aruba, Bonaire, Curaçao, and Trinidad and Tobago, which lie off the coast of Venezuela. In the Western Caribbean off the Yucatàn Peninsula are Cancún and Cozumel, two islands belonging to Mexico.

Along the 2,000-mile Caribbean chain nature has been extravagant with its color, variety, and beauty. Verdant mountains rise from sun-bleached shores. Between the towering peaks and the sea, rivers and streams cascade over rocks and hillsides and disappear into mangrove swamps and deserts. Fields of flowers, trees with brilliant scarlet and magenta blossoms, and a multitude of birds and butterflies fill the landscape. The air, refreshed by quick tropical showers, is scented with spices and fruit.

Yet, what makes the Caribbean islands unique is not simply their beauty or geography but rather the combination of this lovely and exotic scenery and the kaleidoscope of rich and diverse cultures. Like the vibrant landscape they reflect, the people and their cultures have evolved from a wide range of traditions, music, dance, art, architecture, and religions from around the world.

When Do I Want to Go?

In general, cruise lines follow the sun, visiting the destinations during their best weather seasons. Hence, for cruises to some exotic destinations and such seasonal cruise areas as Alaska, the British Isles, Canada, and Antarctica, you have only a two-to-five-month window of opportunity. For the Caribbean, Mexico, Hawaii, and the Orient, among others, cruises are available all year.

Following is a short list of popular world cruising destinations and their cruising seasons.

Africa	Year-round, but mostly May–October for North Africa; November–April for eastern and southern Africa
Alaska	May–September
Asia and the Orient	Mainly October–March

Baltic	May–October
Bermuda	May–October
Black Sea	April–October
Canada	May–October
Caribbean	Year-round
Hawaii	Year-round
India and Southeast Asia	Year-round, but mostly November–April
Mediterranean	March–November
Mexico	Year-round
New England	May–October
Panama Canal	September–May
South America	North Coast, year-round; other areas, September–April
South Pacific	Year-round, but mainly November–April

For every cruise area, there are periods of peak demand known as *high season,* periods of moderate demand called *shoulder season,* and periods of low demand referred to as *low season* or *value season.* Usually demand is highest when optimal weather in the cruise area coincides with those times of year that people want to take vacations. In the Caribbean, peak demand occurs between Christmas and the middle of April, and from June 15th to August 15th. Yet, within the peak season, there are often valleys when prices are likely to be at their lowest for the year, offering you an opportunity to save a bundle. For example, in the Caribbean, during the period immediately after the Christmas–New Year holiday the demand drops, and the first two weeks in January are often priced at value season rates. If you have the flexibility, shifting dates a week or two can sometimes save a lot of money. It's always wise to check out the period immediately before or after your selected dates to know your options.

The January–April market targets seniors and folks from northern climes seeking a respite from the snow and ice. Though the weather in the summer is not as good as in the January–April period, the family market creates high demand during midsummer when school is out of session. When demand tapers off at the end of the high season, there is a transitional, or shoulder, season. Shoulder season gives way to low season as demand for cruises continues to decline.

During high season, cruise ships tend to sail full. This means, among other things, that the cruise will be more expensive (because demand is high), and that the ship will be more crowded. If you are flexible concerning when you can travel, it is usually possible to identify several periods during the year when the weather is predictably good, but where demand is at moderate or low levels. Cruising during these periods provides the best of all circumstances, that is, lower prices, less crowded ships, and good weather. Caribbean cruises in November and early December before Christmas are good examples. The hurricane season is over, prices are low, and cruise ships are significantly less crowded. Early May for Alaska is another good time.

If your travel schedule is not flexible, as in the case of many families, shoulder seasons (early June or late August) may be your best bet. We will revisit the subject of demand in the section How to Get the Best Deal on a Cruise.

What Sort of Lifestyle or Level of Activity Am I Seeking in a Cruise?

As baby boomers enter middle age and relative affluence, and as younger couples and families discover the economy of cruise vacations, the demographics of the cruise market continue to change. This means essentially that the days are over when a 35-year-old might be the only passenger on board without gray hair. On most midmarket cruises of two weeks or less, the passenger population is amazingly diverse. Responding to an ever widening range of energy and interests among these passengers, cruise lines have developed a variety of activities that offers something for almost everyone.

Even with a "something for everyone" philosophy, however, the cruise lines continue to fine-tune their product for certain primary markets. Thus, while Celebrity Cruise Lines might develop programs and activities for younger cruisers, younger cruisers continue to be a secondary market. The line's real ambition is to serve the needs of its primary market, the 45–65 age group. What this means essentially is that a younger person will have a good time on Celebrity, but an over-40 will probably have a better time because the line has effectively built the cruise around his or her preferences.

This subtle distinction between how cruise lines serve their primary, secondary, and even tertiary markets, makes relevant the question, "What sort of lifestyle or activity level am I seeking?"

In each of our cruise line and ship profiles, we have pinpointed the style, tenor, and activity level of the cruises offered. As you compare, look for an activity and social mix that seems right for you, but don't get bogged down in age demographics. A lot of older people are very young at heart and are active, athletic, and like to party, while many young people appreciate the serenity of a more sedate cruise and may spend their entire day reading in a lounge chair.

We should also make the point that the choice to participate in any activities or to party the night away is entirely yours. Do, however, pay attention to the size of the ship. A small ship, serving 250 or fewer passengers, is likely to have only one or two lounges and limited deck space. If you don't care for a full day or evening of shipboard activity, you'll enjoy its low-key ambience. A small ship that suits your tastes is one of the great delights of cruising.

Large ships have the space and resources to offer considerable variety. Carnival Cruise Line, for example, pretty much wrote the book on get-down-and-boogie cruising, but even on a Carnival ship it is possible to enjoy a relaxing cruise experience. Ships carrying 1,000 or more passengers have plenty of places to escape the festivities, if that is your inclination.

Fortunately, most of the ships offer a variety of music for dancing. Many even have separate on-board nightclubs offering different types of music, dancing, and entertainment. All cruise ships in the mainstream have more sedate music in their lounges before dinner as well as a disco that bounces 'til the wee hours.

Cruise lines custom design their promotional brochures to appeal to their target markets. If you identify with the people and activities depicted in the brochure, you probably will feel comfortable and at home on one of that line's cruises. Lines that do not cater to families and children, for instance, do not publish photos of families and kids in their promotional literature. Collect brochures from your travel agent and flip through the pages. Are the passengers in the photos all younger than you, older than you, your age, or do they represent people of various ages? Does the emphasis seem to be on shipboard activities or on the scenery and ports of call? Do you get the feeling that life on board is a 24-hour party, or is the picture presented more mellow and laid-back? An even more accurate gauge, spelled out and easily uncovered, are the facilities of the ship.

What Level of Formality Do I Prefer?

Most cruises give passengers an opportunity to play dress-up. Jackets and ties and sometimes even tuxedos (or at least dark suits) are requested for men in the main dining room on certain evenings. Women wear cocktail dresses and on some ships, evening gowns. While some nights may be more formal than others, most ships have a dress protocol that passengers are expected to observe. (See Dress Codes under the section Preparing for Your Cruise later in Part One.)

Formality, or lack thereof, is yet another way that cruise lines differentiate their offerings. A luxury cruise line targeting extremely affluent passengers will almost always be more formal than a middle-of-the-market line. Family cruise lines and budget lines, not unexpectedly, are the least formal, and adventure-type cruises are usually the most informal of all.

The bottom line when it comes to formality is deciding how much you are comfortable with. There are cruises where you can leave your coat and tie at home, and others where a tuxedo is all but mandatory. The great majority, however, fall somewhere in between, varying the attire from night to night and not getting out of joint if someone breaks the dress code. For example, if a man wears a neat, dark suit and tie instead of a tuxedo for the captain's party, no one will turn him away and half the men in the room will be similarly attired. On the other hand, an informal budget ship might ask passengers not to wear shorts and tank tops in the dining room, especially for dinner, and be strict about it. For 75 percent of all ships, men can get by with a sports coat and would cover all the bases with a sports coat and a dark suit. Dress for women covers a broader range. Slacks or a skirt with a sweater or blouse will suffice for most nights, as will a simple dress. On dressier nights many women shift to dark slacks and tops, nice-restaurant-caliber attire, or cocktail dresses.

After your first cruise you will discover that most cruise passengers don't spend a lot of time worrying about formality. If it's a big deal with you, check out the ship's dress code before you book. If you think you have to invest in a new wardrobe to meet the dress requirements, you should consider another ship.

What Standards Do I Require for Dining and Food Quality?

Food, its quality and the overall dining experience, is cited by most passengers as a critical element of their cruise experience. As it happens, the fare on cruise ships is generally very good. This is quite an accomplishment considering that meals on cruise ships represent the exponential extension of catered banquet dining.

Preparing meals for 300–1,400 persons at a sitting is not easy under any circumstances. To do it at sea with such attention to detail, quality of ingredients and preparation, and beauty of presentation is one of the miracles of cruising. Cruise ships have made an art of serving palatable food to large numbers of diners. Most hotel food and beverage managers, in fact, could learn a lot from cruise ship chefs. Speaking personally, it has been a long time since we have had a banquet meal in a hotel that compared favorably to the meals we have enjoyed on cruises.

The main point to make is that you cannot expect the same finesse and excellence from a galley rolling out hundreds of dinners as you can from an upscale restaurant that cooks dishes to order for a small number of guests. While there are a few ships that rival better restaurants, they are the exception, and they are small ships.

Group dining notwithstanding, food is one of the distinguishing and differentiating aspects of cruising, and the quality of meals and sophistication of the dining experience varies considerably from ship to ship. Though luxury ships serving smaller numbers of passengers in single seatings have the greatest potential for serving memorable meals, midmarket lines like Celebrity have demonstrated that they can approach similar standards of excellence serving much larger numbers.

If you have a very refined palate and eat exclusively in the finest restaurants, you may have trouble finding ships that can meet your dining requirements except in the high end group. If like many of us, however, you dine out fairly regularly in restaurants of varying quality, have an acquaintance with the world's major cuisines, and possess enough common sense to understand the basic limitations of cruise food service, you will find a good selection of cruise ships capable of meeting or exceeding your expectations.

If you dine out infrequently, but enjoy simple, basic foods prepared well, you'll be happier eating on a cruise ship than a pig on the sofa. For those not hung up on gourmet food, there are more cruises to choose from, and even better, they are among the most affordable. When it comes to food, you can play it one of two ways. You can use your cruise dining experience to broaden your culinary horizons, or you can save some bucks by sailing on a ship that specializes in good, but less expensive, American fare.

In the final analysis, a lot of people end up paying for food much fancier than their taste requires. If you are a meat and potatoes person, you may get a better deal putting your dollars into a cabin upgrade on a midmarket line rather than paying upscale prices for fancy food and service on a luxury line.

In recent years cruise lines have tended to put their best foot forward on good dining room meals, or on good buffets, but seldom both.

Holland America and Celebrity are notable exceptions. And almost all lines have cut back noticeably on the midnight buffet except for one extravaganza during the week when the chefs go all out to show off their culinary skills.

Weather and lifestyle have also had a lot to do with changes in cruise ship dining. Because most cruise ships spend all or part of the year in the Caribbean and Mexico, where passengers prefer to stay in their bathing suits most of the day, the lines have found that it makes sense (and saves them money) to go with the flow, so to speak, and have expanded the lido breakfast and lunch. A third reason for the popularity of lido dining is that it gives passengers some relief from the regimentation of imposed dining room hours.

How Gregarious Am I (Are We)?

Generally speaking, it's easier to meet folks on a small ship than on a large one. There are fewer passengers in a more intimate space and you tend to see the same people more often. Conversely, on a large ship, the only folks you see regularly are your dinner table companions (hope you like them!). As an example, we met a nice woman checking in for a seven-day cruise on the 2,300 passenger *Monarch of the Seas.* Though we looked for the woman all week, we never ran into her again. On the larger ships, if you meet somebody you would like to see again, better get their name and cabin number before parting company.

Large ships, however, offer many social settings. The *Monarch* has four or five bars and an equal number of lounges and nightspots. While it is also possible to meet people on shore excursions, in the health club, around the pool, and in the casino, the easiest time to meet them is at various planned activities and games. That's why, if your goal is to meet people, you should participate—whether it's aerobics and line dancing or bridge and a wine tasting. Such activity also helps people with similar interests to coalesce.

The style of a cruise is important. If you are gregarious, you might prefer a ship that emphasizes social events and promotes more of a party atmosphere. If you are more solitary or perhaps taking a romantic cruise with your significant other, you may prefer a ship where the social agenda is less frantic.

Not surprisingly, most cruisers solve the problem of companionship at sea by taking lovers, friends, relatives, or all of the above with them. As on the Ark, the majority of cruise passengers arrive paired up. To an extent, this is attributable to the double occupancy norm for cabins. Solitary passengers must pay a hefty "singles supplement" for the privilege of having a cabin to themselves. Thus, folks arrive two by two. They might be spouses, friends, brothers, sisters, or even same-sex strangers lumped together by a travel agent or the cruise line.

There are, of course, real solitary travelers, some of whom are single. Cruise ships schedule gatherings for single folks to meet, and some try to place single travelers at the same tables in the dining room, but, by and large, you may have to scout around to hook up with other singles.

The Other Passengers: What Kind of People Am I Most Comfortable With?

As common sense suggests, the less expensive the cruise, the more varied the passengers. On an affordable four-day Premier (*Big Red Boat*) cruise, we had retired seniors, middle-aged professionals, 20-something newlyweds, a bowling team from Erie, Pennsylvania, families with small children, a group of pipe fitters, and a number of college students on spring break.

For longer and more upscale cruises of two weeks or more, the cost of passage ensures that the passenger population is somewhat more affluent and perhaps less diverse. On a seven-day Caribbean or Mexico cruise, with midmarket lines such as Royal Caribbean, Princess, Celebrity, and Holland America, you will find more seniors, more professionals, fewer tradespeople, fewer families with children (except during the summer), and fewer people under 25 years of age. Seven-day or longer cruises on the same lines to Alaska and the Mediterranean, which are generally more costly than those to Mexico and the Caribbean, reflect further homogenization of the passengers.

On the most upscale lines, such as Seabourn, Radisson Seven Seas, and Cunard *Sea Goddess*, the average passenger is older (over 55) and affluent. While there is a smattering of young professionals, passengers under 20 are likely traveling with parents or grandparents. Some lines don't take children, or at least discourage their presence because they do not have the facilities or the atmosphere for them. Couples account for 80 percent of those on board. Most singles are likely to be widows or widowers, or mature singles affluent enough to afford the lifestyle.

In our profiles of the respective cruise lines and ships, we have carefully and extensively scrutinized their passengers so you'll know what to expect. We believe the inclusion of this information is one element that makes this book different from other guide books on cruises. If you have strong feelings concerning who your fellow passengers will be, we recommend that you pay close attention to these descriptions.

What Kind of Itinerary Do I Prefer?

When it comes to itineraries there's a world to choose from. You can have mostly days at sea, mostly days in port, or a balance of the two. Your cruise can be educational or just fun. There are theme cruises where shipboard entertainment or education has a central focus, such as a jazz festival, and cruises where the emphasis is on certain activities, such as scuba diving, sailing, or wildlife viewing.

A basic preference to be determined is the ratio of time spent at sea versus the time docked in port. If you are most interested in visiting various ports of call, look for an itinerary that allows for the maximum number of ports. But be aware that when a ship visits more than five ports on a seven-day cruise, some of those port calls are likely to be half-day stops. These port-intensive itineraries are likely to be found most frequently on Mediterranean and Eastern Caribbean Cruises. Compare itineraries for different lines making the same ports of call. A line that gives you more time at each destination most likely has fewer ports of call. When figuring your available time in each port, take into consideration that your ship must clear customs on arrival before passengers are allowed to disembark. If the itinerary indicates that the ship makes port at 8 A.M., it may be 9 or 9:30 before passengers are allowed to go ashore. Prior to leaving port, most ships require that passengers be back on board 30 minutes before sailing, depending on the port. Thus your time in port could be trimmed by an hour or so both coming and going.

Another important consideration, if you want to maximize your time in port, is whether your ship can tie up at the dock or whether it must anchor offshore, necessitating the use of a tender (a small commuting boat) to ferry you to shore. Having to use a tender can take a big bite out of your available time in port. As common sense suggests, the larger the cruise ship, the more likely the need to use a tender. In any event, the published itinerary or a query to your travel agent will provide the information you need concerning tendering.

Many cruise passengers relish the serenity and feel of being at sea. To them, cruising is less about ports of call than enjoying life aboard a moving vessel. These passengers are usually experienced cruisers and in recent years have been very vocal in opposition to cruise lines cramming port after port into their itineraries to attract first-time cruisers (who commonly perceive value in the number of ports on an itinerary). To be sure, it is more difficult to find itineraries featuring days spent at sea than to uncover itineraries with daily port calls. Most three-, four-, and seven-day cruises spend more daylight hours in port than at sea. Longer cruises, typically, feature somewhat more time at sea. When you read an itinerary, days spent underway are shown as "cruising" or "at sea."

A good look at a map highlighting ports of call in the world's cruise areas will give you a sense of the hundreds of ports that cruise ships can work into their itineraries. With the possible exception of the Atlantic coast of Africa, ports in most cruise locations are situated close enough to one another to allow a port visit every day, if that were the way a cruise line wished to structure the itinerary. Fortunately, most cruise itineraries of seven days or more strike a balance. A typical seven-day itinerary, for example, usually includes two days spent entirely at sea. Rarely on a seven-day cruise, however, will the days at sea exceed three. Three or four days of cruising is typical of ten-day itineraries; four to five days on 12–14-day itineraries.

The best buys for those who crave more days at sea are repositioning cruises. They are also the best bargains. These occur at the end of the season in one cruise area when the cruise line repositions its ship(s) by dispatching them to another cruise area where a new season is about to begin. Thus, Princess Cruises repositions some of its Caribbean fleet in April (the end of high season in the Caribbean) to the Pacific Northwest for summer cruises to Alaska. Royal Caribbean at the same time might reposition ships from the Caribbean to Europe or the Mediterranean. While repositioning cruises stop at some ports en route, there is usually a high ratio of days underway to days in port. Because repositioning itineraries are singular and unique, occurring on certain vessels only twice a year, they are more difficult for the cruise line to promote, and, the cost of passage is usually discounted significantly.

Specialized Itineraries and Specialized Ships

Most large-ship itineraries combine a number of days at sea with a number of days in port. Your time either at sea or in port is unstructured, and how to spend it is basically left for you to determine. Specialty cruises, by contrast, zero in on a specific activity or pursuit and make it central to the cruise experience. Some cruises may specialize in viewing whales, others in exploring archeological ruins. Sometimes the activity focus derives from the cruise vessel itself. Smaller, 80–150-passenger cruise ships can dock in small ports and anchor in secluded coves. The ability of these ships to facilitate fishing, swimming, snorkeling, scuba diving, and waterskiing right off the stern (they carry their own sports equipment) can make a difference in the way passengers spend their time.

Traditional, main line cruise ships sometimes offer theme cruises. A theme cruise might consist of cruising with professional football players and watching reruns of famous games, or it might consist of wine tastings, and culinary explorations. A couple of years ago, a normally conservative cruise line ran a Blues Cruise. Some of the line's regular customers booked the Blues Cruise dates without knowing about the theme outing. Once underway, they were aghast to find their usual, dignified fellow passengers replaced by a ship full of foot stomping, denim wearing, blues fans. The moral of the story is a theme cruise is great fun if it's playing your tune, but would be the wrong cruise for you if it were not.

A cruise ship can be the medium for countless activities and themes. Whether you prefer the more typical laissez-faire cruise experience or buy into a more structured or regimented cruise is your choice. When it comes to structure and specialization, cruises run the gamut. For additional information on specialty cruises, see the chapters in Part Three: Cruising Alternatives.

Big Ships vs. Small Ships

Lately, it seems, a week doesn't pass by without a cruise line announcing plans for yet another ship—bigger and, of course, better than the last. But is bigger really better for a cruise? Not necessarily.

Some new words have crept into the cruise lexicon which you will not find in *Webster's*. Their definitions have grown with usage and not everyone agrees on the precise meaning, but these are, more or less, the currently accepted parameters:

Megaliner: a cruise ship with a basic capacity (i.e., two persons per cabin) of 2,000 or more.

Superliner: a cruise ship with a basic capacity of about 1,000 to 2,000.

Midsize: a cruise ship with a basic capacity of 400 to 900.

Small ship: a cruise ship with a basic capacity of under 400.

Boutique ship: a luxury cruise ship with a basic capacity of under 300.

Oceanliner: generally, any ocean-going passenger vessel but tends to be used for former steamships which once sailed transatlantic and in worldwide service and have since been converted into a cruise ship.

Until you sail on a small ship, it may be hard to realize the special pleasures it offers. Small ships in most cruising areas are fewer in number but more diverse in style than larger ones. Small ships range from traditional sailing ships, such as Star Clipper's tall ships, to modern, computer-driven ones like Windstar Cruises', and in the degree of comfort and service from the modest vessels of American Canadian Caribbean Lines to ultraluxurious ships, like Cunard's *Sea Goddess* twins and the new ships of the Silversea Cruise Line. Prices likewise run the gamut from the moderate Windjammer Barefoot Cruises to *très cher* Seabourn Cruises.

Indeed, the spectrum is so broad it is difficult to generalize, yet all small ships are cozy, imparting a warmth that you would never feel on a superliner. The smallest ones are like being on a private yacht, at a weekend house party, or in a country club.

Small ships are people-sized. It's easy to learn the layout on the first day and feel like the ship is home by the second. Life aboard is casual, even on the most luxurious ships. Informality and friendliness go hand-in-hand. With a small number of passengers, a camaraderie among them develops naturally; making friends is easy—an advantage for single travelers. The intimate, congenial atmosphere also enhances the interaction between passengers and personnel, from the captain, who usually operates an open bridge, to the staff and crew, who are likely to call you by name from the first day.

Small cruise ships with their shallow drafts, turn-on-a-dime maneuverability, and small number of passengers can gain access and acceptability to places where large ships cannot go. Their size makes them welcome at private islands and exclusive resorts, and allows them to nudge into shallow bays and hidden coves, accessible only by sea. Their ports of call tend to be offbeat and uncommercialized.

Some small cruisers have bow ramps, enabling them to disembark passengers directly onto beaches or remote villages. Others carry Zodiacs to take passengers into wilderness areas. Some have retractable marinas, allowing passengers to indulge in waterskiing right from the ship; some have glass-bottom boats to view offshore reefs.

A small ship has a certain exclusivity, whether or not its intention is to be exclusive. There is a single, unassigned seating for meals rather than early or late assigned seating as on larger ships. On the more deluxe ships, dining is even at the time of your choosing—that's part of the luxury. There are no crowds, no long lines, almost no regimentation. Best of all, on shore, you do not feel like part of a herd.

Today's superliners and megaliners are self-contained floating resorts with facilities and amenities that operate almost around the clock. The bigger they get, the more the ship becomes the focus; ports of call matter less.

For miniliners, the destinations are key, and sightseeing from the ship is the main activity. They offer more varied and unusual itineraries than larger ships and often feature naturalists and other experts who give talks about the area being visited and even accompany passengers on shore excursions.

Small ships appeal to more experienced, discriminating, and independent travelers, who enjoy the low-key ambience and appreciate what is not available as much as what is. They neither want nor need the hoopla and nonstop activities that typify a day on a large ship. Although a few small vessels have tiny casinos and small-scale entertainment, on most, conversation and companionship replace chorus lines and cabarets.

The smaller size attracts all age groups. Sailing ships, particularly windjammers, draw the young and adventuresome, attracted by the lower price and the opportunity to work alongside the crew. Deluxe ships and those with longer itineraries attract older travelers, with both the time and the means to enjoy them. And even though they may be older, many are young in spirit, with an intellectually curious outlook. They appreciate an island's culture and are eager to interact with the local population, try the local cuisine, and participate in local activities.

Sound appealing? Then consider one of the following three basic types of miniships. Ultraluxurious liners, whose appeal is privacy and pampering, exclusivity and elegance, feature suites of tasteful opulence, gourmet dining, and an evening atmosphere that is often formal. In sharp contrast is the adventure-oriented ship, whose destinations are chosen for their natural beauty, wildlife, or cultural interest and whose activities include hiking, birding, and the like. Usually, their accommodations are modest, their service minimal, and their cooking down-home, with limited choices or set menus served family style. They appeal to people who care little for luxury, but are keenly interested in a participatory travel experience.

A third type strikes a middle ground, offering comfortable but not lavish accommodations, good food, and attentive service. There is some adventure, some history and wildlife, and some time for golf, tennis, and water sports. Evening entertainment includes cards and board games, movies, local talent at ports of call, and guest speakers.

Even with these choices, it's fair to say that cruises on small ships are not for everyone. Some would be bored, others might find them confining. But if you abhor lines or regimentation and operate on your own juices, yearn for a cozier, more intimate on-board environment, or want to try trimming the sails or floating about in indulgent luxury, a small ship might be just right for you. And you just might agree that big is not necessarily better.

Old Ships vs. New Ships

Poets through the ages have praised the beauty of sailing ships. But those who have seen classic cruise ships like the *Rotterdam* and *QE2* enter or leave the harbor have probably been equally captivated by a noble grace that is both massive and subtle. Examine the *Norway* up close and you will notice that there is scarcely a straight line in her. Alas, such ships will never be built again.

There will always be a debate on whether the old or the new is better. The classic ships still in service, as opposed to those that are merely old, offer an ambience that none of the newer ships can duplicate. But the newest cruise vessels have advantages that could only be dreamed of in 1960: consider the 45,000-ton cruise ship *Royal Princess* which pays its way with all outside cabins (152 of them with private balcony), or the *Costa Romantica* and the *Westerdam,* where the *average* cabin is 200 square feet and superbly equipped. Because there are a number of older ships in service that are well maintained and kept up-to-date by their owners, you have a good choice between the old and the new afloat. One way to decide which you prefer is to take a look at what each type of ship has to offer in areas that mean most to passengers.

The first thing you notice in any vessel, old or new, is the external appearance: in brochures, in advertisements, and on that first sight as you approach the ship on sailing day. The newest ships are designed from the inside out. The purpose is to have more and better public rooms and the largest usable deck space. These vessels will spend most of their days in calm seas. None will have to cut through the North Atlantic in winter at full speed to maintain a schedule, so they do not need the fine lines and razor-sharp bows of the *QE2.* Instead, the new designs have squared-off sterns and chunky superstructures that provide many benefits internally, but none externally.

As with some prima donnas, most new cruise ships have one or two good angles that are used in publicity material: mostly profile shots and aerial views showing raked stems and funnels and broad decks for recreation and lounging. But as you approach the ship in a tender or at the pier, you'll see what she really looks like without makeup or a wide-angle lens: a full-figured lady from bow to stern.

Once you get in your cabin, though, you may forget how your ship looks from the outside. The space available to modern interior designers has generally made possible standard, usually larger, cabins for every-one. Some older ships like Commodore's *Enchanted Isle* and American Hawaii's *Independence* (which has 54 different cabin configurations) offer comfortable amounts of space in every cabin, but they can't match the improved bathrooms and the attention that has been paid in newer ships to the use of space and lighting. On a new vessel the cabins will have a TV set that works and good movie programming. On many ships you can even watch CNN or the after-dinner show in your cabin.

Luxury vs. Midprice and Economy Cruises

A friend of ours buying a stereo system was offered a speakers' upgrade for $300 extra. Naturally, he was curious to know exactly what he would get for his additional $300. The salesman showed him a lot of snazzy acoustic graphs that didn't provide much additional information. As it happened, our friend turned down the upgrade. He later discovered that the upgrade speakers were indeed much better, but the quali-tative difference was beyond the human ear's ability to discern. What the extra dollar buys in a cruise is as salient a question as our friend's query about the stereo, and sometimes the answer is just as surprising.

Spending more on a cruise does not, for example, necessarily buy more or better facilities. Some of the most extraordinary lounges, health spas, exercise rooms, pools, lounges, and showrooms are found on the megaships of Carnival and Royal Caribbean Cruise Lines, very afford-able midmarket lines. Dropping big bucks likewise will not ensure that your ship is newer, nicer, or more competently and courteously staffed. Regarding the latter, there is a thin line between being considerate and efficient, and being obsequious and in the way. To get a handle on how much attention you are likely to receive on any cruise, check the ratio of passengers to crew. The lower the ratio the more service you will, or at least should, get.

Sometimes buying a luxury cruise will get you a larger cabin. Seabourn Cruise Line, for example, offers only suites. On the luxury lines, your cabin will almost always have a roomier bath with a tub (and a shower).

When it comes to food, the luxury lines have the edge. Usually they have the advantage of feeding smaller numbers of passengers at a single seating stretched over a couple of hours. This means that passengers arrive at the dining room a few at a time, like at a restaurant on shore. Though some come early and some late, the staggered arrivals allow the galley the flexibility to cater better to individual needs, to provide more choice, and to cook dishes to order. On most midmarket and economy cruises, there are two seatings for each meal; when their seating is called, the passengers blow into the dining room like the Marines hitting the beach on Iwo Jima. Surprisingly, however, the quality of meals on some luxury cruise ships is only marginally better than that of the better midmarket lines. Midmarket Celebrity Cruises makes the dining experience a top priority and turns out meals that compare favorably to some ships that cost much more. What the extra dollars for a luxury cruise generally buy is exclusivity. And for those who can afford it, that's saying a lot.

SPECIAL PEOPLE WITH SPECIAL NEEDS

Some folks require special services or special accommodations in their cruise vacation. If you are a honeymooner, single, disabled, require a special diet, or plan to travel with small children or teens, read on.

Singles

Safety and security, comfort, convenience and companionship, fun and freedom—all are reasons that have made cruise holidays among the fastest growing options available to independent travelers who want to go it alone. And it's understandable.

In today's society, a cruise ship is about the safest, most secure environment anyone can find. A woman, particularly, might hesitate to strike up a conversation with someone in a hotel bar, dine alone in a fancy restaurant, or walk into a nightclub by herself, but such barriers do not exist on a cruise ship.

What's more, on a ship, the fun is at your fingertips—no need to count wine glasses or drive home alone late at night. The nightclub, disco, casino, and theatre are down the hall or a flight up from your cabin.

Relieved of the need for an escort and with ready-made companions for dinner, bridge, or dance lessons, a cruise allows single persons—whether an unmarried 20-something or an 80-year-old spinster, a divorcée, a confirmed or rebounding bachelor, a widow or widower—to vacation on their own terms with the freedom to do as they choose.

The cruise lines' own statistics show that one out of four passengers is single, and with an estimated reservoir of 72 million unattached persons in the United States, it would probably be higher except for one deterrent: cost.

Cruise prices, as we have already said, are based on two people sharing a cabin, just as in most hotels. For one person to occupy a cabin

Cruising for Singles

S = Single cabins available
GSP = Guaranteed share program available
Single Supplement = Percentage of fare based on per person double
  occupancy rate

Cruise Line	S	GSP	Single Supplement
Alaska Sightseeing	Yes	No	175
American Canadian	Yes	Yes	175
American Hawaii Cruises	Yes	Yes	160
Carnival Cruise Lines	Yes	Yes	150 to 200
Celebrity Cruises	Yes	Yes	150 to 200
Clipper Cruise Line	Yes	Yes	150
Club Med	Yes	Yes	150
Commodore Cruise Line	Yes	No	150
Costa Cruise Lines	Yes	No	150
Crystal Cruises	No	No	150 to 200 by category
Cunard	Yes	Yes	Varies by ship
Delta Queen Steamboat	Yes	Yes	175
Dolphin Cruise Line	No	Yes	150
Holland America Line	Yes	Yes	125 to 150
Majesty Cruise Line	No	Yes	150
Norwegian Cruise Line	Yes	Yes	150
Orient Lines	Yes	Yes	125 to 175
Premier Cruise Lines	Yes	No	175
Princess Cruises	Yes	Yes	150% of minimum
Radisson Seven Seas	No	No	125
Renaissance Cruises	Yes	No	$995 per 7 days
Royal Caribbean	Yes	Yes	150
Royal Olympic Cruises	Yes	Yes	150
Seabourn Cruise Line	No	No	Varies by cruise
Seawind Cruise Line	No	No	150 for categories E–M; 200 for categories A–D
Silversea Cruises	No	No	150
Special Expeditions	Yes	Yes	Limited availability in cat. 1 and 2 at 150%
Star Clippers	Yes	Yes	150
Swan Hellenic Cruises	Yes	Yes	Varies
Windjammer Barefoot	No	Yes	175 (some blackout dates)
Windstar Cruises	No	No	150
World Explorer Cruises	Yes	No	130

alone, cruise lines impose a surcharge over the per person double occupancy rate, which can vary from 10–100 percent, depending on the cruise line, ship, itinerary, season, and cabin category. The single's price or single supplement, as the cruise lines call it, is expressed as 110–200 percent.

The most frequent charge is 150 percent for all except suites, which usually go for the full tariff of 200 percent. The rate is always published in the cruise line's brochure; however, that could be only a starting point for you. Your choices are to bring a friend or to avail yourself of one of the following options:

Guaranteed Single Rate   You pay a set price, which is published in the brochure and which is comparable to the low end of a per person double occupancy rate; the cruise line assigns your cabin at the time of embarkation. You do not have a choice, but you do have a guarantee of price and privacy.

You are likely to be assigned an inside cabin, but not necessarily, since traditionally, the cheapest and most expensive cabins sell out first. If you select the slow season (October in the Caribbean) or the start of a new season (May in Alaska) or a repositioning cruise when the ship is not likely to be full, you might luck out and get a nice outside cabin.

Royal Caribbean Cruise Line and Norwegian Cruise Lines offer a guaranteed single fare, which includes air transportation, for all their fleet. Seawind offers it in only one category on the *Seawind Crown*.

Some cruise lines do not show a guaranteed single rate in their brochure, but will accept a reservation when bookings are light. It pays to ask.

Low Single Supplement   A few cruise lines have single supplements of 15 percent or less. Seabourn offers 110 percent on more than half of its cruises; Silverseas has a few at 110 percent and most at 125 percent. American Hawaii adds $100 or about 5 percent in two midpriced categories. In all these cases, you pay slightly more than the per person double rate, but you get privacy, and in the case of Seabourn and Silversea, all the accommodations are deluxe suites and all but a few superdeluxe suites are alike. Orient Lines not only has a low supplement, but, often during its low season (normally summer), the cruise line waves the single supplement altogether as a special promotion.

Flat Rate   Clipper Cruises, Star Clipper, and some other cruise lines simply charge a flat rate for sole occupancy of the cabin. You pay more but are ensured privacy and choice.

Guaranteed Share The cruise line plays travel matchmaker. You pay the per person double occupancy price for a cabin, and the cruise line matches you with a compatible cabin mate (same sex and smoking preference). If the line does not find a suitable mate you get the cabin to yourself without paying an extra premium. The savings are obvious; so are the drawbacks. It's a bit of Russian roulette. You stand a better chance of having a cabin to yourself during a slow season or on a repositioning cruise. Some cruise lines do not show a guaranteed share program in their brochure, but accept a reservation. Ask.

Single Cabin Some older ships have single cabins but the supply is dwindling because new ships do not have them. A single cabin has a set price, but not necessarily comparable to a per person double rate; more likely, a surcharge has already been built into the price.

Single cabins are found on American Hawaii: *Independence* (18); Dolphin: *IslandBreeze* (14); Cunard: *QE2* (145), *Visitafjord* (36); P&O: *Canberra* (161), *Victoria* (22); Norwegian Cruise Line: *Norwegian Star* (49). You need to book early as single cabins go quickly.

Also, some cruise lines allow solo travelers to occupy a less desirable cabin, such as an inside room with upper/lower berths, with a minimal or no surcharge.

Helpful Hands

Golden Age Travellers (Pier 27, The Embarcadero, San Francisco, CA 94111; (415) 296-0151), offers about 300 different cruises a year and provides a cabin mate matching service and a promise of lower supplements based on its bargaining clout. Annual fee to join is $10 per person; $15 per couple.

Travel Companion Exchange (P.O. Box 833, Amityville, NY 11701; (800) 392-1256; (516) 454-0880), offers membership, a matching service, and eight issues of a 40-page newsletter for $99.

The Single Traveler (2849 West Dundee Road, No. 118, Northbrook, IL 60062; tel/fax: (708) 272-6788), is a newsletter that publishes information on special deals, including cruises, for singles.

Finally, watch for specials and find a knowledgeable travel agent to help you. A smart, experienced agent knows which, when, and how cruise lines make special deals for singles and they can often unearth ways that advance purchase and special promotional fares, even though based on double occupancy, can be applied to single travelers.

Other Tips for Sailing Solo   The cruise industry is working hard to get a handle on the singles market but still has a long way to go. If you have romantic inclinations, the probability of finding love at sea varies according to age group. Twenty-somethings should look to the Caribbean on cruise lines like Carnival that target a younger market. Even on these lines, however, the mean passenger age will be above 35.

When you sail alone but want to meet people, be sure to participate in activities, shore excursions, sports. That's the best and easiest way to make new friends. Small ships generally are preferable to large ones because it is easier to mix and the staff takes greater care to ensure that you are part of the ship's social life.

Among small ships, adventure and educational cruises are your best choice; a camaraderie develops quickly among passengers who share a common interest and a certain sense of adventure. For single women, the number of unattached men is likely to be higher than on traditional cruises.

If you're a 40-something or older single woman who loves to dance, take a cruise on a ship with gentlemen hosts—single males, age 50 or older, who act as hosts to dine and dance with all unattached women—no favoritism or hanky-panky allowed. Crystal, Cunard, Delta Queen, Holland America, and Royal Olympic Cruises have them.

Four times annually, Windjammer Barefoot Cruises offers singles cruises. The cruise line all but guarantees a 50–50 break of males and females. It says nothing about ages and does get them all. You also do not get a break on the price—the single supplement is 150 percent—unless you are willing to share.

Another common complaint we hear from single cruisers concerns table assignment in the dining room, and the complaints run both ways. Some singles are discontent because the cruise line has plunked them down with a bunch of married folks. Others are annoyed because they have been seated at a table with other singles and resent the cruise line playing matchmaker. Though the adequacy of the response varies from line to line, your best bet is to submit an advance written request to the line specifically stating your preference in dining companionship. Once on board, if you are disenchanted with your table mates, ask the maître d' to move you.

Honeymooners

If there is a better honeymoon option than a cruise, we can't think of it. There is nothing more romantic than balmy nights and warm sunny days under a Caribbean or Mediterranean sky. Though some prospective honeymooners are concerned about being interned with a legion of regimented strangers, nothing could be further from reality. Your cabin is your honeymoon suite; on most ships it comes with complimentary room service, so you never have to leave unless you want to. You can forget the car, unpack only once, and still visit a number of exotic places. Many cruise lines (with advance notice) will provide you a cozy table for two in the dining room. Even if you do not request a private table, let the cruise line know you are newlyweds. You will probably get some preferential treatment, a bottle of champagne, flowers in the room, a souvenir photo, or even a cabin upgrade.

If you are contemplating a cruise honeymoon, there are a few things you might want to look for. Because most weddings are on Saturday, cruises offering Sunday or Monday departures make for easier logistics. If a private table is important, you should check with the cruise line prior to booking. Some cruise lines do not offer private tables. Check on the availability of bathtubs versus showers if that is important, and finally, make sure that room service is available at all three meals and that there is a full menu from which to choose. Most cruise lines offer room service, but the room service menus are often limited.

Nonambulatory Disabled Passengers

Many people who must use a wheelchair or other physically limiting aids have been able to discover the pleasures of cruising firsthand. Because getting around the ship is such an integral part of the experience, however, you need to be very direct and specific when exploring your options. Many ships have dining rooms, showrooms, public restrooms, or some combination of the foregoing that are not wheelchair accessible. On a few small ships there are no elevators; on others, particularly older ships, the elevators do not service every deck. Most ships require you to bring your own wheelchair. Many ships require that you use a collapsible wheelchair or one that's narrow gauge. Do not count on a lot of wheelchair accessible facilities, least of all passenger cabins. On the most wheelchair accessible ships afloat, no more than two dozen cabins will have wheelchair accessible bathrooms. There is usually no way, incidentally, to get a wheelchair into the bathroom of a regular cabin. If you need the special cabin, plan to book well in advance. If you can get around a little without a wheelchair, check out the tips for the partially nonambulatory disabled below.

If you need to get around in a wheelchair, you will have to depend heavily on the ship's elevators. What you want, therefore, is a ship that has a lot of elevators relative to its complement of passengers. Divide the number of passengers by the number of elevators. The lower the calculated number, the less time you will spend waiting for elevators, all other things being equal.

It is important that you book your cruise through an agency that specializes in travel for the handicapped, or at least has some experience in the field, to get some recommendations from them based on their experience. In this book under each cruise line's Standard Features and cruise ship's Cabin Specifications we have listed the number of wheelchair accessible cabins available. Two references with valuable information are *Wheels and Waves* by Genie and George Aroyan (1993; Wheels Aweigh, 17105 San Carlos Boulevard, Suite A-6107, Ft. Myers Beach, FL 33931) and *Travel Agent Guide to Wheelchair Cruise Travel* by Bill Cushing (1993; TAG Publishing, P.O. Box 1046, Camarillo, CA 93011).

If you power your own wheelchair, as opposed to being pushed by a companion, bring along something to extend your reach while seated. A rubber-tipped pointer like teachers use is good, a collapsible one is ideal. You will need the pointer to reach buttons in the elevator, some light switches, and the like. Likewise, and even in some wheelchair accessible rooms, you will not be able to reach the hanging rod in your closet or some of the higher level storage space without either human help or a prosthetic device that extends your reach.

Make sure that dining rooms, rest rooms, showrooms, lounges, promenade decks, and the pool areas are wheelchair accessible. Determine whether the gangways are wheelchair accessible at all ports of call. If tenders are used, will you be able to board them in a wheelchair? In the dining room, will your table accommodate your wheelchair, or must you shift to a regular chair? If you cannot make the shift yourself, must you have a companion to assist you, or are crew members allowed to assist? How about in your cabin and elsewhere on the ship, in what way may they assist? Will the cruise line require that you sign a medical waiver? Does the line require special documentation from your physician to make a wheelchair accessible cabin available to you? Does it require that you travel with a companion assistant?

No matter how dependable your travel agent is, call the cruise line and double check all of the important arrangements yourself. Finally, the Society for the Advancement of Travel for the Handicapped, (202) 966-3900, in Washington, D.C., serves as an information clearinghouse for disabled travelers.

Partially Ambulatory Disabled

If you use a wheelchair sometimes, but you can walk a little way, you will do fine on most cruise ships large enough to have elevators. You will be able to get around your cabin and into the bathroom on foot. A collapsible wheelchair will enable you to cover the longer distances, say from your cabin to the dining room or showroom. Crutches are pretty iffy on cruise ships, and although walkers are somewhat better, the safest way to get around for the partially nonambulatory is in a wheelchair.

Larger ships, over 22,000 gross tons say, will have wide passageways, spacious public areas, and in all probability, an adequate number of elevators. Smaller ships often have tight passageways, steep stairs, and sometimes no elevators. Older vessels may have bulkhead doors with raised thresholds to negotiate, blocked passageways with steps to the next level, and no elevator access to some decks.

When choosing a cabin, try to get one near the elevators. We also recommend that you book a cabin with a shower (with a metal chair or stool to sit on); many bathtubs on ships are higher/deeper than those we use at home. Most cabins' baths are equipped with sturdy hand grips, but it's always wise to ask.

Depending on your situation, you might want to consider booking an itinerary that cruises primarily on calmer water, like an Inside Passage itinerary to Alaska, or a Mississippi River cruise. If you do cruise on the open sea, cabins situated on lower decks in the center of the vessel are the least susceptible to the motion of the ocean.

Passengers with Sight and/or Hearing Impairments

Many people with sight and/or hearing impairments enjoy cruising. Most travel with a nondisabled companion. Regardless of the presence of a companion, be sure to inform your cabin steward of your disability. In the event of a critical alarm or message, or an emergency situation, he should be instructed to check your cabin immediately to make sure your companion is with you, and to render whatever assistance is required if your companion is absent. If you are hearing impaired and cannot hear a knock at the door, your steward should be given permission, in the event of an emergency, to enter if there is no response to his knock.

Passengers with Diet Restrictions

Diet restrictions usually do not pose a problem on cruise ships. The galley will prepare special meals to your specification and serve them to you at regularly scheduled seatings in the dining room. Orthodox practitioners of religions that mandate verification that a meal is prepared in a certain way should ascertain from the cruise line whether such verification will be possible. All cruise lines request advance notice—two to three weeks—for specific needs. Under the cruise lines' Standard Features, we have provided this information. Also, there is usually a paragraph in the fine print of a cruise line's brochure detailing procedures to follow.

Families with Younger Children

Though some cruise lines are equipped to handle younger children, we do not recommend cruising for kids under five years of age. Cruise lines that really want family business advertise that fact. If you have young children and want them to enjoy the cruise, but do not necessarily want to tend them 24 hours a day yourself, book with a cruise line that specializes in family cruises. Ships from these lines will have special play areas, supervised activities, and sometimes a separate swimming pool for children. Best of all, the chaperoned children's program provides a welcome respite from parenting for mom and dad.

If, however, your rich Aunt Hattie wants to treat you and your nippers to a luxury cruise, don't decline because the ship doesn't have any photos of kids in its promotional brochure. For a variety of reasons, little ones end up on essentially adult cruises and fare reasonably well. While adult cruises will not have a lot of planned activities (perhaps none) for children, your children will revel in the adventure of being at sea.

Usually, however, the children's center will be a sort of sea-going day care or in-cabin baby-sitting. If both in-cabin baby-sitting and room service (or informal dining options) for all meals are available, you've got it made. Sign up for the second seating in the dining room, or if there is only one seating, go late. Let the little ones enjoy room service in the cabin or take them to the buffet or informal dining area. All fed and scrubbed, turn the munchkins over to the sitter as you head for the dining room. Of course, you can take your children to the dining room, but if they are six or under, you may not want to try it more than once.

If your ship has a children's program, your kids will be on the go all the time, if you're lucky, that is. Some children, to their parent's surprise, seriously balk at being dispatched to the children's center. First, they don't know any of these strange kids; second, they've decided to be your little companion for the duration of the cruise. We've seen children who scarcely countenance their parents' presence at home become mom and dad's shadow on a cruise. If you do not want your child permanently

Cruising for Children

This chart includes only those cruise lines with facilities for children; for details, see the cruise line's profile in Part Two. Many cruise lines not included on this chart accept children and offer cruises as appropriate for them as those on the chart, but they have no special facilities for children. Also, note that age limits vary from "no age restriction" to "no children under age 18 permitted." Always check with the cruise line before making plans.

(A) Varies by destination
(R) Reduced third or fourth berth rate, regardless of age
(S) Seasonally
* Varies with ship, consult cruise line
** Under age 10 not permitted

Cruise Line	Age Limit for Child Discount	Air/Sea Rate**	Baby-Sitting Avail.	Special Shore Excursions	Teen Center/ Disco	Playroom/ Youth Center	Youth Counselors
Abercrombie & Kent	(R)	Yes	Some	Yes	No	No	Some
American Canadian Caribbean Line	No disc.	Yes	No	Some	No	No	Some
American Hawaii	18	Yes	Yes	No	Yes	Yes	Yes
Carnival	(R)	Yes	Yes	Some	Some	Yes	Yes
Celebrity	12	Yes	Yes	Yes	Some	Yes	(S)
Commodore	(R)	Yes	Yes	Some	Yes	Some	Some
Costa	No*	Yes	Yes	Some	Yes	Some	Yes
Crystal	12	Yes	Yes	No	Yes	Yes	Yes
Cunard	*	Some	Yes	(S)	Some	Some	Some
Delta Queen	16	Yes	No	No	No	No	No
Disney	NA	Yes	Yes	Yes	Yes	Yes	Yes
Dolphin	12	Yes	Yes	No	Yes	Yes	Yes
Holland America	12	Some	Yes	Some	No	Some	(S)
Majesty	12	Yes	Yes	No	Yes	Yes	NA
Norwegian	(R)	Yes	Yes	Some	Yes	Yes	Yes
Premier Cruise Lines	(R)	Yes	Yes	No	Yes	Yes	Yes
Princess	(R)	No	Yes	Some	Some	Some	(S)
P&O Lines	NA	NA	Yes	NA	Some	Yes	Yes
Royal Caribbean	(R)	Yes	Yes	(S)	Most	Most	Yes
Royal Olympic	12	Yes	Yes	No	(S)	(S)	(S)
Seawind	NA	Yes	Yes	No	(S)	Yes	(S)

attached to you at the hip, you had better get some understanding and agreement before you leave home. Explain how things work, negotiating what time you will spend together and what time you will spend apart. If your children are too young to negotiate deals and enter into family contracts, save the family cruise for another year. If you don't reach an understanding, but still want to take little Ned on a cruise, your only recourse is to plug him into the kids' program as soon as possible and hope he likes it better than hanging out with you.

A word about accommodations: cruise ship cabins are a lot more confining than children's homes, or even most bedrooms for that matter. Your kids will size up your cabin in about ten seconds and figure that there is not much to do there. From that point, they will be obsessed with getting out the door and running loose around the ship. You need to anticipate this response. Set limits with your kids in advance about bedtime, naps, private time for mom and dad, meals, and the plan for each day. Also, while some cruise ships have TVs in the cabins, many do not. When there is a TV, the programming is usually limited to a news channel, some movies, and a channel featuring information about the ship and shore excursions. Therefore, you should bring along some games, books, and toys to keep the children reasonably content when they are in the cabin.

If you can afford it, putting the children in an adjoining cabin is much better than cramming them in with you. This may not be as great an expense as you think, because of airfare. If you get the kids their own cabin, the cruise line will pay for airfare as part of the package. If you elect to bunk the young ones in your cabin, you have to buy their airfare as an "add-on." A few cruise lines (those that have family, i.e, connecting cabins) will even give you a break on a second cabin, especially during the low seasons.

Families with Teens

Teens think cruising is cool and may enjoy everything the ship has to offer except the casino and some lounges. On some ships, teens are even allowed in the disco and other adult areas if they are accompanied by their parents. Ships oriented to families or to the broader market often have designated clubs where the teens can dance and arcades where they can play Ping-Pong, pool, or electronic games. All in all, teens do pretty well on cruise ships. They are old enough to move around the ship without constant supervision, will definitely eat their money's worth of food, and have new experiences they will be telling their friends back home about for the next year.

Television addicted kids should forget about going on a cruise. A cruise is a totally new environment for children—some embrace it with gusto, eager to learn, to find every nook and cranny—others are intimidated and need help. For the right kids, however, it's a fabulous, fun, learning experience.

Because teens can be messy and tend to spend hours in the bathroom, we double our recommendation that you get them their own cabin if you can afford it.

When it comes to teens, anticipation is the name of the game. As with younger kids, do your negotiating and set your limits before you leave home. Finally, though we believe teens are safe on their own on the boat, we suggest you keep them under tight rein when you go ashore. If this is your first cruise and you have any qualms about taking the kids, try going without them first to size up the matter firsthand. They and you might enjoy it more if you are familiar with the territory.

We have included in both the Cruise Line Standard Features and the cruise ship profiles a special section on children's facilities. These references are a start. You may also want to consult Traveling with Your Children (80 8th Avenue, New York, NY 10011; (212) 206-0688), an organization that publishes an annual cruise line report with details down to the last playpen and high chair on all major cruise lines.

Shopping for and Booking Your Cruise

GATHERING INFORMATION

Now that you have more or less outlined your requirements and preferences, the next step is to compare these against the profiles of the cruise lines and cruise ships described in this big, fat book. After you have identified several cruise lines from the profiles that seem to meet your needs, obtain a copy of their respective promotional brochures. Promotional brochures can be obtained from the cruise lines directly by calling or writing, using the phone numbers and addresses listed in the line profiles, or from a travel agent.

A travel agent who specializes in cruises, or who at least sells cruises routinely, can be a good source of information. Many travel agents have cruised extensively themselves and can provide firsthand information about different ships and lines. Also, many travel agents are willing to put you in touch with other clients who will share their thoughts and opinions. Always understand, however, that from a self-interest perspective, it is the cruise line that pays the travel agent a commission on every cruise the agent sells.

In addition to obtaining promotional material from the cruise lines and travel agents, buy several Sunday papers: (1) a newspaper in a primary geographic market for the cruise industry, such as New York, Chicago, Dallas, or Los Angeles, (2) your local paper, and (3) the paper of the largest city within 200 miles of your home. If you live in Louisville, for example, you would buy a St. Louis or Cincinnati newspaper. Reading the travel sections in these papers will give you a good sense of where the deals are. If you live in a medium-sized city like Charlotte, North Carolina, you may uncover cruise deals in the New York or Atlanta paper that beat the socks off anything offered in your local paper.

Finally, here are a number of magazines, periodicals, and Internet sites that you may find helpful:

Cruise Critic/America Online is written and hosted by Anne Campbell, former author of *Fielding's Guide to Worldwide Cruises* and a veteran cruise writer. There are candid ship reviews based on firsthand experience by a team of writers, information on cruise lines, news updates almost daily, information on cruise promotions and best deals, a weekly chat room, and, as she describes them, her own "thoroughly biased" personal recommendations. It also has a new Ports of Call feature by this book's author, Kay Showker. The site is accessed in America Online with the keyword Cruise Critic.

Cruise Week is a weekly cruise industry newsletter which subscribers can receive by fax or e-mail, produced by a knowledgeable editor who has reported on the industry for many years. While it is directed primarily to the industry, consumers who are interested in keeping up with the news about cruising will find it a timely resource. Annual subscription: $99. Write to Lehman Publishing Co., 910 Deer Spring Lane, Wilmington, NC 28409 or call (800) 593-8252; fax: (910) 790-3976; Internet: CruzWeek@worldnet.att.net.

Cruise Reports offers evaluations and firsthand comments on ships by travel agents who have recently cruised on them. The annual subscription rate is $32 for six issues. Write to 88 Main St., Suite 453, Mendham, NJ 07945 or call (201) 605-2442.

Cruise Travel is a magazine completely dedicated to cruising. Though it is unabashedly rah-rah cruising, and critical content is nonexistent, it is nevertheless a good source of information. Its six issues a year also contain ads from dozens of cruise discounters, consolidators, and cruise specialty travel agents. Subscriptions run about $20 a year in the United States, $21 in Canada. Write to P.O. Box 342, Mt. Morris, IL 61054 or call (800) 877-5893.

Ocean & Cruise News reports on cruise industry news and reviews a different ship in each issue. It runs a highly touted, much publicized annual evaluation of cruise lines and cruise ships based on subscribers' votes, which tend to reflect seasoned cruisers' preferences for certain established lines such as Holland America Lines. Write to P.O. Box 92, Stamford, CT 06904 or call (203) 329-2787.

Porthole is a reincarnation of an earlier magazine that was geared to ship buffs. In its new sleek, glossy format, it is by far the most attractive and lively of the magazine on cruises and features a wide range of interesting articles on topics related to cruising by a stable of knowledgeable writers. There is some critiquing. Annual subscription, $19.85. Write to Panoff Publishing Co., 7100 West Commercial Blvd., Suite 106, Ft. Lauderdale, FL 33319-2124 or call (800) 776-PORT; (954) 746-5554; fax: (954) 746-5244.

HOW TO READ A CRUISE LINE BROCHURE

You may be surprised to discover that cruise brochures are very elaborate booklets as opposed to the small hotel brochures that fill the rack at the Holiday Inn. Because cruise brochures contain so much information, we thought we might suggest a systematic approach to evaluating their contents.

Look at the Pictures

Flip through the brochure and look at the pictures. All of the photos have been *carefully* chosen to excite the kind of people for whom the cruise line tailors its product. If the photos grab you, and you identify with the activities depicted, this may be a good cruise line for you. Don't forget to pay attention to the ages of the people in the photos.

Sizing up the Ships

Look at the ships. Are they too big, too small, just about right, or you don't care as long as they float. Most brochures contain a deck-by-deck schematic of the ship. Bypass for the moment any consideration of cabins and concentrate on the layout of the ship, looking for features that may be important to you. If you like to work out, look at the relative size of the exercise room and try to find a photo of it so you can check out the types of equipment. If you have problems walking, make sure the ship has elevators. Because the best views at sea are from the upper decks, pay attention to public areas, both inside and outdoors, particularly on the top two decks and the Promenade deck.

Itineraries

Scrutinize the cruise line's itineraries, making some preliminary selections concerning where and how long you want to cruise. On what days of the week, and at what times does the cruise begin and end? Are these days and times workable for you? Having narrowed things down to a couple of specific cruises, read over the itineraries, observing how much time the ship spends at sea versus time in port. Note also how much of the time at sea occurs during waking hours versus at night. Look at the ports of call. Are there enough ports of call to suit you, or too many, or too few? Is the amount of time allocated for each port adequate, or too short, or too long?

For practice, let's take a look at a Crystal *Harmony* ten-day itinerary from Copenhagen to London/Tilbury.

Day	Date	Port	Arrive	Depart
Sunday	June 4	Copenhagen		6 P.M.
Monday	June 5	Baltic Sea	Cruising	
Tuesday	June 6	Helsinki	8 A.M.	6 P.M.
Wednesday	June 7	St. Petersburg	8 A.M.	
Thursday	June 8	St. Petersburg		6 P.M.
Friday	June 9	Stockholm	4 P.M.	
Saturday	June 10	Stockholm		3 P.M.
Sunday	June 11	Cruising		
Monday	June 12	Oslo	8 A.M.	5 P.M.
Tuesday	June 13	Cruising		
Wednesday	June 14	London/Tilbury	7 A.M.	

The cruise sails at 6 P.M. on a Sunday. This departure timing allows several options. Because most flights from the United States to Europe depart in the late afternoon and evening, you could (if you live in the eastern United States) work most or all of Friday and catch an evening flight to Copenhagen arriving on Saturday morning. You would have most of Saturday and until about 3:30 P.M. Sunday to rest and see Copenhagen. Alternatively, you could fly out Saturday evening and arrive in Copenhagen on Sunday morning with about four or five hours at your disposal before you board. A third possibility, of course, would be to arrive before Saturday and enjoy a more leisurely weekend. The first day at sea is a wonderful start as it gives you a chance to catch up on jet lag and become familiar with the ship.

This cruise calls on four ports, not counting ports of origination and termination. This is fewer than average for a ten-day cruise, but all of the ports are major cities. Crystal gives you a lot of time in each port. In St. Petersburg and Stockholm, you actually remain in port at dock overnight. If you are interested in St. Petersburg and Stockholm, this will work out well. If not, it is a long time to spend in port. Crystal also gives you pretty much full days (8 A.M. to 5 or 6 P.M.) in Helsinki and Oslo. To be very precise, the total cruise is 229 hours, of which you will spend 153 hours (67 percent) at sea and 76 hours (33 percent) in port. However, note that only 71 hours of the 153 hours spent at sea will be during daylight waking hours (between 7 A.M. and 10 P.M., for our purposes).

Rates

Flip to the rate charts in order to determine whether the cruises you like fall roughly within your budget. We do mean roughly: almost nobody pays the brochure rates. About the only thing brochure rates are good for is to provide a base figure for calculating discounts. We list the discounts available and tell you how to get them in the section titled How to Get the Best Deal on a Cruise.

Most cruise lines present their fares in a compact little chart like the one presented below for Royal Caribbean International Cruise Line's *Rhapsody of the Seas'* seven-night southern Caribbean itinerary.

The fares presented are per person based on two persons sharing a cabin (double occupancy). If the per person fare for a cabin on Main Deck, Category F, in Winter/Spring is $1,749, then you and your spouse or companion would pay a total of $3,498 ($1,749 × 2) for the cabin.

If you want to leave your significant other at home and get away by yourself, you will have to pay a singles supplement for the privilege of having the cabin to yourself. For this particular cabin Royal Caribbean charges 200 percent of the double occupancy rate. Because you definitely will not eat as much by yourself as the two of you together could eat, this policy seems a little extreme. Be that as it may, almost all cruise lines exact some sort of singles supplement. (See Singles, pages 62–66 for rate explanation.)

As many as four, sometimes five, persons may share a cabin depending upon the cabin configuration. Rates for the third, fourth, and fifth persons in a room are deeply discounted, sometimes as much as 66 percent off the regular double occupancy fare. Let's say that Tom, Ed, John, and Earl are willing to share a "B" Deck, Category I cabin that goes for $1,599 per person double occupancy. The cruise line will charge the double occupancy price ($1,599) for two of the four men, and the third/fourth person rate of $699 for the remaining two. Thus, the tab for all four would be as follows:

Person 1	$1,599	Cruise Only
Person 2	$1,599	Cruise Only
Person 3	$699	Cruise Only
Person 4	$699	Cruise Only
TOTAL	$4,596	

Rhapsody of the Seas *Rate Chart*

Holiday cruises—add $250 to special holiday cruises. Single Guarantee Program guests add $500.

Cat.	Deck	Description	Base	Season
R	Bridge	Royal Suite, King/Queen	$4299	$4399
A	Bridge	Owner's Suite, 2 Queens	3399	3499
AA	Bridge	Royal Family Suite, Accommodates 8 people	3399	3499
B	Bridge	Grand Ocean View Suite, 2 Twins	3099	3199
C	Bridge	Superior Ocean View Suite, 2 Twins	2499	2599
D	Commodore	Superior Ocean View Stateroom, 2 Twins	2099	2199
E	Main, A, and B	Family Stateroom, Accommodates 6 people/Ocean View	1799	1899
F	Main	Larger Stateroom, Ocean View/2 Twins	1749	1849
H	A	Larger Stateroom, Ocean View/2 Twins	1649	1749
I	B	Larger Stateroom, Ocean View/2 Twins	1599	1699
J	Bridge	Superior Stateroom, Inside	1549	1649
K	Bridge, Commodore, Main	Larger Stateroom, Inside	1499	1599
L	A, B	Larger Stateroom, Inside	1449	1549
M	Bridge, Commodore, Main	Stateroom, Inside	1399	1499
N	A, B	Stateroom, Inside	1349	1449
O	A	Stateroom, Inside	1299	1399
P	A	Stateroom, Inside	1249	1349
Q	B	Stateroom, Inside	1199	1299
S		Single Guarantee Program (provides single occupancy of staterooms—assigned at Royal Caribbean's discretion*)	1799	1949
SH		Special Share Program (pairs you with a person of same sex and smoking preference)	1199	1299
Third & Fourth Person			699	699

Accommodations in categories R–D have a private bathroom, vanity area, closed circuit TV, radio, and phone.

Accommodations in categories E–Q have two twin beds that convert to a queen-size, private bathroom, vanity area, closed circuit TV, radio, and phone.

Rates include port charges. Air transportation and certain taxes and fees ($6.50–12.50 per person per cruise) are additional.

All rates quoted in U.S. dollars, per person, double occupancy.

* Passengers traveling alone who want to select specific accommodations will be charged 150% of the double occupancy price for categories O, P, and Q and 200% for all others.

Length: 915'• Beam: 105.6'• Draft: 25'• Gross tonnage: 75,000 tons • Passenger capacity: 2,000 double occupancy • Total staff: 765 • Cruising speed: 22 knots

† Stateroom has third and fourth
Pullman berth available.

△ Family staterooms can accommodate
six persons.

‡ Connecting staterooms have a chair
instead of a sofa.

⚓ Indicates accessible staterooms.

Categories M-Q have sitting areas with
sofa or chair.

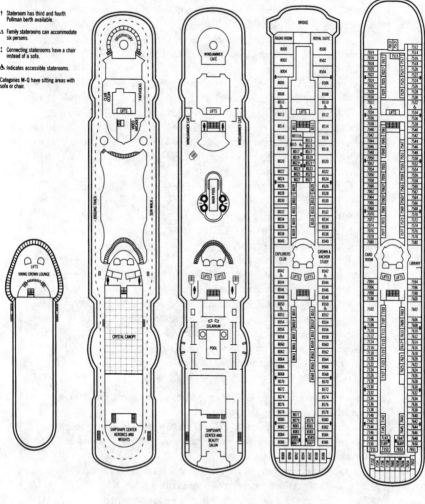

Viking Crown Deck	Compass Deck	Sun Deck	Bridge Deck	Commodore Deck

Royal Caribbean International

RHAPSODY OF THE SEAS℠

Mariner Deck

BROADWAY MELODIES THEATER UPPER LEVEL

LIFTS

GIFTS & SHOP

FASHION & FORMAL

LOGO SOUVENIR

PERFUME

PHOTO SHOP

PHOTO GALLERY

CENTRUM BALCONY

LIFTS

MOONLIGHT BAY LOUNGE

CONFERENCE CENTER

SCHOONER BAR

SHALL WE DANCE LOUNGE

Promenade Deck

BROADWAY MELODIES THEATER

LIFTS

CASINO ROYALE

PURSER'S & SHORE EXCURSION DESKS

CHAMPAGNE BAR

MAIN ENTRANCE

LIFTS

EDELWEISS DINING ROOM

Main Deck

LIFTS

CHAMPAGNE BAR

MAIN ENTRANCE

LIFTS

EDELWEISS DINING ROOM

"A" Deck

LIFTS

LIFTS

"B" Deck

LIFTS

LIFTS

81

Usually, for cruise lines that bundle airfare to the port into the total price of the cruise, the air is normally included only for the two persons paying the double occupancy rate. The cruise line will arrange air, often at a discounted rate, for the third and fourth persons.

If Tom, Ed, John, and Earl want to split the cost of their Royal Caribbean cruise equally, here's the way the finances average out:

Cruise Fare for All Four Guys $4,596
Final Cost Per Person   ($4,596/4) = $1,149

Because most cabins are small with particularly tiny bathrooms and limited closet space, we do not recommend cruising with more than two persons in a cabin unless you have no other choice from a budgetary point of view. If, however, you elect to cruise with extra persons in your cabin, select your roommates with care. Make sure everyone is compatible when it comes to smoking, snoring, bedtimes, and waking times. Most of all, be tolerant and bring along your sense of humor. Start with a cruise in a warm clime so that you can spend more time on deck. Indeed, one reason a cabin on a Caribbean or Mexico cruise is much less significant than in an area of inclement weather relates directly to the amount of time you are likely to spend in your cabin. In the Caribbean, you do little more than sleep and change clothes in your cabin, particularly when it's your first cruise. Finally, pack light.

To repeat, the rates listed in the cruise line's brochure represent the official price, also known as the list price, the rack rate, or the brochure rate. Whatever you call it, it is the highest rate and serves as the base rate from which discounts and special deals are calculated. You should anticipate paying 25–45 percent less depending upon the cruise line, ship, itinerary, time of the year, and general condition of the market. We have much more to say about this later in this section.

Sailing Dates

Next check the sailing dates for the cruises that interest you, making sure that at least some of the dates are compatible with your schedule. But also check the dates around it to see if a slight shift puts you into a lower priced season.

Cabin Category and Ship Deck Plans

Now it's time to look at the different types of cabins available. Many brochures feature a floor plan for several types of cabins showing the size and configuration of the cabin and bath, as well as the placement of the furniture and fixtures. Likewise, some brochures provide color photographs of the different types of cabins.

Though some upscale cruise lines offer only suites, most ships provide a varied choice of cabins. The top of the line and usually on the top decks is the owner's suite or royal suite, generally a palatial affair comparable to the presidential suite in a good hotel with a price that will leave you numb. Next come a small number of one- (or two-) bedroom suites, followed by a somewhat larger number of mini- or demisuites. Suites, particularly on newer ships, often have verandas. Moving down from these deluxe accommodations, you get to the standard cabins, which account for 85 percent or so of the berths on most ships. For most people, outside standard cabins with a window are more desirable (but more expensive) than inside standard cabins without windows.

Standard cabins on the higher decks are considered more desirable because of their lofty view (if an outside cabin) and their proximity to the pool deck (often known as the Lido Deck) and other key public areas. When it comes to cabin price, usually the higher the deck the higher the rate.

Standard cabins on the upper decks on ships built since about 1988 sometimes have special features like private verandas or larger windows, though the size and appointments of standard cabins generally remain the same throughout the ship. As you move down from deck to deck, windows often are smaller. Though the Royal Caribbean International chart does not specify how large the window is or whether or not the view is obstructed, this information regarding obstructions is provided on the rate chart of most lines and should result in the lower-deck cabins having a lower price.

Cabins situated toward the middle of the ship are normally considered more desirable than cabins on either end, because center cabins are closer to stairs and elevators as well as being less affected by the back and forward (pitching) motion of the ship. The side to side (rolling) motion is more pronounced the higher you go and felt least on the lower decks. If you are prone to motion sickness, the most stable cabins of all are located at the water line near the center of the lower passenger decks. But the fact is that on large cruise ships these days, you will feel very little motion of the sea, except perhaps on the highest decks and if you really love the idea of the sea air wafting over you while you sleep, consider a cabin with a veranda. It's a very special treat and worth every dollar.

Before selecting a cabin category, however, you need to acquaint yourself with the deck plan of the ship. Normally, the schematic is, more or less, to scale and is color coded according to cabin category. Relating the Royal Caribbean rate chart above to the ship schematic for the *Rhapsody of the Seas*, you discover that the most expensive accommodations are on the Bridge Deck, the fourth highest of ten decks. The cabins are centrally located mini-suites with verandas, and the Bridge Deck is removed from the sounds of the galley, engines, lounges, pool area, and showroom.

Other things to check on the ship deck plans are the locations of decks where passengers walk or jog. Avoid cabins situated beneath jogging tracks or promenades. Similarly, avoid cabins where the window looks out onto a track or walkway. Pinpoint the location of lounges, showrooms, the casino, discos, and other potentially noisy, late night public areas. Avoid cabins either directly above or below these facilities. Also be aware that engine noise is sometimes audible in lower deck cabins located toward the stern. It should be pointed out that even veteran cruisers have difficulty gleaning much of this information from a deck plan. All of this, however, can be checked out by your travel agent when you book.

Always look at what you get for a few dollars more or a few dollars less in terms of cabin location. In the chart above, for example, you can get an outside cabin on the "B" Deck for only $50 more than an inside cabin on the higher Bridge Deck.

A PRELIMINARY LOOK AT DISCOUNTS AND INCENTIVES

By this stage in the game, you should know whether or not you are interested in a cruise offered in the brochure you are reading. If you see something you like, the next step is to check out the cruise line's price incentives and discounts.

Though the cruise market continues to grow, supply (defined as the number of ships and the number of cabins) has historically run several years ahead of demand. In other words, there are more cabins to fill than people to fill them. With an additional 40,000 cabins coming on line over the next several years, the market has become increasingly competitive, and the cruise lines are having to cut a lot of deals to keep their ships filled. Until demand catches up with supply, a buyer's market will prevail.

Price incentives and discounts offered in the cruise line's brochure come in an assortment of sizes and packages. First, the cruise line divides its calendar into seasons based on levels of demand, weather, known travel patterns, and other circumstances that generate that

PRINCESS CRUISES 🌊

MINI-SUITE WITH PRIVATE BALCONY

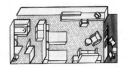

(Category A)

Large bedroom with twin beds, which make up into a comfortable queen-size bed. Sitting room area and private balcony for entertaining. TV. Spacious closets. Refrigerator. Bath with tub and shower.

OUTSIDE DOUBLE WITH PRIVATE
BALCONY

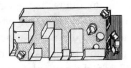

(Categories BA, BB, and BD)

Two lower beds, which make up into a comfortable queen-size bed. TV. Spacious closet. Refrigerator.

OUTSIDE OR INSIDE DOUBLE

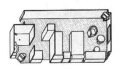

(Categories CC, C, D, EE, E, FF, F,
GG, G, H, I, J, K, L, and M)

Outside staterooms have a picture window. Two lower beds, which make up into a comfortable queen-size bed. Many staterooms with two upper berths. TV. Spacious closet. Refrigerator. GG has a queen-size bed. G has one lower bed and one upper berth, and portholes.

demand. You have probably surmised that high season is the most expensive, followed by shoulder season, and then low season. What you save, however, by cruising in low season as opposed to high season is not all that great for most lines, judging strictly from the published brochure price. In general, if you cruise in shoulder season, you will save 3–6 percent from high season rates. If you cruise in low season, your savings will be in the 6 percent to 10 percent range.

The most important point to make here is that the high, low, or shoulder season fares published in the brochure serves as the base fares to which additional discounts are applied. If you cruise during low season, for example, your base fare will be 6–10 percent below the high season fare. Using this base fare, other discounts can usually be had, driving the cost of your cruise lower still. Also, remember from our previous discussion that the ship will be less crowded and cabin upgrades more readily available during low and shoulder seasons.

After scoping out seasonal discounts, turn your attention to early booking discounts. As the name implies, cruise lines offer fairly substantial discounts to travelers who are willing to book six months to a year ahead. Early booking allows the cruise line to use your money in advance and provides the line with critical information concerning the likelihood of a particular cruise filling. Early booking incentives are most commonly offered as a deep discount (15–45 percent) off the prevailing seasonal rate, or as a two-for-the-price-of-one deal. Two-for-one deals, incidentally, do not normally include airfare. Either way, the early booking incentives are the largest and most certain of the discounts available from the cruise lines directly. You get other benefits too—the cabin of your choice, the most direct air routing, and your dining room seating preference (if the cruise line bases its policy on a first-come, first-served rule). That's the kind of information available in the fine print or will be known by a knowledgeable and experienced travel agent.

In addition to seasonal and early booking discounts, various cruise lines offer on-board incentives, such as cabin upgrades, some amount of credit for purchases on the ship, receptions with the captain, and the like. Sometimes a couple of nights at a hotel at the origination or termination port are packaged as a booking incentive. Almost all cruise lines offer early bird and other discounts (often up to 50 percent) to repeat passengers. Many discounts, including those offered by the cruise lines as well as those offered by travel agents, wholesalers, and consolidators, never appear in the cruise line's promotional brochure. We will discuss these and other discounts in the section titled How to Get the Best Deal on a Cruise.

ROUND-TRIP AIRFARE

Unless you live within a reasonable drive from the port where your cruise originates, you will require transportation to the port city. Until recently, most, but not all, cruise lines included air transportation cost in your cruise fare and promoted it as "Free Air." But times, they are a' changin' and you need to be aware of these changes because they might make a difference in the bottom-line cost of your cruise.

First, check the rate information in the cruise line's brochure to determine whether or not air transportation is included in the price of the cruise. When a cruise line includes air transportation as part of its overall package, they agree to fly you round trip from certain cities known as gateway cities. While these gateway cities vary from cruise line to cruise line, they usually include all major U.S. and Canadian cities and quite a few smaller cities. If your air transportation is part of the cruise package but your gateway city is especially far from the port, the cruise line may levy an air supplement. The air supplement is an extra charge added to your air-inclusive cruise.

What Happened to "Free" Air?

Until recently, cruise lines touted their air/sea packages as all-inclusive travel that included "free" airfare. Nothing, of course, was ever free. The cruise lines were able to build air transportation cost into the cruise fare and call it "free" because of the dollars they saved by buying seats in bulk. By buying well in advance and in large volume, the cruise lines could negotiate big discounts on airfares. These discounts enabled the cruise lines to offer you a complete vacation package, including air transportation plus the cruise for a good price. Now, however, the traditional air/sea package—a cruise with the air transportation and transfers together in one inclusive price—is an endangered species.

Many cruise brochures published after midsummer 1997 reflect a fundamental change in pricing that is gaining strength throughout the cruise industry. To be specific, more and more cruise lines are publishing their rates as "cruise-only" fares and are selling the air transportation as an "add-on." You have the choice, therefore, of buying air transportation from the cruise line or on your own.

The reason for the change is that marketing conditions have radically reduced the availability and size of discounts airlines give cruise lines. Simply put, demand for air travel has increased and the airlines find that they can fill their planes without offering substantially reduced fares. Today, the only way cruise lines can obtain the discounts required to put together a good air/sea package is to buy the airlines' least attractive itineraries, in other words, those flights with late night departures, circuitous routes, multiple stops, etc. An exception are those luxury cruise lines that continue to offer air inclusive cruise packages. These lines are willing to pay the going rate to ensure that their customers get the most direct and convenient flights.

In a corollary development, passengers have discovered that they can get better airfares on their own. In addition to obtaining better fares and more direct routings, passengers who book their own air have the peace of mind of receiving their tickets well in advance. Often in the air/sea packages, air carriers fail to issue tickets until the last minute (in order to get passengers more equally distributed on available flights). As departure time approaches, this practice makes for panicked cruise passengers wondering where their tickets are.

Another irritant to passengers is that flight itineraries arranged by the cruise lines are not always eligible for frequent flyer mileage. When they are eligible, passengers or travel agents usually have to call the airline and provide their frequent flyer numbers once they have their tickets in hand.

These scenarios and others have created nightmares for the cruise lines, for travel agents and for passengers. Much as they may be reluctant to give up their most successful marketing vehicle—one-price-buys-all—many cruise lines have concluded there's greater benefit in "unbundling" the package than keeping it.

In the "unbundled" cruise package, the price of your air "add-on" is calculated from your gateway city and is always printed in the cruise line's brochure. When you buy the cruise line's air add-on, transfers are included. When you purchase your air transportation on your own (or use your frequent flyer award), you can sometimes buy airport transfers from the cruise lines. Carnival, for example, has both a one-way and round-trip transfer which must be booked 14 days in advance; price varies with location. If such an arrangement is not available, you will need to make your own arrangements. All of this may seem a bit complicated, but the good news is that a travel agent can handle all such details for you—and we advise you to let them, particularly if you are buying your first cruise—so that you still end up paying one inclusive price for a "seamless" package. Note also that despite these new realities, the cruise lines usually have lower add-on fares than you can get on your own. Even so, it's always a good idea to comparison shop; your travel agent might be able to do even better.

When air transportation is included, the cruise line, in conjunction with the airline, will determine your flight time and routing. You can request a particular routing through your travel agent or request a change. Many cruise lines maintain "Air Deviation" desks—that's shorthand for the department that handles requests from cruise passengers who want to deviate from the routing they have been assigned. Cruise lines added this service in recent years to help travel agents deal with the increasing number of passenger complaints about their air routing, which the airlines (not the cruise line) control. It will cost you a fee of $50 to make a change (just as it would if you made a ticket change directly with an airline). And it might cost an additional air supplement if no seats are available in the airfare category designation of your ticket, but you will be told those charges at the time of your request for a change.

If you prefer to arrange (and pay for) your own air transportation when you are buying an inclusive air/sea package, you will be able to deduct some allowance from the cruise fare because you are not using the included air transportation. The amount will be shown at the bottom of the rate sheet as "Cruise Only Travel Allowance." As an example, the allowance is usually about $250 on one-week Caribbean cruises.

Price, however, is not the only consideration in buying the cruise line's "air add-on" deal. When a cruise line arranges your air transportation, they also arrange for your luggage to go directly from the airport to the ship. In other words, once you check your luggage at your home airport, you will not see it again until it is delivered to your cabin aboard ship. Similarly, the cruise line will meet your plane and provide you transportation from the airport to the ship. One of the negatives of booking your own air is that you will have to take care of getting yourself and your luggage from the airport to the ship. After the cruise is over, some—but not all—cruise lines provide the same luggage and transportation service for cruise-only passengers as for air-inclusive passengers.

Sometimes, usually during the busier times of the year, the cruise line may fly you to the port city a day in advance. When this occurs, the cruise line normally provides hotel accommodations. If you live in the western United States, and are sailing from an eastern port, it is possible that the cruise line will fly you to the port city on a red eye (i.e., late night) flight. In this event you will arrive in the port city between midnight and 9 A.M. More considerate cruise lines arrange hotel accommodations known as day rooms for you to rest up before boarding your ship later in the day. Similar arrangements are sometimes made for eastern passengers embarking from the West Coast, and for passengers on European or Asian cruises.

Whenever a cruise line puts you in a hotel room, they assume responsibility for getting you from the hotel to the pier. If you know you will be accommodated in a hotel prior to your cruise, pack everything you are likely to need at the hotel in your carry-on bag as you may not have access to your luggage until after you board your ship.

Air transportation provided by most cruise lines is coach. Seat assignments, boarding passes, and upgrades (when available) must be arranged by you through your travel agent.

If you are cruising during the fall (excluding holiday periods) or during some time of year when airfares are frequently discounted in your city, you may want to consider booking your own air to save money. Also, you might want to buy cruise only if you can reach the port via one of the discount airlines like Southwest. If you can book your own air for the same price as the cruise line's air allowance or for a few dollars more, you will be able to choose your airline, assure yourself of a good flight itinerary, accrue frequent flyer miles, and be comforted in having your airline tickets in hand well before your departure date.

If you elect to go with the cruise line's air-inclusive package or buy air transportation from the cruise line as an add-on, take the following precautions:

1. Call early to reserve. Most cruise lines work on a first-come, first-served basis. Passengers are assigned to the airline seats that have been allocated in the cruise line's bulk purchase agreements with specific airlines. Cruise lines contract for a specific number of plane seats for every cruise—when those seats are filled, the cruise line has to scramble to get additional ones. That's when you are likely to get a circuitous route to your departure port.

But let's put this in its proper perspective. First, the airline crunch comes at holiday times—Labor Day, Thanksgiving, Christmas—and can be exacerbated by bad weather and plane delays. You know this from the outset, so if you are planning a cruise during a holiday period, make your plans early, buy your air from the cruise line and save yourself a pile of headaches. As a veteran travel agent advised, "Passengers should seriously consider taking the air/sea package from the cruise line during the winter months, especially if they are flying from a cold-weather gateway. If there are weather or equipment related delays, the cruise line will help air/sea passengers get to the ship. If passengers have booked their own air, they are on their own if they miss the ship. Passengers who insist on doing their own air would be well advised to purchase third party travel insurance that covers trip interruption, delay or cancellation due to weather, or equipment related problems."

2. Ask your travel agent when you can expect to receive your tickets. Most cruise lines note this in their brochures—it's part of the fine print. If not, your travel agent will know from experience or can find out from the cruise line. The normal period is two to three weeks prior to the cruise departure date. Smaller cruise lines are generally better than the big guys about getting documentation to you early.

3. If you have a particular route you want to fly from your hometown to your cruise departure port, tell your travel agent at the time of booking or as soon as you know so that your plane tickets can be issued properly. If upon receiving your plane tickets, however, you find that you have been routed in a manner that requires airport layovers and a change of planes (rather than a direct flight) you may still have recourse: the Air Deviation desk, as explained above.

Finally, as a memory jog from our previous discussion of third, fourth, and fifth persons sharing a cabin, remember that air transportation for these folks is usually not included in the cruise price. If this is the case, third, fourth, and fifth persons can usually obtain air transportation through the cruise line (often at a good price) or make their own arrangements.

HOW TO GET THE BEST DEAL ON A CRUISE

To get a good deal on a cruise (or anything else), you need to know who the players are and how the game is played. How the game is played in this case is determined in large measure by the unalterable reality that a cruise is a time sensitive product. In other words if a cabin is not sold by the time the ship sails, it loses all of its value. This time sensitivity makes selling cruises like playing Beat the Clock. From the time a cruise is announced, the cruise line is on a countdown to get all the cabins sold. The immense fixed and variable expense of keeping a cruise ship in operation makes the sales countdown a high pressure, big stakes endeavor.

From a consumer perspective, the time sensitivity of cruises is a major plus. Any time a seller is in the position of either making the sale or writing off the inventory (empty cabins in this case), there's going to be some wheeling and dealing, and wheeling and dealing almost always benefits the buyer. However, from the outset, we need to stress, if you allow yourself to be influenced only by "getting the best deal" in choosing a cruise, you are likely to end up on the wrong cruise.

The Players: Cruise Lines

The cruise lines have sales offices and will sell you a cruise directly if you do not want to go through a travel agent. But in fact, you will usually get a better price buying from an agent or one of the other players. Cruise lines, to their credit, are loyal to the travel agents who sell their product and will not undercut the prices available to agents. It's not altruism but realism. Not only do the cruise lines not want to bother, but it would not be cost effective for them. It costs a cruise line far more to maintain sales offices to serve the general public than it does to maintain a sales network through travel agencies that are located in every big city and small hamlet across the country. In fact, to approximate the level of distribution provided by travel agents would be prohibitively expensive. In our opinion, the only time that it is better to deal directly with the cruise line is when you are pier hopping. Pier hopping is the term used to describe showing up at the pier, bags packed and ready to go, and then negotiating with the ship's boarding officer for a walk-on rate for whatever accommodation is available. People who have the time and inclination for pier hopping are few.

The Players: Wholesalers and Consolidators

Sam Walton (Wal-Mart) taught all of America that the more of something you buy, the lower the price should be. Businesspeople call it buying in quantity or volume discounting. In cruising, the volume buyers are travel wholesalers and consolidators. These players, booking well in advance, buy large numbers of cabins on specific cruises with the intention of reselling the cabins at a profit. The combination of advance purchasing and volume discounts, coupled with the fact that the cruise lines do not have to pay commissions, allows wholesalers and consolidators to buy at prices substantially below what an individual could hope to obtain. Some cabins are purchased on a returnable basis, meaning that the wholesaler can return cabins that go unsold to the cruise company by a certain date; other cabins are bought on a nonreturnable basis. In this scenario, the wholesaler or consolidator eats any cabins he is not able to sell. The biggest discount available to any of the players in the cruise market go to wholesalers and consolidators who buy cabins in bulk on a nonreturnable basis. Wholesalers and consolidators sell to travel agents and sometimes, as in the case of the Cruise Line, Inc., of Miami, Florida, directly to consumers. If the wholesaler sells a cruise through a travel agency, the wholesaler pays the agent a commission.

However, some cruise lines refuse to turn over their inventories to these middlemen. You should also note that most cruise lines that deal with wholesalers and consolidators are generally lines with large ships, or at best, they promote and offer the best deals on a limited number of ships. At the same time, wholesalers and consolidators focus on a limited number of cruise lines. If they spread themselves too thin over the broad spectrum of cruises, they diminish their clout with specific lines. Keep in mind, it is in the wholesaler's or consolidator's interest to steer you to the ships where they get the best deal. That may or may not be in your best interest.

The Players: Travel Agents

Over 95 percent of all cruises are sold by travel agents. As the name implies, travel agents act as sales representatives of the cruise lines. Unlike wholesalers and consolidators, travel agents do not actually buy cabins, but rather sell from the cruise line's inventory on commission. Like cruise lines and wholesalers, however, travel agents make the most money when they sell in volume.

Some full-service travel agencies specialize in selling cruises while others are cruise-only agencies, meaning that they sell nothing but cruises and cruise-related travel. These latter sell so many cabins for certain cruise lines that they earn what are known in the trade as override commissions. An override commission is like compound interest: it is a commission on a commission. There is usually a minimum volume threshold. Up to the threshold the agency receives the normal travel agent's commission. Once the threshold (in dollar volume sold) is reached, the override kicks in. General travel agencies and independent agencies are able to cash in on the override commissions by joining a consortium, a group of travel agencies that pool their sales to take advantage of the overrides.

Travel agents accrue commissions and overrides in much the same way as airline passengers accumulate frequent flyer miles. Though frequent flyers may have accounts with a number of airlines, they understand that they cannot build up enough mileage to get a free ticket unless they concentrate their business with one or perhaps two airlines. The same theory holds for travel agents selling cruises. To make the most in commissions and overrides they have to push certain cruise lines, known in travel industry parlance as preferred suppliers. If the cruise line that interests you is one of your travel agent's preferred vendors, great. If not, your agent will probably work to interest you in a line with which the agency has such an arrangement.

Because most cruises are sold by travel agents, it is critically important for the cruise lines to develop an extensive system of loyal travel agents. There is so much competition among cruise lines to influence agents that consumers sometimes end up as unwitting pawns in a sales and marketing chess game. Recently, for example, Carnival Cruise Line offered agents a free cruise for two if they booked three cabins on the line's ship, Tropicale, by a certain date. Holland America awards its agencies bonus points, which can be redeemed for chocolate, picnic lunches, or dinners in local restaurants. Incentives like these influence recommendations that agents make and narrow choices for consumers. Mind you, these are all good, reputable cruise lines, but they are not necessarily a good fit for all of an agent's customers. Good travel agents cultivate client relationships, placing the client's needs and preferences first, but some agents go for the sales that net the largest commissions and the most goodies.

To be fair, many agents will sacrifice part of their commission or override to make a cruise more affordable to a good customer. Some agencies that sell cruises in volume routinely take lower commissions in order to underprice other agencies. Understand that in many locations the competition for cruise business among travel agencies is just as keen as it is among cruise lines, particularly with the recent proliferation of cruise only agencies. And now that airlines are cutting back on travel agency commissions, the competition for cruise business will heat up even more.

In the final analysis, buyer beware. You can protect yourself best by developing a long-term relationship with a knowledgeable, reliable travel agent who wants your business and works hard to put you on the cruise that is right for you.

Helping Your Travel Agent Help You   When you call a travel agent, ask if he or she has cruised. Firsthand experience means everything. If the answer is no, either find another agent or be prepared to give your travel agent a lot of direction. Always ask your travel agent who his or her preferred vendors are. Just asking the question will alert the agent to the fact that you are a savvy buyer. Check the agent's recommendations against the information in this guide. Obtain, if possible, the permission to contact other clients who have been on the cruise ship line recommended and ask your friends. Chances are someone you know has sailed on the line.

To help your travel agent to get you the best possible deal, do the following:

1. Determine from brochures, the recommendation of friends, and this book where and when you want to cruise, and what cruise lines seem to offer the kind of cruise that most appeals to you and how much you can afford to spend.

2. Check out the cruise travel ads in the Sunday travel section of your local newspaper and compare them to ads running in the newspapers of one of cruising's key markets (i.e., New York, Philadelphia, Los Angeles, Phoenix, Dallas, Chicago, Boston, Washington, or Atlanta) nearest you. Among the best sources are the Sunday travel section of the *New York Times, Miami Herald, Los Angeles Times,* and *Chicago Tribune.* See if you can find some cruise deals that fit your plans and that include a cruise line you like. Also look at the ads in specialty magazines like *Cruise Travel.*

3. Call the consolidators or retailers whose ads you have collected. Ask any questions you might have concerning their offers, but do not book your trip with them directly.

4. Tell your travel agent about the cruises you find and ask if he or she can get you as good or better a price. The deals in the paper will serve as a bench mark against which to compare alternatives proposed by your travel agent. However, you must always be aware that promotional ads are often bait—in this business as in others—to get your attention. The lead price, as it is known, is likely to be for a limited number of cabins on a particular sailing and not available just any time. This element is probably the trickiest part of trying to get the best deal for yourself. You will notice from reading the profiles in this book and in looking at cruise line brochures, that every ship has 6–20 different categories of cabins—and that's only one ship. A cruise line with four or eight ships has a very wide "berth" in which to maneuver. So often, unless you can pinpoint the date, itinerary, and cabin category being advertised, you could be mixing apples and oranges, and it may be hard to know if you are getting a good deal or not. *Nobody ever said this was easy.*

5. Choose from among the options uncovered by you and your travel agent. No matter which option you elect, have your travel agent book it. Even if you go with one of the offers in the newspaper, it may be commissionable (at no additional

cost to you) and will provide the agent some return on the time invested on your behalf. Also, as a travel professional, your agent should be able to help you verify the quality and integrity of the deal.

HOW THE GAME IS PLAYED: THE SALES COUNTDOWN

Cruise lines work well in advance to schedule cruises and develop their promotional brochures. It is essential for the cruise line to get out of the blocks quickly with their marketing campaigns in order to avoid panic sales, or dumping, as it's sometimes called, as the sailing dates draw near.

Most cruise itineraries and dates are announced 10–14 months in advance. Particularly attractive dates on popular ships sell out well in advance, even without early booking discounts. Likewise, cruises to seasonal destinations like Alaska fill up fast. Usually the last cruises to fill are low and shoulder season cruises to year-round areas like the Caribbean. When it comes to cabins, the highest-priced and the lowest-priced accommodations sell out first.

Until recently, little attention was paid to stimulating early booking. Consequently, many consumers waited for discounts made available at the last minute when the cruise lines hit the panic button. The cruise lines finally wised up, however, reasoning that if they made discounts available as an incentive for early booking, they could generate some cash flow as well as get a much better sense of the sales prospects for each cruise. In the main, this strategy works well, although there continues to be distress selling of cabins during the last six to eight weeks before a cruise sails.

If things work out as planned, the cruise line can, as one executive put it, "nudge the cruise full." What this means essentially is that the marketing department monitors cabin sales continuously throughout the countdown period and introduces sales initiatives as needed to preclude the panic dumping of cabins at the last minute.

Escalating Base Rate Model

To see how this works in practice, let's examine a popular pricing model that has been adopted by several prominent cruise lines. When the cruise is announced, the cruise line advertises a base fare, discounted from the brochure fare by, say, 40 percent. The cruise line warrants that the discounted base fare may increase as the countdown progresses, but will never be lower. Theoretically, therefore, a consumer who books a November cruise in the preceding April would pay less than a passenger who books in June. That passenger, in turn, would pay less than someone booking in August, and so on.

This strategy allows the cruise line and the travel agent to tell the customer that "this cruise will never be cheaper than today." The customer knows at any point in time, that the rate may, repeat may, go up, but will never be lower. The cruise line, for its part, has the option of maintaining the discounted rate if the ship is filling slowly, or raising it incrementally over time as the cruise approaches being sold out. Because this model begins with a lowest ever base rate that may increase as time passes, we call this model the escalating base rate model. It's like the capacity controlled fare raising of airlines.

Giving the pricing model a name is useful because it makes it easier to understand what the cruise line does when nudging is required to fill the ship. Pay attention: what the cruise line tells the customer is that the base rate will never be cheaper than today. That is very different from telling the customer that the base rate is the deepest discount available.

In practice, the cruise line operates two separate pricing systems. The primary system is the escalating base rate system, described above. If everything goes without a hitch and the cruise sells to near capacity, that will be the only system employed. If, however, sales are lagging behind expectations and require a nudge, the line will go to its totally separate and collateral model: the special situations system.

Special Situations System

Special situations represent any number of special, usually time limited and tightly targeted sales initiatives introduced to goose sales. Special situation initiatives run concurrently with, and independently of, the escalating base rate system. Examples of special situation initiatives include a deeply discounted senior citizen's rate, a direct mailing to previous customers offering a big discount, a regional campaign targeting a certain city or geographic area, or a heavily discounted group sales overture to a large company for their executives or employees.

Each special situation initiative is designed to target a carefully selected market segment. The initiatives may run sequentially or concurrently, but as a rule will be short-lived and terminated when the objective of selling out the cruises in question is achieved. What is really important about special situation initiatives is that the discount offered might be much greater than the base rate discount. If you can dig up a special situations discount program, you may have found the lowest possible fare. If the special is advertised in Atlanta and you live in Buffalo, the air component of the package will not be of any use to you.

However, if you can buy the cruise-only part of the special and then arrange affordable airfare from Atlanta, you've got a deal.

A common special situations approach is for the cruise line to join forces with specific travel agents. Just as travel agents have preferred suppliers (cruise lines), which they push harder than other cruise lines, so too do cruise lines have preferred retailers. Often when a cruise is not selling to expectations, the cruise line will enlist the assistance of their favorite, big-volume travel agencies to help move the remaining cabins. Because the cruise line is anxious to sell the cabins, it develops special promotions with these designated agents featuring extra deep discounts and special incentives, such as cabin upgrades or discounted air add-ons. Many of these agencies sell cruises only and field hundreds of 800-number calls each day. If the cruise line gives them an especially juicy deal with which to work, they can sell a lot of cabins in a hurry. Big-volume, cruise-only agencies advertise in *Cruise Travel, Travel & Leisure,* and *Condé Nast* magazines (to name a few), as well as in many large market newspapers.

The Dump Zone

In the cruise marketplace anything can happen. As it turns out, some cruise lines are either not equipped to nudge effectively or are just not very good at it. Sometimes cruise lines that are quite expert when it comes to special situations campaigns do not succeed in filling their cruises. The upshot is that during off-season, particularly, there still may be a goodly number of empty cabins sold at distress prices during the final eight weeks before sailing.

When time is running out, travel agents and cruise lines know that it is much easier and far less logistically complicated to sell a cruise to someone who does not require air transportation to the port city. Florida is a huge market for late breaking deals because of its large retired population and its immediate proximity to the ports. Pacific Coast and New England states likewise enjoy distress sales opportunities.

If you live within easy driving distance of Miami, Ft. Lauderdale, Port Canaveral, Tampa, New York, Galveston, New Orleans, Los Angeles, San Francisco, San Diego, Seattle, or Vancouver (BC), you live in a dump zone. You are well situated to avail yourself of last-minute discounts. Remember, however, that you will have to choose from what is available and will probably have no choice when it comes to cabin selection or dining room seatings.

Discount Alphabet Soup

Before you begin shopping for discounts, pick what type of cruise appeals to you. Once you start looking, don't get sidetracked by price. Instead, stay doggedly on the trail of the cruise that best meets your needs. Never equate cheapest with best, but on the other hand, don't necessarily equate it with worst either.

More than a dozen different types of cruise discounts (in addition to seasonal discounts) are commonly offered. As you encounter these discounts in your cruise shopping, be aware that the catchy marketing come-ons, like "Two-for-One," or "Sail Three Days Free" aren't always what they seem. What the cruise line giveth, in other words, the cruise line sometimes taketh away. For example, a promotion advertising 50 percent off on the second person in the cabin (a frequent gimmick) is nothing more than 25 percent off for both—chances are you could have done better with an early booking discount. The best method of comparing rates, with or without discounts, is to calculate the per diem (per day) cost of your cruise vacation. Add the cost of the cruise plus the cost of your airfare if it is not included, as well as taxes, port charges, and other costs (transfers, etc.) as appropriate. Divide the whole cost by the number of nights that you will stay on the ship or in hotels, if any, provided as part of the package by the cruise line.

Work Sheet

Cruise Cost	_____
Airfare (if not included)	_____
Transfers (if not included)	_____
Other	_____
TOTAL	_____

Total divided by number of nights = _____ per day

Always compare apples to apples. Some cruising areas are more expensive than others. Caribbean cruises should be compared to Caribbean cruises, for instance, not to Alaskan or Mediterranean cruises. Remember also, that cruise lines are not created equal. Comparing a seven-day Commodore (Budget Inn) cruise with a seven-day Silversea (Ritz-Carlton) cruise has no meaning. The cruise line profiles in Part Two will help you understand the differences.

Early Booking Discounts

There are two kinds of early booking discounts; both usually include round-trip airfare. The most common is the discount described above as the escalating base rate model. For marketing purposes, each line has a different name for these discounts. Royal Caribbean International, which pioneered the pricing strategy, calls its program breakthrough rates. Escalating base rates are always capacity controlled and can be withdrawn or escalated without notice. Some other lines that employ capacity control pricing include Carnival, Crystal, Celebrity, Costa, Holland America, Princess, Norwegian, Regency, and most other large ones. The second type of early booking discount is the flat cut-off date. In other words, if you book before the specified date, you get the discount. Princess, Holland America, and most other cruise lines use this kind of discount on certain itineraries.

Discount for Full Payment in Advance

Passengers who pay in full by a specified date (often as much as six to nine months in advance of the cruise) receive a 10–20 percent discount. These discounts are popular with Crystal, Seabourn, Silversea, and others, particularly in the luxury market.

Free Days

Passengers are offered a seven-day cruise for the price of a six-day cruise, or a twelve-day cruise for the price of a ten-day cruise. Variations on the theme include complimentary extra days (with hotel) in the port city before and/or after the cruise, or "book a seven-day cruise and receive a free two- or three-day land package." These are sometimes found in conjunction with the Asian cruises of Orient Cruise Line, among others, and on the Southern Caribbean cruises of Seawind Cruises. Divide double occupancy price by the total number of days offered in the package to get a per diem cost for comparative purposes.

Two-for-One and Second Passenger Cruises Free

The sales hook is that two passengers cruise for the price of one, but there's some tricky math involved. Pick your cruise and cabin category and find the double occupancy price per person, air inclusive, on the cruise line's brochure rate chart. The two-for-one price is this rate less the cruise line's air cost for one person from your gateway city.

Let's say the air-inclusive double occupancy brochure rate is $2,000. Your travel agent will have to call the cruise line to determine what their round-trip air cost is from your gateway city. This amount is subtracted from $2,000 and the remainder is your cruise-only cost for two persons. You then have the option of making your own air arrangements or buying your airfare as an add-on from the cruise line. Celebrity, Princess, Regency, Costa, and Holland America frequently offer two-for-one promotional fares. Two-for-ones work great if you can travel to and from the port city inexpensively on frequent flyer miles or by car. If you have to pay for air, however, crunch some numbers. A little comparative math might demonstrate that a discounted air/sea package is a better deal.

Two-for-one offers come and go with supply and demand. It is often difficult for travel agents—or anyone else—to keep up with them. Normally, two-for-one fares are offered far in advance with a cut-off date to secure early commitments. At other times, they might pop up on very short notice, perhaps less than a month. These tend to be fire sales. Obviously, such fares are intended to boost the cruise line's short-term sales and can be withdrawn at any time.

Flat Rates

This is an early booking program where every cabin in the ship, except probably the owner's suite and most other luxury accommodations, is sold for the same flat rates (one for inside cabins and one for outside cabins) on a first-come, first-served basis. The earlier you book, the nicer your cabin. Flat rates are usually cruise only, but airfare may be purchased as an add-on. Flat rates are frequently offered by Princess, Crystal, and Norwegian Cruise Lines.

X Percent off Second Passenger in a Cabin

In this very common discount offered by many cruise lines, the first passenger pays the double occupancy brochure rate and the second passenger gets 40–70 percent off. Some simple averaging demonstrates that this works out to a discount of 20–35 percent per passenger. Airfare is usually included.

Reduced Rate Air Add-Ons

If you purchase airfare from the cruise line separately (as opposed to included in the cruise price), that is an air add-on. Sometimes cruise lines will couple a discounted cruise-only rate (no airfare) with a very attractive air add-on. This usually occurs when the cruise line is able to negotiate an exceptionally good bulk airfare purchase with an airline from a specific gateway city. In essence, the cruise line is passing some of their savings along to the consumer. Typically, this kind of deal applies only to specific cities and is offered only for a short time. It often results from an airline's slow sales and its need to stimulate air travel from a particular area, as opposed to being a cruise line initiative.

Senior Citizen Discounts

Because seniors have traditionally been the backbone of the cruise market, they are one of the first groups targeted for a discount program if a line is having difficulty filling a cruise. Usually the discount requires that one person sharing the cabin must be at least 55 years old. Size of discount varies, as does the inclusion of airfare.

Kids or Third/Fourth Passengers Go Free or at Reduced Rate

This is a fairly common discount offered by cruise lines like Carnival, Celebrity, and Premier that target families and younger cruisers. Third and fourth persons or children sharing a cabin cruise free or at a substantial discount. Airfare for the third/fourth person or children is often included.

Third/fourth person rates are generally part of a cruise line's basic rate structure (rather than discount or promotional fares). They normally appear in the cruise line's brochure and are applicable year-round. Their promotional use might come into play by being reduced or waived altogether, perhaps during the summer to stimulate family travel or in the shoulder season to stimulate first-timers to buy a cruise when three or four friends can share the cost.

Back-to-Back or Contiguous Segments Discounts

The seven-day cruise is the most popular product offered by any cruise line, as it suits the vast majority of people in terms of time and cost. However, there are people who have both the time and means for longer cruises. To satisfy both groups, the cruise lines have several choices. They may break longer cruises into seven-day segments, enabling a passenger to board in one port and depart from another. Or, they may offer two 7-day segments with different itineraries as one 14-day cruise, offering the second week at a greatly reduced price: for example, a ship departing from Miami that sails one week to the Eastern Caribbean and the next week to the Western Caribbean. By combining the two, the only port repeated in 14 days is Miami, the departure port. Throughout our cruise line profiles we highlight the ships whose itineraries lend themselves to this sort of coupling and who offer attractive discounts for the second segment.

Repositioning Cruises

When a cruise line moves a ship from one cruise area to another, this is called a repositioning cruise—and it represents one of the biggest bargains of the year. Rather than dispatch a ship empty, cruise lines sell their repositioning cruises, and to attract as many passengers as possible, they offer them at very attractive prices. The majority of repositioning cruises are scheduled in spring and fall when the great "migration" of ships takes place—mostly, when ships that have spent the winter on Caribbean, Panama Canal, and Mexico cruises are dispatched to Alaska or to New England/Canada and/or Europe for the summer; and again in autumn, when these ships return.

Repositioning cruises with interesting and unusual itineraries, such as from the Caribbean to New England via the Eastern Seaboard, are not as likely to have as much of a discount as those with few ports of call, such as transatlantic crossings. Those with more days at sea, however, appeal particularly to folks who really love to cruise and cherish having several uninterrupted days or weeks at sea.

Group Discounts

Persons traveling together as a group can almost always negotiate a special group rate. Obviously, the larger the group the better the rate. If the group is large enough, at least one free berth or cabin is customarily provided for the group organizer in addition to the discounted rate. What constitutes a group varies from cruise line to cruise line, but if you have eight or more persons—a family reunion might be an example—traveling together and occupying at least four cabins, you have enough buying power to obtain a discount, some extra amenities, or a cabin upgrade.

Standby Rates

When a cruise line offers deeply discounted standby rates, it publicizes specific itineraries and sailing dates for which the rates are available. The way it normally works, you rank order your ship, departure date, and cabin preferences and send them to the cruise line along with a modest deposit. If one of your preferred dates is available, the cruise line notifies your travel agent 30 days or more in advance. If you are offered your first choice, the deposit is considered nonrefundable. Airfare is not included.

Cabin Upgrades

There are four basic ways to get a cabin upgrade:

1. *Advertised or Unadvertised Specials*   Though usually publicized only to travel agents, cabin upgrade programs provide agents with a powerful selling tool. Upgrades apply to specific sailings and can be guaranteed by the agent and cruise line at time of booking. For the customer, it means that you can buy the cheapest available fare and be upgraded from one to five cabin levels, depending on the promotion and the timing of your booking—and the clout of your travel agent.

2. *Soft Sailing Upgrades*   A soft sailing is a cruise industry term for a specific cruise that looks as if it will sail substantially less than full capacity. Because cruise lines (and travel agents) live or die on repeat clientele, they go out of their way to make your experience as pleasant as possible. What this means among other things is that the line will usually upgrade your cabin if space is available. Booking the least expensive cabin category on a low or shoulder season cruise offers the best opportunity for receiving an upgrade. Early booking an inside cabin on a ship where there are very few inside cabins (study the ship's deck plans) might result in an upgrade to an outside cabin.

3. *Guarantees*   Sometimes, if the cruise is sold out of the cabin category you request, the cruise line will offer a guarantee. With a confirmed booking the cruise line promises to provide a cabin in the category you request or better, but does not specify. You pay exactly the same rate as for the cabin you requested, including any early booking or other applicable discounts. Because guarantees are offered only when the cruise is sold out or oversold in a requested cabin category, chances of getting the upgrade are good. The downside is that you are taking pot luck, and cannot specify where on the ship you prefer your cabin to be.

4. *Paid Upgrades*   A number of cruise lines, particularly on soft sailings, will allow you to buy an upgrade. Sometimes the paid upgrade is a real bargain, as little as $15 per person per cabin category.

Confusion among cruise passengers regarding the availability of discounts often leads to frustration and disappointment as a travel agent wrote to us pointing out:

PLEASE, PLEASE tell people that cabin upgrades are a privilege and not a right. I think I will scream if one more person asks me how to get upgraded, because they all expect upgrades these days. With most ships sailing at [near] 100% capacity, most people have a slim to none chance of getting upgraded—and almost certainly not from an inside cabin to an outside cabin. Many cabin upgrades are given at the time of booking, but "guaranteed cabin categories" do not mean guaranteed upgrades—these are based solely on availability. The only thing that is guaranteed is that they will get a cabin in at least the category they are booked in! Former passengers and people who book the earliest are the most likely to get upgrades, if they become available. If a certain cabin category is that important to someone, they should book it and pay for it, and not hope to be upgraded to it. This is an almost certain prescription for disappointment. Plus, any travel agent that tells [clients] to take a "guaranteed" or "run of ship" rate to increase their chances of being upgraded, is setting up their clients for disaster. The agent may say one thing, but the client hears the word "upgrade" and thinks this is a given. Then when it doesn't happen, the client gets angry with the travel agent and the cruise line.

Free Stuff

From time to time, as part of a specific promotion, a cruise line might offer cameras, binoculars, and other tangible goods as incentives to book. Or this can happen in conjunction with a theme cruise, for example, a photography cruise that's sponsored by a manufacturer of photo equipment.

Organizational Discounts

It is common for cruise lines to develop relationships with travel clubs like the American Automobile Association or with associations such as AARP. Even Sam's Club discounts cruises. Check to see if any special cruise discounts are offered by organizations to which you belong.

Credit Card Programs

Some cruise lines like Carnival have their own credit card programs with participating banks. Whenever you use the credit card, you accrue points or "cruise dollars." The points or dollars can be applied toward a cruise or can be taken as credit to spend on board. Mailings promoting special discounts are sent to cardholders, and sometimes automatic cabin upgrades are offered to cardholders charging a cruise on the card.

Along similar lines, miles accrued on the American Express membership miles program (one mile for every dollar charged) can be redeemed for cruises. At last count, American Express had signed up more than a dozen cruise lines in this program.

Travel Agents' Discounts

We have found that agents selling the same discount program for a particular cruise often quote different prices. Usually the difference is small, 2–5 percent, but might be higher. What's going on here is that some retailers are sacrificing part of their override to lowball the competition. While big-volume cruise-only agencies engage in this practice routinely, local travel agents frequently will knock a few dollars off their commission to retain a good regular customer. Whenever you see an ad that claims "We will beat or match your best offer," that agent is probably rebating some commission to his clients. But be very careful in dealing with agencies that make a practice of undercutting their competition in this manner. Commissions represent an agent's costs and profit. As any smart businessperson knows, if you keep giving away your profit, you will end up with too much red ink.

Cruise Loan Programs

Pioneered by Princess Cruise Lines and copied by others, cruise loan programs have benefited from a lot of publicity in the press and in travel industry media. The cruise lines and travel agents see cruise loan programs as "a perfect tool for taking away one of the clients' biggest stumbling blocks; paying for a cruise vacation in full prior to sailing." Cruise loans also help the cruise lines and travel agents trade the customer up: "Stateroom upgrades and balconies," one ad persuades, "are just a matter of a few dollars more a month."

In essence, you borrow the money for your cruise loan on a revolving line of credit (like most credit cards) and then pay off the loan in fixed installments of 24, 36, or 48 months like a mortgage or a new car loan. The main difference between a mortgage or a new car loan and a cruise loan is that mortgages and car loans are secured by pledging your home or car as collateral. Because there is nothing to pledge as collateral on a cruise loan, the interest rates are higher, much higher. In 1997 the lowest annual percentage rate for a cruise loan was 14.99 percent and ranged as high as 26.99 percent. Loans are administered by participating banks which are not affiliated with the cruise lines. If you are able to secure the lowest interest rate, the monthly payment for a seven-day cruise costing $4,252 per couple, financed over 36 months is $144 per month. Multiplying the $144 per month times 36 months, you will end up paying $5,184 for your cruise.

Lost in the Information Haze

While the discounts described are always there, it is not always easy to find them. With so many cruise lines, so many cruises, and so many discounts and marketing campaigns being promoted simultaneously, the sheer volume of information being placed in the system is sufficient to create a huge mental overload. Deals come and go so rapidly that a travel agency has to be very cruise knowledgeable, well staffed, and computerized to keep on top of things. While the big cruise-only agencies are the best equipped to handle the information flow, even they occasionally get behind.

The National Association of Cruise Only Agencies (NACOA) can provide you with a list of their members in your locale. Discount agencies usually advertise their services widely; however, you should check out the reliability of any agency with whom you do business.

Cruising the Internet for Cruises

If you were to start your Internet voyage in search of cruises by using the word "cruises," you would instantly learn that there are thousands of sites you might investigate. My first search using Alta Vista uncovered 135,451 related sites. When I narrowed it to "cruise vacations," I drew 10,000 locations and with "cruise discounts," 9,000.

So, the first lesson for someone starting out to cruise the Internet for cruises is to realize that there is a sea of information and you can quickly drown in it if you do not know what you are doing or know how to search the net efficiently. And even if you are a wiz at searches, you will still need a great deal of time and infinite patience.

Cyberspace is chaotic. We cannot organize it for you, but we can offer some guidelines that might be helpful to find information about cruises. Essentially, cruise-related information on the Internet is precisely that—information. Lots and lots of information. As of this writing you can get help, ask questions, order brochures but you cannot purchase a cruise directly from a cruise line on the Internet, with one exception. In late September 1997, Renaissance Cruises is scheduled to launch the first on-line direct booking service by a cruise line. Initially, it will be limited to one year-round Mediterranean itinerary and one price/cabin category. On-line customers pay by credit card.

Generally, the information is available from these sources:

- Cruise lines: Almost all the major cruise lines and many of the smaller, specialized ones have their own site on the World Wide Web (www). We have included their web address in the Part II profiles and in Part III when they were available.
- Cruise associations: Trade organizations such as CLIA, Cruise Lines International Association, which have their own web sites.
- Travel agencies: Hundreds of travel agencies have their own web page and others participate through their trade organs.
- Travel publications: Major travel magazines, such as *Travel & Leisure, Travel Weekly;* and book publishers like Macmillan (which publishes this book), have web sites.
- Individuals: Many individuals who are recognized travel experts or who consider themselves experts on cruises or are simply interested in them have created their own sites.
- Subscriber services such as America Online, which has approximately 8 million members, and CompuServe, which has about 3 million, have programs on cruises with content created specifically for them.

In our opinion, you can almost forget about all of them except the first and the last, with a few exceptions in the other categories.

For the most part, cruise line web sites are information-focused. They do not have reservations or sales capabilities; they were not designed for those purposes. The typical site features ship descriptions with cabin and public rooms photos, and itineraries—in other words, about the same material you would find in a brochure. And indeed, you can usually request a brochure by e-mail, sometimes requiring you to give a phone number or an e-mail address before the order can be filled. You will rarely find fares, and when you do, they are likely to be only sample prices. You will find general cabin information but not specific sizes or configurations. Such sites are useful when you know—more or less—where and when you plan to cruise, but the information is, of course, on the host cruise line only.

Some cruise line web sites are well done, fun, clever, and even amusing, and they are getting better all the time. Others are so basic and slow to upload, you would learn more by reading the cruise line's brochure. Often the best ones have special features such as itineraries with links to maps and port information or the facility to search by zip code for travel agencies near you. Often, too, the site is linked to other cruise-related information. For example, American Hawaii Cruises' site is linked to "Whales of the Wild," which lists whalewatching and other nature-oriented cruises. If you have the time, there is no end to the links you can pursue.

The range of information is as broad as it is voluminous and there is no uniformity in presentation or the amount, style, and detail of the information offered. For example, Premier Cruise Lines has a "Cool stuff for kids" tab which leads you to puzzles and a game; while "Cool stuff for adults" gives you a recipe for a "Banana Mama." Royal Caribbean International's site is not only extensive and detailed but it even has an index to facilitate your research. Yet, it's done with a light-hearted touch and includes such features as "Frequently Asked Dumb Questions."

On some of the better sites, such as Windstar Cruises' web page, you can go through a typical day on board, see a sample dinner menu, review itineraries with sailing dates, and read about special fares and onboard credits for Internet users. Its sister company, Holland America Line, offers a cruise match program on its site. By clicking on your preferences in several categories—destinations, ships, ports of embarkation, cruise duration, etc.—certain Holland America cruises with their low to high fares, will be recommended. Carnival Cruises, another sister company to Windstar, with one of the most extensive sites, offers pictures and descriptions of each cabin category, including drawings of cabin layouts—a rare feature. And, it even has a page on employment opportunities with Carnival. The three lines are linked to each other.

Subscriber services have created the best organized, most useful and user-friendly sites of all. For news, guidance and evaluations, the best by far is America Online's "Cruise Critic," which is created and maintained by editor-in-chief and host and veteran cruise writer Anne Campbell and a team of cruise-specialists and knowledgeable persons. Here, you will find candid, continuously updated ship reviews and evaluations on more than 100 ships with descriptions on facilities, activities, amenities, itineraries, and fellow passengers; news on cruise industry developments; and features on everything from seasickness to the latest bargains. The Cruise Critic library contains trip reports and travel tips from AOL members.

Campbell and others host weekly chat rooms and there are message boards for AOL members to ask questions or post their opinions on cruises, ports of call, and related matters. Cruise Critic has a ship finder and cruise selector to help you narrow your choice for selecting a cruise and to pair you with the most appropriate ship and itinerary. This element has not yet been developed to its full potential.

CompuServe subscribers can benefit from the "Cruise Forum" which some reviewers have named the best in cyberspace for its wealth of material prepared by cruise-specialists, particularly travel agents. The extensive library includes detailed ship reviews—often several on the same ship, and message boards, but Cruise Forum does not have the breath of coverage and topics that can be found on AOL's Cruise Critic.

For web sites created by knowledgable individuals, radio talk-show and television personalities Paul Lasley and Elizabeth Harryman have "On Travel," which is essentially a radio on the Internet (you must have audio capability to access the audio). It was the first all-travel audio web site and offers timely coverage on cruises, often from on-location and including conversations with cruise line executives and shipboard personnel.

Cruise Review library (http://www.pagesz.net-isdavis/rtc. html) is compiled by John Davis, who says he is neither a travel agent nor a long-time cruiser. However, he will connect you to a bounty of ship reviews—often several on the same ship reflecting different experiences—and ports descriptions, to cruise line web sites as well as to some travel agent newsletters about cruising.

K. L. Smith's Cruise Letter (http://www.chevychase.com/cruise) is edited by Sharon Jackson, a travel agent in Rockville, Maryland, who specializes in cruises and is the main person responsible for CompuServe's Cruise Forum. The latter is a useful resource for ship reviews, travel tips, information on discounts, and links to cruise lines web sites.

So what's the bottom line? If you want information, cruising the Internet for cruises can be useful and fun. It can also be frustrating and very time-consuming. You will pick up a great deal of information and broaden your knowledge about cruises. You will also learn quickly which sites are worth your while and which are not. Be cautious about the comments made on message boards, forums, and chat rooms from unidentified sources whose reliability you cannot check, as opposed to the host whose credentials you will know.

But when it comes to selecting a cruise, we believe that this book—we say in all modesty—together with cruise lines compendiums and a truly knowledgeable travel agent remain the most efficient and effective way to help you select the right cruise—i.e., the cruise that right for you.

PULLING IT ALL TOGETHER

Now that you know the players and how the game is played, it's time to put your knowledge into action.

Step 1. To Agent or Not to Agent

Your first big decision is whether or not to use your regular, or in any event, local travel agent. This guide, in conjunction with brochures acquired from the cruise lines, Sunday travel sections, and a cruise specialty magazine or two will suffice to enable you to narrow your choices. Even so, a reliable travel agent can contribute immeasurably in offering advice and particularly in facilitating the process. If you have a travel agent who has served you well, and particularly if you give that agent enough business to be considered a good customer, by all means, you should use him or her. If you travel infrequently and don't have a regular travel agent, ask some of your more traveled friends for recommendations. Try to select a travel agent close to your own age or one who shares your same interests and lifestyle. Make sure the travel agency has a good reputation and that the agent with whom you are dealing has had experience in selling cruises. Remember, using a travel agent will not cost you more; the cruise line, not you, will pay any commissions.

Step 2. Narrow Down

Using this book and the other material you have gathered, prioritize your list of lines, ships, and cruises to a manageable four. Be flexible. Also be alert to the possibility of travel agents pushing their preferred suppliers that may or may not be on your list.

Step 3. Scout the Discounts

Using the information you have collected from newspaper travel sections and other sources, share any special deals you have identified with your travel agent. Ask if he or she can do better. Try calling a few high-volume cruise-only agencies on your own. After you have asked about the cruises on your priority list, ask what's the best deal the agency is selling right now. In collecting quotes, always ask for the bottom-line cost in dollars rather than the percentage discount. Repeat the quote to the selling agent and verify what is included in terms of airfare, accommodations, transfers, etc. Take notes.

Do not under any circumstance fall into the trap of buying a cruise simply because it sounds like a great deal. This is particularly true if you are buying your first cruise. Your top priority is to determine which cruise is right for you. Then and only then is it time to start scouting deals. The best way we know to ruin your cruise vacation is to book the wrong ship in an effort to save a few dollars.

Step 4. Buy Early or Buy Late

As you have learned from the foregoing sections, the biggest discounts can usually be had by buying early (four to six months before sailing) or buying late (during the last month). As a first-time cruiser you will have greater choice and peace of mind taking the early bird route. After you have sailed on a few cruises, or perhaps even after your first cruise, you will be in a better position to play the best deal game. But remember, any time you hold out for a deal, you shorten your options on getting the cabin you want, the dining room seating you want, or the airline routing you prefer. In the long run, these will be much more important ingredients in the quality of the cruise you buy than saving another $50 or $100.

Step 5. Give the Seller a Price to Beat

When you've narrowed the field to one or two specific cruises and you are ready to buy, call the four or so retailers who quoted the best prices the first time around. Take the best price you were quoted in the first round and call them all back, saying, "I've been quoted a price of $X for this particular cruise, can you beat it?"

Step 6. Check It Out

When you have struck the best possible deal, share it with your travel agent and give him a chance to match it. If he can't match it, he may be able to verify the deal's integrity or uncover any hidden problems. If the deal is commissionable, have your agent book it. If not, particularly if the agent has invested a lot of time on your behalf, offer him a $50 or $100 consultation fee. This will help bind your relationship and improve the agent's attitude toward working with you in the future.

If you are going it alone and you decide to buy from an agency outside your city or state, try to determine whether the selling agency is bonded and whether it is a member of their local Better Business Bureau (BBB) and/or Chamber of Commerce. Check also to see if the agency is a member of the American Society of Travel Agents (ASTA) or the National Association of Cruise Only Agencies (NACOA) or Cruise Line International Association (CLIA). Membership in these organizations is not a guarantee of ethical business practices, but the organizations have a vested interest in maintaining the good reputation of cruising and try to attract only upstanding members. If in doubt, a call to the local BBB or any of the associations mentioned should confirm what the agency claims.

American Society of Travel Agents (ASTA) (703) 739-2782
Cruise Line International Association (CLIA) (212) 921-0066
National Association of Cruise Only Agencies (NACOA) (305) 663-5626

To find out how consolidators and wholesalers respond to questions concerning their affiliations and accreditations, we called all of the cruise discounters who advertise in *Cruise Travel* and *Condé Nast* magazines. Some agencies were gracious and responsive and seemed to understand that customers have a right to check them out. An amazing number of agencies, however, were surly and entirely nonforthcoming. "Who are you?" and "What do you need to know that for?" were typical responses. Telephone representatives from four agencies said they didn't know the answers to our questions but would call us back. Guess what? We never heard from them again. When you call to check out an agency, accept nothing less than complete courtesy, openness, and cooperation. Life's too short and your cruise is too important to deal with rude salespeople. And remember to show the same respect. Travel agents are busy people. Good ones will work hard for you, but they can also spot someone who is merely on a fishing expedition.

Step 7. Protect Yourself

When you pay for your cruise, use a credit card and insist that the charge be run through the cruise line's account as opposed to the agency's account. This precaution is important. Financially shaky agencies sometimes use customers' deposits and fare payments to settle outstanding agency debts instead of securing the customer's booking. When these agencies fold, the customer is often left with no cruise and no refund. Running the charge through the cruise line's account protects you from the collapse of the travel agency. Paying with a credit card allows you to cancel payment if the cruise is not provided as promised.

If you are shelling out a lot of money for a cruise, protect your investment with travel insurance. While most travel insurance comes with a lot of bells, whistles, and minor coverages, two things should concern you: (1) loss of your paid fare if you must cancel or if your cruise is interrupted, and (2) the potentially huge costs of an emergency medical evacuation. You also want to protect against major medical expenses while traveling if your primary health insurance doesn't cover it.

Though overpriced at about \$5–8 per every \$100 of coverage, travel insurance nevertheless is a prudent expenditure. You can never tell when you might become unexpectedly ill or have a death in the family. On a lesser order of magnitude, you might miss your sailing date because of a flight cancellation or delay.

While travel insurance coverages can be purchased separately, they are usually packaged, or as the insurance industry puts it, bundled. What we recommend is good trip cancellation/interruption coverage coupled with emergency medical evacuation coverage. Trip cancellation/interruption insurance covers you (the insured traveler) and your traveling companion(s) against losses caused by illness, injury, or death. In addition to yourself and your traveling companions, most policies cover losses resulting from the interruption of your trip by the death, serious injury, or serious illness of a close family member back home. American Express and Travelers have a policy that also provides coverage in the event of a business partner's illness, injury, or death.

If you cancel your cruise before leaving home, your trip cancellation/interruption insurance will reimburse you for the full amount you paid for the cruise, less any refund you receive from the cruise line. While cancellation and refund policies vary from cruise line to cruise line, most lines provide a full refund if you cancel 61 or more days prior to your departure date. When you buy trip cancellation/interruption insurance, remember that you are covered only to the extent of your investment. If you are buying a \$1,500 cruise on Princess, in other words, you don't need \$10,000 worth of insurance.

The ideal trip cancellation insurance will allow you to cancel for any reason. Most policies, however, stipulate those situations that qualify for the coverage. At a minimum you should insist on being covered for death, injury, illness, jury duty, court appearances, accidents en route to the airport or pier, and disasters at home, such as a fire or flood. The same coverage applies to your traveling companion(s). If you buy a cruise at the double occupancy rate and your traveling companion has to cancel, your policy should pick up the single supplement, if you want to continue by yourself.

Many policies cover unexpected disasters en route like airline or shipworker strikes, but usually do not cover such things as hurricanes, earthquakes, or other disasters at scheduled ports of call. Cruise lines reserve the right to alter the itinerary once under way to avoid bad weather and other problems.

Unfortunately, the fine print in many policies is tricky. And as you might expect, a number of seemingly innocuous loopholes limit the carrier's obligation. One essential question when buying trip cancellation/interruption insurance is whether it covers preexisting conditions. A preexisting condition is one for which you were treated by a physician in the 60-day period (90 days in Maryland) before the policy was purchased. In the better policies, if the preexisting condition is controlled by medication, it is covered. Be aware, however, that in insurance company language, "controlled" is very different from "treated." If you have high blood pressure and take medication that maintains your blood pressure at normal, safe levels, your condition is controlled. If you have a tumor and are receiving radiation, the carriers would stipulate that you are being treated but that your condition is not controlled. If your tumor caused you to cancel your cruise, the policy would not reimburse you. Because this whole discussion of preexisting conditions (and the language that defines them) is so slippery, we recommend that you question the insurance carrier directly concerning any health problem, obtaining written confirmation if necessary.

Along the lines of preexisting conditions, pregnancy is covered by most policies if you cruise during your first two trimesters. If a complication arises, the policy will pay off. If for some amazing reason you deliver your baby normally while on a cruise, you would not be covered. In any event, many cruise lines will not accept a pregnant passenger in her third trimester and beyond.

Another potential land mine in trip cancellation/interruption insurance is operator failure. What if your travel agent, airline, or cruise line goes belly up? While brochures and most policies say that they will pay in the event of operator failure or default, sometimes failure and default are defined in the fine print as bankruptcy. Because many businesses fail and go under without ever declaring bankruptcy, this is an important distinction. An interesting aside to the operator failure question is that most policies exclude the failure of the company that sold the cruise (usually a travel agent) and/or the company that sold the insurance. If you buy insurance from a travel agency, your coverage will take care of you if the cruise line or airline fails, but won't cover you if the travel agency fails. This is another example of why you should pay for your cruise with a credit card and insist that the charge be run through the cruise line's account instead of the travel agent's.

Trip interruption coverage is sold along with trip cancellation and supplements what you recover from the cruise line if something goes wrong during your trip. If a family member dies, for example, and you have to fly home from a port of call in the middle of your cruise, the interruption coverage will pay for your plane ticket home plus reimburse you for the unused portion of your cruise (less any refund you receive from the cruise line). The same policy would pick up the single supplement of your cabin companion if he or she remains on the cruise.

Bundled with trip cancellation/interruption is emergency medical evacuation insurance. This coverage pays to evacuate you to a place where you can obtain quality medical care. In the Caribbean and other more remote cruise areas, you might prefer not to entrust your care to the local medical establishment. The insurance company in conjunction with a qualified physician usually must verify your condition and authorize the evacuation. Once an evacuation is authorized, the insurance carrier ordinarily selects the means of transportation.

As a rule, emergency medical evacuation insurance does not cover hospital stays, doctors, diagnostic procedures, treatments, or medications, though sometimes medical coverage is bundled with a comprehensive trip cancellation/interruption policy. In any event, check your primary health insurance, Medicare, or HMO to make sure you are covered for medical attention required when traveling abroad. If you are not covered, we recommend that you buy supplemental insurance for your cruise.

If you are going on an upscale cruise and hauling along Rolex watches, gems, and other valuables for dress-up night, check your homeowners policy to determine what your coverage is when you travel. If you find yourself vulnerable, take out a rider. When you travel, carry your valuables on your person as opposed to placing them in checked luggage. Better still, leave them at home.

Travel insurance is available through travel agents and cruise lines but is generally underwritten by insurance companies. The most comprehensive package is the Travel Guard Gold Comprehensive policy, which may be more than cruisers need. Travel Guard also markets a less expensive Travel Guard Cruise and Tour package. Listed below are several of the major carriers along with their policy names and phone numbers.

Access America Service Corporation Access America Cruise Policy,
    (800) 248-8300

American Express American Express Travel Insurance,
    (800) 234-0375

Mutual of Omaha Mutual of Omaha Cruise and Tour,
    (800) 228-9792

The Travelers Travel Insurance,
    (800) 821-2828

When shopping for travel insurance, remember that the language in the brochure is marketing language. The language in the policy legally defines your and the carrier's obligations.

If your cruise line offers its own policy, compare its costs and coverages against one or more of the policies listed above or one offered by your travel agency. If the cruise policy compares favorably, buy it. The cruise line has more of a vested interest in your satisfaction than does an insurance company and will probably be more helpful and less bureaucratic should a problem arise.

When you buy cruise insurance, you need to understand when it begins. Some policies start from the time of deposit; others take effect when the trip actually begins, for example, air/sea—at the airport, at the port, or when you have boarded the ship.

Second, every cruise brochure has fine print explanations regarding payment/cancellation/insurance coverage. Read it. They also have—usually not in fine print but rather in large type to get your attention—a full page on the cruise line's insurance package. Review it carefully and cut through all the hype.

PREPARING FOR YOUR CRUISE

A cruise may be about the easiest vacation you can take when it comes to making preparations because so much is done for you, particularly when you buy an air/sea package. During the cruise, entry formalities are handled by the ship for its passengers in most cases, sparing them the need to fill out immigration forms or to clear customs in each port of call.

In most ports you can simply walk off your ship after it has been cleared by local authorities, spend the day sightseeing, shopping, enjoying a sport or other pleasant pursuits, and return to your ship without having to do anything more than pass through metal detectors for security reasons and show your boarding pass. It's remarkable, if you stop to think about it or compare it to a trip by air visiting similar locations.

The destination of your cruise will make some difference—the more exotic the location, the more you may have need for planning ahead, perhaps for innoculations, visas, and the like. And of course, the weather during your cruise will determine the wardrobe you select.

Such advice may seem obvious to those who have traveled, and if it does, let this information serve simply as a reminder or checklist. Even the most seasoned travelers have been known to pack their cruise tickets in their checked luggage or leave their traveler's checks at home.

CRUISE LINES BROCHURES

The easiest place to start your preparation is by reading the large compendium of the cruise line from which you selected your cruise. It has a wealth of useful information. To be sure, much of it is glossy pictures and promotional puff to entice you to take a cruise, but almost all contain several pages, usually toward the rear, aimed at answering the questions people ask most often.

They are the specifics about dining hours, smoking/nonsmoking provisions, paying for incidentals on board ships, embarkation and sailing times, and similar tips. In this book, too, each of the major cruise line profiles in Part Two includes a chart entitled Standard Features, which will answer similar questions pertaining to a specific cruise line and its ships.

CRUISE LINES VIDEOS

Most cruise lines have videocassettes of the cruise you are taking that they would be happy to send you—for a fee. Most cost about $15. Essentially, it is a promotional video but it will give you an idea of what to expect, particularly if your cruise is to an area of the world in which you have not traveled previously. You will probably receive a flyer from the cruise lines to order the tape directly from a distributor. Vacations on Video (phone (602) 483-1551; fax (602) 482-0785) is a major distributor of cruise videos.

TRAVEL DOCUMENTS

You do not need a passport or visa for cruises in the Caribbean, Alaska, Mexico, Panama Canal, New England, Canada, Bermuda, or Hawaii— that's about 90 percent of the cruises sold in the United States. However, it's a good idea to carry your passport or some documentation that bears your photo because airlines—and even some cruise lines—require a photo identification. What's more, it's always smart to have a passport for travel outside the United States—as much for your returning to the United States as for any reason. If you do not have a passport, you will need to have proof of citizenship, such as a certified copy of your birth certificate. Personally, we would never leave U.S. shores without our passports. It facilitates your travel wherever you are and it's the best identification you can carry. But never pack your passport in your suitcase; carry it with you at all times.

Aliens residing in the United States need to have valid alien registration cards and passports. All non-U.S. citizens must have valid passports and necessary visas when boarding any cruise ship departing from and returning to U.S. ports.

Passengers on most other cruises—in Europe, former Soviet bloc countries, Asia, Africa, South America—are required to have a valid passport and in some cases may need visas. A valid passport usually means one that will not expire for at least six months.

Often, on cruises in these destinations, ship authorities will ask you to surrender your passport when you check in and will keep it until the end of your cruise. This enables them to clear the ship more quickly in foreign ports. In such cases, you do not need to worry about giving over your passport to the ship. The passports are locked away securely and are taken out only if local authorities ask to see them.

TRAVEL REQUIREMENTS

Specific requirements for visas and vaccinations depend on the ports of call on your cruise. Normally, this information will be provided by your cruise line or travel agent. However, obtaining the necessary visas and any other documentation required for embarkation, debarkation, and reentry into the United States is your responsibility and if you do not have the proper documents, you will be denied boarding.

U.S. passengers under 18 years are usually not allowed to board a cruise ship at initial embarkation without proper proof of identification. No refund of the cruise fare will be given to passengers failing to have such identification. Documents that will be accepted as proof of identification vary with each cruise line. You will need to inquire in advance if the information is not provided in the cruise line's brochure, which it usually is—in the fine print.

Children traveling with anyone other than their parents or legal guardian must have permission in writing for the child to travel. Failure to comply with this requirement can also result in denial of boarding.

DRESS CODES AND PACKING

What to pack will be determined to a large extent by your ship and its destinations. Another useful key is the dress code, which is usually explained in the cruise line's brochure, and noted in the Standard Features in each cruise line's profile in Part Two.

There are no limits on the amount of luggage you can bring on board ship, but most staterooms do not have much closet and storage space. More important, since you are likely to be flying to your departure port, you need to be guided by airline regulations regarding excess baggage.

Despite the image you may have about fancy parties and clothes, the reality is that shipboard life is very casual. You will spend your days in slacks, shorts, T-shirts, and bathing suits. Lightweight mix-match ensembles with skirts, shirts, blouse or T-shirts, shorts, and slacks are practical. Colorful scarves are another way to change the look of an out-fit. For women, cocktail dresses are appropriate for evening wear.

Men usually are asked to wear a jacket at dinner. A gentleman who does not have a tuxedo should bring a basic dark suit and white shirt. Add a selection of slacks and sport shirts, one or two sports jackets, and at least two pairs of bathing trunks.

If you are heading for a warm weather cruise—Caribbean, Mexico, Hawaii, Tahiti—pack as you would for any resort destination. Light-weight, loose-fitting clothing is ideal and cotton or cotton blends are more comfortable than synthetic fabrics for the tropics. Include two bathing suits if you are likely to be spending much time in the sun and at the beach. And don't forget a cover-up for the short jaunt between your cabin and the pool or other outside decks, since cruise ships ask passengers not to wear bathing suits in the public rooms.

Take along cosmetics and suntan lotion, but don't worry if you forget something. It will most likely be available in shipboard or portside duty-free shops. Sunglasses and a hat or sun visor for protection against the sun are essential. A tote bag comes in handy for carrying odds and ends, and plastic bags for wet towels and bathing suits upon returning from a visit to an island beach. You might also want to keep camera equipment in plas-tic bags as protection against the salt air, water, and sand.

The first and last nights of your cruise are casual and the nights your ship is in port almost always call for informal dress. At least one night will be the captain's gala party where tuxedos for men and long dresses for women are requested but not mandatory. Another night is a masquerade party; it's entirely up to you whether or not to participate.

Bring your most comfortable walking shoes for shore excursions. Tennis, deck, or other low-heeled rubber or nonskid shoes are recom-mended for walking about the ship, walking up and down gangways, getting in and out of the ship's tenders, if that's necessary, and for sight-seeing. And you will need a sweater for breezy nights at sea or for the air conditioning in the dining room or shore excursion bus. A small flash-light, a fold-up umbrella, and a light jacket are often handy.

Pack as lightly as possible. For a one-week or shorter cruise, you should be able to fit everything you need into one suitcase. But most of all, be comfortable. You do not need to rush out and buy an expensive wardrobe. Obviously, if your cruise is in a cool or cold climate, you will need to plan accordingly. A Baltic or Scandinavian cruise in summer is likely to encounter colder temperatures than you might think—similar to a New England fall, but then can quickly turn to a hot summer day. Plan for layers when the weather is uncertain.

As we mention elsewhere, it's a sound practice to have a small carry-on bag for your medications and cosmetics, and to include a change of clothing for your first afternoon aboard your ship, in the event there is a delay in the delivery of your luggage. Also, bring a fold-away bag to carry all those duty-free bargains that probably won't fit in your suitcase.

Every evening, an agenda for the following day is delivered to your room; it states the dress code for the following evening. It may be:

Casual:	Comfortable daywear such as slacks, shorts, jeans, but some cruise lines will state specifically that T-shirts, tank tops, or shorts are not allowed in the dining room for dinner.
Informal:	Dresses and pantsuits are suggested for the ladies; jackets are required for the men, but ties are optional.
Formal:	Cocktail dresses or gowns for the ladies and tuxedo, dinner jacket, or dark business suit suggested for men; jacket and tie are required.

To some extent, the dress code is determined by the itinerary. An adventure cruise might be three weeks, but not a single night will be formal or even very dressy.

As a general rule, the line up will be like this:

3–4 nights: one formal, one informal, and one or two casual.
7–8 nights: two formal, two informal, two or three casual.
10–14 nights: three or four formal; four or six informal; four or five casual.

You are asked to comply with the ship's stated dress code, if for no other reason than out of respect for your fellow passengers. Generally, the suggested attire is respected throughout the evening or at least until after the shows in the main showroom and the late-night buffet when it is a gala event. Often those who want to stay up late for the disco or casino change to more comfortable dress, if they prefer.

COSTUMES

Some people like to bring an outfit for '50s and '60s night or country and western night, a musical instrument or props for the passenger talent show, or a costume for the masquerade parade. If you don't have room for a costume, the cruise staff can help you make one. There's absolutely no requirement for you to dress in a costume, but if you want to do so, ask your travel agent for theme nights featured on your cruise. The brochures from the cruise line will also tell you about theme nights.

SPORTS EQUIPMENT

If you plan to play golf or tennis frequently, you might want to bring your own equipment, and of course, you'll need the appropriate clothes and shoes. Ships that have golf practice facilities supply the equipment, sometimes for a nominal fee.

Fins and a snorkeling mask, particularly if you have one fitted with your eyeglass prescription, are bulky but will save you a $10 to $20 fee everytime you go snorkeling on your own, but if you buy the ship's shore excursions, the equipment is included. Scuba gear is usually included in dive packages, too, and, except for your regulator, is impractical to bring on a cruise.

Hiking boots, jogging shoes, riding attire and other sporting gear will depend entirely on you and the nature of your cruise. For adventure or expedition cruises, such as to Antarctica, your cruise line will give you ample information about dress and the equipment you might need.

MONEY MATTERS

Another element that makes cruise travel easy: you have already paid for almost everything, particularly if you bought an air/sea package. There are no surprises, no hidden costs. The budget you will make for your trip depends on you. It will cover personal items—hair care, laundry, spa and beauty treatments, drinks, wine with dinner, shopping, gifts, casino, shore excursions, and tips.

These are such personal matters, it's hard to give advice, except for shore excursions and tips, which are covered later in this section. Some people have trouble spending a conservative $50 a day; others can drop $500 in the casino every night and not bat an eye.

Dollars are readily accepted throughout the Caribbean and indeed throughout most of the world, as are traveler's checks and major credit cards. In Europe or Asia, the ship's purser or front office usually offers foreign currency exchange facilities or the ship brings someone aboard to provide the facility in each port of call.

If you do exchange money (it's a great opportunity to teach kids about other currencies—French francs in Martinique, Dutch guilders in

Curaçao, pesos in Mexico) exchange only small amounts for your immediate use. Seldom will you have time to exchange the money back before returning to your ship, and you lose money every time you make the exchange.

Even with U.S. dollars, always carry small denominations—ones, fives, tens. Chances are, if you are owed change, it will be returned in the local currency. Incidentally, U.S. coins are seldom accepted in foreign countries and are impossible to exchange except in quantity at foreign exchange banks. Likewise, with foreign coins when you want to exchange them back into U.S. currency. Most become souvenirs.

Major credit cards have become the currency of travelers worldwide. On cruise, you will often find them the most convenient method of payment for settling your account aboard ship, for shopping at duty-free shops, and for payment of local restaurant or hotel bills. However, do not expect to use them in off-the-beaten-track locations. The Cuna Indians of the San Blas Islands—an exotic stop on Panama Canal cruises—want your greenbacks.

PRESCRIPTION MEDICINE AND OTHER MEDICAL REQUIREMENTS

As with any trip, whether on land or sea, you should have all your required medicine with you and carry it with you in your hand luggage, not packed in your suitcase. As a further precaution, carry copies of your prescriptions with you. The same is true of eyeglasses.

If you have special dietary requirements, you or your travel agent should communicate them to your cruise line at the time you book your cruise. Most ships can accommodate normal requirements of low salt and low fat but more complex ones that require special stores be carried aboard require planning. Do not take anything for granted. Inquire. For example, many ships do not normally stock skimmed milk. In each of the cruise line profiles in Part Two in the section entitled Standard Features, the amount of advance notice a cruise line requires to handle special diets is indicated.

Cruise ships that travel beyond coastal waters are required to have a doctor on board, and most large ships have nurses and impressive, well-stocked medical facilities. The doctor and nursing staff have daily office hours, which are always printed in the ship's daily agenda, and they are always on call for emergencies. There are charges for most medical services, which generally are reasonable.

SUNBURNS

You will need to take precautions against the sun when you are on a Caribbean or Mexican cruise. The sun in the tropics is much, much stronger than the sun to which most people are accustomed. Always use a sunscreen with an SPF of 15 or higher and do not stay in the direct sun for long stretches at a time. Nothing can spoil a vacation faster than a sunburn.

LEARNING THE LINGO

Cruise ships have a language all their own. And while it is not necessary to enroll in a Berlitz course to learn it, becoming familiar with a few terms will be worthwhile so you won't feel lost at sea, if you will forgive the pun.

Passengers don't reserve rooms on a ship, they book *cabins,* which cruise lines sometimes call by a fancier name, *staterooms.* The price level of a cabin is known as its *category.* A cabin rate per person in a double occupancy cabin is called *basis two.*

When you reach your ship, you will board or embark; when it's time to leave the ship, passengers *disembark.* If the ship arrives at a port where it cannot pull into the dock, the ship will *ride at anchor* and passengers are taken ashore in a *tender,* one of the small ancillary vessels that travel on board the ship.

Several terms will assist you in finding your way around the ship. The *bow* is the front of the ship, while the *aft* is the rear, and the center portion is *midships,* or *amidships.*

Heading forward, toward the bow, the right side of the ship, is know as the *starboard* side; the left side of the ship is called the *port* side. Ships have *decks,* never floors. Decks are named after such things as precious stones (Emerald Deck), activities (Sports Deck), places (Monte Carlo Deck), and planets (Venus Deck).

If you've built up an appetite from all this exploring, you can go to the *main seating* (or sitting) and eat early, or the *second seating* and dine late. Some ships have *single seating,* which means that all passengers eat at the same time for all three meals. Other ships have *open seating,* in which case you may sit anywhere—at any unoccupied table or join others. And by invitation, you may even find yourself at the *captain's table.*

On board, there are people to help you decode ship lingo. The purser's office is the information center, usually called *Purser's Square.*

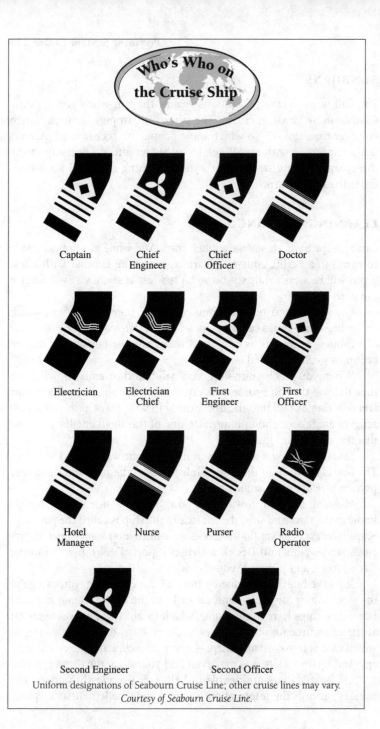

Who's Who on the Cruise Ship

Captain

Chief Engineer

Chief Officer

Doctor

Electrician

Electrician Chief

First Engineer

First Officer

Hotel Manager

Nurse

Purser

Radio Operator

Second Engineer

Second Officer

Uniform designations of Seabourn Cruise Line; other cruise lines may vary.
Courtesy of Seabourn Cruise Line.

The *hotel manager* is in charge of all passenger-related, shipboard services, such as dining, housekeeping, etc. The *chief steward* is responsible for cabin services and *cabin stewards* or *stewardesses* take care of cabins; while the *dining steward* is your waiter. The *cruise director* functions as the emcee and the *cruise staff,* who are his assistants, runs all activities and entertainment and makes sure that you are having a good time. And finally, there's the *captain,* who is in charge of everything.

Cruise lingo is part of the fun, so don't take it too seriously. Here are the most common terms you are likely to encounter.

Add-on	A supplementary charge added to the cruise fare, usually applied to correlated airfare and/or postcruise land tours.
Aft	Near, toward, or in the rear (stern) of the ship.
Air/Sea	A package consisting of the two forms of travel, i.e., air to and from the port of embarkation, transfers to/from the port, as well as the cruise itself.
Amidships	In or toward the middle of the ship; the longitudinal center portion of the ship.
Astern	Beyond the ship's stern.
Basis two	A cabin accommodating at least two persons; also referred to as double occupancy.
Batten down	To secure all open hatches or equipment for sea worthiness while the ship is under way.
Beam	Width of the ship (amidships) between its two sides at its widest point.
Berth	Dock, pier, or quay (key); also, the bed in the passenger cabins.
Bow	Front or forward portion of the ship.
Bridge	Navigational and command control center of the ship.
Bulkhead	Upright partition (wall) dividing the ship into cabins or compartments.

Category	The price level of a cabin, based on location on the ship, dimensions, and amenities.
Colors	A national flag or ensign flown from the mast or stern post.
Course	Direction in which the ship is headed, usually expressed in compass degrees.
Crow's nest	Partially enclosed platform at the top of the mast used as a lookout.
Deck plan	An overhead diagram deck by deck illustrating cabin and public room locations in relation to each other.
Disembark	Depart from the ship.
Dock	Berth, pier, or quay (key).
Draft	Measurement in feet from waterline to lowest point of ship's keel.
Even keel	The ship in a true vertical position with respect to its vertical axis.
Fathom	Measurement of distance equal to 6 feet.
First seating	The earlier of two meal times in the ship's main dining rooms.
Fore	The forward mast or the front (bow) of the ship.
Forward	Toward the fore or bow of the ship.
Funnel	The smokestack or "chimney" of the ship.
Galley	The ship's kitchen.
Gangway	The opening through the ship's bulwarks (or through the ship's side) and the ramp by which passengers embark and disembark.
Gross registered ton	A measurement of 100 cubic feet of enclosed revenue-earning space within a ship (see *Space ratio*).

Hatch	The covering over an opening in a ship's deck, leading to a hold.
Helm	Commonly the ship's steering wheel, but more correctly the entire steering apparatus consisting of the wheel, the rudder, and their connecting cables or hydraulic systems.
Hold	Interior space(s) below the main deck for storage of cargo.
House flag	The flag denoting the company to which the ship belongs.
Hull	The frame and body (shell) of the ship exclusive of masts, superstructure, or rigging.
Knot	A unit of speed equal to one nautical mile per hour (6080.2 feet) as compared to a land mile of 5,280 feet.
League	A measure of distance approximating 3.45 nautical miles.
Leeward	In the direction of that side of the ship opposite from which the wind blows.
Manifest	A list or invoice of a ship's passengers, crew, and cargo.
Midships	(see *Amidships*)
Nautical mile	6,080.2 feet, as compared to a land mile of 5,280 feet.
Open seating	Seating in the main dining room(s) is not assigned.
Paddlewheel	A wheel with boards around its circumference, and, commonly, the source of propulsion for riverboats.
Pitch	The rocking back and forth (bow to stern) motion of a ship that may be felt in heavy seas when the ship is under way.

Port	The left side of the ship when facing toward the bow.
Port charge	Port taxes, collected by the line and paid to a local government authority; it may include other miscellaneous charges, such as gasoline surcharge and fees.
Port tax	A charge levied by the local government authority to be paid by the passenger.
Prow	The bow or the stem (the front) of the ship.
Purser	A senior management position on board ship. In most cases, the purser is like the general manager of a hotel, but in some cases, he or she is more of the financial or administration officer.
Quay	(pronounced "key") A dock, berth, or pier.
Registry	The country under whose flag the ship is registered and to whose laws the ship and its owners must comply; in addition to compliance with the laws of the countries at which the ship calls and/or embarks/disembarks passengers/cargo.
Rigging	The ropes, chains, and cables that support the ship's masts, spars, kingposts, cranes, and the like.
Roll	The alternate sway of a ship from side to side.
Running lights	Three lights (green on the starboard side, red on the port side and white at the top of the mast) required by international law to be lighted when the ship is in motion between sunset and sunrise.
Second seating	The later of two meal times in the ship's dining room(s).
Space ratio	A measurement of cubic space per passenger. Gross registered ton divided by

the number of passengers (basis two) equals space ratio.

Stabilizer	A gyroscopically operated finlike device extending from both sides of the ship below the waterline to provide stability for the ship and reduce its roll.
Stack	The funnel or "chimney" from which the ship's gases of combustion are freed to the atmosphere.
Starboard	The right side of the ship when facing toward the bow.
Stateroom	Cabin.
Steward	Personnel on board ship.
Stem	The extreme bow or prow of the ship.
Stern	The extreme rear of the ship.
Superstructure	The structure of the ship above the main deck or water line.
Tender	A small vessel, sometimes the ship's lifeboat, used to move passengers to and from the shore when the ship is at anchor.
Transfers	Conveyances between the ship and other locations, such as airports, hotels, or departure points for shore excursions.
Upper berth	A single-size bed higher from the floor than usual (similar to a bunk bed), usually folded or recessed into the wall or ceiling by day.
Wake	The track of agitated water left behind a ship in motion.
Waterline	The line at the side of the ship's hull that corresponds to the surface of the water.
Weigh	To raise, e.g., to weigh the anchor.
Windward	Toward the wind, to the direction from which the wind blows.

TIME TO GO

If you have purchased an air/sea package, your cruise begins from the moment you arrive at the airport. Here's how.

CRUISE DOCUMENTS

Normally, you will receive your travel documents—tickets, transfer vouchers, boarding forms, luggage tags, etc.—about two weeks before departure. Some cruise lines, particularly the more deluxe ones and the smaller ones that go to offbeat destinations, begin sending out material a month or more in advance.

Often, this will include information about the ports of call on your itinerary and the shore excursions that are sold on board ship. It will also include a "Welcome Aboard" brochure, which is intended to help familiarize you with your ship. Read it. It will help you in making preparations.

Be sure to bring all cruise documents and literature pertaining to your cruise that you receive from your cruise line or travel agent with you. *Do not* pack them in your luggage. You will have to show your cruise ticket when you check in during initial boarding procedures at the dock.

The final cruise documents will include your airline tickets and cruise tickets. Your travel agent should have checked them before sending them to you. *Check them yourself.* Sometimes, if you have bought your cruise late, the documents will come directly to you from the cruise line. *Check them too.*

Also included will be luggage tags with the cruise line's name and logo. They show spaces for you to list your name and address on one side and the name of your ship, your cruise number and cabin number, departure date and departure port, on the other side. The information you need to complete the luggage tags is always contained in your cruise ticket.

You should attach at least one tag to every piece of luggage you are taking, including your hand luggage. (You would be amazed by the number of people who, in their excitement over travel, leave hand luggage behind on an airplane, in the airport, or on a motorcoach. If you have a tag on it, airline or port personnel will know immediately what to do with it.)

Once you have checked in at the airport, you will not need to deal with your luggage again. Assuming it is properly identified, it will be in your cabin when you board the ship or soon thereafter. If it is not, do not panic. Cruise ships, especially large ones, have thousands of bags to unload and sort as passengers arrive. It may seem like an eternity, but from our experience luggage moves from the airport into your cabin with amazing speed.

But the delay is one of several reasons why you should travel with a small carry-on bag. In addition to your medications and cosmetics, it's a good idea to include a *change of clothing* in your hand luggage for your first afternoon aboard the ship, particularly when you are coming from a cold climate to a warm one. And if you really want to play it cool, you might also include a bathing suit—although there is not likely to be water in the pool while the ship is in port.

AIRPORT ARRIVAL AND TRANSFERS

As soon as you walk off your airplane in Miami, Ft. Lauderdale, San Juan, Vancouver, or any airport of a major departure city, you will find uniformed cruise line representatives, usually with a placard of your ship's name held high. The reps gather all their charges and escort them or direct them to awaiting motorcoach transportation. You will need to have your transfer voucher to board the bus, so keep it in a handy place.

If you do not spot your cruise line representative, ask one of your airline personnel or another cruise line for help. Or simply go to the first airport "red" phone you see and ask for your cruise line representative to be paged, or proceed to the location where motorcoaches pick up passengers to transfer them to the pier.

You do not need to go to the baggage arrival area. Your luggage is being transferred directly from the airplane to baggage conveyors that go directly to trucks engaged by the cruise lines to transfer the luggage of their passengers to the appropriate ship. That's why it is so important for you to fill in your luggage tags properly and put them on your bags.

ADVANCE ARRIVALS OR DELAYED RETURNS

Almost all cruise lines have hotel and sightseeing packages for those who want to arrive in their port of departure in advance of their cruise or to remain there at the end of their cruise. These, too, are described in the cruise line's brochure. Such a decision is strictly a personal matter. Obviously, if you can afford the time and additional expense, it is nice to be able to extend your vacation.

If your cruise begins following a long flight, such as a European or Asian cruise, or from the West Coast to the Caribbean, or the east coast to Alaska, ships normally schedule the first day as a day at sea to give passengers a chance to catch up on jet lag. If not, and the itinerary calls for immediate stops at ports of call, you could consider arriving a day early, although we do not see the point in spending money for a hotel room just to sleep when you can just as easily sleep on your ship and either skip the first day's excursions or take a half-day tour after a few hours of rest.

The time to give the most serious consideration to a-day-in-advance arrival is when you have purchased the cruise-only portion of a cruise and are arranging for your own transportation to the departure port and your travel falls during heavy travel periods—Thanksgiving, Christmas, New Year's, President's weekend—when the weather in the northern portion of the United States traditionally turns bad and flights are delayed.

If you are on an air/sea program, your cruise line has a much greater obligation—although not necessarily a legal one—to get you to the ship when you've been delayed, either by holding the ship's departure or by arranging for a hotel room and getting you to the first port of call. If you are traveling on one of the cruise line's air/sea packages, you are likely not alone but one of many stranded passengers.

The cruise line has your name on a list with the cruise line's representative at the airport and knows to expect you. They are in touch with the airport and your cruise ship and are probably laying out a strategy before you arrive in your departure port. However, if you have chosen to travel on your own, the cruise line has no such record and no obligation to help you, although most will try, if they can. If you arrive a day or so early, you can avoid the potential hassle. Some people might also advise you to arrive early so that you can avoid standing in line to check in. That, it seems to us, is the least valid reason. Lines at the airport and at cruise ship departure gates are a fact of life in today's mass-market travel. If you are so impatient that you cannot stand in a line to check in—even if it takes an hour—without having your blood pressure boil over, then you are probably on the wrong cruise. Let's face it. Megaships have mega passengers and they must be processed one at a time. It would certainly speed up the process if everyone arrived with all their documents filled in properly.

AT THE PIER

If you are lucky, you will be in the first busload of passengers to arrive from the airport and the first in line to check in. But don't count on it. Chances are you will be among several hundred others, and, depending on the cruise line, the day of the week, the size of the ship, and probably some other contingencies, you will stand in line ten minutes to two hours—or at least it could seem like two hours. Pull out a magazine or a book and start reading.

Large cruise lines with large ships do have the procedure down to a system, asking you to line up behind your letter in the alphabet. Despite an occasional glitch, it works well. If there are exceptionally long lines or if you are a hyper type A personality, however, you would probably be better off to repair to the nearest bar for an hour or so. You will have up to 30 minutes before departure to get on the ship. Some cruise lines even let you board up to 15 minutes prior to departure, but we would not suggest anyone cut it that close.

Normally, cruise lines begin processing passengers at 12 noon or 1 P.M. for a departure at 4 or 5 P.M. But often they do not allow passengers to embark earlier than two or three hours before departure in order to have ample time for the previous passengers to disembark and the crew to clean the ship and prepare your cabin.

VISITORS

For security reasons, most cruise lines now have a no visitors policy. If your friends or family want to send you off in style, they can arrange through your travel agent to have a party set up for you, flowers, with wine, and champagne in your cabin, or a birthday cake or anniversary surprise in the dining room.

SETTLING IN

BOARDING YOUR SHIP

Most cruise ships have their cabin stewards/stewardesses—all decked out in uniforms and white gloves—waiting at the gangway to greet you and escort you to your cabin. Your attending escort might give you a quick orientation or will ask you to wait for your regular cabin steward whose name is probably on a small tent card on your dresser/desk along with the ship's literature that is awaiting your arrival. It might also include some postcards and stationery, an agenda for the day's events, and a deck plan.

CHECKING OUT YOUR CABIN

You will want to take a quick look around the cabin to be sure everything is in working order, which it usually is on new ships but not necessarily on old ones. You will need to know how to operate the air conditioning, lights, and the hot water faucets—some new fancy ones are tricky and the water from the tap can scald you. Check for the location of the life preservers, blankets, and pillows—do you have enough? If there's anything missing or not as you requested—twin beds instead of a double—now's the time to report it. If you cannot locate your cabin steward, go to the purser or front desk. If you do not get satisfaction, start working your way up to the *hotel manager*.

HAIR DRYERS/ELECTRIC SHAVERS

Almost all cabins on modern cruise ships have standard 110 AC electrical outlets, so you can use a small hair dryer and an electric razor without needing an adapter. A few older ships are not fitted so conveniently.

LAUNDRY AND DRY CLEANING

Almost all ships have laundry service, but far fewer have dry cleaning facilities. Generally, the laundry service is good and reasonable, but they do tend to use lots of bleach. You can give your articles to be cleaned or pressed to your cabin steward. Usually they are returned in a day, and same-day service is available for an extra fee, as in a hotel. You will find price lists and laundry bags in your cabin.

For safety reasons, however, ships ask that you not use irons in your cabins but most have laundrettes with an iron and ironing board, as well as coin-operated washers and dryers for passenger use. The Standard Features section in each cruise line's profile in Part Two has specific information on the availability of hair dryers and laundrettes.

TELEPHONES AND OTHER COMMUNICATIONS

All but a few cruise ships have telephones in cabins along with instructions on using them and a phone directory. Most phones now have direct-dial to the United States 24 hours a day, but *be aware* of the price. Usually, you will be charged $15 per minute for a ship-to-shore call. Receiving a call or a fax may carry a charge of $5 per minute or more. Cruise lines' policies vary. Some allow you to place collect calls or charge your call to your shipboard account. Recently, Celebrity Cruises installed new technology that enables passengers to dial 800-numbers in the United States directly from their cabins. The price is $9.50 per minute.

If someone wants to reach you at sea, they can telephone the ship by calling 1-800-SEA-CALL, asking for the ship by name and giving its approximate location. Charges for this telephone call will appear on the caller's regular long-distance phone bill. Ship-to-shore telephone and fax services are normally available only when your ship is at sea. When the ship is in port, local shoreside communications must be used.

CHECKING OUT YOUR SHIP

After you have checked out your cabin, it's a good idea to take a tour of the ship. With your deck plan in hand, start at the top and walk the full length of each deck. You might not necessarily remember where everything is, but it will give you a good overview. The ship is going to be your home for the next few days or weeks or more, so it's nice to feel at home as quickly as possible.

CHECKING ON YOUR DINING RESERVATIONS

When you book your cruise, your travel agent should state your dining preference and request your reservations. You may request first or second seating, smoking or nonsmoking areas, tables for two, four, six, or eight. Most cruise lines say they honor requests on a first-come, first-served basis, yet only a few will confirm them in advance. Generally, dining room reservations will only be confirmed by the maître d'hôtel on board.

Royal Caribbean International is one of the few lines that has the dining reservation printed on your cruise ticket. Why, in this age of computers, all of them can't do the same, is a mystery—unless it's to allow the maître d'hôtel to have control for the last-minute shuffling that goes on and to ensure he gets his tips.

You may receive a confirmation card for your dining room seating arrangements upon check-in at the pier, or it may be in your cabin. If not, your first order of business will be to check on them. Even the cruise lines that give you a dining room reservation in advance may still ask you to confirm it with the maître d'hôtel.

Wherever you receive the notice, if it is not what you requested, make a beeline to the maître d'hôtel. Most will be able to accommodate you, although not necessarily on the first night. Sometimes it takes until the next day or so to straighten it out. Rest assured, you will not be the only one. We know of no other single item that causes more consternation than dining room reservations. There are always a few problems on every cruise.

If you have left it to the cruise line or maître d'hôtel to place you randomly at a table and you are unhappy with your dining companions, do not hesitate to ask the maître d'hôtel to change you. His job is to make you happy. A cruise is meant to be fun and enjoyable. Dining is one of its main ingredients. There's nothing worse than having to spend a week dining at a table of people with whom you have nothing in common and with no basis for conversation. And you don't need to.

DINING HOURS

All but the most luxurious ships or the most informal ones have two seatings for the main meals of the day. Generally, they are:

Breakfast
First or Early Seating: 7 or 7:15 to 8 or 8:15 A.M.
Second or Late Seating: 8:15 or 8:30 to 9:15 or 9:30 A.M.

Lunch
First or Early Seating: 12 noon to 1 P.M.
Second or Late Seating: 1:15 or 1:30 to 2:15 or 2:30 P.M.

Dinner
First or Early Seating: 6:15 or 6:30 to 7:30 or 8 P.M.
Second or Late Seating: 8:15 or 8:30 to 9:45 or 10 P.M.

Many ships have open seating for breakfast and lunch and assigned seats for dinner, in which case the hours are likely to be:

Breakfast: 8 to 9:30 A.M.
Lunch: 12:30 to 2 P.M.
Dinner: First Seating: 6:15 or 6:30 to 7:30 or 8 P.M.
  Second Seating: 8:15 or 8:30 to 9:45 or 10 P.M.

If you are an early riser, you will probably be happy with the early seating. If you are likely to close the disco every night, you might prefer the late one. Of course, you will not be confined to these meals as there's usually an early bird coffee, a buffet breakfast, midmorning bouillon, lunch buffet, ice cream on deck, afternoon tea, cocktail canapes, a midnight buffet, and if you are still hungry, there's room service and on some ships a fruit basket in your cabin.

ESTABLISHING SHIPBOARD CREDIT

Most cruise lines have now gone to a cashless system. Upon check-in you will be given a card, just like a credit card, which you will use as your identification card. If you want to establish credit for purchases on board ship, drinks at the bar, wine in the dining room, etc., you need to present a major credit card, American Express, Mastercard, Visa, and sometimes others, either at the check-in desk or the purser's office (you will be told at check-in) to have an imprint made and signed.

On the last night of the cruise you will receive a printout of all your charges for your review. You can choose to pay it with cash or traveler's checks or have it billed to your credit card account, just as in a hotel. The Standard Features in each cruise line's profile in Part Two has an entry listing the credit cards each cruise line accepts for cruise payments as well as shipboard charges.

PREPARING FOR TIME ASHORE

PORT TALKS AND SHOPPING GUIDELINES

All ships offer what are known as port talks—briefings on the country or island and port where the ship will dock. The quality of these talks varies enormously, not only with the cruise line but also with the ship, and depends largely on the knowledge of the cruise director and the importance the cruise line puts on this element of the cruise experience.

For the most part, mainstream cruise lines with large ships do a lousy job with port talks. On the other hand, adventure and expedition cruises give superb talks. Generally, small ships have a better track record than large ones.

In the Caribbean, particularly, the talks on large, mainstream ships are given by staff with little or no real knowledge of the islands. They do little more than spill out a batch of trite information and clichés.

Often the talks are nothing more than shopping tips, and in fact, some are shopping talks sponsored by local stores—a practice that has reached scandalous proportions. Be aware, too, that cruise directors often receive commissions from local stores, even though they will deny it. Their vested interest could color their presentation and recommendations.

There are two simple steps to avoid being misled: First, during the port talk, if the cruise director or anyone else recommends one store to the exclusion of all others, that should alert you to shop around before buying. The store being recommended may actually be the best place to buy, or it may not.

Second, if you have been led to believe there are fabulous buys to be had in duty-free shops on board and in ports of call, forget it. More often than not, you can do as well, if not better, at discount stores and factory outlets at home. Nonetheless, if you are considering sizable purchases, particularly of jewelry, cameras, china, or crystal, bring a list of prices from home with you and do some comparison shopping. But be sure you are comparing like products. Prices in shipboard shops are a good gauge as they are usually competitive with those at ports of call.

In the Caribbean, you can expect to save about 20 percent on such well-known names as Gucci, Fendi, and Vuitton and on French perfumes, which must be sold at prices set by the makers. Any store caught undercutting the price will be dropped from distribution. The biggest savings are on cigarettes and liquor, not because the retail price is so much cheaper, but because you save the hefty U.S. federal and state taxes imposed on them.

SHORE EXCURSIONS: SOME PITFALLS AND COSTS

The sightseeing tours that passengers take at ports of call are termed shore excursions by the cruise lines, and they are the weakest link in the total cruise story, which is unfortunate, given their importance to the overall cruise experience. Shore excursions are available at every stop on a ship's itinerary and in almost all cases they are an additional cost.

The exceptions are adventure and expedition cruises, where shore visits are an integral part of the cruise and indeed are one of the reasons these types of cruises may appear to be more costly than mainstream cruising. Also, cruises in China usually include the cost of shore excursions, not because the cruise lines are suddenly altruistic but because the Chinese set them up that way.

With a rare exception, shore excursions cannot be purchased in advance, which is one of several reasons that make them a weak link. Usually, however, a pamphlet describing the shore excursions offered by your ship is included in the literature your cruise line sends you in advance.

Not all brochures have prices with them, but if you want the prices in order to plan a budget, you can ask for them, either directly from the cruise line or through your travel agent. It may take some effort to get them. We are happy to report, however, that more and more cruise lines do appear to be including prices in their literature. Also, more are publishing pamphlets with tours specific to the itinerary of your cruise, which makes it easier for you to read and decide which of the tours you might want to take.

To maximize the pleasure of your cruise and spend your time in port to your best advantage, read the literature. And also read other books and magazine articles about the ports of call you are visiting. In some locales, you might decide that you prefer sightseeing on your own or enjoying a sport or another activity.

Generally, you buy shore excursions on your ship either from a shore excursion office or, in a few cases, from the purser or cruise director. It has been assumed in the past that people prefer buying their shore excursions on board since, frequently, their interests and plans change once the cruise is under way. However, that assumption may have no foundation in fact. On the contrary, after you have been subjected to the manner in which shore excursions are sold on cruise ships, you might say, as we do: there must be a better way.

Often you will need to make your decision the first night of the cruise and unless you have done your homework—which most people have not—you will be buying blind. We urge you to read your tour literature *in advance of your cruise*. The shore excursion office usually has limited hours, and for the first few days of the cruise the lines for shore excursion tickets, particularly on large ships, are long.

Normally, shore excursions are operated by local tour companies, using motorcoach transportation for 30–50 passengers, depending on the location and the terrain. Most are designed to appeal to the majority of passengers and assume that passengers are on their first visit to the locale, which is another reason they are a weak link.

Shore excursions vary little from cruise line to cruise line and are, for the most part, dull, off-the-shelf, unimaginative, city and/or countryside tours to the best known, instant-photograph sights. And that's a third reason they are a weak link. There are some exceptions. The most notable are the Greek Isles cruises where tour escorts are university graduates and must pass stiff examinations to qualify for their jobs.

Also commendable are the selections by American Hawaii Cruises for the variety of sports and their stress on nature and culture. The worst are the excursions in the Caribbean, which is where most ships cruise. Unfortunately, the cruise lines have shown little interest or effort to improve them or to help local operators improve them.

Throughout this book, we have included some information on shore excursions, but not as much as we would have liked due to space limitations. We tried particularly to point out which cruise lines have the more imaginative shore excursions and to give readers an idea about prices.

As a rule of thumb for ordinary tours, you can expect to pay about $11–13 per hour of touring. In other words, a two- to two-and-a-half-hour city tour will range from about $20–30, a three-hour island tour will be $30–40, and so on. There are many variables, depending on the locale, the number of people on the excursion, local costs, and mode of transport, to name a few.

When the ship arrives in port, the people who have purchased shore excursions are allowed to disembark first and are usually asked to follow a departure schedule in order to avoid a traffic jam at the gangway. This is seldom a problem when the ship pulls dockside as the passengers can be off-loaded quickly. It can be a problem when the ship must tender, however, as it cuts down as much as an hour or more (depending on the size of the ship) on the amount of time you will have in port if you plan to go on your own.

AT THE END OF YOUR CRUISE

TIPPING

There are no hard and fast rules about tipping, but because it causes so much consternation for passengers, cruise lines offer guidelines, which are distributed on board ship; some even publish them in their cruise brochures, in case you want to budget for them in advance. In Part Two, the Standard Features box of the cruise line profiles lists the Suggested Tipping for each line.

The guidelines are very similar, with the budget cruises being slightly less and the luxury cruises being more. You can follow the guidelines or follow your own desire. Ship officers and senior management are never tipped. But for everyone else on the service side that you encounter, tips are their main source of compensation. Only a few luxury and deluxe ships include tipping in the rates; these are noted in the Standard Features of the cruise line profiles, where it pertains.

At the last session the cruise director will hold to tell you about disembarkation procedures, he will also outline the ship's tipping guidelines. There's nothing subtle about the matter of tipping, as there once was. On the last day of your cruise, your cabin steward will leave you a supply of envelopes for distributing your tips and likely a copy of the guidelines. Of late, it's gotten so crass that the envelopes are actually stamped with the titles—Cabin Steward, Dining Steward, Waiter—in case you did not know whom you should tip!

Normally, the tips are made to individuals—your cabin stewards and dining room waiters. On ships with Greek crews, tips are pooled in a common kitty for distribution to include those behind the scenes, such as kitchen staffs. On small ships, particularly adventure ships, tips are also pooled.

You can choose to distribute your tips the last night of the cruise, as most people do, or the morning that you depart. Some cruise lines, particularly the more deluxe ones, will arrange for you to prepay tips. This information is noted in the cruise line profile's Standard Features, where it pertains.

DEPARTING

All good things must come to an end, your captain and cruise director will tell you, and to make the disembarkation as smooth as possible, they will ask you to follow certain procedures. These will be outlined by the cruise director in his final disembarkation talk and repeated frequently on the closed-circuit television in your cabin and on an instruction sheet with the daily agenda. Also on the last day, your cabin steward will give you luggage tags that you are to fill in and attach to your luggage. You are asked to place your luggage outside your cabin door—all but hand luggage—after dinner before you retire.

The luggage tags use a color-coded, alphabetic system that enables the ship to move passengers off in an orderly fashion by cabin locations and by airline departure times for those on air/sea packages, as well as identify the airline on which you are traveling so that your luggage will end up in the correct place at the airport.

Most cruise lines ask that you have your luggage outside your door for pick up by 11 P.M. or midnight, but some are unreasonable, wanting it out by 8 or 10 P.M. If you dine at the late seating, that's before you finish dinner or the show ends. Such early requests are strictly for the ship's convenience—never mind the passengers' inconvenience—because no luggage can be unloaded until the ship docks. Do what's convenient for you and tell your cabin steward what to expect. The last night of a cruise is almost always casual so you can plan your packing accordingly. If you have brought an extra carry-all bag, as we suggested, you will find it very handy for the last minute items you forgot to pack.

Ships normally arrive in port on the last day about 7 or 8 A.M. and need about an hour to clear and unload luggage, which means that no passengers will disembark before 9 A.M. The ship is very eager to get passengers off as quickly as possible. Some people find the disembarkation process so abrupt as to be unpleasant. But do try to remember that another group of passengers will be arriving soon, and the staff and crew have only about four hours to turn the ship around and be all smiles for the next cruise.

Breakfast is served either at normal hours and will have a full menu, or at abbreviated hours with a short menu. Room service is usually not available.

Normally, you will be called to depart by the color of your luggage tags, which, in turn, means the departure time of your flight. In other words, they want to get the earliest departures moving out the soonest.

After you leave the ship, you will encounter varying degrees of chaos depending on the port, but usually you will walk into the baggage holding area where your luggage has been placed according to the letter of your last name. You are responsible for finding it and taking it to customs. In Miami, for example, there are baggage handlers to help you and the customs official stands by the exit door to take the customs declaration form you were given aboard ship to fill in. They may ask to see your passport, so it's wise to have it in a handy place, along with your airline tickets.

After you pass through customs, you give your luggage to the airline representative to board on a truck for the airport—and watch it being loaded along with hundreds of others—and then you find the motorcoach that's going to your airline's departure gate, show your transfer ticket, and climb aboard.

If you are not on an air/sea package, you might be able to board the motorcoach anyway, unless you have a lot of luggage. Otherwise, at busy ports taxis are always standing by.

Sometimes, the airlines with large numbers of passengers on their flights will set up desks at the port to enable you to check in at the dock and proceed directly to your gate at the airport. It's such a sensible arrangement, you have to wonder why it's not the routine.

Part Two

CRUISE LINES
AND
THEIR SHIPS

Best of the Best 97–98

Best Kept Secret:	*Marco Polo* (Orient Cruises)
Best Value-for-Money/High:	*Silver Cloud/Silver Wind* (Silversea Cruises)
Best Value-for-Money/Mid:	*Galaxy* (Celebrity Cruises)
Best Value-for-Money/Low:	*Carnival Destiny* (Carvinal Cruise Line)
Best Overall Luxury Ship:	*Crystal Harmony* (Crystal Cruises)
Best Overall Premium Ship:	*Sun Princess* (Princess Cruises)
Best Overall Budget Ship:	*Mayan Prince* (American Canadian Caribbean Line)
Best Small Ship Experience:	Windstar Cruises
Best Big Ship Experience:	Royal Caribbean International
Best Cabins:	Silverseas Cruises
Best Cuisine:	*Radisson Diamond* (Radisson Seven Seas Cruises)
Best Service:	Seabourn Cruise Line
Best Itineraries:	Cunard
Best Pre-Cruise Literature:	Clipper Cruise Line
Best Enrichment Programs:	Crystal Cruises
Best Entertainment:	Carnival Cruise Lines
Best Sports Facilities:	Norwegian Cruise Line
Best Shore Excursions:	Princess Cruises
Best Family Cruises:	Royal Caribbean International

The *Unofficial Guide to Cruises* will award these categories in each new edition. We invite input from readers to help us in making selections. Please send us your candidates for any of the above categories.

THE HEART OF THE MATTER

This section begins with alphabetical listings of the cruise lines and ships that serve the U.S. and Canadian market. Following the listings are the in-depth cruise line and ship profiles, the heart of this guide. The presentation for each cruise line has three parts: a cruise line profile, standard features, and cruise ship profiles.

Cruise Line Profiles

The opening three to four pages focus on the cruise line and the type of cruises it offers. The Type of Ships, Type of Cruises, Cruise Line's Strengths, Cruise Line's Shortcomings, Fellow Passengers, Recommended For, and Not Recommended For are "at-a-glance" summaries to help you select for further reading those cruise lines of potential interest. Knowing something about who your fellow passengers are likely to be is for some people the best way to spot the right cruise. Learning our recommendations or the cruise line's strengths and weaknesses might be better leads for others.

This summary information is followed by a background on the Line, its Fleet, and Cruise Areas to give you a picture of the company behind the cruise. The section entitled Style defines the cruise experience you can expect on any of the ships of that particular cruise line. Distinctive Features highlights some of the special amenities or facilities the line offers that are innovative or might not be available on other ships.

Rates

The Rates section highlights discounts, special fares, and packages, and provides a range of per person daily (per diem) rates. These figures were derived by averaging cruise-only (no airfare) brochure rates for each class of cabin accommodation on every ship in the line. The calculations exclude owner's suites, presidential suites, and other extraordinary accommodations. The purpose of the rate table is to give you a sense of the most and the least you would have to pay per day for a cruise if you paid brochure rates. If you are a savvy shopper you will almost certainly be able to chip away 5 percent to 50 percent of the listed per diem rate by taking advantage of readily available discounts. As an aside, our average rate is not calculated by summing the highest and lowest rates in the table and dividing by two. The average per diem takes into account how many of each type of accommodation is available in the line's cabin inventory. It should be noted that the Per Diem Rate Table averages rates for all ships of the line.

Past Passengers tells you what you can expect by being a loyal customer, and The Last Word is exactly that—our summary of the line, the big picture and any point that needs to be made or emphasized.

Standard Features

Information on facilities and amenities common to all of a cruise line's ships, such as officers, staff, dining facilities, dress code, cabin amenities, electricity, etc., is all listed on one page for handy reference.

Cruise Ship Profiles

The cruise line's fleet, starting with its flagship or most representative ship, is covered in depth. Sister ships with identical design that represent a specific class or style of ship have been clustered together. Other ships that vary only in degree have been given shorter treatment, along with the suggestion to readers to review all the section for a full picture of the cruise experience that the line offers—a recommendation we would make to any user of this guidebook.

Quality Ratings   To separate ships according to the overall quality of the cruise experience, and to allow you to compare ships from different lines, we have grouped the ships into classifications denoted by numbers 1–10, with 10 being the best rating attainable. The numerical ratings (enclosed in a circle) are based on the quality and diversity of the ship's features and service, taking into consideration the ship's state of repair, maintenance, and cleanliness; the design, comfort, decor and furnishing of public areas; recreational and fitness facilities; meal quality and dining room service; entertainment, activities, and shore excursion programs; cabin comfort, decor, furnishings, and spaciousness; and the hospitality, courtesy, and responsiveness of the officers and crew.

As an aside, we have opted for the numerical ratings (explained above) because some of our colleagues in the travel press have hopelessly muddled the more familiar star ratings. Traditionally, ships have been rated on a scale of one to five stars. This rating system was easily understood by the cruising public and provided the consumer with a quick, easy way to compare the opinions of different critics. Recently, however, some writers have unilaterally changed the scale to 1–6 stars, and in one case, 1–7 stars, effectively precluding any meaningful comparison. We believe that the consumer profits from a standardized rating system. In the absence of any such standardization, however, we have elected to get out of the star business.

Value Ratings   There is no consideration of cost in the quality ratings. If you are a person who wants the finest cruise available and cost is no issue, you need look no further than the quality ratings. If, on the other hand, you are looking for both quality and value, then you should check out the value rating, expressed in letters. The value ratings are defined as follows:

A   Exceptional value, a real bargain.
B   Good value.
C   Absolutely fair. You get exactly what you pay for.
D   Somewhat overpriced.
F   Significantly overpriced.

All value ratings are based on brochure rates. Any discount you are able to obtain will improve the value rating for the ship in question.

A Word about New Ships

It is our policy not to evaluate or rate new ships until they have been in service for at least one year. This allows the new ship to work out kinks and settle into normal operation. Ratings for new ships will be included in revised editions of the *Unofficial Guide*. If you are contemplating a cruise on a new ship, a quick perusal of our ratings and descriptions for other ships in the same cruise line should give you a pretty good idea of what to expect. If a ship has not completed a full year of service as of press time, it will be marked as a "preview" in the ship's ratings box.

A Matter of Reference

Cruise lines profiled in this section are listed on page vii of the Contents. To find listings of specific ships, please refer to the Appendix: "Cruise Ships Index, " pages 804–819.

ABERCROMBIE & KENT
INTERNATIONAL, INC.

1520 Kensington Road, Oak Brook, IL 60521
(630) 954-2944; (800) 323-7308; fax (630) 954-3324
http://www.abercrombiekent.com

TYPE OF SHIP   Small expedition vessel.

TYPE OF CRUISES   Adventurous, education-oriented for sophisticated travelers with an avid interest in nature and wildlife.

CRUISE LINE'S STRENGTHS
- superb enrichment program
- highly experienced expedition leaders
- size and maneuverability of ship
- friendliness of staff and crew
- all-inclusive programs
- Antarctica itineraries

CRUISE LINE'S SHORTCOMINGS
- small, spartan cabins and bathrooms
- limited cabin storage space
- ship subject to vigorous movement in heavy seas

FELLOW PASSENGERS   Professional, retired or semiretired, affluent, well educated, well traveled, usually age 50 and up, in good health and reasonably fit. Flexible, ecology-minded, and intellectually curious. A sizable contingent are Europeans, especially Germans, and other nationalities.

Recommended For   Adventurous travelers who are deeply interested in nature, wildlife, geology, history, and photography, flexible enough to adapt to weather changes and resulting itinerary changes, and fit enough to enjoy hikes in the snows of Antarctica or rides in Zodiac boats on the Amazon. Singles, who will have no trouble making friends aboard this amiable vessel.

Not Recommended For   Disabled travelers, children, and anyone demanding a set routine, entertainment, and luxurious accommodations.

CRUISE AREAS AND SEASONS Antarctica, November–February; Amazon, March–April & October; Caribbean, May; Australia (southern), summer.

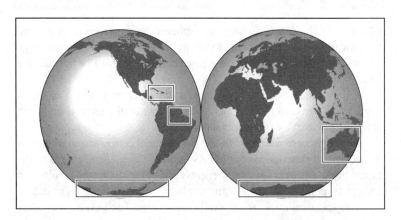

THE LINE Abercrombie & Kent is a prestigious international tour operator specializing in exotic and offbeat worldwide journeys for affluent, sophisticated travelers. Other company programs include barge and river cruises in Europe and on the Amazon, Nile, and Yangtze rivers (see Part Three). In all its programs, the company stresses culture and ecologically sound tourism.

A&K has operated the *Explorer* since 1991. A ship with a venerable history, it is the most experienced vessel sailing in Antarctic waters. Built in 1969 in Rauma, Finland, for the late Swedish travel pioneer, Lars-Eric Linblad, as the *Linblad Explorer* it was the world's first expedition cruise ship. It subsequently sailed as the *Society Explorer* for Society Expeditions.

The *Explorer* has an ice-strengthened hull (with an unrestricted rating from the Norwegian Det Norske Veritas classification society) that allows it to crunch effortlessly through packed ice. Its small size, shallow draft, and bow thrusters increase maneuverability among the ice floes and bergs. When she is not sailing in the Antarctic and South American waters, A&K also charters the vessel to other operators at certain times of the year.

The Fleet	Built/Renovated	Tonnage	Passengers
Explorer	1969/1992	2,398	96

STYLE   High-seas adventure for sophisticated travelers with a thirst for education and enrichment, an interest in wildlife, and the drive to go beyond the predictable to have a rare travel experience designed for a hardy, affluent few.

Cabins are small but adequate; what they lack in luxury is compensated for by the travel experience. The international cuisine is good but not gourmet. Service is friendly and efficient.

Passengers are welcome on the navigational bridge and have access to a coterie of experienced naturalists on the ship's staff, as well as to the expert guest lecturers who are credentialed zoologists, marine biologists, geologists, polar explorers, oceanographers, artists, and photographers.

The socializing focuses around the lectures. Each evening cruisers gather in the lounge over cocktails while the expedition leader and guest lecturers recap the day's events and answer questions. During Zodiac outings and shore landings, the experts lead small groups, pointing out wildlife, geology formations, and points of historical interest.

DISTINCTIVE FEATURES   A small but focused library offers books and maps relevant to the cruising area. The navigational bridge is open to passengers at all times. Passengers receive extensive pretrip information covering the itinerary, clothing requirements, photography tips, and an expedition notebook with reading list. On Antarctic cruises, every passenger is given a parka and backpack. After the cruise, participants are sent a copy of the bridge log and an illustrated voyage diary.

RATES

Highest Per Diem	Lowest Per Diem	Average Per Diem
$521	$159	$253

The above per diems are calculated from the cruise line's nondiscounted *cruise-only* fares on standard accommodations. Per diems vary by season, by cabin location, and by cruise areas.

Note: All tips and shore excursions are included in the cruise fare.

Special Fares and Discounts   Early booking discount of 10 percent with six months' advance purchase. Passengers booking two consecutive sailings get 20 percent off the second cruise.

- Single Supplement: 150 percent in the lower-priced cabin categories; 200 percent for other categories.

Packages
- Air/Sea: All prices include regional transportation within South America; international air is extra.
- Others: None on Antarctica itineraries.
- Pre/Post: All Antarctica programs include a pre- or postcruise stay in the port of embarkation/debarkation, with hotel, meals, and sightseeing.

Past Passengers   Marco Polo is the club for veteran A&K travelers. Small and exclusive by design, it offers a quarterly newsletter, occasional "members-only" trips, a 5 percent discount on land arrangements on most tours, luggage tags, members' priority on new destinations, tailor-made itineraries, a library of A&K videotapes for loan at no charge, and eligibility to compete in the annual Marco Polo Photo Contest. The annual membership fee is $75, with five-year, lifetime, and children's memberships available.

THE LAST WORD   Cruise ships have flocked to Antarctica in recent years, but the *Explorer* has the longest experience sailing in these demanding waters, as well as the most experienced expedition leaders. Because weather conditions are so changeable in this remote part of the world, it helps immensely to have a savvy staff familiar with a variety of alternative landing sites. The Antarctica cruises are intended for serious travelers who cherish the unusual opportunity. Gadabouts and travelers simply wanting to add exotic destinations to their travel list should look elsewhere. (See Abercrombie & Kent International, Inc., Part Three, Amazon River Cruises.)

ABERCROMBIE & KENT/EXPLORER STANDARD FEATURES

Officers Northern European and Filipino.

Staffs Dining, Cabin/Filipino; Cruise and Entertainment/International.

Dining Facilities One dining room for a single, open seating. Buffet breakfast and lunch, a la carte dinner. Breakfast served in the lounge, midmorning bouillon, midnight snacks, and coffee/tea throughout the day. Afternoon tea.

Special Diets Vegetarian, low fat, low salt. Requests must be made in writing at least three weeks prior to sailing.

Room Service Light breakfast. During rough seas, passengers may order other meals from the dining room menu.

Dress Code Casual at all times.

Cabin Amenities Hair dryers, radios, toiletries.

Electrical Outlets 220 AC.

Wheelchair Access None.

Recreation and Entertainment Reading, board games, daily quiz; lounge with bar, piano, small dance floor; films/slide shows in lecture hall.

Sports and Fitness Small gym with reclining bicycle, ski machine, free weights; mixed sauna and shower. Small dipping pool (not used during Antarctica cruises). Stretch-and-tone class offered on deck on sea days.

Other Facilities Gift shop, sundeck, hospital, laundry/pressing service, satellite telecommunications, daily fax news.

Children's Facilities None.

Theme Cruises None.

Smoking Nonsmoking charter flights, dining room, and lounge during lectures and recap sessions.

A&K Suggested Tipping Dining room and cabin attendant tips included in rate. Bar/wine waiters may be tipped at passenger discretion. Extra tips may be contributed to the crew's party and activities fund.

Credit Cards For cruise payment and on-board charges, American Express, Diners Club, Discover, Mastercard, Visa, cash, traveler's checks, personal checks. On-board gift shop purchases, Visa, Mastercard only (separate imprint required).

Explorer

	Quality Rating	Value Rating
Explorer	❸	B

Registry: Liberia	Length: 239 feet	Beam: 46 feet
Cabins: 53	Draft: 13.7 feet	Speed: 12 knots
Maximum Passengers: 96	Passenger Decks: 5	Elevators: none
	Crew: 71	Space Ratio: n.a.

THE SHIP The *Explorer* is a jaunty little red ship, trimmed in white, and built expressly for polar waters, with an ice-strengthened hull, shallow draft, and bow thrusters for optimal maneuverability. The vessel's strong suit is its experience sailing in Antarctica. No other ship has been there longer.

A small flotilla of Zodiac boats is available for excursions among the ice floes and for shore landings. The Zodiacs are lowered over the side of the vessel into the water, and passengers walk down a stairway to board them. At the gangway before leaving the ship, staff members check everyone to be sure they are warmly and safely attired with rubber boots, waterproofs, lifejacket, and so on.

The *Explorer* is an extremely compact but functional vessel, with a main deck with the gangway exit, the reception desk, fax news and notice board, gift shop, dining room and lounge, bar and library.

The lounge is the ship's main socializing area, where evening recap sessions are held and self-service coffee and tea are available throughout the day. One deck up, the lecture hall is used for films and slide shows. Outside the hall is the pool deck where passengers—bundled in wool blankets on deck chairs—read, catch the sun on their faces, or snooze. Another deck up is the open bridge, hospital, and a small gym. A breezy top deck, covered in AstroTurf, is frequented mainly by photographers.

One remarkable feature of the *Explorer* is that nobody gets cabin keys and there are never problems. Still, you should leave expensive jewelry at home; you will not need it and no one would be impressed if you wore it. But for those who insist, safety deposit boxes are provided, free of charge, at the reception desk.

ITINERARIES 14–21 days, Antarctica, from November–February. Tour programs depart from Uruguay, Chile, Argentina, or the Falkland

Islands. Some sailings call at the South Georgia Islands. The ship makes as many landings as possible on the Antarctic Peninsula at such spots as Cuverville, Paulet, and Elephant islands. Each day the expedition leader announces the planned itinerary, but visits are subject to weather conditions.

- *In March–April and September–October*, the *Explorer* cruises the Amazon River on two separate itineraries: an 18-day, nearly 2,300-mile voyage, *The River Sea,* from Belem, Brazil to Iquitos, Peru; or a 10-day itinerary, *Upper Amazon,* which begins at Pevas, Peru and terminates at Manaus, Brazil. Extensions to Machu Picchu and other South American destinations can be added. In May and August, she has several positioning cruises in the Caribbean, visiting Suriname, Guyana, Orinoco River, Curaçao, Bonaire, and Tobago.

Home Port   Varies with itinerary.
Port Charges $96–119 per cruise.

CABINS   Passengers may be surprised initially by the compactness of the *Explorer*'s cabins, but they soon find that all the essentials are provided—adequately, if not lavishly. The beds may be a bit short for six-footers and the water-saving bathroom devices take a little getting used to—in the shower, a lever is pressed to deliver spurts of water lasting about 30 seconds each. All baths have shower only except the Marco Polo Suite, which has the ship's only bathtub.

Storage space is limited (two narrow closets), especially considering the boots, parkas, and other gear most passengers bring on an Antarctic expedition. But everyone does get a porthole (all cabins are outside), small vanity/desk and bureau, and nice touches like extra blankets, hair dryers, toiletries, pitchers of ice water, writing paper, and postcards.

Specifications   53 outside cabins, including 2 suites. Standard dimensions are 160 square feet. Most cabins with twin lower berths (none convert to doubles); a few have bunks; a few are triples. Suites have queen-size beds. No connecting cabins; no singles.

DINING   Mealtimes aboard the *Explorer* are casual, lively affairs, where all passengers are accommodated in a single, open seating. Crisp, white cloths drape the tables, which seat four or seven guests. The international cuisine is refreshingly unpretentious. Meals are ample and satisfying, if not of gourmet standard.

Breakfast is a large buffet with dishes ranging from meusli and fresh fruits to buttery croissants and sticky danish. There's also oatmeal, cold cereals, meats, and made-to-order eggs. For early risers, coffee and rolls are available in the lounge, where bouillon also is served midmorning.

Everyone's favorite meal is lunch, a buffet groaning with soup cooked from scratch, imaginative salads, fresh cold seafoods, hot fish and meat dishes, homemade pastas, breads, rolls, several desserts, and a cheese tray. Teatime, held in the dining room, features cookies and pastries.

Dinner is the only a la carte meal, with three or four choices of appetizer, soup, salad, entree, and dessert. Several nights offer theme menus: French, Filipino, and so on. On one evening, weather permitting, there may be a barbecue/buffet on the sun deck with hot mulled wine.

At both lunch and dinner, wine, beer, and cocktails may be ordered. The wine list is limited but reasonably priced; selections are good and include Chilean and Argentinian wines. Guests who feel peckish at midnight will find snacks and desserts in the lounge.

SERVICE   Genuine friendliness is the hallmark of service aboard the *Explorer.* The Filipino dining room and cabin staff are very pleasant, well prepared, and eager to please. Even though passengers sit at different tables each meal in the open-seating dining room, waiters have a knack for remembering preferences, and the two-person bar staff is equally adept whether mixing cocktails or serving wines. The savvy maître d'hôtel helps passengers mix and is especially considerate of single travelers.

FACILITIES AND ENTERTAINMENT   No formal entertainment or shows are to be found on the *Explorer,* where days are packed with intellectual and physical pursuits like lectures, Zodiac rides, hikes, and wildlife-watching. Every evening, before dinner, passengers gather in the lounge for a recap by the expedition leader, staff naturalists, and guest lecturers.

Socializing resumes here after dinner, sometimes until the wee hours. A passenger may tickle the keyboard; someone may sing; usually, however, guests just mingle for conversation. Sometimes, at night, slides, a film, or a Hollywood movie are shown in the lecture hall, which offers theater seating to accommodate all passengers. The library is a popular spot at any hour of the day.

ACTIVITIES AND DIVERSIONS   Enrichment lectures by expert naturalists, geologists, polar explorers, and authors are well attended. Most talks are accompanied by audiovisuals. Throughout the day, staff and guest speakers mingle with passengers, answering questions or pointing out seabirds and whales from the sundeck. On the bridge, deck officers congenially show passengers the charts and explain the navigational equipment. In the lounge, passengers write postcards, update diaries, and read books from the adjacent library.

One of the hottest areas on the ship is the tiny gift shop, where new items are continuously materializing only to be snapped up by passengers with a seemingly insatiable lust for coffee-table books, jewelry, Patagonia jackets, T-shirts, pins, hats, potholders—anything with the word "Antarctica" on it.

SPORTS, FITNESS, AND BEAUTY   A small gym offers a reclining bicycle, ski machine, and free weights. There's also a mixed sauna with shower. Days at sea, a stretch-and-tone class is offered on deck (weather permitting). There's a small dipping pool but it is not used during Antarctic cruises. There is no beauty salon (despite one being shown on the deck plan in the brochure; it's been converted into storage space), but there are hair dryers in the cabins.

SHORE EXCURSIONS   On the Antarctica programs, as is typical of most expedition cruises, city tours in pre- and postcruise packages and Zodiac trips, landings, and so on during the cruise are included in the price of the cruise.

POSTSCRIPT   Abercrombie & Kent's precruise literature is excellent for helping you prepare for your cruise, but even under the best of circumstances in the Antarctic, you should be prepared for a few rough days at sea, particularly because your itinerary includes a crossing of the unpredictable Drake Passage.

This intimate vessel draws exceptionally interesting, intellectually curious passengers, among whom many lasting friendships are forged during the voyages. But if you do not share a similar thirst for knowledge nor have the flexibility to deal with the frequent changes that are caused by the vicissitudes of the weather and the sea, you could quickly find yourself on the wrong ship—a long way from home.

ALASKA SIGHTSEEING/CRUISE WEST

Fourth and Battery Building, Suite 700, Seattle, WA 98121
(206) 441-8687; (800) 426-7702; fax (206) 441-4757

TYPE OF SHIPS   Six small, informal, cabin-equipped, minicoastal cruising vessels and two day-touring boats.

TYPE OF CRUISES   Casual, close-up, light adventure, with emphasis on scenery and wildlife in coastal areas, seasonally.

CRUISE LINE'S STRENGTHS
- innovative itineraries
- enthusiastic crew
- itinerary flexibility allows extra time for wildlife viewing
- small ships
- cuisine

CRUISE LINE'S SHORTCOMINGS
- small cabins; noisy lower-deck cabins
- some small bathrooms with hand-held showers
- limited shipboard facilities
- lack of evening activities
- lack of discounts on cruises

FELLOW PASSENGERS   Mature, physically active passengers from mid-40s to mid-80s; retired couples and seniors. Passengers tend to be somewhat older on the Columbia River cruises, younger for Alaska cruises. Day cruisers attract a growing number of 30-somethings. Up to 70 percent are college educated or have some college; passengers are well traveled and more intellectually curious about nature, history, and ecology than typical passengers on mainstream cruise ships.

Passengers are outgoing and friendly, and most would rather rise early to catch the sunrise than party late into the night. Most are Americans from California, Florida, New York, Great Lakes region, Pacific Northwest, and Texas; some are from Canada; about 24 percent are repeaters. Regardless of age they like the intimacy and simplicity of a casual cruise to places that larger liners cannot reach.

Recommended For   Small ship devotees; people looking for a light adventure, to experience a region up close instead of passively viewing it from a distance; those more interested in wildlife than nightlife and who like to travel in jeans more than tuxedos; those comfortable in congenial, intimate atmosphere.

Not Recommended For   Travelers who need to be entertained, enjoy a lavish, resortlike experience with emphasis on nightlife; prefer facilities and activities of large ships; gamblers.

CRUISE AREAS AND SEASONS   Alaska and western Canada, April–October; Pacific Northwest and California, March–December.

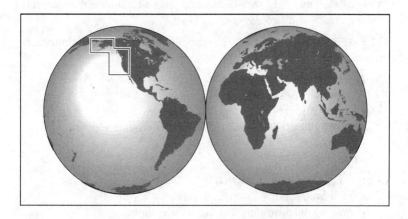

THE LINE   After flying "The Hump" in the China-Burma-India theatre during World War II, Charles B. "Chuck" West moved to Alaska to become a bush pilot. Flying over the remote northern wilderness, he recognized Alaska's great appeal for tourism. In 1946, he organized, sold, and piloted the first all-tourist air excursion north of the Arctic Circle. From that modest start, he built the largest tour company in Alaska-Westours, which he sold to Holland America Line in 1973.

Starting over again at 60, West began building the tour company that has become Alaska Sightseeing/Cruise West. In 1986, he built a luxury touring motor-yacht, or cruiser, for day tours on Prince William Sound. Two years later he purchased a second motor-yacht for day cruises on the Inside Passage.

In 1990, the company acquired its first overnight coastal cruising vessels, and, after major renovation, began service from Juneau to Glacier Bay. Other ships followed at the rate of one a year, as the company dramatically expanded its operations in Alaska, the Pacific Northwest, and California. March 1997 saw the arrival of the line's most luxurious ship, *Spirit of Endeavour* (formerly *Newport Clipper*), which underwent a $4.1 million renovation before entering service. Now the line's flagship, she gives AS/CW a new, more upscale level of cruises. The fast-growing line added six vessels in seven years and has grown to become the largest small-ship cruise company in North America.

The Fleet	Built/Renovated	Tonnage	Passengers
Spirit of Alaska	1980/1995	97	82
Spirit of Columbia	1979/1995	98	80
Spirit of Discovery	1976/1992	94	84
Spirit of Endeavour	1985/1996	99	107
Spirit of Glacier Bay	1971/1994	97	54
Spirit of '98	1984/1995	96	99
Glacier Seas	1976/1994	90	85
Sheltered Seas	1986/1994	95	90

[The last two ships are day-cruisers and have only a brief mention in the text.]

STYLE   Believing that smaller is better on a cruise vacation, Alaska Sightseeing/Cruise West's credo is that responsible travel is to enjoy enriching experiences while causing minimal impact on the environment. The company encourages environmental education and understanding through unusual, up-close experiences, while respecting the wildlife and their natural habitat.

The small vessels can nose into shore for close-up views of scenery and wildlife. The ship's shallow draft and compact size allow them to negotiate intricate waterways, narrow locks, and small marinas inaccessible to larger ships. Their size and casual, intimate atmosphere also make for instant friendships not possible on a large cruise ship.

Four of the seven vessels have bow-landing capabilities, enabling them to pull up to wilderness beaches or shoreside parks. En route, narration and occasional talks by park rangers, historians, and other specialists keep passengers abreast of the history, geology, and wildlife of the areas in which they're cruising. Otherwise, the style on board is unstructured.

With little formal shipboard entertainment, passengers entertain themselves largely by immersing themselves in the scenery and wildlife, reading, playing cards and games, or by socializing with other passengers and the crew.

The cruise line's young, mostly college-age crew is recruited primarily from the Pacific Northwest and Alaska. Their caring attitude and enthusiasm are part of the cruise line's strengths. Another highlight is the cuisine, which is more sophisticated than normally associated with small-ship, light-adventure style cruising.

DISTINCTIVE FEATURES Bow-ramp on *Spirit of Columbia* and bow stairs on *Spirit of Glacier Bay* and *Spirit of Alaska* enable passengers to walk directly onto pristine wilderness areas. Bridge open to passengers.

RATES

Highest Per Diem	Lowest Per Diem	Average Per Diem
$500	$220	$311

The above per diems are calculated from the cruise line's nondiscounted *cruise-only* fares on standard accommodations. Per diems vary by season, by cabin location, and by cruise areas.

Special Fares and Discounts
- Single Supplement: 175 percent of twin rate; single cabins available on *Spirit of Glacier Bay* and *Spirit of Discovery*.

Packages
- Air/Sea: Air add-ons available from up to 75 gateways.
- Pre/Post: Large variety of cruise-tour packages throughout Alaska, with one to nine days of land touring before or after a cruise.

Past Passengers
No past passenger club.

THE LAST WORD AS/CW's American-built and flagged vessels are subject to Federal Maritime Commission bonding and strict U.S. Coast

Guard inspections. Currently, Alaska Sightseeing/Cruise West is the only cruise company offering regular Alaska cruises from Seattle from spring to fall.

The company's focus remains faithful to that of its founder, who envisioned that travelers should be taken on trips in small groups in order to maximize their enjoyment without overwhelming the villages, small ports, and wilderness areas they visit; and that the focus should be outward, on the wildlife, scenery, and culture, rather than inward, on nightclubs, discos, or gambling.

By focusing on the wildlife, such as whales, bears, seals, eagles, and other indigenous species passengers are likely to see, and difficult-to-reach wilderness areas, AS/CW believes it is helping to increase public awareness and support for the protection of our natural treasures.

All the ships in Alaska Sightseeing/Cruise West's fleet are similar in the style of cruises they offer, regardless of their size or degree of luxury. Most passengers try an Alaskan cruise first. If they like the experience, they graduate to cruises in the other areas.

ALASKA SIGHTSEEING/CRUISE WEST STANDARD FEATURES

Officers American.

Staffs Dining, Cabin, Cruise/American.

Dining Facilities One dining room with open seating but meals served at specific hours. Early continental breakfast and 6 P.M. appetizers served in forward lounge. Coffee, tea, fresh fruit available throughout day.

Special Diets Notice required at time of booking; cruise line can accommodate vegetarian, kosher, low-fat, low-salt, and other heart-healthy requests.

Room Service None, except for owner's suite on the *Spirit of '98*.

Dress Code Casual at all times; coats and ties and dresses not required. Most passengers wear jeans, chinos, and layer with shirts, sweaters, and windbreakers when necessary in cooler climates.

Cabin Amenities Air conditioning/thermostat; upper-deck cabins have windows that open. Most bathrooms are small, some with hand-held showers. Reading lights over bed; closets, storage, or drawers under beds. Some cabins have sink and vanity in room, separate from bathroom. Television and phone in all cabins on *Spirit of Endeavour*.

Electrical Outlets 110 AC.

Wheelchair Access *Spirit of '98* has elevator; two cabins for disabled.

Recreation and Entertainment Forward lounge with bar setup, television, small library with reference books of area, informational videos, movies; informal entertainment by crew, occasional talks by historians, park rangers, and other experts. Bridge and other card and board games. Ships stock binoculars but it's wise to bring your own.

Beauty and Fitness Overnight vessels have some fitness equipment, such as stair step machines, exercise bicycles. No beauty/barber shop.

Other Facilities No doctor; at least one crew member on each vessel is trained in "First Response."

Children's Facilities None.

Theme Cruises None.

Smoking No smoking allowed in public rooms or cabins; smoking allowed only on outside, open deck areas.

AS/CW Suggested Tipping $10 per passenger per day. All tips are pooled and shared by nonofficer staff.

Credit Cards For cruise payment and on-board charges, American Express, Visa, Mastercard.

Spirit of '98

	Quality Rating	Value Rating
Spirit of '98	➋	C

Registry: United States	Length: 192 feet	Beam: 40 feet
Cabins: 49	Draft: 9.3 feet	Speed: 13 knots
Maximum Passengers: 99	Passenger Decks: 4	Elevators: 1
	Crew: 26	Space Ratio: n.a.

THE SHIP   The largest and most sophisticated ship in this expanding fleet, *Spirit of '98,* provides considerable comfort. Added to the AS/CW fleet in 1993, she was built in 1984 by previous owners and sailed as the *Pilgrim Belle, Colonial Explorer,* and *Victorian Empress.* The handsome vessel has the profile and interior ambience of a turn-of-the-century river steamer. In 1994, her Victorian profile won her a role in the Kevin Costner movie, *Wyatt Earp.*

   The ship's decor recalls a Victorian country hotel. Square wood columns trimmed with vertical strip mirrors and fanciful wall lamps accent a handsome mahogany and mirrored bar in the forward observation lounge. A similarly designed buffet area in the dining room is furnished in good reproductions. Wingback chairs, leaded glass, old-fashioned brass lamps, and extensive use of interior wood, including hand-rubbed mahogany window casements, help to carry out the Victorian theme. The ship has four decks with all but one cabin on three of them.

ITINERARIES   *The Spirit of '98* cruises from Seattle and Juneau on alternating seven-night voyages, with stops at Ketchikan, Skagway, Haines, Sitka, and sails by Tracy Arm and Misty Fjords National Monument. Two days each way are spent cruising Desolation Sound and the British Columbia coastline.

- *Ten-night adventure cruises*, in April and September, include all the seven-night stops, plus extra time cruising in the maze of forested islands that constitute the Inside Passage, with visits to El Capitan Passage and Sea Otter Sound—spectacular, rarely visited areas west of Prince of Wales Island.

Home Ports   Seattle; Juneau.
Port Charges $135.

CABINS   The all-outside cabins come in a variety of arrangements and for a small ship are quite roomy, with adequate closet and storage for a casual cruise. Recently, all had major renovation and refurbishing in rich Victorian-style colors and fabrics. All cabins are air conditioned, but also have windows that open—a welcome feature on these close-to-shore cruises.

Cabins on lounge and upper decks open onto promenades. Lower-priced cabins on the main deck have windows on the outside hull of the ship, a perceived benefit for those who like to keep their curtains open to enjoy the view, but want their privacy, too.

The ship has an amazingly large, two-room owner's suite on the top bridge deck with picture windows on both sides. The only cabin on the entire deck, just aft of the bridge, it has a sitting area for entertaining, a game and meeting area with table, complimentary bar, television, VCR, bedroom with a king-size bed, and an adjacent bath with a full-size tub. Passengers occupying this cabin may have their meals served en suite.

Specifications   48 outside cabins; 1 suite. Dimensions range from 100–120 square feet. 40 with twins; 2 with upper/lower bunks; 6 with queen. No singles.

DINING   In the Klondike Dining Room, all passengers dine at one seating in a variety of table configurations, including booths next to the picture windows. The dining room has open seating for all three meals, with passengers moving from table to table to break bread with various fellow travelers.

The cuisine is better than one might expect for this type of cruise and it scores high with the passengers. It's classic Pacific Northwest fare, highlighting the region's fresh seafood and local produce and Northwest wines and microbrews, as local specialty beers are known. As with all the line's overnight vessels, bread and pastries are baked on board. Coffee, tea, cocoa, and fresh fruit are available throughout the day.

Early riser's continental breakfast is available in the forward lounge, and full breakfast in the dining room is served at 7:30 A.M. Lunch features soups, salads, and sandwiches, while appetizers served between 6 and 7 P.M. include specialties such as Alaskan Dungeness crab and artichoke dip or baked brie en croute.

Dinner follows at 7:30 P.M., with a choice of seafood or meat in surprisingly sophisticated entrees. Typical choices might be fresh halibut in Dijon sauce, or veal picata with white wine and capers. Among the specialties are Oregon razor clams, lightly grilled with garlic aioli. Razor clams, Dungeness crab, and salmon are widely regarded as the Pacific Northwest's most treasured seafoods. The dishes are as visually pleasing as they are satisfying to the palate.

SERVICE   The young, enthusiastic, mostly college-age crew are friendly, caring, and especially considerate of older passengers. Recruited primarily from the Pacific Northwest and Alaska, the customer service representatives, known as CSRs, perform a wide variety of duties, including cleaning the cabins daily and doubling as the dining room staff.

FACILITIES AND ENTERTAINMENT   Most entertainment is provided by the passengers interacting with each other in conversation, cards, or board games in the lounge or the dining room when it is not in use. There is no pool, casino, aerobics class, bingo, midnight buffet, or napkin-folding classes. The crew provides informal talent and lively entertainment on Crew and Casino nights. The vegetable races are very amusing—and can be lucrative for those who place their modest wagers correctly on such entries as Percy Potato or The Lemon Sisters. A television set is available for evening movies. There are occasional guest lecturers, talks by the cruise coordinator/naturalist, and light musical entertainment by the old-style player piano in the main lounge.

ACTIVITIES AND DIVERSIONS   Unlike many coastal cruise ships, this one has a quiet second lounge with wraparound picture windows at the stern. Called Soapy's Parlor, tea is set up here in the afternoon, and it's a good spot for reading while watching the ship's wake.

On-board activities are low-key, focusing on informal nature talks, movies, and games. The bridge deck has ample space for sunning, viewing scenery, or lounging under an awning. In good weather, it is the venue for a barbecue lunch. In the evening, the forward lounge and bar is the ship's social center. A small area serves as a gift shop where caps, mugs, and similar items are for sale. A shuffleboard and a huge checkerboard, with one-foot squares painted right on the deck, are found on the bridge deck, along with two exercise machines.

POSTSCRIPT   *The Spirit of '98* is a unique vessel which most likely will never be duplicated. Her best features are the period design and decor, the exceptional scenery her cruises offer, and the camaraderie fostered by the young, high-energy crew.

Spirit of Discovery

	Quality Rating	Value Rating
Spirit of Discovery	❷	D

Registry: United States	Length: 166 feet	Beam: 37 feet
Cabins: 43	Draft: 7.5 feet	Speed: 13 knots
Maximum Passengers:	Passenger Decks: 3	Elevators: none
84	Crew: 21	Space Ratio: n.a.

THE SHIP   Built in 1976 as the *Independence* and renamed the *Columbia,* the handsome vessel cruised first along the East Coast, then in Puget Sound, before being acquired and renovated by Alaska Sightseeing/ Cruise West in 1992.

The forward lounge of this three-deck vessel is the ship's social center and cool weather retreat. Nicely decorated in tones of blue, soft grays, teals, and mauves, it has a bar with ample offerings of standard spirits as well as Northwest wines and specialty brews. Furniture is arranged in conversational groupings with blue suede chairs around a bench sofa along the bow windows. These, along with the mirrored ceiling and chrome accents, give it the look of a private yacht, or a small, upscale European-style hotel.

The lounge has good views to both sides and over the bow through a row of tall vertical windows at the front. A door to the bow viewing area is convenient for passengers who want direct outside access without climbing stairs. Standing at the bow, passengers can practically touch the vegetation when the ship noses up to the shoreline. The bridge has a wraparound viewing area and, like all AS/CW vessels, is open to the passengers at most times.

ITINERARIES   The vessel begins her Alaska cruises in early May with a ten-night adventure cruise between Seattle and Juneau. From mid-May–mid-September, *Spirit of Discovery* leaves from Juneau on a series of three- and four-night cruises into Glacier Bay National Park and Sitka. The three-night cruise spends a full day in both arms of Glacier Bay with a Park Service naturalist; the four-night itinerary adds a cruise into untouched wilderness inlets and bays around Admiralty Island, called "Fortress of the Bears" by the Tlingit Indians and Warm Spring Bay. Admiralty Island is home to large concentrations of black bears, grizzly bears, and Sitka black-tailed deer. Whales abound in these waters, as do sea lions and seals.

Home Port   Seattle.

Port Charges   Ten-night Alaska: $135; three- and four-night Glacier Bay: $27.

CABINS   All cabins are outside with large windows and are found on all three decks. Most are small but adequate and furnished with a vanity, desk, and chair, storage and closet space (could use more hangers), and bathroom with showers. Two sought-after smaller cabins, sold as singles, are located amidship on the bridge deck.

The four deluxe cabins on the top level are the most spacious and have a queen-size bed, writing desk and chair, television/VCR unit, and fridge/minibar. All bridge deck and most lounge deck cabins open onto a promenade. Two lowest-priced cabins are on the lower main deck forward, and are reduced in size to fit the curvature of the hull.

Specifications   43 outside cabins; no suites. Dimensions range from 64 square feet (single cabin) to 127 square feet. 34 with twins, 1 with double, 4 queens, 2 with upper/lower berths, 2 singles.

DINING   The Grand Pacific Dining Room, located aft on the main deck, is pleasant and airy, but a bit noisy because it is over the engine room. The food is imaginative and quite good, highlighting freshly prepared Pacific Northwest versions of classic American cooking with fresh local produce and seafood. All passengers dine in one open seating with a variety of table configurations.

Passengers may start the day with an early riser's continental breakfast, followed by a sit-down breakfast, lunch, and 6 P.M. appetizers. Dinner offers a choice of two entrees, which include such delicacies as fresh lingcod wrapped and baked in parchment paper, grilled razor clams in light garlic aioli, or a superb rack of Ellensburg lamb, roasted with Dijon rosemary crust.

SERVICE   Customer service representatives, galley crew, engine crew, and deck hands are young Americans, mostly from the Pacific Northwest—attentive, enthusiastic, and outgoing. Friendships are formed each week between the crew members and passengers, so much so that farewells are often poignant, and many crew members receive holiday greeting cards from passengers for years after their cruise.

SPORTS, BEAUTY, AND FITNESS   Three fitness machines—a stair stepper, exercise bicycle, and rowing machine—are available.

Spirit of Alaska / Spirit of Columbia

	Quality Rating	**Value Rating**
Spirit of Alaska	②	D
Spirit of Columbia	②	D

Registry: United States	Length: 143 feet	Beam: 28 feet
Cabins: 39	Draft: 7.5/6.5 feet	Speed: 12.5/10.5 knots
Maximum Passengers:	Passenger Decks: 4	Elevators: none
82/80	Crew: 21	Space Ratio: n.a.

THE SHIPS   The *Spirit of Alaska* and the *Spirit of Columbia* are identical in size and similar in layout and are, essentially, smaller scale versions of their sister ships.

The *Spirit of Alaska,* built in 1980 as the *Pacific Northwest Explorer,* was extensively renovated when acquired by AS/CW in 1991 and again in 1995. The *Spirit of Columbia* (the former *New Shoreham II* of American Canadian Caribbean Line) is AS/CW's newest acquisition. She made her debut in March 1994 after the line spent more than $2 million to refit and refurbish her in a theme the company calls "Western National Park Lodge." Those familiar with the Ahwahnee Lodge in Yosemite or the Banff Springs Hotel in Banff will have an idea of the ship's interiors.

Both ships have four decks with most cabins on the lower and upper decks and a forward view lounge and dining room on the main deck. The lounge serves as the center of social life and venue for briefings. It has a small bar, a gift shop area, a library of reference works about the area covered by the cruise, a television, and movie videos. The dining room, amidship, hosts all passengers at a single, open seating. The upper deck has an unobstructed walking/jogging circuit and several exercise machines.

On the *Spirit of Alaska,* the bridge deck provides open and covered seating to view the passing scenery and a venue for buffet lunches on good weather days. The ship can get very close to nature, with passengers able to walk directly onto the shore via bow ramp stairs.

Besides her decor, *Spirit of Columbia* has other differences: a large owner's suite with picture windows looking over the bow, three additional suites, a raised wheelhouse with 360° viewing on the bridge deck, and a unique bow ramp. A V-shaped segment of the bow is hinged and, when lowered, forms a ramp with access to the shore directly from the forward passenger lounge.

SPIRIT OF ALASKA ITINERARIES   A ten-night adventure cruise from Seattle to Juneau in spring spends extra time in the Inside Passage, exploring rarely visited areas west of Prince of Wales Island. In addition, the ship visits Desolation Sound in British Columbia, Misty Fjords, Ketchikan, Wrangell, Sitka, Tracy Arm, Frederick Sound, Skagway, Haines, and Glacier Bay. A seven-day version from mid-May until early September explores an area between Ketchikan and Juneau, which large cruise ships normally traverse in less than 24 hours.

- *From late September–October*, *Spirit of Alaska* makes weekly round-trip cruises from Seattle into the lower half of the Inside Passage that lies in British Columbia, exploring protected waterways and wilderness areas, such as spectacular Princess Louisa Inlet, reachable only by boat or floatplane.
- *In Washington*, *Spirit of Alaska* cruises the San Juan Islands; the Puget Sound ports of LaConner, adjacent to the famous tulip fields of the Skagit Valley; and Port Townsend, one of only four remaining Victorian-era seaport towns in the United States.

Home Ports   Seattle; Juneau.
Port Charges   Alaska: $135.

SPIRIT OF COLUMBIA ITINERARIES   Until late November, *Spirit of Columbia* sails weekly from Portland to the twin cities of Clarkston in Washington and Lewiston in Idaho, a round trip of 1,000 miles. Cruising on the rivers offers a different pleasure each season. Spring brings migratory birds, flowers, and fresh greenery in the rolling hills of eastern Washington and Oregon and in the Snake River canyons; fall offers bright foliage in the Columbia River Gorge. Summer has bright sunshine and warm, swimmable water. The seven-day trip has five days of shore excursions, all included in the price.

- *From Portland*, the *Spirit of Columbia* heads eastward through the Columbia River Gorge (declared a National Scenic Area) and traverses the locks of Bonneville Dam, the first of eight. (The river rises 738 feet from the Pacific Ocean to the Idaho border.) At Clarkston, Washington, passengers are transferred to high-speed jet boats for a 140-mile round-trip thrill ride up the Snake River into the heart of Hells Canyon, the deepest gorge in North America.

Home Port   Portland.
Port Charges $107.

CABINS   Both ships have cabins ranging from roomy—for ships of this size—to very small. *Spirit of Alaska's* named suites and deluxe cabins on the bridge and upper decks have small sitting areas and open onto side promenades. The three suites on the bridge deck have oversize double beds and windows on two sides; each can take a third person.

Spirit of Columbia's eleven named suites and deluxe cabins have television/VCR, refrigerator, side tables, and chair. The suites have a double bed; deluxe rooms have twins. The owner's suite has a queen-size bed, bathtub/shower, and a stocked complimentary bar. Cabins on the upper and bridge decks open directly onto port or starboard promenades.

On both ships, main deck cabins are on the short passage between the dining room and the forward lounge, a high traffic area, but convenient for those who want easy access to activities and facilities. Windows in these cabins are on the outside hull of the ship, ensuring privacy.

Lower deck cabins have portlights high on the bulkhead, which allow one to tell day from night but are not for viewing. Baths are small units with hand-held showers and curtains on tracks. Most have twin beds; all have reading lights, closet, and storage under the beds. These cabins, located just above the engine room, can be noisy at night when the ship is underway, but the difference in price from those on the main deck makes them a good buy for budget watchers.

Alaska *Specifications*   12 inside; 24 outside; 3 suites. Dimensions range from 81–130.5 square feet. 26 with twins; 13 with doubles; 7 cabins accommodate third persons; no singles.

Columbia *Specifications*   12 inside; 20 outside; 7 suites. Dimensions from 73.5–176 square feet.

DINING   As with all AS/CW vessels, the cuisine is good American fare emphasizing fresh Pacific Northwest and Alaskan seafood and local produce. The Grand Pacific Dining Room of the *Spirit of Alaska* had a major upgrading and redecorating in 1994, replacing the old, long, family-style tables for a variety of more intimate round and square ones. Tables on the port and starboard side utilize long upholstered banquettes that run bow to stern underneath the windows.

SERVICE   The young all-American staff helps to set the friendly ambience and, regardless of long hours and much work, they remain courteous, enthusiastic, and helpful, especially to seniors. Despite repeated trips through the same region, most retain a sense of awe about the magnificent scenery in which the vessel sails, often joining the passengers on deck with much excitement during close-up wildlife sightings or glacier calvings.

POSTSCRIPT   The Alaska adventures of *Spirit of Alaska* are designed for those with a sense of adventure who want a slice of the real Alaska—seldom-visited areas, unspoiled wilderness, and small ports and villages where the large cruise ships cannot go.

Spirit of Columbia's cruises are filled with historical references to the Lewis and Clark expedition of 1804–06, cultural and adventurous aspects, and the diverse scenery in the region—from the crashing headlands of the Pacific to thick forests, rolling wheat fields, barren hills, and deep canyons.

Readers considering cruises on either *Spirit of Alaska* or *Spirit of Columbia* should review the section on *Spirit of '98* or *Spirit of Discovery* for more details on AS/CW shipboard facilities and services.

Spirit of Glacier Bay

	Quality Rating	Value Rating
Spirit of Glacier Bay	❷	D

Registry: United States	Length: 125 feet	Beam: 28 feet
Cabins: 29	Draft: 6.5 feet	Speed: 10.5 knots
Maximum Passengers:	Passenger Decks: 3	Elevators: none
54	Crew: 16	Space Ratio: n.a.

THE SHIP   The smallest of Alaska Sightseeing/Cruise West fleet, this little coastal cruiser was its first cabin-equipped, overnight vessel. Built in 1971, by the same American shipyard as the *Spirit of Alaska*, the *Spirit of Glacier Bay* was extensively renovated by AS/CW in 1990 and again in 1994. In many ways, she is a smaller version of the *Spirit of Alaska,* but has one less deck and two freestanding cabins on upper deck aft called "The Condominiums." Each has picture windows to the side and aft and are quite private.

The *Spirit of Glacier Bay* has a forward lounge with picture windows lining the port and starboard sides. Underneath each row of windows are upholstered banquettes running the length of the room, and a variety of small cocktail tables and upholstered chairs in the center of the room to accommodate various sizes of conversation groups. There is a television and VCR for showing informational videos and movies and a small bar. The upper deck has an unobstructed circuit for walking and exercise equipment.

The Snug Harbor Dining Room lies amidship, just aft of a short companionway and a block of four larger cabins, with picture windows on the outside hull of the ship. The top deck has good viewing areas from the bow and stern, with a covered area amidships.

ITINERARIES   The *Spirit of Glacier Bay* makes ten-night repositioning voyages in May and September between Seattle and Juneau. Itinerary is the same as the ten-night voyages offered by the *Spirit of Alaska, Spirit of Discovery,* and *Spirit of '98.* Starting in mid-May and continuing through mid-September, the little ship makes a series of two- and three-night voyages from Whittier into Prince William Sound, with visits to College Fjord, Columbia Glacier, Harriman Fjord, and Blackstone Bay. The three-night cruise includes a port call at Valdez.

- *In late March and April,* and again in late September–October, the *Spirit of Glacier Bay* sails weekly round trip from Seattle into Washington state's waterways. The itinerary includes Gig Harbor, a side trip to Mt. Rainier, Sequim, Friday Harbor and Rosario Resort in the San Juan Islands, cruising Hood Canal, the Victorian seaport town of Port Townsend, and the artists' community of LaConner.

CABINS   Half of the *Spirit of Glacier Bay*'s cabins (A) have picture windows and tend to sell out fast. The 15 more economical cabins (B) below deck are smaller, with small portlight windows high in the cabin, not suitable for viewing. Those who suffer from claustrophobia need to be aware of these limitations before booking. These cabins are located just above the engine room and can be noisy at night when the ship is underway.

Having said that, however, these cabins are far more economical than the outside picture window cabins, and budget watchers could save hundreds of dollars by booking one. All cabins are simply decorated and have private bathrooms with showers, air conditioning, and heat control. There are also two popular single cabins far forward on the upper deck.

Specifications   13 inside; 14 outside; no suites. Dimensions, 63–90 square feet. 23 with twins; 2 double; 2 with upper/lowers; 2 singles. 2 cabins accommodate third persons.

DINING   Like the *Spirit of Alaska*, the *Spirit of Glacier Bay*'s dining room, located amidships on the main deck, can accommodate all passengers in one open seating. Tables utilize long upholstered banquettes that run bow to stern underneath the picture windows.

Passengers are usually surprised that the fresh Pacific Northwest fare is better prepared and more sophisticated than one might assume from such a small galley. The menu, similar to the *Spirit of Alaska's*, offers meat dishes, but many passengers, especially those from outside the Pacific Northwest, favor the fresh seafood dishes from local waters.

SERVICE   The young all-American crew, like all AS/CW staff, have a friendly, eager-to-please attitude. On this small a ship, friendships between the young staff and the older passengers are often forged quickly. Officers who are older professionals have the same outgoing manner and keep the wheelhouse open for passengers to visit.

POSTSCRIPT   This is a homey, comfortable little vessel, suited to short cruises. The relaxed ambience, casual dress, and low-key social life on board are appropriate to touring off-the-beaten-track places that the big ships can't reach.

Spirit of Endeavour (Preview)

Registry: United States	Length: 215 feet	Beam: 37 feet
Cabins: 51	Draft: 8.5 feet	Speed: 10.5 knots
Maximum Passengers: 107	Passenger Decks: 4	Elevators: none
	Crew: 30	Space Ratio: n.a.

THE SHIP   AS/CW's new flagship, *Spirit of Endeavour*, was launched in November 1996, following a $4.1 million refurbishing and refitting. Formerly the *Newport Clipper* of Clipper Cruise Lines, the *Endeavour* was built in 1983 by Jeff Boat of Jeffersonville, Indiana.

The *Endeavour* is considered the most luxurious of AS/CW's fleet and one of the more deluxe mini-cruise ships sailing in Alaska. The ship has teak decks and wide companionways and the cabins are large in comparison to the other ships and have wide picture windows. They are equipped with phone, television, VCR, and tiled baths. As with other ships of the fleet, the *Spirit of Endeavour* is air conditioned and has comfortable lounges. The dining room accommodates all passengers at a single open seating.

The recent renovations included refurbishing of all the cabins and public areas, updating of safety features, and the installation of new engines and new bridge electronics. The work also included the installation of new bow and stern designs that increase the ship's fuel efficiency by more than 22 percent. Mounted in front of the ship's bow is now a "bulbous" underwater extension that decreases fuel consumption. This bulbous configuration splits the water, forcing the current up and away from the hull, thereby reducing the bow wake and water resistance.

At the stern, a new stern ferring forces water to flow closer to the surface, creating a "gently rolling wave" that reduces the amount of drag created by the original stern design. The savings in fuel costs derived from the hull modifications are expected to pay for all of the research and design work entailed in about two years of operations. The reduced fuel consumption has ecological benefits as well.

SPIRIT OF ENDEAVOUR ITINERARIES   Between late April and mid-September, the *Spirit of Endeavour* sails weekly on one-way cruises between Seattle and Juneau, with two days cruising Desolation Sound and the Inside Passage including Misty Fjords. Stops are made at Ketchikan, Petersburg, LeConte Fjord, Sitka, and cruising Glacier Bay National Park.

- *In late September through the end of November*, the ship repositions to San Francisco for three- and four-night cruises into the California Wine Country, the Sacramento River Delta, and Sacramento. These cruises are for those less concerned with the miles traveled than with exploring a small but richly diverse area, close in, as only a small ship can provide.

POSTSCRIPT   Of all the company's overnight cruising vessels, the *Spirit of Endeavour*'s clean lines and raked bow make it look most like a mini-version of a cruise ship. Viewing some of the most breathtaking scenery in the world is a major activity on this ship and appeals to a settled type of person looking for quiet social life and relaxed itinerary.

Readers interested in sailing on the *Spirit of Endeavour* should review all of the AS/CW section.

AS/CW's two-day cruisers, *Glacier Seas* and *Sheltered Seas*, are not covered here as their type of cruises are outside the scope of this book. *Glacier Seas* makes one-way, eight-hour crossings of Prince William Sound between Valdez and Whittier, Alaska, from late May–September; *Sheltered Seas*, a sleek, luxury motor yacht, cruises to the "inside" of the Inside Passage between Juneau and Ketchikan, Alaska. For more information, contact the cruise line or your travel agent.

AMERICAN CANADIAN CARIBBEAN LINE

461 Water Street, Warren, RI 02885
(401) 247-0955; (800) 556-7450; fax (401) 247-2350
http://www.accl-smallships.com

TYPE OF SHIPS   Small, no frills, budget.

TYPE OF CRUISES   Light adventure, destination-oriented at an un-hurried pace.

CRUISE LINE'S STRENGTHS
  • innovative small ships
  • imaginative itineraries
  • homey ambience
  • friendly, diligent staff
  • moderate prices

CRUISE LINE'S SHORTCOMINGS
  • minimal service
  • spartan cabins
  • cabin bathrooms
  • limited shipboard facilities
  • sparse precruise information

FELLOW PASSENGERS   Mature, experienced travelers from 40–85; in the summer, retired couples, seniors, most in their mid- to late 60s; similar in winter with the addition of younger passengers in their 40s who enjoy water sports. But even if not all are sporty types, they are all good sports; friendly and unpretentious; most with modest means; college educated, well traveled. Even the PhDs or affluent ones care little for luxury and loathe ostentation, but are keenly interested in the travel experience and particularly in history, wildlife, and ecology. They play bridge and Scrabble and read avidly, favoring such publications as *Travel Holiday*, *Smithsonian*, and *Audubon*. Most come from the U.S. Northeast, Florida, and California.

Recommended For Travelers seeking friendship, companionship, light adventure to unusual destinations at a slow pace, moderate price on a small ship with a family atmosphere. Those who abhor large ships.

Not Recommended For Swingers, hip or hyper superachievers, snobs, sophisticates, or night owls.

CRUISE AREAS AND SEASONS Cruises of 6–15 days, spring–fall, U.S. coastal waterways between Rhode Island and Florida; Hudson River/Erie Canal, New England/Canada, Newfoundland, Labador; small rivers in mid-America; Mississippi byways from Chicago to New Orleans; Great Lakes/New England via the Erie Canal. In winter, Bahamas; Virgin Islands; Eastern/Southern Caribbean and Orinoco River; Belize, Barrier Reef to Honduras and Guatemala.

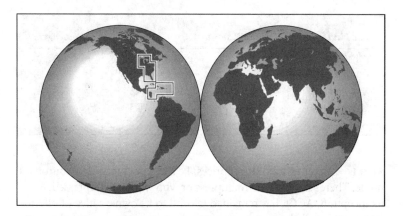

THE LINE Shipbuilder, adventurer, and insatiable traveler Luther Blount designed and built his first small ship in 1964 for cruising the Hudson River, the Erie Canal, and Canada's inland waterways with his friends. In time he developed such a loyal following that he turned his hobby into a business and for the next decade pioneered innovative itineraries, venturing where other passenger ships did not go.

With slightly larger ships launched in 1979 and 1983, he expanded to the Bahamas, the Virgin Islands, and the small islands of the Eastern Caribbean, and added "Caribbean" to the line's name to reflect more accurately its growth. By 1992, when the *Mayan Prince* made its debut, Blount had already pioneered unusual itineraries in Central American waters, the Southern Caribbean, and other U.S. waterways. The *Niagara*

Prince, which has innovative features designed expressly to enable it to travel the full length of the Erie Canal, was launched in 1994; and the *Grande Caribe*, a slightly longer version of ACCL's other ships, is scheduled to be inaugurated in 1997.

Each new vessel has had design improvements, adding larger cabins, utilizing public rooms better, and giving the ships even greater flexibility. But the style of the cruise experience has not changed. ACCL is still a family enterprise; daughter Nancy Blount is the company's vice president and director of operations, and Luther Blount, ever the inventor, and now in his senior years, is still a hands-on president, designing every aspect of the ships, supervising every inch of the building, and scouting new itineraries. His design concepts have been the prototype for many small cruise ships launched in recent years.

The Fleet	Built/Renovated	Tonnage	Passengers
Caribbean Prince	1983	99	83
Grande Caribe	1997	99	100
Mayan Prince	1992	95	90
Niagara Prince	1994	95	84

STYLE   Adventure at budget prices. Leave your Guccis and Vuittons at home. There's no one here to impress or who would be impressed. Since its inception, ACCL has remained faithful to its owner's idea of offering cruises on small ships with an informal, unpretentious atmosphere and limited service or planned entertainment, providing passengers with an intimate, up-close look at the places they visit. The ships have shallow drafts that enable them to go into small tributaries. Bow ramps allow direct access to normally inaccessible places, sailing to secluded beaches for swimming and snorkeling on reefs that passengers can have to themselves. The ships carry a glass-bottom boat, small sailboats, and snorkeling equipment.

ACCL cruises, staffed by American officers and crew, are run like a family outing rather than a conventional cruise. The ships serve surprisingly good food, family-style, in a folksy atmosphere that makes for instant friendships. Limited table service is provided by cheerful, hardworking dining room staff, always ready to bring beverages, second helpings, or deal with special requests. Wine and alcoholic beverages are supplied by the line on special occasions, but basically, passengers bring their own liquor and wine and the ship supplies free setups.

ACCL pioneers new itineraries every year, searching out untapped areas that are strong in beauty, history, flora, and fauna, and provide frequent opportunities for exploring, swimming, and snorkeling.

DISTINCTIVE FEATURES   ACCL's ships, built at Blount's shipyard in Warren, RI, have bow ramps—a Blount innovation and one of the ship's most popular features. Another unusual feature is the retractable pilot house, which allows the vessels to sail under low bridges.

RATES

Highest Per Diem	Lowest Per Diem	Average Per Diem
$237	$104	$152

The above per diems are calculated from the cruise line's nondiscounted *cruise-only* fares on standard accommodations. Per diems vary by season, by cabin location, and by cruise areas.

Special Fares and Discounts   10 percent discount on certain cruises when two cruises are booked back-to-back.

• Third Passenger: 15 percent discount for each occupant of cabin.

Packages
• Air/Sea: On certain Belize, Caribbean, and Panama Canal sailings.
• Pre/Post: Panama; Belize; Bonaire; Trinidad; New Orleans.

Past Passengers   Loyalty is rewarded: after ten cruises with ACCL, a passenger is entitled to a free cruise.

THE LAST WORD   The high number of repeat passengers—up to 68 percent—would seem to indicate that ACCL has found the right formula for a certain type of passenger, namely, those who do not want or need pampering and appreciate the small-ship cruise experience, preferring conversation and friendship to chorus lines and casinos. When new itineraries are announced, they usually sell out quickly.

The whole company reflects the hands-on philosophy of its owners; it does not even use computers for reservations so as not to lose the personal touch with its loyal customers. Those who understand the limitations of a small ship and nature of these cruises enjoy themselves immensely; those who do not may quickly find that they are on the wrong ship.

ACCL's chief shortcoming is one that could easily be corrected—namely, the dearth of information on itineraries, ports of call, and shore excursions sent to passengers prior to their cruise. Tours are not published in advance and passengers receive no supplementary literature describing the places a cruise will visit.

ACCL maintains that itineraries and tours change, but experience will show they do not change that much. It is difficult to understand why ACCL, which has been operating cruises for two decades, handles itinerary information and shore excursions so haphazardly, particularly since its passengers are destination-focused. It is all the more puzzling when you know that ACCL is one of the few cruise lines that does not take a profit on shore excursions. It either includes them in the cruise price or sells them at cost—that's just one of the many features that make ACCL cruises a truly good value.

ACCL Ships Standard Features

Officers American.

Staffs Dining, Cabin, Cruise/American.

Dining Facilities One dining room with open seating; meals served at specific hours only: breakfast, 8 A.M.; lunch, 12 noon; dinner, 6 P.M.

Special Diets Cruise line needs notice at time of booking, but chefs can accommodate basic requests.

Room Service None.

Dress Code Casual at all times; men never need a tie. Gentlemen might bring a jacket and women a dress in case you want to try a fancy restaurant or nightspot in a port of call.

Cabin Amenities Air conditioning/heat; upper deck cabins have windows that can be opened. Very small bathroom with hand-held shower. Reading light; plug for hair dryers. Limited storage space.

Electrical Outlets 110 AC.

Wheelchair Access No designated cabins; *Niagara Prince* has motorized chair for boarding.

Recreation and Entertainment Lounge with bar setup, books and videos; informal entertainment, occasional lectures; bridge and parlor games. No casino, swimming pool, gym, or theatre.

Sports and Other Activities Glass-bottom boat and snorkeling equipment on board.

Beauty and Fitness No facilities. On request, cruise director will make appointments with beauty/barber salons in ports.

Other Facilities Ships have no doctors; *Mayan Prince* has medical room.

Children's Facilities None. Children under 14 not accepted.

Theme Cruises Fall foliage.

Smoking No smoking inside ships; smoking allowed only outside, in open areas.

ACCL Suggested Tipping All tips are pooled and shared by staff; guidelines call for $10–12 per person per day.

Credit Cards None.

Mayan Prince / Caribbean Prince

	Quality Rating	**Value Rating**
Mayan Prince	2	A
Caribbean Prince	2	A

Registry: United States   Length: 175/160 feet   Beam: 38 feet
Cabins: 46/38   Draft: 6 feet   Speed: 10 knots
Maximum Passengers: Passenger Decks: 3   Elevators: none
  92/83   Crew: 18/15   Space Ratio: n.a.

THE SHIPS   The *Mayan Prince* and the *Caribbean Prince*, small sister ships with shallow drafts and flying the American flag, are comfortable but very basic vessels, designed for river and coastal cruises. Although the ships are similar in layout, the *Mayan Prince* was built after maritime fire prevention regulations were issued and, therefore, construction materials such as aluminum and formica have replaced much of the wood seen in the *Caribbean Prince*. Both ships have simple, homey decor.

Both ships have three passenger decks; ceilings are low. At the center of the main deck is the dining room, which serves as an all-purpose room between meals. Forward is a small self-service bar, the cruise director's office, and a small lounge shaped by the bow. It has the ship's only television set, books, and newspapers that are supplied when the ship docks in ports where they can be purchased.

The upper or promenade deck has cabins and a wraparound promenade with small areas at each end of the ship for chairs where passengers sit to read, converse, and enjoy close-up views of passing scenery.

At the bow a flight of steps leads down to ACCL's patented bow ramp, which is put to use when the captain spots a secluded beach in the tropics where passengers can enjoy a swim and snorkeling, or at historic sites along the Erie Canal where there is no dock. The bow on the *Mayan Prince* has extensions and can be made longer than on the line's earlier ships. This enhancement improved the chances for dry beach landings and widened the opportunities for landings in inaccessible places.

Also from the promenade deck, stairs lead to the ship's roof, an open deck with chairs for passengers' use. It has another of ACCL's unusual features: a retractable pilot house, which is removed on trips through the Erie Canal to enable the vessel to pass under bridges along the way. The small room is quite literally dismantled by lifting its roof, folding back its three sides, and disconnecting all the equipment. Then, the captain's chair, console, steering mechanism, and equipment are lowered down to the level of the promenade deck where they are reconnected so that the ship can resume operation. It's quite a scene to watch and leaves you with an I-had-to-see-it-to-believe-it notion.

ITINERARIES The itineraries are divided into two basic seasons, connected by repositioning cruises. In summer, both ships sail on cruises along the inland waterways of New York, New England, and Canada between Rhode Island and Quebec City. The *Mayan Prince* has 6–15-day cruises, starting from Warren, Rhode Island, and traveling through the Long Island Sound, up the Hudson River into the Erie Canal, Lake Ontario, and the St. Lawrence Seaway to Montreal and the Saguenay fjord, ending at Quebec City. Passengers are bused back to the point of origin. *Caribbean Prince* cruises are 12 days.

- *For summer 1997*, the ship sailed on ACCL's first cruise of Newfoundland and Labrador in celebration of the quincentennial of John Cabot's voyage of discovery. It departed from Massena, NY, a few miles from Montreal airport, and called at Quebec before continuing east.
- *In winter*, the *Mayan Prince* offers two-week island hoppers mostly to quiet coves and small ports of the Eastern and Southern Caribbean with stops in the Virgin Islands, St. Maarten, Bonaire, Curaçao, and the Panama Canal, visiting the San Blas Islands and the Darien Jungle. The *Caribbean Prince* cruises the coastal waters of Belize and Central America.
- Repositioning cruises along the intracoastal waters of the eastern seaboard between Florida and Rhode Island are available in spring and fall. Some repositioning cruises sail along the Gulf Coast as far west as New Orleans.

Home Port Warren, RI; ships depart from various ports depending on itinerary.

Port Charges $35–150, depending on itinerary.

CABINS   Small, spartan, but functional cabins are fitted with twin beds on metal frames (*Mayan Prince*), except for three cabins on the lower deck which have double beds. Storage space is limited to four drawers with about one square foot of counter space, a four-foot-high metal cabinet for hanging clothes, and luggage storage under the beds. Cabins have accordian doors that close tight but do not lock, nor do they have keys.

All cabins are outside, except for six budget units on the lower deck. On the *Mayan Prince*, ten cabins open onto the promenade deck; no cabins on the *Caribbean Prince* open directly onto the deck. Other promenade deck cabins have windows that open—a particularly pleasant feature for cruising on U.S. and Canadian waterways when fresh cool air fills the room.

The largest and most desirable cabins are on the promenade deck; those on the main deck are aft of the dining room and kitchen near the stern and are the noisiest. The lower deck cabins do not have windows and are similar to large bunks on a sailboat. Repeat passengers reserve them because they are the quietest quarters on the ship—and you can't beat the price. They are not recommended for anyone who has even the slightest problem with closed-in space, however, regardless of price.

Bathrooms, which are also a Blount creation, are tiny but utilitarian and ingeniously designed. They can best be described as the deluxe version of a "head" on a sailboat or RV. A small—very small—sink with spring taps lets water run for only a few seconds at a time. The hand-held shower is very efficient and can be left in its wall mount when showering; the shower curtain also serves as the "door" to the head. A small trap in the floor lets out water from the shower. The toilet has its own fill-and-flush system that works very well. However, if you do not operate it properly—refilling the water in the bowl after each use—or close the trap in the floor, an unpleasant odor can develop.

Cabins are cleaned daily but linens are changed every third day. Bath towels are changed more frequently or as needed. (The ship does not have laundry facilities.) No room service.

Specifications   6 cabins inside; 39 outside; all have private facilities. Standard dimensions are about 108 square feet. Most have twin lower beds; some can be converted to doubles. Three of the six on the lower deck have two lower berths, one of which is extra wide and therefore could accommodate a third person. No singles.

DINING   One of the biggest advantages enjoyed by a ship of this size is reflected in the food—fresh products and homemade bread and pastries—and the taste. The food is well-prepared American fare; not only is it much better than expected for the ship's category, but it is better than some lines that cost double the price.

Menus are set and posted daily. A frequent request from passengers is to have a choice of at least two entrees. And although they praise the food, they criticize the ships' tendency to serve more fat and high cholesterol foods than desirable, given the predominant age of passengers.

Breakfast is a hearty American one with the main course—eggs, pancakes, etc.—changed daily. Lunch usually consists of a soup (the best I've had on any ship), salad, and dessert; dinner features fish, chicken or meat, vegetables, and dessert. Meals are served family style but the staff is in attendance, eager to fill requests, serving the dessert, beverages, and second helpings. Coffee, tea, and other refreshments and cookies are available in the dining room at all times.

The dining room, which has an open-kitchen galley, has tables for 4, 6, 8, and 10. The square tables for four are used during nonmeal hours for card games. Passengers bring their own liquor and wine, and ACCL provides storage, free setups, and ice. For the captain's dinners on the second and last night of a cruise, ACCL supplies wine and an open bar. Likewise, for Celebration Night when, collectively, the passengers celebrate birthdays, anniversaries, etc., the line supplies wine. Make-Your-Own-Sundae with many varieties of ice cream and toppings is another popular event.

SERVICE   The crew members, young and energetic, are mostly from Rhode Island or neighboring states and they are terrific. They must be something of a jack-of-all-trades as the same teams that clean the cabins attend the dining room. They are cheerful, hard working, and unfailingly polite. They show an eagerness to please and are particularly accommodating to their mostly older passengers.

FACILITIES AND ENTERTAINMENT   Except for television, videotapes, the occasional local talent at ports of call, and visiting lecturers, there is no evening entertainment of the usual cruise variety. Most people on these ships are in bed by 10 P.M. Although the ships have a few shelves of paperbacks, avid readers should bring their own.

Passengers gather in the lounge and by the small bar which has setups and soft drinks for informal predinner cocktails. They prepare drinks themselves with the help of a crew member. After dinner, some are likely to linger for bridge and other card and parlor games or a film.

There is no shop, although the cruise director does open his "boutique" to sell signature shirts, caps, jackets, etc., at least once during the cruise.

ACTIVITIES AND DIVERSIONS   In addition to card and parlor games, some cruises have lecturers. ACCL captains are very knowledgeable about the places the ships visit and often provide running commentary. Those lucky enough to sail on the Hudson River/Erie Canal cruise with Capt. Robert Gifford will have a real treat. He is a dedicated historian and walking encyclopedia on the region. He acts as a guide while piloting the ship through the canal, giving passengers fascinating information they will not find elsewhere.

SPORTS AND FITNESS   On board, one can take a daily walk on the promenade deck; otherwise, sports activities take place on shore and, depending on the itinerary, can include swimming, snorkeling, hiking, and birding.

BEAUTY   On request, the cruise director books appointments with beauty parlors in ports.

SHORE EXCURSIONS   The ships have no excursion desk; on the first day of the cruise, the cruise director distributes a list of tours with brief descriptions. They vary with itineraries and range from $6–30. As an example, Intracoastal cruises have five excursions: a city tour in Baltimore, harbor tour in Norfolk, trolley tour in Charleston, buggy tour in Savannah, and tour of the NASA installations at Cape Canaveral. There is also a walking tour with a local guide in Beaufort, SC, among others. ACCL uses local operators specialized in handling small groups with special interests and avoids standardized tours. The line claims it continuously checks tours and changes them when more appealing ones are found.

POSTSCRIPT   The ships' best features are their staffs, the itineraries, and the camaraderie among passengers—an experience not found on a large ship. To be sure, the ships are basic and utilitarian from stem to stern. At times, you might have the feeling that you are camping. Yet, passengers do appear to be happy and having a good time. Clearly they are the type who are more interested in the ships' destinations than creature comforts.

Niagara Prince

	Quality Rating	Value Rating
Niagara Prince	➋	A

Registry: United States	Length: 166 feet	Beam: 40 feet
Cabins: 42	Draft: 6.3 feet	Speed: 12 knots
Maximum Passengers: 84	Passenger Decks: 3	Elevators: none; chairlift
	Crew: 15	Space Ratio: n.a.

THE SHIP   The newest addition to ACCL's fleet, which made its debut in November 1994, was designed with a dual purpose: to sail through the entire length of the Erie Canal and on coastal waters. Not only does it have a retractable pilot house like its sister ships, but its low profile can be made even lower like a semi-submarine through a new feature in the hull, which owner and designer Blount describes as being similar to letting the air out of a tire.

Riding lower in the water, the *Niagara Prince* can pass under the lowest bridges of the Erie Canal, enabling passengers to travel through the canal from Troy to Buffalo for the first time in over 120 years—a dream-come-true for Blount. (Other ACCL ships travel about three-quarters of the way.) The feature also enables the ship to pass under the low bridge of Chicago into the heart of the city.

Among the *Niagara Prince*'s other new features is a chairlift for passengers who have difficulty negotiating stairs and an enhanced lounge/dining room. Now located on the top deck (it's on the main deck of the other ships), the room has windows at the bow and along the side, enhancing passengers' views from the interior of the ship.

In other aspects, such as cabins, bathrooms, meals, and activity, she is similar to the *Mayan Prince*. There are 40 outside cabins; two inside.

ITINERARIES   In her maiden year, *Niagara Prince* cruised the Mobile and Tennessee rivers, the Tenn-Tom Waterway, and traveled via the Mississippi and Illinois rivers to the Des Plaines and into Chicago. Due to the city's low bridges, the *Niagara Prince* is the first cruise ship able to navigate the Chicago River through the heart of the Windy City. The ship returns to Rhode Island from Chicago via a cruise through the Great Lakes and the Erie Canal.

- *In winter*, the *Niagara Prince* cruises on 12-day itineraries up the
  Orinoco River in Venezuela; to Aruba, Bonaire, and Curaçao; the
  Virgin Islands; and the Bahamas. In spring, the ship returns
  north for a series of mid-America cruises between New Orleans
  and Chicago. From May–mid-July, she transits the Erie Canal on
  a series of 12-day cruises and returns via Chicago to New
  Orleans in October.

Home Port   Warren, RI.
Port Charges $50–100.

POSTSCRIPT   In addition to the features and small-ship experience
that ACCL cruises offer, the *Niagara Prince* is a one-of-a-kind ship sailing a unique itinerary through America's most historic waterways. That
makes it both a great value and a great cruise experience.

Grande Caribe (Preview)

Registry: United States	Length: 182.7 feet	Beam: 39 feet
Cabins: 50	Draft: 6.3 feet	Speed: 12 knots
Maximum Passengers: 100	Passenger Decks: 3	Elevators: none; chairlift
	Crew: n.a.	Space Ratio: n.a.

THE SHIP   ACCL's decision to add another ship was spurred by the
cruise line's double-digit growth for the last five years. Built at Blount
Marine in Warren, like the other ships, the *Grande Caribe* is designed for
coastal cruises from Labrador to the Amazon, and has ACCL's trade-
marks—a shallow draft and bow ramp—guaranteeing access to remote
areas that large cruise ships cannot reach.

The new ship also has a retractable pilot house for passage under
low bridges on inland waterways. A new feature is a stern swimming
platform. It will carry a Blount-designed glass-bottom boat and Sunfish
for its winter cruises in the Caribbean and Central America.

Although the *Grande Caribe* is only a slightly larger version of her
sister ships and similar in most respects, her layout varies in two ways:

the dining room is on the main deck; and the lounge is on the top deck from where passengers can enjoy panoramic views.

The ship is scheduled to sail on Erie Canal/Canada cruises in summer, followed by repositioning cruises in the fall en route to Panama, where she is expected to sail during the winter season.

AMERICAN HAWAII CRUISES

1380 Port of New Orleans Place, Robin St. Wharf,
New Orleans, LA 70130-1890;
(800) 543-7637; fax (504) 585-0694
http://www.cruisehawaii.com

TYPE OF SHIP   Modernized, classic oceanliner.

TYPE OF CRUISE   Destination- and family-oriented, casual and all-American.

CRUISE LINE'S STRENGTHS
- the destination
- friendly staff
- kids' program
- shore excursions
- theme cruises

CRUISE LINE'S SHORTCOMINGS
- aging ship
- lack of amenities in cabins
- small bathrooms
- U.S. and Hawaiian laws inhibiting line's development

FELLOW PASSENGERS   Families with children during summer; honeymooners, seniors, retired couples year-round. Most are experienced travelers, 40 percent have visited Hawaii before, and 60 percent have been on a cruise. The average age is 50+; 20 percent of the passengers are 70+. The median household income is $40,000+. More than a third are celebrating a special event, usually an anniversary.

Recommended For   Families, particularly those with children, first- and second-time visitors to Hawaii; honeymooners; seniors and others who want the most convenient way to see the islands; those looking for a cultural experience and a slower pace. New, shorter cruise segments are designed to attract first-timers, younger travelers, and honeymooners.

Not Recommended For   Sophisticated travelers who prefer luxury, gourmet cuisine, and individual travel. Singles looking for companionship or those looking for 24-hour entertainment, gambling, discos, and fitness activities.

CRUISE AREAS AND SEASONS   Seven days, Hawaii Islands, year-round.

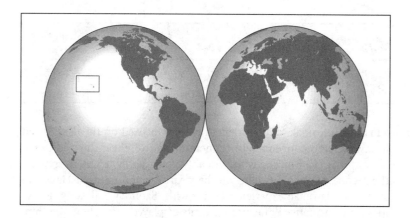

THE LINE   Following a $50 million renovation of its ship by Chicago-based American Classic Voyages (the parent company of Delta Queen Steamboat Company, which acquired American Hawaii Cruises in July 1993), American Hawaii Cruises hopes to turn a liability—its aging ships—into an asset by celebrating its distinguished history, stressing the appeal of traditional cruising, and focusing strongly on the Hawaiian aspect of its name.

Sailing into challenges is nothing new for AHC. Created specifically to cruise in Hawaiian waters at a time when U.S. flag operations had all but disappeared, it took an act of Congress (due to the Jones Act) to get AHC's *SS Independence* (in 1979) and *SS Constitution* (in 1982) recommissioned as American flag vessels. (The Jones Act requires that ships cruising solely between U.S. ports must be American flag vessels, owned by U.S. citizens, built and refurbished in the United States, and staffed with an American crew. AHC's vessels are the only ocean-going cruise ships sailing under the American flag today.) In 1988, when the line was acquired by American-Chinese businessman Peter Huang, health and fitness centers were added along with innovations to attract a younger audience. These included more imaginative and more active, sports-oriented shore excursions, three- and four-day cruises combined with resort vacations, and a more Hawaiian content to the cruises.

Huang also developed the line's strong environmental commitment, particularly for protecting the whales that migrate from Alaska to breed in the warm Hawaiian waters in winter. Whale-watching cruises accompanied by experts are offered.

The Fleet	Built/Renovated	Tonnage	Passengers
Independence	1950/1994	30,090	818

STYLE   Informal, family-oriented cruises focused on the destination in a warm and congenial atmosphere meant to reflect the traditional *aloha* spirit of Hawaii and with a friendly, if not highly polished, crew. By the second day, you are likely to be wearing a muumuu or Hawaiian shirt. The Hawaiian experience begins with "Saturday Sail Away" festivities featuring native floral arrangements displayed throughout the ship, crew members dressed in traditional Hawaiian attire, and traditional island chants and drums to send cruisers on their way.

Upon boarding, passengers receive a lei, the traditional necklace of fresh flowers, to welcome them. During the cruise, the emphasis is on experiencing the Hawaiian culture, with Hawaiian activities, entertainment, educational programs, and Hawaiian regional specialties in the dining room. The atmosphere is casual and so is the dress; there's never a need for a tuxedo and only once—the Captain's Party—for even a tie.

Life on board goes at a slower pace than typical mainstream ships on Caribbean and Mexican itineraries. There are no really late nights—most people are in bed by midnight if not before, and the food, activities and entertainment are geared toward older passengers. At the same time, American Hawaii welcomes kids with its seasonal children's program that keeps them happy and well occupied, and it loves honeymooners and about-to-be-newlyweds with its "Weddings in Paradise" package.

DISTINCTIVE FEATURES   A cultural display created by the Bishop Museum in Honolulu is intended to stimulate passengers' interest and knowledge in Hawaii. A *kumu*, a storyteller and teacher of traditions, is on board every cruise to enhance passengers' knowledge and enjoyment of Hawaiian culture and lore. Children's rates are available on most shore excursions.

RATES

Highest Per Diem	Lowest Per Diem	Average Per Diem
$328	$164	$221

The above per diems are calculated from the cruise line's nondiscounted *cruise-only* fares on standard accommodations. What you will actually pay *should* be *substantially* less (see Part One, How to Get the Best Deal on a Cruise). Per diems vary by season and by cabin location.

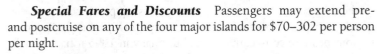

Special Fares and Discounts Passengers may extend pre- and postcruise on any of the four major islands for $70–302 per person per night.

- Third/Fourth Passenger: $695.
- Children's Fare: Ages 17 and under, sharing cabin with two full-fare passengers, sail free through December 20, 1997.
- Standby Fares: Occasionally, there are special rates for Hawaii residents.
- Single Supplement: 160 percent for all categories except suites which are 200 percent. A few cabins in two inside deluxe categories are available as singles for $100 additional.

Packages
- Air/Sea: Yes.
- Others: Golf, special occasion, honeymoon, anniversary. The "Weddings in Paradise" package includes the services of a minister or judge, a lei and haku (floral hairpiece) for the bride and a lei or boutonniere for the groom, a chilled bottle of champagne, two dozen 5 × 7 photos in a keepsake album, live music by Hawaiian musicians, and a wedding cake for two. The cost is $595. A wedding reception may be arranged for an additional fee. Weddings are performed on board in Honolulu prior to departure; only one wedding is scheduled per ship, per sailing. Times for ceremonies are given at the time of the booking. Contact AHC for information on documentation required.

- Pre/Post: Any length hotel stays combined with three-day, four-day, or seven-day cruise.

Past Passengers   Holokai Hui (meaning Seafarer's Club) is the past passenger club and provides special benefits including free cabin upgrade, separate check-in, on-board party, and other features. Passengers are eligible after their second cruise with AHC.

THE LAST WORD   The very factors that helped AHC develop its strong niche (read monopoly)—American built/flag vessels with required American crew (along with the inherent high costs)—are also those that have hampered the line's development. The Jones Act requires that ships cruising solely between U.S. ports be built in the United States. Yet, no comparable ship has been built in the United States in 35 years, and none are being built nor are likely to be built due to high costs. Added to this, gambling—a big money-maker for cruise ships—is forbidden. (That's the law of Hawaii.) Nor is there duty-free shopping; even on the ship, state sales tax is collected on gift shop purchases.

To remain competitive with newer ships, AHC did not raise prices for four or more consecutive years, but finally in 1995 it had to make modest increases. The cruises have broad appeal and could be enjoyed by almost anyone visiting Hawaii, offering the most comfortable way to visit the islands and enjoy some of the local flavor. The new, shorter cruises, introduced in 1996, are designed to appeal to younger travelers looking for more variety in a faster-paced vacation, first-time cruisers attracted by the idea of sampling a cruise without making the investment in a seven-day trip, and honeymooners who are looking for a mid-week departure.

American Hawaii Standard Features

Officers American.

Staffs Dining, Cabin, Cruise and Entertainment: American.

Dining Facilities One dining room in two sections; two seatings/three meals. Breakfast, lunch, tea on deck on one afternoon. Cookies, ice cream, popcorn around the clock.

Special Diets Accommodated with advance notice.

Room Service 24 hours with a limited menu through Bell Station, reached by phone. Cabin attendants on duty from 7:30–11:30 A.M. and 12–2, 5–9 P.M. and cannot be reached by phone while on duty.

Dress Code Casual; tie and jacket for captain's gala requested.

Cabin Amenities Direct cellular telephone service; bathrooms with showers; mirrored vanity. No televisions.

Electrical Outlets 110 AC; shaver and hair dryer outlets in cabins.

Wheelchair Access Two cabins.

Recreation and Entertainment Nightclub, show lounge; three bars, lounges; TV screens in top deck bar; movie theatre.

Sports and Fitness Two freshwater outside swimming pools; Ping-Pong; fitness center; shuffleboard.

Spa and Beauty Beauty/barber shop; massage.

Other Facilities Boutique; hospital; laundrettes/coin-operated machines; conference facilities with audio/visuals.

Children's Facilities Youth center; children's program June–August, enhanced during holidays; children's rates for shore excursions.

Theme Cruises Yes.

Smoking No smoking allowed in public rooms. Smoking permitted in cabins and outside decks.

AHC Suggested Tipping Per person, per day: cabin steward, $3.50; waiter, $3.50; busboy, $1.75. 15 percent added to bar bills.

Credit Cards For cruise payment and on-board charges, American Express, Visa, Mastercard, Discover.

Independence

	Quality Rating	Value Rating
Independence	❹	C

Registry: United States	Length: 682 feet	Beam: 89 feet
Cabins: 421	Draft: 26.5 feet	Speed: 17 knots
Maximum Passengers:	Passenger Decks: 9	Elevators: 4
1,021	Crew: 315	Space Ratio: 37

THE SHIP Following $50 million of renovations, the *Independence* made her first voyage in November 1994, sporting a new logo on her smokestack that looks even more Hawaiian than the familiar red hibiscus used since the line began. The extensive renovations were aimed at creating a more authentic Hawaiian ambience in the decor. Even the rooms and decks were renamed using authentic Hawaiian names. Other major improvements included upgrading the air conditioning, electrical, and pollution control systems and structural repairs and replacements.

The most dramatic changes are found in the elegant Kama'aina Lounge (formerly Independence Lounge) and other public areas on the Kama'aina Deck (formerly Promenade Deck) where, on both sides of the room, 40 feet of windows were added to open up the space with an indoor-outdoor "lanai" environment, creating a more inviting ambience and giving passengers better views of the islands and sea.

A large open area that now houses the Bishop Museum is splendid, and the updated showroom and the lounge are lovely. The Hawaiian lanai effect extends to the aft section, part of which is shaded by canopies. The warmly decorated public rooms display artwork by local artists.

Because the ship originally was designed for three classes of passengers—making some public areas difficult to reach—better access and passenger flow were the primary objectives of the renovations. A grand stairway was added to the pool area aft to connect the ship's three main decks: Kama'aina, Ohana, and Sun. An additional aft stairway allows access to the pool area from the cabins on the lower decks. In addition, the forward elevators were extended to the top two decks. New corridor carpeting with images of dolphins and whales swimming toward the bow is also meant to help passengers orient themselves within the ship.

To make way for new deluxe suites in the former Sports Deck Solarium and on the boat and main decks, the fitness center and conference center were relocated. Handicap-accessible suites were also created, and all cabins were renovated and redecorated.

ITINERARY   Year-round, the *Independence* sails on a seven-day itinerary, departing Honolulu on Saturday evening at 9 P.M., with Sunday at sea, arriving Sunday evening at Kauai and remaining overnight. On Monday evening the ship departs for Maui, Hilo, and Kona and returns to Honolulu on Saturday. Three- and four-day cruises, with Maui as the midweek destination or embarkation point, were introduced in June 1997. They can be combined easily with land packages.

Home Port   Honolulu.
Port Charges and Taxes $85 per passenger.

CABINS   The newly redecorated cabins are very comfortable and storage space more than ample. Concealed compartments and beds as well as fold-out tables are some of the features created by the ship's original designer, Henry Dreyfuss, that have been retained.

The new decor uses brightly colored Hawaiian fabrics from the 1940s and 1950s, with traditional Hawaiian patterns in the bedspreads. Although the bathrooms were renovated, they are smaller than those found in comparable-size cabins on newer ships and the fixtures remain of the 1950s vintage. All cabins have baths with showers and mirrored cabinet, except three top suites on the boat deck which also have tubs; most have a mirrored vanity.

All cabins are equipped with a cellular telephone service that takes advantage of Hawaii's extensive cellular telephone network and enables passengers to phone directly to the U.S. mainland at considerably less cost than is normally the case on cruise ships. You will find instructions in your cabin that explain the system and costs. There are two types of rates: in port at the dock and at sea or anchored offshore. You will be charged for all calls, including credit card and operator-assisted calls. Sample rates at the dock to the continental United States: $2 for first minute, $.75 each additional minute. At sea, all calls: $3 for first minute, $.25 each additional minute.

Room Service is available through the Bell Station (like the bell captain's desk in a hotel) reachable by phone 24 hours a day for beverages, light snacks, and ice. (You might get a recorded message asking you to leave a message.) Cabin attendants are on duty from 7:30–11:30 A.M., 12–2 P.M., and 5–9 P.M.; they are available for all cleaning services, towels, and turn-down, delivery of "Tradewinds," the daily schedule, and general maintenance.

As the cruise line's brochure explains, the ships' original layout for three classes results now in 50 different cabin configurations, which AHC has grouped into 13 different fare categories. The cabins are pictured and described in AHC's easy to use brochure. The bed configurations vary—queen, twins that convert to double, lower and upper pullman-style berths, or single lower sofabed. The *Independence*'s six new solarium suites added on the bridge deck are some of the largest, each with 300 square feet, and have high ceilings, skylights, and windows that open. Two cabins designed for the disabled are located on the Aloha Deck.

Specifications   217 cabins inside, 204 outside; 37 suites. Standard dimensions are 105–205 square feet. 84 with twin; 147 double/queen/king; 131 upper and lowers; 22 singles.

DINING   To give passengers a taste of the islands, menus include a selection of Pacific Rim and Hawaiian regional cuisine along with traditional favorites. Local ingredients—fresh fish, fruit, vegetables, and herbs—are used to ensure authenticity. In addition, a variety of familiar items boast a new spin, such as Maui mango pasta and roasted rack of lamb with Molokai herbs.

Over the years, American Hawaii's cuisine has gotten mixed reviews—from poor to excellent—but of late, the line has been getting higher marks on both quality and variety.

A typical dinner menu includes three appetizers, two soups, two salads, six entrees (with at least one fish, pasta, and vegetarian selection), three desserts, plus a selection of ice creams and sherbets. California and French wines are featured and range from $16 Buena Vista Sauvignon Blanc to $42 Labourne-Roi Meursault (Burgundy).

One notable improvement has been the expansion and redesign of the buffet on the Ohana Deck (upper deck) where breakfast and lunch offer a wide selection of dishes. The buffet has Hawaiian-style indoor-outdoor cooking, and seating areas extend to the swimming pool area, partially shaded by canopies.

Ice cream and sherbet treats are a long-standing tradition. Pu'uwai, meaning healthy heart, is a low-fat, low-cholesterol program available in the dining room. Daily, a Hawaiian cocktail specialty, such as Blue Hawaiian or Mai Tai, is featured for $4.75; in the afternoon a self-service popcorn machine provides a snack.

To accommodate passengers who are off the ship during the regular meal hours, the ship has extended lunch service from 2:30–4:30 P.M., with hot dogs and hamburgers available at the buffet. Coffee and tea, juice and sodas are available 24 hours in the Ohana Buffet.

SERVICE   The young American crew is friendly, courteous, energetic, high spirited, and attentive. Both men and women serve as cabin and dining room attendants and are given high marks for efficiency. Particularly noteworthy are the waitresses in the dining room and on the pool deck. Many of the staff are new employees who need time to train, particularly in the care of small things, like wiping and cleaning deck chairs in the morning and evening, picking up stray trash on the decks, buffing the brass—in other words, an attention to details that make the ship look spiffy and are the hallmark of a well-run ship.

FACILITIES AND ENTERTAINMENT   Evening entertainment is family oriented with local Hawaiian entertainers being standard fare. The Hoi Hoi Showplace on the Kama'aina Deck is the show lounge where performers celebrate Hawaiian traditions with island entertainment and the Ray Kennedy Entertainers perform three Broadway-style shows weekly. Next door, the Hapa Haole Bar re-creates the "tourist" Hawaii of the 1930s and 1940s. "Concerts on the Pacific" by headline entertainer, Doug Dunnell is a nightly feature in the Kama'aina Lounge.

The ship's orchestra is also very good with a range from Elvis to Hawaiian which passengers seem to enjoy thoroughly. On a recent cruise, many passengers seemed to like dancing but had limited opportunities to do so. AHC adds gentlemen hosts to dance with the unaccompanied women on the ship during Big Band cruises.

At the stern, the Commodore's Terrace, a semicircular bar/lounge with an open-air configuration, is one of the most pleasant areas on the ship, offering passengers a 180° view of Hawaii's beautiful scenery. In the evening, the terrace is the venue for low-key entertainment.

Two large television screens are located in the poolside Surfrider Bar on the Sun Deck.

There are no televisions in cabins, and the ship has no casinos as gambling is prohibited in Hawaii. The movie theatre shows current films as many as four or five times daily. Selections and times are listed in the daily program.

ACTIVITIES AND DIVERSIONS   The *kumu*, a teacher of Hawaiian traditions who is on board for every cruise, is an integral part of the passengers' Hawaiian experience. She brings the spirit of *aloha* and talks about island history, music, craft, cultural tradition, lore, and mythology, meeting with passengers at different times throughout the day and evening, choosing appropriate shipboard settings to enhance and illustrate her stories. She teaches them native Hawaiian words, the meaning of the hula dance, and how to play ancient island games, blow conch shells, make leis and other crafts, and play the ukelele. The kumu's study has been added by the main lounge on the Kama'aina Deck.

Exhibits created by the renowned Bishop Museum also enable passengers to learn about Hawaii through displays of ancient Hawaiian games, arts and crafts, traditional garments, natural artifacts, and three-dimensional interactive exhibits on the wildlife and natural history of Hawaii. During whale-watching months from January–March, seminars by experts on nature and wildlife by experts from Pacific Whale Foundation are offered on board.

In addition, the daily program includes games, line dancing, and such unusual activities as instruction in making fabric hibiscus flowers, shell hair combs and earrings, and palm weaving. The ship has a conference center.

SPORTS AND FITNESS   Since the ship is in port every day but one, and so many of the shore excursions are sports-oriented, shipboard sports are limited. The ship has two small swimming pools that were given a much needed renovation during drydock in 1997. The ship also has a small fitness room with a few exercise machines but no daily fitness programs, other than an early morning walk. The open deck space is generous.

On shore, passengers can arrange to go biking, hiking, deep-sea fishing, horseback riding, kayaking on the Huleia River where *Raiders of the Lost Ark* was filmed, sailing, swimming, snorkeling, diving (novices and certified), and windsurfing. The newest golf package provides for play on four islands at some of Hawaii's leading courses.

SPA AND BEAUTY   The beauty salon is small; prices are moderate. The massage schedule fills quickly; you should sign up early to get an appointment.

CHILDREN'S FACILITIES   A supervised children's program is available during the summer months and holidays with organized games, talent shows, crafts sessions, special parties, and other activities for children in two groups: the Keiki ("kids" in Hawaiian) program for ages 5–12 and the "Hui O Kau Wela Nalu," (Summer Surf Club) for teens, 13–17. The ship has an on-board youth recreation center and a full-time recreation coordinator. There are also special kids' rates on most shore excursions.

SHORE EXCURSIONS American Hawaii shore excursions are some of the best of any cruise line and offer enough choices to suit everyone in the family. The ships are in port every morning of the cruise except one.

To help you make your selection, you will find a shore excursion book with color photos, descriptions, and prices in your cabin. A colorful, graphic display center on board shows the 50 or so options currently available. They include beach picnic, submarine and helicopter rides, visits to tropical gardens, macadamia nut farm, working ranch, plantation, the Polynesian Cultural Center, nature parks, craft shops, and local feasts and festivals. You can go biking, hiking, kayaking, and snorkeling and see whales, birds, volcanoes, rain forests, and more. Golfers should inquire about the line's golf package. Prices range from $15–150. Shore excursions cannot be purchased in advance of the cruise.

Particularly noteworthy are those that enable passengers with a sense of adventure to enjoy the less explored areas of Hawaii and experience the state's many natural attractions. You can join a raft exploration of the Na Pali coast, fly over the 5,000-foot rim of the Waialeale Crater in a helicopter, ride horseback along Hawaii's spectacular ocean bluffs, or take part in a kayak trip down the Huleia River in the heart of the Huleia National Wildlife Refuge, site of the opening scenes from the film, *Raiders of the Lost Ark*.

On Hilo, the Hawaii Volcanoes National Park is the big attraction; Old Hawaii: Hilo 100 Years Ago Tour is a quieter, gentler look at Hawaii. The Kauai highlight is a helicopter flight, subject to weather conditions.

Note: Schedule the Haleakala Crater helicopter flight for morning; afternoons are often cloudy and windy and planes cannot fly.

If shore excursions fill up, you can find one on your own as several companies provide them. You could also read up on the islands in advance, rent a car on each island (your ship will make arrangements), and explore on your own.

THEME CRUISES Recently, American Hawaii expanded its theme cruises, offering them almost year-round; inquire from AHC for the exact dates. Whale-watching cruises are traditional from January to March during the height of the season when humpback whales are in warm Hawaiian waters with their young. The cruises are accompanied by experts who give talks about this endangered species. Big band cruises, featuring music of the 1940s and headliner entertainers, are offered throughout the year.

Aloha Festival sailings, mid-September–mid-October, coincide with Aloha Month, the annual fall festival celebrated throughout the islands. Started in 1946 by the Jaycees as Aloha Week, it has become an annual tradition on all the islands to highlight Hawaii's rich cultural heritage. Passengers enjoy special presentations on Hawaiian history, art, music, and dance by distinguished local hula schools, storytellers, and artists who share their expertise and rich talents. These guest performers, known in Hawaii as "living treasures," dedicate their lives to the preservation of Hawaiian heritage. In port, passengers can attend colorful parades and street celebrations.

POSTSCRIPT   When Delta Queen Steamboat Company acquired American Hawaii, it made a commitment to do whatever it took to make its ship first class and the cruise the most authentic way to see the islands and experience their culture. To that end, they have invested large sums in the ship to restore and improve it. Even so, this is not a new ship. Don't expect a fancy two-level showroom and state-of-the-art health spa. Rather, it remains typical of the oceanliners built during its time, when dining rooms and theatre were located on lower decks and bathrooms were small. The ship should be enjoyed as a classic.

The ship is comfortable with a quiet dining room and spacious open decks. It offers a great introduction to the Hawaiian islands and the easiest, most unhurried way to island hop, especially for first-time Hawaii visitors who want to see as much of the islands as possible in a week. And now with the new three-and four-day cruises, it's even easier to have your cake and eat it too by combining a cruise with a hotel stay in a week's holiday.

It also provides a good sampling of cruising for first-timers—you only unpack once—and there's ample time in port for those who worry about seasickness, claustrophobia, or boredom. The first day of the cruise is at sea—a welcome amenity for those who have traveled long distances and are likely to have jet lag.

For old Hawaii hands, the cruise is a new way to see the islands. For experienced cruisers, it's a pleasant cruise and comprehensive visit to the fiftieth state. But if you are looking for excitement, 24-hour entertainment, gambling, discos, fitness activities, and gourmet cuisine, this is not the cruise for you.

CARNIVAL CRUISE LINES

3655 NW 87th Avenue, Miami, FL 33178-2428
(305) 599-2600; (800) 438-6744; fax (305) 599-8630
http://www.carnival.com

TYPE OF SHIPS New, mod superliners and megaliners

TYPE OF CRUISE Casual, contemporary mass market. "Fun Ships" hallmark makes the ship the destination and as central to the cruise vacation as its ports-of-call.

CRUISE LINE'S STRENGTHS
- lavish recreational and entertainment facilities
- new fleet with unusual, innovative interiors
- larger than average cabins for price category
- value
- clear, easy to use literature

CRUISE LINE'S SHORTCOMINGS
- megaliner size
- little relief from crowds and glitz
- lack of outdoor promenade deck
- lines for facilities and services

FELLOW PASSENGERS Broad spectrum from all walks of life, from 3–93. Although Carnival's image is shiploads of young swingers partying day and night (an image Carnival worked hard to cultivate to attract young people to cruising), the mix is more likely to range from Joe Six-pack and his Nike-footed kids to Lester and Alice celebrating their fiftieth wedding anniversary. The cruises lend themselves to families with or without kids, honeymooners, married couples, singles, and seniors. Average age: 43. On a typical cruise, 40 percent are ages 35–55; 30 percent under 35 (including 130,000 kids annually); 30 percent over 55. Seventy percent are first-time cruisers. Most have medium income.

Recommended For First-time cruisers who want an active, high-energy, party atmosphere; young singles and couples; young-at-heart of any age; those who enjoy flash and Las Vegas glitz or similar ambience.

Not Recommended For Small-ship devotees; sophisticated travelers who prefer luxury, gourmet cuisine, and individual travel; anyone seeking quiet or cerebral travel experience; those who consider Martha's Vineyard their ideal vacation spot.

CRUISE AREAS AND SEASONS Bahamas and Caribbean; West Coast/Mexican Riviera, year-round. Panama Canal, Alaska, Hawaii, seasonally. Expanded offering of Alaska and Hawaii voyages.

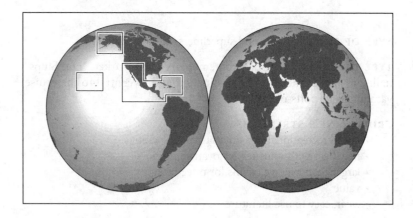

THE LINE In 25 short years, Carnival Cruise Lines went from one ship that ran aground on its maiden cruise to the largest, most influential cruise company in the business, having revolutionized the very nature of cruises along the way. Its story is the stuff of legends.

Ted Arison, a cruise executive based in Florida, and a maverick travel company in Boston bought the *Mardi Gras* (formerly the *Empress of Canada*) in 1972 to offer cruises that would change the steamship business forever. But first, they had to get past three years of losses and near bankruptcy. Then, Arison took over the company, assumed its $5 million debt, bought the assets—the *Mardi Gras*—for $1, and created the "Fun Ship" idea, turning a profit in his first year and adding two more ships.

Arison's aim was to take the stuffiness out of cruising and abandon the elitist image on which classic oceanliners had thrived. He wanted to make cruises fun and available to everyone, but particularly to middle

America, who had never dreamed of a holiday at sea. He hit the right button. Through most of the 1970s Carnival ships continuously broke occupancy records while traditional steamship companies were sinking all around.

Carnival continued to defy conventional wisdom. In the late 1970s when the world was reeling from the oil crisis with fuel prices and ship-building costs spiraling skyward and the very future of cruising in doubt, Carnival ordered a new ship, *Tropicale*, whose technology set new standards for the industry, changed ship profiles, and enhanced Carnival's fun ship concept.

Then, only a decade after its inauspicious beginning, Carnival added three radically new ships—*Holiday*, *Jubilee*, and *Celebration*—that set the trends of the eighties and beyond. The superliners, as they are known, each carrying 1,800 passengers, were not the largest passenger ships that had been built, but their design and madcap decor were so profoundly different from the oceanliners of the past, they could only be called revolutionary. At the same time, Carnival expanded its Caribbean itineraries and added West Coast cruises.

To get ready for the twenty-first century, Carnival is adding eight megaliners, each for over 2,600 passengers, and lifting a few eyebrows with their names. The *Fantasy*, *Ecstasy*, *Sensation*, and *Fascination* were followed in November 1996 by the 101,000-ton, 3,400-passenger *Carnival Destiny*, the world's largest ship. A sister ship is scheduled to debut in 1999 and a third one in the year 2000. Meanwhile, two more ships in the *Fantasy* class will enter service in 1998. Carnival's new ship investment in the 1990s exceeds $4.5 billion.

Under Arison's son, Micky, Carnival's young, aggressive team has pushed cruise vacations as being the universal dream holiday for people from all walks of life, regardless of where they live. Not only have they preached the gospel, they have made the growth happen with smart marketing, advertising, and pricing.

A publicly held company since 1987, Carnival carries upwards of 1.3 million passengers a year, accounting for 28 percent of all cruise passengers boarding from U.S. ports. In 1989, it broadened its base (and spiffed up its image) by acquiring the classic Holland America Line and the chic, upscale Windstar Cruises. Later, it acquired partial ownership in the ultraluxurious Seabourn Cruise Line. All operate as separate companies but the move helped each to sharpen its focus; together, they give Carnival tremendous clout.

In 1996, Carnival Corp. bought part ownership in Airtours, one of Europe's largest tour companies, as a stepping-stone into the European market; and together, in 1997, Carnival and Airtours bought Costa Cruises, Europe's largest cruise line. That purchase will give Carnival approximately 37 percent of the world cruise market. To expand in Asia, Carnival formed a joint venture with Hyundai Merchant Marine to offer cruises for the local Asian market, starting in 1998.

In April 1997, Windstar Cruises, which is owned by Carnival, bought the *Club Med 1*, which is a larger version of the Windstar ships. It will join the Windstar fleet in March 1998. Meanwhile, the cruise line is negotiating to acquire *Club Med 2*, which has different owners than its sister ship.

In recent years, Carnival has introduced departures from new gateways and expanded its focus on families. Its children's program employs one of cruising's largest staffs of trained personnel with 100 child counselors spread over eleven ships on a full-time, year-round basis; additional personnel are brought on during peak periods. Recently, too, a second children's playroom has been added to all the *Fantasy* class ships. Carnival's most recent innovation is a "Vacation Guarantee" that allows a dissatisfied passenger, upon notification to the purser's office, to leave a cruise at the first non-U.S. port of call and get a prorated refund. The aim is to nudge potential cruisers who might be hesitant in trying a cruise.

The Fleet	Built/Renovated	Tonnage	Passengers
Carnival Destiny	1996	101,353	2,642
Carnival Triumph	1999	101,353	2,642
Celebration	1987	47,262	1,486
Ecstasy	1991	70,367	2,040
Elation	1998	70,367	2,040
Fantasy	1990	70,367	2,044
Fascination	1994	70,367	2,040
Holiday	1985/1994	46,052	1,452
Imagination	1995	70,367	2,044
Inspiration	1996	70,367	2,044
Jubilee	1986	47,262	1,486
Paradise	1998	70,367	2,040
Sensation	1993	70,367	2,040
Tropicale	1981/89/94	36,674	1,022

STYLE   Youthful and casual, the Fun Ships have so much action, options, and diversions that the ship itself is the cruise experience. An important part of creating Carnival has been Joe Farcus, an interior architect and decorator, unique in his role among the cruise lines. Farcus is nothing if not original. He believes that people go on vacation to have fun and it's his job to create the surroundings and atmosphere for them to do so. That he has done. If you accept his wild and flamboyant decor as amusing and entertaining, you will find it ingenious. But sometimes, Farcus has gone overboard, you might say. There's so much bombarding the senses, the impact can be more exhausting than exhilarating.

The emphasis on fun is intended to get people out of their cabins and onto decks and into public rooms to see and be part of the action. The wide selection of activity and entertainment aims at attracting a broad spectrum of passengers, but the appeal basically is to the young and young-at-heart adults, couples, honeymooners, and families with children—at reasonable prices. Carnival cruises are poles away from the elegance and formality long associated with luxury cruising.

Another characteristic: perhaps Carnival more than any cruise line has standardized features on all its ships. If you see a water slide on one ship, you can count on its being on the others and a menu with four desserts on one ship will be on others; even the names of the decks on all ships are the same. Not only does the uniformity help keep down costs in this computer age but consistency is reassuring to passengers—and their travel agents.

DISTINCTIVE FEATURES   The ships' design and decor; children's programs; family packages; two late-night buffets; 24-hour pizzerias; alternative casual dining restaurant, state-of-the-art fitness centers; tuxedo rentals. Vacation guarantee.

RATES

Highest Per Diem	*Lowest Per Diem*	*Average Per Diem*
$287	$154	$195

The above per diems are calculated from the cruise line's nondiscounted *cruise-only* fares on standard accommodations. What you actually pay should be substantially less (see Part One, How to Get the Best Deal on a Cruise). Per diems vary by season, by cabin location, and by cruise areas.

All published rates include port fees.

Special Fares and Discounts   Early bird program, called Super Savers, provides discounts up to $700 per cabin on three- to four-day cruises, and up to $1,300 on seven-day cruises, and is capacity controlled.

- Children's Fare: Same as third/fourth person rates, which are deeply discounted. If the children are under 12, the rates are even lower. Passengers younger than 21 years must be accompanied by an adult 25 or older in the cabin. Exceptions apply to married couples and to children who are traveling with parents in a separate cabin.
- Single Supplement: 150 percent or 200 percent, depending on category.

Packages
- Air/Sea: No.
- Cruise/Air Add-on with transfers: Yes.
- Pre/Post: Yes.
- Others: Yes.

Past Passengers   No club. After first cruise, passengers placed on mailing list to get *Carnival Currents*, the line's on-board magazine; special discounts and on-board cocktail party.

THE LAST WORD   Carnival has had an enormous impact on today's cruises, particularly those aimed at the mass market, and when it comes to marketing cruises, Carnival wrote the book. Yet, despite the-girl-next-door cheerleading of Kathie Lee Gifford, who has helped Carnival project the image of universal appeal, a Carnival cruise isn't for everybody. The ships have more glitter than glamour. Some people love them; others think they redefine tacky. For the generation that has grown up in Toys 'Я Us, Texas-size shopping malls, Disney make-believe, and the lights of Las Vegas, Carnival's glitzy, gargantuan ships might feel like home. But if big, brassy, and boisterous is not your style, Carnival is not for you.

Yet, we hasten to add, everyone should take at least one Carnival cruise to see for themselves. The ships are eye-popping and the atmosphere infectious. Even the most staid, button-down party poops are often turned on by the Carnival neon and end up having the time of their life.

CARNIVAL SHIPS STANDARD FEATURES

Officers Italian.

Staffs Dining/International; Cabin/Central American, Asian; Cruise/American and others.

Dining Facilities Two main dining rooms/two seatings for three meals, located on upper decks (*Tropicale* has one dining room). Breakfast and lunch served cafeteria-style on the Lido Deck; two late-night buffets. *Destiny*'s lido restaurant is four-in-one: pizzeria, Asian, Trattoria, American Grill. Seaview Bistro dinner service in lido restaurant.

Special Diets Low salt, diabetic, vegetarian, bland, kosher.

Room Service 24 hours; limited, light menu.

Dress Code Casual; no shorts in evening; two formal nights; tuxedos are not required and semiformal dress is acceptable.

Cabin Amenities Closed-circuit television; safe. Bathrooms with shower; international direct-dial phones. Hair dryers on request.

Electrical Outlets 110 AC.

Wheelchair Access 11–20 cabins, depending on ship.

Recreation and Entertainment Casino, bingo, disco, library (except *Tropicale*); ten bar/lounges (17 on *Destiny*; 7 on *Tropicale*); two-deck show lounges (one-deck on *Tropicale*; three-deck on *Destiny*).

Sports and Other Activities Three outside swimming pools, shuffleboard, jogging tracks (*Fantasy*-class and *Destiny*), Ping-Pong.

Beauty and Fitness Barber/beauty salon, sauna. Nautica Spas on all ships in *Fantasy* and *Holiday* group; full gym, exercise classes, body treatments. (Small spa on *Tropicale*.) Spa fare on menus.

Other Facilities Boutiques, tuxedo rentals, infirmary, drugstore, video of cruise souvenir ($50), and coin-operated laundry facilities.

Children's Facilities Camp Carnival, year-round, with supervised activities for toddlers to teens. No toddler programs on *Tropicale*. Video arcades, water slides, playroom, club/disco for teens, children's menus, high chairs. Baby-sitting arranged for $4 per hour for first child, $2 for each additional child. Passenger under 21 must be accompanied by adult over 25.

Smoking Smoke-free dining rooms and main show lounge.

Theme Cruises None.

Carnival Suggested Tipping Per person, per day: cabin steward, $3; waiter, $3; busboy, $1.50; 15 percent added to wine and bar bill.

Credit Cards Cruise and shipboard charges, American Express, Mastercard, Visa, Discover, Optima.

Fantasy / Ecstasy /Elation / Fascination / Imagination / Inspiration / Paradise / Sensation

	Quality Rating	Value Rating
Fantasy, Ecstasy	6	A
Elation (1998)	Preview	
Fascination, Imagination	6	A
Inspiration	6	A
Paradise (1998)	Preview	
Sensation	5	B

Registry (*Fantasy, Ecstasy*): Liberia
Registry (*Sensation, Fascination, Imagination, Inspiration*): Panama

Length: 855 feet	Beam: 118 feet	Cabins: 1,022/1,020
Draft: 26 feet	Speed: 21 knots	Maximum Passengers:
Passenger Decks: 10	Elevators: 14	2,634/2,594
Crew: 920	Space Ratio: 34	

THE SHIPS   Billed as ships for the twenty-first century, Carnival's eight megaliners have already bedazzled passengers of the 1990s. Their flashy decor and high-energy ambience are something of a Las Vegas-at-Sea, Disneyland, and Starlight Express in one. Passengers are introduced to the ships in atrium lobbies spanning seven decks at the heart of the ship with specially commissioned art of huge proportions. Throughout the vessels there are so many bars, lounges, entertainment, and recreation outlets—all with highly imaginative settings—you need more than one cruise to find them all. It's certain, no one takes a cruise on one of these ships to rest; your senses work overtime.

Except for the decor—each ship has a theme—the vessels are identical in layout and style, and as with all Carnival ships, even the names of the decks are the same.

The *Fantasy*, the first of the group, is the most dazzling with a towering atrium awash in lights and dominated by a 20-foot-high kinetic sculpture by Israeli artist Yaacov Agam, composed of geometric designs rotating on cylinders. Here and in the entertainment areas, 15 miles of computerized lights are programmed to change color—constantly, but imperceptibly—from white to cool blue to hot red, altering the ambience with each change. It's awesome! Its name, *Fantasy*, is an understatement.

The second megaliner, *Ecstasy*, is designed as a city at sea. Carnival watchers have declared her to be the most elegant and sophisticated of the fleet, reflecting a conscious effort to upgrade and tone down the style. Well, maybe. But there's no chance of mistaking this for anything but a Carnival ship, especially when, upon arrival, you are awestruck by the 24-foot-high plastic and steel sculpture in the Grand Atrium. Created by kinetic artist Len Janklow, it is composed of 12 huge cubes flooded in light, each holding 8 small cubes, that appear to be floating in space, and programmed to move clockwise and counterclockwise.

Esctasy's decor takes its inspiration from the heyday of Manhattan's Cafe Society and comes across as urbane and perhaps more refined than some of its sister ships, with exotic woods, Italian marbles, rich carpets, sumptuous fabrics, and a vintage Rolls Royce on the double-width promenade called City Lights Boulevard, which is lined with bars and lounges. The highlights are the Neon Bar, a piano bar with vintage neon signs, and Chinatown Lounge, guarded by huge lion-headed Foo dogs. The inside is meant to resemble a street scene complete with an enormous smoke-belching dragon.

Sensation, the third in the series, most closely resembles the *Ecstasy* with decor that is slightly more sophisticated than its mates, and it uses light, sound, and color to create a "sensual" environment. The public rooms range from elegant to kitsch. Among the latter, the Touch of Class Lounge is a "hands-on" experience with gigantic hands complete with red polished fingernails cupping the entrance, and other hands supporting tables with chairs and bar stools shaped like hands.

Fascination, the newest of the group, takes our fascination with Hollywood, particularly of the 1930s, 1940s, and 1950s, as its theme with a mix of homage and spoofs—and kitsch galore. There is the Puttin' on the Ritz Lounge, Bogart's Cafe, and Passage to India Lounge on Hollywood Boulevard, the entertainment promenade. But the real showstoppers are the 20 life-size mannequins of movie legends— Marilyn Monroe, Bette Davis, John Wayne, and other stars—posed here and there, as they might be in real life. At the Stars Bar, you find Gary Cooper and Rita Hayworth, and in the Tara Library, Vivien Leigh and Clark Gable.

The interiors place a little less emphasis—but only a little—on special effects than some of her sister ships and use 20 varieties of marble and eight rare woods. The Grand Atrium is dramatic with bands of purple neon edging each of the seven decks that rise from the main lobby and is centered by an enormous sculpture, Nucleus, by British artist Susanna Holt.

Artist Len Janklow let his imagination run into outer space when he created the 24-foot-high sculpture that dominates the *Imagination*'s atrium. Composed on four rotating towers of stainless steel and clear plastic, the forms contain images of space ships, space stations, and other futuristic technologies. His is only one of the many works of art commissioned from five artists whose imaginations carried them from powerful seascapes to mythical tales of ancient Greece and Egypt.

Architect Joe Farcus's fertile imagination was also working overtime creating the decor of the bars and lounges. Among the favorites are Shangri-La, a night spot for music and dancing, and Mirage, the sing-along piano bar. But most innovative are the ship's 24-hour pizzeria, the first on any Carnival ship—now a feature on all of them—and an adjacent bar featuring draft beer from around the world.

Farcus's concept for the *Inspiration* was inspired by the arts, particularly music. Throughout, the decor uses musical icons, themes, and motifs—from a bigger-than-life replica of Elvis's guitar in the disco to the elegant Chopin Lounge with a piano, of course, and a wall of violins in the Promenade bar that Strauss would have loved. The ship has a similar multideck glass-domed atrium and dramatic centerpiece, a promenade lined with lounges and bars, and the similar sports and recreation features of the *Fantasy* group.

ITINERARIES

Fantasy   Three- and four-day Bahama cruises, year-round, departing from Port Canaveral on Thursday and Sunday to Nassau and Freeport. Bahamas cruises have a full day at sea, instead of a beach party on a Bahamian island, a popular feature which most other ships offer. When passengers remain on board, they spend money in the bars and casino. The additional revenue helps Carnival keep down the price of its cruises and its bottom line.

> *Home Port*   Port Canaveral.
> *Port Charges* $75–85.

Ecstasy   Three- and four-days, year-round, Bahamas and Western Caribbean, from Miami. The three-day cruise departs on Friday to Nassau; four-day cruise departs on Monday to Key West and Playa del Carmen/Cozumel; both cruises have a day at sea.

Home Port   Miami.
Port Charges $75–85.

Elation   Beginning April 1998, the ship will sail year-round, on seven-day Mexican Riviera cruises from Los Angeles to Puerto Vallarta, Mazatlan and Cabo San Lucas.

Fascination   Seven days, year-round, Eastern and Southern Caribbean, departing from San Juan on Saturday to St. Thomas, St. Maarten, Dominica, Barbados, and Martinique. As an island sampler, particularly for those on their first visit to the Caribbean, the *Fascination's* itinerary is one of Carnival's best, reflecting the Caribbean's cultural diversity and offering contrasts between highly developed St. Thomas and St. Maarten and off-the-beaten-track Dominica, historic Barbados, and seductive Martinique. At the same time, it provides plenty of shopping, sports, and dining options plus a full day at sea.

Home Port   San Juan.
Port Charges $109.

Imagination   Seven days, year-round, Western Caribbean, departing from Miami on Saturday to Playa del Carmen/Cozumel (remaining until midnight), Grand Cayman, Ocho Rios, and three days at sea.

Home Port   Miami.
Port Charges $109.

Inspiration   Seven days, year-round, Eastern and Southern Caribbean, departing on Sunday from San Juan to St. Thomas, Guadeloupe, Grenada, and two new ports of St. Lucia and Santo Domingo. As an island sampler for those who have visited the Caribbean in the past, the *Inspiration's* new itinerary is one of Carnival's most interesting. Not only does it showcase the region's cultural diversity, but it also includes Santo Domingo, one of the best kept secrets in the Caribbean.

Home Port   San Juan.
Port Charges $109.

Sensation   Seven days, year-round, Eastern Caribbean, departing on Saturday from San Juan to St. Thomas and St. Maarten, with three days at sea.

Home Port   San Juan.
Port Charges $109.

Paradise   n.a.

CABINS   As with all Carnival ships, the 12 cabin categories include some of the largest standard cabins and junior suites of any ships in their price category. They are finished in light oak woodwork, and although the colors vary some from ship to ship, the furniture and decor are essentially the same—basic and comfortable. On the *Fantasy*, for example, the colors are gray and orange with gray carpeting that has red, purple, green, and blue pinstripes that pick up the tiny flecks of these colors in the bedspreads.

Almost all cabins have twin beds that convert to king-size ones—a Carnival innovation that was quickly copied by other cruise lines for almost all of their new ships. The cabins have phones with international direct dial; a desk/dressing table; closed-circuit television with channels for movies, cartoons, and some satellite programs depending on the ship's location; stereo music; and wall safes. Outside cabins have picture windows.

The bathrooms are particularly well designed with roomy shower stalls. They have soap but no gift toiletries; hair dryers are available on request. Closet space is adequate for the short, warm weather nature of the cruises.

Specifications   383 inside cabins, 564 outside; 54 suites with verandas (28 suites with bathtub Jacuzzi). Standard dimensions, 183–190 square feet; 947 with twin convertible to double; 19 inside with upper and lower berths; no singles. All have wheelchair accessible cabins.

DINING   Each ship has two dining rooms with two seatings for three meals. The rooms are located on an upper deck and have large windows with good views. Dinners often have themes, such as Caribbean night and French night, with music, menus, and costumed waiters in keeping with the theme.

Both restaurants have round tables usually for eight people in the center of the room but the sides are lined with rectangular tables, which are sometimes difficult to get in and out of. The *Ecstasy's* Wind Star and Wind Song dining rooms get more kudos for their stylish decor than its earlier sister. The whole group gets criticized for a high noise level. Also, the ships no longer have wine stewards; wine is served by waiters and busboys who are not familiar with the selections.Breakfast and lunch are served cafeteria-style on the Lido Deck and there are two late-night buffets. *Fantasy's* Windows on the Sea is one of the group's most attractive restaurants with colorful pastel parasols, brass highlights, and etched glass. On the *Ecstasy*, the Panorama Bar and Grill has floor-to-ceiling windows and a playful ambience with signal flags and indirect blue neon lighting. *Fascination's* Coconut Grove Bar and Grille, with fabrics and flooring of a tropical theme, has imitation palm trees as columns and a bamboo bar and tables.

After testing an alternative casual-dining concept on the *Holiday* and *Jubilee* for several months, Carnival added "Seaview Bistros" fleetwide in early 1997. The bistros offer an array of specialty salads, pastas, steaks, and desserts—along with a daily chef's special—served in a cafe-like setting. The bistros operate each evening from 6–9:30 P.M. in a designated area of the casual lido restaurant used for breakfast and lunch. They have a distinctive atmosphere, with personal touches such as tablecloths, preset silverware and floral arrangements on the tables. And, while service is buffet-style, waiters are on hand to refill drink orders and food requests. The bistros are meant to handle about 100–150 people but double that number or more can be accommodated when the need arises.

Carnival was never known for its cuisine, but in the past few years it has made a real effort to upgrade the quality, selections, and variety of its cuisine with commendable results. A typical dinner menu has three juices, four appetizers, three soups, two salads, two fish choices, three entrees of beef, chicken, or turkey, five desserts, plus a variety of ice cream and sherbet, cheese, and beverages. At least one of each course is marked as spa fare which has lower calories, sodium, fat, and cholesterol. Breakfasts and lunches in the dining rooms have equally elaborate selections.

SERVICE   Dining staffs generally get good marks, but cabin attendants get mixed reviews. Passengers will find that cruise directors and their staff are very professional, but the cruise director on ships of this size is in little evidence except when he is on stage. Recent passengers on the *Fantasy* report that contacting their friendly room steward or the purser's desk by phone was nearly impossible. They also complain that on boarding the *Fantasy*, they encountered some orientation problems. Rather than being escorted to their cabins, they were greeted upon arrival, handed ship diagrams, and directed to find their cabins on their own.

The bottom line on service: ships of megaliner size offer many wonderful facilities and services, but personal service is not among them.

FACILITIES AND ENTERTAINMENT   One of the most distinctive features of the *Fantasy* group is an indoor promenade on only one side of the ship that serves as an "entertainment boulevard" lined with bars, lounges, disco, casino, and nightclubs. Called the Century Boulevard on the *Fantasy*, the promenade has the Cats Lounge, whose decor takes its cue from the long-running Broadway show, and Cleopatra's, a piano bar with every ancient Egyptian art cliché known to man.

At one end of the Boulevard, the spectacular, two-deck Universal show lounge stages nightly entertainment on the scale of a Las Vegas show with well-endowed, feathered, long-legged showgirls (and men) in the Broadway musical vein, and it's outstanding. At the stern is the opulent Majestic Bar with a king's ransom of marble and an entire wall of onyx. Through the bar, you enter the flamboyant Crystal Lounge where red and white lights nearly blind you. Here you can catch the Midnight Special, a naughty cabaret with comedians and a variety of musical and other artists. The casinos, each with over 200 slot machines, 20 blackjack tables, roulette, and other games, are among the largest afloat.

On the *Fascination*'s Hollywood Boulevard, the most amusing place is Bar 88, named for the 88 keys on a piano and decorated with huge neon-lit keys at the door and on the columns between tables that are shaped like tiny pianos. At the Passage to India Lounge, the two life-size elephants that greet you are only a prelude to the inside draped with an elaborate Indian ceremonial cloth, British colonial-style mahogany chairs, a statue of a multiarmed Hindu deity, a domed shrine holding a silhouette of Buddha, mosaic tiles on the ceiling, and floral carpets on the floor. The Puttin' on the Ritz Lounge, with black decor inspired by Fred Astaire's top hat in his famous dance number, offers late-night comedy acts and a vocalist.

Fascination's Palace Lounge in shimmering golden beige and silvery pink with painted clouds decorating the walls, had the most technologically advanced stage at sea when she was introduced and its Tribute to Hollywood was one of the best shows anywhere. It combined classic Hollywood numbers, such as Marilyn Monroe's "Diamonds Are a Girl's Best Friend" and performers dancing in the style of Fred Astaire and Ginger Rogers, with contemporary numbers danced to the music of Whitney Houston and Michael Jackson. The lasers in *Tommy* were wild and a takeoff of Madonna raised some eyebrows.

On the *Sensation*, the Michelangelo Lounge, one of its most popular gathering spots, combines soft gray, yellow, and black in its furnishings and uses classic features such as Ionic columns, Greek designs, and ceiling frescoes. The bar and dance floor are marble. The Polo Lounge, in traditional polo colors and motifs, was designed for those seeking a quiet spot—all the ships have at least one such lounge.

ACTIVITIES AND DIVERSIONS   The ships have the usual array of activities—bingo, singles party, newlywed game, passenger talent show, beer chugging, and other competitions, horse racing, bridge and other card games, ballroom and country line-dance classes, masquerades, wine and cheese party, sing-alongs, and more. There are tours of the galleys and the bridge, first-run movies daily and more than the usual number of boutiques. The library-lounge, especially the mahogany paneled Explorer's Club on the *Ecstasy*, is one of the loveliest rooms in the Carnival fleet.

SPORTS AND FITNESS   Three swimming pools, one with a slide, Ping-Pong, shuffleboard, and volleyball are available, and pool games are staged almost daily. On Caribbean and Mexican cruises, depending on the ports, you can play golf, go sailing, horseback riding, biking, hiking, snorkeling, diving, and windsurfing.

The 12,000-square-foot Nautica Spa on the Sports Deck is a full-fledged gym with state-of-the-art equipment and trained instructors to help passengers use them. Or one can choose from an array of jazzercise, exercise, and aerobics classes. The Sun Deck has a 500-foot outside, uninterrupted jogging track and separate locker rooms, dressing rooms, and shower facilities for men and women, six whirlpools, saunas, and steam rooms—all included in the cruise price. Instructors will also create a fitness regimen for you to do at home.

SPA AND BEAUTY   The beauty salon and spa, operated by the Steiner Group, a British-based company, has nine private rooms for body and facial treatments—facials, pedicures, massage, herbal packs, and more—which carry a charge and can get to be an expensive indulgence.

CHILDREN'S FACILITIES   Camp Carnival, which handles over 130,000 kids fleetwide annually, is a year-round program with a wide array of activities supervised by trained counselors for kids in four different age groups: Toddlers (2–4), Juniors (5–8), Intermediate (9–12), and Teens (13–17). Children enjoy puppet making, finger painting, and learning the alphabet and numbers; older children have pizza parties, bingo, charades, Twister, scavenger hunts, lip sync, and more. Teens have their own scheduled activities from disco parties and star search contests to evening deck parties. All ships have video arcades, wading pools, water slides, two playrooms, teens' club/discos, special children's menus, and high chairs.

Recently, Carnival added a second children's playroom to the *Fantasy*-class ships as part of the ongoing expansion of Camp Carnival fleetwide. The new playrooms, designed to accommodate kids 5–12, are stocked with age-appropriate toys, games, and puzzles, including such popular pastimes as air hockey, foosball, and "pop-a-shot" basketball, along with the latest high-tech video games. The original playrooms on these ships are now geared specifically toward the toddler set.

Camp Carnival operates from 9:30 A.M. to 10 P.M. At 10 P.M., baby-sitting in the form of slumber parties in the children's playrooms is available and can be arranged through the purser's office for $4 per hour for the first child, $2 for each additional child. The toddler program is not available on the *Tropicale*.

SHORE EXCURSIONS   On Bahamas cruises of the *Ecstasy* and the *Fantasy*, the shore excursions offered by the ships are standard and mundane. You can easily tour Nassau on your own, taking a walk in Historic Nassau or using public transportation. Nassau and Freeport offer swimming and snorkeling at beautiful beaches, art galleries, pretty gardens, and shopping in Nassau at the straw market and duty-free stores on Nassau's Bay Street (only one block from the port), and at the International Market in Freeport.

Although Carnival has recently increased its shore excursions, offering a much greater variety than in the past, in general, they are standard tours that often, you can take on your own (with the possible exception of Dominica, which might be difficult but not impossible to arrange in advance). Dockside, plenty of vans with driver/guides are eager for your business and ready to design a tour to your liking. Prices may vary depending on your ability to bargain and the driver's eager-ness for your business, but do agree on a price in advance.

POSTSCRIPT   The ships are innovative but they seem more like a theme park than a cruise ship. The dearth of quiet lounges makes it dif-ficult to get away from the constant blast of high energy. The *Fantasy* was the first of the new megaliners to sail on short cruises and is well suited for them, attracting as they do high numbers of first-time cruisers who want to pack lots of activity into a short time.

An air/sea package is recommended for *Fantasy* cruises as the Orlando airport, where most passengers arrive, is about an hour's drive from Port Canaveral where the ship departs. There is no public trans-portation between the two; those traveling on their own need to hire a taxi or rent a car. On the other hand, those who book "cruise-only" can buy Carnival's transfer package. Also, if you buy the Orlando package, you can plan to take the Spaceport USA bus tour that is included in the package on the day you sail. In that way, the full morning can be spent at Spaceport USA, about 20 minutes from Port Canaveral. A late lunch is available on the ship up until 3:30 P.M.

Holiday / Jubilee / Celebration

	Quality Rating	Value Rating
Holiday, Jubilee	➎	B
Celebration	➎	B

Registry (*Jubilee, Celebration*): Liberia
Registry (*Holiday*): Panama

Length: 728/733 feet	Beam: 92 feet	Cabins: 726/743
Draft: 25 feet	Speed: 21 knots	Maximum Passengers:
Passenger Decks: 9/10	Elevators: 8	1,800/1,896
Crew: 660/670	Space Ratio: 32	

THE SHIPS   When the *Holiday* was unveiled in 1985, its decor was so different it was called zany. Micky Arison, Carnival's chairman, called it a "Disney World for adults." For those accustomed to the sleek lines of traditional ships, the ship's boxy look took some getting used to, but it was the inside innovations that revolutionized the very concept of cruising, making the ship with its four decks for Recreation and Entertainment as much the destination as its ports of call.

The most startling change was the main promenade deck. Instead of encircling the ship as had been typical of passenger ships, the deck runs double-width down only one side—a feature that became standard on all of Carnival's megaliners. Called Broadway on the *Holiday*, with as much glitter as the neon on its namesake, it serves as a meeting place and thoroughfare with bars, nightclubs, casinos, disco, and reminders of Broadway like a traffic light, street lamps, authentic 1934 vintage bus, and Times Square.

Now, after a decade during which larger and even more flamboyant ships have been added to Carnival's fleet, the *Holiday* is regarded as traditional. That may be pushing credibility somewhat, but it's amazing how quickly passengers have become comfortable with the new ideas the *Holiday* introduced. What's more, the innovations keep coming.

In December 1994, the *Holiday* debuted a $1 million entertainment complex with cruising's first virtual reality machines. The *Holiday* was quickly followed by the *Jubilee* and the *Celebration*. The trio are identical in almost all aspects except decor. Each follows a theme, more or less, with the *Jubilee* taking its inspiration from historic, romantic England, with the main promenade called Park Lane, a Victorian gazebo bar, a Trafalgar Square, and Churchill's Library. Throughout the ship, a generous use of wood makes the *Jubilee* a bit more mellow than other Carnival ships. The Atlantis Lounge, the main showroom with art deco interiors, and the Sporting Club, the casino with golden slot machines, etched glass, and golden mirrors, are standouts.

The *Celebration* is a tribute to New Orleans at Mardi Gras, complete with Bourbon Street, an outdoor cafe, bistro, a New Orleans streetcar named—you guessed it—Desire, and nightly, a Dixieland band tunes up before dinner on Bourbon Street. Sculpture by Israeli artist Yaacov Agam greets passengers in the lobby and his wall pieces decorate main areas and stair landings. But the most dramatic art is the work by San Francisco artist, Helen Webber, whose sculptured aluminum kites hang on wires the full six decks of the stairwells. The *Celebration*, like the other ships, has at least one quiet corner—Admiral's, a library and writing room dedicated to the great oceanliners of the past with models, pictures, and memorabilia.

ITINERARIES

Holiday Three- and four-day cruises, year-round, Baja California, departing from Los Angeles every Friday on three-day cruises for Ensenada, and every Monday on four-day cruises to Catalina Island and Ensenada. Both cruises have a full day at sea.

Home Port Los Angeles.
Port Charges $75–85.

Jubilee Through April 1998, seven days, Mexican Riviera, departing from Los Angeles on Sunday for Puerto Vallarta, Mazatlan, and Cabo San Lucas, with three days at sea.

- *Mid-May–mid-September,* seven days, Alaska, between Vancouver and Seward/Anchorage and including College Fjord, Columbia Glacier, Lynn Canal, Skagway, Juneau, Ketchikan, and the Inside Passage. The ship will offer 12-day Hawaii cruises between the two seasons in April–May and September–October.

Home Port Los Angeles.
Port Charges $109.

Celebration   Seven days, year-round, Western Caribbean, round-trip from Tampa on Sundays to Grand Cayman, Playa del Carmen/Cozumel, and New Orleans; or round trip from New Orleans on Fridays to Tampa, Grand Cayman, Cozumel, and back to New Orleans. Passengers boarding in Tampa spend a day and evening in New Orleans; those boarding in New Orleans enjoy a day in the Tampa Bay area. Both itineraries enjoy three days at sea. Carnival is the only cruise line to have this interesting and unusual itinerary—two foreign ports and two U.S. gateway cities—for the Western Caribbean. Each locale is distinctive and offers a day in port completely different from the other ports.

Home Ports   Tampa; New Orleans.
Port Charges $109.

CABINS   For all the unconventional elements on the ships' activity decks, the cabins on the *Holiday* trio are downright sane and larger than most ships in the same price category. Outside cabins have picture windows while those inside have back-lighted windows of the same size, making the cabin seem larger and alleviating some of the closed-in feeling of an inside cabin. The cabins are furnished with twin beds that can be converted to kings, and have ample closet and drawer space in cabinets of genuine wood. Specially commissioned artworks decorate the walls and add a touch of class.

A renovation of the *Holiday* with refurbishing of furniture, carpeting, and cabin bathrooms was completed in late 1995.

Holiday *Specifications*   279 inside cabins, 437 outside; 10 suites with whirlpool bathtubs. Standard dimensions, 180 square feet. 683 with twin beds convertible to kings; 27 inside, 10 outside with upper/lower berths. No singles. 15 wheelchair accessible.

Jubilee *and* Celebration *Specifications*   290 inside cabins, 443 outside; 10 suites with whirlpool bathtubs. Standard dimensions, 185 square feet. 709 with twin beds convertible to kings; 16 inside, 8 outside with upper/lower berths. No singles.

DINING   The *Holiday* group features the same menus as the *Fantasy*-class ships with two dining rooms serving three meals. Recently, Carnival significantly upgraded and expanded food service in the lido area on all its ships, a result of passenger preference for more casual breakfast and lunch choices. Now for breakfast and lunch different specialties are being offered each day in addition to the standard favorites, such as scrambled eggs or hot dogs and hamburgers. Particularly popular are the new, made-to-order pasta stations and expanded salad bars. Also available throughout the day in the lido are cookies, ice cream, and frozen yogurt. Staff in the lido area has been doubled to provide extra service. Wine bars on the Promenade decks have also been added.

FACILITIES AND ENTERTAINMENT   The Lido Deck on these ships has acres of open space and a swimming pool with a 14-foot-high spiral water slide that has now become a Carnival signature on all its ships. A more secluded pool is at the stern, and a kids' pool is on the deck below. The ships have Nautica Spas with separate facilities for men and women and a jogging track. Decks throughout are covered with Burmese teak.

Somewhere it has been written that Carnival offers 103 different activities and that might not be too far off. They run from wine tastings and auctions to knobby knee contests—you would be amazed by how many people join in!

In the evening, there's bar hopping and people watching on Broadway, Park Lane, or Bourbon Street and action in the casino or the electronic game room. One of the favorite spots on all three ships is the piano bar, but *Celebration*'s Red Hot Piano Bar wins the all-time kinky honky-tonk award. Red walls glow under red lights and the bar is shaped like a red piano with the ivories as the bar counter, and the music is—red hot. Lest the action here not be hot enough for you, a spiral staircase leads directly up to the casino on the deck above.

The ships also have huge theatres spanning two decks where Broadway-style musicals and Las Vegas–type shows are staged twice nightly. Seats are terraced on six levels so all 1,000 revelers have unobstructed views.

Camp Carnival, the year-round program for children available on the *Fantasy*-class ships, operates on the *Holiday* trio also, offering an array of supervised activities for four separate age groups. But for now, only the *Holiday* has Carnival's latest innovation—an extraordinary, one-of-a-kind entertainment complex designed for kids of all ages.

Set in Blue Lagoon, the smaller of two show lounges on Broadway, the facility incorporates cutting-edge electronic game technology. The games range from high-tech thrillers to more traditional favorites like pinball and air hockey, but the main attractions are two virtual reality machines. These games immerse players in a three-dimensional gunfight with high-resolution graphics and 32-channel digital sound, and R360, where players strap themselves in for an aerial dogfight while the machine spins them 360 degrees and upside down. Prizes are awarded to winners. Charges for playing the games are posted directly to passengers' shipboard accounts. The Midnight Special, a late-night cabaret show formerly featured in the Blue Lagoon, was moved to the larger Americana Lounge.

SHORE EXCURSIONS   All Carnival ships offer similar shore excursions at common-rated prices. Most are standard, off-the-shelf type of tours that you can usually take on your own. The main—and often only—reason to book any through the ships is convenience.

POSTSCRIPT   The *Holiday*, *Jubilee*, and *Celebration* set the course for Carnival for the decade and had an incalculable impact on cruising. Zany, yes. Successful? You bet. Probably because they were so new and different and Carnival had the nerve to defy convention in so blatant a way, passengers took to them enthusiastically—and still do. Whether or not the Carnival product is your cup of tea, these ships are worth a try for the fun and innovations in cruising that they offer at affordable prices.

Carnival Destiny

	Quality Rating	Value Rating
Carnival Destiny	8	A

Registry: Panama	Length: 893 feet	Beam: 125 feet
Cabins: 53	Draft: 27 feet	Speed: 22.5 knots
Maximum Passengers: 3,400	Passenger Decks: 12	Elevators: 18
	Crew: 1,070	Space Ratio: 38

THE SHIP   The *Carnival Destiny*, the largest cruise ship ever built and the first too wide to transit the Panama Canal, made her debut in November 1996 with quite a splash. When the planning began five years ago, Carnival employees were asked to submit their wish list of things to enhance the new ship. Apparently, they got most of their wishes.

The *Destiny* has Carnival's first doubled-decked dining room; a show lounge spanning three decks; a double-width promenade lined with lounges and bars; a mall-style shopping area; a 9,000-square-foot casino; 17 bars and lounges, four swimming pools and an expansive Nautica Spa; a retractable glass dome over the swimming pool area; and sports and recreation facilities similar to the *Fantasy* group. The pool area, with a stage for entertainment, has teak decks cantilevered in an amphitheater arrangement. Virtual World is high-tech virtual reality game center.

The configuration of *Destiny* is a departure from other Carnival ships in that the entertainment and recreation decks are situated between accommodations decks. The two lowest passenger decks have only cabins; they are followed by three decks of public rooms; and then five accommodations decks of cabins and suites with balconies. Also, in an effort to avoid big rooms and long corridors that would reinforce the ship's huge size, public rooms are broken up by spanning two or three levels. The arrangement is often confusing, however.

Despite her size—nearly three football fields in length and gigantic from the outside when seen at berth—*Destiny* does not seem as large from the inside as some of her *Fantasy*-class cousins. This is primarily due to the layout and the decor, which has quieter, softer, and toned-down—sometimes even tony—interiors compared to Farcus's flamboyant creations on other Carnival ships.

The Rotunda, a nine-deck atrium with four glass elevators and a glass dome, is the ship's focal point. An enormous marble and onyx mural of abstract geometric forms suggesting skyscrapers decorates the walls. But instead of the huge sculptures found on the *Fantasy*-class ships, *Destiny*'s atrium has an attractive lobby bar at its base, creating a great meeting place which helps to humanize the huge space.

ITINERARIES   Seven days, year-round, alternating Eastern and Western Caribbean, departing from Miami to San Juan, St. Croix, and St. Thomas, or Miami to Playa del Carmen, Cozumel, Grand Cayman, and Ocho Rios. Both itineraries offer three days at sea.

> ***Home Port***   Miami.
> ***Port Charges*** $109.

CABINS   *Destiny*'s cabins are the largest—220–260 square feet for standard ocean-view cabins—and most attractively furnished of all the Carnival ships. All cabins have hair dryers, safes, and interactive television. Cabin numbers pinpoint your deck as well as location: forward, aft, or a midship. Each section has its own elevators.

Sixty percent of the standard outside cabins have small balconies, all with clear front panels for unobstructed ocean views. Unfortunately, they do nothing to absorb sound. This and the lack of sufficient soundproofing makes the cabins noisy. Ocean-view cabins have a sitting area with sofa and coffee table.

The veranda cabins create a new category of standard cabins for Carnival that, although larger, are comparable in price to the standard outside ones on the *Fantasy*-class ships. Family cabins are located near the children's play facilities.

Note: We have received complaints about inadequate soundproofing between cabins (which may have as much to do with the boisterous nature of *Destiny* passengers as with cabin walls). Particularly to be avoided are the cabins on Deck 6 forward which are directly above some lounges that are in full swing most of the night.

Specifications   515 inside cabins, 432 outside with verandas; 48 suites with verandas, some with bathtub Jacuzzi. Standard dimensions, 220–260 square feet; all cabins with twins convertible to double; 4 inside with upper and lower berths; no singles. There are 25 wheelchair-accessible cabins.

DINING   The Galaxy and Universe restaurants—Carnival's first bi-level dining rooms—have an open feeling and the additional space allows for more widely spaced tables. Nonetheless, the noise level is high. Both dining rooms enjoy ocean views.

The two-deck Sun & Sea, the casual lido restaurant, dressed in shades of green with yellow, hand-blown Murano glass and hand-painted ceramic tile decorating the walls and countertops, serves a variety of foods in different settings, thus creating alternative dining options at no additional charge. The Trattoria is the setting for pasta and other Italian dishes made to order; Happy Valley features Chinese cuisine, stir-fried to order; and The Grille, a third specialty corner, serves hamburgers and hot dogs. The service has also been upgraded with waiters available to bring dishes and beverages to tables. The newest addition, the "Seaview Bistro," offers an array of specialty salads, pastas, steaks, and desserts—along with a daily chef's special—in a cafe-like setting. The bistro operates each evening from 6–9:30 P.M. in a designated area of the lido restaurant with a bistro atmosphere and touches such as tablecloths, preset silverware, and flowers on the tables. And, while service is buffet-style, waiters are on hand to refill drink orders and food requests.

For more alternatives, there is a 24-hour pizzeria, and on Promenade deck, a patisserie, attractively appointed with cherrywood counters and windowed banquettes along the walkway.

FACILITIES AND ENTERTAINMENT   In the evening, you are likely to run out of energy before you run out of choices. The big, flashy Millionaire's Club, said to be the largest casino afloat, has 321 slot machines and 23 table games. In the lavishly decorated Apollo Bar with hand-cut mosaics depicting Greek gods, the revolving piano enables the pianist to shine a spotlight on you or anyone else eager to test one of the microphones mounted in the center of each table.

At the whimsically decorated Downbeat where a 20-foot trumpet and French horn are suspended above the stage, you can sit on clarinet-shaped barstools or at glass tables that rest on oversized sections of horns to listen to the band.

In the Point After Dance Club, tricolored neon lights snake across the ceiling above a bilevel floor and over 500 video monitors flash pictures and computer-generated graphics around the room. But a staircase by the dance floor takes you down to the elegant Onyx Room, a more sedate club where back-lit alabaster panels glow softly beside a neon and glass dance floor.

The three-deck Palladium show lounge is the most technologically sophisticated on any cruise ship, according to Carnival. The additional deck below the seating levels allows the orchestra pit to be retracted, and the space above enables backdrops, special lighting equipment, and even performers to be "flown" offstage via cables. A Venetian glass chandelier hangs from the dome; at show time, when the lights dim, the chandelier goes high-tech with fiber-optics.

To achieve the three decks of seats (for 1,500 people), some sacrifices were made. The main floor is almost level, making viewing beyond the first few rows difficult for anyone but an NBA player. Also, balcony rails partially block some views. The big production shows, *Formidable*, styled after a French-style revue, and *Nightclub Express*, which opens at the Cotton Club and races through half a dozen other settings, are up to Carnival's usual topnotch quality.

If you are still looking for something to do, you can visit Virtual World, a game center with virtual reality and other electronic games or the All Star Bar, decorated with its celebrity memorabilia, including tables bearing authentic autographs of star athletes and featuring seven big-screen televisions broadcasting different sports events simultaneously.

SPORTS, FITNESS, AND BEAUTY The *Destiny* has four pools, including a children's pool, and seven whirlpools. Two pools have swim-up bars and another has Carnival's trademark water slide—but three decks high and 214 feet long. A retractable dome covers the aft deck and pool.

The two-level Nautica Spa and health club covers 15,000 square feet. One level has a beauty salon, massage rooms, Jacuzzis, and sauna and steam rooms with floor-to-ceiling windows. The second level has an aerobics room and a juice bar. The spa offers hydrotherapy bath, aromatherapy, and other body treatments. There is also a "Nouveau Yu Health Environment Capsule," an egg-shaped, temperature-controlled capsule designed to induce relaxation.

The gym has a wide array of equipment, including bikes, treadmills, step and rowing equipment, and 16 Keiser machines. Instructors lead exercise classes and can be hired as personal trainers for the week. There is also a one-eighth-mile jogging track on the Sun Deck.

CHILDREN'S FACILITIES   Children have a two-deck-high, 1,300-square-foot indoor/outdoor play center, complete with a jungle gym and pool. See *Fantasy* profile for information on Carnival's children program.

POSTSCRIPT   *Carnival Destiny* is Carnival's most beautiful ship to date, but there's no getting around it—it's big and noisy, and for now, at least, seems to attract people who are eager to party, day and night. That may reflect the excitement generated by its being the first of the new cruise ships over 100,000 tons and will probably simmer down when the novelty wears off. Nonetheless, the ship is definitely not for bookworms, fans of boutique hotels, or those in search of a quiet, laid-back vacation. Also, the signage could be improved as the layout, unlike on Carnival's other ships, can be confusing. One frustrated passenger was heard to remark at the end of a week's cruise, "I've spent most of my time trying to find my way around." Yet, the bottom line is this: The *Carnival Destiny* has met with such passenger enthusiasm that Carnival has already ordered two more just like her.

Tropicale

	Quality Rating	Value Rating
Tropicale	❸	B

Registry: Liberia	Length: 671 feet	Beam: 85 feet
Cabins: 511	Draft: 23.3 feet	Speed: 22 knots
Maximum Passengers: 1,400	Passenger Decks: 10	Elevators: 8
	Crew: 550	Space Ratio: 36

THE SHIP   When Carnival launched the *Tropicale* in the 1980s, it was the first new cruise ship built in almost a decade and it came with many new features: all same-size cabins, except for 12 suites; all cabins with large picture windows instead of portholes; greatly expanded deck space for sports and other activities; and twin beds that could be converted to kings—a feature copied throughout the cruise industry.

As the forerunner of the superliners and yet scaled down in both size and activity, *Tropicale* is the right combination for many people.

ITINERARIES   Ten and 11 days, winter, Southern Caribbean, from San Juan to St. Thomas, Martinique, Barbados, Grenada, St. Lucia, St. Barts, Antigua, and St. Maarten; or St. Thomas, St. Barts, St. Lucia, and Aruba, with a partial transit of the Panama Canal, followed by Ocho Rios before returning to San Juan.

- *In April*, she sails on 14-day Panama Canal positioning cruises, departing from San Juan to St. Thomas, Panama Canal, Caldera, Costa Rica, Acapulco, Puerto Vallarta, and San Diego, with eight days at sea; or, the reverse.
- *In April–May*, the ship is Hawaii-bound for either 11 or 12 days from Ensenada or Vancouver to Kauai, Maui, Hilo, Kona, and Honolulu; or, reverse. Both itineraries spend one day at sea.
- *In spring of 1998*, the *Tropicale* is scheduled to begin her new life for Carnival Cruises Asia; itineraries have not be announced.

Home Port   San Juan.
Port Charges $149.

CABINS   The *Tropicale* was refurbished in 1994, when the decor was brightened to give it more of the ambience of the superliners. As with all Carnival ships, the *Tropicale* has 12 categories of cabins and similar furnishings.

Specifications   172 inside cabins, 307 outside; 10 suites. Standard dimensions, 150–160 square feet. 479 with twins convertible to kings; upper/lower berths, 15 inside, 5 outside. No singles. 11 wheelchair accessible.

DINING   The *Tropicale* has one dining room, located on a lower deck. When the ship sails full, the room is crowded and noisy. As with all Carnival ships, theme nights—Mexican, Caribbean—feature music and colorful presentations of the food by the waiters.

ENTERTAINMENT AND FACILITIES   The *Tropicale* has seven bars and lounges, including a piano bar, but it has neither a cinema nor a library. The energy level on the *Tropicale* is low-key and many of the shipboard activities generate only mild interest, although the median age is about 43. Bingo, country line-dancing, and the casino are likely to draw the biggest crowds.

POSTSCRIPT   The *Tropicale* is scheduled to enter Asian service in 1998 for a new company, Carnival Cruises Asia, which Carnival formed in 1996 with a South Korean company to cater to the local Asian market.

CELEBRITY CRUISES

5201 Blue Lagoon Drive, Miami, FL 33126
(305) 262-6677; fax (800) 437-5111
http://www.celebrity-cruises.com

TYPE OF SHIPS Stylish superliners and megaliners.

TYPE OF CRUISE Moderately priced deluxe; ample activity at comfortable pace; emphasis on quality.

CRUISE LINE'S STRENGTHS
- cuisine
- well-designed, spacious ships
- two ships on Bermuda cruises
- dining room service
- children's program
- value for money

CRUISE LINE'S SHORTCOMINGS
- lack of outside, wraparound promenade deck
- excessive promotion of on-board shopping
- boarding procedures
- loud deck music on some ships

FELLOW PASSENGERS Moderately affluent, late-30s to 60s in high season; ages lower in off-season. Typical passenger is 48 years old, married, and has a household income of $50,000+. He/she tends to be an educated, experienced traveler, who understands quality, owns a house in a relatively affluent suburb, and has college-age children. Fifty percent have taken a cruise before, and of this group, 20–30 percent are repeaters with Celebrity. Due to the line's sailing regularly from the northeast United States and having the largest share of the New York/Bermuda market, 70 percent of passengers live on the East Coast; the balance come from the Midwest and West Coast.

Recommended For Middle to upper-middle income travelers in their 40s and up, whether on their first or tenth cruise, who appreciate good service and cuisine and want the recreational and entertainment variety of a large ship at an easy pace. Those with children during the holidays.

Not Recommended For small ship devotees; those seeking intellectual travel experience.

CRUISE AREAS AND SEASONS Bahamas, Caribbean year-round; Alaska, Bermuda, in summer; Panama Canal, spring, winter, and fall.

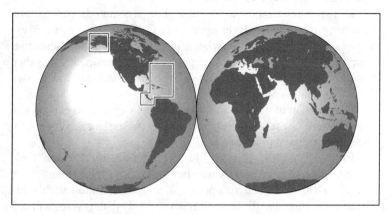

THE LINE From its inception in 1989, Celebrity Cruises' objective has been to offer deluxe cruises for experienced travelers at affordable prices. At first, no one believed it could be done; they were all the more skeptical because the new cruise line was being created by the owners of Chandris Cruises, an established company long associated with economically priced cruises for budget-conscious travelers.

Yet, in less than three years, Celebrity Cruises achieved its goal. What's more, it did it better than anyone imagined. Almost overnight, word spread that a Celebrity cruise was the best value for money of any cruise, offering as much or more than many cruises selling for considerably higher prices.

Quickly, too, it became apparent that Celebrity Cruises was much more than a new cruise line. It was a completely new product, sporting a new generation of ships that had been designed for the traveler of the 1990s and setting new standards of service and cuisine in its price category. To their admirers, Celebrity's initial three ships define the ideal size of a cruise and combine the right measure of contemporary design elements and decor with touches of traditional cruising.

Not one to rest on his laurels, John Chandris, the chairman of Celebrity Cruises and nephew of the founder, took up another challenge. In 1992, Celebrity teamed up with Overseas Shipholding Group, one of the world's largest bulk-shipping companies, to form a joint cruise company to build a new class of ships for the twenty-first century. The *Century*, the first of the three ships, was unveiled in December 1995; the *Galaxy*, the second, in 1996, and the *Mercury* in 1997. Once again, Celebrity's ships were winners.

Known as the *Century* series, these ships accommodate 26 percent more passengers in 48 percent more space than Celebrity's first generation of ships and have the very latest in entertainment and interactive communications systems designed by Sony Corporation, among other new features. Even though the new ships are more spacious and deluxe, Celebrity is maintaining its mid-price level.

The addition of the new ships has enabled Celebrity to expand the areas where it cruises, doubling its capacity in Alaska and offering its first summer season in Europe in 1998.

In June 1997, Celebrity and Royal Carbbean International took cruise watchers by surprise when they announced their intention to merge. Celebrity expects to operate as a separate brand with John Chandris remaining at the helm, though it's likely that its ships will sail on new itineraries next year. The $1.3 billion deal will result in a fleet of 20 ships when all the ships of the two lines, now under construction or on order, enter service by the year 2000.

The Fleet	Built/Renovated	Tonnage	Passengers
Century	1995	70,000	1,740
Galaxy	1996	77,713	1,870
Horizon	1990	46,811	1,354
Mercury	1997	74,000	1,870
Zenith	1992	47,255	1,374

STYLE From the handsome deep blue and white exteriors with their distinctive signature stacks to the elegant interior decor, Celebrity's ships have style, combining the glamour of traditional cruising with a fresh, contemporary look. That integration of modern and classic can be seen in the art on display by famous contemporary artists, such as David Hockney and Roy Litchenstein, and ancient artifacts from Greece.

On its first ships, introduced at a time when atriums were becoming cruise ship architectural standards, Celebrity chose instead to use the space for public rooms, giving passengers an array of entertainment and recreation options similar to the megaliners but without their glitz. Small, separate lounges, each with its own ambience and entertainment, offer a variety that appeals to a broad range of tastes.

The ships were also designed with a view to passenger comfort and flow. For example, the Rendezvous Lounge amidships provides a place where passengers can mingle before and after dinner—intended to reduce the usual crowds waiting for the restaurant or show lounge to open.

Celebrity distinguished itself from its competitors by giving top priority to serving superior cuisine. To that end, the line hired as its food consultant Michel Roux, an award-winning master French chef, who operates a Michelin three-star restaurant, a catering service, and other food enterprises in England. Roux helped design the ships' kitchens, trained chefs, and worked with the ships' food suppliers to ensure year-round quality. After launching the new cruise line, Chandris created a separate company with staff trained by Roux to handle Celebrity's catering.

For Celebrity, Roux created a sophisticated but unpretentious cuisine intended for people with refined palates, placing the stress on quality rather than quantity, although the quantity is there, too, and establishing a new standard for its competitors. In the restaurants, dinners are accompanied by live piano background music.

DISTINCTIVE FEATURES   Sony communications and entertainment system. Computer room on *Galaxy*. Shipboard passenger-service manager who is more father-confessor than concierge. Children's program and specially priced shore excursions. Martini bars. AquaSpa packages may be booked in advance. Celebrity's unusual ten-year agreement with the Bermuda government that allows two Celebrity ships to call at Bermuda regularly throughout the summer, a highly coveted position due to the island's popularity with travelers. The ships sail on different Bermuda itineraries and have preferred berthing in Hamilton.

RATES

Highest Per Diem	Lowest Per Diem	Average Per Diem
$485	$128	$256

The above per diems are calculated from the cruise line's nondiscounted *cruise-only* fares on standard accommodations. What you actually pay *should* be *substantially* less (see Part One, How to Get the Best Deal on a Cruise). Per diems vary by season, by cabin location, and by cruise areas.

All published rates include port fees.

Special Fares and Discounts Early bird discounts, called Five Star rates, represent some of the best values in cruising. The fares are time-sensitive, capacity-controlled, advance purchase plans offering up to 50 percent discounts on cruise-only rates for all ships; deluxe cabins and suites are not included. Base rates for seven-day cruises, starting from $925 for inside cabins and $1,025 for outside ones, also have the option of upgrades for an additional low cost.

Two itineraries, such as the *Century*'s Eastern and Western Caribbean, can be combined at a special rate.

- Third/Fourth Passenger: Yes.
- Children's Fare: Yes.
- Single parents: Seasonally.
- Single Supplement: 150 percent or 200 percent, depending on category.
- Guaranteed single rate.

Packages
- Cruise/Air Add-on with transfers: Yes.
- Others: Anniversary, honeymoon, family.
- Pre/Post: Yes.

Past Passengers The newly revamped Captain's Club is open to all passengers after their first Celebrity cruise, with payment of a one-time fee of $35 for a lifetime family membership. The club offers special discounts on cruises, promotional packages, cabin upgrading on certain advance purchases, and other savings. Members receive Captain's Club baggage tags, club pins, newsletter, video of ship or destination, advance notices on special offers, priority check-in and disembarkation, and private cocktail party during their cruise.

THE LAST WORD   Celebrity Cruises has been one of cruising's real success stories. It came up with the right formula at the right time: classic cruising, updated for contemporary lifestyles, and available at reasonable prices. Its immediate success resulted from exceeding everyone's expectations and reflected the extensive planning and testing that went into the ships. The line set and has maintained unusually high standards for its price range. The exception is Celebrity's selection of Caribbean shore excursions. They are off-the-shelf tours, adequate for those visiting the Caribbean for the first time, but for experienced cruisers for whom the line was designed, the tours fall short of Celebrity's own high standards. Their redeeming feature is that Celebrity is one of the few cruise lines to have reduced rates for children.

In sum, almost anyone would enjoy a cruise on a Celebrity ship, but first-time cruisers with cultivated tastes and experienced cruisers who seek higher levels of comfort and service than are commonly available on ships in this price range will be the most appreciative of their value.

CELEBRITY SHIPS STANDARD FEATURES

Officers Greek.

Staffs Dining, Cabin/International; Cruise/European, American.

Dining Facilities One main dining room with two seatings for three meals; midnight buffet; indoor/outdoor lido buffet breakfast and lunch. *Century* class has two-level dining room.

Special Diets Request at time of booking.

Room Service 24-hour menu; butler service in suites.

Dress Code Casual but not sloppy during the day; informal in evening with two nights formal or semiformal.

Cabin Amenities Direct dial phone; bath with shower; suites with marble bathrooms, whirlpool tubs, terry robes. Television with CNN and music channels. Hair dryers on *Century* class. All *Galaxy* cabins have minibars and the upper category cabins have VCRs.

Electrical Outlets 110 AC.

Wheelchair Access See Cabin section for each ship.

Recreation and Entertainment Card room/library; casino; two-deck show lounge; bars/lounges; disco; video game room. Bingo, lotto, horseracing, culinary demonstrations, wine tasting, fashion show, arts and crafts. High-tech entertainment center on *Century* class.

Sports and Other Activities Two outside swimming pools; exercise classes, walks, golf putting, dance lessons, Ping-Pong, deck and swimming pool games.

Beauty and Fitness Barber/beauty salon; health club, gym, and sauna; jogging track on Sun Deck; spa with beauty treatments.

Other Facilities Boutiques; hospital; laundry and dry cleaning services; meeting facilities on *Century* class. No passenger-operated washers or dryers.

Children's Facilities Playroom; teen disco; baby-sitters; year-round, age-specific programs with counselors.

Theme Cruises Occasionally.

Smoking Smoking is not permitted in dining room or Celebrity Theater. Other public rooms have designated areas.

Celebrity Suggested Tipping Per person per day: cabin steward/butlers, $3; dining room waiter, $3; busboy, $1.50. 15 percent service charge added to all beverage checks.

Credit Cards Cruise/on-board charges, American Express, Mastercard, Visa, Discover/Novus.

Horizon / Zenith

	Quality Rating	Value Rating
Horizon/Zenith	8	B

Registry: Liberia	Length: 682 feet	Beam: 95 feet
Cabins: 677/687	Draft: 24 feet	Speed: 21.4 knots
Maximum Passengers:	Passenger Decks: 9	Elevators: 7
1,660/1,690	Crew: 642/670	Space Ratio: 34.5

THE SHIPS The *Horizon* and the *Meridian* (which was sold recently), launched Celebrity Cruises in 1990. Except for decor and minor adjustments, the *Horizon* and *Zenith*, the third ship, are twins, constructed at the same shipyard, Meyer Werft, in Papenburg, Germany. The vessels' similarity was a deliberate strategy to facilitate passengers' familiarity and comfort with the fleet and, of course, to help keep costs down. The differences in the two ships are in the details and decor.

Spacious and open, *Horizon*'s ultramodern clean lines give it an almost futuristic look that is tempered by the decor of natural and pastel colors and soft leather chairs. Two design teams—from Greece and England—created its distinctive interiors. Original art on the walls and displays of ancient artifacts add to the feeling of quality—a characteristic reflected throughout the fleet.

The public rooms are positioned on four spacious decks. Those on the entertainment deck are connected by an inside promenade that, in one section, has floor-to-ceiling windows looking out to sea and flooding the area with light.

Building on the quick acceptance and success of the *Horizon*, Celebrity Cruises made only a few enhancements in the *Zenith*, which was completed in record-breaking time using CAD, computer-aided design. Michael and Agni Katzourakis, who created the interiors for the *Horizon* and many other luxury ships, designed the cabin interiors. London-based John McNeece, another cruise ship interior design veteran, did the public rooms. In contrast to the *Horizon*'s cool sophistication, the *Zenith* has a warm, inviting ambience through the lavish use of fine wood and rich fabrics of soothing colors.

The *Horizon* and *Zenith* are fitted with navigation parameters for maneuvering St. George's harbor in Bermuda, adding to Celebrity's flexibility in deploying its fleet. Both ships also incorporate safety features that exceed the requirements of international legislation and national authorities. The extra safeguards added an estimated $1 million to the cost of each ship.

HORIZON ITINERARIES   In winter, Eastern and Southern Caribbean, with 10- and 11-day cruises from Ft. Lauderdale, departing Friday to St. Maarten, St. Lucia, Barbados, Antigua, and St. Thomas; or, Monday to Curaçao, La Guaira, Grenada, Barbados, Martinique, and St. Thomas. Both itineraries have four days at sea. For summer 1998, the *Horizon* sails on a new itinerary, departing weekly on Sunday from New York to Bermuda and calling at Hamilton and King's Wharf.

Home Ports   Ft. Lauderdale, winter; New York, summer.
Port Charges   Included in price.

ZENITH ITINERARIES   Winter, 10–16 days, transcanal between San Juan and Acapulco via St. Thomas, Curaçao, Aruba, Cartagena, Panama Canal, Puerto Caldera, and Huatulco, or reverse itinerary, with three days at sea. Or, between Ft. Lauderdale or New York and Acapulco, via Port Canaveral, Cozumel, Grand Cayman, Cartagena, San Blas, Panama Canal, Puerto Caldera, and Huatulco; four days at sea.

• *In summer*, seven days, Bermuda, departing from New York on Saturday to Hamilton and St. George; two days at sea. In April and October, she sails on seven-day positioning cruises between San Juan and New York.

Home Ports   San Juan, winter; New York, summer.
Port Charges   Included in price.

CABINS   Handsomely fitted in light wood, the spacious, well-designed cabins reveal the planning and attention to detail that went into them. For example, all the built-in furniture has been finished with rounded corners and edges for safety and durability. Space, maximized by the arrangement, is generous with two full-length closets (larger on the *Zenith* than on the *Horizon*) and plenty of drawers. Bathrooms, larger than average for ships in this price range, have generous counter space. Almost 75 percent are outside cabins. The decor is colorful and cheerful but easy on the eyes. New technology installed recently enables passengers to dial (800) numbers in the United States directly from their cabins. The price is $9.50 per minute (most ships charge $15 per minute). All cabins are also equipped with the Celebrity Network, which enables you to order breakfast, room service, and wine for dinner, review your account, and request other services directly from your cabin television.

Lengthening the ninth, tenth, and eleventh decks on the *Zenith* provided space for ten suites and deluxe cabins more than on the *Horizon* and for larger royal suites. Suites have marbled bathrooms with whirlpool tubs and excellent showers. Most have a king-size bed and a sleeper loveseat. The suites are roomy and have butler service, but unless you can easily afford the difference in cost, the true value is in the standard cabins.

Cabin stewards or stewardesses can be summoned via phone. Cabins are cleaned and bathroom linens changed twice daily. Butler service is available in the suites.

On the *Zenith*, the cabins on Europe Deck aft near the playroom are to be avoided in the summer and holidays when there is likely to be a large number of children aboard—unless, of course, some of them are your kids.

Horizon *Specifications* 144 inside cabins, 533 outside; 20 suites. Standard dimensions are 172 square feet; 473 with twin (273 convert to doubles); 64 double/king; third/fourth persons available; no singles.

Zenith *Specifications* 146 inside cabins, 541 outside; 22 suites. Standard dimensions are 172 square feet; 462 with twin beds (260 convertible to doubles); 74 double/king; third/fourth persons available; no singles.

DINING The highly praised cuisine, developed by master French chef Michael Roux, was a major contributor to the line's immediate success. Roux's credo is to use the best quality products and to keep menus seasonal, changing them every three months. To maintain his demanding standards, Roux sails on each ship several times during the year.

Food presentation gets as many accolades as the preparation. A typical lunch menu offers a choice of four appetizers, two soups, two salads, two cold and three hot entrees, a selection of vegetables, and four desserts plus ice creams, sherbet, and cheeses.

Dinners have as many choices with the addition of a special menu by Roux. Every menu includes at least one dish designated as lean and light; there is a separate, full week's vegetarian menu. Wines to accompany each meal or wine by the glass are suggested on menus. Wine prices are moderate to very expensive.

Celebrity eschews the themed nights for dinner—French, Caribbean—which other lines offer and which are more show than substance in authenticity. Rather, Celebrity features such themes for the midnight buffets when chefs are better able to do justice to ethnic cuisine and the setting changes to enhance the experience.

Dining Room Service is exemplary and the gracious ambience is enhanced by piano music at lunch and dinner. Although the dining room seats 840 passengers at a time, its "H" layout with a raised center lessens the feeling of being in a huge room. Nonetheless, when the ships are full, which they usually are, the room is crowded as the tables are close together. A limited number of tables are for two; most are for four, six, or eight.

Breakfast and lunch in the Windsurf Cafe offer a variety of hot and cold selections. Unfortunately, when the ships are full, long lines tend to develop, particularly on days at sea when passengers do not need to be up for early shore excursion departures. Celebrity has attempted to relieve the problem by having waiters at the buffet lines to carry your tray to your table. For the most informal setting, hamburgers and hot dogs are cooked to order at the Grill, immediately outside the Windsurf Cafe, where pleasant outdoor seating is available on the Lido Deck.

SERVICE   Celebrity has distinguished itself from other cruise lines in the mid-price range with service, particularly in the dining room. However, on a recent cruise we noticed some decline in service standards following the introduction of new personnel from Eastern Europe. (Former communist countries were not exactly the ideal milieu for learning the fine points of gracious living.) They are extremely pleasant and eager to please, but their lack of experience shows. Among the line's innovations is a passenger service representative whose sole job is to solve life's little problems. She or he is usually found in the main lobby, ready to give a helping hand.

FACILITIES AND ENTERTAINMENT   The ships have a variety of lounges for peace or pleasure, with entertainment ranging from a sing-along piano bar and dance music in the lounge to Broadway-style productions in the two-deck show lounge. Among the most popular spots is the Rendezvous, a lounge amidships convenient to the dining room. Crowded for cocktails, it is a great people-watching spot anytime. Harry's Tavern, fashioned after a Greek taverna, takes on a more raucous atmosphere with karaoke and musical entertainment.

The *Zenith*'s Fleet Bar (called America's Cup on the *Horizon*), one of the most attractive rooms afloat, is a top deck club-like piano bar with a small dance floor and a wide expanse of windows. It's everyone's favorite for drinks and dancing. Enlarged considerably on the *Zenith* from its sister ship, the lounge is light and cheerful by day, softly aglow at sunset, and sophisticated and stylish in the evening. Both *Zenith* and *Horizon* also feature champagne and caviar service, offered in the observation lounge, as well as martini bars.

Evening entertainment is balanced between specialty numbers, such as acrobats, comedians, magicians, and big production shows; all qualify as family-appropriate. In the bilevel show lounge, which doubles as a meeting room, most seats have good sight lines. During a week's cruise, two big stage productions are presented. They are not Celebrity's strong suit.

From the upper level, passengers can walk aft to the casino, which offers blackjack, roulette, and slot machines, or to the shops and disco. From the lower level, they pass the library, card room, piano bar, and main lounges.

ACTIVITIES AND DIVERSIONS   Scheduled activities have been greatly increased over the years and now offer such an incredible array, it would be virtually impossible for one person to do it all. But the variety ensures there is enough to suit most every passenger. Choices range from exercise and dance classes to contests and karaoke. The week's activities might include a singles' party, poolside Island Night, honeymooners' champagne party, a jazz concert, and seminars on cuisine, the stock market, stress management, and estate planning, to name a few. Art auctions draw only mild interest. First-run movies are shown daily in the show lounge during afternoons and a variety of not-so-new ones on cabin television; a week's schedule is provided in your cabin.

SPORTS AND FITNESS   The ships have wide open decks with plenty of space for deck chairs, even when the ships are full, and quiet corners for reading, sunning, or snoozing, but shaded areas are limited. There are swimming pool games, Ping-Pong, trapshooting, darts, shuffleboard, and golf putting. In port, the line offers golf and snorkel programs and other sports, depending on the port of call.

The ships have large, well-equipped fitness centers and a one-fifth-mile jogging track on their sunny top decks, but no outside, wraparound promenade deck. Use of the facilities, saunas, and exercise classes, which are offered several times daily, is included in the cruise price. There is a full-fledged fitness program with four or five activities scheduled daily.

SPA AND BEAUTY   The ships' spas, operated by the Steiner Group of London, have barbershops and beauty salons, and offer massage, facials, and body treatments for additional fees. These services are expensive, as they are on all cruise ships, but particularly for ships in the Celebrity price range. Spa and fitness programs may be booked in advance.

CHILDREN'S FACILITIES   During summer and major holidays, all Celebrity ships feature special daily programs for four different age groups: Ship Mates (3–6 years), Celebrity Cadets (7–10 years), Ensigns (11–13 years), and Teens (14–17 years), all supervised by youth counselors.

The young kids enjoy painting and drawing, songs and dances, movies, and other activities appropriate to their age. Celebrity Summer Stock is a chance for young thespians to participate in theatrical shows with dances and costumes. The Young Mariners' program gives children a look at day-to-day operations of a ship and the chance to meet the captain and learn navigation by the stars.

Junior Olympics offer water volleyball and basketball, golf putting, Ping-Pong, and other games. At meals, kids can join their peers at the Celebrity Breakfast Club, and at dinner, order from their own menu in addition to the regular one. The program also has activities for families to enjoy together and a special masquerade parade.

SHORE EXCURSIONS   On *Horizon*'s winter itinerary, Catalina Island, off the southeast coast of the Dominican Republic, gives passengers the much-enjoyed day-at-the-beach, included frequently on the itineraries of other ships in the region. Catalina is a short distance from the famous resort Casa de Campo, one of the Caribbean's largest layouts, with excellent golf, tennis and polo facilities.

In summer, *Horizon* and *Zenith* sail weekly from New York to Bermuda, one of the cruise world's most popular destinations—neat, clean, orderly, interesting, and offering something for everyone. It is unique as a cruise destination. In Bermuda, the ships offer island tours, glass-bottom boat and snorkel trips, sailing, and nightlife tours. Most tours are three hours and range from about $30–40. Children's rates are about 30–40 percent lower.

Bermuda also is easy to tour on your own. Depending on your interests, you can visit historic forts, museums, art galleries, craft shops, duty-free shops, the Aquarium, and the lovely Botanic Gardens. With advance planning, tennis and golf can be arranged. The National Historic Trust has excellent walking tours. Rental cars are not allowed in Bermuda; taxis are available. Mopeds, or scooters, are the most popular way to get around.

POSTSCRIPT   The *Horizon* and *Zenith* continue to exceed expectations. The *Zenith* has two of the best warm weather itineraries available.

In winter, it visits some of the most interesting ports in the Eastern Caribbean and is ideal for those who have already taken more standard Caribbean cruises. In summer, both ships sail to Bermuda, a cruise well suited for families. Well planned from the outset, the ships are comfortable, stylish, and an ideal size, providing broad appeal and offering a good all-around cruise experience and value for money.

Century / Galaxy / Mercury

	Quality Rating	Value Rating
Century	❼	B
Galaxy	❿	A
Mercury (November 1997)	Preview	

Registry: Liberia	Length: 807/865 feet	Beam: 105/105.62 feet
Cabins: 875/935	Draft: 25 feet	Speed: 21.5 knots
Maximum Passengers:	Passenger Decks: 10	Elevators: 9/10
1,750/1,870	Crew: 843/909	Space Ratio: 40

THE SHIPS *Celebrity* got a jump on the next millennium with the December 1995 debut of the *Century*, the first of a new fleet designed for cruising in the twenty-first century. The $320 million ship, constructed at the same German yard as the *Horizon* and *Zenith*, has the same designers, John McNeece and Agni and Michael Katzourakis, as well. *Galaxy*, the second of the three sister ships, was launched in December 1996 and the third, *Mercury*, is scheduled to arrive in early November 1997.

Three years of meticulous planning went into creating the new breed with more than ten design teams working in tandem with *Century*'s builders to achieve a comfortable, inviting, integrated design. With 48 percent more space than her sister ships but only 26 percent more passengers, the *Century* and *Galaxy* are very spacious and have one of cruising's highest passenger-space ratios in their category. They have large entertainment and activity areas and generous-size cabins.

Public rooms run the gamut in style from an elegant wood-paneled bar to a futuristic disco.

Sony Corporation of America has designed a communications and entertainment system to put passengers on the information superhighway as well as the high seas. Along with an array of sophisticated entertainment options and interactive video services, the Sony music, pictures, and electronic publishing divisions provide their products and expertise. Sony Signatures sells Sony merchandise in *Century's* boutiques.

Century's focal point is a three-deck Grand Foyer encircled by a spiral staircase and topped with a dome ceiling of painted glass, lit as if by sunlight during the day and as a starlit sky in the evening. The piazza has a waterfall with changing fiber-optic images, marble floors, warm burled woods, brass trim, and suede-upholstered furniture. Nearby are boutiques along the Boulevard and Tastings, a wine and coffee piano bar.

The *Galaxy* is essentially *Century's* twin in layout but slightly larger, with some significant differences and new features that reflect improvements over her sister ship. The most noticeable is *Galaxy's* atrium with a 40-foot-high video panel projecting constantly changing images (instead of *Century's* waterfall). Also new is "Sony Wonder," a permanent high-tech center where free computer classes are given. You can learn to navigate the web, take "DOS for Dummies" and preview different software. Sony is also developing a program that allows passengers to send and receive e-mail from ports.

The *Galaxy's* best new feature is a retractable glass dome, known as a magrodome, covering one of the two swimming pools and the surrounding deck area. It now has an indoor/outdoor grill and bar area, Oasis, which should prove to be the most popular area of the ship.

The ships also have multilevel, multipurpose observation lounges that become discos in the evening. One of the ships' two atriums, positioned aft and spanning three decks, opens onto the casino, Rendezvous Lounge, the dining room's foyer, and a champagne bar.

The *Century* group, like its predecessors, have outstanding, multi-million-dollar art collections, virtually contemporary art museums-at-sea. The focus for the *Century* is contemporary masters; that for the *Galaxy*, the avant-garde. The collections, which include established and emerging artists over a broad range, were assembled by Christina Chandris, the line's curator and fine art advisor, and in the case of the *Galaxy*, in collaboration with the Marlborough Gallery of New York.

ITINERARIES

Century Year-round, seven-day cruises alternating between the Eastern and Western Caribbean, departing on Saturday from Ft. Lauderdale to San Juan, St. Thomas, St. Maarten, and Nassau; or Playa del

Carmen/Calica, Grand Cayman, Cozumel, and Key West. Both itineraries have two days at sea.

Home Port   Ft. Lauderdale.
Port Charges   Included in price.

Galaxy   In winter, seven-day Eastern Caribbean, departing weekly on Saturday from San Juan to Catalina (Dominican Republic), Barbados, Martinique, Antigua, and St. Thomas, with one day at sea.

- *In summer,* seven-day Alaska cruises, from Vancouver via Inside Passage to Glacier Bay or Hubbard Glacier, Skagway, Haines, Juneau, and Ketchikan. In addition to the standard sightseeing tours, the ship has great outdoor shore excursions that enable passengers to see Alaska according to their interests and level of skill, from walking tours to kayaking, mountain biking, sportsfishing, and more.
- *In April–May and October–September,* she sails on 15- and 17-day positioning cruises from Ft. Lauderdale to Cozumel, Grand Cayman, Panama Canal, Puerto Caldera, Acapulco, Cabo San Lucas, San Diego, and Los Angeles, with six days at sea; or reverse; and West Coast/Alaska cruises from Los Angeles and San Francisco.

Home Ports   San Juan, winter; Vancouver, summer.
Port Charges   Included in price.

Mercury   For her maiden year in winter, seven-day Western Caribbean cruises, departing on Sunday from Ft. Lauderdale to Key West, Cozumel, Playa del Carmen/Calica, and Grand Cayman, with two days at sea.

- *From late May–mid-September,* seven-day Alaska cruises, alternating north- and southbound itineraries between Vancouver and Seward via the Inside Passage. In April and October, two-week transcanal cruises between San Juan and Los Angeles.

Home Ports   Ft. Lauderdale, winter; Vancouver, Seward, summer.
Port Charges   Included in price.

CABINS   Each deck has its own color scheme, with cabins on each deck using complementary colors for carpeting and bedspreads. The spacious cabins have soothing colors combined with windows framed in rosewood that convey a posh but comfortable look, pleasing to the eye. On the *Century,* all cabins have built-in vanities, generous closet and drawer space, large bathrooms with showers, hair dryers, minibars, televisions, and other Celebrity standards.

Celebrity Network enables passengers to use interactive cabin television to order breakfast or room service, book spa appointments, and buy shore excursions. You can also gamble (charged to the room), order merchandise from shops, and watch pay-per-view movies (including adult-only selections). Interactive televisions are also located throughout the ship to provide information as well as entertainment.

While cabins on the *Century* are similar to those on the *Zenith* and *Horizon*, on the *Galaxy* they were redesigned somewhat to accommodate more features. As a result, some storage space has been lost; the drawer space, particularly, is inadequate. All have minibars and and the upper category cabins have VCRs. Both ships have posh penthouse and royal suites and all the suites have marble bathrooms, whirlpool tubs, verandas, and butler service.

Century *Specifications* 304 inside cabins, 571 outside; 52 suites, 61 suites and deluxe cabins with verandas. Standard dimensions, 172 square feet; 806 with twin beds, all convertible to doubles; third/fourth persons; no singles. 8 wheelchair accessible.

Galaxy/Mercury *Specifications* 296 inside cabins, 639 outside; 50 suites and 170 mini-suites with verandas. Standard dimensions, 184 square feet; 877 with twin beds, all convertible to doubles; third/fourth persons; no singles. 8 wheelchair accessible.

DINING *Century*'s stylish Grand Restaurant, the main dining room, comes with several innovations—Celebrity's first two-tiered dining room with a majestic staircase that leads to a colonnaded center aisle reminiscent of Karnak Temple in Egypt; its baroque decor creates the ambience of the golden age of the great oceanliners. There are twin galleys; each prepares the food for half of the dining room and, in that way, provides speedier service, consistent temperatures, and freshness. Other dining areas are the casual Veranda Grill, adjacent to the pool area, and the Islands Café with four buffet stations and two bars. There is an afternoon tea buffet in the Café in addition to Celebrity's traditional Elegant Tea.

The Orion Restaurant on the *Galaxy* is quite different from the *Century*'s dining room. The second tier is larger to accommodate the ship's additional capacity and the overall decor is lighter, more contemporary, and less pretentious than her sister ship. The room's focal point is an enormous backlit ceiling panel of a hemisphere with continents superimposed.

One of *Galaxy*'s major new features is the Oasis, the casual dining restaurant. The traditional indoor section, divided into small areas, is very attractive and inviting; the outdoor section has a garden setting surrounds a small swimming pool and is covered by a magrodome, which is particularly appealing when the ship is in Alaska. Look for Michel Roux to open Celebrity's first alternative-dining restaurant in this pretty spot.

SERVICE   Celebrity continues to distinguished itself from other cruise lines in the mid-price range with the quality of service, particularly in the dining room where the dedication to European-style service is one of these ships' best and most rewarding features.

FACILITIES AND ENTERTAINMENT   The two-deck Celebrity Theater for Broadway-style revues and cabaret shows has a sloping orchestra section and cantilevered balconies providing unobstructed views of the stage. The show lounge has the state-of-the-art capabilities of a Broadway theatre, including a revolving stage, the ability to handle multiple scenery backdrops, an orchestra pit that rises and lowers, sophisticated lighting, and other special effects.

The Crystal Room (called The Savoy on *Galaxy*), a low-key night club for evening dancing, has an art deco motif of etched-glass panels, luminous alabaster dome ceiling, rotating bronze globe, and a color scheme of red, black, and gold that recalls chic New York of the 1930s. The Savoy's art deco design has a jungle motif for its late-night cabaret and Fortune's Casino has the full roster of games. There is also a champagne bar. The Rendezvous Square, next to the dining room, is similar to the Rendezvous Lounge on the other Celebrity ships—a lively place for cocktails or socializing before and after dinner.

High atop the *Century* is Hemisphere (Stratosphere Lounge on the *Galaxy*), an airy sunlit observation lounge by day that transforms into a futuristic "disco under the dome" at night, when with movie-like special effects, window blinds drop automatically, etched-glass room dividers illuminate one by one, and a special table "glows." The hemisphere then rises—light emanating from within—and like something out of a science fiction film, the dance floor appears. Telescopes are placed around the room's edge for stargazing between dancing and socializing.

On the *Galaxy*, the Stratosphere has three sections: the outer one next to the floor-to-ceiling windows is a quiet zone by day for viewing the passing scenery and reading; the middle-level is ideal for cocktails at sunset; while the innermost area can be used for meetings during the day with the use of pulldown screens to separate it from the other parts of the lounge. In the inner area, the mosiac wood flooring of the room is exquisite and reflects the quality of the materials and workmanship throughout the ship. In the evening the inner room becomes the disco where sophisticated equipment transforms the space into a completely different environment and offers a terrific multicolored laser light show.

Michael's Club on the *Century* is an intimate lounge fashioned after a private gentlemen's club, paneled in rich woods and furnished with cushy leather chairs and couches. On the *Galaxy*, the room is very contemporary in decor and lacks the cachet of its sister ship. On both ships, the clubs have been given over to the latest fad of cigar smoking, including craftsmen to demonstrate cigar making, an art which Columbus and the early conquistadors learned from the Caribbean's native Indians. The *Galaxy* also has a martini bar.

A multipurpose conference center has flexible walls that fold into wall pillars, allowing for use as a conference center, cinema, meeting room, library, or card room. The center's high-tech equipment includes keypads in the armchairs that can be used for responses to questions or for interactive movies. On the *Galaxy*, plans are afoot to have a daily shipboard-produced television show with news and interviews in the manner of *Good Morning America*.

ACTIVITIES AND DIVERSIONS   As on Celebrity's other ships, scheduled activities are many and varied to appeal to a wide range of passengers. The week's activities include exercise and dance classes, contests, singles' party, honeymooners' champagne party, karaoke, to name a few. There might be art auctions and seminars on cuisine, the stock market, and estate planning. First-run movies are shown daily on cabin television; a week's schedule is provided in your cabin. There are also adult pay-per-view movies on your cabin television. The ships have video game rooms with more of Sony's state-of-the-art equipment.

SPORTS AND FITNESS   The spacious ships have 62,000 square feet of open decks and sports, such as a golf simulator, Ping-Pong, volleyball, basketball, darts, and a jogging track. The *Century*'s two swimming pools have cylindrical waterfalls that are flanked by a bridge and rimmed with teak benches.

SPA AND BEAUTY   The Health and Fitness Club is one of the best-equipped gyms at sea with a hydropool, saunas, and steam rooms and a gym with cardiovascular machines and weight stations. Personal trainers are available to create individualized aerobics and training programs. There is the full range of stretching, pulling, and rowing machines plus ongoing aerobics classes.

The spacious AquaSpa, one of the most popular features of Celebrity's new trio, has serene surroundings inspired by Japanese gardens and bathhouses and offers a wide range of beauty and health treatments. The most unusual is Rasul, a treatment based on an Oriental ceremony with a seaweed soap shower, medicinal mud pack, herbal steambath, and massage.

Not to be missed is the tranquilizing thalassotherapy treatment taken in a 115,000-gallon pool with waterjet massage stations. Spa treatments are expensive for Celebrity's price category, but that doesn't deter passengers who seem happy to pay for being pampered. The spa treatments may be booked in advance of your cruise.

CHILDREN'S FACILITIES   With every ship, Celebrity's children facilities get better. The Fun Factory on *Galaxy* is a 1,600-square-foot playroom, and there's a kids' splash pool. As on the line's other ships, there are supervised daily programs for four different age groups: Ship Mates (3–6 years), Celebrity Cadets (7–10 years), Ensigns (11–13 years), and Teens (14–17). Junior Olympics offer water volleyball, basketball, Ping-Pong, and other games. The teens have a private lounge with a dance floor plus Cyberspace, a video game room. At meals, kids can join their peers at the Celebrity Breakfast Club, and at dinner, order from their own menu in addition to the regular one. The program also has activities for families to enjoy together and a special masquerade parade.

POSTSCRIPT   Celebrity's new class of ships lives up to their advance billing, combining gracious European service with modern decor, high-tech wizardry, and enough glitz to keep them competitive as they sail into the next century. Those who prefer large ships for their high-tech, high-energy entertainment, extensive children's facilities, state-of-the-art exercise equipment, along with pampering in mammoth spas and dining in large elegant restaurants, will be pleased with this trio.

CLIPPER CRUISE LINE

7711 Bonhomme Avenue, St. Louis, MO 63105
(314) 727-2929; (800) 325-0010; fax (314) 727-6576
http://www.clippercruise.com

TYPE OF SHIPS   Small, first class.

TYPE OF CRUISE   Destination-oriented, light adventure, low-key, intellectually stimulating cruises for nature- and culture-oriented travelers on the byways of the Americas.

CRUISE LINE'S STRENGTHS
- itineraries
- cuisine
- accompanying naturalists and experts
- small size and maneuverability

CRUISE LINE'S SHORTCOMINGS
- aging ships
- lack of room amenities and service
- limited shipboard activities
- shallow-draft vessels in open sea or turbulent waters

FELLOW PASSENGERS   Relatively affluent, educated, usually professionals, often retired and semiretired, and likely to be part of a university alumni group. They come from throughout the United States having a distinct preference for small ships—often after trying a big ship—for the camaraderie, intimate ambience, and small number of passengers.

They are not bargain hunters or looking for last-minute specials. Rather, they are mature (over 50), well-traveled, low-key, and often, seasoned cruisers and Clipper repeaters.

Most are ecology-minded and intellectually curious. Some prefer remote, relatively unknown areas; others seek destinations closer to home with strong cultural and natural history appeal, particularly places where small ships have access but large ships must pass by.

Recommended For   Experienced travelers who like the cozy ambience of a country inn where people are recognized by name; big-ship refugees turned off by mainstream cruises and seeking quieter, more substantial travel experience; those with inquisitive minds who travel to learn.

Not Recommended For   Night owls, swingers, party seekers, unsophisticated travelers; people who want to be entertained and have only marginal interest in history and nature; those who like to dress up in showy finery.

CRUISE AREAS AND SEASONS   Caribbean, South America, Central America, Panama Canal, Europe, and Antarctica in winter; Eastern Seaboard, New England/Canada, Great Lakes, West Coast, Mexico, and Alaska in spring, summer, and fall.

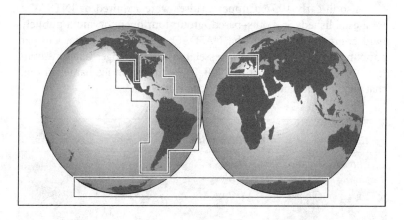

THE LINE   Founded in 1982, Clipper Cruise Line launched its first ship the following year to fill a niche: providing culture- and nature-oriented cruises on comfortable small ships along the historic byways of the United States and the Caribbean. Central America and other parts of North and South America were added as the line expanded.

Built in Indiana and Florida, the ships are U.S.-registered and have American crews. Their shallow drafts and turn-on-a-dime maneuverability, designed primarily for coastal cruises, enable them to sail into places where larger ships cannot go. Their smaller size provides an intimacy and sense of place often missed on large ships. Destinations are as diverse as the hidden fjords of Alaska and the antebellum South along the Intracoastal Waterway.

The ships cruise mostly during the day, stopping for passengers to tour an island, hike in a rain forest, enjoy a secluded beach, or snorkel in reef-filled waters right from the ship. Nights are often spent in port with everyone going ashore for an evening with the local folks. Absent but not missed are casinos, discos, staged entertainment, and the organized diversions of large ships.

Some Clipper cruises visit places for their cultural appeal, focusing on an area's history and regional identity, and including guest lecturers to add depth to the experience. Others explore coastal areas with natural history appeal. They are accompanied by naturalists and scientists, and Zodiacs (motorized, inflatable rubber rafts) extend passengers' reach into inaccessible areas.

In spring of 1997, the line ventured into European cruises for the first time, cruising the 100-passenger *Switzerland* on Holland's waterways.

Also in early 1997, Clipper Cruises were acquired by INTRAV, a long-established, St. Louis–based, group tour operator and a publicly held company traded on the NASDAQ. At the same time, Clipper announced plans to add a new vessel, the 121-passenger *Clipper Adventure*, to begin service in April 1998. The ship has an ice-hardened hull that enables it to sail from the Arctic to Antarctica.

The Fleet	Built/Renovated	Tonnage	Passengers
Clipper Adventurer	1975/1997	4,364	122
Nantucket Clipper	1984	1,471	102
Yorktown Clipper	1988	2,354	138

STYLE Clipper cruises stress destinations rather than shipboard fun and games. The small nature of the ships provides for a cordial shipboard ambience that resembles a country inn. Passengers experience a more personalized cruise than large ships can offer. The ships are just the right size for mingling—small enough for getting to know people and large enough to ensure an interesting mix. The congenial atmosphere and shore excursions taken as a group make it easy to meet everyone in the course of a week and for a certain camaraderie to develop effortlessly among the passengers. The convivial American crew, most fresh out of college, helps to establish the friendly atmosphere.

Life aboard is casual, unregimented, and leisurely paced with none of the organized activities or nightlife that typify mainstream cruise ships. The experience is enhanced by the presence of naturalists and experts who, in addition to their seminars, add to the passengers' enrichment with informal talks during shore excursions and over cocktails at the end of the day.

The cruise line is particularly proud of its role in providing environmentally responsible travel, maintaining that the size of its ships and the nature of its cruises make a minimal impact on the places the ships visit.

DISTINCTIVE FEATURES Historians, naturalists, and other experts travel as guides on the ships; Zodiac landing crafts are carried aboard. Excellent literature is sent in advance for trip preparation. A consumer protection plan, which Clipper pioneered, guarantees that all passenger funds are held in a bank escrow account monitored by the Federal Maritime Commission.

RATES

Highest Per Diem	Lowest Per Diem	Average Per Diem
$436	$192	$283

The above per diems are calculated from the cruise line's nondiscounted *cruise-only* fares on standard accommodations. Per diems vary by season, by cabin location, and by cruise areas.

All published rates include port fees.

Special Fares and Discounts Discounted fares are available only occasionally for special promotions.

- Third Passenger: Specific rate for each cruise, quoted in brochure.
- Single Supplement: Specific single rate for category, two cabins on each cruise, quoted in brochure; otherwise, 150 percent of brochure rate on other cabins, provided they are available.

Packages
- Air/Sea: For some departures.
- Others: No.
- Pre/Post: Alaska; train tours combined with Sea of Cortez, Northern California, and Pacific Northwest, among others.

Past Passengers   Clipper has a high number of repeaters, which the line calls Clipper Alumni. They are the first to receive information on new itineraries and often make up as much as 73 percent of such cruises. Some cruises are offered to them exclusively; occasionally, special reunion cruises are arranged as a personal invitation from Clipper's president. These popular cruises are enhanced with hotel overnights with a banquet, special shoreside events, complimentary shore excursions, or open bar. Repeat passengers are acknowledged on every cruise at the captain's party. Second- to eighth-time cruisers receive gifts—wine, flowers—ninth time and up get discounts of $200–400 per cabin.

THE LAST WORD   Clipper does not attempt to duplicate what large cruise ships offer and should not be compared to them. Clipper cruises are for people who recoil at the notion of today's popular cruises on megaships. Yet, with all the attractions of a small ship-access, camaraderie—anyone who does not fit into Clipper's rather country club, somewhat academic atmosphere could quickly feel out of place.

CLIPPER SHIPS STANDARD FEATURES

Officers American.

Staffs Dining, Cabin, Cruise/American.

Dining Facilities Single-seating dining room for three meals with open seating, buffet breakfast in lounge, and occasional lunch buffet on Sun Deck. Self-service coffee and tea in dining room.

Special Diets Accommodated with advance notice.

Room Service None.

Dress Code Casual but smart; coat and tie recommended for special occasions or going to fashionable restaurants in ports of call.

Cabin Amenities Radio, but no television or phones; bathrooms with showers; no tubs or other amenities.

Electrical Outlets 110 AC.

Wheelchair Access None.

Recreation and Entertainment Seminars by naturalists, anthropologists, and historians; photographing, bird-watching onshore and en route.

Sports and Other Activities Swimming, snorkeling, beach walks, and wilderness and rain forest hiking. No swimming pool aboard.

Beauty and Fitness None; beauty and barber shop services generally available in port.

Other Facilities No laundry service.

Children's Facilities None.

Theme Cruises Fall foliage, golf, art.

Smoking No smoking allow in any interior areas, including cabins, at any time. Smoking permited only on outside decks.

Clipper Suggested Tipping Tips are pooled. $9 per passenger per day, placed in an envelope and deposited in a box at cruise's end. No service charge is added to wine or bar bill.

Credit Cards For cruise payment, Mastercard and Visa for reservation deposits only; for on-board charges, American Express, Mastercard, Visa.

Nantucket Clipper / Yorktown Clipper

	Quality Rating	Value Rating
Nantucket Clipper	❹	C
Yorktown Clipper	❹	C

Registry: United States	Length: 207/257 feet	Beam: 37/43 feet
Cabins: 51/69	Draft: 8 feet	Speed: 9.5 knots
Maximum Passengers:	Passenger Decks: 3/4	Elevators: none
102/138	Crew: 32/40	Space Ratio: n.a.

THE SHIPS   U.S.-built and flying the American flag, the *Nantucket Clipper* and the slightly larger *Yorktown Clipper* are almost identical twins. With their shallow drafts, the ships glide into small places as easily as they tie up in small ports, sailboat-filled harbors, and coves.

The *Nantucket Clipper* has three passenger decks and the *Yorktown Clipper* four decks, including a spacious top Sun Deck aft of the bridge—a comfortable place to take up residence while watching the world go by. Cabins and lounges are nicely decorated with quality furnishings and fabrics. No glitter, no glitz.

Both ships have a single forward observation lounge and bar on the center deck that is the homey social center including a full-service bar and a small library. Three sides of the cheerful room have large picture windows trimmed with light wood. Textured fabric and neutral colors with pastel accents give the lounge a warm, contemporary look. After a few days, the room takes on the familiar air of a club where passengers pass the time in conversation, reading, writing notes or postcards, or simply watching the passing scenery. It is also the scene for enrichment lectures. An early breakfast buffet, afternoon cookies, and hors d'oeuvres at cocktail time are served here daily.

ITINERARIES   Both ships sail on a series of 6–15-day itineraries that change every month or so, but in a year's span, one or the other would have traveled in spring through fall from Canada and New England, along the Eastern Seaboard to the Caribbean, northern South America, Central America, and the Panama Canal, and journeyed up the Pacific coast, taking in Baja California, some rivers of the Northwest, and Alaska.

Nantucket Clipper *Itineraries*   In winter in the Caribbean, the Yachtsman's Caribbean is a seven-night cruise, round trip from St. Thomas through the U.S. and British Virgin Islands, stopping at St. John, Jost Van Dyke, Tortola, Virgin Gorda, and the Salt and Norman islands.

- *In spring*, Antebellum South cruises sail along the Intracoastal Waterway between Jacksonville and Charleston, followed spring to fall by 7–14-day itineraries of Colonial America, Chesapeake Bay, Northeast United States, Eastern Canada and Nova Scotia, St. Lawrence Seaway, and the Great Lakes. In September–October, she offers two, seven-day Fall Foliage on the Hudson River cruises, round trip from New York City, and a third in October that sails from New York to Washington D.C., taking in the Hudson River and the Chesapeake Bay.

Home Port   Varies, depending on itinerary.
Port Charges $75–125.

Yorktown Clipper *Itineraries*   Winter cruises of six, seven, and ten days focus on the southern Caribbean, departing from St. Lucia or Grenada to cruise the Grenadines, often called by yachtsmen the most beautiful sailing waters in the world; and from Curaçao to Trinidad, taking in Bonaire, the Orinoco River, and Tobago. Other cruises transit the Panama Canal, visiting the San Blas islands, the remote Indian villages of the Darien Jungle, and Costa Rica's Pacific coastal parks and rain forests en route.

- *In April*, the ship heads north to Baja California, Northern California, and the Pacific Northwest, then travels through the Inside Passage to Alaska for the summer, with various itineraries. In May and September, an 11- or 13-day Folklore and Natural History of British Columbia and Southeast Alaska cruise sails from Seattle to Ketchikan, delving into the lore of the native Americans of this area. From May–August, she offers seven-night cruises between Ketchikan and Juneau.
- *From September–November*, she offers a series of trips that combine rail travel with cruising and include the Pacific Northwest, Santa Fe, the Grand Canyon, and San Francisco.

Home Port   Varies, depending on itinerary.
Port Charges $75–125.

CABINS   All six categories of cabins are outside, and all but those in the lowest category have picture windows, providing for pleasant viewing of the passing scenery.

Cabins on the Promenade Deck open directly onto an outdoor wraparound deck (as on river steamboats) rather than interior corridors. Though these have an airy feel and provide direct access to the passing scene, some passengers might prefer the more traditional arrangement of cabins that open onto a central corridor. On the *Yorktown*, another four cabins on the Sun Deck are the largest and most private.

The cabins are small but adequate for a casual cruise. They are well lighted, well designed in terms of space with ample storage, and appear more spacious because of a large wall mirror. Beds are either parallel or at right angles, the latter resulting in more floor space. The furnishings have a clean, modern look, with pastel curtains and bedcovers in peaches, blues, and greens, closets and dressers in light wood, and pastel landscape paintings on the wall. The bathrooms have showers only—no tubs—and are small with limited shelf space and a mirror surrounded with bright, clear, theatre-style dressing room bulbs.

Cabins do not have telephones or televisions; radios, however, provide wake-up calls, ship information, and music. The absence of TVs and phones is meant to add to the get-away-from-it-all nature of the trip. Some cabins get the noise of the hydraulic lift used to raise and lower the gangplank each time the ship docks. Also, there is no convenient place to dry wet clothes, short of hanging them on the railing outside the cabins on the Promenade Deck.

There is no room service. Services such as laundry, beauty shop, and barbershop are available in port. The ships have no nurse or doctor aboard; however, the vessels are almost always close to a shore in case of medical emergency. The lack of these services or an elevator and the difficulty of walking on steep gangways make the ships unsuitable for physically disabled persons.

Specifications   All outside cabins; no suites. Standard dimensions range from 122–139 square feet. All have two lower beds; no singles. None are wheelchair accessible.

DINING   The dining room, situated on the lower deck, has large picture windows and pleasant, understated decor reflecting quality. Passengers dine all together at set times at a single, open seating at round or square marble-topped tables, which, for dinner, are covered with white cloths.

The food is good American cuisine prepared by a staff headed by a chef trained at the prestigious Culinary Institute of America and features excellent soups, good quality beef, fresh seafood, vegetables, and fruit.

The meals are presented in a straightforward manner by the young, cheerful staff. Selections are not as extensive as on larger ships—dinner menus offer two entrees—but the food has the flavor of having just been prepared in your own kitchen. All menus feature a regional specialty. A good but small, moderately priced selection of wines is available.

An early bird light breakfast is served in the lounge and lunch buffets are offered on the Sun Deck when the weather permits. Snacks, including fresh fruit, are available throughout the day, and in the afternoon trays of just-baked chocolate chip cookies are set out in the Observation Lounge. You can tell when their arrival time is approaching as passengers begin to mill about in anticipation about 4 P.M. The bar in the lounge is open at 11 A.M. and closes at midnight.

SERVICE The staff is a clean-cut bunch of young men and women, dressed in their all-American red or blue T-shirts and white slacks or skirts. They are cheerful, attentive, friendly, and unfailingly polite. Most come from the U.S. heartland where Clipper Cruises is based and are college students who sign on for a full year. They take care of the restaurant, bar, and cabins, working 12 hours a day, six days a week—and smiling through it all.

FACILITIES AND ENTERTAINMENT There are daily seminars on board by naturalists, historians, or other experts on the places visited by the cruise, and follow-up sessions for discussions after the visits. The naturalist also acts as a guide for those who want to take nature walks, bird-watch, and learn more about the local environment. On days at sea, there is usually a movie in the dining room in the afternoon.

Often, a local folklorist or other interesting character comes on board for a lecture, discussion, or entertainment, depending on the itinerary. The cruise director uses mealtime or the pre- or postdinner interval for briefings about the next day's adventures. Frequently, evenings are spent in port, giving passengers an opportunity to check out the local nightlife. Otherwise, after dinner, passengers gather in the lounge for chats over drinks or to watch video movies on the two television sets in the dining room. The majority of passengers are in their cabins by 10 P.M.

ACTIVITIES AND DIVERSIONS Deck space is adequate for a destination-oriented ship and most people use it to laze in the sun, read, or watch the world go by—often through their binoculars. Activity centers around the destination, whether it is a tour of a historic town, a game of golf, or a hike in the woods. There are no organized fun and games as on a large ship.

SPORTS AND FITNESS   Walkers can circumnavigate the Promenade Deck and when the ships tie up at night, as they often do, many passengers take a walk into town. Depending on itinerary and weather, snorkeling can be enjoyed directly from the ship, and scuba diving, windsurfing, deep-sea fishing, golf, or tennis can be arranged. The ships have no pools, whirlpools, exercise equipment, or fitness centers.

SHORE EXCURSIONS   Cruises usually call at ports seldom visited by other ships and often tie up at small, out-of-the-way marinas and yacht harbors, enabling passengers to explore remote islands and out-of-the-way coastlines on foot. Where the ship cannot dock, passengers go ashore or exploring by Zodiac. Generally, such excursions are included in the price of the cruise. In more urban areas, the ships often tie up within walking distance of the main cultural attractions and offer better-than-standard tours at additional but reasonable costs.

POSTSCRIPT   Although the adventures are light and seldom out of earshot of civilization, many of the itineraries do entail walking, wet landings, and climbing in and out of Zodiacs in remote areas. Some itineraries involve traversing open sea for short stretches, and with the *Clippers'* shallow drafts of only eight feet, passengers may have a bumpy ride for several hours. Because the ships do not carry doctors and do not have elevators, they are not able to handle passengers with physical limitations or health problems.

The precruise information and briefing papers which Clipper Cruise Line sends to its passengers in advance of the cruise are thorough, some running the length of a book. Not only are these excellent reference materials, but they also reflect the cruise line's commitment to making their cruises a stimulating and enriching travel experience passengers can savor long after the cruise has passed.

Clipper Adventurer (Preview)

Registry: Bahamas	Length: 330 feet	Beam: 53.5 feet
Cabins: 63	Draft: 16 feet	Speed: 14 knots
Maximum Passengers: 122	Passenger Decks: 4	Elevators: none
	Crew: n.a.	Space Ratio: n.a.

With the acquisition of Clipper Cruise Line by the St. Louis–based tour company, INTRAV, in April 1997, Clipper also acquired the 122-passenger *Clipper Adventurer*, which is scheduled to begin service in April 1998.

The *Clipper Adventurer* is the former *Alla Tarasova,* an expedition vessel with an A-1 Super Ice-class rating, built in 1975 in the former Yugoslavia. Prior to joining Clipper Cruises' fleet, she will undergo a complete renovation under the supervision of her captain, Hasse Nilsson, the well-known, former master of the *Linblad Explorer* and the first captain to take passengers through the Northwest Passage. The remodeling will include the addition of a window-lined observation lounge, a library with bar, sauna, gymnasium, and beauty salon.

The ship has all outside cabins, with twin lower beds and private bathrooms. The dining room seats all passengers at one seating; service is to be provided by Clipper's all-American staff.

The *Clipper Adventurer* is expected to be one of the most comfortable expedition ships in the market and is equipped with a fleet of eight Zodiac landing craft for exploring hard-to-reach locations from the Arctic to Antarctica.

The inaugural voyage of the *Clipper Adventurer* will be a ten-night cruise of the Iberian Peninsula, Madeira, and Morocco, as well as the Canary Islands. Other itineraries of her maiden season, designed by Captain Nilsson, include Scandinavia, Russia, Greenland, the Atlantic Coast from Halifax to Port Everglades, and the Amazon River. The ship will be in Antarctica for the 1998–1999 season and voyages ranging from 7–21 nights.

CLUB MED

40 West 57th Street, New York, NY 10019
(212) 977-2100; (800) CLUB MED; (800) 258-2633;
fax (212) 315-5392
http://www.clubmed.com

TYPE OF SHIPS   World's largest cruise ships with sails.

TYPE OF CRUISE   Casual, sports-oriented all-inclusive vacations with easy lifestyle for active, upscale vacationers.

CRUISE LINE'S STRENGTHS
- cabins
- unlimited water sports
- itineraries
- carefree, international ambience

CRUISE LINE'S SHORTCOMINGS
- language and cultural collisions
- cuisine
- entertainment
- limited use of sails

FELLOW PASSENGERS   Club Med ships attract a range of passengers whose profiles change depending on the cruise, season, and location. Typically, passengers range from 30–60 years old. The majority are couples, but groups of singles, some seniors, and a few honeymooners are also aboard. Forty percent have been on other cruises, 20 percent are repeaters with Club Med ships, and 20 percent are first-timers who are particularly attracted to Club Med because they see it as being more active and adventurous than standard cruises which they shun. Surprisingly, only 40 percent of passengers have been to a Club Med village; they find similarities but they see the cruise as more upscale, slower-paced, and less group-oriented.

Club Med 1 has somewhat different passengers from Club Med 2 due to location and itineraries. Club Med 1, which sails in the Caribbean and

Mediterranean, has more Europeans. In the Caribbean from January through March, approximately 30 percent are American, but at times they can be as few as 20 percent. Summer sailings in the Mediterranean have more Americans, sometimes as high as 50 percent. *Club Med 2*, based in Tahiti, attracts Asians, particularly young Japanese and Australians, as well as Europeans and North Americans.

The American contingents on *Club Med 1* are mostly active, urban professionals from northeast cities—doctors, lawyers, and executives ranging from 27–50 in age. They are sporty and travel-wise but not fussy. They are not bargain hunters shopping for the lowest price. They weekend at the Hamptons, dine at neat little restaurants, and belong to tennis or squash clubs. They are more interested in water sports and visiting less-traveled islands than lavish eating or shopping.

Recommended For   Francophiles and those who fall into the French ambience with ease; sailing buffs but not hard-core sailors; Club Med village alumni or those who like the Club Med concept but want more luxury; and those who want to brush up on their French.

Not Recommended For   Anyone who is not comfortable in a French milieu, or who prefers a more familiar American atmosphere and large ships.

CRUISE AREAS AND SEASONS   Seven days, Caribbean in winter, Mediterranean in summer; transatlantic cruises, spring and fall. Tahiti, year-round.

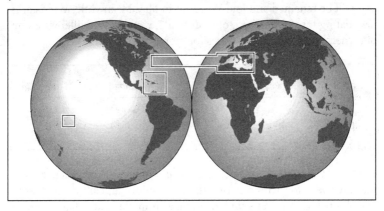

THE LINE   In 1990, after two decades of spreading the gospel for all-inclusive resort vacations and their easy lifestyle, Club Med took its formula to sea in the world's largest sailboats that have all the facilities of a cruise ship.

Stretching the length of two football fields and rigged with five 164-foot masts and seven computer-monitored sails, the ships marry twentieth-century technology with the romance of yesteryear at sea. They sail like a dream, no listing or heeling—and no officers on deck. The officers are on the bridge watching their computers.

Club Med ships have the same design as the Windstar vessels, but they are one-third larger and carry more than double the number of passengers. Those who have experienced both quickly recognize that even among small ships, size makes a big difference. The Club Med ships have the same open, nautical feeling and are free of glitz, but with more than 300 passengers they lose much of the intimacy that makes the smaller version so appealing.

Now for the first time, Club Med is treating its cruise ships like what they are—cruise ships—and is trying to get away from the notion that they are merely a seaborne version of its villages. But because the ships are more deluxe than the villages, the innovative resort operator is reaching beyond the ready-made market of village devotees to court experienced cruisers as well as noncruisers who have never been to Club Med.

In April 1997, *Club Med 1* was purchased by Windstar Cruises, whose owning company is Carnival Cruise Lines. The ship will leave the Club Med fleet in March 1998 at the end of her winter Caribbean season and will be renamed and join Windstar in May. Meanwhile, Windstar is negotiating for the purchase of *Club Med 2*, which has a different group of owners. (See Windstar Cruises for more information.)

The Fleet	Built/Renovated	Tonnage	Passengers
Club Med 1	1990	14,000	376
Club Med 2	1992	14,000	396

STYLE   Club Med cruises are basically a French product, an all-inclusive vacation with a twist—the same informal, carefree ambience that Club Med veterans will recognize from stays at villages but in deluxe surroundings with cruise ship amenities. They will also recognize the GOs—Gentils Organisateurs—who are unique to Club Med. They are the social hosts and hostesses who keep the action and smiles going day and night.

Most of the GOs are French or other Europeans or Americans who speak very good French. Like all good den mothers, their first task upon your arrival aboard is to familiarize you with the layout of the ship and to answer your questions. They organize shipboard activities and can usually give you valuable tips on the best bars and restaurants to visit in ports of call.

For those who have little or no experience with sailing, the spacious rooms, understated nautical decor, and easy camaraderie with the staff create a relaxed ambience that makes it easy to imagine you are on your own yacht, a feeling Club Med encourages. But Club Med's alluring promotional brochures with the ship in full sail notwithstanding, there are no yachts for 390 people.

On the other hand, people who normally go to resorts, on scuba diving trips, or would like a leisurely paced holiday in the sun, get just about all this—sports, destinations, sun, relaxation, and a French ambience—in one package when they sail with Club Med. The price of a cruise, like its villages, is all-inclusive and up-front, and the cruise experience is consistent no matter when you sail.

The dress code is about as varied as the passengers. On the two gala night dinners during the week, guests who are inclined to wear beaded dresses and tuxedos, do so; those into ethnic fashions bring out their turbans and caftans. But for the most part, casual is the order of the day and casual chic the rule of the evening.

DISTINCTIVE FEATURES   All outside cabins; sports platform at the stern opens to become a private marina. Mauritian stewards.

RATES

Highest Per Diem	Lowest Per Diem	Average Per Diem
$483	$96	$254

The above per diems are calculated from the cruise line's nondiscounted *cruise-only* fares on standard accommodations. Per diems vary by season, by cabin location, and by cruise areas.

Special Note: All tips are included in the cruise fare on the *Club Med 1* and the *Club Med 2*.

Special Fares and Discounts   From time to time Club Med offers specially priced cruises, but it does not discount prices.

- Single Supplement: 50 percent additional charge, subject to availability.

Packages
- Air/Sea: Yes.
- Others: Honeymoon; golf; cruise and Club Med village combinations.
- Pre/Post: Yes.

Past Passengers   No special club or promotions.

THE LAST WORD   Most passengers like the informality and sociability of the GO concept, giving them a deeper sense of involvement in the cruise experience and leaving them with memories of people as much as places. The camaraderie also encourages some reluctant passengers to participate more in activities—to take a snorkeling lesson or blunder at learning to windsurf.

On the other hand, the constant interaction between the young and bouncy GOs and passengers creates a summer camp atmosphere that is not for everyone and can easily annoy some who have paid several thousand dollars for the cruise.

The GO team is bilingual in English and French, but French is the primary language of the ship. Language can get to be a problem for English speakers who are not up to the communications challenge, don't like to depend on sign language and gestures to communicate with fellow travelers, or who might feel there isn't an equal balance of English and French spoken during shows, activities, and excursions.

Obviously, the language problem can vary with the staff—some are more careful to translate during shows and activities than others. And, it goes without saying, the amount of English—or any other language— spoken during a voyage is likely to depend on the number of non-French-speaking guests sailing on a particular cruise.

Club Med is aware of the problem and claims to be addressing it, but basically its attitude is: theirs is a French-European product and passengers should know that before they come aboard. The cruise is, after all, an experience where Americans might lunch with people from Normandy, snorkel with a group of Italians, and share drinks with a couple from Austria. That's all meant to be part of the attraction.

Club Med would like passengers sailing in the Caribbean, for example, to feel they are getting a taste of Europe—without crossing the Atlantic. And with the passenger mix, they do. Whether it works for you depends on you and, perhaps, the passengers from the other side of the Atlantic. But when half the passengers are middle-aged French people whom one person described as "solid, vin ordinaire bourgeoisie," and the other half are an equally unsophisticated mix of Americans and other nationals, the twain, alas, seem never to meet. If most of the Americans do not speak French and the French do not converse in English, a them-versus-us situation can develop, and that, obviously, is not what Club Med has in mind.

So, if you go with realistic expectations and do not buy into the romanticized illusions, you will probably have a wonderful time, and who knows, it might be very romantic, even like being on your own yacht.

CLUB MED STANDARD FEATURES

Officers French and International.

Staffs Dining/French, Mauritian; Cabin/Filipino, Mauritian; Cruise/*Club Med 1*: French, other European GOs (Gentils Organisateurs); Cruise/*Club Med 2*: French, American, Japanese, Australian GOs.

Dining Facilities Two ocean-viewing dining rooms with single seating, unassigned at dinner. One a la carte; one buffet for breakfast and lunch. Open-air cafe and one bar serves continental breakfast; another bar serves afternoon tea with French pastries.

Special Diets Request at time of booking.

Room Service 24-hour with limited menu.

Dress Code Relaxed, casual attire such as Bermuda shorts, deck shoes, polo shirt, and blazer; two formal gala night dinners.

Cabin Amenities Bath with shower, television with remote control, radio, minibar, safe, ship-to-shore telephone, terry robes, hair dryer.

Electrical Outlets 110/220 AC.

Wheelchair Access None.

Recreation and Entertainment Three bars and lounges, nightclub, casino, piano bar, disco.

Sports and Other Activities Two swimming pools; aerobics and exercise classes daily; water sports platform with snorkeling, windsurfing, and waterskiing. Boats for diving excursions for certified divers.

Beauty and Fitness Beauty salon, fitness center, sauna, tanning salon, spa treatments, whirlpools.

Other Facilities Boutique, observation deck, laundry, no dry cleaning service.

Children's Facilities Under 12 not accepted; no youth programs.

Theme Cruises *Club Med 1*, golf.

Smoking Nonsmoking sections in restaurants; smoking allowed in all public areas.

Club Med Suggested Tipping Tips not permitted.

Credit Cards For cruise payment and on-board charges, American Express, Mastercard, Visa.

Club Med 1 / Club Med 2

	Quality Rating	**Value Rating**
Club Med 1, Club Med 2	⑥	C

Registry: Bahamas	Length: 617 feet	Beam: 66 feet
Cabins: 186/191	Draft: 16 feet	Speed: 12/15 knots
Maximum Passengers:	Passenger Decks: 6	Elevators: 2
405/403	Crew: 178/181	Space Ratio: 34/36

THE SHIPS   Under combined sail and diesel power at 14 knots, rigged with five 164-foot masts and seven computer-monitored sails, these ships cut quite a picture on the high seas. Shallow drafts allow them to enter small harbors and protected waters where large ships cannot go.

Built at a French shipyard in Le Havre by French naval architects, the Club Med vessels, like Windstar, have American computers that can control the ship to heel less than two degrees. Electric engines provide quiet, auxiliary power. The handling of the ship appears to be effortless.

The twin ships are spacious and have eight Burmese teak decks. The interiors by the well-known European designer, Albert Pinto, evoke an understated luxury reflected in the meticulous craftsmanship, the use of fine mahogany, quality fabrics, and leather, reminiscent of the classic sailing ships. Crisp, simple, white and blue decor predominates, with brass, chrome, glass, and mirror accents.

The ships are open to their surroundings, even inside. A glass roof covers half the main lounge, bathing the area in light. Long walls of windows, plus open-air and enclosed sections for the two aft bars, afford refreshing views of the sea and shore. The light and openness add a special touch.

Language problems aside, the most appealing features of the cruise are its French-international atmosphere and the extras, such as wine with lunch and dinner and an elaborate lobster bake on the beach. These along with water sports and gratuities are covered in the cost.

In the Caribbean, the ship calls at a port each day and sails through the night. Unfortunately, passengers get very little opportunity to experience the pleasure of sailing under canvas. Passengers disembark daily for planned shore excursions, snorkeling and sunbathing at the beach, or to sightsee on their own.

CLUB MED 1 ITINERARIES   Seven-day Caribbean cruise, November–late February 1998, from Martinique on five alternating itineraries: 1. St. Lucia, Tobago Cays, Bequia, Mayreau (in the Grenadines), Barbados, and Carriacou; 2. Los Roques, Blanquilla, Carriacou, Barbados, and Mayreau; 3. Les Saintes, St. Barts, Virgin Gorda, Jost Van Dyke, St. Thomas, and St. Kitts; 4. St. Lucia, Union, Grenada, La Blanquilla, Trinidad, and Mayreau; 5. Les Saintes, St. Maarten, Tintamarre, San Juan, Virgin Gorda, and St. Kitts. An occasional jazz cruise sails the Caribbean.

> **Home Port**   Martinique.
> **Port Charges**   Included.

CLUB MED 2 ITINERARIES   Three-, four-, and seven-day cruises, French Polynesia. Three days: from Bora Bora to Rangiroa and Papeete; four days: from Papeete to Moorea, Raiatea-Tahaa, and Bora Bora; seven days: from Papeete to Moorea, Raiatea-Tahaa, Bora Bora, and Rangiroa.

> • *Club Med 2* will reposition to the Carribbean in December 1997 and take over *Club Med 1*'s itineraries, beginning in March 1998.

> **Home Ports**   Papeete (to December 1997); Martinique (from March 1998); Cannes (summer).
> **Port Charges**   Included.

CABINS   Large comfortable, and handsomely decorated in navy blue and white with hand-rubbed mahogany cabinetwork, the cabins are all on the outside with twin portholes. They are fitted with twin or king-size beds, a mahogany desk, large mahogany-framed mirrors, ample closets, closed-circuit television, radio, safe, minibar, and ship-to-shore telephone, which is also used to order room service. The teak-floored baths have showers, hair dryers, and fluffy bathrobes.

Two large suites are on the top deck next to the captain's quarters. They have sitting areas and large baths with circular showers, toiletries, hair dryers, and color-coded towels for each occupant. *Club Med 2* has five suites with red, blue, and yellow decor.

The television has four channels—one in French, one in English, one giving information on the day's port of call, and one in whatever language is needed, depending on the passenger makeup. Movie selections are modest at best. No satellite television.

Guests are welcomed on board with a fruit basket in their rooms, along with complimentary champagne, fresh flowers, and bottled water.

(Note: the first bottle of water is free, but replenishments carry charges.) Breakfast can be enjoyed in the cabin—a first for Club Med and one of the ways the ships are more deluxe than the villages. There is 24-hour room service and laundry service is available at an extra charge. Cabins and public areas are very quiet.

The choice cabins are on D (Da Balaia/Desirade) Deck; those below on C (Cancun/Caraibes) share the deck with the watersports platform. The rooms with three and four bunks are on B (Bali/Borneo) Deck.

Club Med 1 *Specifications* 186 outside cabins; 2 suites; 15 double bed, 152 twins (24 convertible to doubles); 23 cabins accommodate 3 passengers; 6 have 4 beds. Standard dimensions, 188 square feet. No singles.

Club Med 2 *Specifications* 191 outside cabins; 5 suites; 124 twin (31 kings; 55 convertible to doubles); 23 cabins accommodate 3 passengers; 4 have 4 beds. Standard dimensions are 188 square feet. No singles.

DINING Dinner aboard ship is a serious affair that can last up to three hours. The ships have two ocean-view dining rooms, each with different menus. On the *Club Med 1*, the Odyssey (called Le Grand Bleu on *Club Med 2*), an open-air veranda cafe on the top deck, serves casual breakfast, luncheon buffets, and theme dinners featuring different cuisines from around the world. La Louisiane on *Club Med 1* (called Deauville on *Club Med 2*) is a more intimate, formal dining room. The a la carte menu offers several choices for each course—another distinction from Club Med villages, which have buffets.

Both restaurants have waiter service and single, unreserved, unassigned seatings at tables for two or more with continuous service during dining hours. Officers and staff dine with passengers. American passengers, unaccustomed to lengthy meals, say they would prefer to have the option of a more casual restaurant for dinner.

Both ships feature French cuisine. Buffets include an array of freshbaked breads and croissants, and the salads and entrees at lunch—fish, veal, pasta, curries—are good and abundant but not gourmet. There are European touches, such as cheese carts and café au lait. Along with French cuisine, *Club Med 2* serves Japanese specialties, even for roomservice breakfasts.

In the Club Med tradition, complimentary wine of the Club's private label, beer, and bottled water accompany both luncheon and dinner. An extensive wine list is available in La Louisiane for an additional charge.

Although continental breakfast from room service comes at no extra cost, lunch, dinner, and snacks from the room-service menu cost extra and are pricey. The quality of the food is not always comparable to that served in the dining rooms. Afternoon tea with French pastries is served daily with music in the chic, navy-and-white-checked piano bar with indoor and outdoor tables.

The sometimes uninspired food is not up to the level one might expect of a deluxe French ship. On the other hand, Club Med villages have never been gourmet havens, either.

SERVICE The Club Med stamp on the service is obvious. The officers are French and the crew, Filipino. The Mauritian staff, dressed in impeccable white shirts, shorts, and socks, handle the dining and hotel duties and continually hear praise for their friendly, professional service. The energetic, tan, and attractive GOs who make up the cruise staff are headed by the Chef du Village, the cruise director. They are easily recognized by the striped French sailor blouses they wear. These cheery camp counselors do it all—work the reception desk, run the activities, instruct in sports, and provide entertainment. During their off hours, they dine, play, and hang out with passengers.

FACILITIES AND ENTERTAINMENT The Topkapi Piano Bar, one of five bars, is the most popular on-board meeting place for afternoon tea or after-dinner drinks. It serves drinks (at higher-than-average prices) throughout the evening; happily, waiters do not push to sell drinks as on many ships. On *Club Med 2*, the Topkapi Bar was expanded and doubles as the ship's nightclub—a change made as a result of feedback from passengers on the *Club Med 1*.

A small but fully equipped casino with English female croupiers offers roulette, blackjack, and slot machines. Blackjack and roulette lessons are taught in the afternoon.

A lounge that doubles as a theatre has a bar, stage, bandstand, and dance floor. Each evening after dinner there is a different show or program here by the GOs, displaying their talents in song and dance—some more entertaining than others and all of it amateurish. Because passengers become friends with the GOs during the cruise, some of it can be fun, watching them hoof away and mouth the words to the taped songs. But, as one person described it, you feel like the audience during parents' weekend at a junior college, and some passengers, thinking that at these prices they paid for more professional entertainers, might not be amused.

Those who like to kick up their heels make their way to the chrome and glass disco with its lighted dance floor or the Fantasia nightclub, which is hidden on the bottom deck next to the engine room behind an unmarked door. Perhaps as a result of its location, the only evening it seems to be crowded is for the weekly show performed by the GOs.

At least one night of the cruise is Carnival Night on the *Club Med 1* in the Caribbean. That's the time to get out your costumes or your ingenuity or both. You don't have to participate, but most passengers do and seem to enjoy it in spite of themselves.

ACTIVITIES AND DIVERSIONS   Scrabble, bridge, Trivial Pursuit, dance contests, and karaoke are some of the organized daytime diversions along with sightseeing and sports. There is a small and limited multilanguage library and card tables with leather chairs in a lounge. The boutique carries cruise wear, perfumes, accessories from some of the top European fashion names, and Club Med gear.

SPORTS, FITNESS, AND BEAUTY   Each ship's Nautical Hall is a teak sports platform at the stern that unfolds into the sea to become a marina from which passengers can enjoy watersports when the ship is at anchor. The vessels carry sailboards, sailboats, snorkel fins, and masks, and provide waterskiing, windsurfing, sailing, and snorkeling instruction at no extra charge. They also carry two 130-horsepower ski boats and scuba equipment to take certified divers with their C-card on diving trips. The scuba program is one of the line's best values.

The less ambitious can take up positions on the chaise lounges around the two outdoor swimming pools—one fresh and one saltwater. Canvas-clad deck chairs are set about over three decks. Even when the ship is full, there is plenty of space to lounge. The supervised fitness center has a treadmill, stationary bicycles, and weight training equipment. Passengers so inclined can exercise 24 hours a day while enjoying a panoramic view from the top deck. Aerobics, stretching on AstroTurf, and water exercise classes in the pool are held daily on the top deck or on the beach. Several decks below is a pine sauna and massage room. Skeet and Ping-Pong are also available.

Club Med 2 has a reduced fitness center to accommodate the golf simulator (one of the few activities not included in the fare), which enables passengers to play some world-famous courses. (Presumably, this feature was added for Japanese passengers.) For serious pampering, *Club Med 1* has licensed massage therapists and offers mineral and moisturizing whirlpools and jet hydrotherapy, seaweed baths, back and leg treatments, massage therapy, saunas, and an ultraviolet tanning salon with tanning tables. Both ships have a beauty salon that offers hair and facial services. All beauty services and treatments cost extra.

SHORE EXCURSIONS   Both half-day and daylong excursions are organized by Club Med at most ports and are accompanied by a local guide and GO. The ships do not always dock in ports, but rather, tender passengers in some of the smaller islands and remote locations. Shore walks, beach trips, and the weekly lobster fest are included in the fare; commercial port excursions are not and can be costly.

The literature on shore excursions is in French and priced in francs. On Caribbean cruises, excursions costs $19–96. Among the best and most popular excursions are the catamaran cruise in Jost Van Dyke and the helicopter flightseeing tour in St. Thomas.

On Mediterranean cruises, there are unusual tours, such as a helicopter ride over Corsica, and others where you can discover one of the real advantages of cruising—visiting places that are either difficult or impossible to reach by any other means.

Shore excursions are probably less important on Club Med's itineraries than on mainstream cruises particularly in the Caribbean and Tahiti because most of the islands visited are sun spots with splendid beaches and exquisite waters filled with beautiful reefs, and the main attraction is water sports.

THEME CRUISES   Six-night golf cruise from Martinique on the *Club Med 1*.

POSTSCRIPT   Nonsmokers should be aware that smokers are in the majority on *Club Med 1* and have the run of the ship. Restaurants have nonsmoking sections, but smoking is allowed in all public areas. The ship is equipped with a good ventilation system that seems to combat the smoke.

Don't forget to bring along a French-English dictionary, unless, of course, you are fluent in French.

COMMODORE CRUISE LINE

800 Douglas Road, Suite 700, Coral Gables, FL 33134
(305) 529-3000; (800) 237-5361; fax (305) 654-9031
http://www.commodorecruise.com

TYPE OF SHIP   Classic, midsize oceanliner.

TYPE OF CRUISE   Casual, informal, unpretenious, budget priced; a cruise for all ages.

CRUISE LINE'S STRENGTHS
  • high value for low price
  • outstanding staff
  • family cabins
  • varied entertainment

CRUISE LINE'S SHORTCOMINGS
  • age of ship
  • noise level
  • rushed port visits

FELLOW PASSENGERS   A variety of passengers—first-timers, newly-weds, families, older couples, singles, young retirees, senior citizens, and experienced cruisers of all ages—might make up the mix on any given cruise. With New Orleans as home port, the majority are likely to come from Louisiana and neighboring Texas, Mississippi, and Alabama, and others from the Midwest and California. In spring and fall, the median age is about 49; it drops to mid-40s in summer and winter holidays, when more passengers travel with children and younger couples increase.

The majority of passengers are professionals or in management; 58 percent are college graduates. Average household income is $52,000 per year; male/female ratio is almost equal. About 25 percent are retired; on any given cruise, about a quarter are seniors. Fifty-four percent have cruised before; 46 percent are first-timers; 98 percent say they would cruise again.

Recommended For   Budget-conscious first-time cruisers, families, and others seeking an easy, laid-back vacation with dependable service and plenty of activity in a friendly, informal atmosphere.

Not Recommended For   Passengers seeking a sophisticated or intellectual travel experience or the floating resort facilities of a superliner.

CRUISE AREAS AND SEASONS   Western Caribbean and Central America, year-round.

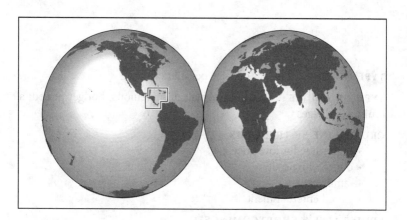

THE LINE   Begun in 1966, Commodore Cruise Line was one of the true trailblazers in offering weekly cruises from Miami to the Caribbean. Building to a fleet of three vessels, dubbed the "Happy Ships," it sailed on these routes, developing a solid reputation for tried-and-true cruises, for more than two decades. The line became known for theme cruises—Oktoberfest, Mayfest, Country and Western—which it also pioneered.

In 1987, Commodore was acquired by Effjohn International, a Scandinavian company that operates one of the world's largest passenger fleets, and was merged first with Bermuda Star Line and later with Crown Cruise Lines, a company in which Effjohn has ownership. Through it all, Commodore maintained its separate identity and moved away from the stiff competition of the new megaliners in Florida to New Orleans where, until recently, it had the only Caribbean cruises departing weekly, year-round.

In late spring of 1995, Commodore Cruise Line was acquired by a group of Miami investors, headed by travel industry veteran Fred A. Mayer, a founder of Regency Cruises and former head of Exprinter, a tour and cruise wholesale company. One ship, *Enchanted Seas*, is on a long-term lease to World Explorer Cruises.

The Fleet	Built/Renovated	Tonnage	Passengers
Enchanted Isle	1958/1994	23,500	726

STYLE   Comfortable like a pair of favorite slippers is the way some passengers describe a Commodore cruise. It provides a relaxing vacation at affordable prices with plenty of activities in a congenial atmosphere, appealing to middle Americans of all ages who know and want good value. Many of its repeaters have tried the highly publicized large ships with nonstop activity, but prefer the warm, more restful atmosphere of a Commodore cruise.

Except for theme cruises when the passenger mix and ambience might vary, Commodore aims at providing dependable, satisfying cruises for a broad spectrum of vacationers year-round. While the majority of passengers range from 45–60 in age, over the years, the line's audience has become younger, if anything, as cruising has reached wider audiences. At the same time, the over-60s seem to have a swell time, although some opt to stay on board during ports requiring a tender. Groups account for approximately 40 percent of its passengers. Repeaters are encouraged with special fares for members of the newly created past passenger club.

DISTINCTIVE FEATURES   Elaborate theme nights on all cruises. On its Key West/Western Caribbean itinerary, the ship remains overnight in Cozumel.

RATES

Highest Per Diem	Lowest Per Diem	Average Per Diem
$208	$135	$154

The above per diems are calculated from the cruise line's nondiscounted *cruise-only* fares on standard accommodations. What you will actually pay *should* be *substantially* less (see Part One, How to Get the Best Deal on a Cruise). Per diems vary by season, by cabin location, and by cruise areas.

Special Fares and Discounts   Commodore's early booking discounts of up to $150 per cabin are available when reservations and deposits are made 90 days prior to sailing. Also, see Past Passengers below.

- Third/Fourth Person: $350.
- Single Supplement: Rates range from 135 percent to 200 percent, depending on cabin category, and include air transportation.

Packages
- Air/Sea: Yes.
- Others: Honeymoon includes cabin with double bed, welcome cocktail, bottle of champagne, bottle of wine with dinner, photograph, fresh fruit basket, and bouquet of flowers.
- Pre/Post: Yes, plus annual four-day Mardi Gras/New Orleans package.

Past Passengers   Club Commodore frequently offers loyal fans special sailings with discounted rates and special events on board.

THE LAST WORD   If you know what to expect, Commodore's cruises are among cruising's best values and a good choice for first-time cruisers who are awed by the very notion of taking a cruise. They appeal most to budget-minded, value-conscious, middle- and upper-middle-class travelers from middle America, and are an affordable option for honeymooners on a budget. For seniors who like plenty of daytime activity and nighttime entertainment, Commodore is a comfortable choice. The ship shows its age despite recent facelifts, but the line must be doing something right as they sail almost full year-round with loyal fans who return time and again and newcomers attracted by the price. They get what they pay for; there are no surprises. The new owners, who took over in July 1995, expect to add more ships. Stay tuned.

COMMODORE STANDARD FEATURES

Officers European, Scandinavian, and others.

Staffs Dining, Cabin/International; Cruise/American.

Dining Facilities One main dining room, two seatings for three meals with open seating for breakfast and lunch; breakfast, lunch, and midnight buffet in Harbor Grill on Promenade Deck.

Special Diets Requests must be made three weeks in advance of sailing.

Room Service 24 hours.

Dress Code Casual by day; casual or informal in evening; formal suggested but not required for captain's welcome and farewell dinners. Shorts not allowed in dining room for dinner.

Cabin Amenities Phone; closed-circuit television has two channels with first-run movies; baths with shower, most superiors also have tub.

Electrical Outlets 110 AC.

Wheelchair Access Public areas ramped; cabins modified.

Recreation and Entertainment Casino; disco; nightclub; show lounge; cinema and theatre; observation lounge, library, video game room, card and meeting room. Bingo, bridge, dancing classes, horse racing, arts and crafts classes.

Sports and Other Activities One outdoor swimming pool; Ping-Pong, pool games, trapshooting, exercise, aerobics. No wraparound deck.

Beauty and Fitness Beauty/barber shop, massage, small exercise room.

Other Facilities Boutiques, medical facilities, laundry service.

Children's Facilities Youth counselors during summer and holidays. Small video/game room. Commodore Cuddly mascot to entertain kids.

Theme Cruises Newly expanded; music and comedy to Cajun cooking and more.

Smoking Smoke-free dining room; public rooms have smoking and non-smoking sections.

Commodore Suggested Tipping Per person per day: cabin steward, $3; dining room waiter, $3; busboy, $2; and per week, head waiter, $4; 15 percent of check is added to wine and bar bills.

Credit Cards For cruise payment and on-board charges, American Express, Discover, Mastercard, Visa. No cash used during cruise; instead, passengers are billed and tab settled at end of cruise.

Enchanted Isle

	Quality Rating	Value Rating
Enchanted Isle	❸	A

Registry: Panama	Length: 617 feet	Beam: 88 feet
Cabins: 369	Draft: 28 feet	Speed: 20 knots
Maximum Passengers:	Passenger Decks: 9	Elevators: 3
84	Crew: 330	Space Ratio: 33

THE SHIP   The spacious ship has a warm ambience set by the congenial staff, starting with the captain. Thanks to its size, passengers enjoy more personalized service than is found on large ships. The ship has large cabins, some holding up to five people, which are popular with families, especially when coupled with the low prices.

Enchanted Isle (formerly the *Bermuda Star* and *Veendam*) is almost a twin of the *Enchanted Seas*, which is now under lease by World Explorer Cruises. The two ships were built in 1957 at the same time in the same shipyard—Ingalls Shipbuilding Corporation of Pascagoula, Mississippi. After a year's absence serving as a floating hotel in St. Petersburg, Russia, and a facelift at a shipyard in Poland, the ship returned to Caribbean service in late 1994.

The ship has a variety of public rooms and lounges and ample deck space. The plainly decorated public rooms are in good shape, and the air conditioning functions well, considering the age of the ship. Some cabins have seen better days, although recent refurbishing has improved them. On the other hand, passengers seem to have a good time and are not too concerned about the decor.

The Promenade Deck holds most of the public rooms and runs the full length of the ship from the casino at the fore to the main pool at the stern. The side decks are teak and spacious, but they do not encircle the ship completely. The ships' limited number of elevators requires long walks from some cabins, which can be hard for less-than-hearty passengers.

ITINERARIES   Seven days, Western Caribbean, year-round. The ship sails weekly on Saturday from New Orleans to Playa del Carmen, Cozumel, Grand Cayman, and Montego Bay, with three days at sea.

Occasionally, the ship departs from this itinerary and visits Puerto Cortes and Roatan in Honduras, instead of the two Mexican ports in the regular schedule.

Home Port   New Orleans.
Port Charges $90.

CABINS   Comfortable and spacious, depending on category, the cabins have ample closets and storage space for two, perhaps three persons, but are cramped for four. More than 75 percent are outside; most top-priced cabins have bathrooms with tubs; others have showers only. Some bathrooms have a bidet. The water is steaming hot and the spotless bathrooms were retiled in fall 1996 when all the cabins were refurbished.

The usual desk or bathroom amenities, such as stationery and shampoo, are not provided. The number of electrical outlets is limited; one accommodates a hair dryer. Reading lights set into the wall beside the bed provide plenty of light.

Some cabins on the Boat and Sun Decks have views partially obstructed by lifeboats, but they are not indicated on the deck plan. Cabins on the lowest deck do not have elevator access.

Room service offers continental breakfast and a limited menu of soups, salads, and sandwiches.

Specifications   72 inside cabins, 286 outside; 72 for third/fourth persons; 2 singles. Standard dimensions, inside or outside, 152 square feet; deluxe and superior, 191–293 square feet. Large variety of configurations: some twins with upper and lower berths; some with twin beds convertible to doubles; some connecting cabins.

DINING   The cuisine has gotten mixed reviews in the past, mainly for its lack of consistency. However, a new chef seems to be performing miracles, with many passengers saying they are repeaters because of the good food.

Menus are more limited in the number of selections than on more expensive ships but certainly adequate. A typical dinner menu offers choices of two juices, two appetizers, three soups, three salads, four entrees with vegetables, cheese, three desserts, and beverages. Second helpings are available upon request. Light cuisine is offered at every meal.

The low lighting in the main dining room is meant to create a warm ambience, but instead, it just makes it hard to see, and the noise level is uncomfortably high. Most seating is at round tables for eight in close proximity to one another; some banquettes and smaller seats are in corners. No smoking is allowed in the dining room.

The service in the dining room gets as high marks as the food, although it is sometimes rushed. The maître d'hôtel and the dining staff seem genuinely eager to offer a pleasant dining experience, but the noise level and crowded tables make their task a difficult one.

The Harbour Grill on the Promenade Deck offers indoor/outdoor dining for breakfast and lunch buffets in a cheerful and comfortable atmosphere. The inside bar features happy-hour hot snacks, as well. The outside area has a full-service bar, covered entertainment area, and poolside grill. Burgers and hot dogs with all the trimmings are prepared on deck daily at lunch, and an "ice cream parlor" along with cookies and prepared sandwiches opens in the afternoon. During summer and holidays, pizza, tacos, burgers, and a child's plate are offered. Midnight buffets are attractive but ordinary.

SERVICE Passengers lavish praise on the staff and service—among the best of any ship offering weekly Caribbean cruises. Without question, Commodore's staff is its biggest asset.

The crew is efficient, thorough, pleasant, and accommodating. They have an average of 10 years' service; some have been with the line over 20 years. It is not uncommon for repeat passengers to request a specific room steward or waiter. Bar service is excellent and bartenders more than willing to accommodate unusual requests.

You get the impression they like their jobs and the company they work for. (The staff and crew are allowed to invite family members to cruise with them after being with the company three months. That makes for happy campers!) The positive attitude is reflected in the way the staff and passengers interact so well. By the end of the cruise, most of the staff are able to call passengers by their first names.

Ground personnel are also applauded. In addition to transferring passengers who book flights through the cruise lines, the uniformed representatives at the airport in New Orleans are praised for their courtesy and help to those who make their own arrangements, giving them clear, concise directions regarding transportation to the dock.

FACILITIES AND ENTERTAINMENT Each day and evening are meant to reflect the place being visited.

Theme nights are extremely popular and some passengers plan their packing around them, with costumes for Mardi Gras night and poodle skirts and bobby socks for the 1950s hop. The ship's orchestra is excellent and entertainment by an array of singers, magicians, and comedians is well done, keeping passengers coming back each night.

The lip sync show, games with audience participation, and horse races draw the biggest crowds. Unlike most ships, the *Enchanted Isle* lets passengers "purchase" horses for the week and the "owners" are given materials to decorate them—some take their decorated horses to dinner! The casino, with an adjacent bar, offers slots, blackjack, and roulette.

Each lounge has its own personality—one quiet and intimate; another open and loud—with enough variety to suit all. The Mid Ocean Lounge, the main showroom, has seating on a gradual decline toward the center floor, somewhat like a theatre. It is more than adequate for most activites and has good sight lines except for some seats blocked by pillars. The sides, on higher levels, have a full-service bar and large windows offering spectacular daytime views in air-conditioned comfort.

The Spyglass Lounge on Sun Deck is a quiet retreat with the best view of the front of the ship. It is popular with older passengers who enjoy the quiet piano/cocktail music, but it seems to take first-timers a few days to find it. Relaxed and intimate, the room is pleasantly decorated. Its bar opens in late afternoon, and there is music before dinner. The disco on the Sun Deck is supposed to close at 2 A.M., but most nights it remains open until well after 4 A.M. for dancing to current rock/rap hits. Bartenders and waiters stay until the last passenger is ready to call it a night.

ACTIVITIES AND DIVERSIONS   During the days at sea, there is usually a talk by a guest expert or a special feature on topics as varied as wine tasting and napkin folding to finances and the stock market. Game show addicts come in large numbers for Commodore's own version of Liar's Club, Family Feud, Newly Wed/Not So Newly Wed Game, Jeopardy, and for country line-dancing. Ice carving is also popular and includes a photo session and information on ice-carving history.

The television movies, changed daily, are good quality and often first-run, Academy Award winners. The ship has a pleasant, airy card room with four tables, a small video game room, and a theatre (always cold) where movies are shown when the ship is in port. The theatre has a small stage with piano and is used as a gathering place for shore excursion participants.

The small library has a very limited selection of books and odd checkout hours. Passengers who plan to read during their cruise should bring their own material. The boutique offers daily specials on souvenir T-shirts and similar gifts and offers a 50 percent discount on liquor.

SPORTS, FITNESS, AND BEAUTY   One outside swimming pool (tiles need replacing) is on the Promenade Deck. Deck chairs are supplied on the Promenade Deck but not elsewhere, however, no one seems to mind if passengers take their own chairs to quiet spots.

A beauty salon, a barber shop, and a massage room are tucked away down low on the Theatre Deck. Massages are popular and should be booked early. The small fitness center is similar to that at a low-budget hotel with three stationery bicycles. Morning toning, stretching, and aerobics classes and guided jogging around the ship are offered. There are no sauna or spa treatment facilities.

CHILDREN'S FACILITIES   The ship does not have facilities exclusively for children. Games and activities are held in the library, card room, outside decks, swimming areas, and in the theatre. Up to four youth counselors come on board during the summer months to coordinate activities when there are at least 15 youths on a cruise. In 1997, Commodore introduced Commodore Cuddly, its new bear mascot, to entertain young passengers. The mascot has three different outfits: A Commodore outfit for greeting guests; a tee-shirt with epaulets for shipboard activities; and a nightshirt for a tuck-in service for junior passengers.

SHORE EXCURSIONS   Cannot be booked in advance. The ship offers a selection of tours and sports at prices typical for the Caribbean, ranging from $30 for a two-hour Cayman Island tour to $80 for a seven-and-a-half-hour visit to Tulum from Playa del Carmen with return by ferry to Cozumel. Passengers complain that some excursions are rushed and they need more time in port.

Port talks vary in substance. The presentation on Cozumel is very helpful, with good tips on shopping and restaurants. For Grand Cayman and Jamaica, the port talks push jewelry shopping to the point that it is obvious someone receives a hefty commission to promote particular stores.

In Grand Cayman, tenders are used to convey passengers to shore, as is the case with most ships calling here. In Cozumel, on/off boarding is quick and easy. Here, horseback riding, an introductory scuba course, and dive excursions for certified divers are available.

THEME CRUISES   Commodore has new, expanded theme cruises from music and comedy to Cajun cooking and more. Oktoberfest and Country and Western are standards; others, such as Rock 'n' Roll, Arts and Crafts, and Stop Smoking cruises are occasional.

POSTSCRIPT   A word of caution: During embarkation, black soot from smokestacks has been known to cover the ship's open decks and soil clothes. At sea this is not a problem. The officers and staff are somewhat lax about attendance by passengers at the compulsory lifeboat drill.

Commodore ships are not megaliners, but then, you don't pay mega bucks. They are a good, solid value; first-time cruisers, especially those on a budget, get their money's worth. Some cabins require a lot of walking to reach stairs and elevators. Some passengers complain about the lack of religious services on board. But all in all, the ships can be recommended as long as people know what to expect: superior service, good (not great) food, entertainment, and plenty of activity. Then, too, the ships' itineraries visit some of the Caribbean's most popular ports.

COSTA CRUISE LINES

World Trade Center, 80 SW Eighth Street, Miami, FL 33130-3097
(305) 358-7325; (800) 327-2537; fax (305) 375-0676

TYPE OF SHIPS   New modern superliners and traditional oceanliners.

TYPE OF CRUISE   Mainstream, mass market designed for Europeans as much as North Americans, hence more European in service and ambience.

CRUISE LINE'S STRENGTHS
- cabins
- Italian style and service
- new fleet with a distinctive style
- friendly crew
- itineraries
- dining room cuisine

CRUISE LINE'S SHORTCOMINGS
- noise level in dining rooms
- excessive announcements
- mediocre buffets
- language problems
- lack of consistency

FELLOW PASSENGERS   Costa has two seasons: Caribbean from late fall to early spring and Northern Europe, Mediterranean, and Norwegian fjords from spring through fall. As a result, it has two sets of passengers. In the Caribbean on the *CostaRomantica*, 80 percent of the passengers are from North America and typically average 45 years in age with an annual household income of $50,000+. A chorus of Italian-American fans and newlyweds are attracted by the line's Italian style that offers a bit of Italy in the Caribbean. Most have cruised before and come from Florida, the Southeast, the Northeast, and to a lesser extent, the Midwest and West Coast.

In Europe, 80 percent or more are Europeans who have likely traveled abroad, perhaps cruised before. Among the North Americans, average ages and places of origin are about the same as the Caribbean cruisers, but those on a European cruise would be inclined to rent a car and drive through Europe on their own instead of traveling on an escorted tour. They enjoy traveling with and meeting people from other countries.

Since Costa's European cruises are often a bit longer than seven days and cost more on a per diem basis, passengers are likely to be older, more affluent, and in the mind set of a European visit rather than a Caribbean holiday in the sun. This, however, is not necessarily true of the Europeans on board Mediterranean cruises.

Recommended For Italophiles; first-time cruisers and less experienced travelers who want to try a more European ambience but with the typical facilities of a large ship; and repeat cruisers who simply want to try something different.

Not Recommended For Those who like small ships, an all-American atmosphere, and prefer to travel with fellow Americans.

CRUISE AREAS AND SEASONS Caribbean, Mediterranean, Greek Islands, Holy Land, Black Sea, Northern Europe, Norwegian fjords, Baltic, Russia, South America, transatlantic cruises.

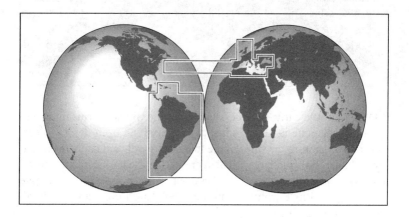

THE LINE Genoa-based Costa Crociere, the parent company of Costa Cruise Lines, has been in the shipping business for over 100 years and in the passenger business for over 40 years. Now the fifth largest cruise line in the world, it was one of the earliest lines to sail on one-week

Caribbean cruises from Miami when it began in 1959, and the first to introduce an air/sea program in the late 1960s.

Yet, despite its long Florida-Caribbean association, in 1993, Costa changed course to become a more Europe-focused cruise line. Out of its six ships only two sail from U.S. ports and only in the winter season. The balance of its fleet is positioned mostly in Europe, catering to Europeans. In 1993, Costa Crociere broadened its European base further by selling 24 percent of the company to Croisieres Paquet, a French firm belonging to the Accor Hotel/Chargeurs group, which owns Paquet Cruises.

Costa launched the 1990s with four new ships costing more than $1 billion and meant to serve a broad spectrum of passengers. The ships have a distinctive style that is a marked departure from the classic oceanliners of its older fleet. They combine modern and classic qualities with interesting new design features. The 76,000-ton *CostaVictoria*, added in 1996, is its largest ship to date. In 1997, Carnival Cruise Lines and its European partner, Airtours, purchased Costa Crociere, the parent company of Costa Cruises Lines.

The Fleet	Built/Renovated	Tonnage	Passengers
CostaAllegra	1992	30,000	810
CostaClassica	1991	53,700	1,300
CostaMarina	1969/1990	25,000	770
CostaRiviera	1963/1994	35,000	924
CostaRomantica	1993	53,700	1,356
CostaVictoria	1996	76,000	1,950

STYLE   In the early 1980s Costa coined the phrase "Cruising Italian Style" to celebrate its Italian kinship in everything from design to cuisine and to capture the spirit of the fun and friendly atmosphere created by its Italian staff and largely Italian crew. Then, when Costa introduced its new ships at the dawn of the 1990s, it replaced the concept, despite its success, with "Euroluxe," embracing a more European style in an effort to broaden the line's appeal.

Perhaps it helped Costa establish its dominant position in Europe, but it was neither understood nor well received by its North American fans. Costa quickly returned to applauding its Italian connection. Yet, the confusion it caused still plagues the line and some old fans remain unconvinced.

The new ships are Italian, designed and built in Italy by Italians, with floors and walls of fine Italian marble, splendid wood cabinetry, designer fabrics and linens, and Italian art throughout. But rather than the familiar, classic Italian look, they reflect the sophisticated architecture and decor of modern Italian designers, often regarded as trendsetters in their field.

Life on board is made to seem *molto Italiano* from the pasta and espresso to Italian lessons, Italian cooking classes, Italian ice cream, pizzas in the pizzerias, and toga parties. Yet for all the trimmings, the Italian ambience has been diluted, principally because Costa ships no longer have all-Italian crews, although Italians are in key management positions.

The ships are very much "today" with gyms and spas and fitness programs, and Costa's shore excursions in the Caribbean stress outdoor activities. One of its most popular innovations is Serena Cay (Catalina Island, off the southeast coast of the Dominican Republic), Costa's "private" island where passengers on Eastern Caribbean cruises spend a day at the beach. The island is near the sprawling resort of Casa de Campo, which has, among its many facilities, a tennis village, two of the Caribbean's best golf courses, horseback riding, and polo.

DISTINCTIVE FEATURES   Pizzerias serve free hot pizza throughout the day. On Caribbean cruises couples can renew their wedding vows in a special shipboard ceremony.

RATES

Highest Per Diem	Lowest Per Diem	Average Per Diem
$446	$131	$245

The above per diems are calculated from the cruise line's nondiscounted *cruise-only* fares on standard accommodations. What you will actually pay *should* be *substantially* less (see Part One, How to Get the Best Deal on a Cruise). Per diems vary by season, by cabin location, and by cruise areas.

Special Fares and Discounts   Andiamo Fares provide discounts of 10–25 percent, depending on the category, for bookings 90 days in advance.

- Children's Fare: Same as third/fourth passenger fares.
- Single Supplement: 150–200 percent.

Packages
- Air/Sea: Yes, mostly as add-on programs.
- Others: Spa, seniors, honeymoon, family.
- Pre/Post: Yes, in Amsterdam, Florence, Rome, Venice.

Past Passengers The line does not have a repeat passengers club, but it does send periodic mailings to past passengers, announcing new itineraries and offering them special discounts.

THE LAST WORD Costa's expansion has been bumpy, and the avalanche of criticism regarding quality, Euroluxe, and the radically different look of the *CostaClassica* didn't help. The worst seems to be behind them, judging from recent reports, but some work is still needed, particularly in establishing consistency in the product.

To its credit, Costa has dared to be different in style and in the markets it pursues, preferring to be number one in Europe, where it has a strong base and years of experience, rather than struggling to survive in the fierce competition of the Caribbean. The strategy all but guarantees that when you take a Costa cruise, whether it's a Caribbean or a Mediterranean cruise, the experience increasingly will be European or international, rather than one catering primarily to American tastes.

From spring through fall, when Costa blankets Europe, it is said that more than 28 percent of all those taking a cruise in Europe are cruising on a Costa ship. Some Americans welcome the opportunity to take a European vacation with Europeans and take pleasure in the multinational encounter. Others see it as a deterrent, reacting negatively to the lack of cohesiveness about the cruises that this situation often creates. They're turned off by cliques in lounges and bars and the steady stream of announcements—for bingo, shopping talks, shore excursions—in five languages, even though English-speaking hostesses are on board to cater to North American passengers.

COSTA CRUISES STANDARD FEATURES

Officers Italian.

Staffs Dining/Italian, other European, Asian, Central Americans; Cabin/International; Cruise and Entertainment/International.

Dining Facilities One main dining room, two seatings for three meals, midnight buffet featuring Italian cuisine; indoor/outdoor buffet breakfast and lunch. *Victoria* and *Romantica* have pizzerias and pastry cafes.

Special Diets Should be requested four weeks in advance.

Room Service 24 hours; butler service in suites with full service for meals from dining room menus.

Dress Code Casual; informal evenings; two nights formal/semiformal.

Cabin Amenities Phone, radio, private shower, hair dryer, safe, T.V.; suites have whirlpool bath, minibar, and veranda (except *Marina*).

Electrical Outlets 110 AC; 110/220 AC on *Marina*.

Wheelchair Access Six cabins on *Classica*, *Romantica*, and *Victoria*; eight on *Allegra* and *Marina*.

Recreation and Entertainment Casino; bars and lounges with nightly entertainment; showrooms on *Classica* and *Romantica*; disco; dance and Italian lessons; bingo; bridge; horse racing, library; card room.

Sports and Other Activities Two outside swimming pools, *Classica* and *Romantica* (one, *Allegra* and *Marina*). Exercise classes, snorkeling lessons, paddle tennis, Ping-Pong, deck and pool games.

Beauty and Fitness Barber shop and beauty salon, spa, sauna, European beauty treatments, fitness centers, jogging track, whirlpools.

Other Facilities Boutiques, medical facility, laundry and dry cleaning services, meeting room, chapel, synagogue on *Classica*.

Children's Facilities Costa Kids year-round; baby-sitters. See text.

Theme Cruises Yes.

Smoking Smoking in designated public areas.

Costa Suggested Tipping Per person per day: cabin steward, $3; waiter, $3; busboy, $1.50; head waiter, $1; 15 percent gratuity added to all beverage bills (including mineral water in the dining room).

Credit Cards For cruise payment and on-board charges, American Express, Diners Club, Discover, Mastercard, Visa.

CostaRomantica / CostaClassica

	Quality Rating	Value Rating
CostaRomantica	7	C
CostaClassica	4	C

Registry: Liberia	Length: 718/723 feet	Beam: 98 feet
Cabins: 678/654	Draft: 24/25 feet	Speed: 20 knots
Maximum Passengers: 1,782	Passenger Decks: 10	Elevators: 8
	Crew: 650	Space Ratio: 42/41.

THE SHIPS   The *CostaRomantica* and its twin, *CostaClassica*, are almost identical in design and layout. These spacious ships with public rooms located on the upper four decks have the ultramodern Italian interiors that use a king's ransom of marble, dramatic glass window walls, futuristic sculptures, clean lines, sharp angular shapes, and fine art to create a new look for cruise ships reflecting modern trends in Italian design, radically different from traditional European oceanliners.

Perhaps because the *Classica* was so new and different from classic cruise ship design, the initial reaction from Costa's American fans was not favorable. For some people, the decor was harsh with the extensive use of marble and severe lines rendering the interiors cold, while in other areas, the furnishings were too ornate and radical. The white marble stairways with metal trim look so antiseptic, they resemble a hospital more than a cruise ship.

Costa took heed and with the *Romantica* made some design changes that used more warm wood paneling, particularly by the elevators and stairwells, warmer fabrics, and other refinements that resulted in the interiors being more approachable. (Perhaps as a further indication, Costa recently gave the *Classica* a new role. It is no longer paired with the *Romantica* for the Northern American market during the winter Caribbean season; instead, it has been replaced by the new *Costa Victoria*.)

The ships' layouts are similar and easy to follow, with one lounge or public space flowing to the next and creating an overall sense of openness and harmony. Decks are named after European cities.

Passengers are introduced to the *CostaRomantica* in the ship's dramatic Grand Lobby, set low on the Copenhagen Deck, which is dedicated entirely to cabins, as are the deck below and the two decks above. White-gloved room stewards are on hand to escort passengers to their cabins. The background music of Vivaldi and Pavarotti is meant to underscore the start of a week of "Cruising Italian Style."

The lobby's dramatic centerpiece is a moving sculpture by Susumu Shingu, the Japanese sculptor selected to create the artwork installed in Genoa in 1992 to commemorate the Columbus Quincentennial. The sculpture is a suspended mobile with panels that move continuously and change color against the lobby's Cararra marble walls and floors.

The heart and social center of *CostaRomantica* is the Piazza Italia and Grand Bar on the Verona Deck—an atrium that doesn't seem like one because it is fully furnished as a lounge, with a small bandstand and dance floor to one side and a long bar on the other. The spacious lounge is the favorite gathering spot for prelunch and predinner drinks, as it is a short walk from the dining room, aft. Encased in soft green Venetian stucco walls, the lounge offers a quietly elegant setting with jacquard fabrics in greens and blues against dark teal carpeting, enhanced with fresh greenery all about.

Called Piazza Navona on the *Classica* where rust and coral tones are used, the lounge has ultramodern, sharply angular chairs and sofas, and a skylight ceiling trimmed with dark wood, somewhat like shoji screens. Forward are meeting rooms, the library, chapel, card room, and the ground floor of L'Opera, the bilevel show lounge.

From the Piazza Italia, a double stairway at the center of the lounge leads up to the Vienna Deck and the next most popular spot—Romeo's Pizzeria and Juliet's Patisserie. Forward are shops on the Via Condetti, named for Rome's most fashionable shopping street.

The top deck of the *Romantica*, with swimming pools and spa, has a new group of suites over the bridge in the area occupied by the spa on the *Classica*. Reducing the spa area on the *Romantica* and adding the suites was the major layout change between the two ships.

COSTAROMANTICA ITINERARIES

- *December–April*, seven days, alternating Eastern and Western Caribbean, departing from Ft. Lauderdale on Sunday for Key West, Playa del Carmen/Cozumel, Ocho Rios, and Grand Cayman; or San Juan, St. Thomas/St. John, Serena Cay/Casa de Campo, and Nassau; both have two days at sea. At Serena Cay,

only passengers participating in the ship's shore excursion may
disembark at Casa de Campo; likewise, at Playa del Carmen. In
late November and December, 10- and 11-day cruises with a
similar itinerary include a partial transit of Panama Canal.
- *May–October*, seven days, Western Mediterranean, from Genoa
to Naples, Palermo, Tunis, Palma de Mallorca, Barcelona, and
Marseille.
- *In May*, 15-night transatlantic positioning cruise, eastbound,
Ft. Lauderdale to Genoa; and in October, 14 nights, westbound, Genoa to Ft. Lauderdale.

Home Ports   Ft. Lauderdale; Genoa.
Port Charges $111.50, Caribbean; $140–160, Europe.

COSTACLASSICA ITINERARIES

- *May–October*, seven days, Eastern Mediterranean, from Venice on
Sunday to Bari, Italy and to Katakolon, Santorini, Mykonos,
Rhodes, and Kithira in Greece.
- The *Classica*'s winter Caribbean itinerary sails in the Eastern
Caribbean from Guadelupe and is sold in Europe only.

Home Port   Venice.
Port Charges $140–160, Europe.

CABINS   Spacious and well designed, the cabins are these ships' best
feature. Standard cabins are unusually large and fitted in cherrywood
furnishings including a dresser/desk unit with a large mirror, bedside
tables with lamps, a control panel for lights by the bed, ample closet
space, and two chairs, one of which opens into a bed suitable for a child
or teenager.

A rather elegant touch is the white curtain extending the width of
the room, which can be raised and lowered to cover the oversized porthole; so, too, are the designer amenities and high-quality bed and bath
linens. All cabins have television with CNN, radio, safe, direct-dial satellite phone, and hair dryer. The 24-hour room service offers a modest
menu of sandwiches and beverages.

Of the 24 suites added to the *Romantica*, the 6 largest—all named
for famous operas—are located above the ship's bridge on the Monte
Carlo Deck and have floor-to-ceiling window walls for stunning views
of ports and sea. The remaining 18 are spacious junior suites but under-
mined by noise from the jogging track overhead. More desirable is a
group of ten large suites amidships on the Madrid Deck, with verandas

large enough for chaise longues. The *Classica's* ten suites also have verandas.

All suites have phones in the bathroom, large whirlpool bath, separate shower, double vanity and spacious sitting area with minibar (there's a charge), and daily fresh fruit. Their decor is enhanced by authentic tapestries, handwoven bedspreads, and Renaissance art. Butler service is available to enjoy full service for any meal from dining room menus, complete with set table, en suite.

CostaRomantica *Specifications*   216 inside cabins, 428 outside; 16 suites, 18 mini-suites. Standard dimensions are 174 square feet inside, 200 square feet outside. 340 with twin beds; 56 with queen. 126 inside cabins, 116 outside take third and fourth persons; no singles.

CostaClassica *Specifications*   216 inside cabins, 428 outside; 10 suites with veranda. Standard dimensions are 150–200 square feet. 158 with twin beds (152 convertible to double), 121 queen. 359 cabins take third and fourth persons; no singles.

DINING   The Botticelli Restaurant on the *Romantica*, similar to its counterpart, the Tivoli, on the *Classica*, is a beautiful room, laid out almost entirely in off-white and brown Carrara marble with coffered ceilings that create a palatial effect without glitz. Light, elegantly designed wicker-backed chairs sit at round tables, most seating eight, dressed in starched white tableclothes with fine china, glassware, and fresh flowers.

Lovely as the room may be, the lack of carpeting on the floor or fabric on the walls, unfortunately, causes the noise level to be extraordinarily high. After discovering the problem on the *Classica* (the noise level at the center of the room is so high it's difficult to have a conversation with people at the same table), more acoustical material was added, particularly in the ceiling, to dampen the noise in the Botticelli. It helped some, but not enough. The tables on the side toward the back of the room get less noise. Two wings at the entrance are designated as smoking areas.

The restaurants on both ships have movable panels at the side, which are faced with a variety of scenes—a European city, landscapes, or Italian gardens—that create a different ambience for each evening. The panels were designed by Giorgio Cristini, the set designer for Milan's famous La Scala Opera House.

Dinner menus do not have as many selections as some ships in Costa's price group, but the choices are ample and of good quality with a good balance of Italian and other European dishes and American favorites. A different pasta is featured at lunch and dinner, which American audiences, particularly, rave over.

A typical dinner menu offers three appetizers, two soups, one salad, a pasta, three entrees plus a vegetarian one, three or more desserts, plus ice cream, sherbet, cheese, and fresh fruit. The presentation is always attractive. With advance notice, your waiter or maître d'hôtel will prepare special requests, particularly if they fall within his Italian repertoire.

Il Giardino, the Lido Cafe for indoor breakfast and lunch buffets, was slightly redesigned to improve serving problems encountered in the *Classica*'s La Trattoria. Unfortunately, it did nothing to help the food. For those who want a nice breakfast or lunch, the selections in the dining room are superior by far. Il Giardino's decor, however, creates one of the ship's prettiest, informal settings with its rattan chairs dressed in English country-styled fabrics against aquamarine glass walls and fine wood floors. The setting for the midnight buffet is moved around, depending on the weather and the theme.

Adjacent to the Lido Cafe, the Terrazza Cafe was reproduced from the *Classica*'s popular Alfresco Cafe, the most pleasant location on the ship from dawn to dusk. Set with wicker chairs and tables under an airy, high-peaked, canvas canopy, it provides a cool, inviting outdoor setting for breakfast and lunch or any time of day.

The other big hit, one flight below, is Romeo's Pizzeria where pizza is served throughout the day without additional charge (although you might want to buy a glass of wine or beer with which to wash it down). Romeo's neighbor, Juliet's Patisserie, open from 9 A.M. to midnight, has cakes and ice cream without charge and espresso (with a charge). Afternoon tea with fabulous desserts is served daily, and from 10 P.M. to midnight, a small cart dispenses Italian ice cream.

SERVICE A change with a major impact for Costa in recent years has been in the makeup of the crew. No longer are the ships all Italian as they once were, but rather, they are multinational, little different from the crews found on most other cruise lines. As a result, Costa has lost an edge that once truly distinguished it from the pack. Italian officers are still in command of its ships and Italians fill the supervisory roles in the restaurant but the flair and fun that Italian waiters, particularly, are able to create is often missing.

The hotel and dining staff come from India and Asia, the Caribbean, Europe, and Central and South America. Many speak little or no English. The service is attentive, friendly, and good—often, very good, but for those who have known Costa over the years, the *ambiente* isn't the same.

The cruise staff is a cheerful bunch running daily activities and bingo, but you'll be lucky if you ever see the cruise director, except on stage to open the nightly show.

FACILITIES AND ENTERTAINMENT   The variety of evening entertainment during the week is meant to appeal to the line's multinational passenger mix. The *Romantica's* main show lounge, the L'Opera Theater, is a modern interpretation of a classic, horseshoe-shaped concert hall. Red and royal blue carpets ringed by plush royal blue velvet seats against a wall of blue mosiacs, and brass railing for gold accents, help to create the glamorous atmosphere of a European theatre. There's even a foyer and bar, similar to those in a theatre or a concert hall. Most, but not all, seats have good sight lines and the hard, stiff ones in the balcony are a boon to back sufferers. L'Opera (Coloseo on *Classica*) has shows nightly with two new extravaganzas added recently.

The *Romantica's* spectacular casino with Venetian stucco walls inlaid with gold accents has as its centerpiece a large crystal chandelier surrounded by a circular crown of recessed molding. Columns are covered in mosaics and complement a large mosaic mural by noted artist Sambonet entitled *Amazonia*. A rounded bar sheathed in briarwood and set against a blue marble backdrop is stunning. The casino offers blackjack, roulette tables, and slot machines.

At the stern the Tango Ballroom, a multipurpose lounge with a large dance floor, becomes a nightclub with live music and a high-energy ambience. The room in deep blue has one wall of emerald green marble behind the bar and window walls for great ocean views, a particularly lovely, quiet daytime retreat.

The Diva Disco, high atop the ship, is a daytime observation and cocktail lounge as well as the late-night hot spot. The expansive views from the floor-to-ceiling windows reflect in mirrored walls and create incredible, almost funhouse scenes of sea and ports throughout the entire room.

Everyone's favorite night is the toga party when passengers don their Roman creation from sheets, which the ship provides. It's positively remarkable how many different ways passengers think of to make togas, and silly as it sounds, almost all passengers get into the spirit of it and have a great time.

ACTIVITIES AND DIVERSIONS   Daytime diversions fill the agenda with dance and Italian lessons, gaming lessons by the casino staff, bingo, bridge, backgammon, culinary demonstrations, port and shopping talks, horse racing, and Costa's amusing version of the Not So

Newlywed Game. A video game room is part of the teen center and there's a library and card room. Movies are shown on cabin television.

The full-service conference center offers a flexible layout of one large meeting room, two smaller rooms, audiovisual equipment, moveable leather chairs equipped with armrests and flip-top desks, and a board room for 20. The center has its own front desk like a hotel registration counter, which meeting planners applaud.

SPORTS, FITNESS, AND BEAUTY The _Romantica_ has two outdoor pools separated by Costa's distinctive yellow stacks. As with the _Classica_, the main pool is located at the stern and is surrounded by three terraces of teak decks with lounge chairs for sunning. There are four Jacuzzis (two on the _Classica_). The second pool is inlaid with ceramic tiles; suspended above it is another Susumu moving sculpture in red metal, which changes shape when it is moved by the wind.

The Carcalla Spa on the _Classica_ has floor-to-ceiling windows providing views of the sea while exercising. _Romantica's_ spa, reduced in size, was relocated along the sides of the stack. In addition to weights, lifecycles, and treadmills, the spa has sauna, steam, and massage rooms, and a beauty salon offering personalized programs and combination packages for hair and body treatment, from $99–299.

A partial deck above the swimming pools has a jogging track and open spaces for sunning. An area beneath the Divi Disco, which is cantilevered above the deck, makes a great hideaway—for those who find it—for sunning or snoozing in stylish cabana chairs with high rattan hoods.

CHILDREN'S FACILITIES Costa Kids, a year-round program available on Caribbean and European cruises, offers daily activities geared to two age groups: Costa Kids Club for ages 5–12 and Costa Teens Club for ages 13–17. A full-time youth counselor is available on each ship year-round; additional counselors are added when there are more than 12 children on a cruise and on holiday sailings.

Activities at the Youth Center include Nintendo competitions, bridge and galley tours, arts and crafts, a scavenger hunt, Italian language lessons, bingo, board games, captain's Coke-tail and pizza parties, ice cream socials, face painting, cartoons, and movies. The _Classica_ also has a teen center. At sea, Costa Kids Club hours are 9:30–11:30 A.M., 2–5 P.M., and 8–10 P.M. The hours may vary depending on itinerary and ports of call.

European cruises have three clubs: Baby Club for ages 3–6; Junior Club, ages 7–12, and Teens Club, ages 13–17. The Baby Club offers a fables and tales hour, handcrafts, games, and ice cream parties; Junior Club has aerobics, puppet theatre, mini-olympics, and team treasure hunts; Teens Club offers sports and fitness programs, guitar lessons, video show productions, a rock-and-roll hour, and more.

In Europe, baby-sitting service for ages 3–6 is available at no charge on *CostaClassica*, *CostaRomantica*, *CostaAllegra*, and *CostaMarina*. On Caribbean cruises, there is a charge of $8 per evening for one child and $10 for two, and the service is subject to staff availability.

SHORE EXCURSIONS   *CostaRomantica* Caribbean cruises are port-heavy, classic itineraries to the most frequented islands of the region. The line offers standard, off-the-shelf excursions at slightly higher prices than their competition; brochures with prices are available.

On the *Romantica*'s Eastern Caribbean itinerary, the ship does not arrive in San Juan until evening, when shops are closed and only night-club tours are available. Generally, these tours are of poor quality and not worth the price, but if this is your first visit to San Juan, it is probably the best way to sample some of its nightlife, which is terrific.

The *Romantica* stops at Serena Cay where Costa developed facilities for a fun day at the beach with games and water sports. Alternatively, you can take an optional tour to Casa de Campo, one of the Caribbean's largest resorts with excellent facilities. The ship sells excursions for tennis, horseback riding, and golf there. The golf package is expensive but the Peter Dye twin courses are ranked among the best in the world. The line also offers a deep-sea fishing trip (Dominican waters are considered among the best fishing waters in the Caribbean) and a scuba and snorkeling program in selected Caribbean ports.

Generally in Europe, depending on the ships and their itineraries, Costa's shore excursions are as varied as her cruises. Excursions range from a walk to a glacier in Norway to a trip to the pyramids in Egypt. For most locations, only one or two tours are described in the brochures and no prices are listed, making it difficult to plan. The itineraries are port-intensive, with rarely more than one or two days at sea in a week's cruise.

POSTSCRIPT   On the last night of the cruise, passengers are asked to place their luggage outside their cabin doors by 10 P.M., which is a convenience only for the ship's crew and an unnecessary inconvenience for passengers, especially those on late seating. A midnight deadline is standard; ask your steward for guidance.

For those considering two consecutive cruises, for example, the one-week Eastern Caribbean cruise followed by a Western Caribbean trip, the menus and entertainment are rotated on a seven-day basis, and therefore, repeated the second week.

Whether in Europe or the Caribbean, the ships make seemingly endless announcements in several languages, beginning at 8 A.M. on the days the ships are in port. Since 95 percent of this information is posted in the daily agenda, the constant intrusion would seem to be unnecessary and detracts from the appeal of the cruises.

CostaRomantica and *CostaClassica* were built to serve both Americans and Europeans but that might be an impossible goal. Dividing their time between the Caribbean in winter and Europe in the summer has been a logical solution. (It's also a financially prudent one; in Europe in summer, the line can charge higher prices and, as yet, the pressure to discount has not spread to Europe.) The split personality has clearly changed Costa's product. As long as you know this from the outset, you should have an enjoyable cruise. If you take advantage of Costa's frequent promotional fares, you will get good value, too. Music lovers might want to ask about the special "Fiesta Magnifica" cruises featuring performances by well-known Italian singers on *CostaRomantica*, which Costa added in 1997 for the first time.

CostaAllegra / CostaMarina

	Quality Rating	Value Rating
CostaAllegra	⑤	C
CostaMarina	⑤	C

Registry: Liberia	Length: 613/572 feet	Beam: 84 feet
Cabins: 405/383	Draft: 27 feet	Speed: 22/19 knots
Maximum Passengers:	Passenger Decks: 8	Elevators: 4
1,066/1,026	Crew: 450/385	Space Ratio: 37/32

THE SHIPS Built from a freighter hull, *CostaAllegra* is an unusual-looking cruise ship from its bow to its cutaway stern that is almost all glass. Indeed, the elaborate use of glass, allowing natural light to stream through the ship, gives it an open, airy feeling from the floor-to-ceiling windows of the dining room to the glass walls and transparent dome over the disco and spa.

Not the smallest of the fleet, but smaller than Costa's newest duo and with a more intimate ambience, *CostaAllegra* is distinctively contemporary Italian in the design and decor, though not as radical as the *CostaClassica* and in some ways more interesting. Here, glass and mirrors combined with water have been used to create visual effects that enliven the ship's interior.

For example, the pool deck has a long, glass-bottom "canal" for water to flow from the whirlpool to the swimming pool. On the deck below refracted light ripples through the glass ceiling of the elegant Murano Bar and the glass atrium. Further visual interest is created from the integration of art in the ship's layout. The eight passenger decks are named for impressionist artists—from the top, Manet, Rousseau, Degas, Modigliani, Lautrec, Gauguin, and van Gogh. Each level has reproductions and stylized murals taken from the artist's work. Marble, too, is used but more sparingly than on the *Classica* or *Romantica*.

The *CostaMarina*, a former cargo liner built in 1969, is similar to the *Allegra* in many ways, starting with its odd profile with her glass-walled stern capped by a dome, and the easily recognized cluster of upright yellow stacks with the big Costa "C" on them. Completely rebuilt by Costa in 1990, *CostaMarina* was designed by the *Allegra's* architect, Guido Canali, and has his signature use of glass and water to reflect and flood the ship in light.

The *CostaMarina* also has a three-deck glass-walled atrium located aft and a glass-domed roof above the Galaxy nightclub. Its waterfall cascades over a slanted glass wall from the Sports Deck to the Laguna Deck and empties into a very small swimming pool with two Jacuzzis. Underwater glimpses of the pool can be seen through portholes in the Casino Lounge on the Marina Deck below.

The ships' layouts are easy to follow. Most of the public rooms are on the top three decks, while cabins are on the lower three as well as the center deck, which they share with the dining room. Unlike the *Allegra* or any other ship at the time she debuted, the *CostaMarina* has an escalator, the first on a cruise ship. It takes passengers from the Marina Deck to the dining room, one flight below.

On the *Allegra*, passengers arrive on the Lautrec Deck, directly into a large, three-deck atrium lobby, which during the day is bathed in sunlight from a skylight that reflects on a tall, ultramodern glass sculpture that dominates the space. The walls of the atrium are covered with hand-painted watercolors of the Commedia dell'Arte, depicting a visual history of theatre in Italy.

The *Allegra's* modest size allows for fewer lounges and bars than her bigger sisters, but enough to provide the entertainment and activities of a modern cruise. On the Degas Deck, a show lounge anchors the forward end and a nightclub the stern. In between is the casino, some elegant shops around the Piazzetta Allegra with a patisserie and bar, the light-filled Murano Bar, a card room, and a handsome, little-used library with only a few books.

One flight up, the Rousseau Deck has suites at the bow and a swimming pool with a waterfall and bar, the Yacht Club Buffet, and the Crystal Club under the dramatic glass geodesic dome that is easily spotted in the ship's profile. The floor-to-ceiling windows make it a popular observation lounge by day and a lively disco at night.

The top deck accommodates a greenery-filled spa behind the bridge, plus a second level with a solarium, spa treatment rooms, children's center, and a jogging track along the swimming pool's overlook. The ship also has a chapel and meeting room.

COSTAALLEGRA ITINERARIES May–October, 7–13-day cruises in Europe; in May, Northern Europe and Baltic; in June, Iceland, North Cape; June, July: Norwegian fjords; May, July, August: Baltic, Russia; September: positioning cruise, Amsterdam to Genoa; September, October: Spain to Portugal.

- *November–April, Allegra* winters in the Eastern Caribbean. The cruises are sold in Europe, primarily to Europeans.

Home Port Genoa.
Port Charges In Europe, $140–160.

COSTAMARINA ITINERARIES May–September, 7–11-day cruises in Europe. In May, nine days, Genoa to Amsterdam; June–September, seven days, Baltic, Russia, and Norwegian fjords; September, ten-night positioning cruise, Copenhagen to Genoa.

- *December–April: Marina's* winter South American cruises are sold only in Europe.

Home Port Genoa.
Port Charges $150–175.

CABINS The *CostaAllegra* has 14 categories of cabins with almost as many inside rooms as outside. *CostaMarina* has eight categories with more inside cabins than outside ones—unusual for new ships. All cabins are on the lower four decks except for eight suites and eight inside cabins designated as wheelchair accessible, which are located on a higher deck. Likewise, the *Allegra* has eight cabins for wheelchairs with ramp access and wide bathroom doors. On both ships these special cabins have bathrooms with grab bars.

The cabins are not as large as those on Costa's newer ships, but they are well designed and comfortable with pleasant decor and ample drawer and closet space. All have twin beds, desk and dresser, phone, safe, television/radio, hair dryer, bathroom with shower, and natural light from oversized portholes.

Allegra's 13 suites are on the Rousseau Deck forward, with the three grand suites just under the bridge at the bow, enjoying the same view as the captain. They have a separate living room and bedroom, a second smaller bedroom, marble bath with Jacuzzi tub, and separate shower. The ten slightly smaller suites have a sitting area with sofa and chairs, Jacuzzi tub and showers, as well as a veranda. *Marina's* eight suites have bathrooms with tubs and verandas and are tastefully furnished in deep blue against pale wood and white walls with contemporary art.

Cabin service repeatedly gets high marks as efficient and attentive. The room service menu even has pizza in the evening.

CostaAllegra *Specifications*   187 inside cabins, 205 outside; 13 suites. Standard dimensions are 146–160 square feet. Grand suites with sitting area and bar. 378 with twin beds (268 convertible to doubles); 116 third and fourth persons; 6 singles; 8 equipped for disabled.

CostaMarina *Specifications*   203 inside cabins, 183 outside. Standard dimensions are 140–170 square feet. 283 with twin beds; 80 double/king; 8 suites; 15 three/four persons; 14 singles.

DINING   The *CostaAllegra's* Montmarte Restaurant, resembling an elegant European restaurant, is dressed in textured fabrics of gray on burgundy lacquered chairs. Walls with huge portholes frame the sides and panels of glass at the stern flood the room with light. Tables seating four to eight are set about the room, divided by glass panels and live greenery, and a baby grand piano provides background music. The *CostaMarina's* spacious, attractive Crystal Restaurant is also at the stern with windows on three sides to enjoy views of the sea and scenery. Both ships' restaurants offer two seatings and a midnight buffet.

The cuisine is predominantly Italian and served in a European style with frequent tableside preparations and beautiful presentation. The pasta, which is prepared fresh, is always a favorite and always on the menu for lunch and dinner, along with a wide variety of other continental selections. The Pasta Festival, a poolside feast on the day at sea, is an-all-you-can-eat pasta lover's dream with a half dozen or more different pastas being made continuously. Dinner menus are similar to those of other Costa ships, offering about the same number of choices—ample but not extravagant.

Unlike the criticism which greeted the *Classica* and *Romantica*, the breakfast and lunch buffets in the *Allegra*'s indoor/outdoor Yacht Club seem to have gotten it right with good food and lots of variety. The attractive facility has wicker chairs with blue-striped cushions, wooden tables inlaid with blue panels, and miniature replicas of old sailing ships to carry out its nautical theme. Afternoon tea is served and cabin service is available from a limited menu.

SERVICE The *CostaAllegra* has Italian officers, dining room supervisors, and head waiters, but a mix of nationalities throughout the ship and among the cabin crew. All get good reviews for friendly, attentive, and efficient service.

FACILITIES AND ENTERTAINMENT Activities, sports, and entertainment are not as elaborate on the *CostaAllegra* and *CostaMarina* in Europe as on Costa's ships in the Caribbean, and given the port-intensive nature of its European itineraries and largely European mix of its passengers (who are more attuned to friendship and conversation), they do not need to be.

But certainly enough goes on during the day and evening for those who prefer their shipboard activity at a relaxing pace with most of the standards, such as bingo, fashion show, card and parlor games, and poolside fun. The evening offers low-key shows in the showroom and music for dancing in several lounges and the disco. Quality varies but in general the individual performers and the ship's cruise staff are most popular.

Shops, meeting rooms, a library, a card room, and hairdressers are also on board. Supervised children's activities are available as on other Costa ships.

SPORTS, FITNESS, AND BEAUTY In addition to the pool and whirlpool, *Allegra* has an open-to-the-sun jogging track on the top deck and the spa has exercise equipment—each in its own little garden environment with light streaming in from the glass ceiling overhead. There are sauna, steam room, massage, beauty salon, barber shop, and beauty treatment rooms. There is a charge for beauty treatments but none for the use of exercise equipment. The *Marina* spa and fitness center are likewise on the top deck with similar facilities, but it does not have a jogging track and the deck space is more limited.

POSTSCRIPT When the *CostaAllegra* was introduced, Costa was still finding its way back to the right road from the wrong turn it had taken with its ill-fated "Euroluxe" idea and the less-than-successful introduction of the *CostaClassica*. The *CostaAllegra*, perhaps because she is smaller with a friendly and lively *ambiente*, seems to have helped the line's reputation. The *CostaAllegra* gets consistently good reviews for food and service.

Passengers adverse to smoking should note that areas are designated as smoking or nonsmoking on the ship, but some European passengers flout the restriction—defiantly. Readers considering a cruise on the *CostaAllegra* or *CostaMarina*, or any Costa ship for that matter, should review the entire section on Costa Cruises to be familiar with the line's services and facilities.

CostaVictoria

	Quality Rating	**Value Rating**
CostaVictoria	❹	D

Registry: Liberia	Length: 824 feet	Beam: 105.5 feet
Cabins: 973	Draft: 19.5 feet	Speed: 23 knots
Maximum Passengers: 2,250	Passenger Decks: 12	Elevators: 12
	Crew: 800	Space Ratio: 38.5

THE SHIP Costa's newest ship, which made her debut in June 1996, is the line's first megaship. Designed by well-known naval architect Robert Tillberg, she is not only the largest passenger liner built in Germany, but she is also the largest catering to the European market. Yet, despite her size, she was designed with a shallow draft and exceptional maneuverability and can call on smaller ports of call as well as pass through the Panama and Suez Canals.

Ultra modern and sophisticated, *CostaVictoria* emulates the style set by *CostaClassica* and *CostaRomantica*, but is larger and carries almost a third more passengers. The extra size allows for some dramatic designs and more choices in dining and entertainment.

The main entrance, the circular Planetarium Atrium, is one of two atria and the ship's focal point. It spans seven decks and has four glass elevators connecting the main lobby with the pool deck above. It is capped by a large glass dome that allows sunlight to penetrate the ship, reflecting off the colored glass sculpture by Milan artist Gianfranco Pardi, on the lowest level (Deck 5). Deck 5 also has the purser's office, shore excursion desk, and a piano bar. All but 1 of the 12 passenger decks are named after Italian operas.

The most dramatic room of all is the Concorde Plaza, an observation lounge at the bow. It spans four decks and has a floor-to-ceiling glass wall providing spectacular ocean views. The area is designed as an Italian piazza, a signature feature found on all Costa ships. Opposite the expanse of windows is a marble dance floor adjoined to a center stage; its backdrop is a waterfall inspired by Leonardo Da Vinci's drawings of the moon eclipsing the sun. The plaza is decorated in shades of blue, silver, and gold; all colors inspired by the sun, the moon, and the stars. The lounge serves as an elegant area for socializing, special shipboard events, and evening entertainment, including cabaret shows, games, bingo, and port lectures.

Other public rooms include a disco, a children's playroom, teen's club, an arcade of boutiques, a library, card room, chapel, and a trio of conference rooms equipped with audio and video, overhead, and computer projections.

ITINERARIES In winter, the *CostaVictoria* sails from Ft. Lauderdale, every Sunday on alternating seven-night itineraries to the Eastern and Western Caribbean. The Eastern one visits San Juan, St. Thomas/St. John, Serena Cay/Casa de Campo, and Nassau; the Western one goes to Key West, Playa del Carmen, Cozumel, Ocho Rios, and Grand Cayman. Both have two days at sea. At Serena Cay, only passengers participating in the ship's shore excursion may disembark at Casa de Campo; and likewise, at Playa del Carmen.

- *In late March*, she makes a 16-night eastbound transatlantic voyage to Genoa. From spring–fall she cruises on seven-night eastern Mediterranean cruises from Venice.

Home Ports Ft. Lauderdale; Venice.
Port Charges n.a.

CABINS The majority of cabins are located on the upper decks. Sixty percent are outside cabins with a porthole or large square window. The cabins are small compared to those on the *Classica* and *Romantica* and none have private balconies. *CostaVictoria* is the line's first ship to have a minibar, safe, hair dryer, and interactive television in every cabin category.

Standard cabins range from 120–150 square feet. All have direct dial telephones and are fitted with sliding doors that separate the living area from the bathroom. The bathrooms are circular in design, with rounded shower stalls and vanity areas. The six top suites and 14 mini-suites, located forward on the pool and sports decks, are decorated in Laura Ashley fabrics and trimmed in pearwood. They have sitting areas, whirlpool baths, walk-in closets, and queen beds, plus one upper berth and a murphy bed, thus accommodating up to four people. Butler service is provided.

The *CostaVictoria* is equipped with a unique "fan coil" system that allows each cabin to be refreshed with its own recycled air or with air coming from outside the vessel. In this way, the air of cabins of smoking passengers will not be mixed with the air of nonsmokers' cabins.

Specifications   386 inside, 578 outside; 20 suites; 6 wheelchair accessible.

DINING   *CostaVictoria* is the first of Costa's vessels to have two dining rooms: Fantasia Restaurant, located aft, and Sinfonia Restaurant, amidship. Both are decorated with marble and pine walls with glass chandeliers by Murano, famous Italian glass blowers. Both restaurants have large picture windows that allow for port and sea views. Scenic murals, as in the dining rooms on the *Romantica* and *Classica*, transform the windows from ocean views by day to Italian scenes by night. Unfortunately, the food cannot go through the same transformation. It's not up to the standard of the *Romantica* and *Classica*.

The multipurpose Tavernetta Lounge, a glass-enclosed area with a bar, lively entertainment, and dancing, doubles as an alternative restaurant at no extra charge; reservations are required. The walls are decorated with ten oil paintings of earlier Costa passenger ships by Bermuda-based marine artist Stephen Card.

For informal dining, the ship has an indoor/outdoor buffet for breakfast and lunch. Bolero, the indoor buffet, is surrounded by glass windows that overlook the water, furnished with rattan chairs around light marble tables on teak wood floors, and decorated in light colors. The outdoor Terraza Café, similar to one on *Classica* but much larger, is protected by a large white conopy, said to be the largest of its kind, made by Canobbio, an Italian firm specializing in circus tents and sports arena coverings. Other dining options include two buffets, a pizzeria, ice cream bar, and grill.

FACILITIES AND ENTERTAINMENT   The two-deck Festival Show Lounge is decorated in rich reds with Tivoli lights twinkling in the ceiling. The stage can be raised up to three feet for variety and large production shows or lowered for dancing. Sight lines for those in the rear are poor.

The Grand Bar Orpheus, with mirrored columns and a marble-topped bar trimmed in rare, blue Brazilian marble, is a popular spot for cocktails and after-dinner espresso and cappuccino. It is connected by a curved glass stairway to the big, bright Monte Carlo Casino one deck above. Just outside the casino is Capriccio Lounge, an intimate piano bar whose walls are adorned with floor to ceiling mosaics that tell a tale. They were created by Italian painter Emilio Tadini.

The cruises feature theme nights, such as Notte Romantica, the lively Festa Italiana, and the rollicking Roman Bacchanal.

SPORTS, FITNESS, AND BEAUTY   At the top of the ship is the Solarium, a viewing and sunning area with large steel pipes that give off continuous mists of cold water. There are two outdoor pools surrounded by six whirlpools and two shuffleboard courts. A special feature on this deck is the Wimbledon Tennis Court, a miniature tennis court utilizing smaller racquets and balls. It can be converted into a basketball or volleyball court.

The Pompeii Spa has an indoor swimming pool adorned with a large mosaic at its center. It is surrounded by Roman columns in mosaic tile and teak wood lounge chairs. The spa has a Turkish bath, saunas, massage, Thalassic therapy, hydrotherapy, and other beauty treatment rooms. A 1,312-foot jogging track connects the spa to the gymnasium, which is equipped with weight training equipment and an aerobics room. This is the first ship to carry products from Tuscany's chic Terme di Saturnia. There is a beauty salon.

CHILDREN'S FACILITIES   The Peter Pan's Children Club is the center for children's activities. There is a disco and teen's club with a dance floor, video games, four computer stations, and a large television monitor. The room can also be used as a mini-theatre.

POSTSCRIPT   *CostaVictoria* is in the style of Costa's newest fleet, sporting modern Italian design and workmanship. But her cabins are small compared to the older ships. This, combined with the lack of cabins with verandas—a strong trend on all new ships—leaves one wondering how she will fare in the fiercely competitive Caribbean market where she winters. If you are a longtime Costa fan and go expecting this ship to be like the *CostaRomantica*, or to have the *ambiente* of the

CostaRiviera when she sailed in North America, you will be disappointed. It's a different product.

COSTA CRUISE LINES EUROPEAN FLEET

CostaRiviera   Costa Cruise Lines' oldest vessel is marketed primarily toward Europeans in Europe. A popular ship familiar to Costa fans in North America for more than a decade, helping to define "Cruising Italian Style," *CostaRiviera* was seconded to the ill-fated American Family Cruises and modified to serve as its first ship. After that line's demise, the ship was returned to Costa service in Europe. She now sails from Venice, May–November, on seven-day cruises to Greece and the Eastern Mediterranean, and from November–March, she goes west on 10- and 11-night cruises to the Canary Islands, giving Costa a program of Mediterranean cruises year-round. Although the ship was renovated after it was returned to Costa service in 1994, some of the facilities that were added for children by American Family Cruises were retained, enhancing the ship's attractiveness for families with children. Further renovations more recently installed new carpeting, bedding, full-length mirrors, and television in all cabins.

CostaPlaya   (formerly *Pearl of Scandinavia*) sails from the Dominican Republic. The cruises are sold only in Europe. Part of the agreement when Costa was bought by Carnival/Airtour was to remove the ship from the Costa fleet. No word on its ultimate disposition had been announced at press time.

CRYSTAL CRUISES

2121 Avenue of the Stars, Los Angeles, CA 90067
(310) 785-9300; fax (310) 785-3891

TYPE OF SHIPS   Modern, luxury superliners.

TYPE OF CRUISE   Modern version of glamorous, traditional cruising with a touch of California glitz, for upscale, sophisticated travelers.

CRUISE LINE'S STRENGTHS
- impeccable service
- beautifully designed ships
- large number of cabins with verandas
- alternative restaurants
- globe-roaming itineraries

CRUISE LINE'S SHORTCOMINGS
- two sittings in main dining room
- some cabins with restricted views
- limited closet space; some small bathrooms
- inadequate seating capacity in alternative restaurants

FELLOW PASSENGERS   Professional, retired or semiretired, experienced travelers, likely to be owners, entrepreneurs, and top-level executives rather than their staffs, 45–70 in age. Typical passenger is an affluent, active, fashion-conscious, friendly 55–60-year-old couple or mature single.

Recommended For   Travelers who care about quality and appreciate style with a bit of flash, and who want the facilities of a large ship; urbane first-time cruisers who can afford it.

Not Recommended For   Anyone not comfortable in a tony, sophisticated ambience.

CRUISE AREAS AND SEASONS   Caribbean, Mexico, Panama Canal in fall, winter, and spring; South America, China/Orient, and Asia in fall,

314

winter; World Cruise in winter; Europe and Alaska in summer; and South Pacific in autumn.

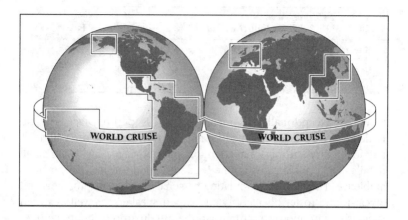

THE LINE Two years before its first ship made its debut in 1990, Crystal Cruises promised that it would return the golden age qualities of the grand oceanliners, with their elegance and personalized service, to modern cruises for the "upscale mass" market—a notion that appeared to be an inconsistency in terms. The new line not only delivered on its promise, but *Crystal Harmony*, its first ship, turned out to be even better than its advanced billing. Quickly it become the ship by which others in its class—or aspiring to be in its class—were measured.

And therein lies the tale. There were no other ships in its class. Crystal Cruises created a niche all its own: *Crystal Harmony* is the size of most superliners, but it carries one-third less passengers. (Some comparable-size ships carry double the number of passengers.) As a result, *Crystal Harmony* offers the best of all possible worlds—the facilities of a large ship with the personalized service of a small vessel, and with the spaciousness that even some of the most luxurious ships cannot match.

The *Crystal Harmony* was built in Japan by Mitsubishi Heavy Industries, a subsidiary of Nippon Yusen Kaisha, the Japanese shipbuilding giant known for its technologically advanced ships and the owner of California-based Crystal Cruises.

On the technical side, the ship incorporates state-of-the-art engines, radar, and navigational equipment. The refrigeration system, whose unique design is a closely held secret of the owning company, maintains fish, fruits, and vegetables in an almost fresh state for long periods at a time. For passengers, the luxurious vessel offers comfort and an array of amenities that go far beyond the norm. Ironically, *Crystal Symphony*, a twin of *Crystal Harmony*, was built in Finland, rather than Japan for cost-saving reasons.

The Fleet	Built/Renovated	Tonnage	Passengers
Crystal Harmony	1990	49,400	940
Crystal Symphony	1995	51,044	940

STYLE   Exceptionally spacious ships with superliner facilities and Rodeo Drive style are designed for affluent travelers who are willing to pay for luxury and personal attention and appreciate quality in small details. The cruises provide fine food and good service in a gracious ambience. They feature stimulating personal enrichment programs and a year-round roster of celebrity and expert speakers, as well as varied itineraries with more structure than the ultraluxurious, boutique lines but less formality than some older luxury ships. Generally, itineraries include more days at sea than is the norm so that passengers have time to enjoy fully the luxury and pampering that Crystal offers—a feature appreciated most by experienced cruisers.

DISTINCTIVE FEATURES   Few lines provide as many thoughtful features as does Crystal. These include two specialty restaurants at no additional cost; gentlemen hosts to dance and socialize with women traveling alone; close-captioned television for the hearing-impaired; free self-service laundry room on each deck; business service center with audiovisual equipment, fax machines, and other office equipment, secretarial and translation services; take-out laptop computers; air-conditioned tenders with toilets.

RATES

Highest Per Diem	Lowest Per Diem	Average Per Diem
$835	$303	$493

The above per diems are calculated from the cruise line's nondiscounted *cruise-only* fares on standard accommodations. What you will actually pay *should* be *substantially* less (see Part One, How to Get the Best Deal on a Cruise). Per diems vary by season, by cabin location, and by cruise areas.

Special Fares and Discounts   Crystal has an advance purchase discount program that ranges from 10–30 percent, depending on the cruise, and may be used with other promotional rates and Crystal Society savings.

- Third Passenger: Minimum fare for cruise.
- Children's Fare: Under 12, half fare when with two full-paying adults.
- Single Supplement: Crystal's single's fare, introduced in 1996, begins at 115 percent of the double occupancy rate for the lowest categories and is applicable to advance-purchase discount rate.

Packages
- Air/Sea: Yes.
- Others: Honeymoon.
- Pre/Post: Yes.

Past Passengers   Crystal Society, the past passenger club, has been revamped. Beginning in 1998, the program offers a progressive set of amenities based on an incremental number of cruises. In other words, the more often you cruise, the richer the rewards. Some of the benefits are complementary business and first-class air upgrades; confirmed stateroom and penthouse upgrades; shipboard credits from $200 to $800 per couple; free cruises in staterooms and penthouses, limosine transfers, prepaid gratuities, and private luncheon and dinner parties.

Passengers are automatically enrolled after their first Crystal cruise and receive members-only financial bonuses with every subsequent cruise. The higher reward levels—5–30 cruises, 50, 70, and 100 cruises—are given special privileges ranging from stateroom and air upgrades to free two-week cruises in a penthouse. All members receive an exclusive 5 percent savings off cruise fares, an additional 5 percent savings for reservations made while on a cruise, priority check-in at the pier, a Crystal Society travel bag, membership card, recognition pin, a quarterly newsletter, and, beginning with the tenth cruise, a complimentary bottle of wine and fresh flowers on every cruise. In addition to the annual President's cruise, several cruises are designated as Crystal Society Sailings and feature a personal escort, exclusive special events, and special gifts.

THE LAST WORD   Crystal Cruises identified a market of experienced travelers (but not necessarily experienced cruise passengers) who were not being served by other cruise lines. With the *Crystal Harmony*, the line created a new cruise product that set new standards of luxury in service and surroundings for large ships and has followed it up with the even more luxurious *Crystal Symphony*. For those who can afford the cruises, they will get quality all the way. And when you compare Crystal's quality and extra amenities to other lines in the same price bracket, you will find Crystal's cruises are among cruising's best value.

CRYSTAL SHIPS STANDARD FEATURES

Officers Norwegian and Japanese.

Staffs Dining/European; Cabin/International; Cruise/American.

Dining Facilities One main dining room, two seatings for three meals with open seating for breakfast and lunch; buffet breakfast and lunch on Lido Deck; alternative dinner restaurants; midnight buffet; tea.

Special Diets Requests should be made when reservations confirmed.

Room Service 24-hour menu; butler service on Penthouse Deck.

Dress Code Casual by day; casually elegant in the evening with two formal evenings per week of cruising.

Cabin Amenities Direct-dial phone with voice mail, television with CNN and ESPN, VCR; stocked minibar; safe; bathroom with tub, two hair dryers, robes, suites with marble bathrooms and whirlpool tubs.

Electrical Outlets 110/220 AC.

Wheelchair Access Four on *Harmony*; seven on *Symphony*.

Recreation and Entertainment Casino, disco, nightclub, show lounge, piano bar, coffee/wine bar, cinema/theatre, six lounges, observation lounge, card/meeting room, video game room, smoking room. Guest lecturers, area specialists, celebrities. Bingo, bridge, dancing, and crafts classes.

Sports and Other Activities Two outdoor swimming pools, one with retractable roof, two Jacuzzis, teak deck for walking/jogging, paddle tennis, golf clinics and practice corner, deck and pool games.

Beauty and Fitness See text.

Other Facilities Boutiques, concierge, hospital, laundry/dry cleaning, valet service, laundrettes, video camera rentals, meeting facilities, business service center.

Children's Facilities Playroom, baby-sitters, youth programs.

Theme Cruises Yes.

Smoking Public/dining rooms nonsmoking except in designated areas.

Crystal Suggested Tipping Per person per day, cabin stewardess, $3.50; waiter, $3.50; busboy, $2. $5 per person per meal in alternative restaurants; 15 percent added to bar bills.

Credit Cards For cruise payment and on-board charges, all major credit cards. Aboard ship, charge system, and bill settled at the end of the cruise.

Crystal Harmony / Crystal Symphony

	Quality Rating	Value Rating
Crystal Harmony	⑩	C
Crystal Symphony	⑩	C

Registry: Bahamas	Length: 781/791 feet	Beam: 97/99 feet
Cabins: 480	Draft: 25 feet	Speed: 22 knots
Maximum Passengers: 1,010	Passenger Decks: 8	Elevators: 9
	Crew: 545	Space Ratio: 52.6/54.3

THE SHIPS Gleaming white inside and out, *Crystal Harmony* is a symphony of Japanese technology and artistry, European service and tradition, and American flair for fun and entertainment. The elegance is in its simplicity, clean lines, and extraordinary attention to details.

Its spaciousness—one of the highest ratios of passenger-to-space of any ship afloat—quality, and luxury are evident from the moment you step on the ship. The decor has a bit of glitz but is always in good taste. It was created by Swedish, Italian, and British design teams and swayed by Japanese artistic understatement. A harmony of quiet colors and quality furnishings, it sets fine fabrics and textures against marble and woods accented with brass and stainless steel. A generous use of glass lightens the interiors and gives them an airy ambience.

Passengers' introduction to the ship is the Crystal Plaza, an atrium lobby with cascades of crystal (it's actually lucite) lights, stairways, and railings that seem to float in space. They are outlined with brass fixtures against white marble walls, and here and there are accents of deep green suede, fresh greenery, hand-cut glass sculpture, and a waterfall. To one side is a crystal—what else—piano that seems to sum up the feeling of opulence the ship conveys. The beautiful lady has many lounges for many purposes and moods. The prettiest room and one of the most handsome lounges on the high seas is the Palm Court, an airy space in white and mint green with graceful palms under skylights. It takes on the atmosphere of a traditional palm court in the afternoon for tea when the tables are laid with crisp linens and gleaming silver and a harpist strums in the background. Forward of the Palm Court is the fabulous Vista Lounge, a trilevel observation lounge with white leather chairs on sky blue carpets and floor-to-ceiling windows that stretch around a 270° view.

Crystal Symphony, which was introduced in May 1995, is essentially a twin of the *Crystal Harmony* with alterations that are improvements on the first ship. Among the enhancements, the Crystal Cove Lounge, Crystal Plaza, and Lido Cafe have been doubled in size; the casino and shopping arcade expanded; and video room added.

In other changes, a spiral waterfall highlights *Symphony's* atrium and its basic color scheme is beige and light green, in place of *Harmony's* blue.

One of the most noticeable—but least successful—alterations is the popular Palm Court, which has been moved forward, enlarged, and combined with the Observation Lounge, rather than having them as separate lounges as on the *Harmony*. The *Harmony's* Palm Court wins hands down.

Other important changes are in the cabins—all outside and about a third more cabins have verandas than on the *Harmony*—and all with larger, better-designed bathrooms. The two alternative restaurants have new locations; both were enlarged.

HARMONY ITINERARIES   January–May, 6–15 days, on a wide variety of cruises, from Los Angeles and Acapulco via the Panama Canal to Barbados, New Orleans, or San Juan, with a break in late January and February for three South American cruises between Barbados and Buenos Aires.

- *May–September*, Alaska, 6–11 days, from Los Angeles and Vancouver to Anchorage; September to November, 8–19 days, crossing to the Orient via Hawaii, Japan, and Hong Kong to Sydney; and November–January, 11–14 days, Australia, New Zealand, and the South Pacific, returning in December via Hawaii to Acapulco.

Home Ports   Los Angeles, Barbados, and other ports, varying with season and itineraries.

Port Charges $50–195, depending on area and cruise duration.

SYMPHONY ITINERARIES   11–101 days, on around-the-world, Europe, and Panama Canal/Caribbean cruises.

- *In September and October*, the *Symphony* makes her debut on four ten-day fall foliage cruises of New England/Canada from New York, followed by December and January cruises from Los Angeles to Barbados and Ft. Lauderdale via the Panama Canal.

- *Her world cruise* departs Los Angeles in mid-January and sails west, taking a new southern hemisphere route. It is available in seven segments of 11–19 days, via Hawaii to New Zealand and Australia, followed by Hong Kong to Singapore via Vietnam, and on to India, the Suez Canal, and Athens to London in late April.
- *From late April–November*, *Symphony* summers in Europe on 10–16-day cruises of the Mediterranean, Northern Europe, Baltic Sea, and Black Sea.

Home Ports   Los Angeles and other ports, depending on season and itinerary.

Port Charges $110–695, depending on cruise.

CABINS   Large, comfortable, and handsomely appointed with fine fabrics and high quality furnishings, the well-equipped cabins have sitting areas. Standard cabins have adequate closet and storage space, although some complain that hanging space is limited for long voyages. Early complaints about insufficient drawer space and small bathtubs have been corrected. Large down pillows and comforters on beds, plush robes, fluffy towels, fine toiletries, and a voice-mail facility on the direct-dial telephone reflect the line's attention to detail. All cabins have fresh flowers, two hair dryers, and television with CNN and ESPN.

More than half of all cabins have private verandas. Unfortunately, some cabins (Categories G, Horizon, and Promenade decks) have views obstructed by lifeboats. They are, however, noted in Crystal's cruise book as "limited" or "extremely limited" views and priced accordingly.

The ship's ultimate luxury is found on the all-suites Penthouse Deck, where a concierge is in attendance. Penthouse suites have large bedrooms and sitting areas and luxurious marble bathrooms with Jacuzzi bathtubs. The four most extravagant suites cover 948 square feet.

The posh suites are attended by four European-trained, white-gloved butlers and six Scandinavian stewardesses. The young men, dressed in formal attire (some will find this pretentious) are as competent as they are eager to serve. They will unpack your bags (and repack them at cruise end), arrange a party or a full dinner in your suite, and attend to other special requests. Nightly at cocktail time, they serve hors d'oeuvres and pour the drinks from your fully stocked bar. During a day at sea, all passengers are given a ship tour when they can visit all the different cabin categories—a useful sales gimmick for when you select the cabin for your next cruise! And should the impulse seize you to do just that, there is a "cruise consultant" on board to take your booking, normally, at a nicely discounted price—a practice many cruise lines now follow.

The *Symphony*'s standard cabins, roomier than on the first ship, have been improved. It would be hard to imagine more comfortable cruise ship cabins in a standard category. All are outside, and 278 cabins, or about a third more cabins than on the *Harmony*, have verandas with overall dimensions of 246 square feet. The other standard cabins cover 202 square feet and have large picture windows. All have a seating area with a loveseat. Some of the suites on Penthouse Deck have slightly different arrangements than those on her sister ship, allowing for larger closets. The *Symphony*'s bathrooms of standard cabins have been redesigned, enlarged, and greatly improved. All have two sinks in a six-foot counter, bathtubs as well as showers, and larger closets with more hanging and drawer space. All 64 Penthouse Deck suites have verandas.

Harmony *Specifications* 19 inside cabins, 461 outside; 198 with veranda. Standard dimensions are 196 square feet. 62 penthouse suites with verandas measuring 360 or 492 square feet. No singles. All twins convert to queens or kings.

Symphony *Specifications* 480 outside cabins, including 64 penthouse suites with verandas and 278 deluxe cabins (246 square feet) with verandas; 138 deluxe (202 square feet) no verandas; 7 wheelchair accessible.

DINING Super in quality and stunning in presentation, *Crystal Harmony*'s cuisine is one of its strongest features and on par with fine restaurants in New York and Los Angeles. It is served on fine china and tableware by waiters who are as polished as the silver.

The spacious peach and blue dining room with floor-to-ceiling windows and modern crystal chandeliers is elegant and well designed, providing for more space than usual between tables—a feature that helps to keep the noise level down. There are also a greater than normal number of tables for two.

Dinner menus, which are placed in cabins in advance, are greatly varied during the cruise. Typically, they include a choice of four appetizers, three soups, two salads, pasta, five entrees of fish, poultry, and meat, vegetables, and an array of desserts.

Perfect *Harmony* selections of lighter fare and low-salt, fat, and sugar choices are also available. The maître d'hôtel often asks passengers for their favorite dishes as the kitchen will prepare special requests with advance notice. The extensive wine list has over 150 varieties.

The *Symphony*'s dining room is spacious and attractive, perhaps slightly more subdued than the *Harmony*'s. On an early sailing, the kitchen did not seem to have its act together quite yet, but the problems that come with a new operation should be smoothed out quickly, especially now that Crystal has appointed as its executive corporate chef, Toni Neumeister, one of cruising's most celebrated chefs, who was formerly with Royal Viking Lines.

The ship's most innovative features—and a first for cruising—are the intimate, alternative dinner restaurants, Kyoto and Prego, available at no extra cost to all passengers, in addition to meal service in the main dining room. Prego features Italian fare; Kyoto serves Japanese specialties, presented in traditional manner, and other Asian cuisine. Each restaurant has its own kitchen where food is cooked to order. Reservations are required; be sure to make yours early because both are enormously popular.

The *Symphony's* alternative restaurants, Prego offering Italian cuisine and Jade Garden serving Chinese fare, are located on Deck 6 instead of Deck 11 as on the *Harmony*, giving passengers easier access to the restaurants and the entertainment areas on the same deck. Each has a separate entrance.

The *Symphony's* Prego, double the size of its counterpart on the *Harmony*, probably ranks as the Number One attraction on the ship. Handsomely decorated and meant to suggest Venice by the use of deep blue, red, and cream, the room has banquettes and high-back chairs around the tables for four and six. The Italian specialties are outstanding—so much so that the restaurant has a waiting list almost every night.

The Jade Garden, with a tiny water garden at the entrance, does not measure up to *Harmony's* Kyoto in decor, ambience, or cuisine. The restaurant's decor uses a white hard finish and bright lighting that seem more appropriate for a computer room than a dining room. The cuisine, heavier and oilier than Americans are accustomed to in Chinese food, cannot compare to the Japanese specialties served in Kyoto.

The level of service and cuisine in the dining room and alternative restaurants are meant to compensate for the lack of the single sitting dining room, which is traditional on luxury ships. (Diehards consider this Crystal's unforgivable sin.) In addition to their novelty, the alternative restaurants have a hidden charm: Even with lots of space to roam aboard ship, dining daily in the same surroundings on a long cruise can sometimes become boring. Having the two restaurants for a change of ambience and cuisine is a great bonus.

The indoor/outdoor Lido Cafe serves breakfast, midmorning bouillon, and lunch. The Bistro has coffee and pastries for late risers and wine and cheese during the day. Luncheon and themed buffets are often set up around the pool and are very popular. The Trident Bar, an extension of the Neptune Pool swim-up bar, offers hot dogs, hamburgers, and other poolside snacks, and there's a bar for ice cream and frozen yogurt. The Lido Cafe on the *Symphony* was one of the major improvements. By moving the alternative restaurants to their new location on Deck 6, there was space to double the size of its counterpart on the *Harmony* and add a second buffet counter, and, at the same time, connect the Lido Cafe to the aft deck for indoor/outdoor seating for breakfast and lunch.

A sumptuous tea is served daily in the pretty Palm Court, and weekly the Crystal Plaza is the setting for a dessert extravaganza set to Mozart. And should you still suffer hunger pains, your cabin attendant would have already replenished the fruit in the basket in your cabin and will bring you any item on the extensive room service menu. You also have the option of dining in your cabin with the meal being served course by course. Another popular corner is the attractive Bistro Cafe where snacks, coffees, teas, and desserts are served during the day. Charming French bistro prints that hang on the wall are reproduced on the pottery used in the Bistro. On several sailings, the cruise line features a wine and food festival with guest chefs and wine experts.

SERVICE   Both ships have among the highest crew-to-passenger ratios in cruising. The well-trained staff is young, cheerful, and eager to please, and service is thoroughly professional and consistently excellent throughout the ship. For the most part, the dining room staff are Italian, Spanish, and Portuguese; cabin attendants, Filipino; and the cruise and entertainment staff, American. A European-style concierge and purser service is available 24 hours a day.

FACILITIES AND ENTERTAINMENT   Cocktails in the Vista Lounge, the piano bar, or the wood-paneled Avenue Saloon (enlarged on the *Symphony*); one of the entertainment lounges with dance music; or a classical concert by a harpist or trio might precede dinner. A cabaret show with headliners in Club 2100, and two nightly full-scale, high-quality, Broadway-style productions in the Galaxy show lounge are offered in the evening. Local entertainers are often brought on board during the ship's stays in ports of call. One evening is a masquerade party.

The Starlite Club, which replaced the *Harmony*'s Club 2100 and disco, is one of *Symphony*'s most attractive lounges with blue and gold, art deco interiors. It is used for the captain's cocktail and past passenger parties, pre- and postdinner cocktails and dancing. In the late evening, it becomes the disco, depending on passenger preference during each sailing.

The Galaxy Lounge, the ship's main show lounge, offers an eclectic array of first-rate productions that might range from classical ballet to a Broadway revue. Crystal has its own production team, Gretchen Goertz and Kathy Orme, who create all the production shows including choreography and costume design and who are very original and very good. For the *Symphony*'s maiden season, the pair created two excellent productions: the *Symphony of Nations*, something of a tribute to the countries the cruise line visits, is a tour de force with costume changes representing about 40 countries around the world. *Some Enchanted Evening,* a new show, featuring the songs of Rodgers and Hammerstein, debuted on both ships in 1997.

Crystal Harmony boasts the first and only casino-at-sea operated by Caesar's Palace of Las Vegas. The casino (enlarged on *Symphony*) has Roman columns at the entrance and toga-clad dealers and offers blackjack, slots, and roulette. Among the papers sent to passengers prior to sailing is an application for credit at the casino.

ACTIVITIES AND DIVERSIONS   Cultural and destination-oriented lectures by experts, political figures, and diplomats on the region of the cruise are a regular afternoon or after-dinner feature. Card and other games are part of daytime activities along with dancing classes, golf clinics, and arts and crafts. The well-stocked library has videos as well as books. The Hollywood Theatre with high-definition video projection and hearing-aid headsets runs films each afternoon and evening, in addition to films and other programs on cabin television. For further diversion, there are the pricey temptations with familiar designer names in the pretty shops on the Avenue of the Stars.

SPORTS, FITNESS, AND BEAUTY   A lap pool has adjacent whirlpools and an indoor/outdoor swimming pool has a swim-up bar and a retractable roof for use during inclement weather. There is generous open deck and sunning space, along with Ping-Pong, shuffleboard, pool games, golf, and the only full-scale paddle tennis court at sea. A wraparound, unobstructed teak deck on Deck Seven is used for walking or jogging.

The large salon/spa on the top deck has ocean views, health club facilities with exercise equipment, aerobics and other exercise classes throughout the day conducted by an instructor, and separate steam rooms and saunas for men and women at no charge. You can also have a personally developed cuisine program. The salon offers an array of pricey body and facial treatments, from a 35-minute massage for $69, to a half-day Crystal Creation for $200, to a customized "weight loss" package of ten hours spread over three sessions, for $500.

CHILDREN'S FACILITIES Youth programs with counselors are provided only when the cruise line is informed in advance that a sizable number of children will be on board. Baby-sitting services can be arranged privately with crew members for about $5 per hour.

SHORE EXCURSIONS Shore excursions are sold on board, but certain ones can sometimes be purchased in advance. Details are in the shore excursion brochure sent to passengers prior to their cruise. Tours tend to be expensive, depending on the locale, and range mostly from $30–50 for half-day; $80–115 full day.

Efficient service in air-conditioned tenders in ports where tendering is available is a much appreciated amenity. The concierge and excursion desk are helpful in suggesting and arranging port programs for those who want to be on their own. Crystal provides good maps and information about each port of call.

POSTSCRIPT The two ships probably have enough differences that repeat passengers will have their favorite, but in fact, they are enough alike that Crystal's growing number of loyal passengers, along with any first-timer, can find happiness on either ship.

CUNARD

555 Fifth Avenue, New York, NY 10017
(212) 880-7500; (800) 5-CUNARD (528-6273); fax (212) 949-0915
http://www.cunardline.com

TYPE OF SHIPS Cunard's fleet, from small, ultraluxurious ships to large superliners, reflects the diversity of today's cruising.

TYPE OF CRUISES Along with the diversity offered by its ships, Cunard offers a range of destinations and durations, from warm weather vacations to scheduled transatlantic summer service, to cruises around the world and to the four corners of the globe for affluent, experienced, and demanding travelers. After a reorganization in 1996, Cunard has been reoriented to be an all-luxury cruise line, all with Cunard's British pedigree.

CRUISE LINE'S STRENGTHS
- name recognition
- distinctive ships
- worldwide itineraries
- fine accommodations, cuisine, and service

CRUISE LINE'S SHORTCOMINGS
- aging fleet
- mixed products
- evening entertainment on *Sun* and *Sea Goddess*

FELLOW PASSENGERS With its variety of ships and ports of call, Cunard attracts a broad spectrum of passengers from first-timers eager to visit many ports to veteran cruisers who seldom leave their ship, but mostly the fleet attracts affluent, mature, and experienced travelers. Depending on the time of the year, the makeup is American and British, with large contingents of Europeans on certain ships. Generally, the line has a healthy repeat factor of up to 50 percent on some ships, with a few favorites drawing as high as 90 percent on certain cruises. The loyal fans are well traveled, well heeled, and demanding.

The *QE2* attracts a very different crowd on its world cruise than on its transatlantic service. On the world cruise, they are mostly affluent, older passengers who take long winter vacations. During the summer, they may be all ages, incomes, and walks of life, many families with children, and people attracted simply by the notion of taking an ocean voyage on the famous ship.

Recommended For Those who enjoy a certain amount of formality and tradition, abhor glitz, are accustomed to luxury, and are willing to pay for it. Sophisticated travelers who appreciate luxury and fine cuisine.

Not Recommended For Those not comfortable in elegant ambience and who prefer a casual or nonstop party atmosphere.

CRUISE AREAS AND SEASONS Caribbean, round-the-world in winter; transatlantic May–December; Europe, spring–fall; South America, Orient, Bermuda, South Pacific, New England/Canada, Panama Canal, and Africa seasonally.

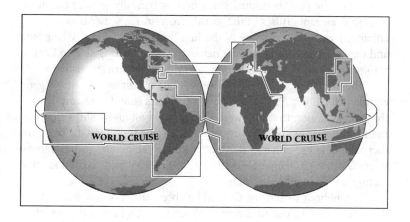

THE LINE Cunard Lines, with a history stretching back 157 years, sailed into 1997 as almost a new cruise line with new management, a new organization, and a new direction. Yet, the experience of reinventing itself is nothing new for Cunard. With the postwar birth of the jet age and the demise of transatlantic passenger service, all traditional steamship companies like Cunard had to adapt to the new realities to survive. Some converted their ships for modern cruising, some built new ships, and some bought or merged with other cruise lines. Cunard took all these actions and more.

During the era of the grand oceanliners, Cunard Lines was best known for its queens—particularly, the *Queen Mary* and *Queen Elizabeth*, which set the standard of elegance at sea for decades. *Queen Elizabeth 2* made her debut in 1969, at the moment when storm clouds had gathered over the future of transatlantic service.

In 1971, Cunard was acquired by Trafalgar House, a multinational conglomerate headquartered in London, but throughout the decade there were doubts as to whether the line would survive. Having the only remaining oceanliner on regular transatlantic service helped keep her going. In 1982, the *QE2* was pressed into Her Majesty's service during the Falkland Islands War. For Cunard and the *QE2*, it might have been a blessing in disguise, giving the ship a new lease on life with the publicity and a much needed refurbishing by the British government prior to her return to passenger service.

In the 1980s Cunard moved to corner the luxury market, first by acquiring the *Sagafjord* and *Vistafjord*, traditional oceanliners that had long epitomized luxury cruising, and in 1986 the ultradeluxe *Sea Goddess* twins, the first "boutique" ships built specifically to offer the most exclusive, elegant cruises in the world. Then, in 1994, her position was enhanced with the purchase of the highly acclaimed *Royal Viking Sun* and the prestigious Royal Viking name. It was something akin to British royalty with Norwegian bloodlines marrying an American aristocrat.

Then in 1996, Trafalgar House was taken over by the Norwegian company Kvaerner ASA, which now is Cunard's parent company. Under the reorganization that followed, Cunard sold off all its ships that did not fit into the luxury category, and at the same time the *QE2* was further remodeled to enhance her luxury appeal, eliminating some cabins to reduce the passenger total from 1,750–1,500, and created single-seating dining in all restaurants.

Throughout its history, Cunard has been an innovator with a long list of firsts in response to changing lifestyles. The *QE2* was the first ship to have a full-fledged spa at sea. Recognizing the impact of the electronic revolution on people's lives, including their holidays, Cunard installed the first computer learning center on the *QE2*, a satellite edition of world news delivered daily to passengers, and a CD-ROM library.

The Fleet	Built/Renovated	Tonnage	Passengers
Queen Elizabeth 2	1969/87/94/96	70,327	1500
Royal Viking Sun	1988/1993/96	38,000	740
Sea Goddess I	1984/95/97	4,250	116
Sea Goddess II	1985/95	4,250	116
Vistafjord	1973/83/94/97	24,492	736

STYLE   The legendary *Queen Elizabeth 2* has a style all her own. She is the only passenger ship that sails the Atlantic on a regular schedule, which she does from May–December and does so with three levels of service. She also sails on an annual world cruise from January–April. The weeks in between are taken up with short cruises, usually in the Caribbean and Europe.

To many, the *QE2* is the ultimate cruise experience. A city at sea, she dwarfs all but the newest megaliners. She is proud, elegant, formal, and as British as—well, yes—the queen. In December 1994, Cunard returned the *QE2* to service before her $45 million renovation had been completed and got socked with one of the worst publicity batterings anyone could remember. Nonetheless, the renovations, and more recent ones in 1996, made the *QE2* practically a new ship, updated and ready for the next century.

Cunard's four other luxurious ships—all perennial award winners—started with different owners and have distinct features, but they share some in common. All four ships—*Royal Viking Sun*, *Vistafjord*, *Sea Goddess I*, and *Sea Goddess II*—have mainly Norwegian officers and European dining and hotel staffs, single-seating dining, and top-of-the-line luxury service with a certain amount of formality. Dress during the day is casual, but gentlemen are required to wear jacket and tie for dinner and several nights of the week call for formal attire.

The ships sail on diverse itineraries. Because they offer longer and more expensive cruises, they attract affluent, mature, and experienced travelers accustomed to the best. Often, they stress enrichment programs, featuring experts in different fields.

The *Royal Viking Sun* makes an annual world cruise in the winter and has a diverse global itinerary for the remainder of the year. The spacious and graceful *Vistafjord* maintains the ambience of traditional cruising. The small, exclusive *Sea Goddess* twins trade on unabashed snob appeal, offering highly personalized service and an unregimented atmosphere to give passengers the feeling of being in an exclusive private club.

DISTINCTIVE FEATURES   Golden Door fitness instructors on several ships; gentlemen hosts to dance and dine with unaccompanied women on *QE2*, *Vistafjord*, and *Royal Viking Sun* year-round. *QE2* computer learning center, 18-car garage, florist, kennel, tuxedo rental, CD-ROM library, and bookshop. *Royal Viking Sun*, air-conditioned tenders, pool with swim-up bar, gold-plated bathroom fixtures in penthouse suites, the first croquet court-at-sea, same-level tender access, and walk-in closets. *Sea Goddess*, water sports marina at stern and all-inclusive prices.

RATES

Ship	Highest Per Diem	Lowest Per Diem	Average Per Diem
QE2	$669	$198	$402
Royal Viking Sun	$1,010	$329	$607
Sea Goddess I & II	$933	$450	$608
Vistafjord	$822	$305	$457

The above per diems are calculated from the cruise line's nondiscounted *cruise-only* fares on standard accommodations. What you will actually pay *should* be *substantially* less (see Part One, How to Get the Best Deal on a Cruise). Per diems vary by season, by cabin location, and by cruise areas.

Special Note: All tips and beverages (including alcoholic drinks) are included in the cruise fare on *Sea Goddess I* and *Sea Goddess II*. All tips are included in the fare on *Vistafjord*, *Royal Viking Sun*, and *QE2*.

Special Fares and Discounts

• Early booking discounts of 20 percent available fleetwide.
• Children's Fare: Third/fourth person fares.
• Single Supplement: QE2, 175–200 percent; world cruise, 115–200 percent based on cabin grade. *Royal Viking Sun*, 125–140 percent; *Vistafjord*, 150 percent. *Sea Goddess I* and *II*, none.

Packages

- Air/Sea: Yes.
- Other Packages: Yes.
- Pre/Post: Yes.

Past Passengers   Cunard World Club, the past passenger program, was revised in 1997 to cover its passengers worldwide. The Skald Club and Cruise Miles programs have been discontinued. Enrollment kits for World Club were sent to more than 80,000 passengers who had sailed with Cunard since 1992. Passengers are automatically enrolled into the new program at one of the three levels; Bronze, for two to four cruises; Silver, five to seven; and Gold, eight or more cruises, or more than 100 days of Cunard cruising.

Club benefits included on-board credits and social events for repeat passengers. "Privileged Pricing" fares are 20 percent lower than published brochure fares and are available on the *QE2*, *Royal Viking Sun* and *Vistafjord*. These fares may be combined with the additional 5 percent on-board discount, for savings of up to 25 percent on all cruises, except world cruises and *Sea Goddess I* and *II*.

On-board credits are issued per cabin: Bronze, $100; Silver, $150; Gold, $200, and are automatically added to members' shipboard accounts. They may be applied toward the purchase of luxury goods and services including spa treatments, shore excursions, and boutique items. Space-available upgrades are offered also to Silver and Gold members prior to sailing.

Sea Goddess past passengers are given an incentive to bring along their friends and family on a cruise. Past passengers receive gift certificates for a 10 percent discount on their next cruise for each cruise of six days or more that they recruit, and every friend or family member gets a 10 percent discount certificate for their next cruise. Past passengers can use up to four certificates (40 percent discount) on their next *Sea Goddess* cruise.

THE LAST WORD   Cunard is best known for its luxury, but if you don't understand the differences in the levels of luxury, it can be somewhat misleading. Each ship is a different product and in the case of the *QE2*, there are differences within the ship. For example, the popular image of the *QE2* is glamour, grand luxury, and haute cuisine. For those who take the highest-priced suites and deluxe cabins and dine in the Grills, the picture is accurate—but that's less than 30 percent of the total passengers. On the ship's transatlantic run, the *QE2* has three levels of service determined by cabin category, which is a polite way of saying three classes based on price. Each category is assigned specific restaurants and cocktail lounges and entrance is restricted accordingly. You will learn quickly what class distinction means when you try to dine or even have a cocktail in a bar that's not in your class. The redeeming factor is that all the entertainment, sports, recreational facilities, and, of course, shops are available to all passengers without any restrictions.

Cunard is now accepting reservations for the millennium cruises on all five ships. A $1,000 per person deposit is required.

QE2 Standard Features

Officers British.

Staffs Dining, Cabin, Cruise/British, European, and International.

Dining Facilities Single seating in all five dining rooms for all three meals; informal Lido Cafe for breakfast, lunch, and midnight buffet; pavilion snack bar.

Special Diets Diabetic, low calorie, low cholesterol, low salt, and vegetarian available.

Room Service 24-hour room service.

Dress Code Formal/informal for dining, depending on evening.

Cabin Amenities Radio, direct-dial telephones, 20-channel television with CNN. Bathroom with tub and shower in mid- and top categories. Refrigerators, walk-in closets, verandas.

Electrical Outlets 110 AC.

Wheelchair Access Ramp access, four cabins with wheelchair access, bathtubs with grab bars, wide doors, low sills, special bathrooms.

Recreation and Entertainment Casino, cabaret, Broadway revues. Life Enrichment seminars, guest lectures by experts. Queens Room, Grand Lounge, five bars, disco, computer learning center, bingo.

Sports and Other Activities Indoor/outdoor pools, deck sports, golf putting and driving net, jogging track, paddle tennis, Ping-Pong.

Beauty and Fitness Spa, fitness center, gym. See text.

Other Facilities Cinema/theatre; launderette, laundry/dry cleaning service, library, hospital, tuxedo rental shop, foreign exchange; 18-car garage, florist, kennel, shops, boardroom, chapel/synagogue.

Children's Facilities Teen center, video, supervised children's play-rooms, nursery, nannies, baby-sitting service.

Theme Cruises See text.

Smoking Designated areas in public rooms.

QE2 Suggested Tipping All gratuities included; however, additional tipping allowed.

Credit Cards For cruise payment and on-board charges, American Express, Diners Club, Discover, MasterCard, Visa.

Queen Elizabeth 2

	Quality Rating	Value Rating
Queen Elizabeth 2	❽	D

Registry: England	Length: 963 feet	Beam: 105 feet
Cabins: 779	Draft: 32.75 feet	Speed: 28.5 knots
Maximum Passengers: 1,500	Passenger Decks: 12	Elevators: 13
	Crew: 1,015	Space Ratio: 36

THE SHIP   *Queen Elizabeth 2*, Cunard's flagship, is the lone survivor of a long, rich history of ocean travel, and the only ship still providing regularly scheduled transatlantic service. Her new look after a $45 million facelift in 1995 and another $18 million in 1996 emphasizes her uniqueness—a grand oceanliner with the flexibility to provide a modern cruise experience.

The *QE2's* renovations were so comprehensive, with major remodeling of the layout and style of almost all public areas, she is practically a new ship. The new interiors were created jointly by John McNeece, Britain's leading designer of cruise ship interiors, and MET Studio, an architectural and design firm that worked with James Gardner, the original designer and master planner for the *QE2*.

In addition to improved passenger flow throughout the ship, the designers have given her new and fresh decor, facilities, and ambience that address today's lifestyle while retaining the ship's distinctive character. By cleverly integrating the history of the *QE2* and Cunard into the new decor, the designers created a ship as modern as the twenty-first century and, at the same time, a floating museum named Heritage Trail which has 24 exhibits that underscore her traditions. A guide to the collection and escorted tours are available.

Public lounges and other rooms are laid out across three decks—Quarter, Upper, and Boat—with new links and stairways to let traffic flow naturally and to reflect the changes in passengers' activities at different times of day as they shift from place to place and from daytime to evening. Areas were also opened up to bring the outside in, so passengers are always aware of the sea.

Activities are set along well-defined decks with the flow fore and aft, as on a classic oceanliner, and never reaching a dead end.

Clearly delineated promenades echo the grand promenades of the earlier Queens. In the reception areas, on the stairwells, between decks, and along the promenades are the museum's heritage displays.

Passengers' first view of the *QE2* is the Midships Lobby, a two-story atrium on Deck Two with elegant decor in rich mulberry and green set against honey-colored cherry wood trimmed in bronze and banquettes covered in suede. A four-part mural by artist Peter Sutton depicting the history of Cunard and the *QE2* covers the circular walls of the atrium; the bell from the first *Queen Elizabeth* and the *Spirit of Atlantic* statuette are on display.

ITINERARIES   Essentially the *QE2* has two seasons: Winter, world cruise; summer, transatlantic. In between, she sails on short cruises from New York to Bermuda and Caribbean or from Southampton to Europe.

- *January–April:* *QE2*'s 1998 around-the-world cruise departs from New York on Jan. 6 and Ft. Lauderdale on Jan. 8 westbound for a total of 104 days. The ship will break with *QE2*'s traditional route of the past decade, taking the southern route around Africa (instead of through Suez Canal) and calling en route at Mombasa, Durban, Cape Town, St. Helena, and Dakar. The voyage is also available in 14 segments of 11–41 days. Some optional land programs en route are China, five days; Vietnam, overnight; and African Safari, overnight. Among the bonuses, passengers on the full world cruise get first class air transportation and those who sail 48 days or more receive $2,000 on-board credit; all gratuities are included.

- *April–December:* From mid-April–mid-December, she sails between New York and Southampton on a regular schedule, approximately twice monthly in both directions, on six-day voyages. Intermittently, she has four- to ten-day cruises in Northern Europe and Mediterranean; and three-day weekend cruises, five-day Bermuda cruises, and six-day New England/Canada cruises from New York; and 11–16-day cruises to the Caribbean and Panama Canal.

Home Ports   New York; Southampton.

Port Charges $215–260 world; $185 transatlantic; $65–360 others.

CABINS   The *QE2*'s cabins have never looked better. They are also more comfortable and convenient. All cabins throughout the ship were refurbished with handsome decor and all bathrooms have new tiles, vanities, showers and baths, sinks, and toilets. In the 1996 renovations, more than 100 cabins were taken out of service, reducing the number of passengers to enable all passengers to dine at one time—a measure of a luxury ship.

The *QE2* has a complex arrangement of cabin categories that is different for the world cruise and the transatlantic service. Because where you dine is determined by the category of your accommodations, it is important to understand precisely what you are buying. In principle, it means that when you pay more, you get more.

For the world cruise, the ship offers 22 categories—of which the top 8 plus the 5 named suites dine in the Queens Grill. On the transatlantic and short cruises in Europe and the Caribbean, there are fewer categories—of which the top four, one deluxe single, and the named suites dine in the Queens Grill. The next group, ultradeluxe, is split between the Queens, Princess, and Britannia Grills, and so on down the line.

Even so many categories do not begin to reflect the variety of configurations. Essentially, the top two decks, Signal and Sun Boat, have the largest, most luxurious suites with verandas and penthouse service, an extra level of service with butlers whose duties range, from arranging parties en suite and serving canapes in the evening, to arranging for priority disembarkation and customs and immigration preclearance, to expediting luggage delivery to a designated area of the pier.

The ultradeluxe cabins are amidship on the Sun, One, and Two decks, and the other categories are, more or less, distributed fore and aft on Two and Three decks as well as the two lower decks. All cabins have television with 24-hour CNN, information, and movies. The cabins that Cunard calls Grill and deluxe class have refrigerators, VCRs, and bathrooms with tub and shower; those called premium have bathrooms with shower only. In the most recent renovations, the bathrooms of 55 penthouse suites were remodeled with new sinks and counters and marble walls.

Specifications   146 inside single and double cabins, 635 outside singles and doubles; 4 luxury suites. Standard dimensions not available. 700 with 2 lower beds; 62 singles. Some cabins for disabled available.

DINING   One area of major change is the restaurants. There are now seven; all were extensively refurbished and some were moved and renamed. Cunard maintains that the food has been upgraded, as well, but some passengers have taken exception to that claim. The most recent change, and one intended to add to the ship's luxury appeal, is that all dining rooms now have single seating for all meals.

The Mauretania Restaurant (formerly on Upper Deck) is now on Quarter Deck, amidship, and in 1997, had a million-dollar refurbishing that gave it a new look and the food upgraded. Named for an early Cunard ship, the *Mauretania*, the room has photographs and a 1907 telegraph from its namesake. On display is a 15-foot model of the ship, one of the largest museum items on the Heritage Trail.

The Caronia Restaurant (formerly the Columbia Restaurant on Quarter Deck) is on Upper Deck, forward, and named for another Cunard ship whose opulence was legendary. The room has two commissioned works of art: the centerpiece, *White Horses*, a sculpture by artist Althea Wynne, depicts four horses riding waves, emblematic of the British seamen's term for white caps; the other is a painting of the *Caronia* in a Caribbean setting by artist Jane Hum. Dubbed the Green Goddess for the color of her hull, the *QE2*'s decor uses a lot of green. At the entrance, the new Crystal Bar serves as a lounge for patrons of the Princess Grill and Britannia Grill restaurants, as well as the Mauretania.

The Princess Grill (formerly Princess Grill Port) and the Britannia Grill (previously Princess Grill Starboard) are basically in the same location, Quarter Deck forward, but the entrances were changed. Now, each has a separate entrance from the Crystal Bar. The renaming of the latter was to pay tribute to Cunard's first ship, *Britannia*. A model of the ship is displayed in the Heritage museum group entitled, Samuel Cunard and the Paddle Steamers.

The Queens Grill was refurbished, but still has understated decor. The Erte drawings were removed (why remains a mystery). It is the smallest of the dining rooms and only passengers booked in Queens Grill class may dine there or have a drink in the Queens Grill Lounge.

With the exception of the Queens Grill, where the cuisine is meant to be of the highest gourmet standard and patrons enjoy tableside preparations, menus in the other dining rooms are the same. The rooms' size and ambience probably differ more than the food. Menus offer a selection of hors d'oeuvres, three soups, a sorbet refresher, five entrees, two salads, four or five desserts, cheese, ice cream, sherbet, and fruit. There are recommended wines and a spa menu.

The lido is the ship's most obvious bow to today's changing lifestyles. It was totally transformed into a spacious, informal, buffet-style restaurant, providing an alternative setting for breakfast, lunch, and the midnight buffet, and a bar serves coffee and drinks throughout the day.

Floor-to-ceiling windows wrap around the aft end and open to the outside deck, giving the room a light and airy feeling, which is enhanced by the white, beige, and mint green decor and bleached wood furniture. Two murals by Italian artist Giancarlo Impiglia are meant to capture the QE2 cruise experience with lifelike scenes of passengers lingering on deck, talking to the captain, sunbathing poolside, and sipping champagne.

To make way for the Lido Cafe, a pool and glass magrodome were removed and replaced with stairs leading down to the One Deck lido area and the new Pavilion, a glass-enclosed bar and grill where snacks and drinks are served.

SERVICE   The officers are British, but the hotel and cabin staffs are mostly Europeans and many are women. The level of dining room service rises along with the dining room and price. For those in Grill class, the service is meant to be luxurious. For the other passengers, the service is, well, British. But to be fair, after years of bad or indifferent service, improvements are noticeable. Most passengers say the service is friendly and attentive.

FACILITIES AND ENTERTAINMENT   Updating the lifestyle on the QE2 was at the heart of the 1994 renovations as seen particularly on Upper Deck with the Golden Lion (formerly Theatre Bar) near the theatre and casino. A large pub in the classic English tradition and decorated in mahogany and red and green plaid, it is meant to be the ship's informal social center with an upright piano, television, karaoke, and the traditional dart board on the wall. The pub offers 14 different lagers, stouts, and draught beers from Denmark, Ireland, Germany, Holland, the United States, and of course, Great Britain. Other beers representing the QE2's ports of call are added from time to time.

The classy Grand Lounge, the showroom for big-name entertainment, was completely changed and improved. Gone are the twin stairs that lead up to the shopping mezzanine. Instead, there is a modern, fully equipped, and curtained stage with state-of-the-art lighting, a new dance floor, improved sight lines, and additional seating in a room ablaze in red with black and gold trim.

The popular Yacht Club, with handsome nautical decor and America's Cup memorabilia, was expanded to create an observation lounge and bar during the day and a sophisticated nightclub and disco in the evening. The expansion has drawn criticism from some who liked the Club small and cozy, but anyone seeing it for the first time will find it delightful. With the magrodome removed, passengers get a sweeping view of the ocean from the Club; its removal also added sunning space on the new teak deck, along with the deck sports.

On Quarter Deck, the Chart Room bar (formerly Midships Bar) showcases some of Cunard's nautical antiques with a collection of gold-edged antique charts, an antique burr walnut chart chest, and the chronometer from the *Queen Elizabeth*. An electronic world map behind the bar shows the ship's course. A piano from the *Queen Mary* provides music for cocktails and after dinner.

The Queens Room has retained its dignified best. The bust of Queen Elizabeth has a new velvet backdrop, the lighting and sound system were upgraded, and there's new furniture and regal blue and gold draperies. The "Royal Connection" is showcased in exhibits of the Queen's Standards presented to the ship by Queen Elizabeth II, which include photographs and portraits of the Queen and Queen Mother.

The room is the setting for afternoon tea and for ballroom dancing, now part of the evening entertainment. Gentlemen, if you forget your formal attire, not to worry. The QE2 has a tuxedo rental shop. Ladies, if you need a partner to dance, gentlemen hosts are on board for precisely that purpose.

The QE2 always has a variety of dance music in the different lounges and a lineup of celebrity performers. A recent schedule included Bill Cosby, Peter Duchin and his orchestra, Dick Clark, Marvin Hamlisch, and the Yale University Whiffenpoofs.

ACTIVITIES AND DIVERSIONS   With her variety of lounges and public rooms, the QE2 has always been able to provide a wide array of activities. Your day could begin early with exercise in the fitness center or jogging on your own. You can take a lesson in the computer learning center or attend any number of seminars and workshops in the redesigned theatre, which now functions as a lecture hall and conference facility, as well as a cinema.

The Life Enrichment Program with seminars, workshops, and lectures by experts is part of every cruise, and there's the usual shipboard bingo, horse racing, arts and crafts, and beauty demonstrations. If yours is a theme cruise, you might have the additional attraction of jazz or classical music concerts.

The QE2 has the only library at sea staffed by a full-time professional librarian. Now doubled in size with a new book shop, it has more than 6,000 books, hundreds of videos, and a multimedia reference library for passengers to access the latest reference material on CD-ROM. Designed to bring a contemporary atmosphere to the traditional library, it has red leather seats and desks to provide ample space for passengers to use the library's new facilities.

SPORTS, FITNESS, AND BEAUTY   The ship has indoor and outdoor pools, and deck sports include a golf putting and driving area, shuffleboard, Ping-Pong, and a jogging track.

Supervised exercise classes are available daily in the fitness center and gym on Deck Seven, while the spa on Deck Six has sauna, massage, and a variety of beauty and body treatments. The barbershop and beauty salon, operated by Steiner of London, are on Deck One.

Incidentally, the QE2 has one of the largest, best-equipped hospitals of any ship afloat. Hopefully, you would never need it, but when you are halfway around the world it's comforting to know it's there.

CHILDREN'S FACILITIES   Club 2000 is the teen center on upper deck and there is a supervised children's playroom and nursery.

SHORE EXCURSIONS   Passengers receive small booklets with summary information. They are cruise-specific, with thumbnail sketches of an itinerary's ports of call.

THEME CRUISES   Throughout the spring to winter season, the QE2 runs a series of theme cruises that vary from year to year but are likely to include such topics as art and antiques, big band and nostalgia, Broadway goes to sea, classical music, culinary summit at sea, gardening, jazz, murder mystery, natural history, opera, and theatre at sea. Inquire from Cunard for a current schedule.

POSTSCRIPT   The QE2 renovations have practically made her a new ship. And while she now looks chic and contemporary and better prepared for the twenty-first century, she actually seems more in the tradition of a great liner than when she first appeared in her formica gloss of the 1960s. Yet, for all her changes, she remains the same—a unique ship with a mystique no other ship can duplicate. This underscores an often noted fact that other cruise lines spend over $3 billion annually on promotion, but over the years, tests show that the only passenger ship that the man on the street can recall by name, unaided, is the QE2.

With her reputation and aura, it is probably a given that passenger expectations run higher about the QE2 than any other ship. That all but ensures some passengers with inflated fantasies will be dissatisfied; skeptics may be surprised, if not thrilled, and most will be happy that they, too, can say they have sailed on the Queen.

ROYAL VIKING SUN, SEA GODDESS I & II, VISTAFJORD STANDARD FEATURES

Officers Norwegian.

Staffs Dining and Cabin *RVSun*, *Vistafjord*/Scandinavian and International; *Sea Goddess I & II*/European and American.

Dining Facilities One dining room with single seating for three meals; *Sea Goddess* with open seating. Casual indoor/outdoor cafe for lunch buffets and pizza. Alternative Italian restaurant, *RVSun*, *Vistafjord*. *Sea Goddess*, complimentary wine, liquor, and beverages.

Special Diets Available upon request.

Room Service 24-hour room service; full menus. *Sea Goddess*, full 24-hour meal and beverage service.

Dress Code Casually chic by day; informal and formal for evenings.

Cabin Amenities Television, VCR, direct-dial phone, walk-in or large closets, radio, hair dryer, refrigerator. *Sea Goddess*, all suites with sitting room, stereo, stocked bar, refrigerator, bathroom with tub.

Electrical Outlets 110 AC.

Wheelchair Access *RVSun*, four cabins, wide bathroom doors, bathtubs with grab bars; *Vistafjord*, six cabins.

Recreation and Entertainment Casino, card room, lectures, bingo, bridge, dance lessons, gentlemen hosts (except *Sea Goddess*). *RVSun*, *Vistafjord*, nightclub, four bars/lounges. *Sea Goddess*, piano bar. See specific ships.

Sports and Other Activities Golf simulator on all but *Sea Goddess*. *Vistafjord*, outdoor and indoor pools. *RVSun*, two pools, roque, quoits. *Sea Goddess*, outdoor pool, whirlpool, water sports platform.

Beauty and Fitness Spa, gym, barber/beauty salon, saunas, exercise class. Walking/jogging deck on all ships except *Sea Goddess*.

Other Facilities Medical facility, library/writing room. *RVSun* and *Vistafjord*, book and video library, launderette, concierge, boutiques. *Sea Goddess*, valet.

Children's Facilities *RVSun*, youth counselors seasonally.

Theme Cruises Year-round selection.

Smoking Designated areas in public rooms.

Suggested Tipping Gratuities included in cruise fare on all ships.

Credit Cards For cruise payment and on-board charges, American Express, Diners Club, Discover, Mastercard, Visa.

Royal Viking Sun

	Quality Rating	Value Rating
Royal Viking Sun	⑨	D

Registry: Bahamas	Length: 673 feet	Beam: 95 feet
Cabins: 380	Draft: 23.5 feet	Speed: 21.4 knots
Maximum Passengers: 758	Passenger Decks: 8	Elevators: 4
	Crew: 450	Space Ratio: 51.3

THE SHIP   The pride of Royal Viking Line when she made her debut in 1988, *Royal Viking Sun* was the prize of Cunard's purchase in 1994. With it, Cunard also acquired rights to the Royal Viking name, one of the most respected in travel—from its inception in 1970, *Royal Viking* set the standard for modern luxury cruising for Americans for two decades.

Of all the modern ships introduced in the 1980s, the *Royal Viking Sun*, designed for gracious living at sea, lived up to her advance billing for luxury, elegance, and innovation. Built at Wartsila Marine in Turku, Finland, the *RVSun* is one of the most spacious cruise ships ever built. The penthouse suites are palatial and even the standard cabins are as large as suites on many other ships. There is an array of beautiful, comfortable lounges and special treats, such as walk-in closets in cabins, the first on a cruise ship, a swim-up bar in the main pool, a lap pool in the health spa, an electronic simulator of famous golf courses, and the first croquet court afloat.

The *RVSun* also has some unusual technical features, same-level jetways for easy access to docks or tenders; air-conditioned tenders with stable catamaran hulls and equipped with radar and sonar, lavatories, and bar; and two high-speed man-overboard (MOB) boats.

Clean lines and uncluttered decor reflect the *RVSun's* Scandinavian origins. Fine wood and high quality fabrics in quiet colors echo quality throughout the ship. Public rooms and facilities are on two center and two top decks, and cabins are spread over seven of the ship's eight passenger decks.

ITINERARIES   Worldwide and round-the-world cruises.

- *January–April:* World cruise departs from San Francisco, 104 days, and is also available in 12 segments ranging from 18–55 days. The itinerary includes 38 ports of which 12 are maiden calls in such places as Cambodia, Vietnam, and the Andaman Islands. Among the bonuses, passengers on the full world cruise get first class air transportation and those who sail 48 days or more receive $2,000 on-board credit; all gratuities are included. The *RVSun* spends three days in Hong Kong and makes overnight calls at Sydney, Perth, Bangkok, Madras, Bombay, Haifa, and Venice.

• *April–September:* At the end of her world cruise, the *Royal Viking Sun* sails on a series of cruises from Ft. Lauderdale and/or New York before making a transatlantic voyage to begin her European summer, roaming from the Mediterranean to the Baltic, North Cape, and Ireland on 5–15-day cruises. In September, she sails to the Black Sea from Venice.

• *October–December:* In September, she leaves from Athens on a 78-day Asia odyssey, composed of five consecutive, 12–19-day cruises that depart from Bombay, Singapore, and Hong Kong. The final leg departs from Sydney to San Francisco. In December, the ship has two West Coast cruises from San Francisco to Acapulco.

Home Ports   Various ports, depending on itinerary.

Port Charges $195–240, world cruise; $75–700, depending on cruise.

CABINS   The *RVSun's* large, handsomely appointed accommodations come in a dozen categories of four basic types: penthouse suites, deluxe, and standard outside and inside cabins. All but 25 cabins are outside and have large windows. Penthouse suites and deluxe cabins, which account for more than one-third of the accommodations, have verandas.

The cabins are airy with pastel decor and dark wood cabinets with a mirrored dresser/desk. All have television, VCR, three-channel radio, phone, mini-refrigerators, locking drawers, walk-in closets, and robes. Almost all have bathrooms with tub and shower. All but a few have twin beds that convert to kings and most have a small sitting area with a love seat, table, and chair. There are launderettes on two cabin decks. Room service is available around the clock.

The largest, most luxurious suites are on the top two decks, creating an exclusive penthouse of suites with butler service. The suites have dividers to separate the bedroom from the sitting area. The elegant Owner's Suite with a whirlpool bath surrounded by picture windows facing the sea was also a cruise ship first.

Specifications   25 inside cabins, 355 outside including suites; 18 Penthouse suites; 1 Owner's Suite; 122 with verandas; 48 deluxe. Standard dimensions, 191 square feet. 368 cabins with 2 lowers, convertible to doubles; 2 with single lower. 4 wheelchair accessible cabins.

DINING   Superb cuisine is the ship's hallmark. Traditionally, menus are rotated on a 30-day cycle, although that could change with itineraries, and offer a choice of specialties from around the world, supplemented by the freshest ingredients at each port of call.

The elegant main dining room in coral and mauve accommodates all passengers at a single seating for breakfast, lunch, and dinner. The large room, which spans two-thirds of Promenade Deck, is divided into three sections: forward, middle, and aft. The largest, most desirable section, aft, is encased with large windows on three sides, providing an almost unobstructed 180° view of the sea and scenery.

The forward section is a little smaller and perhaps a bit more intimate. Both sections have raised center areas that offer sea views, regardless of table location. The connecting middle section is narrow and least desirable, but it has the attraction of being connected by a winding staircase to the popular Compass Rose Room and bar on the deck above. The tables, mostly large and seating eight or ten people, are set with fresh flowers and fine china, crystal, and silverware. There are some small tables for two, four, or six, often by the windows.

For dinner a chef's special menu along with suggested wines, is featured nightly. The full menu offers three appetizers, three soups, two salads, a sherbet refresher, four entrees (fish, chicken, veal, beef), selections of vegetables, cheese, three desserts, ice cream, and fresh fruit. There is also a light menu with calorie counts.

The Garden Room and Cafe is the alternative venue for breakfast and lunch. The cheerful room has a wall of windows and skylights that look aft to the deck and the sea. You have the option of eating in the light and airy cafe or outside on the adjacent deck. Hot dogs, hamburgers, and sandwiches are served at the Pool Bar.

The Venezia, which replaced the Royal Grill adjacent to the Garden Room, is the alternative restaurant featuring Italian cuisine. In addition to the extensive menu, there are daily chef's specials. There is no additional cost; reservations are required. The room holds 60 people; therefore, passengers may make only one reservation per cruise. They can, however, put their name on a standby list.

SERVICE   The officers are Norwegian and set the tone with their friendly, open manner. Most of the dining and hotel staffs are Scandinavian and Northern European, many of whom came to the Sun from other Royal Viking Line ships. Cabins are attended by Scandinavian stewardesses, and indeed, it was Royal Viking Line that established this custom 20 years ago; it seems to define luxury cruises today. The young women are as pleasant and thoughtful as they are efficient and thorough.

FACILITIES AND ENTERTAINMENT   Norway Deck, devoted entirely to public rooms, is anchored by lounges at both ends. The Norway Lounge forward is the main lounge and accommodates all passengers at one time. In addition to the stage, it has a bandstand and a dance floor. During the day the pink and coral room is used for various activities, such as a Skald party, lecture, bingo, or afternoon tea. In the evening, there might be a concert by a classical performer, a colorful production show, the big band sound for dancing, entertainment by well-known stars, or the captain's party. Entertainment is not *RVSun's* strong suit.

The Compass Rose Room, amidship, is a comfortable cocktail lounge with piano music and an adjacent bar with a cruvinet for premium wines by the glass. Here, stairs wind down directly into the dining room below. The Compass Rose is also the place for the midnight buffet. Next door, the casino has slot machines, blackjack, and roulette.

The Midnight Sun Lounge, aft, is a multipurpose lounge with a high-tech video system. Here you might enjoy parlor games in the afternoon and come back in the evening for drinks when it is a piano bar or after dinner when it's a nightclub with cabaret and comedy.

On Sky Deck above the bridge, the Stella Polaris Lounge is an observation lounge with 180° of wraparound windows facing the bow. Here, even the seats at the bar have clear views of the sea. It's a popular vantage point from which to watch a transit of the Panama Canal or view the fjords of Norway. On days at sea, it is the scene for an elegant tea with white glove service, and in the evening, it becomes a romantic setting for music and moonlight.

ACTIVITIES AND DIVERSIONS   The *RVSun* offers an excellent enrichment program of port and theme lectures featuring distinguished speakers whose expertise might range from art and antiques to wine and world affairs. The Starlight Theatre on Norway Deck shows films twice daily and is used for lectures and enrichment programs. The Dickens Library has a diverse selection of reading material; nearby, the card room can be divided into separate areas for private parties. There is also an arcade of smart boutiques.

The plush Oak Room is reminiscent of a men's club with comfortable, leather chairs in an intimate, wood-paneled setting. It makes a cozy daytime retreat or just the place for an after-dinner drink. The room has a wood-burning fireplace, but . . . well, that's a story in itself.

To ensure safety, its builders spent more than $100,000 to enclose the room with fire walls and to install an individual smoke detector and sprinkler system, automatic fire doors, heat sensors, portable fire extinguishers, a locked glass screen, and a television camera for 24-hour surveillance from the bridge. Still, the fireplace cannot be used. After approving the fireplace during construction, the U.S. Coast Guard reversed its decision when the ship sailed—such is the caprice of bureaucrats.

SPORTS, FITNESS, AND BEAUTY Bridge Deck has a wind-sheltered swimming pool with a whirlpool and a swim-up bar and is surrounded by a sunning area. Its location amidship and separate from the ship's other sport facilities is somewhat unusual.

Topside you will find the croquet court and golf practice area, but the computerized golf simulator is seven flights down on the lowest passenger deck. Shuffleboard, Ping-Pong, and quoits are available on Norway Deck, and a lovely teak deck for walking or jogging wraps around Promenade Deck.

On Scandinavia Deck, the bright and airy spa surrounds an outdoor lap pool on three sides. The spa with floor-to-ceiling windows has a gym with exercise equipment, an aerobics area, and a professionally trained staff to put you through your paces. There are sauna and massage rooms and the beauty salon offers a full line of hair, face, and body treatments. It has a variety of pricey salon and spa packages.

SHORE EXCURSIONS The *RVSun's* shore excursions are as varied as her itineraries. The packet of information sent to passengers in advance of their cruise has a shore excursion booklet for planning purposes. In addition to the concierge, the ship's shore excursion office is a full-service travel office.

POSTSCRIPT The *Royal Viking Sun* is luxury cruising on a large liner at its best. Little wonder that she has had an unprecedented acceptance from discerning, cosmopolitan travelers for her comfort, cuisine, facilities, itineraries, and impeccable service. The *RVSun* was designed for globe-roaming cruises and is ideal for her annual round-the-world voyage. The itineraries during her European summers are very port intensive. Travelers who prefer more days at sea will probably find the transpacific cruises and segments of the world cruise, the cruise around South America, and transcanal cruises more satisfying. The best deals are the transatlantic trips in late spring and fall, which, if booked early enough, offer large discounts and glorious days at sea.

Vistafjord

	Quality Rating	Value Rating
Vistafjord	⑧	C

Registry: Bahamas	Length: 628 feet	Beam: 82 feet
Cabins: 375	Draft: 27 feet	Speed: 20 knots
Maximum Passengers: 677	Passenger Decks: 9	Elevators: 6
	Crew: 379	Space Ratio: 35

THE SHIP   A spacious ship designed for long cruises and gracious living, the *Vistafjord* was launched by the vanished Norwegian American Cruises in the 1970s, and acquired by Cunard in 1983. She is a classic luxury liner, with the tasteful look of quiet grace, beautiful, distinctive interiors created at a time when expensive hardwoods were used lavishly.

The ship is known for its excellent European-style service and friendly Norwegian officers and Scandinavian crews. Its consistent quality and level of luxury has enabled it to attract discerning, well-heeled passengers for more than three decades and retain an unusually high number of repeaters.

The *Vistafjord's* large number of loyal fans cruise frequently and feel like she is their ship. American and British passengers predominate but there are also sizeable numbers of Germans—enough for the ship to be bilingual. All announcements are made in English and German and all printed materials appear in both languages. Depending on the itinerary, there might be other Europeans aboard, making for a cosmopolitan ambience. The majority of passengers are over 60 years in age, and activities are geared to them.

In 1994, the *Vistafjord* got a $15 million facelift that added 11 luxurious suites, a cozy Italian restaurant, a new public address system, a new purser's office with an interactive scan map to help you find your way, and other improvements throughout the ship. More renovations were scheduled to be made in spring 1997.

ITINERARIES   Spring–fall, Europe and Mediterranean; Winter, Caribbean and Panama Canal.

- *September–December:* Mediterranean from Barcelona to Greece, Turkey, Black Sea, and the Holy Land; Venice to Genoa; Naples to Lisbon, Canary Islands, and Morocco. December: Transatlantic, from Lisbon to Ft. Lauderdale via the Caribbean.
- *January–February:* 14 or 15 days, changing itineraries from Ft. Lauderdale to Caribbean; to Panama Canal and Los Angeles, including Solar Eclipse cruise, February 20, 1998, from Ft. Lauderdale to Los Angeles via Panama Canal.
- *March–April:* from Los Angeles to Hawaii and South Pacific.
- *May–August:* Normally, *Vistafjord* spends the summer in Europe sailing on 10–18-day cruises in the Mediterranean, Black Sea, Iberia, Baltic Sea, and Norwegian Fjords.

Home Ports   Various ports, depending on itinerary.
Port Charges $65–375.

CABINS   *Vistafjord's* tastefully decorated rooms come in 17 different categories and 10 configurations which are well illustrated in the ship's brochure. Some cabins with connecting doors can be combined to create a two-room suite with a separate sitting area. The cabins are large; most are furnished with twin beds (some convert to king), one or two chairs and a cocktail table, a large mirrored dresser with locking drawers, a mini-fridge, and generous closets. All cabins have television, radio, and soundproof walls. Ninety percent of the bathrooms have tubs as well as showers. Terry robes are supplied and your basket of fresh fruit is replenished daily.

All of the *Vistafjord's* cabins have new furnishings, most have new bathrooms, and two-thirds were completely remodeled during the 1994 renovations. Two basic color schemes were used: blue and white floral coordinated with a herringbone blue upholstery, and coral and white floral with a herringbone coral upholstery.

Each of the 11 deluxe suites added on the newly created Bridge Deck has a private balcony. Two of the suites are duplexes with huge living rooms, as well as private Jacuzzis, saunas, and exercise rooms. Four cabins on main and upper decks were modified to accommodate handicapped passengers.

All *Vistafjord* cabins are equipped with safes, refrigerators, hair dryers, and VCRs. The telephones have caller recognition, a beeper system for calling stewards, an automatic wake-up-call system, and a 911 call button for emergencies.

Cabins are attended by Scandinavian stewardesses who are as amiable as they are capable.

Specifications   54 inside single and double cabins, 321 single and double outside; 17 suites with private balcony. Standard dimensions, 175 square feet. 73 single cabins for disabled available.

DINING   The Dining Room is the last word in understated decor. Bright, cheerful, and spacious, it easily holds all passengers at one seating. Its sea-foam green decor is complemented by tables set with new, gold-trimmed white china. The ship has open seating for the three meals.

The ship's cuisine consistently receives high marks for variety, preparation, and presentation. The very best quality products—fresh when possible—are used. The cuisine is international and sophisticated, with fish a main feature and delicate pastries a highlight. A typical menu will have three appetizers, two soups, two salads, four entrees, four desserts plus a diabetic dessert, selections of cheese, fruit, and a vegetarian menu. The ship's wine cellar is well-stocked with American and European wines.

The waiters are excellent, but surprisingly, they do not have busboys or attendants to help them. Some may find that this results in somewhat slow service, but on a ship of this type, service is never meant to be rushed. Dining is one of the main activities of the day and is meant to be enjoyed at a leisurely pace.

The *Vistafjord's* popular Lido Cafe, now enclosed in glass, has been improved by the addition of its own galley which offers early morning coffee and fresh-baked rolls, as well as buffet breakfast and lunch. Luncheon buffets feature hot and cold dishes along with hot dogs and hamburgers. Frequently, lunch has a specialty theme highlighting a particular cuisine. An ice-cream parlor was also added. But the most important new addition was Tivoli, an alternative restaurant, situated on the top level of Club Viking, a bilevel lounge and nightclub on Promenade Deck aft. Dressed in elegant black, red, and beige decor, Tivoli features fine Italian cuisine and has its own wine list.

In oceanliner tradition, the ship serves hot bouillon daily on deck at 11 A.M. Afternoon tea is offered in the ballroom, often with a fashion show, and at the Lido Cafe. A late-night snack is laid out in the dining room at 11 P.M. Room service, available 24 hours, offers selections from dining room menus during meal hours and a light-fare menu at other times.

FACILITIES AND ENTERTAINMENT   Evening entertainment is surprisingly varied and belies the ship's somewhat staid image. The ballroom is the main showroom where nightly entertainment might be a Broadway-style musical revue or variety show, an updated version of a

Gilbert and Sullivan operetta, or a guest vocalist, juggler, or magician. One night is likely to be a presentation of sea chanties by the crew; another might feature a folkloric group from the port of call. The large room has a dance floor that draws a crowd when there's big band music before dinner and after the show. Gentlemen hosts are on hand to dance with the unaccompanied women. A small casino next door has blackjack tables and slot machines.

Forward on the same deck, the Garden Lounge is frequently the setting for classical concerts—an opera potpourri, chamber music, piano concert by a guest artist—as well as special parties and dancing. The room has been completely refurbished with appointments that enhance its garden ambience.

One flight up on Promenade Deck, the cozy Club Viking has two levels connected by a spiral staircase and offers piano music at noon, the ship's trio at cocktails, and a nightly cabaret with a singer or two or a jazz combo. After the show, it becomes the late-night disco.

ACTIVITIES AND DIVERSIONS   The ship offers full days of activities. The gentlemen hosts are available for dance classes and afternoon teas, as well as for dining and evening ballroom dancing. Daily, there's bridge with the instructors organizing duplicate games, arts and crafts sessions, bingo, chess, Scrabble, backgammon, discussions on wines from the ship's cellars, astrology sessions, daily lectures by guest experts, a tour of the bridge, and a great variety of recorded music on your cabin radio and television channels.

On Veranda Deck between the North Cape Bar and the library and card room is the theatre where current films are shown and guest lecturers make their presentations.

The *Vistafjord*'s residential-style library, furnished with leather love seats and wing chairs, has a video library with some 400 titles and a CD-ROM search system, along with a small business center with a credit card–operated fax machine and word processors.

SPORTS, FITNESS, AND BEAUTY   The *Vistafjord* has one outdoor and one indoor swimming pool, Jacuzzis, shuffleboard, Ping-Pong, and a golf putting area. There is a wraparound deck for walking and jogging (seven times around equals a mile); a roof was built recently over the Sports Deck to allow for expanded activities. The spa has a range of daily exercises. A Spa Menu is available, as well. The beauty salon and barbershop offer mud wraps, massage, and other beauty and body treatments.

POSTSCRIPT   The *Vistafjord* offers cruising at its most traditional and caters to an older crowd of seasoned cruisers. Anyone unaccustomed to its more formal ambience might easily be bored. While the ship is not a mecca for swingers, singles, or even couples under forty, those who find an itinerary they like and who want low-key luxury and topnotch service without pretension while they sail to distant lands would be suitable candidates. There is ample activity between ports and you will be in the company of others who are well read and well traveled. There's a lot to be said for that, too.

Sea Goddess I / Sea Goddess II

	Quality Rating	Value Rating
Sea Goddess I	⑨	D
Sea Goddess II	⑨	D

Registry: Norway	Length: 350 feet	Beam: 47 feet
Cabins: 58	Draft: 14 feet	Speed: 15 knots
Maximum Passengers:	Passenger Decks: 5	Elevators: 1
116	Crew: 89	Space Ratio: 37

THE SHIPS   The opening picture in the *Sea Goddess* brochure shows one of the ships in the background with a handsome waiter in a starched white uniform—complete with white gloves—wading through the water carrying a tray of chilled champagne to a passenger floating on a mat by the shore. Improbable as it may seem, that could be you. All you need is money and attitude.

Sea Goddess is the good life—or perhaps, the good life people dream about. It's the ultimate sybaritic fantasy. Luxurious surroundings, gourmet cuisine, lazy days, indulgent spa care, romantic evenings, and people catering to your every whim. Divine decadence, as one writer has called it.

The *Sea Goddess* twins were designed for no other purpose than to offer the most exclusive, luxurious vacations at sea. Sea Goddess Cruises, launched in 1984, was the first boutique cruise line, as those with small luxury ships are known. The ships set the standard for luxury in the 1980s, introducing the all-suite concept to cruise ships, and they became the model on which other small ultradeluxe ships that followed were based. Cunard acquired the twins in 1986.

The *Sea Goddesses'* cabins, decor, itineraries, cuisine, standards of service, and activities were all planned to meet the expectations of a select group of very affluent people, providing them an unregimented ambience to give the feeling they are part of an exclusive private club—and indeed, in many ways, they are.

Over the years, *Sea Goddess I* and *II* have attracted a band of loyal fans and held a niche in the luxury market which none of their competitors have been able to do in quite the same manner. The size of the ships is the key. With a small number of passengers and high ratio of staff, exclusivity is assured and highly personalized service all but guaranteed. The natural camaraderie among passengers is evident, almost from the first day. Without effort, a clubby atmosphere develops and friendships are made easily. By the second day, you recognize virtually everyone. By the end of the week, you have probably met them all—on a shore excursion, sharing lunch, over drinks, or in a casual chat on deck.

Sea Goddess passengers are obviously affluent—successful business people, high-level managers, entrepreneurs, professionals, new money rather than old; experienced with luxury; self-assured but not stuffy; active but not fanatic about fitness. They range in age from mid-30s–mid-60s or more; almost all are couples and likely to be on a honeymoon or celebrating a birthday or anniversary.

They are more likely to care about enjoying fine dining, fine wines, and living the good life than delving deep into its refinements. About half will have sailed on a *Sea Goddess* before, and depending upon the area of the cruise, about half will be North Americans with the remainder Germans, Scandinavians, Swiss, and other Europeans.

The ships' interiors, created by the well-known Scandinavian designer Petter Yran, are marked by sophisticated, understated luxury. Elegant and cozy at the same time, the decor employs the highest quality fabrics in muted pastels against marble, fine wood, and brass trim and accented with contemporary art and Oriental rugs. Huge bouquets of flowers are everywhere.

Actually, the luxury of a *Sea Goddess* cruise begins before you leave home. About a month prior to your departure, you receive a navy velvet box with a leather passport case, luggage tags, and a personal preference request form. It asks you to specify which spirits you will require in your suite (included in the tab and replenished at your request), the type of books and magazines you prefer, and your preference of twin or double bed. You are advised the social director will happily arrange private car tours or golf and tennis at ports of call, and you are invited to note the appointments you might need in the hair salon or with the masseuse. Robin Leach couldn't do better.

SEA GODDESS I ITINERARIES   The ship prolongs her Mediterranean summer through October, sailing on varied seven-day itineraries from Venice, Athens, Istanbul, Rome, and Barcelona before departing for the Caribbean on a nine-day transatlantic cruise from Tenerife to St. Thomas.

- *November–December:* In 1997 for the first time in her 14-year history, the ship offers a series of three- and four-night cruises from St. Thomas in November, returning to her traditional seven-night cruises in December. The short cruises can be combined with two or three nights at the Ritz Carlton Hotel in St. Thomas. The three-night cruise sails to St. Barts and Jost Van Dyke; the four-night one calls at St. Barts, St. Maarten, and Virgin Gorda.
- *January–April:* 10- and 11-day Orient itineraries taking in Indonesia, Malaysia, Thailand, and Vietnam. In April, she returns to the Mediterranean via Singapore, Bombay, and Haifa. Shore excursions at selected ports are included in the cruise price on most cruises.

   Home Ports   Various ports, depending on itinerary.
   Port Charges   Included on most itineraries.

SEA GODDESS II ITINERARIES   After her Mediterranean summer and fall, the ship sails to East Africa for a series of cruises in November. In December, she continues to the Orient, where she spends the winter, returning to the Mediterranean for the summer. On most cruises, shore excursions at selected ports are included in the cruise price.

   Home Ports   Various ports, depending on itinerary.
   Port Charges   Included on most itineraries.

CABINS   Accommodations—all outside suites of identical size— are found on all four of the ships' passenger decks. Smaller than the cabins found on some of the newer luxury ships, they are nonetheless comfortable and beautifully appointed in a harmony of soft colors and built-in shelves and cabinets of light wood.

They have a bedroom and sitting room that can be divided by a curtain. The sleeping area is next to a large picture window, which some people prefer (suites often have the lounge next to the window) as it avoids having guests walk through one's bedroom or disturbing your cabin mate who might be sleeping. The lounge area has a sofa, chair, and coffee table with extensions for converting it into a table for dining en suite. The suites have full bathrooms with tub and shower, but they are small. They are, however, stocked with ample toiletries, piles of thick towels, and terry robes. There are three full-length closets but they, too, are small.

All have telephone, radio, refrigerator, remote-control television, VCR (more than 400 video titles are available from the library at all times), key-card door lock, safe, good lighting, and a bar stocked with the drink preferences you listed. Upon arrival you will find a bowl of fresh fruit and a vase of fresh flowers. Cabin attendants are European stewardesses, cheerful and efficient.

Specifications   58 outside suites; dimensions, 205 square feet. All suites with twin beds convert to double; no singles. Cabins for disabled available.

DINING   The luxury of a *Sea Goddess* is most radiant in its dining experience. The Dining Salon, a sea of pink and white tranquility any time of day, offers one open seating for three meals, meaning that patrons may dine when they want, with whom they want. An intimate corner table for two is accommodated as easily as a party of eight.

Dinner, the highlight of the day, is a leisurely affair in a stylish, sophisticated, and romantic atmosphere with soft background piano music. Orders are prepared individually as in a restaurant and served with premium wines and champagne. They are beautifully presented and graciously served at tables set with elegant, fine china and crystal and fresh flowers. The house wines (no additional charge) are excellent and represent labels from around the world. Other fine wines are available at additional cost.

Sea Goddess fans insist the cuisine is the best of any cruise ship (those partial to the competition say the same about their favorites, too). The menus are imaginative and varied with entrees ranging from the esoteric—medallions of reindeer—to traditional. Like the pounds of caviar that seem to come from a bottomless well, foie gras and truffles are used liberally as well. Ingredients are fresh, often purchased locally, and meats are of the highest quality. When you find the entrees not to your liking, you may order something not on the menu. Indeed, you are expected to request your favorites.

Buffet breakfast and lunch are served at the casual, umbrella-shaded Outdoor Cafe topside. Full meals served course by course in your suite are available around the clock. If you want champagne and caviar at 3 A.M. or 3 P.M.—no problem.

SERVICE   Pampered service is the hallmark of a *Sea Goddess* cruise. From the moment you step aboard, you are in something of a never-never land where your every wish or whim is cheerfully granted. And no doubt some people make outrageous requests, if for no other reason than to see if they can be fulfilled. They can.

The dining and cabin staffs are mostly young Europeans—polished, professional, and personable. A service charge is included in the cruise price and tipping is discouraged.

FACILITIES AND ENTERTAINMENT   Activities and entertainment are low-key and minimal. The *Sea Goddess* passenger is not one who needs entertainment, and indeed, many are attracted to the ships precisely for their unregimented ambience and lack of scheduled activities.

The Main Salon, next to the reception area, is an all-purpose lounge, used during the morning for exercise classes or meetings and in the evening for cocktails and after-dinner drinks and dancing. One flight up, the Club Salon, a smaller lounge, is the setting for afternoon tea. Some gather for a nightcap in the piano bar; others might try their luck in the small casino or browse in the library.

SPORTS AND FITNESS   The ships are best in warm weather where life on the open teak decks—from the topside sun deck to the pool and hot tub or in quiet corners—is relaxed and leisurely from sunrise to sunset. Nearby, a white-jacketed waiter waits unobtrusively for your slightest nod. A platform at the stern can be lowered to the level of the sea for passengers to snorkel, swim, and enjoy other water sports from the ship. The ships carry windsurfing boards and speed boats for waterskiing.

The spa has a minigym and is staffed by a fitness professional who schedules several exercise sessions daily for all levels of ability and is available for personal consultation. Spa cuisine is served at lunch and dinner.

POSTSCRIPT   All *Sea Goddess* cruises provide roundtrip economy air transportation from 116 North American gateways and business class for transpacific flights. Cruises include complimentary shore excursions. The cruise's all-inclusive nature—drinks, tips, and tours paid for up-front—is a key attraction. It underscores the fact that people on holiday, even when they can afford extra expenses, don't want to be bothered with them.

DELTA QUEEN STEAMBOAT COMPANY

30 Robin Street Wharf, New Orleans, LA 70130|
(504) 586-0631; (800) 543-1949; fax (504) 585-0630
http://www.deltaqueen.com

TYPE OF SHIPS   Classic steamboats.

TYPE OF CRUISES   River cruises through America's heartland.

CRUISE LINE'S STRENGTHS
- the steamboats
- the setting
- value
- turn-of-the-century atmosphere

CRUISE LINE'S SHORTCOMINGS
- limited shipboard activities
- small cabins on the *Delta Queen*

FELLOW PASSENGERS   There's likely to be a mix of ages, nationalities, families, couples, singles, and grandparents traveling with grandchildren. And they are likely to be a cosmopolitan group—Norwegians, Dutch, British, Germans, Canadians, and Americans. Average age is 62 years—mostly retired, with annual incomes over $35,000—but average age drops on shorter trips that usually include more families. There are honeymooners in their 20s or a middle-aged couple also honeymooning, and repeaters who are river and *Delta Queen* buffs who have sailed on the steamboats more times than they can remember. A surprising number live close to the river and come to cruise in order to enjoy it in a different way. Fifty-five percent have been to Alaska; about 70 percent have cruised one of the upscale, traditional lines.

Recommended For   Anyone interested in American history, culture, and literature or just good, old-fashioned values regardless of age. Those who enjoy the relaxed pace and the proximity and visibility of the shoreline that river cruises offer. Dixieland jazz fans. The gentle motion of the paddle wheeler and the locale of the cruises appeal most to seniors, but those same elements would also attract anyone uneasy about ocean voyages or straying too far from home.

Not Recommended For Sophisticated travelers expecting European-style elegance, elaborate cuisine, and polished continental service. Those who don't enjoy a certain amount of hokum. Families with young children because there are no children's facilities. Those who need large-ship amenities, such as cabin television.

CRUISE AREAS AND SEASONS Mississippi, Atchafalaya (Louisiana), Cumberland, Tennessee, Ohio, Arkansas rivers, year-round.

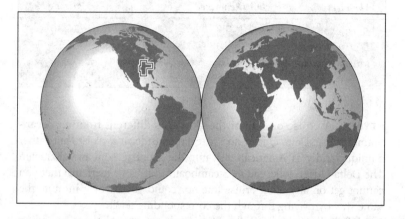

THE LINE Delta Queen Steamboat Company is the nation's oldest flag line. Of the five authentic steam-powered paddle wheelers left in the United States, those belonging to Delta Queen are the only ones offering overnight accommodations and traveling the full length of the country's inland river system.

The forerunner of the Delta Queen Steamboat Company was founded in 1890 by Capt. Gordon C. Greene, who pioneered the concept of river cruise vacations, and his wife, Mary, who was also an accomplished river pilot and steamboat captain. The couple and their sons owned and operated 28 different steamers over the years. After World War II, Tom Greene purchased the *Delta Queen* in California, remodeled her, and inaugurated her on the Mississippi River cruises in 1948. A decade later, he sold the company, and in 1973, the new owners changed the company's name to Delta Queen Steamboat Company. In 1976, it built the *Mississippi Queen*, which is twice as large as her sister steamer. The company, not to mention steamboating on the Mississippi, got a big boost in 1979, when then-President Jimmy Carter traveled down the river on the *Delta Queen*.

This line is now owned and operated by American Classic Voyages, which also owns U.S.-flagged American Hawaii Cruises. In June 1995, the owning company added the *American Queen*, the largest steamboat ever built, celebrating her debut with the 125th anniversary of the Great Steamboat Race in New Orleans when the three vessels appeared together for the first time.

The Fleet	Built/Renovated	Tonnage	Passengers
American Queen	1995	4,700	436
Delta Queen	1926/1984	3,360	174
Mississippi Queen	1976	3,364	420

STYLE   A cruise on one of the *Queens* is different from an ocean-bound cruise. Delta Queen doesn't even consider it a cruise, but rather a unique and very American visit into the country's soul and character. The Delta Queen folks call it "Steamboatin'." It's an experience that you cannot get on any other cruise line nor could you savor it in quite the same way by driving through the corresponding territory.

While floating down the Mississippi on one of these "wedding cakes" at a lazy nine knots per hour, rocking in a veranda chair, and thinking about the history this great river has witnessed, visions of Huck Finn and Tom Sawyer are sure to occur. Sounds corny, but you will be no different than the thousands of folks who have come before you.

It's a nice feeling of nostalgia, particularly in the early morning when a mist hangs over the shoreline and the only sounds are the low hum of engines and the red paddle wheel churning through the river's muddy brown water. Mark Twain called it "too thick to drink and too thin to plow." He also described the early morning magic on the mighty Mississippi as having a "haunting sense of loneliness, isolation, remoteness from the worry and bustle of the world. The dawn creeps in stealthily, the tranquillity is profound and infinitely satisfying."

After breakfast, the cruise staff's perky "Riverlorian" relates colorful bits of river history. Later, your boat, festooned in red, white, and blue flags, arrives in a river port town with its calliope (the steamboat's organ-like keyboard instrument with whistles sounded by steam or compressed air) in full song. Most likely, you are met by the mayor and a host of other town folks who welcome passengers personally and offer directions. That, too, is part of the experience you are not likely to get on other cruises.

DISTINCTIVE FEATURES   The paddle wheel; the calliope; *Delta Queen*'s authentic interiors; Dixieland jazz; Southern specialties; immersion in life on the Mississippi in the last century.

RATES

Highest Per Diem	Lowest Per Diem	Average Per Diem
$540	$141	$313

The above per diems are calculated from the cruise line's nondiscounted *cruise-only* fares on standard accommodations. Per diems vary by season, by cabin location, and by cruise areas.

Special Fares and Discounts   Early booking bonus of up to 15 percent available on select cruises.

- Children's Fares: One child 16 years or younger cruises free in some cabins on the *Mississippi Queen* and *American Queen*, when sharing cabin with two full-fare adults.
- Single Supplement: 150–175 percent, depending on ship and cabin category.

Packages
- Air/Sea: Yes.
- Others: For theme cruises, such as Kentucky Derby.
- Pre/Post: Stopover packages in New Orleans, Memphis, St. Louis, Minneapolis/St. Paul, and other main ports.

Past Passengers   *Delta Queen* boasts a 35 percent repeat passenger rate. Its past passenger group is called the Paddlewheel Steamboat Society of America. Members receive a newsletter, the *Paddlewheeler*, a special champagne reception aboard ship; advance notice of schedules; and discounts in the Steamboutique gift shops.

THE LAST WORD   For most passengers, the real destination of these cruises is the steamboats themselves. From the Huck Finn picnic lunch to the foot-stomping Dixieland jazz, it's a homespun, star-spangled slice of Americana and most people love it.

As a vacation, the riverboats have universal appeal and transcend age. On a recent cruise, an under-40 couple had in tow their 8- and 12-year-old sons on their spring break. They got a daily lesson in American history on the boat and in ports of call. But the boys also enjoyed romping around the Mississippi shoreline, a la Huck Finn. Then, one night in the lounge, the older boy was seen playing chess with a passenger who was 96 years old.

DELTA QUEEN SHIPS STANDARD FEATURES

Officers American.

Staffs Dining, Cabin, Cruise/American.

Dining Facilities One dining room with two seatings for three meals daily, plus tea and moonlight buffet; open seating breakfast.

Special Diets Diabetic, kosher, low calorie/cholesterol, low salt, and vegetarian, should be requested with cruise reservations.

Room Service Continental breakfast served in cabins upon request.

Dress Code Casual but neat during the day; fashionable dress for evening—jacket and tie for men, dress or stylish suit for women.

Cabin Amenities Some cabins with brass beds, Tiffany-style windows, veranda, sitting area, baths with shower, writing area. *American Queen*, emergency call buttons by bed; suites and deluxe cabins have tubs.

Electrical Outlets 110 AC.

Wheelchair Access Companion required. See text.

Recreation and Entertainment Jazz, big bands, cabaret, and Broadway stage revues in lounges; riverboat shows; Mardi Gras party; bridge, bingo; calliope concerts; craft and cooking demonstrations; sing-along.

Sports and Other Activities Jogging on deck; shuffleboard; kite flying; Ping-Pong.

Beauty and Fitness Small exercise room, whirlpool; aerobics; beauty salon and barbershop on *American Queen* and *Mississippi Queen*.

Other Facilities Gift shop; *American Queen* and *Mississippi Queen* conference center, fax service, bank, library, theatre on *AQ* and *MQ*.

Children's Facilities None.

Theme Cruises See specific ships.

Smoking *Delta Queen*, smoking on outside decks only; *American Queen* and *Mississippi Queen*, smoking section in lounges.

Delta Suggested Tipping Per person per night, waiter/waitress, $3.75; busboy, $2.50; cabin attendant,$3.75; dining room captain, $2.50; 15 percent of bill for wine steward; $3.50 per bag for porter.

Credit Cards For cruise payment and on-board charges, American Express, Discover, Mastercard, Visa. Only gift shops set up to take cash. Traveler's and personal checks can be cashed at purser's office.

Delta Queen

	Quality Rating	Value Rating
Delta Queen	❸	C

Registry: United States	Length: 285 feet	Beam: 58 feet
Cabins: 87	Draft: 7.5 feet	Speed: 9 knots
Maximum Passengers:	Passenger Decks: 4	Elevators: none
174	Crew: 75	Space Ratio: 19

THE SHIP The Delta Queen fleet is the only remaining example of the thousands of paddle wheel steamers that once plied the nation's inland rivers. But unlike her present sisters, which are reproductions, the cozy *Delta Queen* is the genuine article, one of a kind. She has the warmth of a bed-and-breakfast inn surrounded by a white picket fence. Her small-town friendliness mirrors the heartland river ports where she calls.

From the outside, this waterborne piece of history looks rather ordinary except for her paddle wheel. Inside, however, she will enchant you with her Tiffany-style stained glass, brass fittings, and rich, polished woods from another era. Simply knowing the *Delta Queen* is the real thing makes you appreciate every ceiling molding and creak in the floor. There's simply no other cruise vessel like her and there never will be because passenger vessels can no longer be built with wood. Indeed, *Delta Queen*'s elaborately crafted superstructure that adds so much to her character was almost her undoing. The saga to save her reads like the "Perils of Pauline."

In the 1920s, the *Delta Queen* was one of two steamers commissioned by the California Transportation Company to be built for use as luxury overnight travel on the Sacramento River between Sacramento and San Francisco. Their steel hulls were fabricated at Isherwood Shipyard in Scotland, then broken down and shipped to California for reassembly. The wheel shafts and cranks were forged at the Krupp Plant in Germany—the Krupp insignia is still there. Her American-built superstructure was crafted from pine, oak, teak, mahogany, and Oregon cedar.

The *Delta Queen* and her twin, *Delta King*, were launched in 1927—and soon became famous for their deluxe appointments—at the astounding cost of $875,000 each. The *Delta Queen* might have died as other steamships did in the following decade, but at the outbreak of World War II, the U.S. Navy took her over, painted her battleship gray, and used her to ferry troops across San Francisco Bay to and from ocean vessels in the harbor. After the war, during the founding conference of the United Nations, the *Delta Queen* carried delegates from 51 nations on sightseeing excursions.

At the war's end, the U.S. Maritime Commission put the boat up for auction. Tom Greene, president of Cincinnati-based Greene Line Steamers, the forerunner of the Delta Queen Steamboat Company, got her for $46,250, a fraction of her original cost. Greene had the vessel crated and towed by ocean tug 5,378 miles in a 37-day trip to New Orleans via the Panama Canal. From there, she went up the Mississippi and Ohio rivers under her own steam to Pittsburgh where she was refitted and remodeled to her original state. She made her Mississippi debut in June 1948.

Again in 1962, the *Delta Queen's* demise was imminent when Betty Blake, her public relations director, revived the old tradition of steamboat races—a ploy to gain publicity for the venerable steamer. It worked. Then in 1969, the *Delta Queen* was once more at death's door when the federal government's new safety standards banned wooden vessels due to their fire hazards. Blake organized a lobbying campaign that resulted in countless letters and petitions from fans and a two-year exemption from Congress—a special status she still enjoys.

The riverboat was overhauled to make her fire resistant, but time ran out and in November 1970, she made what was supposed to be her last docking in New Orleans. Then, by another act of Congress, the *Delta Queen* was saved and listed on the National Register of Historic Places. More than a million dollars was spent to update her sprinkler system, install electronic smoke detectors, and give her a fire-resistant painting and in 1989, she was designated a National Historic Landmark.

To veteran ocean cruisers, a trip on the *Delta Queen* takes a bit of reorientation. The small, intimate boat is like a country inn that just happens to be floating through America's heartland. Upon embarking, passengers are greeted by slick riverboat dandies and Southern belles in hoop gowns—looking as if they stepped from the pages of *Gone with the Wind*. The reception sets the tone for the cruise.

Unlike a large cruise ship that takes at least a day to figure out, the *Delta Queen* takes less than an hour. At the speed of 6–8 miles per hour, the ship averages 100 miles a day (the same distance may take only 90 minutes in a car), but after a day, distance and speed become irrelevant. Life aboard is a tonic for stress. No need for sea legs or concern about seasickness, either. Immediately, you notice the steamboat's hush—scarcely a murmur.

Soon passengers find a favorite spot on deck to take in the passing scenery that changes from forested banks and marshy coves to high bluffs (binoculars are helpful) and to watch the lively commercial traffic moving in a constant parade of barges and towboats, heaped with huge loads of grain, coal, scrap iron, and fuel.

The approach to each river port becomes a major event. The *Delta Queen*'s throaty whistle and cheerful tunes from the 93-year-old calliope announce her arrival and draw people down to the river. (Her calliope, built in 1897 by the T. J. Nichols Plumbing Company of Cincinnati, was originally on the showboat, *Water Queen*, which sank in 1937.) During docking operations, people ashore share news, weather, and scenic highlights with passengers lining the rails; passengers, in turn, relay their experiences about traveling on the *Delta Queen*.

The engine room, which is open at all hours and welcomes visitors, is a highlight for most passengers. The boat's engineers keep fresh coffee ready for those who come to see the operation—immense pistons pushing huge beams mounted to an axle, causing the giant red paddle wheel to turn.

ITINERARIES   3–12 days, year-round, America's heartland rivers. Lower Mississippi cruises depart from New Orleans and spotlight the Old South, visiting cities like Baton Rouge, Natchez, and Vicksburg. Upper Mississippi cruises sail between St. Louis and St. Paul and make stops in Missouri, Iowa, Wisconsin, and Minnesota.

- Ohio River cruises depart from Cincinnati or Pittsburgh and call at small towns in Indiana, Kentucky, Ohio, and West Virginia. Other itineraries include the Cumberland/Tennessee and Atchafalaya Rivers.
- The *Delta Queen* traveled on the Arkansas River for the first time in 1994 and now offers six 7–14-night itineraries. Two other new programs have expanded her geographic scope farther west than ever. One departing from Galveston, TX, sails to New Orleans on the Intracoastal Waterway.
- *Delta Queen* is celebrating her seventieth birthday in 1997 with her first cruise on the Kanawha River in 50 years, her first ever all the way to Charleston, WV. In October, she has her first Illinois River cruise since the 1970s. She also has six-night Fall Foliage cruises between St. Louis and Ottawa, IL (near Chicago) and eight-night Cajun Culture cruises round-trip from New Orleans.

Home Port   New Orleans.
Port Charges $60.

CABINS   Cabins fall into eight categories, all outside and all with private showers. Hair dryers are allowed. Of the six suites, four have large picture windows framed by stained-glass panels, a conversation area, queen-size bed, bathtub, and shower; the other two have smaller sitting areas and shower only. The suites are furnished with antiques while the homey standard cabin furnishings range from good reproductions to collectibles, along with such touches as patchwork quilts, brass wall sconces, and wooden window shutters. A few standard cabins have double beds; the remainder have twins.

The lowest price categories of cabins have upper and lower berths. All are compact, which is to say, small but comfortable and clean. They range in size from 44 square feet for the smallest quarters to 68 square feet for midpriced cabins to 135 and 156 square feet for the top brackets. Some are named after famous guests, including Lady Bird Johnson and Princess Margaret.

Cabins on two of the three decks face onto wide promenades dubbed the "front porch of America" with their inviting white rocking chairs. The third group of rooms on cabin deck open inside onto the quiet central Betty Blake Lounge, but they have outside views through windows topped with stained glass.

Bathrooms are small but functional; many have sinks just outside their bathroom door. There's a dresser and instead of a closet, clothes are hung on an open rack with brass rods.

Specifications   87 outside cabins; 6 suites. Standard dimensions, 100 square feet. 58 with twin beds; 10 with double; 19 with upper and lower berths.

DINING   The Orleans Dining Room on the main deck offers two seatings. Tables are mostly for four, although some are for two and six. Wide windows line the walls on two sides, presenting a panorama of the river. A piano player entertains with old favorites throughout dinner.

At embarkation, a Grand Sailing buffet is laid out with an array of seafood and other delicacies that would make a New Orleans chef proud. Apart from a continental breakfast in the Forward Cabin Lounge on the cabin deck, meals are served in the dining room, with choices from the menu or buffet at breakfast and lunch.

The breakfast buffet offers oatmeal, grits, fruit, sugar-cured ham, and eggs Benedict Cajun (with crawfish sauce). Pancake flavors range from pecan to raspberry. Southern specialties like biscuits and sausage gravy can be ordered from the menu.

Menus feature good ole American favorites—steak, beef stew, ribs, catfish, fried chicken, roast duck, roast lamb—and some Southern recipes you might find in a New Orleans restaurant. Portions overall are relatively small yet sensible for those who sample all five courses, and preparation ranges from good to excellent.

One of the four entrees at each meal is labeled Traditional River Fare. It might be creamy red beans or rice with Cajun sausage and ham chunks or crawfish pie, and such southern delicacies as hushpuppies and batter-fried dill pickles. Vegetables lean to traditional southern style include mustard greens, black-eyed peas, or stewed okra, as does dessert-cobblers, strawberry shortcake and peanut butter pie, with pecan pie topping the list of sins.

In addition to an early bird continental breakfast, the Forward Cabin Lounge has coffee and iced tea available all day, afternoon tea, and a moonlight buffet at 10:30 P.M.—not as elaborate as those on sea-going cruise ships but with an interesting array of desserts, fruits, and several hot items, including a seafood dish.

SERVICE   Cabin stewardesses keep everything neat as a pin. Turndown service includes a praline or mint on your pillow. Cabin service, like all the service aboard, is cheerfully provided by fresh-faced, young midwesterners. Overall, the staff seems to be a well-integrated, clean-cut, and happy family. Their attitude is infectious and genuinely appreciated by the passengers.

FACILITIES AND ENTERTAINMENT   The revered *Delta Queen* is pretty laid back, offering simple pleasures. You won't find a television and the only telephone is for ship-to-shore communication. Despite images of riverboat gamblers and high-stake poker games, there's no casino here; you'll have to settle for bingo.

The Forward Cabin Lounge, distinguished by mirrors, dark green carpeting, and wooden pillars topped with white Ionic capitals, is a popular spot to pass the time relaxing on a couch with your feet propped on a footstool and watching the passing scenery through the windows. The lounge also has tables for playing cards and dining. From the shore excursion desk, you can check out a pair of binoculars, free of charge.

The centerpiece of the *Delta Queen* is the Grand Staircase, which takes you from the Forward Cabin Lounge up to the Texas Lounge on Texas Deck. An ornate bronze filigree railing, scrolled lattice work, and hardwood paneling accent this impressive set of steps covered in red floral carpeting and crowned by an elegant Tiffany crystal chandelier.

Although the *Delta Queen* is casual—evening gowns are best left at home—this staircase makes a fitting backdrop for a grand entrance by any lady dressed in flowing skirts.

At the entrance to the Texas Lounge is a flag-draped display with the plaque recognizing the *Delta Queen*'s landmark status. The wood-paneled Texas Lounge's piano bar is a magnet for the sing-along crowd. You can also come here to get popcorn, a hot dog off the rotisserie, or hors d'oeuvres at cocktail hour. Wide windows circle the room and provide the ideal setting for picture-perfect views of the river and sunsets.

The Orleans Dining Room, which is the boat's largest room, doubles as the entertainment lounge in the evening. After second-seating dinner, tables are rearranged to make room for a stage. Entertainers dazzle audiences with rousing ragtime piano, Dixieland jazz, or banjo strummin'. When the show is over, passengers are invited to dance or join the Night Owl Society for music in the Texas Lounge. The wholesome entertainment is in keeping with the character of the boat, and passengers get involved in festivities, and hokey contests. But this is not really a late-night crowd; most are in bed by 11 P.M.

ACTIVITIES AND DIVERSIONS   The daily schedule is not jam-packed with activities, but there is enough to do, including some things you would never encounter on an ocean cruise—flying kites from the Sun Deck, for example. If you're musically inclined—or even if you're not—you can try your hand at the vintage steam calliope also on the Sun Deck. Everyone who bangs the keyboard gets a commemorative certificate marking the achievement.

Other daytime activities include card tournaments, lessons on the history of the *Delta Queen*, radio trivia games, pilot house tours, wine and cheese parties, old-fashioned sing-alongs, a Mardi Gras costume party, champagne receptions, and walking and jogging to the music of the calliope. Talks by the Riverlorian are well attended.

The Betty Blake Lounge, named for the lady who helped save the *Delta Queen*, is a softly lit parlor filled with armchairs and sofas, writing desks, bookcases, and framed memorabilia. It's a good place to curl up with a book, play a board game, do needlework or write a postcard, which you can have canceled with a *Delta Queen* postmark at the purser's office, just outside the Betty Blake Lounge. It's a fun souvenir of America's only moving post office on inland waterways.

Should you need a wake-up call in the morning, you can get a rap on your door by signing on the purser's blackboard. Next door is a gift shop, exercise area with bikes and other equipment, and shore excursion office.

SHORE EXCURSIONS   Stops at tiny river towns and bustling cities include visits to a wide array of heartland attractions including antebellum southern plantations, the boyhood home of Mark Twain, the Gateway Arch in St. Louis, historic Civil War sites, a variety of museums, and much more.

THEME CRUISES   Cruises are tied to themes almost year-round. The perennials are the Kentucky Derby in May, the Great Steamboat Race in June, Good Old Summertime in July and August, and Fall Foliage in October and November. Recently, the number of educational theme cruises with experts have been increased and are detailed in the new supplement to its brochure, *Steamboatin' University*. With them, the Line hopes to attract more passengers looking for a learning experience as well as a great vacation.

POSTSCRIPT   The *Delta Queen* has been called a romantic anachronism; there is nothing else like her. To cruise on her is to experience another time. Her small size and the leisurely pace of her cruises are conducive to meeting and chatting with fellow passengers wherever you sit. It's a small-town atmosphere that might not suit everyone.

Mississippi Queen

	Quality Rating	Value Rating
Mississippi Queen	⊕	C

Registry: United States	Length: 382 feet	Beam: 68 feet
Cabins: 207	Draft: 8.5 feet	Speed: 10 knots
Maximum Passengers: 420	Passenger Decks: 6	Elevators: 2
	Crew: 165	Space Ratio: 8

THE SHIP   If the *Delta Queen* is a country inn floating on the river, her larger sister, *Mississippi Queen*, is a stately Victorian showboat where Matt Dillon and Kitty would seem quite at home. Proud and wedding cake pretty, she rolls down the river like the grandest float in a holiday procession. On board, it's the Fourth of July—a red, white, and blue celebration of Americana amid the Victoriana. And for good measure, one day lunch is always an old-fashioned barbecue picnic with catfish, chicken, spareribs, and all the trimmings.

Polished brass railings, beveled mirrors, crystal chandeliers, and white wicker chairs supply the turn-of-the-century elements in the decor, yet behind her steamboat trappings, the *Mississippi Queen*, a fairly new vessel, offers six decks of comfort and any number of modern cruise ship amenities, such as a pool and hot tub topside, six lounges and bars, a small gym, elevators, cabin telephones, cabins with private verandas, and a beauty salon.

Make no mistake, even with her many modern-day cruise ship comforts, the *Mississippi Queen* is a true steamboat, powered by an authentic steam engine. You can assure yourself that her huge red paddle wheel is not just for show but functions when you visit the Paddle Wheel Bar on Texas Deck. There, floor-to-ceiling windows at the stern look out over the continuous turning of the paddle wheel's bucket planks that drive the vessel.

ITINERARIES   3–14-day cruises on the Mississippi, Ohio, Tennessee, and Atchafalaya rivers from late January–late December. Cruises depart from New Orleans, Memphis, St. Louis, St. Paul, Chattanooga, Cincinnati, Pittsburgh, and Louisville.

Home Port   New Orleans.
Port Charges $60.

CABINS   The modern side of the *Mississippi Queen* is probably best appreciated in her cabins. All accommodations have air conditioning, wall-to-wall carpeting, telephones, and private bathrooms. Standard cabins are small, compact, and have tiny bathrooms with showers. Suites and outside deluxe cabins have private verandas but only suites have bathrooms with tubs and showers. All cabins are named after river towns, states, Civil War battles, and the like and have historical art hanging on the walls pertaining to the name. Cabin attendants attend rooms twice daily to replenish towels and ice.

Specifications   72 inside cabins, 135 outside; 26 suites (68 with verandas). Standard dimensions are 123 square feet. 167 with twins; 20 with double; 20 with upper and lower berths; 1 wheelchair accessible.

DINING   The dining room serves three meals in two seatings with menu choices similar to those on the *Delta Queen*. Menus are rotated according to the length of the cruise—every seven days on weekly cruises, every ten days on ten-day cruises. Dinner offers several selections in each of five courses—appetizers, soup, salad, entree, and dessert. Some well-known southern dishes, however, have the chef's own twist and may not follow tradition. Don't be too surprised, for example, if a Mississippi Mud pie is a large chocolate chip cookie with ice cream, topped with hot fudge.

A light lunch buffet in the Grand Saloon, a late-night buffet in the Upper Paddlewheel Lounge, and an all-day, help-yourself, old-fashioned hot dogs and ice cream treat on the upper deck's open-air Calliope Bar (with a real calliope) are other options to stave off hunger pains. Room service for continental breakfast is available daily and may be ordered the previous night, although delivery may not always be prompt.

FACILITIES AND ENTERTAINMENT   Entertainment is G-rated and genuine with an emphasis on big band hits of the 1940s and 1950s, Broadway show favorites, ragtime, and foot-stomping Dixieland jazz. The band plays nightly for dancing in the Grand Saloon.

The *Mississippi Queen*, as on its sister ships, features a Riverlorian who entertains passengers with tales from the past, historic tidbits about the river, and explanations of the current activity on the river—all meant to be an essential part of the steamboating experience.

SHORE EXCURSIONS   Shore tours are an additional charge and are purchased on board unless arrangements have been made by a tour group. The tours in each port last about three hours and costs range from about $5–30 per person per excursion.

POSTSCRIPT   For those who prefer more amenities and a larger ship, the *Mississippi Queen* with her Victorian style, added comfort, and extra activity are probably an acceptable trade-off for the charm and unique quality of the *Delta Queen*.

Readers who are planning to cruise on the *Mississippi Queen* should review all the sections on the Delta Queen Steamboat Company to have a full picture of the cruise experience the Line offers.

American Queen

	Quality Rating	Value Rating
American Queen	⑧	C

Registry: United States	Length: 418 feet	Beam: 89.3 feet
Cabins: 222	Draft: 8.5 feet	Speed: 10 knots
Maximum Passengers:	Passenger Decks: 6	Elevators: 2
481	Crew: 180	Space Ratio: n.a.

THE SHIP   This new paddle wheeler made her debut in June 1995 by retracing the route of the first steamboat to travel the nation's inland rivers from Pittsburgh to New Orleans in 1811. With her arrival, the Line increased its capacity 70 percent with one stroke.

Constructed at the McDermott Shipyard in Amelia, Louisiana, the *American Queen* is the largest passenger vessel built in a U.S. shipyard in over four decades and took three years to complete.

No expense was spared in recreating the luxurious setting of yesteryear. The new vessel merges the best features of the *Delta Queen*, which she dwarfs, the Victoriana of the *Mississippi Queen*, whose size she exceeds, and the grand style of the most famous nineteenth-century steamboats with modern shipbuilding technology and some of today's cruise ship amenities. Her white exterior is laden with gingerbread filigree and a huge red paddle wheel turns at the stern. Inside, amenities include a swimming pool, gym, conference center, movie theater, and elevators.

The vessel is powered by two 1930s Nordberg steam engines from the *Kennedy*, a dredge belonging to the U.S. Army Corps of Engineers. The engines were salvaged after 12 workers labored three weeks to remove them from a Mississippi swamp where they had been abandoned. Each of the rebuilt engines generates 750 horsepower to drive the boat's 50-ton paddle wheel.

The *American Queen* is about 109 feet from the waterline to the top of its 70-foot-high fluted stacks which make quite a show. The stacks have 12-foot-tall flutes, and the pilothouse, which has a six-foot-high rooster weathervane, can be lowered via a hydraulic elevator to about a 55-foot height to enable the ship to pass under some of the low bridges along her routes.

ITINERARIES   Three- to seven-day cruises on the Mississippi, Ohio, Tennessee, and Atchafalaya rivers. Cruises year-round depart from New Orleans, Memphis, St. Louis, St. Paul, Chattanooga, Cincinnati, and Pittsburgh.

> **Home Port**   New Orleans.
> **Port Charges** $60.

CABINS   Cabins are designed to give a sense of a Victorian bedroom with period wallpaper, floral carpets and fabrics, brass fixtures, etched glass, and furnishings of either genuine antiques or good reproductions. Even the modern plumbing and electrical fixtures are disguised as antiques. Each cabin is individually named after a noted river town or historic steamboat.

Seven categories of cabins are distributed on all but the lowest passenger deck. Some cabins have bay windows, 98 cabins have verandas. Three-fourths of the cabins are outside; some have windows or private verandas, but most have double french doors. Standard cabins in the B and C midrange categories are considerably larger than on her sister ships.

The cabins are also more "senior friendly" with larger bathrooms, emergency call buttons by each bed, and levers, rather than handles, on doors. Details, such as these, will impress you throughout the ship.

Specifications 54 inside cabins, 168 outside; 24 suites with veranda. Standard dimensions are 141 and 190 square feet. 208 with twin beds; 6 with doubles; 8 singles; 9 wheelchair accessible.

DINING In creating the interiors, the designers borrowed liberally from famous steamboats of the past, particularly the 1878 *J. M. White*, called the most graceful and spacious steamboat of her time. Her celebrated dining saloon, which Mark Twain described as "dainty as a drawing room; when I looked down her long, gilded saloon, it was like gazing through a splendid tunnel," has been copied for the *American Queen* and named the J. M. White Dining Room.

Located on main deck, the lowest passenger deck, the dining room is two decks high with tall windows and ornate fretwork arches. A dropped ceiling in the middle divides the room and gives each half a narrow, soaring appearance. On each side of the dropped ceiling is a vaulted space with two huge mirrors in spectacular gilt frames, dating from the 1880s. Diners enjoy music played on the 1895 rosewood grand piano—one of the 200 or more antiques that accent the Victorian decor throughout the vessel. Completing the setting are the traditionally attired staff—an all-American crew and unfailingly cheerful, hardworking, and eager to please.

FACILITIES AND ENTERTAINMENT A lounge and bar at the entrance to the dining room joins the lower levels of the lobby and Grand Saloon, where nightly entertainment is staged and a band plays for dancing. Designed as an idealized opera house in a small river town circa 1880, the theatre has a proscenium stage and is lined with private box seats around the perimeter of the second story balcony.

In honor of Twain, whose *Life on the Mississippi* captures the essence of steamboating, the long narrow corridor around the upper level of the dining room has been named the Mark Twain Gallery. Books and curio cases filled with exhibits on regional birds, wildlife, steamboat history, and river memorabilia line the room. The gallery, with its Tiffany lamps and writing tables, is both a museum and library. Window areas provide cozy nooks to sit and read, write letters, or watch the passing show of the river's ever-changing scenery.

Forward from the gallery to starboard is the Gentlemen's Card Room, a book-lined masculine retreat in cherry wood and leather meant to resemble Teddy Roosevelt's library. The cases are filled with books typically found in a late-nineteenth-century home, with many first-person accounts of exploration and how-to books of the last century. It also has one of the boat's two television sets, tucked away behind cabinet doors.

To the port side is a Ladies Parlor, a delicate Victorian drawing room in light woodwork and the setting for afternoon tea, meant to be a contrast to the macho card room. From the gallery to midship is the purser's lobby and the grand gilded staircase under a spectacular filigreed ceiling, another element taken from the *J. M. White*. Beyond is the upper level of the Grand Saloon. Beyond the theatre is the lively Engine Room Bar at the stern overlooking the paddle wheel. The engine room viewing area is open to passengers round-the clock, and the engineers, proud of the vessel, seem never to tire of chatting and answering questions.

Forward on Texas Deck, the new steamer has the cruise line's signature, Front Porch of America, complete with swings and rockers. Up top, Promenade Deck has a full-circuit walkway and the Calliope Bar aft. Stairs behind the bar lead up to topmost Sun Deck with its Crow's Nest observation platform, small exercise room, and bathing pool, which is essentially a large hot tub. The Observation Deck also has a full-circuit promenade (seven times around equals a mile). For those who prefer to relax and watch the world go by, binoculars are available for loan. As on the *Delta Queen*, a number of cabins are open onto promenade decks. Although the *American Queen* is much larger than its historic sister, such touches provide a sense of community and make it easy for passengers to meet and mingle.

As with the other two vessels, a Riverlorian is an integral part of the passenger experience and holds court in the Chart Room on Observation Deck where passengers will find authentic old piloting instruments and navigational charts as well as the boat's 1,500-pound solid bronze fog bell. At the end of her inaugural season, the names of all inaugural passengers were engraved on the bell and each received a small replica of it.

POSTSCRIPT   The Delta Queen's brochure has easy-to-read deck plans for all three ships, accompanied by detailed descriptions of the cabin layout, furnishings, and facilities.

Readers who are planning to cruise on the *American Queen* should review the whole section on the Delta Queen Steamboat Company to have a full picture of the cruise experience the line offers.

Disney Cruise Line

**210 Celebration Place,
Suite 400,
Celebration, FL 34747-4600;
(407) 939-3727;
fax: (407) 939-3750
http://www.disneycruise.com**

TYPE OF SHIPS   New megaliners.

TYPE OF CRUISES   Family-oriented mainstream cruises combined with Disney World vacation, designed for all ages.

CRUISE LINE'S STRENGTHS
- Disney name recognition
- New, innovative ships
- Imaginative entertainment
- Children's facilities
- Cabins

CRUISE LINE'S SHORTCOMINGS (to be determined)

FELLOW PASSENGERS   Similar to the folks who visit Disney parks, which is to say, a cross-section of the country from 3–93.

Recommended For   Families with children or grandchildren of all ages. But, like the Disney parks themselves, the new line has designed its cruises to appeal to adults without children, too. It's a Disney product for kids of all ages.

Not Recommended For   Anyone who isn't enraptured by Disney.

CRUISE AREAS AND SEASONS   Bahamas, year-round.

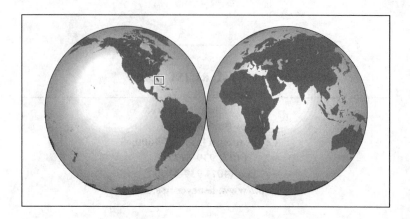

THE LINE   If the past is prologue, when Disney does something, it usually does it in a big, spare-no-expense way. So, get ready for the new Disney Cruise Line to make a huge splash in March 1998, when its first ship, *Disney Magic*, is launched.

What you will see then and in November, when her twin, *Disney Wonder*, is introduced, will be the end result of three years of intensive planning. From the outset, Disney assembled a team of highly respected veterans of the cruise industry and put them together with Disney's unrivaled stable of creative talent and dozens of the world's best-known ship designers. Together, they conceptualized and created the Disney ships, recognizing that every detail would be critical to the line's success.

Their task was to design a product that would have every adult on board feeling like the vacation was intended for them, and at the same time, give every kid the feeling that the vacation was created for them. The results will probably surprise most people; whether or not they will please all of them remains to be seen. My guess is that they will.

The first surprise will be the appearance of the Disney ships. They are classic and innovative at the same time. The exteriors are based on traditional lines, reminiscent of the great oceanliners of the past, but even there, you will find a Disney twist or two. Inside, they will be up-to-the-minute in technology and full of novel ideas for dining, entertainment, cabin design, and fun and entertainment facilities for people of all ages. Even the cruise terminal built for Disney's exclusive use at Port Canaveral was an integral part of the overall strategy; namely, to make embarkation and debarkation—revealed to be a negative aspect of crusing by Disney's market research—experiences that are entertaining and enjoyable.

Disney's plan has been to create a "seamless vacation package" combining a three- or four-day stay at Disney World with a three- or four-day cruise. Disney Cruise Line passengers will be met at the airport by Disney staff and transported to the terminal in easily identifiable Disney Cruise Line vehicles. During the ride, they will watch a video preview of the cruise. At the port they will enter a terminal that has been designed to showcase the ship to arriving guests (often terminal buildings obstruct the view). To allow a smooth embarkation, Disney has taken the "seamless vacation" a step further. There will be no lines to check in for your cruise. When your cruise is packaged with a stay at a Disney hotel, you will check in once. The same key that unlocks your hotel room door will open the door to your cruise ship cabin. Each evening on board you will dine in a different restaurant, each with a different motif, but your waiters and dining companions will move with you.

Some of the ways that the ships will cater to their varied constituencies will be in facilities, services, activities, and programs designed specifically for adults without children, seniors, and honeymooners. For example, in addition to the themed restaurants, the ships have an alternative restaurant, swimming pool, and nightclub for use by adults only, and entertainment choices will range from family musicals to adults-only improv comedy.

Overcoming another cruising negative—the hassle of tendering passengers—was also an important consideration for Disney in selecting its private Bahamian island that is included on all cruises; namely, finding one with deep water where facilities could be built for their ships to pull dockside.

The Fleet	Built/Renovated	Tonnage	Passengers
Disney Magic	1998	85,000	1,750
Disney Wonder	1998	85,000	1,750

DISTINCTIVE FEATURES   Three themed restaurants with "rotation" dining; sports bar in a funnel; children's deck; cabin design; port terminal; split bathrooms; seamless travel packages.

RATES Weeklong packages pair a visit to Walt Disney World in Orlando, unlimited admission, with a three- or four-night cruise; or, a seven-day, cruise-only package.

Highest Per Diem	Lowest Per Diem	Average Per Diem
$463	$145	$262

The above per diems are calculated from the cruise line's nondiscounted *cruise-only* fares on standard accommodations. Per diems vary by season, by cabin location, and by cruise areas.

Special Fares and Discounts n.a.

Packages
- Air/Sea: Yes.
- Others: Yes.
- Pre/Post: Yes.

THE LAST WORD Cruise experts have questioned whether Disney can fill its ships when kids are in school, but Disney officials have no doubts. A year before the new vessel had even left the shipyard, Disney had received 2,000 requests for the 875 cabins available for the maiden voyage. Disney estimates that if 1–2 percent of the 30 million annual visitors to Disney's resorts and parks buy a Disney cruise vacation, the *Disney Magic* would sell out in its first year.

DISNEY SHIPS STANDARD FEATURES

Officers European.

Staffs Cabin, dining/European, Cruise/American.

Dining Facilities Three themed family restaurants with "rotation" dining; alternative adults-only restaurant; indoor/outdoor cafe for breakfast, lunch, snacks, and buffet dinner for children; pool bar/grill for burgers, pizza, and sandwiches; a patisserie; ice cream bar; health-conscious cuisine.

Special diets On request; health-conscious cuisine program.

Room Service 24 hours.

Dress Code Casual by day; casual and informal in the evenings.

Cabin Amenities Direct-dial telephone with voice-mail messaging; both tub and shower; television; safe; hair dryer; minibar stocked for fee.

Electrical Outlets 110 AC.

Wheelchair Access Yes.

Recreation and Entertainment Showroom, theatre, nightclub, comedy club, family nightclub, adult nightclub, sports bar, lounges.

Sports and Other Activities Sports deck; basketball; batting and driving range; paddle tennis; family, sports, adult pools; Ping-Pong, shuffleboard.

Beauty and Fitness Spa with sauna, steam rooms; beauty salon.

Other Facilities Self-service laundrettes; photographic services including one-hour processing and camera and video recorder rentals; laundry, dry cleaning, and valet services; satellite phone services; modern medical facilities; guest services desk; 24-hour front desk service; fax and secretarial services; conference facilities.

Children's Facilities Age-specific supervised children's program, year-round youth counselors; children's drop-off service in evenings; private baby-sitting services; teen club.

Smoking Smoking not allowed except in special areas.

Disney Suggested Tipping Waiter: 3-night cruise, $10; 4-night, $14; assistant waiter, $6 and $8. Cabin steward: 3-night cruise, $10.50; 4-night, $14; 15 percent service charge.

Credit Cards For cruise payment and on-board charges, all major credit cards.

Disney Magic / Disney Wonder (Preview)

Registry: Bahamas
Cabins: 875
Maximum Passengers: 2,400

Length: 964 feet
Draft: 25.3 feet
Passenger Decks: 11
Crew: 945

Beam: 106 feet
Speed: 21.5 knots
Elevators: 12
Space Ratio: 48

THE SHIPS *Disney Magic* and *Disney Wonder* are modern cruise ships with long, sleek lines, twin smokestacks, and nautical styling that recalls a classic ocean liner but with instantly recognizable Disney signatures. The colors—black, white, red, and yellow—are clearly those of Mickey Mouse. Look closely and you'll see that the figurehead is a 15-foot Goofy, swinging upside down from a boatswain's chair, "painting" the hull.

The interior decor combines nautical themes with art deco inspiration but Disney imagines are everywhere, from the more subtle use of Mickey's familiar profile in the wrought iron balustrades to the bigger-than-life bronze statue of Helmsman Mickey rising from a pedestal at the center of the three-deck Grand Atrium. (What a photo op!) From the atrium lobby a grand staircase sweeps up to shops that feature Disney Cruise Line themed clothing, collectibles, jewelry, and sundries.

The ship's layout has two lower decks with cabins, three decks with dining rooms and showrooms, then three decks of cabins, and two sports and sun decks with separate pools and other facilities for children and families and for adults without kids.

ITINERARIES Three- or four-day cruises sail round-trip from Port Canaveral to Nassau, a daylong stop at Disney's private island, Castaway Cay in the Abacos. The four-day cruises add a day at sea. The cruises are combined with a visit to Walt Disney World in Orlando into weeklong packages. Or, they can be taken back-to-back as a seven-day cruise-only.

Home Port Port Canaveral.
Port Charges Included in cruise price.

CABINS The Disney twins have spacious cabins and suites. About three-fourths are outside and almost half of those come with verandas.

The ships offer 12 cabin categories from standard to deluxe, deluxe with veranda, family suite, one- and two-bedrooom suite, and royal suite. Categories are similar to those at Walt Disney World hotels. Passengers who choose to spend three or four days at a Disney resort are matched with a cabin in a comparable category.

The design of the cabins, particularly, reveals Disney's finely tuned sense of the needs of families and children and offers a cruise industry first: a split bathroom with bathtub/shower and sink in one room, and toilet, sink, and vanity in another. This configuration, found in all but the standard inside cabin category, is designed so that any member of the family can use the bathroom without monopolizing it entirely. All bathrooms have both tub and shower.

The decor uses wood paneling generously and has unusual features such as bureaus designed to look like steamer trunks—a nod to tradition. The cabins also have direct-dial telephone with voice-mail messaging; television; hair dryer; and a minibar which is stocked for a fee. All cabins sleep at least three and many can accommodate up to six. In some cabins, pull-down Murphy beds allow for additional daytime floor space.

Specifications   186 inside, 689 outside; 385 suites with verandas, 82 family suites, 16 1-bedroom suites, 2 2-bedroom suites, 2 royal suites; 14 wheelchair accessible. All cabins accommodate 3; inside up to 4; deluxe with verandas up to 4; family and 1-bedroom suites up to 5.

DINING   Dining promises to be Disney's most innovative area. The ships have three different family restaurants plus an alternative restaurant for adults only. Each night passengers will move to a different family restaurant, each with a different theme and different menu, taking along their table companions and wait staff with them. In each of the restaurants, the tableware, linens, menu covers, and waiters' uniforms have been designed specifically to fit the theme.

Lumiere's, named for the candlestick character from *Beauty and the Beast*, is an elegant, French-styled venue featuring continental cuisine served against a mural depicting Disney's *Beauty and the Beast*; while Parrot Key dishes up Caribbean-accented food in a tropical setting. But it's Animator's Palate, a concept restaurant reflecting the creative genius of Disney animation, that is the "pièce de résistance" of Disney's *Magic*. Diners will have the impression that they have entered onto a sketch in black-and-white, as though it were the beginning outlines of an artist's inspiration and, over the course of the meal, the dining room will transform itself through the use of fiber optics into a full-color extravaganza. The waiter's costumes, also, will change gradually from black-and-white to color, and even the dessert will be a "great colorful explosion."

Palo, the casual Italian restaurant named for the pole that gondoliers use to navigate Venice's canals, is the intimate, adults-only alternative restaurant, located high in the ship. Here, diners will enjoy expansive sea views and watch the chefs cook up Italian specialties. There's no extra charge, but reservations are required.

Other dining options include an indoor/outdoor cafe serving breakfast, lunch, snacks, and a buffet dinner for children; a pool bar and grill for hamburgers, hot dogs, pizza, and sandwiches; a patisserie; an ice cream and frozen yogurt bar; 24-hour room service; and a cuisine program for health-conscious passengers.

FACILITIES AND ENTERTAINMENT   Disney promises that the ships' nightly entertainment will be "unlike any other in the cruise industry" and will feature top-quality Disney-produced shows with Broadway-calibre entertainers, cabaret, and an adult-oriented lecture and enrichment program.

Walt Disney Theater, a 1,000-seat theatre with an orchestra pit and superb acoustics, will stage a different show or musical production each night, with Broadway-quality actors, singers, and dancers. In the smaller Buena Vista Theater with full screen cinema and Dolby sound, passengers can watch live shows and a variety of first-run movies and classic Disney films.

Studio Sea, modeled after a television- or film-production set, is a family-oriented nightclub offering dance music, family-oriented cabaret acts, passenger game shows, and multimedia entertainment. The art deco Promenade Lounge offers a haven for reading and relaxation by day and cocktails and piano music by night. The ESPN Skybox, a sports bar in the ship's forward, decorative funnel, will offer the best view on the ship along with the latest scores.

Beat Street is an adult-oriented evening entertainment district with shops and three themed nightclubs—Rockin' Bar D with live bands playing rock and roll, Top 40, and country music; Off Beat, a comedy club showcasing live talent nightly; and Sessions, a casual yet sophisticated place to relax and enjoy easy music.

Disney ships have no casinos. Disney says their research showed its target markets were not interested in gambling at sea.

ACTIVITIES AND DIVERSIONS   Disney diversions are geared to three types of cruisers: children, families, and adults.

A day at Castaway Cay, Disney's 1,000-acre private island, always on the last day of the cruise, is meant to provide the ultimate escape—almost as if you had landed on a deserted island. Ashore the natural environment and beauty of the island, which Disney says it was careful to preserve, will prevail—not a theme-park atmosphere. The island has miles of white sand beaches surrounded by beautiful water. A pier was built at Castaway Cay to allow easy and convenient access for passengers.

There is a protected lagoon for water sports and rentals for power boats, sailboats, kayaks, paddleboats, and floats. Nature trails and bike paths are planned. Supervised children's activities, dining facilities offering an barbecue with food cooked on the island rather than transported from the ship, an entertainment stage with live Bahamian music, and shops will anchor families and kids to the main beach area.

Slightly removed from the action, adults have a long, peaceful sweep of sugary sand to themselves. There is a bar serving drinks and they can enjoy a massage in one of the private cabanas on the beach with shuttered doors that open to the sea.

SPORTS, FITNESS, AND BEAUTY   Of the three top-deck pools, one, with a Mickey Mouse motif and a water slide, is intended for families, another is set aside for team sports, and the third is exclusively for adults. At night the pool area can be transformed into a stage for deck parties and dancing.

The 8,500-square-foot ocean-view Vista Spa and salon, situated above the bridge, is outfitted with Cybex exercise equipment and has a an aerobics room, thermal-bath area, saunas, and steam rooms. It is supervised by a qualified fitness director and offers exercise instruction, massage, and beauty treatments.

The Sports Deck has a paddle tennis court, Ping-Pong, basketball court, shuffleboard, and a batting and driving range. There is also a full promenade deck for walking and jogging.

CHILDREN'S FACILITIES   Kids have more than 15,000 square feet of space—almost an entire deck—with playrooms and other facilities. The children's programs of age-specific activities including challenging interactive programs and play areas supervised by a squadron of trained youth counselors, are expected to be the most extensive in the cruising world. The ships will also offer a children's drop-off service in the evening as well as private baby-sitting services.

Oceaneer's Adventure is the name of the overall children's program. Oceaneer's Club (ages 3–8) is themed to resemble Captain Hook's pirate ship, with plenty of places to run, climb, and perform. Oceaneer's Lab (ages 9–12) has more high-tech play such as video games and internet access. Jammin' is a separate area for teens themed after a trendy coffee bar (as in *Friends*) and has a game arcade.

POSTSCRIPT   Disney Cruise Line expects to attract a high percentage of first-time cruisers, counting on Disney's reputation for quality, service, and entertainment to dispel noncruisers' doubts about cruise vacations. At the same time, a great deal of time and effort was spent up front to ensure that the ships were designed to appeal to adults—with or without children—as much as to accommodate children and families. It remains to be seen if the product stands up to the test. Stay tuned.

DOLPHIN CRUISE LINE

901 South America Way,
Miami, FL 33132
(305) 358-2111;
(800) 222-1003;
fax (305) 358-4807
http://www.DolphinCruise.com

TYPE OF SHIPS   Classic, midsize oceanliners.

TYPE OF CRUISES   Casual, informal, unpretentious, budget-priced cruises for all ages.

CRUISE LINE'S STRENGTHS
- value
- friendly ambience
- service and crew

CRUISE LINE'S SHORTCOMINGS
- aging ships
- evening entertainment
- limited cabin amenities

FELLOW PASSENGERS   Wide range of passengers—first-timers and experienced cruisers, groups, and loyal Dolphin fans of modest means and all ages.

Recommended For   Bargain hunters, singles, honeymooners, retirees, first-time cruisers, and families with young children who want a basic, low-cost cruise in an informal, casual shipboard environment.

Not Recommended For   Those seeking a sophisticated or intellectual travel experience or jazzy megaliner ambience.

CRUISE AREAS AND SEASONS   Bahamas, Caribbean, Panama Canal, year-round; New England/Canada, summer.

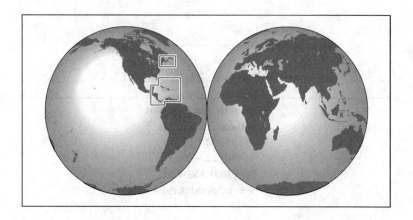

THE LINE Dolphin Cruise Line, formed by two Greek shipowners in 1979, launched its first cruise in 1984 to offer short, budget-priced cruises from Florida to the Bahamas. When the line started, it had a hard time going up against the giants of Bahamas cruises, but low prices and affordable packages that combined the cruises with visits to Disney World or Miami, helped the line compete.

Building on its success, the line added two ships and expanded its universe to other areas of the Caribbean and the Panama Canal. In 1996, it sold the *Dolpin VI*, its first ship and namesake, and replaced it with the larger *IslandBreeze* (formerly the *Festivale* of Carnival Cruises).

After securing its niche in the budget cruise market, Dolphin charted a new course in 1993 by creating Majesty Cruise Line, a separate company, to cater to upscale travelers. In early 1997, Majesty was acquired by Norwegian Cruise Line and will be absorbed by them at the end of the year.

Also in early 1997, Dolphin Cruise Line was acquired by Cruise Holdings, Ltd., a privately held investment group which owns or operates seven cruise ships, including the *Seawind Crown* of Seawind Cruise Line. The purchase is part of Cruise Holdings' long-term strategy to buy the vintage ships which are becoming available as they get replaced by new megaliners, with the goal of offering budget-priced cruises on mid-size ships. Dolphin Cruise Line is expected to continue operating as a separate entity under its present name.

The Fleet	Built/Renovated	Tonnage	Passengers
IslandBreeze	1961/78/86/97	38,175	1,146
OceanBreeze	1955/1992	21,486	776
SeaBreeze	1958/1991	21,000	840

STYLE   Friendly, comfortable, easy-paced, and economical, Dolphin Cruises are suitable for all ages and ideal for vacationers who want a week of sun and fun in the popular islands of the Caribbean.

For active adults, the ships have diving and snorkeling programs, as well as golf and tennis on-board instruction and play in port.

For families, Dolphin offers attractive prices for the third to sixth person sharing a cabin, and offers a year-round supervised children's program, Camp Dolphin. In the renovation of the *SeaBreeze*, cabins with adjoining doors were created especially for families; on the *Oceanbreeze*, pullman beds and a children's playroom were added.

The three ships have friendly staffs and crews, good but not gourmet food, fun activities, entertainment, and casinos. There are no pretensions, no surprises.

DISTINCTIVE FEATURES   Special children's prices on shore excursions.

RATES

Highest Per Diem	Lowest Per Diem	Average Per Diem
$398	$84	$159

The above per diems are calculated from the cruise line's nondiscounted *cruise-only* fares on standard accommodations. What you will actually pay *should* be *substantially* less (see Part One, How to Get the Best Deal on a Cruise). Per diems vary by season, by cabin location, and by cruise areas.

Special Fares and Discounts   Sailaway early bird discounts; 50 percent savings on two consecutive cruises; Mastercard credits.

- Children's Fare: Low third/fourth person rates.
- Single Supplement: 150 percent of double occupancy rates.

Packages

- Air/Sea: Documents sent two weeks after final payment is received, regardless of how early final payment is made. Dolphin has a toll-free number for air/sea passengers needing information on date of travel.
- Pre/Post: Miami, Orlando, Florida Keys.
- Others: Honeymoon, wedding, anniversary.

Past Passengers   Club Dolphin provides discounts to members who have taken at least one cruise with the line.

THE LAST WORD   The three ships are different in size and origin, but these differences are of little significance now under one company because the cruise experience they offer is similar. Facilities and daily agendas are standardized and many of the public rooms and decks on the three ships have the same names.

Dolphin Ships Standard Features

Officers Greek

Staffs Dining, Cabin/International; Cruise/American and European.

Dining Facilities One main dining room, open seating for breakfast, some lunch, two seatings for dinner; midnight buffet; lido restaurant for breakfast, lunch, and some late buffets.

Special Diets Requests must be made in advance.

Room Service 24 hours.

Dress Code Casual by day; casual or informal in evenings; jacket and tie appropriate for some evenings; formal suggested but not required for captain's gala and farewell nights.

Cabin Amenities Telephone, three-channel radio, vanity mirror.

Electrical Outlets 110 AC.

Wheelchair Access Some cabins available.

Recreation and Entertainment Casino, disco, nightclub, show lounge with nightly entertainment, dance classes, horse racing, games, arts and crafts, bingo, singles parties, wine tasting, ice carving, library, video game rooms, masquerades.

Sports and Other Activities Outdoor pool (3 on *IslandBreeze*), wraparound promenade, whirlpools (except *IslandBreeze*).

Beauty and Fitness Beauty/barbershop, massage, sauna, exercise classes.

Other Facilities Boutique, medical, laundry services.

Children's Facilities Camp Dolphin, year-round daily program and youth counselors; children's menu. No baby-sitting service.

Theme Cruises Jazz, country and western, 1950s.

Smoking Designated smoking/nonsmoking in public areas.

Dolphin Suggested Tipping Per person per day, cabin steward, $3.50; waiter, $3.50; busboy, $1.25. Wine stewards and bar bill are tipped on services-rendered basis.

Credit Cards For cruise payment and on-board charges, American Express, Discover, Mastercard, and Visa.

IslandBreeze

	Quality Rating	Value Rating
IslandBreeze	③	B

Registry: Bahamas	Length: 760 feet	Beam: 90 feet
Cabins: 580	Draft: 32 feet	Speed: 22 knots
Maximum Passengers: 1,432	Passenger Decks: 8	Elevators: 4
	Crew: 612	Space Ratio: 33

THE SHIP   At one time the *IslandBreeze* could boast of being the sixth largest passenger ship in the world; now it is dwarfed by megaliners. But for many people, the ship's smaller size is just right. *IslandBreeze*, with its bright, festive decor, still has the feel of a real ship, and passengers like that, too.

Completed in 1961 by Union-Castle Line as the Transvaal Castle, a one-class mailship that ran between England and South Africa, she was bought by Carnival in 1977 and rebuilt for Caribbean cruising. In 1996, she was acquired by Dolphin Cruise Line under a seven year charter/purchase agreement and renamed. Despite her age, the ship is in good condition after having had a $10 million refurbishing and refit in May 1997, which included some upgrading and refit to meet the 1997 SOLAS safety at sea requirements.

The *IslandBreeze* has one dining room, which is located on a lower deck, five bars and lounges, a show lounge, a cinema where movies are shown daily, and a spa.

ITINERARIES   Mid-December–mid-April, 1998, she will sail on two unusual and innovative alternating seven-day Eastern/Southern and Southern/Eastern Caribbean cruises round trip from Santo Domingo, leaving on Sundays. The Eastern loop calls at Barbados, St. Lucia, Guadeloupe, St. Maarten, and St. Thomas; the Southern itinerary visits Curacao, Caracas, Grenada, Martinique, and St. Croix. At other times during the year, the ship is chartered to Thomson Holidays in the Mediterranean for the British market. (The purchase agreement with Carnival stipulated that the ship could sail in the Caribbean only four months of the year.)

Home Port Santo Domingo.
Port Charges $141.50.

CABINS The ship has 12 cabin categories ranging from suites to upper/lower berth cabins. Most are furnished with twin beds, bedside lights, chair, two large chests of drawers, two full-size closets, and telephone and radio, but no television. Bathrooms have showers and some retain their original fixtures.

Specifications 308 inside cabins, 272 outside. Standard dimensions, 132 square feet. 352 with twins; 146 queens; 39 inside, 5 outside, upper/lower berths; 14 singles. None are wheelchair accessible.

DINING The large Continental Dining Room is broken down into a series of rooms through the use of columns and partitions. Both the food and service get the highest marks, especially given the low fares.

Breakfast and lunch are usually open seatings, while dinner has assigned seating at tables for two to eight persons. Dinner menus are typical of the line's offerings with five appetizers, three soups, two salads, two fish dishes, four meat and game entrees, three desserts, plus assorted ice creams and sherbets. Spa selections, lower in calories, sodium, cholesterol, and fat, and a special children's menu are offered. The dining room lunch menus are almost as extensive as dinner menus.

Breakfast and lunch in the Lido Restaurant are not elaborate but certainly adequate, while the midnight buffet is both fancy and extensive.

SERVICE The hard-working international crew gets consistently high marks for good service and an eagerness to please.

ENTERTAINMENT AND FACILITIES There are shows in the Copacabana Lounge, the main showroom, and Le Cabaret Nightclub almost nightly. The ship also has a casino and disco. The Gaslight Lounge, with large comfortable chairs, is divided from the casino by rich wooden panels that give the room the air of a cozy club—a great place for late night drinks and coffee. Movies are shown in the theatre, and television sets in public areas continuously play cruise videos of the previous day's passenger activity—previews aimed at getting you to buy a video to show the folks back home.

ACTIVITIES AND DIVERSIONS The ship has lots of outdoor deck space where passengers can relax in solitude or join the fun and games. The daily program offers the usual array of diversions—aerobics, contests, port talks, swimming pool games, and bingo. There's Ping-Pong and shuffleboard. The homey library is sometimes used for small meetings as is the larger Tradewinds Lounge.

SPORTS, FITNESS, AND BEAUTY   The ship has three swimming pools, gym, massage, and sauna; there is also a beauty salon.

CHILDREN'S FACILITIES   Camp Dolphin is a children's program with a variety of daily supervised activities that are billed as a learning experience as well as fun and games. Youth counselors are on board for every cruise and numbers are augmented during the summer and holidays. There are also children's menus. A Dolphin brochure details the daily programs and menus. There is no baby-sitting service. Dolphin offers attractive prices for the third to sixth persons sharing a cabin.

OceanBreeze / SeaBreeze

	Quality Rating	Value Rating
OceanBreeze/SeaBreeze	3	B

Registry: *OceanBreeze*: (Liberia), *SeaBreeze*: (Panama)
Length: 604/605 feet   Beam: 78/79 feet   Cabins: 384/423
Draft: 29 feet   Speed: 20 knots   Maximum Passengers:
Passenger Decks: 9   Elevators: 2   946/1,150
Crew: 310/400   Space Ratio: 28/26

THE SHIPS   Having been extensively renovated and well maintained, these ships with spacious cabins and public rooms enhanced by lots of brass and teak, belie their age. Originally built in 1955 as the British-flag *Southern Cross* for round-the-world voyages, the *OceanBreeze* was the *Monarch Star*, *Calypso*, and *Azure Seas* before its acquisition by Dolphin Cruise Line in 1992. At one time or another, she has served as a satisfying getaway for seasoned travelers or as a pleasant introduction to cruising for neophytes.

The *SeaBreeze* was built in 1958 as Costa Line's transatlantic flagship, *Federico C,* and was the *Star/Ship Royale* of Premier Cruise Lines before being taken over by Dolphin in 1989. This popular ship caters primarily to couples, honeymooners, and families attracted by her low prices.

The budget-class ships have attractive facilities and furnishings. The atmosphere is casual and the attire informal except for two gala nights when formal attire is requested but not required. She is the only traditional cruise ship sailing on Bahama cruises from South Florida; experienced cruisers will appreciate such features as shaded promenade decks with wooden deck chairs and a promenade that almost encircles the ship.

The *SeaBreeze's* appeal starts with the ship's silhouette, which is handsome and sleek. At the stern, four sun decks rise successively to offer ample sitting and sunning space. Happily, the space on two of the decks is used for outdoor dining. Festive awnings provide a pleasant setting for breakfast, lunch, or drinks. Inside, public rooms have tasteful decor in eye-catching color combinations with reflective metal ceilings, mirrored pillars, and plants. On both ships, elevators give access to all but the top deck and the lowest one, which houses the disco.

OCEANBREEZE ITINERARIES Following her New England/Canada summer cruises from New York, she will offer a repositioning cruise to Florida in October 1997, followed by a short series of cruises from Ft. Lauderdale to the Bahamas, Key West, and Western Caribbean, alternating departures on Friday for a three-day weekend cruises to Nassau and Key West; with Monday departures to Playa del Carmen, Cozumel, and Key West.

In November, she will begin sailing year-round on seven-night Western Caribbean/Panama Canal cruises round trip from Montego Bay departing on Sunday to Cartagena, Panama Canal, San Blas Islands, and Puerto Limon, with two days at sea.

Home Ports   Ft. Lauderdale; Montego Bay.
Port Charges $94.50–197.50, depending on itinerary.

SEABREEZE ITINERARIES   Seven days, year-round, Eastern and Western Caribbean. The ship departs from Miami every Sunday on alternating itineraries for Nassau, San Juan, and St. Thomas/St. John; or for Playa del Carmen/Cozumel, Montego Bay, and Grand Cayman. Both itineraries have three days at sea. The two itineraries can be combined into a 14-day cruise at considerable savings for the second week.

Home Port   Miami.
Port Charges   7 days, $127.50; 14 days, $225.

CABINS   Both ships have 11 categories of cabins—all comfortable with modern decor in pastels and colorful prints. The *OceanBreeze's* standard cabins are fairly similar in size and are equipped with good lighting and ample storage space. The suites have sitting rooms with double sofas, television, king beds, and bathrooms with tubs and hair dryers.

The *SeaBreeze*'s standard rooms are compact with functional storage space. Spacious upper-level cabins have sitting areas, extra storage space, queen beds, and tubs. On both ships, standard cabins have phones, radios, and baths with showers, but no television.

OceanBreeze Specifications   150 inside cabins, 226 outside; 12 suites. Standard dimensions are not available. 39 inside, 82 outside with twin beds; 27 inside, 65 outside with double; 80 inside, 80 outside with upper and lower berths.

SeaBreeze Specifications   161 inside cabins, 263 outside; 7 suites. Standard dimensions are not available. 93 inside, 154 outside with twin beds; 53 inside, 90 outside with double bed; 32 family cabins; 24 upper/lower berths; 2 singles. None wheelchair accessible.

DINING   Both ships have their main dining rooms on a lower deck, as is typical of older ships. The *OceanBreeze*'s Caravelle Restaurant is an attractive, pleasant setting with mostly open seatings for breakfast and lunch, and assigned seats for dinner. Tables accommodate two to ten people.

The food is good and sometimes very good, and gets high marks for presentation as well—features that are all the more outstanding in this price range. Dinner is accompanied by live piano music and the occasional fiesta atmosphere of a singing maître d'hôtel and dancing waiters. Dinners are themed around French Night, Italian Night, and Caribbean Night with menus featuring a few dishes to highlight the theme and waiters dressed in costumes to suggest the locale.

The ships offer standard breakfast and lunch buffets in an indoor-outdoor setting. The midnight buffet in the *SeaBreeze*'s Bacchanalia Restaurant gets higher marks than that featured on the *OceanBreeze*, which on a recent cruise was less than inspiring with standard cold cuts, salads, and one or two hot dishes. Room service is limited to Continental breakfast.

SERVICE   Service is the ships' best feature. The cheerful cruise staffs create a convivial spirit and atmosphere, and the friendly, courteous international crew delivers service that ranges from very good to excellent, despite an occasional language lapse.

On a recent *OceanBreeze* cruise, the service in the dining room was nearly flawless—well paced, efficient, cheerful with attention to detail. Waiters and busboys remembered the thoughtful extras—a second glass of iced tea, samplings of other courses on the menu. Others, too, deserve praise—the smiling, ever-helpful members at the purser's desk, the cheery waiters at one of the bars, the jovial officers-of-the-watch at the gangway, to name a few.

FACILITIES AND ENTERTAINMENT The *OceanBreeze's* Rendezvous Lounge, the main showroom on Promenade Deck, has a central area arranged like a cocktail lounge with seating at small tables with two or three chairs, and raised areas on the side for better viewing.

Evening shows in the main showroom fulfill their purpose—however predictably—offering Las Vegas–style revues and variety shows with a singer joined by the requisite leggy dancers, comedian, juggler, or magician. On a recent cruise, however, several shows lasted over 75 minutes, making them something of an endurance test. Of course, you are not required to stay until the end. In 1997, the ship offered some special cruises with Latin music and entertainment, with an eye to attracting the increasingly affluent Latin community in South Florida.

The Mayfair Lounge, a piano bar, along with the photo gallery and gift shops separate the show lounge from the lively two-story casino, which offers slot machines, blackjack, craps, and roulette. A small disco is on the bottom deck, while the Boat Deck has Cafe St. Tropez. Cafe Miramar, another lounge/bar, has music nightly.

Midweek and usually while berthed in port, a gala deck party is set on three aft decks and includes dancing, games, contests, and an ice-carving demonstration. Cookies and ice cream, fresh fruit, and desserts are served.

The *SeaBreeze* offers similar Las Vegas–style entertainment in its dazzling Carmen Lounge, the main showroom. The room, which has good natural light in the day and cheerful orange upholstering, is usually a quiet corner for daytime reading and relaxing indoors.

Other entertainment includes dancing in the the Royal Fireworks lounge or relaxing and socializing in the charming piano bar. A small casino offers table games and slot machines, or one can visit the Agitato Disco.

ACTIVITIES AND DIVERSIONS Daily activities are similar to the standard fare on most Caribbean cruise ships: quizzes and games, dance classes and bridge tournaments, a fashion show and perfume seminar, a mileage pool, visits to the bridge, skeet shooting, basketball, horse racing, bingo, service club meetings, golf driving, passenger talent shows, masquerade parties, ice carving and food demonstrations, and even an occasional jazz concert.

During a week's cruise, seven different films are shown, each usually four times per day, in the large theatre (which is also used as a meeting room). The small library has paperbacks and a few hardcovers—all with limited check-out times. If you plan to catch up on reading, bring your own. There are video game and card rooms. The boutiques offer daily specials.

SPORTS, FITNESS, AND BEAUTY The *OceanBreeze's* small outdoor pool and hot tubs are found on Bridge Deck; deck space and lounge chairs are adequate.

The *SeaBreeze* offers four decks of sitting and sunning areas and a pool, but its best feature is a wide outdoor promenade deck encircling the ship. The deck is ideal for an early-morning walk or jog (six laps equal one mile) and deck chairs and shaded reading space provide an alternative to sunbathing. The ship also has basketball, shuffleboard, and Ping-Pong, as well as pool games.

Both ships have beauty/barber shops, massage rooms, whirlpools, morning toning, stretch and aerobic sessions, and small gyms with stationary bikes, rowing machines, and weights.

CHILDREN'S FACILITIES Camp Dolphin is the children's program, with special menus, games, and activities. Youth counselors are on board year-round to plan and supervise children's activities. The *Ocean-Breeze* has a children's playroom, while the *SeaBreeze* has family cabins.

SHORE EXCURSIONS The selections are off-the-shelf tours similar to those offered by the majority of cruise ships, but the prices are often more moderate than some of Dolphin's competitors and the line offers special, low prices for children. Sample tours on the *SeaBreeze* are Old and New San Juan, two and a half hours, $19; and the Flamenco Night Club in San Juan, $39; other shore excursions offer sightseeing to archeological sites in Mexican ports, such as Chichen Itza by bus, $77 adults, $39 children; Tulum/Xel Ha, $69 adults, $35 children; and horseback riding in Cozumel, $68 adults, $34 children.

POSTSCRIPT Both ships provide comfortable, budget-class cruises with good service, ample daily activity, and port-intensive itineraries that would appeal to first-time cruisers and to experienced cruisers on a tight budget.

HOLLAND AMERICA LINE

300 Elliott Avenue West, Seattle, WA 98119
(206) 281-3535; (800) 426-0327; fax (206) 281-7110; (800) 628-4855
http://www.hollandamerica.com

TYPE OF SHIPS   Modern superliners.

TYPE OF CRUISES   Essence of traditional yet modern, high-quality mainstream cruises.

CRUISE LINE'S STRENGTHS
- tradition and experience
- outstanding crew and service
- easy-to-like ships
- consistent quality and style
- worldwide itineraries
- impeccable condition of ships

CRUISE LINE'S SHORTCOMINGS
- show lounge entertainment
- shore excursion cancellation policy
- lack of busboys in dining rooms of newest ships
- service problems on new ships; communication problems with dining staff due to language

FELLOW PASSENGERS   Mature, experienced travelers and families who seek comfort and consistency and who appreciate quality and a high level of service. They prefer a refined environment and select cruises by their destinations. Many are retired or semiretired business owners with some college education, executives, and professionals, but the range is from young nurses and secretaries on their first cruise to affluent seniors who cruise often to honeymooners, young families, and some handicapped travelers.

They are interested in learning about other cultures and like to have a choice of activities and the companionship of fellow passengers. They are social-minded, well-mannered, outgoing but not loud.

They enjoy traveling with old friends and making new friends. They are conservative, careful with money and seek good value as well as quality. Often they view a cruise as an opportunity to celebrate a special occasion, a wedding anniversary, or to hold a family reunion.

The average age is mid-50s in winter and younger in summer, but also varies by length of cruise and itinerary, i.e., a seven-day Alaska and seven-day Caribbean cruise on the same ship attract different ages and incomes. Over 55 percent are couples; 50 percent are groups—as different as business organizations, tour groups, or square dancing and stamp collecting clubs.

Recommended For Those who enjoy cruise traditions and want a quality experience in a refined environment but like the facilities and range of choices available on new superliners. Small ship devotees open to trying a large ship. Former budget cruisers ready to move up to higher quality.

Not Recommended For Swingers, party seekers, late-night revelers, trend seekers, or pacesetters.

CRUISE AREAS AND SEASONS Caribbean, Panama Canal, year-round; Alaska, Europe, New England, and transatlantic in summer; Hawaii in spring and fall; World Cruise in winter; Asia seasonally.

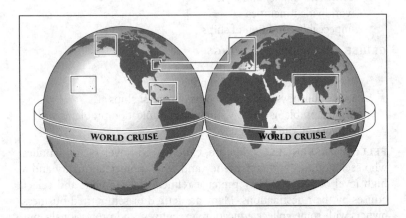

THE LINE Holland America, which has been carrying passengers since 1871, is one of the few lines to make the transition from a classic steamship company to a modern cruise line successfully—and did it better than most. Even though it had to sail through rough seas to get there, the line managed to keep its identity and traditions intact and, at the same time, develop a modern mainstream product that is now the leader of the pack.

The turning point in its modern reincarnation came in the early 1980s when the line introduced the *Nieuw Amsterdam* and *Noordam*, the forerunners of today's superliners. They were considered revolutionary at the time due to such features as a square stern that provided 20 percent more open deck space, two outdoor heated pools, fully equipped gym, spa, and whirlpool, coded cards rather than keys to open cabin doors, and television for in-cabin movies—all features that have become standard on new ships.

In 1988, Holland America took its next big step, buying the beautiful new *Homeric* (from the now defunct Home Lines), renaming it the *Westerdam*, and giving it a $84 million stretch job, and acquiring the unusual Windstar Cruises. The following year Holland America, Windstar Cruises, and Seattle-based Westours, which pioneered tours and cruises to Alaska, were acquired by Carnival Cruise Lines.

Given the sharp contrast in styles, many wondered what might happen to Holland America. As it turned out, it was a brilliant marriage that enabled Holland America to continue its expansion, introducing a quartet of new ships in the 1990s that were even more stunning than their trendsetters of the 1980s. It also enabled the line to expand in Alaska, return to Europe after nearly two decades, and increase the number of its longer cruises—all factors critical to HAL's retaining its large reservoir of loyal fans.

Holland America's newest ships, *Maasdam*, *Ryndam*, *Veendam*, and *Statendam*, are the result of a wish list drawn up by their designers and the Holland America Line staff. They combine the classic elegance of an oceanliner with state-of-the-art technology and have such features as multideck atriums, fountains, Jacuzzis, jogging tracks, and theatres Broadway could envy. They are the first of the HAL fleet to have private verandas.

In 1996, all the fleet was reflagged in the Netherlands after a change in attitude by the Dutch government and resolution of longstanding labor problems.

In 1997, Holland America introduced a new class of ships, starting with the 62,000-ton *Rotterdam VI*. Accommodating 1,320 passengers, with a cruising speed of 25 knots—20 percent faster than today's average—she gives the line a new flexibility in creating itineraries. Slightly larger twins are scheduled for delivery in 1999.

The Fleet	Built/Renovated	Tonnage	Passengers
Maasdam	1994	55,451	1,266
Nieuw Amsterdam	1983	33,930	1,214
Noordam	1984	33,930	1,214
Rotterdam VI	1997	63,000	1,316
Ryndam	1994	55,451	1,266
Statendam	1993	55,451	1,266
Veendam	1996	55,451	1,266
Westerdam	1986/1990	53,872	1,494
Unnamed	1999	65,000	1,440
Unnamed	1999	65,000	1,440

STYLE   Classic but contemporary cruises blending Old World traditions with modern lifestyles, HAL cruises offer the full range of activity expected on large, mass-market ships. Outstanding service by a warm and friendly staff is the line's hallmark, as is a refined setting, such as dining tables with Rosenthal china, crystal, and fresh flowers. The pace is leisurely and designed for experienced, mature travelers and families, who are its mainstay.

The line is making a concerted effort to attract younger passengers, partly by expanding on-board sports and fitness facilities, adding sports bars and ESPN programming, and beefing up its children's program, Club Hal. On shore, the line has added new sports and adventure-type excursions for active passengers on Alaska and Caribbean cruises and "Just for Kids" adventure and learning excursions in Alaska.

As part of this strategy, in January 1997, Holland America bought the uninhibited 2,400-acre Bahamian island of Little San Salvador, which it renamed Half Moon Cay, and is developing as its private island to be included on all Caribbean itineraries for the 1998 Caribbean season. Located between Eleuthera and Cat Island, the island is less than 100 miles southeast of Nassau. The cruise line is initially creating a $16-million facility on 45 acres fronting a gorgeous white sand beach. It promises to be one of the most elaborate and attractive private island destinations offered by any cruise line. Ships anchor offshore and tender passsengers ashore.

There are three areas—an arrival marina and plaza built to resemble the ruins of an old Spanish fort, a shopping area in the style of a West Indian village, and a food pavilion—all connected by walkways and a jitney tram. The market area will have quality shops, an ice cream parlor, coffee shop, bar, and art gallery. There will be a children's playground, a wedding chapel, and a post office which sells Bahamian stamps and has its own postmark. Passengers will get a barbecue lunch featuring West Indian selections. The sports center will offer snorkeling and diving on nearby reefs, Sunfish sailing, banana boat rides, and other water sports, as well as activities such as volleyball and basketball. Parts of the island have been designated as a bird sanctuary by the Bahamian National Trust; nature trails will lead hikers to areas with the best birdwatching.

Holland America ships have the feel of real ships, not just floating hotels, and emanate quality. The fleet, with the space and elegance for longer cruises for which it was designed, shares many characteristics that reinforce its traditions: art and antiques, integral to the decor and reflect Holland's association with trade and exploration in the Americas; Dutch officers and Indonesian crews, continue to link Holland's historical ties to Asia; and the Crow's Nest, an observation bar on the top deck, is inspired by the lookout station on the tall mast of the company's old sailing ships.

DISTINCTIVE FEATURES   Escalators on the newest ships. No-tipping-required policy. Self-service laundry and ironing rooms. On-board upholstery and carpentry shops. On-board traditions such as good libraries, fresh flowers throughout the ships, fruit basket in cabins, separate card rooms for smokers and nonsmokers, hot hors d'oeuvres at cocktails, a call to dinner by chimes played by a nattily uniformed steward passing through the ship. World cruise specials such as logo-embroidered robes, commemorative gifts, personalized stationary. Private Bahamian island.

RATES

Highest Per Diem	Lowest Per Diem	Average Per Diem
$643	$171	$335

The above per diems are calculated from the cruise line's nondiscounted *cruise-only* fares on standard accommodations. What you will actually pay *should* be *substantially* less (see Part One, How to Get the Best Deal on a Cruise). Per diems vary by season, by cabin location, and by cruise areas.

Special Note: Tips are included in the cruise fare on all Holland America ships, although additional discretionary tipping for exceptional service is permitted.

Special Fares and Discounts   KIS (Keep It Simple) is a program for early booking discounts offering up to 45 percent savings. Membership Miles, a program with American Express, offers redeemable mileage in the form of upgrades and discount dollars.

- Third/Fourth Passenger: Low rates.
- Children's Fare: On most seven-day cruises, special flat rate of $335 per child, ages 2–17, as third/fourth persons sharing parents' room.
- Single Supplement: 135–190 percent of double rate or specific published rate for certain cruises; guaranteed share program.

Packages
- Air/Sea: Yes.
- Pre/Post: Yes.
- Others: Weddings and renewal of vows onboard.

Past Passengers   Mariner Club members receive letters and promotional materials approximately five times a year, offering special discounts and cabin upgrades on selected sailings, amenities, recognition, theme cruises, and occasional cruises with HAL's president. New enhancements include baggage tags, separate check-in, Mariners party hosted by the captain, photos and special certificates for third to tenth cruise, medallions for 40,000 miles (silver) to 250,000 miles (platinum), and more.

THE LAST WORD   Holland America puts itself in the premium category, between luxury and economy, but in fact, it's at the high end of premium, a hair's breath from luxury, and *deluxe* by any standard. The refinements and thoughtful touches it offers, unavailable on comparably priced ships, reflect what traditional, stylish cruising is all about.

HAL's consistency—even the names of most public rooms are the same throughout the fleet—has helped it build a large, loyal following. To them, a certain sameness is a virtue. They do not find the predictability boring; rather, they see it as reassuring. It's the type of passengers Holland America wants and gets. If you are of this bent, you will find the ships to be the top in their class. Their price in relation to quality, particularly when you take advantage of early-bird savings, makes Holland America one of the best values in cruising.

HOLLAND AMERICA LINE STANDARD FEATURES

Officers Dutch.

Staffs Dining/Dutch supervisors, Indonesian staff; Cabin/Filipino and Indonesian; Cruise/American and others.

Dining Facilities One dining room, two seatings. Indoor/outdoor lido restaurants for casual buffet breakfast and lunch; taco, pasta, and ice cream bars.

Special Diets Kosher; low sodium, low cholesterol, low fat; vegetarian; sugar-free desserts; baby foods. Request 30 days in advance.

Room Service 24-hours.

Dress Code Casual or informal with two formal/semiformal nights per week of cruise. Tuxedo rental service available.

Cabin Amenities Television; hair dryers, direct-dial phone. Suites and deluxe cabins have VCR, whirlpool bath, and minibar.

Electrical Outlets 110 AC (110/220 AC *Noordam, Nieuw Amsterdam*).

Wheelchair Access 20 cabins on *Rotterdam VI*; 4–6 cabins on all others.

Recreation and Entertainment Theatre for movies and lectures; show lounge; nightclub; casino, bars, and lounges; karaoke; masquerades; sing-alongs; crew show; culinary demonstrations; kitchen tours; bingo, card games; bridge; pool games; dance classes; library.

Sports and Other Activities Two outdoor pools; tennis, golf putting, volleyball, Ping-Pong.

Beauty and Fitness Beauty/barbershop; saunas; massage; fitness program; gym with professional instructors; jogging track; practice tennis.

Other Facilities Religious services; medical facilities; laundry/dry cleaning service; laundry rooms; meeting room. Credit card phones.

Children's Facilities Club Hal year-round youth program with counselors and age-specific activities for three age groups; "Just for Kids" adventure and learning shore excursions.

Theme Cruises See specific ships.

Smoking Designated smoking areas in public rooms; some, such as card room, library, and theatre, are designated no smoking.

Holland America Suggested Tipping No-tipping-required policy; crew are forbidden to solicit tips, but allowed to accept them. No gratuity added to bar bills.

Credit Cards Cruise and on-board charges, American Express, Discover, Mastercard, Visa; no cash.

Maasdam / Ryndam / Statendam / Veendam

	Quality Rating	Value Rating
Maasdam	❾	A
Ryndam	❼	C
Statendam	❽	B
Veendam	❼	C

Registry: Netherlands	Length: 720 feet	Beam: 101 feet
Cabins: 663	Draft: 24.6 feet	Speed: 22 knots
Maximum Passengers: 1,627	Passenger Decks: 10	Elevators: 8
	Crew: 571	Space Ratio: 43.4

THE SHIPS   The four ships—*Maasdam*, *Ryndam*, *Statendam*, and *Veendam*—introduced a new class of ships in the 1990s that set the style and standard for Holland America into the next century. They combine Old World tradition with state-of-the-art technology and provide an imposing yet inviting ambience. The spacious ships differ in decor, which gives each a somewhat different personality, but they are identical in layout and offer almost identical facilities and activities.

Built at the Fincantieri shipyard in Monfalcone, Italy, the interiors were designed by the Dutch firm, De Vlaming, Fenns, and Dingemans (VFD), which was responsible for the *Nieuw Amsterdam*, *Noordam*, and *Westerdam*, and has helped to establish the look and layout that have become Holland America's signature.

In the public areas for the new group, VFD drew from Holland America's maritime history to capture the golden age of Dutch shipping, but in a contemporary context. Integrated into the decor are multimillion dollar collections of art and artifacts from the seventeenth, eighteenth, and nineteenth centuries, reflecting the worldwide exploration of the Dutch. These are combined with contemporary art commissioned for each ship to enhance their modern image; together, they turn the ships into floating art galleries.

In their choice of materials, too, the world was VFD's emporium using whatever was interesting—woolen fabrics from Holland, leathers from Germany, France, and England, glass from Italy. Cabins were made in Finland, a Danish company supplied the teak, and the furniture was built in Slovenia. The galley equipment and refrigerators came from the United States.

The public rooms span two decks on Promenade and Upper Promenade in an asymmetrical pattern, rather than along traditional straight corridors, thus allowing for bars and lounges of different sizes.

The *Maasdam*, the fifth ship in the company's history with the name, is a far cry from the first *Maasdam*—a 1,705-ton, double-masted iron steamship that carried 8 first-class and 288 steerage passengers and 1,500 tons of cargo. It sailed the Atlantic monthly from 1872 to 1884 at a speed of 10 knots. Today's computer-piloted *Maasdam*, moving at more than twice that speed, has only one class and facilities beyond what anyone could have even imagined in those days.

Passengers are introduced to the *Maasdam* by a three-deck atrium on the Lower Promenade Deck, reached by an escalator from the Main Deck. Under a ceiling of mirrors and fiber-optic lights, the atrium sparkles with a dazzling 30-foot glass sculpture, *Totem*, by Italian artist Luciano Vistosi. Inspired by Holland America's long association with Alaska, the sculpture contains thousands of pieces of glass that catch the light and cast specks of color on nearby surfaces. The best place to see it is from the stairs that rim the atrium and lead to Upper Promenade.

The atrium is slightly off the ship's center line. To one side is the small Java Cafe for espresso and cappuccino, and the Wajang Movie Theatre for movies, lectures, and religious services. It has adjacent meeting rooms, equipped with audiovisual facilities.

The atrium sculptures on the *Statendam* and *Ryndam*, whose decor is more rococo than that of the *Maasdam*, are classic in style, but alas, bulky and out of scale with their setting, if not artistically pretentious. On the *Statendam*, it takes the form of a huge fountain with a bronze statue of three huge mermaids rising from the sea. On the *Ryndam*, it is a tribute in marble (all five tons of it!) to sea legends with an oversized sea dragon entwined around the top and an undersized boat at the bottom with an improbable mermaid on its bow. The *Statendam*, another fifth generation HAL ship to bear the name, was voted "1995 Ship of the Year" by the Ocean and Cruise Liner Society. More baroque than the other ships and often eclectic, the interiors range from conservative to bizarre, blending textures and earth tones with classic European and exotic Indonesian motifs.

The *Veendam*, the most stylish of the group, has the same layout as the *Maasdam* but with different color schemes, furnishings, and artwork. Rather than the large fountain as the centerpiece of the atrium, the *Veendam* features a glass sculpture, as on the *Maasdam*, but with a different design. Adjacent to the atrium and sculpture is the Crystal Terrace.

ITINERARIES

Maasdam 10–14 days, Caribbean, Panama Canal, winter; transatlantic, spring and fall; Eastern/Western Mediterranean, Morocco, Western/Northern Europe, Baltic, British Isles, summer and fall.

- *November–March:* 10- and 13-days, Panama Canal transit between Ft. Lauderdale and Acapulco via Half Moon Cay (HAL's new private island in the Bahamas), Panama Canal, Golfo Dulce, Puerto Caldera, Puerto Quetzal (Guatemala), and Santa Cruz Huatulco (Mexico), or reverse.

Home Ports Ft. Lauderdale and other ports, depending on itinerary.
Port Charges Not available.

Ryndam 7–11 days, Caribbean, Panama Canal, Alaska.

- *October–March:* Ten days, Eastern/Southern Caribbean from Ft. Lauderdale on three itineraries: St. Kitts, Martinique, Trinidad, Roseau/Cabrits (Dominica), St. Thomas, and Half Moon Cay; or St. Maarten, Castries/Soufriere (St. Lucia), Barbados, Basse-Terre/Pointe-a-Pitre (Guadeloupe), St. John/ St. Thomas, and Nassau; or Nassau, St. Thomas, St. Maarten, Castries/Soufriere, Barbados, and Half Moon Cay.
- *Solar Eclipse Cruise:* Ten days, departs February 22, 1998 from Ft. Lauderdale to St. Maarten, Barbados, Guadeloupe, St. John/St. Thomas, and Half Moon Cay.
- *May–September:* Seven days, Alaska between Vancouver and Seward via Ketchikan, Juneau, Sitka, Glacier Bay, and College and Harriman fjords; or reverse.

Home Ports Ft. Lauderdale, winter; Vancouver, Seward, summer.
Port Charges $145–161, Caribbean; $110, Alaska.

Statendam 7–21 days, Caribbean, winter; Hawaii, Panama Canal, spring and fall; Alaska, summer.

- *November–December 1997:* Ten days, an unusual combination of the Western, Southern, and Eastern Caribbean with the Bahamas, departing from Ft. Lauderdale to Curaçao, Bonaire, Grenada, Roseau/Cabrits (Dominica), St. John/St. Thomas, and Nassau.

- *In January 1998*, combines Eastern/Southern Caribbean to St. Kitts, Martinique, Trinidad, Roseau/Cabrits (Dominica), St. Thomas, and Half Moon Cay.
- *Solar Eclipse Cruise:* Ten days, departing Ft. Lauderdale on February 21, to Aruba, Bonaire, Curaçao, St. John/St. Thomas, and Half Moon Cay.
- *May–September:* Seven days, Alaska from Vancouver to Juneau, Skagway, Glacier Bay, Ketchikan, and Inside Passage.

Home Ports   Ft. Lauderdale, winter; Vancouver, summer.
Port Charges $145–161, Caribbean; $85–94, Alaska.

Veendam   7–13 days, Eastern Caribbean, winter; Panama Canal, spring and fall; Alaska, summer.

- *October–December 1997:* Seven days, alternating Eastern and Western Caribbean itineraries from Ft. Lauderdale on Sunday to Key West, Playa del Carmen/Cozumel, Ocho Rios, and Grand Cayman (beginning 1998, Half Moon Cay replaces Key West); or to St. Kitts, St. John/St. Thomas, and Nassau (1997)/Half Moon Cay (1998).
- *Solar Eclipse Cruise:* Ten days, departing on February 23, 1998 from Ft. Lauderdale to Curaçao, Bonaire, Grenada, Roseau/Cabrits (Dominica), St. John/St. Thomas, and Half Moon Cay.
- *May–September:* Seven days, Alaska, from Vancouver to Juneau, Skagway, Glacier Bay, Ketchikan, and Inside Passage.

Home Ports   Ft. Lauderdale, winter; Vancouver, summer.
Port Charges $120–161 Caribbean; $85–94, Alaska.

CABINS   Comfortable, contemporary furnishings of light wood and clean lines are combined with continental touches. Standard cabins are almost 30 percent larger than comparable ones on other ships of similar category. Large mirrors lighten the room and add to their spacious feeling. In many, curtains separate the sleeping area from the sitting area; 77 percent are outside cabins.

The decor fashioned by Holland America's senior interior designer, Kym Anton, uses two basic color schemes—peach or blue. Customized floral prints with patterns reminiscent of Indonesian batik are used for the curtains and bedspreads. Standard cabins have original art portraying a Dutch theme by Seattle-based Kathy Haines Dench, who produced 500 monoprints for the three ships. Suites have original paintings and serigraphs depicting Dutch landscapes, cityscapes, and seascapes by California artist M. Rees Marlatt.

All cabins have hair dryers, direct-dial phone with computerized wake-up service, multichannel music system, and closed-circuit television. Full-length double closets and deep chests of drawers—nice features for long cruises—provide ample storage space.

Standard cabins have sofas and 70 percent have sofa beds. All outside cabins have bathtub and shower. Suites and deluxe cabins have veranda, minibar, VCR, and whirlpool bath. Each suite also has a small private dining area and receives laundry and dry cleaning service without additional charge.

Specifications   148 inside cabins, 485 outside (including 120 deluxe cabins and 29 suites with verandas). All with twin beds convertible to queen. Standard dimensions are 186 square feet, inside cabin; 196 square feet, outside cabin. 16 deluxe/36 standard outside have connecting doors for family suites. Some upper/lower berths and single cabins. 6 wheelchair accessible.

DINING   The ships' crowning glories are their dazzling Rotterdam Dining Rooms. Surrounded on three sides by floor-to-ceiling windows that embrace the sea and scenery and span Promenade and Upper Promenade Decks, the rooms are a harmony of elegance and tradition with modern technology. The two levels are connected by a grand curved staircase on which all are happy to make a grand entrance.

On the *Maasdam*, a fountain of antique marble from Argentina is the centerpiece of the lower level. High above on the ceiling is a canopy of a thousand morning glories of blown glass from Murano, Italy. Centered between the two decks is a border of tiny, fiber-optic "florets" programmed to change color, and thus alter the mood of the room.

As one passenger on a recent cruise was heard to say, "The room is so beautiful it takes your breath away."

The room is large but remarkably quiet; diners can converse in normal voice and hear the chamber music coming from the upper-level music balcony from which the ship's musicians serenade dinner guests. The secret: In addition to being spectacular to look at, the glass ceilings absorb sound.

A large number of tables have either window or balcony seats. A microphone at the captain's table on the main floor allows him or other speakers to address the entire room; guests on the upper level may view the speaker on television monitors. Both sides of the upper level have small dining rooms—the King's and Queen's rooms—for small groups and private parties.

On the *Maasdam*, the dining room is decorated in shades of red, accented by blue. Four large, colorful linen screens depicting day and night by Danish artist Bjorn Wiinblad, cover the walls on both decks. (Wiinblad also created the lido's ceramic panels and other works.)

Dining here and on all Holland America ships is more elegant and menu choices are more extensive than on most of today's mainstream cruise ships. The tables are set with white Rosenthal china bearing a gold Holland America Line logo, silver tableware, wine coolers, and vases of fresh flowers on starched linen tablecloths.

A typical dinner menu offers a choice of seven appetizers (six cold, one hot), three soups (two hot, one cold), three salads (five dressings), six entrees, including a vegetarian selection and a light and healthy one, plus selections of imported cheese and fruit, six desserts, pastries, three ice creams, and light and sugar-free desserts. New light and healthy fare along with new menu selections including more than 50 signature dishes have also been added.

Responding to passengers' preference for a casual, flexibly timed breakfast and lunch, Holland America has worked to perfect the lido buffet, outdoing its competitors in quality, choice, and presentation. No better example can be found than the pleasing, informal setting of the *Maasdam*'s Lido Restaurant with its floor-to-ceiling windows and warm teal and coral interiors. The buffets offer hot selections, prepared to order, along with cold treats. *Ryndam*'s Lido Restaurant has a light and cheerful setting with colorful abstract ceramic paintings on the wall and a whimsical yellow neon stripe across the ceiling.

More lunch choices—hot dogs, hamburgers, pasta, satay, and tacos—are available by the lido pool. An ice cream bar is a daily specialty at no extra charge. Sandwiches and desserts after normal dining hours and coffee and tea are available here 24 hours a day. On days in port, food is available by the pool, often with extended hours (up to 5 P.M. at times) for passengers returning from tours. Hot hors d'oeuvres with Indonesian tidbits are served in public rooms before dinner and a popular Indonesian buffet in the lido is a weekly event—all HAL standard features. And should you still suffer hunger pains, the 24-hour room service menu has been expanded and your steward freshens the basket of fruit in your cabin daily.

SERVICE   HAL's efficient Dutch officers and friendly Indonesian and Filipino crew are a winning combination. Unobtrusive service by an unfailingly gracious, smiling, and attentive staff is the hallmark of Holland America and one of the principal reasons the cruise line has so many loyal fans. It is also worth noting that the supervisory personnel in the dining rooms are officers and many of the staff and crew have been with Holland America for many years.

Most cruise ships simply play chimes and make an announcement over the public address system, but on this quartet, as on all Holland America ships, you are summoned to dine by a uniformed steward who passes through the ship playing dinner chimes. (Those old enough to remember will be reminded of the page boy in the Philip Morris cigarette ads.)

It grieves us to report that HAL's much-heralded service has slipped in the course of introducing four ships in less than three years, requiring an army of new employees who need more training. Hopefully, as they settle in, this situation will improve. Language is a problem. We have received complaints about communications problems, particularly in the dining room, due to employees' limited knowledge of English.

FACILITIES AND ENTERTAINMENT   The *Maasdam* and her sisters each have five lounges, often with the same names, and offering similar entertainment and activities. The Promenade Deck is anchored by the two-deck main show lounge and designed by Joe Farcus, who is known for his innovative, flamboyant ship interiors for Carnival Cruise Lines, Holland America's owning company. Farcus's mission was to enliven the entertainment arena of Holland America's new generation of ships while maintaining their continuity with the rest of the fleet.

In the *Maasdam's* Rembrandt Show Lounge, Delft ceramic tiles are the main design element, and are set against brocaded fabrics, gold-tinted mirrors, and mahogany paneling, to recall the era of the seventeenth-century Dutch master, whose portrait is etched into the glass doors at the entrance. Called the Vermeer Lounge on the *Ryndam* in honor of the seventeenth-century Dutch master, Jan Vermeer, Farcus made the tulip his theme, marking the 400th anniversary of the introduction of tulips to Holland in 1594. Designed in art nouveau style, it is reminiscent of the great movie palaces of the 1930s, with lacy mahogany woodwork and silver columns amid dozens of luminescent tulips.

For the Van Gogh Lounge on the *Statendam*, Farcus took his inspiration from the artist's classic *Starry Night*. Special effects, sound, fiber-optic lighting, and even the drawing of the curtain are computerized. Staircases frame the thrust stage, which has a revolving platform to allow for set changes. The *Veendam's* show lounge, called the Rubens Lounge, is named after the celebrated sixteenth-century Flemish painter, Peter Paul Rubens, and features glass sculptures in the style of Rubens. It recently debuted a new production show, *Las Vegas Nights: A*

Musical Trip down the Strip, with an improved sound system and lighting and lavish costumes by designer Bob Mackie.

The lounges offer Broadway-style shows featuring the ship's own entertainers along with jugglers, singers, and others, similar to the entertainment on other mainstream cruise ships. Big production shows have never been Holland America's strong point, although recently a concerted effort has been made to improve them. Not to worry, the ships have an abundance of other entertainment.

Down the hall from the show lounge balcony on Upper Promenade is the Ocean Bar, an animated lounge with music by a combo. Here Matthys Roling, one of Holland's best known artists, created her signature "drapery" art using a rich beige and red fabric to drape the ceilings and walls. William Heesen, a famous Dutch glass sculptor, added his talent designing the objects on the tables and bartop. His son, Bernard, was responsible for the glass artwork in the nearby Piano Bar, adjacent to the casino. This oddly shaped bar is designed around a piano with two adjacent semicircles with tables and curving sofas—a setting conducive to popular sing-alongs. Lights in the cozy bar are programmed to change, altering the ambience of the room.

The casino offers blackjack, Caribbean poker, roulette, dice, and slot machines. Outside the casino, kinetic artist Yaacov Agam created a computer display wall with 32 monitors programmed to show thousands of constantly changing images, many representing great works of art. Farther aft, the Explorer's Lounge is pleasant for a quiet, after-dinner drink, accompanied by the Rosario Strings—a Holland American tradition. The lounge on the *Ryndam* has a stunning mural of a seventeenth-century Dutch harbor filled with ships. The venerable cigar ceremony by the lounge's attractive Filipino hostesses—a long-time HAL exclusive—was recently extinguished, knowing it was only a matter of time before women's libbers and antismoking advocates would protest.

The Crow's Nest on Sports Deck is an observation lounge by day with 270° of angled windows overlooking the bow—an ideal vantage point for viewing a transit of the Panama Canal or the scenic splendors of Alaska. At night the lounge becomes the disco. Joe Farcus designed this room on the *Maasdam*, *Ryndam*, and *Statendam*. On the *Maasdam*, Farcus's interiors are meant to reflect the majestic scenery of the Pacific Northwest and Holland America's long Alaska connection. On the walls, dark green "ubatuba" granite is capped by white marble with jagged edges to simulate snowcapped mountains and triangular lighting resembles stylized evergreen trees. Large sections of the floor are made of slices of oak trees, about 12 inches in diameter, pieced together like a mosaic; the pattern is repeated in the tabletops. In the ceiling a wave-like pattern is meant to suggest the northern lights and gives the disco an atmosphere of fantasy in the evening.

Light fixtures have a sketch of the *Halve Maen*, or *Half Moon*, the sailing ship of Dutch explorer Henry Hudson (after whom New York's Hudson River was named) and Holland America Line's corporate symbol.

On the *Veendam*, the Crow's Nest was designed by Dutch architect Frans Dingemans as a multipurpose area divided into a trio of distinct spaces; a garden-like room with rattan chairs and greenery, just right for afternoon tea; the nautical Captain's Area with its rich suede and leather armchairs, which can be partitioned off for private parties; and the disco.

SPORTS, FITNESS, AND BEAUTY   The new ships' upper decks are designed for today's active passengers. At the center of a 112-foot span of teak deck on Navigation Deck is one of two outdoor swimming pools. One deck up on the lido, the second swimming pool, along with whirlpools and a wading pool, have a sliding glass roof that can cover the area in cool weather—a great asset for Alaska cruises. The pool is framed on one end by a bar and on the other by a tiled wall with a bronze sculpture of five playful dolphins by British artist Susanna Holt.

The topside Sports Deck has two practice tennis courts (except on the *Statendam* where the space is given over to a jogging track). A wide teak deck encircling Lower Promenade Deck has space for deck chairs, as well as walking and jogging (four laps equal one mile). Passport to Fitness is a fleet-wide program with daily exercises and other activities that awards points to participants, who, at the end of the cruise, can redeem them for prizes, such as a belt pack, and T-shirt.

ACTIVITIES AND DIVERSIONS   Throughout the day and evening the ships offer a broad range of activities from lectures, bridge tournaments, and dance lessons, to bingo, golf putting contests, and even kite flying. There are movies (complete with popcorn) and daily religious services. The most unusual diversion are guided tours of the ship's valuable art and antiquities collections. The ships also holds art auctions of contemporary works, but don't be taken in by the sales pitch. Remember, if the bargains being touted sound too good to be true, they probably are.

The ships have large comfortable card and puzzle rooms, a shopping arcade, and libraries with floor-to-ceiling windows. The *Maasdam*'s library has a series of paintings of the five *Maasdams* in Holland America's history, by Bermudian self-taught artist, Stephen J. Card. In the forward staircase on the *Ryndam*, oil paintings of the three previous *Ryndams* are also by Card.

On its European cruises, the *Maasdam* features a series of lectures on such diverse subjects as personal finance, contemporary European life, and the art of the Old World, as part of its Cultural Companion lecture series.

The Ocean Spa, at the forward end, has a beauty salon and fitness center with steam rooms, saunas, rooms for massages and facials, and a juice bar. The gym has ocean views and is equipped with treadmills, step machines, rowing machines, Lifecycles, and a Hydra fitness circuit with ten different resistance machines. In front of the spa is a large outside teak deck where aerobics and other exercise classes are held.

CHILDREN'S FACILITIES All HAL ships have year-round full-time youth coordinators and additional ones are added during holidays and summer. They organize and supervise programs designed to be age appropriate in three groups: 5–8 years, 9–12 years, and teens.

Daily activities for children ages 5–8 may include storytelling, games, arts and crafts, charades, ice cream parties, and more. Those ages 9–12 might learn golf putting, have dance lessons or theme parties, participate in deck sports, or compete in scavenger hunts, Ping-Pong, or karaoke. Teens enjoy the teen disco, dance lessons, arcade games, sports, card games, trivia contests, bingo, and movies.

All have pizza and Coketail parties and ship tours. The ships have wading pools, activity rooms with video games, and children's menus, which include such favorites as hamburgers, hot dogs, and pizza.

On the first night of each cruise, kids and their parents meet the youth coordinator who outlines the program. At sea, there is at least one activity in the morning, afternoon, and evening; none are scheduled while the ship is in port. Baby-sitters are available on request, but not guaranteed. The service is provided by staff volunteers at $5 per hour per child.

SHORE EXCURSIONS Holland America/Westours, which marked its 50th anniversary in 1997, has been the leader in Alaska travel and has a wide range of programs from cruising up close to glaciers on dayboats to traveling by rail on the domed McKinley Explorer. In Ketchikan, you can have a five-hour sightseeing/flightseeing combination for $180, go kayaking or sportsfishing, pan for gold for $32, or play golf in Juneau for $55. HAL's fleet offers two itineraries in Alaska with every Inside Passage cruise highlighted by a visit to Glacier Bay National Park.

Every HAL Alaska cruise also calls at Sitka and offers visits to the Alaska Raptor Rehabilitation Center, dedicated to rehabilitating bald eagles and other injured birds to return to the wild. Recently, Holland

America Line/Westours donated $1.2 million to help the center buy 17 acres and the building it had been leasing from the University of Alaska. Long-term plans call for adding an interpretive center with trails and ponds and a natural history display.

In the Caribbean, the Line offers 175 shore excursions throughout 30 Caribbean ports. Most are standard, off-the-shelf offerings and rates are moderate to moderately expensive. Flightseeing is available frequently and certified scuba divers are able to enjoy their sport in most locations, with a three-hour snorkeling trip in St. Thomas starting as low as $20.

Twenty tours are designated "environmentally sensitive" and recently the line added a new series of eco-tours that focus on the islands' nature, history, and culture—designed to help passengers better understand the islands. These range from rain forest hikes led by a forest preserve guide to air tours to view the archeological wonders of Guatemala and Mexico's Yucatan. Costs range from $17–175 per person.

Nature lovers can take a two-mile guided hike in the rain forest on Dominica; the five-hour tour costs $39 per person. On Martinique, the Valley of the Butterflies, a two-and-one-half-hour tour visits a plantation dating back to the seventeenth century, where an amazing butterfly greenhouse displays every lifestage of these beautiful insects, for $49.

The shore excursions on European cruises can be pricey on any cruise line, but HAL's seem to be a bit higher than its closest competitor. You can save by taking the standard city tours on your own and buying only those shore excursions that are unique or that visit unusual attractions that are difficult to reach on your own.

Be very sure of your tour choices before you purchase them. In addition to the cruise industry's standard policy of no refunds for cancellations 24 hours prior to a tour, Holland America charges a 10 percent fee for canceling anytime after you have purchased any tour.

POSTSCRIPT HAL has a no-tipping-required policy, but in fact so many passengers leave tips, it calls the policy into question. If you want to tip, use the guidelines for other ships in its category, namely, $2–3 per day for your dining steward and a similar amount for your cabin attendant.

The dining rooms of HAL's newest ships no longer have busboys and some passengers—but not all—complain that it has had a negative impact on service, making it slower and less efficient. We have also noticed a slip in service during the shakedown period of introducing four ships in three years. Language barriers may account for much of the problem; lack of training is also evident.

Westerdam

	Quality Rating	Value Rating
Westerdam	**8**	B

Registry: Netherlands	Length: 798 feet	Beam: 95 feet
Cabins: 747	Draft: 75.5 feet	Speed: 22 knots
Maximum Passengers: 1,773	Passenger Decks: 9	Elevators: 7
	Crew: 642	Space Ratio: 36.4

THE SHIP   The *Westerdam*, the largest ship in Holland America's fleet, is not one of the new superliners but she fits with them well. Close in size but longer by 78 feet and slightly narrower, she has 114 more cabins but fewer decks, and a lower space-to-passenger ratio, although the *Westerdam* is certainly a spacious ship, as moviegoers were able to see in *Out to Sea*, the 1997 comedy with Jack Lemmon and Walter Matthau.

When Holland America bought the *Westerdam* in 1989, she was only three years old and had already been hailed as one of the most magnificent ships of the decade, combining the style and refinement of great oceanliners with state-of-the art facilities—a description that fits HAL's new group, too.

To increase her capacity from 1,000–1,476 passengers and fit her with facilities that are standard on Holland America's fleet, the company spent $84 million to have the ship stretched by inserting a 130-foot central section. This provided the space to add a two-tiered show lounge, more bars, a sports deck, fitness facilities, and library and to enlarge the restaurant and second buffet.

Comfortable, classy, and contemporary without glitz, the *Westerdam* is dressed in pastels—soft blues, greens, lilac, peach—with lovely woods, enhanced by art and antiques related to Holland's seventeenth- and eighteenth-century trading tradition, big flower arrangements, and other traditional HAL touches.

Most of the public rooms are on Promenade Deck, anchored by the casino and several lounges forward and the bilevel Admiral's Lounge aft. The Amsterdam Dining Room is located on the lowest of the passenger decks, where there are also a few cabins. The main section has an interesting wood and plexiglass ceiling, rather like a geodesic dome over the center of the room. Even if the room is not as spectacular as those of

HAL's new trio, dining on the *Westerdam* is just as much a treat and consistently praised by passengers. As on all HAL ships, dining is elegant and menu choices extensive; tables are set with Rosenthal china bearing HAL's gold logo on starched linen tablecloths, silver tableware, and fresh flowers.

The *Westerdam* has not one but two lido restaurants giving Holland America the opportunity to make the most of its superior buffets. You can have breakfast and lunch in the pleasant settings of the verandah by the pool on Sun Deck or the Lido Restaurant by the pool on Upper Promenade and come back in the evening for the late-night buffet.

ITINERARIES   Seven days, Caribbean, winter; New England/Canada, summer.

- *November–July:* Seven days, from Ft. Lauderdale on Saturday to St. Maarten, St. John/St. Thomas, and Nassau, with three days at sea. In 1998, to Nassau, San Juan, St. John/St. Thomas, and Half Moon Cay.
- *August–October:* Ten days, from New York to New England and Eastern Canada for fall foliage season.

Home Ports   Ft. Lauderdale; New York.
Port Charges $129.

CABINS   The *Westerdam* has 15 categories of cabins and can boast of having some of the largest standard cabins at sea—most with comfortable sitting areas. Minimum cabins are only slightly smaller and suites are more than double the average size. Most are fitted with twin beds of which more than a third can be converted to queens, and all have ample drawer and closet space. The comfortable decor follows the same soothing colors used throughout the public rooms. All cabins have telephone, closed-circuit television, and fine toiletries, and all outside cabins except a few lower-priced ones have bathrooms with tub as well as shower.

Specifications   252 inside cabins, 495 outside. Standard dimensions are 200 square feet for outside cabins. Some upper/lower berths; no singles. 4 wheelchair accessible.

FACILITIES AND ENTERTAINMENT   Entertainment and other activities on the *Westerdam* are similar to those on her sister ships. Promenade Deck has a cluster of lounges and bars to suit most any mood at any time of day. In the Peartree Club, an orchestra plays for predinner cocktails. Later in the evening, it becomes the late-night disco. Next door, the Saloon, the piano bar dressed in red and resembling a classy turn-of-the-century New York bar, is usually filled with a sing-along crowd. Across the way, the Big Apple has a small dance floor.

As on all Holland American ships, the Explorer's Lounge, which has the ambience of a private club, is one of the most popular spots for afternoon tea, predinner cocktails, or after-dinner coffee and liqueur sipped to the music of the Rosario Strings. Decorated in deep moss green with an abundance of fine wood trim, it is one of the ship's most inviting lounges. Next door, the Book Chest is a delightful spot for those who want a quiet place to read in cool comfort.

Across the way, the Ocean Bar, where you can get a view of the sea from every table, is the best people-watching corner on deck because everyone passes en route to the Queen Lounge, a multipurpose room with evening entertainment, and the Admiral's Lounge, the main showroom.

A guided tour of the ship's valuable art and antiquities collections always draws a crowd. The list of items in the collection runs four pages. The ship holds art auctions of contemporary works, but as we have warned elsewhere, don't be taken in by the sales pitch—it's very unlikely that you are getting a bargain.

ACTIVITIES AND DIVERSIONS   At the forward end of Sun Deck is the theatre, a particularly pretty room with plush gray velour seats and deep blue carpets and walls, where current films are shown daily (complete with popcorn). The theatre is also used for religious services, meetings, and lectures. Other daytime activities are as varied as bridge tournaments and dance lessons to karaoke and bingo. From time to time the ship hosts music festivals and photography cruises. As with all HAL ships, the *Westerdam* has a year-round children's program.

SPORTS, FITNESS, AND BEAUTY   The Sports Deck has an unobstructed 40-by-40-foot jogging track, glass windbreaker walls, and two practice tennis courts. One flight down on Sun Deck, a retractable roof covers the swimming pool, two Jacuzzis, and a bar.

The fitness center on Navigation Deck offers exercise equipment, saunas, and massage rooms, but the beauty salon and barbershop are in a separate location on Promenade Deck near the boutiques.

POSTSCRIPT   On *Westerdam's* New England/Eastern Canada cruises, HAL has introduced a super new excursion in Quebec—a "progressive dinner" that enables passengers to dine around the city in small groups and have a guided tour of Old Quebec beginning with a cable car ride. Appetizers and cocktails are served at the first restaurant, dinner and wine at the second, and dessert and coffee at the third. Passengers are given several choices for each course. Restaurants are selected to reflect the city's current favorites.

Even with the new ships, some HAL fans continue to rate the *Westerdam* as the best of the fleet, lavishing praise on the food and service and appreciating the congenial atmosphere on board. Readers who are considering a cruise on the *Westerdam* should review the entire section on Holland America Lines to have a full picture of the cruise experience it offers.

Noordam / Nieuw Amsterdam

	Quality Rating	Value Rating
Noordam	❼	C
Nieuw Amsterdam	❼	C

Registry: Curaçao	Length: 704 feet	Beam: 89 feet
Cabins: 607	Draft: 26 feet	Speed: 19 knots
Maximum Passengers:	Passenger Decks: 9	Elevators: 7
1,350	Crew: 542	Space Ratio: 28

THE SHIPS   The twin ships, *Noordam* and *Nieuw Amsterdam*, were the forerunners of the *Maasdam* group, and therefore, are not so different, particularly in having the array of special features for which Holland America is known. Identical in deck plan, the *Noordam* followed the *Nieuw Amsterdam* after a year, with only minor changes.

Trendsetters a decade ago, the spacious ships came with square sterns and 20 percent more outside deck space than had been customary for ships of their size, and introduced many features that are commonplace on cruise ships today. The ships could also boast that all door sills were flush with the floor, rather than the toe-stubbing raised ones that had been standard on traditional oceanliners, and they were the first cruise ships to use small, energy-saving, fluorescent light blubs (9 watts instead of 70 watts), unknown to the general public in 1982.

The interior decor, created by the same Dutch design firm responsible for the *Maasdam* group, laid the basis for the Holland America look, tastefully blending traditional and modern styles using museum-quality art and artifacts to underline Holland and Holland America's history. The theme of the *Nieuw Amsterdam's* art collection is the Dutch West India Company of the seventeenth century, and that of the *Noordam's* is the Dutch East India Company. Huge fresh flower displays add a touch of class.

A great deal, too, was borrowed from the *Rotterdam*, Holland America's flagship, until her retirement in 1996—most particularly, the broad teak promenade with the unusual width of 15 feet, that encircles Upper Promenade Deck. It is wide enough for old-fashioned, cushioned wood deck chairs and still has ample space for two or three people abreast to pass or joggers to make their rounds. Perhaps no feature, often absent on new superliners and megaliners, is more appreciated by people who love to cruise. The promenade, particularly on nice weather days at sea, lives up to its name as something of a Main Street with passengers strolling, lounging, reading, napping, leaning against the rail watching the water, or watching people—helping them to connect with each other and the sea.

Most public rooms are on Promenade and Upper Promenade decks, and in Dutch tradition, are always as spotless and efficient as they are comfortable and inviting. As with the *Maasdam* group, the designers gave the interiors a sense of intimacy by creating many lounges and bars and laying them out in an asymmetrical pattern; but otherwise, the layout of the twins is very different from those of the newer *Maasdam*.

ITINERARIES

Nieuw Amsterdam Itineraries South America, Southern/Western Caribbean, fall–winter; Alaska, summer; Panama Canal, May and November.

- *On September 24*, from Vancouver, a new 62-day Grand Orient and South Pacific voyage, available in segments, followed in November by a 15-day Panama Canal voyage and an 11-day Southern Caribbean cruise.
- *December and April:* 11 or 10 days, from Ft. Lauderdale to Curacao (1997), Aruba, Cartagena, San Blas Islands, Panama Canal, Puerto Limon (Costa Rica 1997), and Half Moon Cay (1998).
- *January–April:* Caribbean/South America, 16 days, between Ft. Lauderdale and Valparaiso, Chile via Rio de Janeiro on both southbound and northbound itineraries. The two itineraries can be combined.
- *Summer:* Seven days, Alaska, from Vancouver via the Inside Passage to Ketchikan, Juneau, Glacier Bay, and Sitka.

Home Ports   Ft. Lauderdale, Rio, Valparaiso, winter; Vancouver, summer.
Port Charges $125, Alaska; $185–190, transcanal; $180 South America.

Noordam Itineraries   Central America, Western Caribbean, fall–winter; Alaska, summer; Panama Canal, April and November.

- October–December 1997: 7–11 days, Panama Canal, Caribbean, from Tampa to Key West, Playa del Carmen/ Cozumel, Ocho Rios, and Grand Cayman, with two days at sea.
- 1998: Seven days, Western Caribbean, from Tampa to Grand Cayman, Santo Tomas de Castilla (Guatemala), Playa del Carmen, and Cozumel/Mexico, with two days at sea.
- Summer: Seven days, Alaska, from Vancouver on Saturday via the Inside Passage to Ketchikan, Juneau, Glacier Bay, Sitka, and back.
- April and October: 10–17 days, positioning cruises between the Caribbean and Los Angeles through the Panama Canal.

Home Ports   Tampa; Vancouver.
Port Charges $145, Caribbean; $125 Alaska; $185, transcanal.

CABINS   The twin ships have 13 cabin categories of five basic types, found on eight of the nine passenger decks. They are among the largest of any cruise ship in their category and have a homey look with light wooden cabinets and printed fabrics inspired by Indonesian batik. They were created by Holland America's senior interior designer, Kym Anton, who also fashioned the cabins of the *Maasdam* group.

All cabins have phones, closed-circuit television, and multichannel music, a combination makeup table/writing desk, built-in corner or night tables with drawers and light switches controlled from the bed, a full-length door mirror, and ample closets. Wall and floor construction were given extra insulation for soundproofing. Four cabins on each ship were rebuilt in 1989, specifically for disabled persons.

Specifications   194 inside cabins, 411 outside cabins; 20 suites with picture window and king-size bed. Standard dimensions are 152 square feet inside and 178 square feet outside. 485 cabins with two lower beds (87 convert to queen); 50 with queens; 72 with two lower/two upper beds; 142 have bathtubs and showers; no singles.

DINING   The *Nieuw Amsterdam* Manhattan Dining Room (the Amsterdam Dining Room on the *Noordam*) is on the Main Deck, one flight below Promenade. With floor-to-ceiling windows lining the walls and overlooking the sea, the one-deck-high room is more conventional than the awesome rooms on the newest ships. Nonetheless it's a class act from start to finish with just as many HAL special touches—fresh flowers, soft lighting, heavy silverware, starched linens, fine china and crystal, a super Indonesian crew, and dinner music by the Rosario Strings. The dining room generally has one seating at lunch and two seatings at dinner with elaborate and varied HAL menus to tempt you.

The indoor/outdoor Lido Restaurant overlooks the pool at the stern of Promenade Deck (rather than three decks higher as on the *Maasdam* group), and offers full breakfast and lunch buffets brimming with choices. It extends outside to the Lido Terrace for hamburgers and hot dogs, make-your-own tacos, and an ice cream bar for do-it-yourself sundaes—all at no additional charge. The lido is also the setting for the midnight buffet and the weekly Indonesian buffet. Lest you worry about being hungry, a traditional Royal Dutch Tea is served in the afternoons, 24-hour cabin service is available, and your room steward freshens your fruit basket daily.

SERVICE   Indonesians form most of the service crew in the dining room and cabins, while Filipinos—a more outgoing and chatty lot—provide the ship's musical entertainment and bar service. Many have long years of service and all are unfailingly polite and efficient. After a few days, you will understand why they are HAL's biggest assets.

FACILITIES AND ENTERTAINMENT   With so many lounges, something is going on to please most everyone, every evening. The Stuyvesant Lounge named for Peter Stuyvesant, the Dutch governor of New Amsterdam (today's New York), is a big lounge that spans two decks. Its balcony has its own bar and overlooks the outdoor, wraparound promenade of Upper Promenade Deck on the port and starboard sides. The main showroom, which has the look of a large cocktail lounge more than a theatre, is richly appointed with red carpets and wood-lined walls.

The *Noordam*'s Admiral Lounge, one of the most stunning rooms at sea, has a replica of the stern of a seventeenth-century Dutch East India Company ship, which forms the backdrop for the stage. The spacious lounges are used for many daytime activities as well as nightly shows. Handsome as they are, unfortunately, sight lines are not great.

Pearl Street (Canal Street on the *Noordam*, both well-known streets of old New York), leads forward to Henry's Bar and the Hudson Lounge, popular late-night gathering spots with deep upholstered seats and floor-to-ceiling windows, a small dance floor, live music, and a long bar. As on all HAL ships, one of the favorite rooms is the handsome

Explorer's Lounge, where you can enjoy afternoon tea and after-dinner coffees to the music of the Rosario Strings. The Crow's Nest Lounge, high on the top of Sun Deck, is an observation perch by day and another late-evening rendezvous. The Hornpipe Club in a cluster of lounges adjacent to the small casino, and it doubles as a disco.

ACTIVITIES AND DIVERSIONS During the day, the ships offer standard activities—pool games, dance classes, movies in the Princess Theatre, bridge, horse racing, and bingo. For fitness folks, there is the Passport to Fitness program, a jogging track, a health spa with rowing machines, bicycles, weights, and other exercise equipment, and trained professionals to help you use them. The ships also have year-round supervised children's programs as do other HAL ships.

POSTSCRIPT The *Noordam* and *Nieuw Amsterdam* are mainstream ships, but with above-average service and accommodations at reasonable rates. They are low-key and informal, attracting mostly couples, a sprinkling of singles, and groups of young people traveling together. Holland America seems to understand better than any line that little things mean a lot to experienced cruise passengers and go a long way in gaining the loyalty of new ones. Perhaps it results from more than a century of experience.

Rotterdam VI
(Preview)

Registry: Netherlands	Length: 722 feet	Beam: 103.5 feet
Cabins: 575	Draft: 29.8 feet	Speed: 23 knots
Maximum Passengers: 1,350	Passenger Decks: 10	Elevators: 8
	Crew: n.a.	Space Ratio: 34.7

THE SHIP Although Holland America's other new ships are outstanding, the new *Rotterdam VI*, the line's sixth ship to bear the name, is being eagerly anticipated and expected to be the crème de la crème of the line, upholding Holland America's tradition with timeless grace as she sails into the twenty-first century.

When the *Rotterdam VI* debuts in late 1997 (replacing the recently retired *Rotterdam V*), she will be designated as the line's flagship, setting new standards in ship design, as her predecessor did four decades ago.

She is the first of a new class of larger ships for HAL, to be joined by two sisters in 1999. The three ships are intended to be the fastest cruise ships on the high seas, giving HAL new flexibility in designing their itineraries. They also have more deluxe cabins with verandas.

Rotterdam VI has a specialty restaurant reminiscent of an elegant Venetian dining room, a lounge that evokes the seafaring heritage of Holland America, and a special concierge desk for suite passengers.

The exterior lines of the ship are less angular, with softer, more rounded edges, but like the *Rotterdam V* she has two funnels aft. The interior style was inspired by her predecessor but not copied from it. It evokes the classic elegance of the grand oceanliners, incorporating some of her namesake's rich interiors and elements of her 1930s art deco style.

Rotterdam VI has many features that have proven popular with passengers on HAL's four newest ships in the *Statendam* class. F.C.J. Dingemans, the principal architect, describes the new *Rotterdam*'s interiors as an evolution of what he created for the other four ships, with a similar layout of the public rooms, enabling passengers to recognize immediately that they are on a Holland America ship. There is a three-story atrium (oval in shape instead of octagonal); a larger lido restaurant; a magrodome over the lido pool. Susanna Holt's bronze dolphins cavorting near the Lido Deck pool on the other ships is a family of sea lions on this one.

In other ways, Dingemans says, *Rotterdam VI*'s design represents a new era; as the flagship, it needed to be distinctive. More use of woods and darker colors give the ship a more classic feel. Works by world-class artists, commissioned specifically for the new vessel, and museum-quality antiques that evoke the Dutch maritime tradition of Holland America are an integral part of the decor.

Rotterdam VI differs from the *Statendam* class ships in several ways. Because the ship is designed to be speedier than the others, the hull is longer. Passenger capacity is higher—1,320 instead of 1,266 passengers. And there are three staircases instead of two—in effect, passengers are never more than about 125 feet from a staircase, making it easy to get from your cabin to the public rooms.

ITINERARIES The *Rotterdam VI* makes her maiden voyage in Europe, sailing October 6 on a 12-day Eastern Mediterranean cruise. She will offer two 12-day Eastern and Western Mediterranean itineraries, followed by a 23-day Mediterranean and transatlantic cruise. On December 15, she departs on a seven-day sail from Ft. Lauderdale to Puerto Cortez, Cozumel, Grand Cayman, and Half Moon Cay, where the *Rotterdam VI* will inaugurate HAL's new million-dollar private island.

- *January–April:* After two Caribbean holiday cruises and a 14-day Panama Canal voyage, the ship departs from Ft. Lauderdale on January 19, on a 97-day world cruise, available in segments.

Home Port   Ft. Lauderdale and other ports, depending on itinerary.
Port Charges $131–185, Caribbean; others, n.a.

CABINS   Standard cabins are a roomy 185–195 square feet. Another 120 deluxe cabins with 245 square feet, have verandas with chaise lounge, whirlpool bathtub, VCR, and refrigerator, among other amenities.

Navigation Deck 7 has 40 suites, all with verandas and a private concierge—a new feature for the line. Two of these suites are for handicapped passengers; four are penthouse suites with a living room and large dining area, bedroom and dressing areas, and a separate steward's entrance. At the concierge desk passengers may settle accounts, book shore excursions, and have special requests filled. The deck has a private lounge accessible by key card; it can be converted into a private function room. Special glass walls permit views out into the corridor but when privacy is needed for a private function, an electric current is applied to the high-tech glass, turning it opaque.

Specifications   117 inside cabins, 541 outside; 40 suites; 160 cabins with verandas; some adjoining cabins. 498 standard cabins with twin beds; 618 with convertible twins or queen beds; 284 with third and fourth berths. No singles. 20 cabins for disabled.

DINING   The elegant two-level dining room, similar to those of the *Statendam* group, is aft on the Promenade and Upper Promenade Decks, and has the trademark high ceiling of Venetian glass. On the back wall is a giant mural by Dutch artist Klaas Posthuma, reminiscent of the wall treatment in *Rotterdam V's* Ritz Carlton room.

The ship's new dining feature is a specialty Italian restaurant where passengers dine by reservation, at no extra charge, in an opulent room reminiscent of a baroque villa in Venice. The room is dressed in black with gold-framed mirrors in the ceiling, black and gold columns along the walls, and glass Venetian candelabras in the alcoves. It seats about 90 people and is divided into three intimate areas. Tables have an innovative design with a moveable top that allows people sitting in the banquettes to get in and out of their seats easily.

In the informal surroundings of the large Lido Restaurant, passengers can enjoy a full breakfast and lunch or have hot dogs and hamburgers, grilled to order, and tacos from the self-service bar. There's also the HAL standard make-your-own ice cream sundae bar along with tea and coffee throughout the day.

FACILITIES AND ENTERTAINMENT   The Ambassador's Bar (Upper Promenade Deck) is also linked to Holland America's past with a dance floor in the style of the Ritz Carlton room and a ceiling similar to one on the old *Nieuw Amsterdam*. The atmosphere is that of a friendly harbor pub with nautical decor enhanced by the woodwork which resembles the planking of old ships.

The room also has replicas of items from the old Holland America building in *Rotterdam*—a copy of the sculpture of Henry Hudson's ship, *Half Moon*, that crowns the roof, and a replica of an ornate lamppost that stands outside the building, now the Hotel New York. The piano in the bar is on a turntable, with a moveable wall that allows for different configurations, from a small piano bar to a large room for dancing.

The Crow's Nest (Observatory Deck forward) is a multipurpose room with a "Tea Area," decorated with porcelain and silver reminiscent of Holland's Golden Age of shipping, and a "Captain's Area," with leather chairs and old ship models. At the center is a circular bar and a dance floor that becomes the disco at night.

The larger Explorers' Lounge, outside the upper level of the dining room, focuses on the maritime heritage of Italy as well as Holland, in a large mural of Renaissance Venice. The lounge has a dance floor made of Italian marble in a floral pattern.

The two-level main show lounge which anchors the forward end of the Promenade decks has state-of-the-art sound and lighting equipment, with a rotating stage and hydraulic lifts; there is a dance floor in the center of the room. The decor, meant to reflect the opulent age of sea travel, is in deep red, burgundy, and orange. The theatre curtain is hand-painted satin in shades of maroon, gold, and black. From the ceiling hang huge lamps like giant, upside-down umbrellas etched in gold, and along the sides are gold and black statues holding large candelabras.

CHILDREN'S FACILITIES   The Sports Deck has a children's playroom, complete with craft-making areas, video games, and a teen disco. When there are only a small number of kids on the cruise, the space can be converted into a relaxing place for morning coffee or afternoon snacks.

POSTSCRIPT   Like her predecessor, the *Rotterdam VI* appeals most to traditionalists who remember—and those who would like to imagine— the era of the grand oceanliners. Yet, anyone who appreciates style and tradition will enjoy her. *Rotterdam* cruises will be fairly dressy affairs. Men are asked to wear jackets in public areas after 6 P.M. and there are usually two formal evenings a week, more during long cruises. Readers who are considering a cruise on the *Rotterdam VI* should review the entire Holland America Line section for a full picture of the cruise experience it offers.

MAJESTY CRUISE LINE

901 South America Way, Miami, FL 33132
(305) 530-8900; (800) 532-7788; fax (305) 358-4807
http://mmink.com/mcl.html

TYPE OF SHIPS   New, midsize.

TYPE OF CRUISE   Mainstream, deluxe, short, and weeklong cruises.

CRUISE LINE'S STRENGTHS
- stylish ships
- cuisine
- deluxe amenities in cabins
- Boston-to-Bermuda exclusive

CRUISE LINE'S SHORTCOMINGS
- evening entertainment
- slow dining room service
- nickel-and-dime charges

FELLOW PASSENGERS   On short Bahamas cruises, as many as two-thirds might be Floridians. On weekly summer Bermuda cruises, a large percentage comes from the Boston/New England area. Most are couples from 35–55; some singles and seniors and a few families. A typical passenger is age 45 or more, some college education, married, business or professional with an income of about $50,000.

Recommended For   First-time cruisers and those who prefer a low-key atmosphere to the high-energy, party atmosphere that typifies other short cruises to the Bahamas. Anyone looking for a short getaway in the sun in a casual but stylish environment or who wants nonsmoking cabins.

Not Recommended For   Rowdies, late-night revelers, anyone who is happiest on a jeans-and-beer weekend or who is uncomfortable in a classy ambience.

CRUISE AREAS AND SEASONS   Bahamas, Western Caribbean, and Panama Canal.

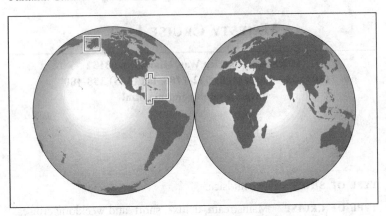

THE LINE   Formed in 1991 by the owners of budget-class Dolphin Cruise Line when a brand new ship became available, Majesty Cruise Line was designed to fill a niche: deluxe cruises for affluent travelers on short Bahamas cruises. The $220 million *Royal Majesty*, built in Finland, made her debut in 1992. In her first year, she established some cruising "firsts"—the first to have a totally smoke-free dining room, to designate 25 percent of its cabins as smoke-free accommodations, and to offer on-board "Kick-the-Habit" seminars for those who want to quit smoking.

It was also the first cruise line to offer a four-night cruise of the Western Caribbean, combining Key West with Cozumel and Playa del Carmen/Cancún. Heretofore, the itinerary was covered by five- to seven-day cruises. It was the first and is still the only cruise line to offer regularly scheduled cruises in summer from Boston to Bermuda. The program is based on a ten-year contract between the cruise line and the Bermuda government.

In March of 1997, Majesty acquired a second ship, *Crown Majesty* (formerly *Crown Dynasty*) from Cunard and in the same month, the two ships which are similar in style and vintage, were acquired by Norwegian Cruise Line. Majesty Cruise Line will cease operations at the end of December 1997; the ships will be renamed *Norwegian Majesty* and *Norwegian Dynasty* and become part of the NCL fleet.

The Fleet	Built/Renovated	Tonnage	Passengers
Crown Majesty	1993	20,000	752
Royal Majesty	1992	32,400	1,056

STYLE   It's mainstream cruising, but a cut above the large ships that dominate short cruises between Florida and the Bahamas. Classy and casual at the same time, these smaller ships (small in comparison to the megaliners) do indeed have the virtues and charm of other small ships: It's easier to learn your way around and get about. With fewer passengers, there are seats in the lounge for shows, no long waits for tenders or at disembarkation, and an absence of crowds in the lobby, casino, or just before the restaurant doors swing open at dinner. You are more likely to get personal attention and enjoy some feeling of intimacy.

Glowing from stem to stern under excellent care, the *Royal Majesty* is the toniest ship on the Florida-Bahamas route. The ship with her splendid decor is very comfortable and offers about any facilities you might want on a short cruise along with deluxe amenities you might not expect. There are thoughtful touches like the canvas-shaded areas on the open pool deck for comfortable outdoor sitting. The quality and presentation of the food is above average.

DISTINCTIVE FEATURES   No-smoking cabins; ironing boards and signature robes in all cabins; Saturday night "Royal Feast."

RATES

Highest Per Diem	Lowest Per Diem	Average Per Diem
$277	$122	$232

The above per diems are calculated from the cruise line's nondiscounted *cruise-only* fares on standard accommodations. What you will actually pay *should* be *substantially* less (see Part One, How to Get the Best Deal on a Cruise). Per diems vary by season, by cabin location, and by cruise areas.

Special Fares and Discounts   "AdvanSaver" rate, a capacity control-type discount, offers up to 40 percent on early bookings.

- Children's Fares: Low third/fourth person rates.
- Single Supplement: 150 percent of double occupancy rate.

Packages

- Air/Sea: Air-sea packages also available for third and fourth persons in a cabin.
- Pre/Post: Miami, Orlando, Florida Keys.
- Others: Wedding, honeymoon.

THE LAST WORD The smaller size and refined decor of these ships make them a refreshing change from the glitzy megaliners, wherever they cruise.

For profiles of the ships, see Norwegian Cruise Lines, *Norwegian Dynasty* and *Norwegian Majesty*.

NORWEGIAN CRUISE LINE

7665 Corporate Center Drive, Miami, FL 33126
(305) 436-4000; (800) 327-7030; fax (305) 436-4120
http://www.ncl.com

TYPE OF SHIPS   Modern superliners, unique oceanliner, new mid-size liners.

TYPE OF CRUISES   Contemporary, mainstream, with stress on sports and fitness, themes, and special interests.

CRUISE LINE'S STRENGTHS
- entertainment
- sports and fitness facilities and activities
- dining options
- theme cruises
- 50 percent nonsmoking cabins
- innovative ships
- spacious standard cabins
- guaranteed singles rate

CRUISE LINE'S SHORTCOMINGS
- overselling luxury of product
- uneven dining room service
- loud deck music
- poor bathrooms on new ships

FELLOW PASSENGERS   Norwegian Cruise Line is the everyman's cruise line with attractive ships in whose environment anyone can feel comfortable. Passengers, mostly from the United States and Canada, represent a very broad segment of people from all walks of life. They have an estimated $35,000+ average annual income per person and come mostly from California, Florida, and New York, along with a sprinkling of Europeans and other nationals.

They are often attracted by NCL's highly acclaimed shipboard entertainment, theme and special interest cruises, and sports programs.

They are a diverse group and include young professionals, families, special interest groups, and incentive winners.

Recommended For   First-time cruisers, active travelers of all ages who want an all-around fun vacation. Joiners. Repeaters and middle-income travelers who like the entertainment and recreational variety of a large ship—but not as large as a megaliner. Those whose special interests relate to sports and music, particularly jazz and country. Those who vacation with their children.

Not Recommended For   Gourmands. Snobs or seasoned travelers with five-star expectations. Sedentary, passive travelers.

CRUISE AREAS AND SEASONS   Bahamas, Caribbean, year-round; South America, winter; Bermuda, Alaska, Europe, spring and summer; Mediterranean, fall; Panama Canal, May and September.

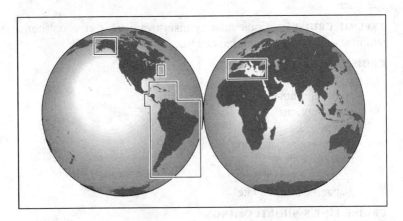

THE LINE   Three decades ago on December 19, 1966, the Sunward sailed from Miami to Nassau with 540 passengers on the first three- and four-day cruises to be offered by Norwegian Caribbean Line on a year-round basis between Miami and the Bahamas and with it, NCL was born. Little did the cruise line or anyone else realize where such a small step would take them, but today, those cruises—the first packaged for the mass market—are credited with launching modern cruising. In the intervening years NCL, which later changed its name to Norwegian Cruise Line, played a major role in shaping today's cruising, bringing many innovations to the experience.

Owned by a Norwegian family who has been in the steamship business in Scandinavia since 1906, Norwegian Cruise Line was begun by the grandson of the original company's founder, Knut Kloster. Within five years of its start-up, NCL had acquired three brand-new ships, pioneered weekly cruises to many Caribbean destinations, and introduced a day-at-the-beach on a private island in its itineraries—a feature soon copied by most of its competition.

Yet, for all its innovations and list of firsts, nothing quite equaled in excitement and impact NCL's purchase of the *Norway* in 1980. After buying her as the *France* for $18 million, NCL spent $100 million to transform her from a great oceanliner to a Caribbean cruise ship, setting in motion the trends that have completely transformed cruising.

At the time the *Norway* was the largest passenger ship afloat with capacity for 2,000 passengers. Her size—the first megaliner—enabled NCL to create a completely new shipboard environment, which turned the ship from a vessel for transportation into a floating resort with restaurants, bars, lounges, entertainment, and sports facilities to keep active passengers in motion almost 24 hours a day. Former passengers and steamship buffs were outraged but the *Norway* turned out to be a magnificent ship.

Later in the decade a series of costly expansion decisions, including the acquisition of Royal Viking Line and Royal Cruise Line, were made by Kloster Cruise Ltd., NCL's parent company. The debt-encumbered company was weakened, and the way was opened for more aggressive lines to take over its pacesetting role. Now it's playing catch-up, re-creating itself with a fleet of new ships that has taken the line in a new direction.

Beginning with the *Norwegian Sea* in 1988, NCL introduced new, midranged superliners, carrying 1,000–1,400 passengers, going against the trend of its competitors who were adding larger and larger megaliners. In addition to the flexibility that the midsize ships give NCL, the line has styled the ships to appeal to more upscale passengers who want the facilities of a large ship but are turned off by the size and impersonal nature of megaliners.

NCL's new fleet has many innovations that have put the line back into its role as a trendsetter. Among the most notable are the dining options with alternative dining; sports bars with live broadcasts of CNN, ESPN, and major sporting events; and separate sitting areas in standard cabins, an amenity usually reserved for deluxe accommodations. At the same time, NCL spent $63 million on renovations to ready the *Norway* for the 1990s and beyond, adding new features and restoring the classic ones. NCL has won a well-deserved reputation for outstanding entertainment, ranging from comedy clubs and cabaret stars to

Broadway shows, which the line introduced to cruising when it acquired the *Norway*.

Traditionally, NCL has blanketed the Caribbean, but in 1994, it introduced Alaska cruises with great success, followed by Europe and the return of the *Norway* to special transatlantic runs. After the demise of Royal Viking Line and Royal Cruise Line, two of their ships went to NCL. The additional ships have enabled NCL to strike out in new directions and reclaim the role of innovator with two more "firsts."

In May 1997, NCL became the first cruise line ever to base a ship in Houston for year-round cruises to the Western Caribbean. Dubbed Texaribbean Cruises, NCL expects to draw on Houston's location as the gateway for ten states with 75 million potential cruise passengers. This region has the country's highest concentration of 45–75 year olds—cruise lines' prime target group. At the same time, Houston, the world's eighth largest port, has built a state-of-the-art facility on a 15-acre site at the head of Galveston Bay for the *Norwegian Star* to call home.

Then, in 1998, NCL will become the first of the major mainstream cruise lines to base a ship in southern South America—which NCL has dubbed Alaska South—for the winter season. *Norwegian Crown* will sail on six 14-day cruises between Chile and Argentina, marking the first time an NCL ship has sailed south of the equator.

And as further evidence that it has roared back from the brink, NCL took over Majesty Cruise Line's two ships, now scheduled to join NCL's fleet in late 1997; placed an order for a 2,000-passenger ship; and took an option to buy the unfinished hull that had been intended to be a sister ship to Costa Cruises' new *CostaVictoria;* and announced plans to stretch two ships and rename three ships in a move to streamline the fleet.

The Fleet	Built/Renovated	Tonnage	Passengers
Leeward	1992/1995	25,000	950
Norway	1960/79/93	76,049	2,032
Norwegian Crown	1988/97	34,250	1,050
Norwegian Dream	1992	48,000	1,754
Norwegian Dynasty	1993	20,000	752
Norwegian Majesty	1992	32,400	1,056
Norwegian Sea	1988	42,000	1,504
Norwegian Star	1973/91/95/97	28,000	1,200
Norwegian Wind	1993	48,000	1,758

STYLE   NCL has always been at the heart of mainstream cruising, with attractive ships and a congenial atmosphere in which anyone can feel comfortable. The ships reflect a contemporary lifestyle and offer a wide range of activities for all ages, almost around the clock, with special emphasis on sports, music, and entertainment, and a yearlong calendar of theme cruises, usually with a sports or music focus.

Responding to changing lifestyles while trying to attract more upscale passengers, NCL has added an array of thoughtful amenities and "signature" items in recent years. These include a full luncheon buffet served upon embarkation on all ships, upgraded menus with new, contemporary dishes, expanded room service menus, and ice cream parlors that dish out goodies every afternoon at no charge. Le Bistro, an informal cafe in the style of Miami's trendy Art Deco district, is a popular alternative restaurant at no extra charge, on all the fleet. Another big hit is the Chocoholic Buffet, a weekly dessert extravaganza.

Some new elegant touches include wine stewards (while some of NCL's major competitors have eliminated them) and strolling musicians in the dining room at dinner; fruit baskets and deluxe bathroom amenities packages in cabins; and pool and beach attendants to provide fluffy beach towels and iced towels to cool sunbathers. All dining rooms are designated nonsmoking. Fifty percent of NCL's cabins are nonsmoking and are all on one side of the ship so the corridors are smoke-free as well; NCL was the first cruise line to accommodate nonsmokers to such a degree. In the casinos, specific blackjack tables are reserved for nonsmokers. Also, cabins are equipped for the hearing impaired on the newest ships.

NCL's Sports Afloat is the most comprehensive year-round sports and fitness program of any cruise line. The ships have fully equipped fitness centers, basketball/volleyball courts, aerobics classes, golf practice facilities, NCL Olympics, and an incentive program that awards passengers for participating. SuperSport cruises are theme cruises designed around a particular sport with sports celebrities and specialists on board.

NCL's water sports programs offer shipboard instruction combined with hands-on experience in ports of call. All ships have snorkeling programs and can arrange scuba excursions for card-carrying certified divers. NCL's dive program on the *Norwegian Wind* in Alaska—yes, Alaska—has been a big hit. Great Stirrup Cay, NCL's private Bahamian island, has an expanded roster of activities.

For kids, NCL has an extensive program with supervised activities available year-round on all ships. Kids under two sail free.

DISTINCTIVE FEATURES   Chocoholic buffets; dive program and other offbeat excursions in Alaska; single/open seating for two meals; alternative dining; official cruise line of Improv; full-scale Broadway shows; sports bars; music and sports theme cruises. Nonsmoking cabins; cabins equipped for the hearing impaired. Guaranteed baby-sitting.

RATES

Highest Per Diem	Lowest Per Diem	Average Per Diem
$500	$100	$209

The above per diems are calculated from the cruise line's nondiscounted *cruise-only* fares on standard accommodations. What you will actually pay *should* be *substantially* less (see Part One, How to Get the Best Deal on a Cruise). Per diems vary by season, by cabin location, and by cruise areas.

Special Fares and Discounts   NCL's LeaderShip fares, available through travel agents, are capacity-controlled fares offering up to 50 percent discounts.

There are two basic prices for each cruise—one for an inside cabin and one for an outside cabin, excluding penthouses and suites. On seven-day cruises, outside cabins are $100 per person more than inside cabins, and upgrades are available at just $15 per person per category. On a three- or four-day cruise, an outside cabin is $50 more per person than an inside one and upgrades are $10.

NCL's LeaderShip vAIRiations Desk handles requests for upgrades, stopovers, and flights on specific airlines, air and cruise documents, air/sea bookings; a final request for deviations must be in writing or faxed. A nonrefundable $50 per person service fee, plus fare differential, if applicable, is assessed.

- Children's Fare: Third/fourth person's fares. Children under two travel free.
- Single Supplement: Guaranteed singles rate.

Packages
- Air/Sea: Yes.
- Pre/Post: Yes.
- Others: Yes.

Past Passengers Latitudes is NCL's past passenger club, which provides members with expedited check-in and priority embarkation, private captain's reception, daily *New York Times,* fax, bridge and galley tours, special Latitude cruises with $100 on-board credit, members' events, gifts, and upgrades. Special discounts on select cruises; newsletter; Latitude Customer Service phone line.

THE LAST WORD In recent years, NCL has had a litany of problems and financial woes that caused its quality to slip and its competitors to outpace it in results, expansion, and innovation, but now, after the downsizing of its owner company, an improvement in its bottom line, and a return of a management that led NCL successfully in the past, NCL's outlook has brightened.

NCL might be described as a work in progress. It has made so many changes and innovations it's hard to keep up. As part of its new strategy to separate itself from its competition with their megaliner fleets, NCL is making a virtue out of having midsize ships. It is offering more amenities that appeal to a more upscale, cosmopolitan, and stylish audience and is striving to provide a more personal cruising experience, stressing the romance and fantasy of cruising.

Is it working? Certainly the product has improved and the line appears to be back on track. Its latest innovations—homeporting in Houston and wintering in South America—are refreshing but untested. Stay tuned.

Norwegian Cruise Line Ships Standard Features

Officers NCL ships/Norwegian; Majesty ships/Greek.

Staffs Dining and Cabin/International; Cruise/American. On *Norwegian Dynasty*/British, Filipino, and International.

Dining Facilities *Crown, Star, Dynasty, Majesty* one dining room; *Leeward, Norway, Sea,* two; *Wind, Dream* three—all with two seatings. Embarkation lunch; Chocoholic, midnight buffets; Le Bistro, Sport Bar & Grill; ice cream parlors; *Majesty* pizza parlor.

Special Diets Vegetarian, low calorie, kosher.

Room Service 24-hour room service.

Dress Code Casual for day, informal in evening. One formal night on short cruises, two on seven-day, with formal or semiformal attire.

Cabin Amenities Deluxe toiletries; radio; phone; refrigerator in suites; bathrooms with tub; sitting areas in standard cabins on newest ships; television with CNN, ESPN, and NBA. Fruit baskets. Majesty ships: hair dryer, robe, ironing board.

Electrical Outlets NCL ships, 110 AC. Majesty ships, 110/220 AC.

Wheelchair Access All NCL ships have cabins, ramp access, bathtubs with grab bars. Ten cabins on *Norway*. Majesty ships, four cabins on each.

Recreation and Entertainment Six or seven lounges; sports bars; Broadway shows, Las Vegas–style revues, comedy; nightclub; disco, casino; library. Wine tastings; singles, honeymooner parties; video arcade (except *Norway*). Majesty ships: piano bar; observation lounge/panorama bar; card/game room. Gentlemen hosts on *Crown*.

Sports and Other Activities Sports Afloat program with basketball, volleyball, Ping-Pong, golf practice. Private island with rental equipment. Snorkeling; scuba for certified divers. Two swimming pools (one on *Leeward, Star, Dynasty, Majesty*); jogging track.

Beauty and Fitness Aerobics, fitness center, sauna, jogging track, barber/beauty salon. Posh spa on *Norway*.

Other Facilities Boutiques, medical facilities, dry cleaning/laundry. Conference rooms.

Children's Facilities Year-round program with youth coordinators; counselors added seasonally. Guaranteed baby-sitting. Majesty ships: Kid's splash pool; playroom; *Dynasty*, youth and teen centers.

Theme Cruises See text.

Smoking Nonsmoking cabins; four NCL, two Majesty ships with non-smoking dining room. Public rooms have nonsmoking sections.

NCL Suggested Tipping Per person per day, waiter and cabin steward, $3; busboy, $1.50; 15 percent added to bar tabs.

Credit Cards For cruise payment and on-board charges, American Express, Visa, Mastercard.

Norway

	Quality Rating	Value Rating
Norway	❻	B

Registry: Bahamas	Length: 1,035 feet	Beam: 110 feet
Cabins: 1,016	Draft: 35.5 feet	Speed: 18 knots
Maximum Passengers: 2,370	Passenger Decks: 12	Elevators: 11
	Crew: 900	Space Ratio: 38

THE SHIP   The *Norway* is one of a kind. A great lady with classic lines and lots of character. When NCL bought the *France* in 1979, she had been mothballed for five years. But at $18 million, she was considered a steal. Her high-quality equipment and workmanship were unrivaled. To build one like her today would cost a $1 billion.

NCL spent $100 million to transform her into the *Norway*. She is a city-at-sea in every way with more staff than many ships have passengers. Her size, history, and character enabled NCL to feature headline-grabbing specials that few ships could imitate, such as NBC's *Today Show*, which broadcast from her for a week.

The *Norway* is the very definition of urbane elegance and comfort. Now after a two-stage $63 million renovation, she is updated for the 1990s. At the same time, she regained much of her physical beauty that had made her a legend as the *France*.

In the first phase, two glass-enclosed top decks and a forward observation deck, 124 upper-category luxurious cabins, a huge spa, fitness center, and jogging track were added. The most recent work, directed by well-known Scandinavian designers, Petter Yran and Bjorn Storbraaten, concentrated on restoring and preserving her classic beauty and design features, such as the irreplaceable bronze murals, gold and silver wall treatments, and some of the art from the original *France*. Only the new Monte Carlo Casino shows any contemporary glitz.

ITINERARIES   Seven days, Eastern Caribbean, winter, plus Western Caribbean on selected cruises and two transatlantic crossings.

- *Norway* sails every Saturday from Miami to St. Maarten, St. John, St. Thomas, Great Stirrup Cay (NCL's private out-island), and three days at sea. Her intermittent Western Caribbean cruises go to Ochos Rios, Grand Cayman, Playa del Carmen/Cozumel, and Great Stirrup Cay.

- *In summer and fall*, the ship makes two transatlantic crossings between Miami/New York and Southampton/Le Havre.
- For the first time, *Norway* will offer a six-month series in Europe from April 18–October 24, 1998.

Home Port   Miami.
Port Charges $111.50–180.

CABINS   Most, but not all, cabins are roomy with big closet and storage space. There are 20 cabin categories spread across ten decks. The top six categories, located mostly on the top three decks, offer concierge service. All cabins on the port side of the ship are nonsmoking ones.

The cabins on the original decks have been restored with graceful charm and will appeal to those with traditional tastes. They have attractive new appointments of quality materials in soft pastels. Such special items as the art deco vanities with three-sided movable mirrors were retained. Many rooms, too, have exquisite, glass-inlaid armoires from the original first-class cabins. All cabins display one of seven commemorative posters issued in 1994 to celebrate the ship's heritage. Some of the *France*'s original cabins with gold leaf and bronze fixtures were left intact.

Of the two decks added in 1990, Sun Deck houses 32 penthouse suites and Sky Deck has 84 deluxe cabins and suites with floor-to-ceiling windows; almost half have verandas. Two large owner's suites and two grand deluxe suites decorated in royal blue and white are located at the bow of the two decks; not all are alike. Some have floor-to-ceiling windows and wraparound balconies, others have Jacuzzi, but all have living room, bedroom, dressing room, and refrigerator. The two owner's suites on Viking Deck are the original ones from the *France*; they have two bedrooms and two full bathrooms. All cabins have television with CNN and ESPN available on a 24-hour basis.

Specifications   371 inside cabins, 475 outside; 170 suites. Standard dimensions, 150 square feet; 503 cabins with 2 lower beds; 369 with double/queen bed; 124 with upper and lower berths; 10 wheelchair accessible.

DINING   The *Norway* has two beautiful dining rooms. The Windward dining room, the forward of the two, was the first-class Chambord restaurant on the *France*, noted for its expanse unobstructed by columns. The famous room looks as splendid as it did the day the ship first sailed. Patrons still descend the glamorous staircase at the entrance and are seated amid gold and bronze murals on three sides. The main change in the room is overhead. The former grand golden dome has been redesigned into a star-filled night sky. The results work well.

The Leeward Restaurant, near the stern, has been renovated with more contemporary decor and may appear to be the more dramatic of the two. It has a spiral staircase leading to a mezzanine, reopened in the 1990 renovations. Service and food are the same in both dining rooms and seating is based on cabin location rather than category. Passengers booked in the forward cabins are assigned to the Windward; those in aft cabins are in the Leeward.

The Great Outdoor Restaurant, the al fresco eatery overlooking the stern, has a new, tonier country club look and a teak ceiling with overhead fans. It is the setting for the buffet breakfast and lunch, and often on theme cruises, such as the country music ones, for special deck parties. But the food here is not up to the dining room's.

Le Bistro, NCL's alternative restaurant designed in an art deco style reminiscent of Miami's trendy South Beach, serves dinner accompanied by contemporary taped music. There is no additional charge, but there is a special fee for tips. The restaurant, open to all passengers including children, accommodates 140 on a first come, first served basis. Wines are available by the glass.

The *Norway* has theme evenings such as the popular Viking Night with elaborately decorated dining rooms, staff dressed in traditional Viking attire, and a menu of Scandinavian specialties. A replica of a Viking ship is the centerpiece of the midnight buffet. SS France Night is meant to evoke the grand style of cruising's past.

The *Norway* was the first to get NCL's upgraded cuisine with new menus, expanded room service menus, and the wildly popular Chocoholic Buffet. This dessert extravaganza has chocolate concoctions of every kind, even chocolate pizzas, as well as espresso, cappuccino, and a variety of teas, ice cream, and more than 25 toppings. Several afternoons a white glove English high tea is served in *Norway*'s classic art deco lounge, Club Internationale, with musical accompaniment. For late night snacks, there might be a Caribbean deck party.

Passengers do not seem to agree on the *Norway*'s cuisine. Some say the food is excellent, others say it is good but not exceptional, while others express disappointment.

SERVICE   There's no agreement on service, either. Some passengers say it's wonderful, others say service is NCL's weakest link, particularly in the dining room. Most give the highest marks to cabin attendants. On a ship of this size, it is not unusual to have such varying opinions. People, after all, come with their own experiences and expectations. One waiter or barman can make all the difference. However, putting together the mix of opinions, the bottom line seems to be that the service is uneven, whether in the dining room, bars, or cabins.

FACILITIES AND ENTERTAINMENT   NCL spends more money on entertainment than any other cruise line, and it shows. It has some of the best entertainment on the high seas. The line has its own producer and director, Jean Ann Ryan, who travels extensively in search of talent.

The *Norway*, particularly, has the space and facilities to handle big time entertainment. The current Broadway show is *Crazy for You*. There's variety as much as quality. In addition to the Broadway shows and Las Vegas–style revues and top-name entertainers, there's music for dancing, disco, piano bar, and comedy.

Most of the action, except for spa and sports, is found on two central decks—International and Pool decks. The Saga Theatre, remodeled and more glamorous than ever, is used to stage blockbuster Broadway shows and revues. The stylish Checkers Cabaret is actually not from the original *France*, although it looks as though it could be, but rather it was created by the famous designer Angelo Donghia, who orchestrated the ship's conversion in 1980. It retains its panache with its distinctive red-and-black checkered carpet and stylized silver palm trees.

Of all the *Norway*'s lounges, the Club Internationale, one of the most stylish, sophisticated, and comfortable rooms afloat, reflects best the splendor of the *France*. Once the first-class smoking salon spanning two decks, the high-ceiling lounge has floor-to-ceiling windows, plush sofas, and fabulous art deco touches such as the light fixtures—all carefully preserved. It makes an ideal setting for the high tea in the afternoon. At other times, it is a sophisticated bar with jazz and the mellow sounds of a trio.

The big, flashy million-dollar Monte Carlo Casino is completely new. Decked out in art deco, it has floors of black granite, mirrored walls, and colorful signs from a bygone era, along with a rainbow of magenta, hot pink, crimson, and royal blue. Ten replicas of antique slot machines are by the entrance, not to be overshadowed by 200 of the latest models.

Down the corridor from the casino, past the shops, is the North Cape Lounge, popular for entertainment at all hours and now brightened with a new bar. And a flight down on Viking Deck, Dazzles, the disco (where the indoor tourist-class swimming pool used to be) goes to the wee hours.

ACTIVITIES AND DIVERSIONS   Somewhere it's been written that the *Norway* has 80 or more different activities for passengers to enjoy on a cruise. Between the entertainment, sports, and recreational activities on any given day, that is not an exaggeration. They run the gamut from art auctions, bingo, and samba and line dancing classes, culinary demonstrations, bridge, trapshooting, word puzzles, parlor games, and a fashion show. Next door is the card room where you can brush up on bridge or find partners for Scrabble.

SPORTS AND FITNESS   The *Norway*'s sports and fitness facilities are outstanding as is its famous Roman Spa. The ship has more than 65,000 square feet of outdoor decks—a mecca for sun worshippers but lean on refuge for those who prefer the shade. To help correct this, a shaded area for outdoor lounging was created behind the bridge on Fjord Deck. Also, lounge chairs now have extensions or hoods that can be used to block the sun overhead. Pool attendants are on hand to help you find a lounge chair and hand out an iced towel when you need to cool down.

The fitness center, basketball court, and volleyball court are found on Olympic Deck, along with a jogging track that encircles the deck (one-sixth mile). The fitness center offers floor-to-ceiling windows with panoramic views of the sea along with workout equipment and daily classes covering everything from morning stretch routines to power walks, aerobic dancing, and swimnastics. Topside, the Sun Deck has a tremendous amount of open deck space and a pool and bar between the ship's stacks.

NCL's Sports Afloat is the most comprehensive year-round sports program of any cruise line with sports and fitness activities tied to shipboard improvement programs and hands-on activities in port. Super-Sports theme cruises are designed around a popular sport—golf, tennis, baseball, running, and others—with specialists and sports celebrities on board who offer performance tips and participate in events with passengers—all at no extra cost. The staff holds NCL Olympics and In Motion On The Ocean incentive awards program with redemption tickets for every sports activity, including health and exercise classes, in which passengers participate, offering prizes such as T-shirts and fanny packs.

SPA AND BEAUTY   The Roman Spa, one of the first luxurious spas-at-sea, was added during the 1990 renovations and covers 6,000 square feet on Dolphin Deck, the lowest passenger deck. It has 16 treatment rooms for body wraps, aromatherapy, and other beauty treatments, eight massage rooms, four herbal therapy baths (cruising's first), cardiovascular exercise equipment, two steam rooms, two saunas, seven showers and four body-jet showers, a Jacuzzi for eight people, and a gym. It also houses a beauty salon, a shallow pool for aquacize classes, and a juice bar. The dining rooms offer a spa menu as well.

Designed and managed by Steiner of London, the spa has a staff of European-trained specialists. Meant to evoke a luxurious Roman bath—the Romans never had it so good—the spa has a large central area like a forum with white columns supporting high-arched ceilings and maroon leather lounges with gold-trimmed pillows along the sides for relaxing. There's a Gladiators training room complete with Stairmasters, bikes, rowing machines, and even a computerized fitness-analysis machine; and bubbling Jacuzzi. You don plush robes in one of the oh-so-clever dressing rooms (determined by whether you're an Antony or Cleopatra).

Passengers can try the spa experience for one hour or be pampered from head to toe for the day or week—at a price, of course, and none of it cheap. Treatments include a Nu Yu facial, a soothing face, neck, and shoulder massage followed by two different masks, one mud, the other a hydrating mask; thalassotherapy, a water-jet massage and seaweed treatment; and reflexology, a tension-releasing foot massage. There are daily water-exercise classes, steam treatments, facials, pedicures, and manicures.

CHILDREN'S FACILITIES   An extensive year-round children's program is offered on the *Norway* with youth coordinators to plan and supervise daily activities for children of all ages. The line publishes a special brochure on its children's program that lists the activities for four specific groups: junior sailors (age 3–5), first mates (6–8), navigators (9–12), and teens (13–17).

At the Coketail party, kids meet the captain; for the masquerade ball, they are given special help in making costumes; their tour of the bridge is conducted by a Norwegian officer; and during the day at the beach, the children have treasure hunts, races, and games. The ship publishes a daily *Kids' Cruise News* and *Teen Cruise News*. The ship has a children's playroom and an ice cream bar.

Guaranteed baby-sitting is available from noon to 2 A.M. for $8 per hour for the first child, $1.50 each additional child from the same family for a four-hour minimum; double on Christmas and New Year's Eve. Kids under two sail free. (Essentially, it mirrors the airlines' policy which allows children under two to fly for free.)

SHORE EXCURSIONS   At least one of the shore excursions in each port puts an unusual spin on the standard, off-the-shelf tours. Generally prices are moderate, ranging from $20 for a two-hour island tour of St.

John to $79 for a flight over the British and U.S. Virgin Islands; some have reduced prices for children.

Great Stirrup Cay, NCL's private island in the Bahamas, is one of the ship's most popular stops. It has an array of activities and equipment, including catamaran-style paddleboats with glass-bottom viewing panels, kayaks, sailboats, and Stingray vu boards (like "boogie" boards with a glass viewing port). Don't forget to bring insect repellent. The Dive-In snorkeling program is available at the island with instruction. The *Norway* also offers a scuba program for certified divers with a "C" card during calls at St. John and St. Thomas. Golf can also be arranged in St. Thomas.

Due to its size and draft, the *Norway* often anchors at sea and tenders passengers ashore. But thanks to its big tenders, *Little Norway I* and *II*, transfers are easy and swift. The tenders ride at the bow of the *Norway* and although they are 80 feet long and weigh 55 tons each, they can be raised and lowered in minutes by two giant cranes. Each carries 400 people and can transfer passengers and crew ashore within an hour or so after anchoring. At Great Stirrup Cay, passengers disembark directly onto the sand through lowered hydraulic front doors.

THEME CRUISES   A list of the *Norway*'s theme cruises with dates is available in NCL's cruise book. The music ones include country, Dixieland jazz, blues, rock, oldies, and big band; SuperSports are football, basketball, baseball, and hockey.

POSTSCRIPT   The *Norway* is a ship for all ages but a cruise on her will be enjoyed most by those who can appreciate her unique qualities. She has a large, loyal fan club; it is not unusual to find passengers who have sailed on her 10 or 20 times. Now spiffed up with her recent renovations, she has much to offer.

Norwegian Dream / Norwegian Wind

	Quality Rating	Value Rating
Norwegian Dream	❼	A
Norwegian Wind	❽	A

Registry: Bahamas	Length: 754 feet	Beam: 94 feet
Cabins: 879	Draft: 22 feet	Speed: 21 knots
Maximum Passengers: 1,754	Passenger Decks: 10	Elevators: 7
	Crew: 483	Space Ratio: 33

THE SHIPS   The twin ships, *Dreamward* and *Windward*, recently renamed *Norwegian Dream* and *Norwegian Wind,* were designed for people who want to know that they are on a ship at sea. At almost every turn, walls of glass instead of steel let you see the ocean and make the connection with the outdoors. It's a nice feeling that too many modern cruise ships have lost. But, having said that, you will also find that these ships have broken the mold on cruise ship design with unusual features, inside and out.

From the exterior at the bow and the stern, all five upper decks are open and step down on a slant, which helps to give the profile a more sleek appearance than most new large ships. Inside, there is no soaring atrium or grand entrance upon first encounter. Rather, from the entrance hall on Promenade Deck, you step into an elevator or take the stairs two decks up to the reception area on International Deck, where you will find the purser's and shore excursion desks. It's an unusual arrangement, indeed.

But the ships' most innovative designs are in their dining arena— four small dining rooms instead of one or two traditional large ones. The smaller rooms have several tiers, which has the effect of breaking up the space into more intimate settings and at the same time enables all the diners to enjoy extensive views through acres of panoramic windows. Topside, the Sun Deck is also tiered, creating the opportunity to use the space in the evening when it becomes something of an amphitheatre for entertainment. The *Dreamward* was the first ship to have a Sports Bar and Grill, filled with banks of television screens for live satellite broadcasts of ESPN, NBA, and NFL programs.

The spacious, airy ships have identical interiors, including the names of the decks and even the names of public rooms and suites. In early 1998, both ships are scheduled to be "stretched" by the insertion of a 130-foot midsection which will increase the capacity of each by 40 percent and add 256 cabins, new lounges, and improved children's and other facilities.

The interiors have the trademark of their well-known Norwegian designers, Petter Yran and Bjorn Storbraaten, who are masters at creating a comfortable, contemporary setting that is casual and elegant at the same time through the use of quality fabrics, fine woods, and marble, and a judicious use of brass or metal trim.

Because these twins have so much windows and glass, the outdoor setting becomes part of the indoor decor. The light that floods the interiors gives them a lively atmosphere, which is enhanced by the open, free-flowing public spaces, particularly on International and Star Decks where one lounge seems to merge into another, rather than being cut up into separate rooms, as on most ships. The idea is that the absence of walls helps people to mingle and socialize more than when they are separated into lounges.

NORWEGIAN DREAM ITINERARIES   Seven days, Western Caribbean, winter; Bermuda, summer; New England/Canada, fall.

- *November–February,* the ship sails weekly on Sunday from Ft. Lauderdale to Grand Cayman, Playa del Carmen (to drop off passengers), Cozumel, Cancún, and Great Stirrup Cay (NCL's private Bahamian island) for beach & barbecue day, with two days at sea.
- *Mid-May–November,* 12- and 14-day cruises of Europe and the Mediterranean.
- *December–April,* seven days, Southern Caribbean from San Juan.

Home Ports   Miami; New York.
Port Charges $115.50–219.50, depending on itinerary.

NORWEGIAN WIND ITINERARIES   Seven days, winter; Alaska, summer.

- *October–December, 1997,* the ship departs on Saturday from San Juan to Barbados, St. Lucia, St. Barts, Tortola (optional ferry to Virgin Gorda), and St. Thomas, with one day at sea. Or, Aruba, Curaçao, Tortola, and St. Thomas, with two days at sea.

- *May–September*, the ship departs weekly on Monday round trip from Vancouver on two itineraries: to Skagway via the Inside Passage, Juneau, Haines, Sawyer Glacier, and Ketchikan; or, the same ports with Glacier Bay instead of Sawyer Glacier. There are positioning cruises in April and September between San Juan and Vancouver, and a five-day Pacific Coast cruise between Vancouver and Los Angeles.
- *October–April, 1999,* the ship departs from Miami on Sunday for the Western Caribbean.

Home Ports   San Juan; Vancouver.
Port Charges $78.50–237.50, depending on itinerary.

CABINS   The twin ships offer 13 categories of cabins and almost all are on the lower five of the ten-deck ships. All cabins on the port side are nonsmoking ones; 16 cabins are equipped for the hearing impaired and six are wheelchair accessible.

For ships in the midprice category, they have four significant, distinguishing features: 85 percent of the cabins are outside ones with large windows; cabins are larger than average in the standard category; all have a sitting area with a table and a sofa chair or love seat that converts to a third bed; and they have a curtain to separate the sleeping quarters from the living area. Such amenities as these are normally reserved for deluxe and higher categories.

There are some trade-offs. The bathrooms are small, particularly the shower stall, and storage and drawer space is insufficient. Space around the beds is a bit tight, but having separate sitting and sleeping areas compensates. Almost all cabins are fitted with twin beds that convert into a queen and have remote-control, multichannel television with CNN and ESPN, radio, telephone, and a hair dryer. Cabin stewards keep the cabins in tip-top shape with twice daily service. The top-category suites include six owner's suites and 48 penthouse ones with balconies. Most have refrigerators and floor-to-ceiling windows. They are served by a concierge who pampers the occupants with complimentary luxury amenities like wine and hors d'oeuvres daily.

Specifications   92 inside cabins, 430 outside; 6 grand deluxe suites; 48 penthouse suites with balcony; 47 suites. Standard outside dimensions, 160 square feet. 531 cabins with 2 lower beds convertible to queen; 76 with third and fourth berths. No singles; 6 wheelchair accessible; 16 hearing impaired.

DINING   The ships' biggest innovations are their dining options. Each of the three dining rooms has its own personality and distinctive setting, and a fourth is an informal dinner cafe. All have the same menus and food is prepared from a central kitchen.

Tables and dining rooms are assigned for dinner only (in two seatings); other meals are open seating. Thus, passengers can choose from any of the three rooms for breakfast and lunch and enjoy their distinctive character. Having these choices helps to make the cruise a more personal experience. The diverse settings make dining more fun and interesting, and having meals with open seating gives passengers a chance to meet more of their shipmates.

The Terraces on International Deck, aft, is the largest dining room, and, as the name implies, it is terraced on three levels, separated by greenery and connected by twin stairways. The arrangement, with views onto other tables, reminds some people of a supper club in vintage Hollywood movies. A large mural covers the back wall but it has to compete for attention with the splendid views diners enjoy through the wall of glass at the stern.

Four Seasons, the second dining room on the same deck amidships, is bordered on the port side by a glass wall that brightens the room and draws your eyes to the sea. The room does not span the width of the ship; rather, it is separated from a corridor and lounge by etched-glass panels.

Sun Terraces, two decks up on Sun Deck aft, is the smallest of the three dining rooms and is casually appointed in light wood and wicker. It is set on three narrow terraces with walls of glass on three sides that extend up and overhead. Light, mint green window shades are rolled into place when the sun is glaring down directly at the diners. The view is across the aft swimming pool to the sea. NCL's alternative restaurant, Le Bistro, serves dinner from 7 P.M. to midnight and is open to all passengers on a first-come, first-served basis at no additional charge. The cozy, informal cafe has a daily pasta dish prepared tableside and other light fare. Wine by the glass is available. Le Bistro operates like a restaurant; there are no assigned seatings or meal times. The dining rooms and Rendezvous Lounge offer espresso and cappuccino.

Topside, the Sports Bar and Grill, decorated with sports photos and memorabilia, doubles as an alfresco restaurant where an informal breakfast and lunch buffet is served. In the evening, passengers are treated to fresh popcorn when they gather to watch sports events carried on the bank of television monitors. Free ice cream and frozen yogurt are available each afternoon at poolside, and if you aren't watching the calories, you can pig out at the Chocoholic Buffet.

The ships had start-up problems on the food side, but of late, both food and service have been getting higher marks, although still uneven. With everything else about the ship being a quality act, it's reasonable to expect the food to be no less.

SERVICE   Generally, the ships are praised for good to excellent service in the cabins, dining areas, bars, and lounges. Calls for room service snacks are delivered quickly.

FACILITIES AND ENTERTAINMENT   As on other NCL ships, the fabulous entertainment is the highlight of the cruise, with passengers often giving the shows standing ovations. *Dreamgirls* was the opener for the *Norwegian Dream;* it now features *42nd Street. George M* played in the *Norwegian Wind*'s Stardust Lounge, the main showroom with a large proscenium stage framed in lights. On alternate nights there are Las Vegas–style variety shows. The *Norwegian Wind*'s lineup also features the first circus revue on the high seas. The room is well laid out in four tiers, providing comfortable seats and clear sight lines from most locations. The lounge has a dance floor and might offer music for dancing before and after the shows.

Lucky's, a horseshoe-shaped piano bar with a dance floor, is a popular stop between the show lounge and casino, further along on the portside. The casino is surprisingly small for this size ship and has a balcony with a few gaming tables. The informal Rendezvous Lounge, across from the Four Seasons Dining Room, is an open bar along the corridor, similar to an outdoor cafe, and as its name indicates it is a good meeting spot and people-watching corner. Next door is the small library and a conference room.

The other centers for evening action are on Sports Deck, anchored by the Sports Bar at the stern and the Observatory Lounge at the bow. With floor-to-ceiling windows on three sides, it's the ideal perch for viewing Caribbean sunsets on the *Norwegian Dream* or the Alaskan wilderness on the *Norwegian Wind*. The lounge draws the largest crowd when it becomes the late-night disco. The Sports Deck's open space is sometimes used for outdoor parties.

ACTIVITIES AND DIVERSIONS   As with all NCL ships, a wide range of daytime activities is available and runs the gamut from art auctions and bingo to dance classes, bridge tours, culinary demonstrations, and pool and parlor games. Regarding art auctions, as we have warned elsewhere, you have to know what you are buying and not be taken in by the sales pitch. Generally, if the bargains being touted sound too good to be true, they probably are.

SPORTS, FITNESS, AND BEAUTY   For active folks, the Sports Deck is your mecca where you will find two golf driving ranges and an instructor to give you some tips. One of the two outdoor pools is within putting range, and one flight up on Sky Deck you'll find the basketball and volleyball court. A second small pool is on International Deck at the stern.

The fitness center has a gym, plenty of equipment, and aerobics and other exercise classes to work off the sins of the Chocoholic Buffet. There's an extra-wide wraparound walking/jogging track on Promenade Deck for good measure. The fitness center also has spa services with massage, sauna, whirlpool, and Jacuzzi. The beauty salon is forward, next to the observation lounge.

The forward end of the pool has another of the ships' innovative designs—teak decks, separated by decorative greenery, step up in five levels on which sunbathers can relax on comfortable lounges, up above the pool as on a grandstand, and watch the fun and games. It's a novel design but maybe not the best. And it's definitely not the quietest part of the ship. On some evenings the setting is used as an amphitheater for special outdoor events and dancing.

As with all NCL's fleet, snorkeling instruction is offered while the ships are at sea and hands-on experience is available at ports of call. The dive program in Alaska is a big hit. The ships have year-round sports and fitness programs as well as theme cruises that focus on a particular sport-golf, tennis, baseball, running, and others—with specialists and sports celebrities. An active or retired NFL player is on board for most seven-day cruises.

CHILDREN'S FACILITIES   The ships have video arcades on the Sports Deck and Kids Korner children's playrooms on the International Deck. The supervised youth program is available seasonally and divided into four groups, according to age. The wealth of activities offered in its children's program is detailed in a special NCL brochure.

SHORE EXCURSIONS   In Alaska, the *Norwegian Wind* offers some of the best offbeat excursions of any mainstream cruise line. One of the most popular is its Dive into Adventure program for snorkeling and diving. It attracts a wide variety of passengers and helps to dispel the myth that cruising is a sedentary affair. It's also something to tell the folks back at the office. Not many people can say they have been scuba diving in Alaska. At the end of the excursion, participants shiver out of their wet suits and jump into the heated pool on Sun Deck.

Other programs available are glacier hiking; mountain biking; 11 miles of trekking through a forest; a six-hour hike outside Skagway; and a three-hour sea-kayaking excursion in two-person sea kayaks from Juneau where you are likely to see a whale close enough to feel its spray when it surfaces. Flightseeing trips from Juneau to a remote lodge pass over vast ice fields that stretch for over a thousand miles. It's awesome.

The more exotic tours are limited to small groups; you must book early. Alaska shore excursions are expensive, regardless of which cruise line you sail. Those who operate them have high costs and a very short season. Some sample prices of the adventure excursions are (per person): six-hour hike to Denver Falls in Skagway, $79; three-hour sea-kayaking in Juneau, $68; snorkeling in Ketchikan, $45; flightseeing with the Juneau Taku Lodge, $168.

POSTSCRIPT   The *Norwegian Dream* and *Norwegian Wind* are well suited for novice and experienced cruisers as well as younger passengers. They are most likely to appeal to upscale, active professionals who want a casual, relaxing vacation in a quality environment, with good entertainment and a choice of restaurants and activity. First-time cruisers, particularly men, who do not realize how much there is to do on a cruise and those who think they'll be bored or don't want to miss Sunday football, have it made on these ships with their Sports Bar. And for one-upsmanship in the office, they can tell about going diving in Alaska.

Norwegian Sea

	Quality Rating	Value Rating
Norwegian Sea	❺	B

Registry: Bahamas	Length: 700 feet	Beam: 96 feet
Cabins: 763	Draft: 21 feet	Speed: 20 knots
Maximum Passengers: 1,798	Passenger Decks: 9	Elevators: 6
	Crew: 630	Space Ratio: 27

THE SHIP   NCL's preparation for the 1990s began in 1988 with the debut of the *Seaward*, recently renamed *Norwegian Sea*, the line's first brand-new ship in two decades. It was also the first of the midsize range that NCL decided to pursue, rather than the megaliners of its competition.

The *Norwegian Sea* was seen as a class act from her first unveiling. Styled by two of Scandinavia's best-known designers, Robert Tillberg and Petter Yran, she has a contemporary, glamorous look with handsome appointments of quality fabrics and furnishings, clearly aimed at an upscale audience, for passengers who want the facilities of a superliner but in a warm, inviting ambience.

The designers also created a spacious feeling by opening up the ship and providing splendid seascapes with floor-to-ceiling windows in lounges and four novel, glass-enclosed stairways—two on each side of the ship—that flood the interiors with light. Throughout, the prevailing colors are muted pastels, accented by brass and mirrored walls. Particularly appealing are the small lounges, which provide pleasant corners for drinks, conversation, and relaxation.

ITINERARIES   Seven days, year-round, alternating Eastern and Southern Caribbean. The *Norwegian Sea* has a new itinerary that departs from San Juan on Saturday, alternating weekly to Santo Domingo, Barbados, Dominica, Antigua, and St. Thomas; or to Santo Domingo, St. Lucia, St. Kitts, St. Maarten, and St. Thomas; each itinerary enjoys one day at sea.

> ***Home Port***   San Juan.
> ***Port Charges*** $117.50.

CABINS   The ship offers 16 categories of cabins, with the six pricier types on the three upper decks and the others on the three lower decks. Compared to NCL's newer ships, the *Norwegian Sea's* cabins are something of a disappointment in terms of size, being smaller and without sitting area in standard cabins. Most are fitted with twin beds and all are equipped with hair dryers and television for movies and 24-hour CNN and ESPN. All port-side cabins are designated as nonsmoking. During the 1995 renovations, four new suites were added, two each on Promenade and Star Decks.

> ***Specifications***   243 inside cabins, 513 outside; 7 suites. Standard dimensions, 122 and 140 square feet. 462 with 2 lower beds (convertible to queen); 290 with 2 lowers and third/fourth berths; no singles; 4 wheelchair accessible.

DINING   The ship has two dining rooms—Four Seasons and Seven Seas—both on main deck. Both offer open seating for breakfast and lunch and assigned seating for dinner, and both have strolling musicians and complimentary espresso and cappuccino.

A popular venue is the stylish Big Apple Cafe, the Lido Restaurant with panoramic sea views at the stern and outdoor patios along each side, decked out with marble-top tables and garden awnings. It is the place for informal buffets at breakfast, lunch, afternoon tea, supper, and midnight. Le Bistro, which replaced the former Palm Tree restaurant, is an informal cafe for Italian specialties. There is no charge, and dinner hours are flexible.

FACILITIES AND ENTERTAINMENT   A group of contingent lounges share the area at the stern on Sun Deck. The elegant Observatory Lounge has cushy leather seats for a comfortable view of the seascape through picture windows; Gatsby's is a wine bar, also with sea views; and Boomer's is the disco.

International Deck, the entertainment level, is centered by the two-deck Crystal Court dominated by a crystal and water sculpture—water cascades from nine crystal columns suspended from a mirrored ceiling two decks overhead and falls into four lighted pools of different sizes and at different levels made of African marble fashioned by Italian stonecutters. To one side is Oscar's, a stylish piano bar with a Hollywood theme, and Everything under the Sun, the shopping arcade. Anchoring the forward end is the Cabaret Lounge, the main showroom that, for its maiden year, featured the Broadway blockbuster, *A Chorus Line*, and now shows *Grease*.

The glamorous Stardust Lounge, a second main lounge for dancing and entertainment, has concentric circles radiating from the large dance floor and is reminiscent of nightclubs pictured in vintage Hollywood movies. By skillfully placing the stage and dance floor to starboard, the designers were able to preserve the daytime views off the stern. The large Monte Carlo Casino with European elegance instead of the Vegas glitz of most cruise ship casinos, is another of NCL's breaks from the mainstream.

ACTIVITIES AND DIVERSIONS   The Promenade Deck is encircled by a very spacious, unobstructed outside deck (one-quarter mile) with a nonslip metal surface rather than the usual teak decking. (The ship was built for a bargain price of $128 million; some assume this deck was one of the compromises made to meet the low price.)

Topside, the ship has a large sunning and lounge area with a 42-foot pool, one of the longest on any cruise ship; a second pool that has overhead sprinklers and a shallow side for lounging, and twin hot tubs. Also within short range is Lickety Splits where ice cream is dished out in the afternoon. One flight up, a sun deck forms a balcony along the periphery of the pools; at the forward end is the fitness center, a golf driving range, and Coconut Willy's, the pool bar. Porthole is a kid's playroom on one of the lower cabin decks.

POSTSCRIPT The *Norwegian Sea* has been a success for NCL since she was introduced in 1988, consistently recording some of the highest customer satisfaction ratings in the fleet. She is a classy ship with wide appeal for all ages and her itineraries offer a broad range of the Caribbean's diversity. Readers planning a cruise on the *Norwegian Sea* should review the whole NCL section to have a full picture of the cruise experience the line offers.

Leeward

Leeward	**Quality Rating** ⑥	**Value Rating** B
Registry: Panama	Length: 524 feet	Beam: 82 feet
Cabins: 475	Draft: 18 feet	Speed: 21 knots
Maximum Passengers: 1,150	Passenger Decks: 9	Elevators: 4
	Crew: 400	Space Ratio: n.a.

THE SHIP The *Leeward*, which made her debut in 1995, was originally built in 1992 as the cruise ferry *Viking Saga* of Effjohn International and has been leased by NCL for four years with an option to renew. As part of the agreement, Effjohn spent $60 million to turn the Scandinavian ferry into a Caribbean cruise ship, all but rebuilding her to make cosmetic and structural enhancements inside and out.

The *Leeward* has a sleek modern look, particularly at the bow, looking more like an oversized yacht than a ferry. The same well-known Norwegian naval architectural firm, Yran and Storbraaten, which have been responsible for other NCL vessels, was in charge of the conversion, helping to ensure her compatibility with the fleet.

Typical of the designers' work, the ship's interiors are pleasing to the eye and use pastel colors along with stone, wood, and marble accents. A small reception area houses the passenger service desk, shore excursion desk, and shops. Adjacent to the reception area are the main staircases and elevators. At the center of the staircase is a pillar of stained glass that reflects soft blue and purple hues, the dominant colors used throughout the ship.

Most of the *Leeward*'s public areas are on the International Desk.

ITINERARIES   Bahamas, Western Caribbean, year-round.

- The *Leeward* sails from Miami on Friday on alternating itineraries of three-day cruises to Nassau and Great Stirrup Cay, NCL's private Bahamian island; or to Key West and Great Stirrup Cay. On four-day cruises, she sails to Cozumel and Key West.

Home Port   Miami.

Port Charges $78.50 on three days; $88.50 on four days.

CABINS   The *Leeward* offers 14 categories of cabins, all located on the lower six decks. They are among the largest of any ship in the short-cruise market; all but a few have sitting areas and refrigerators. Two-thirds of the cabins are outside; all those on the port side are nonsmoking. The spacious cabins are well designed for three- and four-day cruises. They are appointed in burled orange and charcoal gray with natural wood cabinetry and equipped with television for movies and 24-hour CNN and ESPN. All except the top category have bathrooms with shower only; all have NCL's deluxe bathroom amenities package and fruit baskets. The majority of cabins are fitted with two lower beds that can be arranged as a queen-size bed. Most lower category cabins can accommodate third and fourth passengers. Some cabins are equipped for the hearing impaired.

Two owner's suites have private balconies and Jacuzzi baths and the eight deluxe penthouses have separate bedroom and living room as well as balcony. A third group of six suites, along with the owner's suite, fit into the fan shape of the bow on Norway Deck and enjoy lovely views.

Specifications   157 inside cabins, 318 outside (including 211 deluxe); 6 suites, 2 owner and 8 penthouse suites with balcony. Standard dimensions, deluxe outside, 175 square feet. Majority with twins convertible to double; 15 upper/lower berths; no singles; 5 wheelchair accessible.

DINING   Passengers have the option of four dining areas, along with the flexibility of open seating for breakfast and lunch in the dining room and assigned seats for dinner—a NCL trademark.

The ship's two dining rooms are both located at the stern on two widely separated decks, enabling each to have an expanse of windows overlooking the sea on three sides. Diners also enjoy the entertainment of strolling musicians and services of wine stewards. The dining rooms can be divided for private dining for groups. Like the dining rooms on several other NCL ships, they are named Four Seasons (Promenade/Deck 4) and Seven Seas (International/Deck 7).

The *Leeward* has two alternative dining facilities: the Sports Bar and Grill, with a bank of television screens for viewing live broadcasts of ESPN and major sporting events is the casual indoor/outdoor venue for breakfast, lunch, and snacks; Le Bistro, a small, casual restaurant, serves Italian fare for dinner. It has flexible hours and is open to all passengers at no charge, by reservation, from 7 P.M. to midnight. The two restaurants are located across from one another on Sports Deck (Deck 8), along with the swimming pool and other sports facilities. Passengers can expect to have a full embarkation luncheon buffet and another of NCL's innovations—the Chocoholic dessert buffet.

FACILITIES AND ENTERTAINMENT   NCL's hallmark entertainment, including a full-scale Broadway show and music revues, is part of the lineup for the two-deck Stardust Lounge that anchors the forward end of the ship on International Deck. The current feature is *The Pirates of Penzance*. The theatre is configured with rows of curved couches and seats, but sight lines are restricted for those seated in the back of the balcony.

The Monte Carlo Casino, just off the show lounge, is decorated in a stylish, Roaring '20s theme in black with hot-pink murals. The casino has its own bar and in a quiet, separate corner, the Tradewinds Lounge, with a dance floor, is accessible from the casino. Conference rooms with audiovisual equipment designed for corporate meetings and incentive groups are on the same deck. Topside, Gatsby's is a piano bar with intimate seating areas that face expansive windows. It shares the aft section with an observation lounge which becomes the disco at night. The forward area has a basketball court and an observation deck.

ACTIVITIES AND DIVERSIONS   The swimming area on the Sports Deck is surrounded by a large area of teak decks for sunbathing and lounging. The ships has a children's pool, Jacuzzis, a well-equipped gym and fitness center with saunas, a full-service spa, and a beauty salon. Promenade Deck has a wraparound deck for walking or jogging. At Coconut Willy's, a tropical bar by the Sun Deck pool, you can enjoy the music of a Caribbean band.

The line's Sports Afloat program, water sports activities at Great Stirrup Cay, NCL's private island, and its diving programs are all available on the *Leeward*.

Trolland, a kid's playroom on Sports Deck, has a two-story castle, among other attractions, and is home base for a year-round kid's program.

POSTSCRIPT   With the never-ending parade of new megaliners and the demise of many cruise lines with midsize ships, NCL is almost alone in the midpriced, midsize market. The young fleet with its added amenities—standard cabins with separate sitting areas, some of the best entertainment at sea, good fitness facilities, and exceptional sports programs—offers outstanding value. The line appears to be on target for attracting a more active, upscale market. Food still needs improvement and consistency.

Norwegian Crown

	Quality Rating	Value Rating
Norwegian Crown	**7**	B

Registry: Bahamas	Length: 614 feet	Beam: 92.5 feet
Cabins: 526	Draft: 24 feet	Speed: 22 knots
Maximum Passengers:	Passenger Decks: 10	Elevators: 4
1,054	Crew: 470	Space Ratio: 32.6

THE SHIP   The spacious *Norwegian Crown*, the former *Crown Odyssey* which NCL inherited from the now defunct Royal Cruise Line, was built in 1988. Her quality decor by the noted interior design team, A and M Katzourakis, is a modern interpretation of classic architectural elements with stunning art deco design. In the public rooms, marble, fine woods, original art, antiques, chrome, mirrors, stained glass, smoked glass, reflective ceilings, and brass finishes were used with abandon. There's a bit of glitz but it's very well done. In 1997, NCL's signature alternative restaurant, Le Bistro, was added, and renovations were made.

The central foyer on Marina Deck houses the reception desk, shore excursion office, and sundries shop. A small gallery with fine reproductions of antique masterpieces found in the great museums of Athens, Cairo, Europe, and New York leads aft to the Seven Continents Restaurant.

The reception area is connected to the Odyssey Deck by a grand circular staircase of glass trimmed with brass and polished stainless steel. At the foot of the stairway is a six-foot spherical sculpture in bronze by the Italian sculptor Arnaldo Pomodoro. A continuous mosaic of back-lit stained glass panels in art deco geometric patterns extends the full height of all the stairwells.

The grand stairs wind up to the Monte Carlo Court, a large piano bar and lounge adjacent to the casino. The Court is the ship's social hub where passengers gather for cocktails and conversation.

ITINERARIES   Europe, summer and fall; Western Caribbean, winter; South America, winter.

- *December–March*, 1997, seven days, from Miami, departing on Saturdays to Grand Cayman, Roatan, Cancún, Cozumel, and Key West, with one day at sea.
- *Beginning 1998, from January–March*, the ship will be based in South America, sailing on six, 14-day "Alaska South" itineraries between Santiago, Chile and Buenos Aires, Argentina, with three days at sea. Among the highlights will be the fjords of southern Chile and the glaciers of Beagle Channel. One positioning cruise departs Miami on January 3 for Chile via the Panama Canal and Grand Cayman, Puerto Limón, Salinas, Ecuador, Lima, and Arica and Antofagasta, Chile. The return departs Santiago on March 14. Both itineraries enjoy five days at sea.
- *In April and November*, the *Norwegian Crown* departs from Port Canaveral to Bermuda and from May–September, from New York to Bermuda.

Home Ports   Miami; Santiago; Buenos Aires; various European ports, depending on itinerary.
Port Charges   Vary.

CABINS   The *Crown* offers 18 categories of cabins on seven decks. Outside cabins outnumber inside ones four to one and more than half of the bathrooms have tubs. Most cabins are large and even the smallest cabins have 154 square feet and the same basic amenities as the bigger ones.

All cabins have full vanities, two mirrored closets, tie and shoe racks, hand-varnished, solid hardwood furniture and cabinetry, locked drawers, good lighting, and works of art by contemporary Greek artists. Bathrooms are either marble or fully tiled and have large mirrors and recessed toiletry shelves; no hair dryers. Many of the bathtubs are mid-size. All cabins have direct-dial phones and television with CNN and other satellite channels.

The 16 luxury suites on Penthouse Deck are lavish. Each has a furnished private veranda with a sliding glass door, sitting room with a convertible sofa bed, refrigerator, walk-in closet, marble bathroom with whirlpool tub, and butler service. Four apartments can be combined with an adjacent unit by connecting doors to provide more than 1,000 square feet.

The apartments are named after exotic destinations, such as Bali and Tahiti, and the names are evoked in their decor with original paintings and antiques from the locale. Glass partitions separate the sitting and sleeping areas. Beds in the Superior AB Suite category fold into the wall to create a small meeting room.

Specifications   114 inside cabins, 342 outside; 16 apartments with verandas; 20 superior deluxe suites; 34 junior suites. Standard dimensions, 165 square feet. 456 cabins with two lower beds (52 convertible to doubles); 70 with twin queens; 112 cabins third person; 19 third/fourth guests; no singles.

DINING   Seven Continents Restaurant on Marina Deck is the elegantly appointed main dining room, built on two levels with a sunken central section under broad Tiffany-style stained glass domes. The room is trimmed with lacquered woods, beveled glass panels, picture windows with ocean views, and has an ivory grand piano for soft dinner music. Normally, the two seatings are open for breakfast and lunch and assigned for dinner. Dinner menus offer an assortment of regional dishes to complement the ports being visited. Spa cuisine selections have also been added. The noise level when the restaurant is full can be high. There is a midnight buffet and weekly Chocoholic Buffet.

The Yacht Club, decorated with photographs of America's Cup sailing competitions, is an indoor/outdoor bar and restaurant on the Odyssey Deck, offering a buffet breakfast and lunch, afternoon snacks, and cocktails. The Yacht Club opens onto the swimming pool with an expansive deck at the stern.

FACILITIES AND ENTERTAINMENT   Evening entertainment includes NCL's signature Broadway shows and musical revues in the multitiered Stardust Lounge, the main show lounge, where the art deco interiors have walls finished in soft mulberry suede and a tiered ceiling of smokey gray mirrors arranged in a sound wave design. The back wall of the lounge with opaque crystals in Lalique-style glass panels carries the theme further. The lounge has a deep sloping floor that provides good views from almost every seat.

The stage can be lowered to aisle level to become a dance floor. Next door, the intimate Rendezvous Bar is popular for predinner cocktails and the casino offers blackjack, roulette, Caribbean poker, and slot machines.

The ship's crowning glory, you might say, is the Top of the Crown on the highest deck, a circular observation lounge and bar with a dance floor and floor-to-ceiling windows that ensure sweeping, unobstructed views in three directions. A quiet retreat for reading and viewing the scenery during the day, in the evening the Top of the Crown becomes a disco with a sunken, illuminated dance floor of heavy glass and a mirrored ceiling; two domed skylights reveal twinkling stars above. Gentlemen hosts are on board to dance with the ladies.

ACTIVITIES AND DIVERSIONS   Daily activities include outdoor sports, bingo, and wine tasting classes. The Lido Deck is different from most ships as it has mostly cabins, except for the aft section. It also has the two-tiered Coronet Theatre with a full-size screen where current films are shown daily. The theatre is also equipped with individual writing tables and simultaneous-translation equipment. The theatre is used for seminars and conferences as well as for religious services. For the European series, guest lecturers are on board along with colorful folkloric dancers and others board in various ports of call to provide cultural entertainment.

SPORTS, FITNESS, AND BEAUTY   Penthouse Deck has a pleasant teak sunning area and at the stern, a splash pool and two whirlpools. An abstract stainless steel sculpture entitled *Wings* dominates the center of the Penthouse pools. The six-foot piece, lit from above, was created by contemporary Italian artist Carlo Mo.

Deep in the ship on the lowest level is an Indoor Pool Deck—a feature of traditional oceanliners but unusual on modern ships. It has a fitness center and spa with a full-time director. There is an indoor swimming pool for use when the *Crown* is in cold climes, two whirlpools, a mirrored gym with Universal exercise equipment, men's and women's saunas and massage rooms, and a juice bar. The beauty salon offers herbal therapy and other beauty treatments.

POSTSCRIPT   The *Norwegian Crown* is a spacious, comfortable ship and does not seem crowded even when it's full. She fits well in her new home at NCL; having been built for worldwide cruising, she should be a real asset when she heads to South America.

Norwegian Dynasty (Crown Majesty)

	Quality Rating	Value Rating
Norwegian Dynasty	❻	B

Registry: Panama	Length: 537 feet	Beam: 74 feet
Cabins: 400	Draft: 18 feet	Speed: 18.5 knots
Maximum Passengers: 856	Passenger Decks: 8	Elevators: 4
	Crew: 320	Space Ratio: 24

THE SHIP   One of the prettiest of the 1990s, with a sleek, contemporary profile and an unusual interior, the *Norwegian Dynasty* was built in Valencia, Spain, and first operated by the short-lived Crown Cruise Lines and then by Cunard. She was acquired by Majesty Cruise Line in March 1997, and then by NCL.

Designed by Scandinavian architect Peter Yran, who created the interiors of the luxurious *Sea Goddess*, the *Norwegian Dynasty* has a cheerful, open ambience with walls of glass, plenty of deck space, and expansive sea views. The interiors are contemporary with art deco inspiration in soft muted colors in some contexts and vibrant colors in others. All are enriched with teak and other fine wood, marble, murals, and paintings. The warm interiors and quality of furnishings convey a deluxe small ship feeling. Indeed, the combination—small enough to be cozy, but large enough to offer modern cruise ship amenities and facilities—is the ship's primary attraction and enables passengers to enjoy a congenial, less crowded shipboard atmosphere, along with good entertainment, and friendly, attentive service by a Filipino staff.

The layout of the ship is unusual, if not unique. The greenery-filled and balconied five-deck atrium lobby in glass, marble, and brass is aft, rather than amidships. Also, it is on the starboard side rather than at the center, which permits a near solid bank of windows to tower from Deck 4 to Deck 8. The walls of glass flood the interiors with natural light and look out at spectacular sea views, helping to connect passengers with the sea. From the base of the atrium on Deck 4 (actually, the third of seven passenger decks), music from a baby grand piano fills the lobby and helps set the tone. One flight up, Deck 5, is devoted entirely to public rooms and is anchored at both ends by lounges with unusual layouts—

they are oriented to the port side horizontally, facing large picture windows. (Rather than the usual arrangement with lounges facing the bow or the stern.) The multilevel show lounge, for example, is a semicircular room with its stage and dance floor on the port side; the arrangement is meant to provide for closer viewing of the stage. Between the two lounges are shops on the Via Veneto, a large casino, and the popular Alexander's Bar.

In another innovation, four of the main public rooms are stacked vertically at the stern allowing for large windows in virtually every area; the decks are connected by outdoor stairways and open decks. The result is a bright, open atmosphere, expansive views of the sea, and plenty of deck space.

ITINERARIES   Alaska in summer; Panama Canal, winter.

- *October–April:* Ten and eleven days, between Montego Bay and Acapulco on two unusual itineraries. The 11-day departs on Wednesday from Montego Bay, visits San Andres and Puerto Limón, transits the Panama Canal, and calls at Golfito, Costa Rica, and Acajutla, El Salvador, with four days at sea. The ten-day itinerary departs from Acapulco for Puerto Quetzal (Guatemala), Puerto Caldera (Costa Rica), Panama Canal, San Blas, Cartagena, and three days at sea.
- *Late May–early September:* Seven days, from Vancouver on Monday, northbound, and from Seward, southbound. Both itineraries call at Juneau and Ketchikan, and cruise Hubbard Glacier. Northbound the ship calls at Sitka; southbound it substitutes Skagway for Sitka and adds Wrangell.
- Between the Alaska and Panama cruises, the ship offers positioning cruises in May and September.

Home Ports   Ft. Lauderdale; Vancouver; Seward.
Port Charges $89.50–197.50, Panama; $189.50, Alaska.

CABINS   The *Norwegian Dynasty* has nine categories of cabins over five decks with about two-thirds outside. Cabins have nice appointments in mauve, blue, and green pastel patterns with light wood furniture and brass fixtures. A large window makes the cabin seem larger than it is. All cabins have television, satellite phones, radios, safes, and card-key door locks. Closet space is good, but drawer space is minimal. Cabins are fitted with twin beds that can be made into a queen. Bathrooms are small but they have large medicine cabinets, mirrored doors and vanities, and very large cotton towels.

Deluxe cabins and suites have sitting areas with large windows and refrigerators. Ten suites come with private balconies. The four wheel-chair accessible cabins have large bathrooms with grab bars and wide doorways. The housekeeping by amiable and attentive Filipino stewards is very good.

Specifications 125 inside cabins, 263 outside, including 31 deluxe and 12 suites (10 with private verandas). Standard dimensions 137–146 square feet. 351 cabins with 2 lower beds covert to double; 36 with 2 lower and 2 upper berths; 3 with 1 lower and 1 upper berth; no singles.

DINING The main dining room has a skylight and large panoramic windows overlooking the ocean on three sides, providing natural light and sea views for all passengers and a pleasant ambience for dining. There are two seatings for breakfast, lunch, and dinner.

Although tables are close, the noise level is low. The room, decorated in muted colors with lively, contemporary art, has a variety of table configurations separated from service areas by frosted glass.

Above the dining room on Deck 6 is the wicker-decorated Marco Polo Cafe, a casual indoor/outdoor cafe where breakfast, lunch, and dinner buffets are served. No dishes are cooked in the area and selections are limited. In the afternoon, ice cream is available at no charge. The cafe, a bit more elegantly decorated than the norm for a lido cafe, opens onto a two-deck outdoor lounge area where passengers may eat. The 24-hour room service has a limited menu.

FACILITIES AND ENTERTAINMENT Above the Marco Polo Cafe is the Kit Kat Club, a lounge with live music at different hours of the day and used for informal gatherings, games, and movies; it becomes the disco in the evening. It has a full-service bar and can be divided into two sections for meetings.

The activities on *Norwegian Dynasty* start with exercise sessions in the morning. Port talks, trivia contests and other games, horse racing, and bingo draw a crowd in the afternoon.

Alexander's Bar, a quiet retreat adjacent to the casino, is a favorite gathering place for early evening cocktails and after-dinner drinks. Tastefully decorated in muted pastels, the room is separated from the main thoroughfare by frosted glass and wood paneling, giving it a private yet airy feeling. Next door, the casino offers slot machines, black-jack, and roulette.

The Rhapsody Lounge, the main show lounge, offers Broadway-style revues. Valentino's, a lounge with pretty decor highlighted by a waterfall sculpture, has a bar and dance floor; it has musical entertainment and an occasional cabaret show in the evening. Some daytime events, such as afternoon tea, are held here, too. The cozy library has good sea views and a selection of current paperbacks and magazines. The Rainbow Room is a youth and teen center near the swimming pool on Deck Eight. The ship also has a video game arcade.

SPORTS, FITNESS, AND BEAUTY   A wide outside promenade encircles Deck 5, providing an uninterrupted track for walking or jogging. It has lounge chairs for relaxing and enjoying the sea. The topside spa with large forward windows over the bow is a spacious health club with state-of-the-art exercise equipment, bicycles, rowing machines, an aerobics area, and juice bar. A full-time instructor conducts aerobics and stretch classes. The spa has a beauty salon with hair and body treatments, two saunas, and steam and massage rooms. Next to the spa is a swimming pool, Jacuzzis, and a bar. A second jogging track rims the pool on an overhang and windscreens line the perimeter of the deck.

POSTSCRIPT   Despite the growing number of seasoned cruisers who prefer smaller ships, their choices in the midprice range are limited. As one of the few midsize ships built in this decade, the *Norwegian Dynasty* helps to fill the void. She offers an attractive, modern, alternative not only to big ships to the old ships that predominate in her size and price range and to the expensive boutique ships, which account for most of the small new ships. NCL takes over the ship in late 1997, and does not anticipate making any immediate changes in the on-board services or itineraries.

Norwegian Majesty (Royal Majesty)

	Quality Rating	Value Rating
Norwegian Majesty	❼	C

Registry: Panama	Length: 568 feet	Beam: 91 feet
Cabins: 528	Draft: 20.5 feet	Speed: 21 knots
Maximum Passengers:	Passenger Decks: 9	Elevators: 4
1,509	Crew: 500	Space Ratio: 31

THE SHIP With the fanfare one might expect for royalty, when she made her debut in 1992 as Majesty Cruises' *Royal Majesty*, the ship got her send-off in New York by Liza Minnelli—who else?! Intended to appeal to affluent passengers—the ship has five baby grand pianos—*Norwegian Majesty* has an understated elegance that is casual and classy at the same time.

The stylish interiors have the mark of their creators, Michael and Agni Katzourakis of Athens, well-known designers noted for other handsome ship interiors for Celebrity Cruises and other lines. They minimize glitz and create a refined, harmonious environment that achieves elegance in its simplicity and clean lines. Every lounge on every deck has the pleasing aura of a fine hotel—that just happens to float. The contemporary decor uses soft colors, an abundance of natural wood, and leather sofas with glass, mirror, and fresh, lush foliage accents. A touch of tradition is added to the modern look by glass-encased models of old sailing vessels.

The ship is well laid out with public rooms on three decks with passenger cabin decks and many quiet corners in between. Characteristic of several forward lounges are walls of sloped windows. Passengers step almost directly into the two-deck atrium amidships, which serves as the main lobby with the front desk, shore excursion office, and other offices. Aptly called Crossroads, the large circular lobby with windows spanning two decks has a white marble floor bordered with deep blue carpeting, steps up to a white marble island with banquettes, and a white baby grand piano as its centerpiece.

Countess Deck is entirely devoted to public areas. Off the lobby a corridor with chairs and sofas serves as an unofficial smokers' club because it leads aft to the smokeless dining room. Forward from the lobby past two boutiques and Treasured Moments, the photographer's shop, one finds a small library, card room, and meeting room. Small lounges border a large V-shaped piano bar at the center that is connected to Royal Fireworks, a multipurpose lounge and bar with panoramic windows fronting an observation deck.

ITINERARIES Three- and four-night cruises, October–May, Bahamas; six- and seven-night cruises, May–October, Bermuda.

- *On three-night cruises*, the ship departs from Miami on Friday for Nassau and Key West. On four-night trips, she departs Miami on Mondays to Nassau, Playa del Carmen/Cozumel, and Key West, with one day at sea.

- *From May–October*, the six- and seven-day Bermuda cruises depart from Boston on Saturdays and Sundays to Bermuda with four days in St. George's and two days at sea. The Sunday departures are meant to attract honeymooners.

Home Ports   Miami, October–May; Boston, June–September.
Port Charges   Three-night cruise, $98.50; four nights, $103.50.

CABINS   Twelve cabin categories range from royal suites to inside cabins with lower and upper berths. About 71 percent are outside and 25 percent are nonsmoking—the first cruise ship to devote so many cabins to this category. Standard cabins are modest in size and designed with clean, uncluttered lines and finished in natural wood with tasteful furnishings in reds, browns, and greens. Most have twin beds, separated by a chest of drawers, but surprisingly, less than a third convert to doubles. A desk unit with drawer space and dressing mirror and a trio of closets provide further storage space. Each cabin has a mounted television carrying CNN, cable sports, shipboard notices, and movies. Bathrooms have showers and a large sink with ample counter and shelf space and a hair dryer. Among the deluxe amenities in all cabins are robes, premium toiletries, and a built-in ironing board—an unusual feature.

Upper category suites and cabins have a minibar, queen beds, and large ocean-view windows. Forward on Duchess Deck, a group of cabins span an unusual half-moon contour overlooking the bow. The two Royal Suites sport marble baths and offer 24-hour butler service.

Specifications   185 inside cabins, 343 outside; 16 suites. Standard cabins measure 120–140 square feet. 487 cabins with two lowers (134 convert to doubles); 41 with double beds; 171 with three berths; 129 with four berths; all suites accommodate 3 persons; 4 wheelchair accessible.

DINING   The Epicurean Restaurant is an impressive room in lavender and ivory with wraparound, full-length windows over the wake. Diners enjoy live piano music from another of the white baby grands on a small island at the center. Most tables are set for four or six, contributing to the room's intimate feeling. The booth seats, however, are set a bit far from the table, forcing shorter diners to lean forward to reach the table. It was the first smoke-free dining room on a major cruise ship.

The food, from the crisp bacon at morning buffets to the salads, sandwiches, and even the hot dogs at lunch, is excellent. Dinner particularly is a treat, beginning with an impeccably set table with monogrammed dinnerware and table linens—a touch of class lost on most mainstream cruise ships—and exquisite presentation.

Breakfast and lunch buffets are served inside in the casually elegant Cafe Royale. Attractively furnished in light wood and wicker barrel chairs with a wall of sloping windows, the room is tight for buffet lines; fortunately, there is an outdoor dining area near the pool, as well. The buffets are above average for their wide range of hot and cold dishes, daily specialties, and selections of cakes, pastries, muffins and breads. The Cafe Royale is connected to the Royal Observatory, a handsome observation lounge and bar on the deck below.

Piazza San Marco Grill, a second serving area on Majesty Deck in a partially covered outdoor area, has good burgers, hot dogs, and excellent pizza as well as ice cream, between-meal snacks throughout the day, and special late-night buffets (not to be confused with the daily midnight buffet). The grill is adjacent to sunning areas and the outdoor pool. The cruise starts with a welcome-aboard buffet, and there is a champagne breakfast, specialty coffee lounge, and room service.

SERVICE   The crew is made up of 34 nationalities and in general, requests, such as extra pillows, the replacement for a lost cabin key, or additional postcards, are met with amazing speed. Except for the dining room, the service throughout the ship is good.

FACILITIES AND ENTERTAINMENT   The Palace Theater is the show lounge on one level with a steeply tiered floor very much like a theatre, as its name implies. Designed in warm shades of gold, rust, and blue, with a circular stage, it has excellent sight lines from almost every seat and offers the novelty of sitting areas behind the stage itself and facing aft over the ship's stern and wake.

The ship's other entertainment venues include the handsome Polo Club, a popular piano bar and lounge, next to the casino. Decorated in teal and peach, the bar serves a variety of coffees as well as drinks. The large casino offers gaming tables and walls of slot machines.

One deck up, the trendy disco, a large, open area with a wall of wraparound windows, functions as a lively sports bar with 16 television sets during the day and as a disco at night. For at least one late night it's the setting for a "singles mingle." Another double duty lounge, Royal Fireworks, with its walls of sloped windows, serves as a quiet area or as a meeting room for groups during the day and a lounge for dancing before and after dinner. The Observatory Panorama Bar is another attractive lounge with walls of windows around half of the room.

Trimmed in rich natural wood and brass, it has plush seating in groups of four at marble-topped cocktail tables.

On the summer cruises to Bermuda, the ship is not allowed to stage big production entertainment nor is the casino opened. Instead, the ship offers excursions to local nightclubs. Another option is an evening cocktail cruise along the pretty shores of Bermuda.

ACTIVITIES AND DIVERSIONS   Daytime offerings on board are noteworthy, especially considering the busy pace of a three-day cruise. There are bridge tours, Ping-Pong tournaments, bridge and Scrabble games, fruit and vegetable carving demonstrations, napkin-folding and dance classes, and a grandmothers' gab fest. The ship has shops, card room, library with good books, conference room, and small boardroom. There's a wine tasting class one afternoon in the Royal Observatory and a poolside fashion show with outfits from the ship's boutique.

SPORTS, FITNESS, AND BEAUTY   Active passengers can stay busy and in shape in the gym, working out while enjoying ocean views. The gym has state-of-the-art exercise equipment, including Life Circuit machines and a Nordic Track, and a separate mirrored studio where exercise and dance classes are offered. There is a jogging track on the perimeter of Princess Deck. Aerobics are available and there's early morning Tai Chi, golf driving, and Ping-Pong.

The topside pool deck has one of the ship's best features. Bordered by flowering plants and wooden trellises, the pool area is partially covered by two large white canvas tarps shaped like sails, stretched artistically over the corners of the swimming pool, providing shade in open-air areas for those who want to avoid the direct sun. The spa has two whirlpools, saunas for men and women, and massage. A small beauty parlor offers facials and spa treatments in addition to beauty care.

CHILDREN'S FACILITIES   Kids are offered activities and goodies such as special movies, bridge tours, treasure hunts, magic tricks, and children's menus.

The Little Prince play area has the feel of a day-care center, with its own kiddies' pool, playground rides, a ball slide, and a permanent puppet theatre, all done in primary colors. There's even a short kiddies' sink in the bathroom. Older kids have a video arcade with a dozen game machines.

SHORE EXCURSIONS   On the Bahamas cruise, the ship offers standard, off-the-shelf tours. Bermuda cruises give passengers the opportunity to explore the island leisurely on their own or on tour. The ship spends four full days in St. George's, in front of King's Square, which has shops, the historic St. Peter's church, and motor scooter rentals (the island's most popular form of transport) only a few yards away. The picturesque town is ideal for a walking tour and convenient to beaches and sightseeing but not to Hamilton, which is at the other end of the island. There are no car rentals in Bermuda; you either travel by scooter, taxi, or walk.

Among the excursions available are sailing and a visit to the Bermuda Aquarium Museum and Zoo. The ship's Club Nautica program offers snorkeling, scuba diving, and deep-sea fishing excursions.

POSTSCRIPT   NCL takes over the ship in late 1997, and does not anticipate making any immediate changes in the on-board services or itineraries. Along with the purchase of the ship, NCL has inherited Majesty's much-coveted Boston–Bermuda summer cruises.

Norwegian Star

	Quality Rating	Value Rating
Norwegian Star	6	C

Registry: Bahamas	Length: 676 feet	Beam: 83 feet
Cabins: 424	Draft: 24 feet	Speed: 20 knots
Maximum Passengers:	Passenger Decks: 9	Elevators: 5
1,200	Crew: 390	Space Ratio: n.a.

THE SHIP   Built originally as the *Royal Viking Sea*, she was the *Royal Odyssey* under the defunct Royal Cruise Line. In May 1997, after major renovation, she became the *Norwegian Star*, sailing from her new home base in Houston, Texas to the Western Caribbean.

Among the latest enhancements are the addition of NCL's signature alternative restaurants, Le Bistro and Sports Bar, as well as a new Art Deco–themed casino, children's playroom, and video arcade. In addition to the refurbishing of all cabins, the ship's maximum capacity has been increased from 848 passengers (based on two per cabin) to 1,200 passengers by the addition of third and fourth berths in almost 200 cabins.

This classic oceanliner has a light, contemporary ambience by Yran and Storbraaten, the well-known Scandinavian design team who created the decor on the luxurious *Seabourn* and *Sea Goddess* twins, as well as other NCL ships. The designers use lovely textured fabrics, which favor subtle pastels. The overall effect is an airy, inviting ambience with a fresh, modern look of elegant simplicity that retains the ship's classic lines.

Marina Deck serves as the reception center with the purser's desk, shore excursion office, photo shop/gallery, and boutiques. The reception and information desk area has been enlarged.

ITINERARIES   Western Caribbean, year-round.

- The *Norwegian Star* sails on Sundays, year-round, on seven-day "Texaribbean" cruises from Houston with an innovative itinerary to Cozumel, Calica (a port on the Yucatán coast next to Xcaret about ten miles south of Playa del Carmen), and Roatan (Honduras), with three days at sea.

Home Port   Houston.
Port Charges $115.50.

CABINS   The *Norwegian Star* has 16 categories, from large suites to deluxe inside cabins, located on five passenger decks. Most cabins are outside with large picture windows and have bathrooms with big tubs and showers. All are equipped with television with CNN and other satellite channels, direct-dial phone, three-channel radio, and hair dryer. They have full-length mirrors, generous closet space and storage, and a security-lock drawer. Mini-refrigerators are available in seven upper categories.

The ships' most luxurious accommodations are the deluxe suites on the Penthouse Deck. Each suite has a bedroom, a separate sitting room, floor-to-ceiling windows, large bathroom with tub and shower, television and VCR, plus a refrigerator, bar, and sliding glass doors opening onto the veranda.

Specifications   71 inside (22 deluxe), 323 outside; 9 penthouse suites with verandas, 10 deluxe suites, 42 superiors. Standard dimensions 140–200 square feet. All with two lower beds (49 convertible to doubles); 200 third/fourth persons.

DINING   The Seven Continents Restaurant, the main dining room on Viking Deck, serves three meals in two seatings. Menus are the same as those of other NCL ships. It is also the setting for late-night buffets. The elegant decor has tapestry fabrics covering the chairs; handmade Murano glass chandeliers and wall sconces provide soft light.

The ship's dining alternatives include Le Bistro, an informal cafe offering Italian and continental fare, added during the latest renovation; the Sports Bar which serves breakfast and lunch buffets; and the King Bar Grill serving light lunch and snacks. On the new "Texaribbean" cruises, the ship is offering a Tex-Mex barbecue and other special festivities.

FACILITIES AND ENTERTAINMENT   The Fjord Deck is the center of nighttime action with the show lounge and casino. One flight up on Promenade Deck is the Sports Bar which becomes a disco.

Topside, the Top of the Star Lounge at the bow is three bars in one—an elegant observation lounge, a piano bar, and a premium wine bar. Dressed in tranquil shades of gray, blue, and ivory and decorated with maps and astronomy charts, the bar has 180 degrees of floor-to-ceiling windows, a favorite roost for cocktails at sunset.

Directly aft is the enlarged Midnight Sun Lounge, which has the look of a summer garden with a lattice ceiling and peach walls, beige carpet, and Italian rattan furniture. Morning coffee and lunchtime salad bar are served here. It also has a parquet floor for dancing, which makes the multipurpose lounge popular at almost any hour. A theatre on the lowest deck shows current films and is used for lectures and religious services.

SPORTS, FITNESS, AND BEAUTY   The fitness center has been expanded and improved. It has exercise equipment and an aerobics area; sauna and massage rooms for men and women; juice bar; and full-time fitness instructors. Other facilities include a Ping-Pong court, golf practice net, and a beauty salon and barbershop. The wind-sheltered swimming pool on Fjord Deck has plenty of deck space for games and relaxing.

POSTSCRIPT   The Houston-based ship should prove to be a boon for Texans and their neighbors, providing both economy and convenience. Readers planning a cruise on the *Norwegian Star* should review all the Norwegian Cruise Line section for a full picture of the cruise experience the line offers.

ORIENT LINES

1510 SE Seventeenth Street, Suite 400, Ft. Lauderdale, FL 33316-1716
(305) 527-6660; (800) 333-7300; fax (305) 527-6657

TYPE OF SHIP   Updated, midsize oceanliner.

TYPE OF CRUISE   Affordable, destination-intensive, light adventure with first class amenities, fine cuisine, and refined ambience.

CRUISE LINE'S STRENGTHS
- stylish ship
- attentive crew
- alternative dining venue
- itineraries
- singles policy
- price
- dock-level gangway door
- expert lecturers on longer voyages
- precruise information

CRUISE LINE'S SHORTCOMINGS
- limited room service
- shore transport in some remote/primitive locations
- limited on-board shopping
- extra payment for upgraded shore accommodations and tours

FELLOW PASSENGERS   In the short time that Orient Lines has been in operation, it has attracted a certain type of passenger—mature, experienced, inquisitive, friendly, and interested in the line's off-the-beaten-track itineraries. On longer cruises passengers range in age from 50–70, with average annual incomes of about $75,000, and are retired or semi-retired, business owners, managers, or professionals. They come mainly from the West Coast, Arizona, Texas, New York, Florida, Canada, and Great Britain, but some cruises might include other Europeans, Australians, and South Africans. Many are experienced cruisers, but many, too, are first-time cruisers who have traveled frequently in the past on foreign group tours and were drawn to their Orient cruise by its strong destination focus. In 1994, with the introduction of summer Mediterranean cruises, however, the line saw a noticeable drop in age from an average age of 55 to the 35–54 group and an almost tripling of passengers from the Midwest and Northeast.

Recommended For   Orient now has two separate seasons, each with a different appeal. On the longer, winter-season cruises, seasoned travelers, whether or not experienced cruisers, who have interest and curiosity to appreciate exotic destinations but like to travel in comfort and style. Small-ship devotees who want to sample a cruise on a larger ship but not a megaliner. Travelers who want a cruise to be something of a learning experience in luxury. From May–October, first-time cruisers, families, honeymooners, those who want a combined land and sea vacation package in Europe.

Not Recommended For   Unsophisticated or inexperienced travelers and those seeking a high-energy, holiday-at-sea, party atmosphere.

CRUISE AREAS AND SEASONS   In winter, Antarctica, New Zealand, Australia; Southeast Asia/Java Seas; India, Indian Ocean, Egypt, and Africa. In summer, Mediterranean, Greek Isles, and Black Sea.

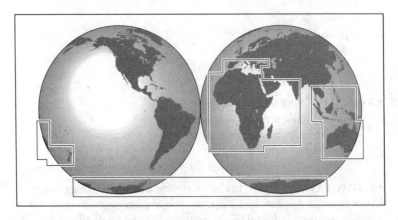

THE LINE   Orient Lines originated in 1991 when its CEO, Gerry Herrod, a British entrepreneur and tour and cruise line veteran, bought the former Russian liner, *Alexandr Pushkin,* for about $25 million. The ship, built in East Germany in 1965 for the Soviets, who hoped to generate hard currency by cashing in on the growing cruise market, was one of four sister ships with ice-strengthened hulls. They had the additional duty of serving as Soviet troop ships and spy ships intercepting Western intelligence signals.

In 1991, after being in a Singapore Yard for minor repairs, the *Alexandr Pushkin* was put up for sale when the Soviets could not pay their bills. After two years of rebuilding by Orient Lines, the ship was transformed into a luxury liner at a cost of $75 million and reappeared as the *Marco Polo*. At the same time, the new cruise line was launched with a goal to offer upscale cruises for experienced travelers to exotic, offbeat parts of the world at reasonable prices. In the second year the mission changed somewhat when the line found great success in a summer Mediterranean program. The Mediterranean itineraries have broadened the age base of its passengers, attracting many in their 30s and 40s, as well as the geographic one, finding new fans from the Northeast and Midwest.

The Fleet	Built/Renovated	Tonnage	Passengers
Marco Polo	1965/1993	22,080	800

STYLE "Adventure in elegance" is one way Orient Lines' *Marco Polo* has been described. From the start the line differentiated itself from most mainstream cruise lines by focusing on its destinations, giving as much weight to developing unusual itineraries as to the facilities of the ship, while providing all the comforts and fine cuisine of a deluxe ship. While daytime activity calls for casual dress, evenings during full days at sea tend to be elegant in the fashion of a luxury ship.

Meant to be an all-encompassing experience, the *Marco Polo*'s winter cruises include detailed port briefings, lectures by distinguished guest speakers and experts in the areas the ship cruises, and extended pre- and postcruise hotel stays with sightseeing in ports of embarkation and disembarkation. Some itineraries feature shipboard performances by local groups to showcase the unique culture of the regions visited. Passengers are sent well-written, well-researched briefing materials prior to their cruise.

DISTINCTIVE FEATURES Gentlemen social hosts (except on Mediterranean cruises); local cultural performances; topside helipad and helicopter; on-board videotaping of workshops for replay on the ship's TV channel; low single supplement. First ship to sail on seven-day New Zealand cruises between Christchurch and Auckland due to special permission from New Zealand government. One of only two luxury ships to be given permission to cruise Antarctica.

RATES

Highest Per Diem	Lowest Per Diem	Average Per Diem
$420	$66	$198

The above per diems are calculated from the cruise line's nondiscounted *cruise-only* fares on standard accommodations. What you will actually pay *should* be *substantially* less (see Part One, How to Get the Best Deal on a Cruise). Per diems vary by season, by cabin location, and by cruise areas.

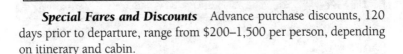

Special Fares and Discounts   Advance purchase discounts, 120 days prior to departure, range from $200–1,500 per person, depending on itinerary and cabin.

- Combination savings for two or more cruises taken in sequence have savings of up to 28 percent.
- Single Supplement: 25 percent on all cabin categories except A and suites. Frequently the line offers special promotions in which single supplement is waived.

Packages
- Air/Sea: Yes.
- Pre/Post: Yes. Orient Lines cruises are designed as cruise tours with two- to six-day pre- and/or postcruise hotel stays in major gateway cities.
- Others: Yes.

Past Passengers   After their first cruise on the *Marco Polo*, passengers are given free membership in the Polo Club and receive information on new itineraries, the club magazine, discounts on cruises, a handsome travel bag for their next cruise, $25–75 on-board credit, depending on length of cruise, bottle of wine in their cabin, and VIP party with the captain on board the ship.

THE LAST WORD   The *Marco Polo* is a midsize ship by today's standards; nonetheless, it is one of the largest ships cruising to exotic destinations on a regular basis. Her size enables her to provide upscale comforts and a full range of shipboard facilities, while her passenger capacity provides a larger base over which Orient Lines can spread costs. Therefore, the line is able to offer cruises at prices considerably lower than most of its competitors, which generally have smaller deluxe ships.

The *Marco Polo* has a significant advantage: superior stability. On this ship, originally designed for long, fast, blue-water passages, with an ice-strengthened hull, waves of 12 feet are hardly noticeable.

Orient Lines cares about single travelers. In addition to having gentlemen hosts on board every cruise to dine and dance with unaccompanied women passengers, the line offers one of the lowest single supplements in cruising, as well as occasional singles promotions, during which the supplement is waived. Also, it is fastidious in matching up participants in its guaranteed share program.

Children are rare aboard the *Marco Polo* but as a result are treated like royalty. On a recent cruise the only child on board, a precocious 12-year-old, toured the engine room, was given a ship's uniform complete with officer's hat, name tag, and commander's stripes, had free run of the bridge, and was even allowed to steer the ship.

ORIENT LINES STANDARD FEATURES

Officers Scandinavian, European.

Staffs Dining, Cabin/Filipino; Cruise/American and British.

Dining Facilities One dining room with open seating for breakfast and lunch and two seatings for dinner with assigned tables; multipurpose lounge used for buffet breakfast, lunch, tea. Specialty dinner restaurant.

Special Diets Accommodated with 30 days' advance notice.

Room Service Continental breakfast, cabin attendants on call.

Dress Code Casual by day; several formal nights.

Cabin Amenities Direct-dial phone, television with VCR, ship programs, radio, hair dryer, toiletries. Safes, bathrobes, and slippers in upper category cabins; small refrigerators in suites. Deluxe suites with sitting room, marble bathroom with tub and shower, and stocked minibars.

Electrical Outlets 110/220 AC.

Wheelchair Access Two cabins.

Recreation and Entertainment Four lounges; port/country lectures by experts; piano and/or string trio music for cocktails and after dinner; nightly entertainment; local folkloric dancers in port; library; card room.

Sports and Other Activities Small outdoor swimming pool, Ping-Pong.

Beauty and Fitness Beauty salon/spa; massage; exercise equipment; Jacuzzis; saunas.

Other Facilities Shops; medical unit. Zodiacs, helicopter; landing pad and meeting room.

Children's Facilities No special facilities.

Smoking One smoking dining room and one nonsmoking; smoking permitted in designated wing of main lounge bar during shows, but not during lectures and briefings.

Orient Suggested Tipping Per day per person $8 pooled for cabin steward, waiter, and busboy; 15 percent of bar bill.

Credit Cards For cruise payment and on-board charges, American Express, Mastercard, Visa.

Marco Polo

	Quality Rating	Value Rating
Marco Polo	❼	A

Registry: Bahamas	Length: 578 feet	Beam: 77 feet
Cabins: 425	Draft: 27 feet	Speed: 18 knots
Maximum Passengers:	Passenger Decks: 8	Elevators: 4
850	Crew: 350	Space Ratio: 27.6

THE SHIP   A lovely vessel with traditional, classic lines, the *Marco Polo* has been enhanced by her handsome art deco interiors created by the well-known design firm of A and M Katzourakis of Athens. Reminiscent of grand liners of the 1920s, pastel furnishings throughout are set against etched and beveled glass, brass, chrome, and rich wood, accented by Thai and Burmese antiques and prints, along with some modern paintings selected by the owner.

The *Marco Polo* is a comfortable ship designed for long cruises. Originally intended for service with the Soviets in the Arctic Ocean, her hull is specially strengthened for icy waters and ice floes, with many extra frames added. After her initial shakedown cruise, some modifications to her hull were made; notably, a new gangway door was cut to allow passengers to enter the ship at the same level as most docks and piers. This avoids a long walk up a steep gangway.

Most cabins are on the main deck, one deck below the Belvedere Deck, which accommodates most of the public rooms and includes the main lobby, three of the four entertainment lounges and bars, the casino, and a library with over 1,000 volumes.

Because of the ship's traditional design, there are numerous outside vantage points, especially on the upper deck forward and the Promenade Deck aft, for viewing ports of call; photographing flying fish, dolphins, and other wildlife; and watching sunsets.

ITINERARIES   5–28 days, year-round, on contiguous itineraries, extending through Asia from New Zealand to Kenya and the Mediterranean and Black Sea; others via South Africa to Antarctica.

- *From January–April* the *Marco Polo* usually cruises in Asia. She is the first foreign cruise ship ever allowed to sail New Zealand waters, stopping in numerous ports. The cruises—seven-day itineraries between Christchurch and Auckland—were made possible by the New Zealand government's waiving of its cabotage laws. Extended stays in Auckland and/or Christchurch are available in conjunction with them.

- *In late April*, the *Marco Polo* sails through Indonesia to Bali and Singapore; a second leg cruises from Singapore to Bombay; and another via the Indian Ocean to the Mediterranean.

- *From May–October,* she offers some of her most popular cruises, focused mainly in the Eastern Mediterranean but with intermittent ones that take in Italy, the Riviera, Spain, plus a fall highlight that combines Egypt and a Kenya safari.

- *In December and January* every other year, the ship offers Antarctica cruises. Antarctica sailings have fewer passengers (only 450 allowed by authorities compared to the ship's normal complement of 600–800), and include scientists and expert lecturers, wildlife viewing from Zodiacs and the ship's helicopter, and visits to scientific stations.

Home Ports   Varies with itineraries.
Port Charges   To be announced.

CABINS   Being an older vessel, the *Marco Polo* has a large variety of cabin sizes and configurations. Almost 70 percent are outside; those in the upper A–D categories have large picture windows.

Cabins are light and handsomely appointed with light wood furniture and pastel bedspreads, curtains, and carpeting. Most are a comfortable size for long cruises with ample drawer and closet space, mirrored dressing table with pullout writing desk, and good reading lights. All have a telephone with international direct-dialing, radio, television with two channels for movies and one for ship programs, bathroom with shower, built-in hair dryer, and complimentary toiletries. Upper category cabins are provided with bathrobes, slippers, and safes. Deluxe suites have a large sitting room, separate bedroom, large marble bathroom with tub and shower, and fully stocked minibars, replenished without charge. Junior suites and some deluxe cabins come with a sitting area and bath with tub and shower. Family cabins have curtain-divided sleeping areas.

Cabins on Sky Deck, including the junior suites and deluxe cabins, and ten cabins on the upper deck have views partially obstructed by lifeboats suspended above the deck below; these are noted on the deck plan in the cruise line's brochure. The two deluxe suites and some other cabins on the upper deck and Promenade Deck have windows that face out over deck areas; however, silvered one-way glass prevents outsiders from seeing in.

Passengers on the *Marco Polo* can enjoy their airy cabins and their amenities all the more when they learn that the old *Alexandr Pushkin's* troopship cabins were only 7 feet wide, 20 feet long, with bare steel walls, 18 berths per cabin in triple bunk beds, and one shower per hundred Soviet troopers!

Specifications 131 inside cabins, 288 outside; 6 suites. Standard dimensions 140–180 square feet. 388 cabins with 2 lower beds (42 convertible to double beds); 28 accommodate third passenger; 10 accommodate 4. Suites and some upper category cabins have double/queen-size beds, some have twin beds convertible to doubles. 2 cabins are wheelchair accessible.

DINING Fine cuisine and exemplary service in elegant surroundings with tables set in fine china, crystal, and fresh flowers make dining one of the ship's best features. The Seven Seas Restaurant on Bali Deck is a large formal room dressed in mauves and grays. Breakfast and lunch have open seating, but there are two seatings for dinner along with assigned tables.

The dining room, entered from the central foyer graced with large abstract oil paintings and oriental statues, has a central, slightly raised area with a handsome art deco circular ceiling, which is separated from the lower outer sides by glass partitions. By the windows on either side of the room are booths and tables for two to ten persons. Floor-to-ceiling mirrors on the inside walls help to create a spacious feeling. The dining room is no smoking.

Through a new association with the Cafe Royal, the renowned London establishment, Orient Lines now offers a special "Evening at the Cafe Royal" menu on each cruise. In addition, chefs from the Michelin-starred restaurant regularly appear on board to create featured dishes.

Dinner menus usually offer three appetizers, two soups, four entrees, and a selection of two or three desserts, cheeses, and fruits. Lighter selections are indicated on the menu. Each menu also comes with a vegetarian and a healthy low-fat, low-salt choice. The wine list offers a selection of vintages from South Africa, Australia, Argentina, and Chile, as well as California and Europe. The wine list is reasonably priced from $10 and up.

Raffles is the place for casual breakfast and lunch buffets. It has a bright, attractive setting with large picture windows and looks out onto the pool deck. Afternoon tea is served here as well as in the Palm Court. An awning outside of Raffles shades the ice cream and dessert bar at lunch. There are tables and chairs with large umbrellas for outdoor seating around the pool.

About two nights a week, Raffles is transformed into an elegant alternative dining room for 75 passengers (reservation required) serving Oriental and Asian cuisine prepared by specialty chefs. The menu changes each evening; the dinners are very popular and usually fully booked. There is a $15 charge per person which includes wine; additional tipping is discretionary. Incidentally, the forward part of Raffles seats more people and has a ceiling that reverberates the sound; some passengers may prefer the quieter tables at the aft end of the room.

Other than continental breakfast, room service dining is not officially available, except in case of illness. This is a deliberate policy of the line but nonetheless a surprising one for a deluxe ship. The line maintains that the fine dining experience which the ship offers is best enjoyed in the dining room. Perhaps, but not all passengers would agree, especially after a long and tiring day on tour when, understandably, some may prefer to eat in the comfort of their cabin. Despite the official policy, however, passengers report that most cabin stewards are happy to bring food to the cabin on request. Another point: on tour days the dress is invariably casual for dinner, and the atmosphere in the dining room more relaxed.

SERVICE   The tone of the *Marco Polo* is set by its friendly, service-oriented Scandinavian officers, lively British and American cruise staff, and well-trained, hard-working Filipino crew, who win high praise from passengers for their attentiveness and cheerful disposition. Cabin staff know passenger names minutes after their arrival, and address them by name throughout the cruise—that seems to make an indelible mark on passengers.

FACILITIES AND ENTERTAINMENT   The Ambassador Lounge on Belvedere Deck is the main showroom where local entertainment brought on board in different ports of call is featured. Invariably, they are highlights of the cruise and are generally better than the musical revues and variety shows staged by the ship on nights at sea. Other on-board entertainment might include a classical concert, piano recital, and Filipino crew show. Many of the cruise staff also double as performers.

The lounge, divided into three sections of curved divans, slopes gently in large steps toward the stage and bandstand and provides good sight lines (except behind a few pillars, or if the room is completely full). Large windows span both sides of the room, and at the rear a marble-topped bar with a chrome railing has floor-to-ceiling mirrors on either side. Diamond-shaped smoked glass and brass wall lighting fixtures, together with royal blue carpets and blue decor, give the room a look that is straight from the 1930s.

The Polo Lounge, between the show lounge and main lobby, is a popular piano bar for predinner cocktails and late evening relaxing; it is also used for afternoon bridge. Tastefully decorated in pastels, leather sofas, and a large floral centerpiece, it has as its focus a cream-colored baby grand piano encircled by a bar.

Le Casino, aft of the main lobby, has roulette, blackjack, slot and video poker machines, and its own elegant art deco, white marble bar and black leather swivel chairs. Photos of famous entertainers hang on the side walls and behind the bar.

Tucked in the sides off the casino are a small card and game room and a well-stocked library with large comfortable leather armchairs and big picture windows. One can browse through the large selection of books, and local and international newspapers are provided when they are available. Guidebooks for the many countries visited by the *Marco Polo* are also provided.

Along the windows between the main lobby and casino is the Palm Court, a small open room with marble-topped tables and wicker chairs. It is a pleasurable retreat for afternoon tea or a quiet drink and conversation. On the opposite side of the ship from the Palm Court are two small boutiques.

The Charleston Club on Promenade Deck aft is one of several multi-purpose lounges, used for bingo, t'ai chi, painting lessons, cocktails, late-evening music and dancing, and midnight pizza. At the entrance, glass doors open onto a lounge in pastel, with a white baby grand piano and small bandstand, a marble-topped bar, and a dance floor. The lounge is popular as a late-night gathering spot, particularly for the cruise staff and a small group of passengers. *Marco Polo* passengers, by and large, are not a late-night disco crowd.

ACTIVITIES AND DIVERSIONS   On the *Marco Polo* (except Mediterranean cruises), specialized lectures by experts on the region of the cruise are highlights and are well attended by passengers. The roster might include such famous people as Sir Edmund Hillary; noted wildlife expert Peter Alden, who has led wildlife and birding expeditions to 105 countries and is recognized in the *Guiness Book of Records* for having seen, recognized, and listed more birds than anyone—a mind-boggling 5,000 or more species; and Dr. Donna Pido, an anthropologist who lived with the Masai for six years and worked as an advisor on the film *Out of Africa*.

Neither lectures nor workshops are presented on the Mediterranean cruises due to the port-intensive nature of these itineraries.

Several gentlemen hosts are also on board all cruises (except Mediterranean) for the ladies traveling on their own to enjoy conversation, dancing, dining, and other shipboard activities in pleasant company.

Among the other diversions are tours of the bridge, bridge and backgammon lessons and tournaments, origami (Japanese paper folding), up-close magic workshops, white elephant sales, passenger talent (or lack thereof!) shows, service club meetings for Lions, Kiwanis, Rotary, and so on, fashion shows, joke contests, and other activities.

SPORTS, FITNESS, AND BEAUTY   On Pool Deck just outside of Raffles is a small (15 feet long) swimming pool with teakwood benches on three sides and a small stage used for fashion shows and entertainment in the evening. There is also a poolside bar. An open deck at the stern and on the sides has old-fashioned wooden steamer chairs. Ping-Pong and shuffleboard are available.

A fitness center and spa on the upper deck has a mirrored exercise room and small gym with treadmills, stationary bicycles, rowing machine, stair steppers, weight machines, and free weights; aerobics, exercise classes, and t'ai chi (especially designed for stretching, relaxation, and low-impact exercise) are offered. There are separate saunas for men and women and three outside Jacuzzis on Sky Deck. From time to time, the ship offers fitness theme cruises.

The beauty salon, operated by the Steiner group of London, offers a full range of pampering services, such as facials, massage and hydrotherapy, with prices comparable to other Steiner-cruise ship salons. Most are an expensive indulgence.

Upper deck also has a jogging track that goes around the ship. It consists mostly of a narrow rubberized path that goes behind the lifeboats. Near the bow the path is on teak decks for about 150 feet, with a good view over the bow. For walkers, Promenade Deck has a one-fifth-mile course laid out between the Charleston Club and the bridge gangway. It is all on teak decks and provides unobstructed views of the sea.

SHORE EXCURSIONS   All cruises feature pre- or postcruise packages and are particularly popular given the distances most passengers travel to reach the ship. Most cruises also include an unusual highlight in their land portion. For example, a cruise/safari in Kenya visits the home of Isak Dinesen (Karen Blixen), the author of *Out of Africa*, along with three days of wildlife viewing in Amboseli National Park at the foot of 19,340-foot Mt. Kilimanjaro.

Typical short shore excursions might include a snorkeling trip to a protected reef in the Seychelles, a visit to see the famous Komodo dragons of Indonesia, a city tour of Durban, South Africa, including the botanical garden and university, or a visit to a nature preserve in Madagascar to see lively, leaping lemurs.

Having the helipad is not only a reassuring feature in case of an emergency in some remote part of the world and for scouting ice conditions in Antarctica, but on the New Zealand programs passengers can board their flightseeing excursions directly from the ship.

Note: Shore transport in some remote/primitive locations (e.g., Zanzibar) is of necessity not top of the line; because of this some shore excursions are not appropriate for passengers with limited mobility. Also, an extra fee for upgraded shore accommodations and tours may be charged but is worth the cost in some third world locations.

POSTSCRIPT   Orient Lines publishes excellent cruise brochures, which are easy to read and understand. The most important features, special events, and workshops for every cruise are highlighted in a quick, easy-to-spot format. Precruise literature with detailed information on shore excursions and trip planning, sent to passengers a month in advance of their sailing, is outstanding.

Writing in 1298, Marco Polo opened his famous *Travels* with the words: "Ye kings, princes, nobles, townsfolk and all who wish to know the marvels of the world, have this book read unto you." If he were writing today, he might say, "All ye who wish to know the marvels of the world, take a cruise on the *Marco Polo*."

P&O CRUISES

10100 Santa Monica Boulevard, Los Angeles, CA 90067
(310) 553-1770; (800) PRINCESS (774-6237); fax (310) 284-2857

TYPE OF SHIPS   New superliners and classic oceanliner.

TYPE OF CRUISES   Very British; budget to moderately priced and deluxe with worldwide itineraries.

CRUISE LINE'S STRENGTHS
- well-organized ships, aboard and ashore
- nonrepeating itineraries with vast number of ports
- distinctive British character
- excellent daytime programs and nighttime entertainment

CRUISE LINE'S SHORTCOMINGS
- small serving portions
- limited fresh salads and pastas
- limited buffet selections

FELLOW PASSENGERS   Mostly British, all ages and incomes, many cruising together for years on voyages from Britain and the Mediterranean. Americans, Australians, and New Zealanders make up a sizable minority on round-the-world voyages.

Recommended For   Anglophiles who like British humor, food, interests. On the round-the-world voyage, the well-traveled who like traveling with the well-traveled.

Not Recommended For   Americans who are not enamored with all things British; who might not appreciate the fiercely loyal passengers who in turn might not appreciate Americans who do not conform to British ways.

CRUISE AREAS AND SEASONS   England to Northern Europe, Iberian Peninsula, Atlantic islands, and Mediterranean in summer; some

Caribbean in winter prior to annual round-the-world voyage, Panama Canal to Pacific, Australia, and New Zealand; return via Southeast Asia, Suez Canal, and Mediterranean or via South Africa.

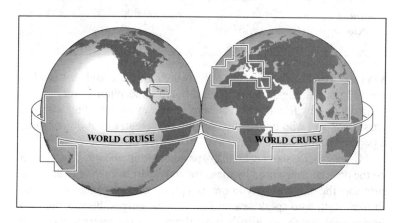

THE LINE The official name of P&O Cruises is the Peninsular and Oriental Steam Navigation Company, which has a direct link to the original company founded in 1837. Always a British-based shipping line, its principal routes traditionally served the empire, i.e., India, Ceylon, Malaysia, the Far East, Australia, and New Zealand.

After World War II, new routes were opened via North America and across the Pacific, and by 1960, P&O had merged with the Orient Line to form P&O-Orient Lines and finally P&O Cruises. Princess Cruises, Los Angeles, is the North American subsidiary of P&O S.N. Co. London.

In April 1995, P&O Cruises introduced the *Oriana*, its first brand new ship in more than two decades. With its arrival, the line made a major repositioning of one ship and added air-sea cruises in the Mediterranean for its mainly British audience. In fall of 1997, P&O replaced the retiring *Canberra* with Princess Cruises' *Star Princess* and changed her name to *Arcadia*.

Now, P&O Cruises is concentrating on three principal programs: cruises departing from Southampton, those based in the Caribbean in winter, and the annual round-the-world voyages. The latter retain a special colonial flavor because many of the older passengers had connections with the British colonies, and some of the staff and crew have years of service with the line. Many Australians, retired or on long service leave, use the ships to travel to and from Britain.

The Fleet	Built/Renovated	Tonnage	Passengers
Arcadia	1989/1997	63,500	1,470
Oriana	1995	69,000	1,800
Victoria	1966/86/97	28,000	714

STYLE   The British style cannot be overemphasized and that is what most of the passengers want. The on-board atmosphere is very social, helped along by friendly British officers who enjoy mingling with the passengers and who host many tables in the restaurants at dinner time, a popular feature of these ships.

Unless there is a non-English-speaking group aboard, English will be the only language used by the crew, and, apart from the Indians, it is probably the only one they know, except, of course for members of the Purser's staff, who speak several European languages. Besides the very British cooking, things British shine through in the reserved nature of some of the passengers, very precise timing for all activities, fondness for a pint (of beer or lager) before lunch, afternoon tea, British humor as found on imported public television programs in the United States and in less familiar music hall humor, cricket matches, and fascination with sports and politics. Most of the passengers do not like change, so not much has changed aboard the line's ships in many years.

DISTINCTIVE FEATURES   The British ambience, proper afternoon teas, excellent port lecturers well versed in local history and culture, classical pianists, social interaction with the British officers, Sunday (Anglican) church services with a passenger/staff choir.

RATES

Highest Per Diem	Lowest Per Diem	Average Per Diem
$708	$280	$392

The above per diems are calculated from the cruise line's nondiscounted *cruise-only* fares on standard accommodations. Per diems vary by season, by cabin location, and by cruise areas.

Special Fares and Discounts
• Third/Fourth Passenger: 50 percent of minimum rate, based on inside upper/lower berth, on *Victoria*.

Packages
• Air/Sea: Yes.
• Pre/Post: Yes.

Past Passengers   P&O's past passenger club is called The Posh Club. You must take a cruise to qualify and there's an annual fee of £30.

THE LAST WORD   With its new ships, P&O has more to offer the American market, but still its basic appeal is to those who really like all things British. P&O cruises such as the summer cruises in Northern Europe or a segment or all of the round-the-world voyages attract serious destination cruisers. On the other hand, the shorter cruises from England to sunny destinations attract largely sun worshipers escaping Britain's lousy climate.

P&O also operates the *Fair Princess*, which sails from Australia to the South Pacific, but the cruises are marketed in a very limited way in the United States.

P&O Cruises is represented in the United States by its sister company, Princess Cruises. Its headquarters office is P&O Cruises, 77 New Oxford Street, London WC1A1PP; Tel. 071-800-2222.

P&O Ships Standard Features

Officers British. For *Arcadia* British officers transferred from *Canberra* but ship not being re-registered at this time.

Staff Dining, Cabin/Indian, also British, European. Cruise/British.

Dining Facilities One dining room with two assigned seatings. Two restaurants on *Oriana* with same menus. Buffet breakfast and lunch at indoor/outdoor facilities, and on *Oriana* and *Arcadia*, buffet dinner sometimes offered in the evening.

Special Diets Request at time of booking.

Room Service Early morning coffee, tea, and biscuits; sandwiches/snacks.

Dress Code Jacket and tie on most nights at sea; some formal evenings when most men wear tuxedos or dinner jackets and women don cocktail and long dresses.

Cabin Amenities Television, radio; BBC news; phones; high percentage of bathtubs on *Oriana* and *Victoria*. *Oriana* cabins have refrigerators and safes. *Victoria* due to have television added.

Electrical Outlets 220 AC.

Wheelchair Access Ten cabins on *Arcadia*, eight on *Victoria* and *Oriana* in various price categories.

Recreation and Entertainment Card room, library, casinos, many bars, show lounge and cabarets, classical pianists, disco, dance classes, bingo, whist (similar to bingo), bridge, evening quiz games, art, crafts, lecturers.

Sports and Other Activities One outdoor pool, one inside on *Victoria*; two on *Arcadia*; three on *Oriana* (one dedicated for children); exercise classes; deck tennis; cricket matches; Ping-Pong; deck and pool games.

Beauty and Fitness Barber/hairdresser; gym and sauna; wraparound deck, mostly for walkers—and lots of them.

Other Facilities Shops; well-equipped hospital; self-service laundries; laundry/dry cleaning services; meeting rooms; cinema.

Children's Facilities Excellent children's programs; programs for teenagers.

Theme Cruises Astronomy, bridge, bird-watching, classical music.

Smoking Designated areas but not strict.

P&O Suggested Tipping Per person per day, cabin steward, $1.50; dining steward, $1; assistant steward on *Victoria*, $.50; section wine stewards, $1; 10 percent added to bar bills.

Credit Cards Currency on board is pound sterling; for on-board charges, American Express, Diners Club, Mastercard, Visa.

Oriana

	Quality Rating	Value Rating
Oriana	❾	C

Registry: Britain	Length: 853 feet	Beam: 105 feet
Cabins: 914	Draft: 26 feet	Speed: 24 knots
Maximum Passengers:	Passenger Decks: 11	Elevators: 10
1,975	Crew: 760	Space Ratio: 38.4

THE SHIP The *Oriana*, which made her debut in April 1995, was built to cater primarily to the British market, but she should have a certain appeal to North Americans as well. She is a beautiful ship. Although she is big, new, and modern, the *Oriana* has the feel of a classic liner in its interior design and decor. No flashy neon or glitz here.

On the contrary, the interiors are as fine and refined as tea in a well-mannered British parlor. The walls are adorned with classic oil paintings, watercolors, historic documents, and ship models. And the ship has something that many large ships catering to the American market lack, namely, an inviting calm where it is easy to relax, with lots of nooks and crannies where you can sit and read, sip a beverage, write a postcard, and let the world go by. It's cruising as it should be.

Much thought has been given to maintaining P&O's loyal passengers, and many of *Canberra*'s distinctive features can be found in the new ship. For instance, the *Oriana* has a large number of singles and four-berth cabins, known as "friendly fours" for economical cruising and for families. Even *Oriana*'s profile, while updated, has a distinctive *Canberra* look, right up to the aft twin funnels.

The wide range of public rooms—17 in all—allows all types of passengers to establish themselves in comfortable and familiar surroundings. The ship maintains the tradition of a vast amount of open deck space for British sun worshipers and those who take their daily "constitutional," as well as two main dining rooms and outstanding facilities for children.

ITINERARIES After her world cruise, *Oriana* sails from Southampton from April–December, taking in the Iberian Peninsula, western Mediterranean, and North African ports in spring, late summer, and fall; Scandinavia and the North Cape, in midsummer; the eastern

Mediterranean and the Holy Land through November; then she heads across the Atlantic to the Caribbean in December. The majority of the cruises last 14 or 15 nights, but there are shorter 12-night trips and longer ones exceeding three weeks.

- *In early January*, the *Oriana* sails on her world cruise, which is probably the one that interests North Americans most. It also attracts Australians and New Zealanders traveling to and from their respective countries. The ship's 24-knot cruising speed permits ambitious itineraries.

Home Port Southampton and various other ports, depending on itinerary.

Port Charges All port charges included; airport departure tax is not.

CABINS In spite of all the continuity with the past, the cabins on the *Oriana* are more luxuriously appointed. They are spacious with lots of storage space and all have private facilities; some have bathtubs, telephones, televisions, and refrigerators; suites have large bathrooms with bathtubs.

The *Oriana* has 11 categories of cabins and an especially wide range of configurations, including a large number of single cabins—a rarity on today's megaliners. Almost all cabins, including suites, are on the three middle decks.

Specifications 8 suites, 16 deluxe cabins, 628 doubles, 114 singles, 6 three-berth, 40 four-berth cabins; 94 cabins with balconies; 8 wheelchair accessible.

DINING Unlike on modern cruise ships, the two main restaurants, the Peninsula and the Oriental, with two sittings for three meals, maintain the steamship tradition of fore and aft restaurants deep down in the hull but with large view windows. And like her sister vessels, the service staff is mainly Indian with some British and Europeans.

The cuisine is British—very British—which means lots of meat and potatoes, and sauces but few salads. The soups are excellent; but a typical English breakfast, with kippers and such, takes some getting use to.

On occasion, however, you might see items on the menu that are so strange, you will wonder how much of a British heritage Americans really have. For example, for the ship's annual Robert Burns Night in honor of the famous Scottish poet, only a Scotsman would understand the menu that features "Royal highland haggis with champit tatties 'n' bashed neeps and wee drap o' the cratur." (That translates as sausage with mashed potatoes and turnips in a sauce with a drop of whiskey—

scotch, of course.) And instead of reggae, calypso, and baked Alaska, there was "cloutie dumpling wi' a glayva bro," a dessert of fruitcake steamed in a cheesecloth and glazed with a scotch whiskey liqueur served to the accompaniment of bagpipes. Well, it's different. But rest assured, most nights the menus are easy to understand, if a little boring.

The Conservatory, the alternate restaurant with indoor/outdoor seating on the Lido Deck, serves informal buffet breakfast and lunch, with a much improved arrangement as well as a better selection than aboard the old *Canberra*. This area can get very crowded at peak lunch hours, so the best time to eat there is after 1:30 P.M.

SERVICE Throughout the ship, service by Indian stewards who know how to cater to British passengers, is very good. These Indian stewards, with more forthcoming personalities and a better command of English, have replaced some of the Goanese who formerly predominated in the service staff. Many British officers host tables at dinner, a very popular feature.

FACILITIES AND ENTERTAINMENT Public rooms range over two principal decks to create a variety of different atmospheres catering to the class-oriented British society. Many of them reflect, in style and name, the company's 160-year history. Entertainment options include classical music in the elegant Curzon Room, cabaret shows in the Pacific Lounge, the large production show in Theatre Royal, the state-of-the-art show lounge, and Harlequins, the disco.

In addition, there is the Lord's Tavern, the on-board "pub," with a cricket theme, the living room–like Anderson Lounge (named for one the founders of P&O) for after-dinner coffee and drinks; a separate cinema for films and special lectures; and the spacious Crow's Nest, an observation bar and lounge, similar but much larger than the hugely popular observation lounge on the *Canberra*, with the same deep wraparound windows for outstanding viewing and a trio playing dance music before and after dinner. The Monte Carlo Casino is off to the side of the Anderson Lounge and very small compared to any on the big ships sailing the Caribbean.

ACTIVITIES AND DIVERSIONS P&O offers an elaborate program of daytime and evening activities from traditional games such as bingo to art, craft, bridge, and dance classes, classical music, quizzes, elaborate shows, and cabaret. The line is known for having an excellent series of port lecturers, who are not only very knowledgeable, but can be counted on to have a dry, British sense of humor; they would never dream of giving the shopping sales pitches that typify many cruise ships in the

Caribbean. The library, with comfortable wing chairs, is supplied by *Ocean Books*, the same organization which supplies the *QE2*.

SPORTS, FITNESS, AND BEAUTY   The *Oriana* has acres of open deck and lots of activities for enjoying it, including deck tennis, deck quoits, shuffleboard, golf nets, trapshooting, and more. Cricket matches between the passengers and officers are always popular. Adult and children's pool games are a major spectacle. The wraparound mezzanine permits many hundreds to watch the fun. One of the ship's two outdoor pools is 42 feet long, said to be the largest afloat. A wide promenade with deck chairs shaded by overhanging lifeboats is a favorite place for passengers to take their daily walks. The *Oriana* has a large health spa with aerobics, a gym, Jacuzzis, sauna, massage, beauty and therapy rooms, and a hair salon.

CHILDREN'S FACILITIES   P&O is highly praised for its children's program. Separate spaces are allocated for young and teenage passengers with good supervision and well-designed programs. Children have their own pool and lido area well away from the two adult pools. Kids eat at an early sitting, with or without their parents present. For parents who are night owls, there is a staffed night nursery.

POSTSCRIPT   Although the *Oriana* is brand new, it operates in the P&O tradition, catering primarily to its loyal British market. But Americans who like the British style (without necessarily being total Anglophiles); or who are turned off by the glitz, loud music, and constant commotion of today's megaliners and yearn for the tranquility which cruising is meant to have, will be happy on this ship. They are likely to find that about 10 percent or so of the passengers will be other Americans of like sentiment.

Victoria

	Quality Rating	*Value Rating*
Victoria	❺	B

Registry: Great Britain	Length: 660 feet	Beam: 87 feet
Cabins: 370	Draft: 28 feet	Speed: 21.5 knots
Maximum Passengers:	Passenger Decks: 10	Elevators: 4
778	Crew: 417	Space Ratio: 38.2

THE SHIP The *Victoria* (formerly named *Sea Princess*) was the last liner built for the now defunct Swedish American Line. It's a dual-purpose vessel that made summertime transatlantic voyages and long cruises for the top end of the American market. When bought by P&O in 1978, her cabins were increased to help make her pay and one funnel was removed, spoiling her handsome profile.

For a time, she cruised from Australia, then from England, and for a period for Princess Cruises until that P&O subsidiary began to take delivery of its brand new and much larger ships. After several years of cruising from Southampton and making an annual round-the-world cruise, the *Victoria* moved to the Mediterranean when the new *Oriana* arrived in April 1995. Now, she has returned to Southampton.

The *Victoria* retains much of her fine Scandinavian design and Scottish workmanship in the layout of the public rooms, with wood paneling and decorative features all over the ship. She is nothing short of lovely inside and out, with maritime artwork touting P&O's long history mounted throughout the public spaces. Her original cabins are spacious and nearly all outside, while the newer cabins are more functional and include some inside rooms.

ITINERARIES The *Victoria* is based in Southampton for cruises to the Atlantic Isles and the Mediterranean. The majority of the cruises are for 14 nights and destination-oriented toward the western Mediterranean, with occasional voyages into the Black and Red seas and the eastern Mediterranean. For the winter months, the ship also cruises in the Caribbean from Barbados. The 15-night itineraries vary to include Caribbean ports, two partial transits of the Panama Canal, and one voyage up the Amazon as far as Manaus.

- Transatlantic positioning voyages link England with Barbados at the beginning and end of the winter season. Because of price and the price competition among cruise ships departing from U.S. ports, the Caribbean cruises attract mainly British passengers who like to cruise on a British ship.

Home Ports Southampton; Barbados.
Port Charges Included.

CABINS The ship has spacious cabins in the top categories. Only the highest categories have televisions, while all have radios and phones. The original cabins are much better designed and appointed than the ones added 20 years ago. For instance, they have small entrance foyers and small sitting areas. Many cabins, including some single ones, have bathtubs. The premier AA category cabins on A Deck are named after famous P&O liners, and each decorated with a print of the ship.

Specifications 370 cabins, 84 inside, 286 outside; 22 singles (inside and outside). Cabin size from 138–467 square feet. Beds are not movable. Cabins A17, A96, A97, B16, B17, B68, B117, and B118 are wheelchair accessible.

DINING The ship has one dining room with two sittings for three meals. The food is mostly straightforward, British-style fare, catering to middle-class British tastes. The best choices are the soups, roasts, the lunch time curry, cheese board, and desserts. Americans will find the portions smaller than on most ships, but the British often choose five to seven courses. The salads and vegetables are only fair, and pasta lovers will find very little variety.

The service, by Indians, is good. After all, Indians have served aboard British ships since the dawn of steam navigation. One large plus is that many officers, including those of junior rank, host tables at dinner.

SERVICE The stewards are British, European (many living in Britain), or Indians, and service is on the formal side and generally quite good. The British tend not to demand a lot of extra service; you may find the response to your requests met with a certain reserve. Nearly all passengers take early morning coffee or tea and that means being awakened at 7:00–7:30 A.M.

FACILITIES AND ENTERTAINMENT The ship has several good house bands for low-key dance music and good show lounge entertainment, plus the excellent classical pianists and the usual battery of cabaret acts. *Victoria* has a wonderful split-level night club, the Starlight Lounge. The casino has blackjack, roulette, slots, and a craps table.

ACTIVITIES AND DIVERSIONS Daytime entertainment is varied and runs from bingo to some of the best port lectures in the business. P&O prides itself on providing participatory activities by taking on excellent bridge, art, craft, and dance instructors. On the longer voyages, passengers' artwork is put on display and the craft classes produce many attractive gift items. The ship has proper theatres for showing full-length films, travel documentaries, and slides. Even for non-cricketers, the passengers-officers cricket match is the sporting event of the voyage.

SPORTS, FITNESS, AND BEAUTY The outdoor pool is the scene for games for adults and children. Deck quoits, using a traditional rope or newer rubber ring, is popular as are Ping-Pong and shuffleboard, all with organized competitions. The British are sun worshipers, so deck chairs go fast on the initial days of warm weather cruising.

The beauty salons are professionally operated by a concessionaire with a long P&O association. Exercise classes are popular, but the gym does not have the sophistication of newer ships. The British love to walk and you will see them in droves after breakfast. *Victoria*, designed for the North Atlantic, also has an indoor pool and sauna.

CHILDREN'S FACILITIES   The British know how to take care of children on ships, and excellent facilities, activities, and supervision by matrons are provided. The more children, the more fun it is at the planned activities in the playroom, the pool, the deck games, and Coke-tail parties, one of which the captain hosts. Children have an early sitting if the parents wish to eat dinner at the regular adult sittings. There's a special children's tea and programs for teenagers.

SHORE EXCURSIONS   The ship provides a wide variety of shore excursions, both standard and unusual; the latter to appeal to the many repeat passengers. Because of P&O's long cruising experience, excursions are very well organized. with the deputy captain on the dock at departure. Passengers become well versed in port attractions by highly informed port lecturers, not shopping promoters. Several of the lecturers have been with the company for many years and have wide knowledge and excellent slides to share. The local guides, of course, will vary. Excursions are fairly priced.

THEME CRUISES   With regular art, bridge, craft, and dance instructors, theme cruises are offered only occasionally. Bridge is probably the most popular although a noted astronomer or show personality may also be announced in the brochures.

POSTSCRIPT   P&O knows exactly who its market is, and the P&O regulars flock to these very British ships, ready to fall into their favorite routines rather than try something new, other than a new port, perhaps. The new passengers are usually first-time cruisers who have come by word of mouth or through a newspaper promotion, as no one living in Britain could fail to identify P&O. The *Victoria* gets a uniformly upscale passenger, one who also is more interested in destinations, hence the emphasis on Mediterranean ports.

Arcadia

	Quality Rating	Value Rating
Arcadia	❺	C

Registry: Liberia	Length: 805 feet	Beam: 105 feet
Cabins: 735	Draft: 27 feet	Speed: 19.5 knots
Maximum Passengers:	Passenger Decks: 12	Elevators: 9
1,652	Crew: 600	Space Ratio: 43

THE SHIP   After Princess Cruises merged with Sitmar Cruises in 1988, Sitmar's *Fair Majesty*, then under construction, was renamed *Star Princess* and launched as a Princess ship. In September 1997, she was scheduled to move to P&O Cruises, the cruise line of Princess Cruises' owner, and again, given a new name, *Arcadia*.

The lady has all the dazzle of any of the superliners built in the 1980s. Passengers are introduced to the spacious ship in the Garden Court, a three-story balconied atrium lobby with a kinetic stainless-steel mobile by California artist George Baker. The enormous computer-controlled sculpture is only part of the ship's million-dollar, museum-quality, contemporary art collection.

From the lower deck of the Garden Court, a wide spiral stairway with glistening, brass-trimmed glass balustrades floats up to other decks where there are bars, cafes, lounges, a casino, a glittering shopping arcade, and the new Century bar which replaced *Star Princess's* Serendipity. The ship now has the feel of a classic ocean liner. Light background music from a white grand piano on the first landing of the spiral stairs fills the air and sets the tone.

If the atrium lobby isn't dazzling enough, head for the top deck and the Windows on the World, a circular room, 80 feet in diameter, above the bridge. An observation and entertainment lounge, it has floor-to-ceiling windows with 270 degrees of views and makes an ideal roost from which to enjoy the scenery. In the evening the lounge becomes a nightclub with cabaret entertainment and dancing under the stars.

And that's only the bottom and top decks. On the decks in between, there is a cascading waterfall in the dining room, and on the Lido Deck there are two swimming pools, four Jacuzzis, and another waterfall!

ITINERARIES   The *Arcadia* makes her P&O debut on December 23, 1997, with a 12-night Christmas/New Year's cruise from Southampton to Iberia and the Mediterranean. On January 5, 1998, she sails eastward from England on a 92-day world cruise via Suez, Southeast Asia, Australia, New Zealand, South Pacific, the west coast of the United States, and Panama Canal. Many of P&O's British and Australian passengers sail on the world cruise part of the way and return home by air, so they have time to visit friends and relations in the "old country" or "down under." Americans are more likely to be aboard this cruise than any of the ship's other cruises. Following her return to Britain in the spring of 1998, she will begin her first season of European cruises from Southampton.

Home Port   Southampton and various other ports, depending on itinerary.

Port Charges   Included.

CABINS   *Arcadia* offers some of the largest standard cabins of any ship in its price range and two-thirds are outside ones. They are located on six of the 12 decks in 17 categories of 4 basic types: inside and outside doubles (with large picture windows); mini-suites with veranda; and suites with verandas.

All have direct-dial telephone, safe, refrigerator, walk-in closet and separate dressing area, key card for door, color television with CNN, and four-channel radio. They are fitted with twin beds that convert to queens.

Specifications   165 inside, 560 outside cabins (including 36 mini-suites and 14 suites with private balconies). Standard dimensions, 188 square feet. 598 cabins with 2 twins that convert to queens; 64 singles; 36 cabins with third and fourth berths; 10 wheelchair accessible.

DINING   The main dining room with a waterfall at its entrance, is a pretty room decorated in rich reds and wood. It is divided into a series of cozy nooks, with tables for two to ten, and offers two seatings for three meals.

Menus are similar to those on other P&O ships and are always available for review at bars and posted around the ship. In general, the selections for each course are ample, but the size of the serving portion will seem small to some Americans, since P&O's traditional British passengers tend to eat more courses, but less of each.

Other dining venues include a casual indoor/outdoor buffet restaurant for breakfast and lunch—the buffet has been extended and redesigned—and a pizzeria that serves made-to-order pizzas throughout the day; both are on Lido Deck, convenient to the swimming pools. The patisserie on a lower deck has specialty coffees along with fresh pastries; in the evening it becomes a bar with a band and dance floor.

FACILITIES AND ENTERTAINMENT A two-level main showroom on Promenade Deck is the venue for revues. At midship, the casino (somewhat reduced in size in the recent renovations to make space for the addition of a card room) has blackjack, craps, roulette, and slot machines. The Oval, a cricketing theme pub which has replaced the former Entre Nous lounge, is a small lounge offering live music and dancing. A lounge on Sun Deck is used for daytime activities and a late-night disco and cabaret.

You will find bridge and other games in the card and game rooms, and a quiet place to read in the recently refurbished library. One flight down is the shopping arcade that opens onto the third deck of the atrium. The theatre shows current and classic films and also functions as a conference center.

Of the two pools on Lido Deck, one has a swim-up bar, and the other has a waterfall and four satellite whirlpools. One flight up on Sun Deck, you will find an outdoor running track (a one-sixth-of-a-mile circuit), paddle tennis, deck cricket, and deck quoits. The fitness center, located on the lowest deck, has a gym with an array of exercise equipment and an aerobics area. It also has a beauty/barber shop and sauna and massage rooms.

CHILDREN'S FACILITIES The youth and teen activities centers are open daily and have a playroom, a small swimming pool, video games, jukebox, television, game tables, a nursery facility, and a new room for teenagers.

POSTSCRIPT *Arcadia* will not begin life with P&O until December 1997, after renovations have been made and certain P&O features have been added to make her more "British." It remains to be seen if she will enjoy as much popularity with her predominately British patrons as she did with Princess's fans. We bet she will.

Readers planning a cruise on *Arcadia* should review all the P&O Cruises section for a full picture of the cruise experience the line offers.

PREMIER CRUISE LINES

400 Challenger Road, Cape Canaveral, FL 32920
(407) 783-5061; (800) 327-7113; fax (407) 783-4925
http://www.bigredboat.com

TYPE OF SHIP   Renovated oceanliner.

TYPE OF CRUISES   Family-oriented short cruises to the Bahamas combined with visits to Walt Disney World.

CRUISE LINE'S STRENGTHS
- children's programs
- festive presence of Looney Tunes characters
- staff and service
- entertainment
- some large family cabins

CRUISE LINE'S SHORTCOMINGS
- noise level
- abundance of children
- cuisine

FELLOW PASSENGERS   The family market is Premier's specialty; not surprisingly, the typical passenger is a vacationing family in the 30–44 age group with children and a household income greater than $35,000.

On the other hand, there are so many definitions of family, that the passenger mix can be quite varied. There are traditional nuclear families with two children, as well as single parents, grandparents traveling with grandkids, and blended families with stepchildren.

During school holidays, the number of children on board is higher but is rarely more than 30 percent of all passengers. Often there's mom, dad, grandma, grandpa, and little Jennifer—four adults for one child. More surprisingly, many passengers have no children and more than 5 percent are on their honeymoon! There are also retired couples, groups, and even winners of incentive programs.

Passengers most often come from the Southeast, New York–Boston, and New York–Philadelphia corridors, Chicago area, and California. And there are also passengers from around the world—a likely result of Disney World's worldwide fame and attraction. About 30 percent of the passengers taking the cruise only are repeaters, while 15 percent combine the cruise and Orlando/Disney program.

Recommended For Families and couples, especially first-time cruisers who seek an informal, short cruise with all the amenities and activities of a large ship, and those who simply want to try a cruise.

Not Recommended For Sophisticated travelers seeking a sedate, adults-only atmosphere.

CRUISE AREAS AND SEASONS Bahamas and Key West, year-round.

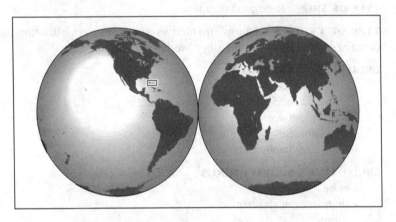

THE LINE Premier Cruise Lines, better known to many as the Big Red Boats, is a success story that happened almost overnight. The success was all the more surprising because no shortage of pundits told its founders that their brainchild wouldn't work, citing poor facilities in Port Canaveral, an insufficient local population to support year-round cruises, and the great distance from Port Canaveral to Nassau, among other reasons. But the founders recognized an enormous untapped reservoir of potential cruise passengers in visitors at Walt Disney World, the nation's biggest tourist attraction, and the Kennedy Space Center.

Premier Cruise Lines was formed in 1983 by Bruce Nierenberg, a brilliant maverick of cruise marketing who has left his imprint on several cruise lines, and Bjornar Hermansen, a financial and administrative whiz with whom he had worked at another cruise line. With the backing of the former Greyhound Corporation (now the Phoenix-based Dial

Corporation) they bought a ship to use on short excursions between Port Canaveral and the Bahamas. They created packages combining Premier's three- and four-night cruises with three nights of "free" deluxe accommodations in Orlando, three days' admission to the Disney theme parks, free tour of Spaceport U.S.A. at Kennedy Space Center, special airfares, plus the use of a rental car with unlimited mileage for a week. The packages were priced so reasonably, who could afford to stay home!

Eager to live up to the "star" billing it designated for itself with its *Star/Ship* name, Premier painted the ship's hull bright red with orange and yellow trim (outrageous! cried the traditionalists) and gave the interiors quality, comfortable decor along with cabins for families, some for up to five persons, and amenities such as bath items usually found in deluxe hotels.

Next, they created something for everyone to ensure the cruises had universal appeal: a full-time youth program for the under-17 set, SeaSports for fitness folks, and topnotch entertainment, a casino, theatre with first-run movies, piano bar, and disco for night owls. They even put champagne and double beds in some cabins for honeymooners. And plenty of good food for everyone.

In 1986, Premier doubled its capacity by adding the *Star/Ship Oceanic*, a popular ship that had belonged to now-defunct Home Lines. Later, Premier replaced one of its ships with the larger *Star/Ship Atlantic*. At the same time, it got the coveted position as the Official Cruise Line of Walt Disney World from the Disney organization, which allowed Premier to have Disney characters and special Disney touches on board and generated enormous publicity.

In 1993, the Premier terminated the Disney agreement and went with Looney Tunes under a licensing agreement with Warner Brothers Consumer Products. The Looney Tunes bunch—Bugs Bunny, Sylvester, Tweety, and friends—take a more prominent on-board role than did the Disney characters. Premier also gave the *Oceanic* a $17 million facelift and also revamped some of the on-board activities to make them learning as well as fun experiences and to provide an environment for family interaction. Five separate, supervised programs are tailored for age groups from tots to teens.

In March 1997, Cruise Holdings, Ltd., a privately held investment group and the parent company of Seawind Cruise Line and Dolphin Cruise Line, bought Premier Cruise Lines as part of its strategy to acquire older, midsize traditional ships. Premier, like its sister cruise lines, will continue to operate under its own name. The *Star/Ship Atlantic* was sold in 1997.

The Fleet	Built/Renovated	Tonnage	Passengers
Star/Ship Oceanic	1965/1993	40,000	1,132/1,500

STYLE   Families with children set the rhythm of the Big Red Boat. Although excellent supervised programs keep junior sailors occupied for good portions of the day, there always seem to be plenty of kids in the ship's show lounges, hallways, and other public areas. Knowing they have only three or four days to take advantage of all the activities and facilities the ship offers, passengers try to cram in as much as possible, including a Bahamas shore excursion or two.

The atmosphere is friendly and fun-filled, and well after a family's normal bedtime, the energy level remains high, with show lounges still buzzing and cruisers of all ages piling their plates at the midnight buffet. The cheerful, energetic cruise staff goes all out to make passengers happy and they obviously have a good time themselves.

DISTINCTIVE FEATURES   With their celebrity aura, the larger-than-life Looney Tunes characters tend to dominate Big Red Boat memories of kids and adults alike. Bugs, Daffy Duck, Yosemite Sam, Road Runner, and the crew make frequent appearances, posing for pictures, signing autographs, and popping up in the dining room. Televisions in the cabins show their cartoons, and the gift shop brims with Looney Tunes stuffed animals and other souvenirs.

Looney Tunes tuck-in, an optional bedtime service provided by a selected character, is an extra touch. The deluxe tuck-in package ($40 one child, $75 for two) includes a character-printed pillowcase, plush Looney Tunes toy, and a photo of the event.

RATES

Highest Per Diem	Lowest Per Diem	Average Per Diem
$236	$112	$180

The above per diems are calculated from the cruise line's nondiscounted *cruise-only* fares on standard accommodations. What you will actually pay *should* be *substantially* less (see Part One, How to Get the Best Deal on a Cruise). Per diems vary by season, by cabin location, and by cruise areas.

Special Fares and Discounts   Under the early booking discount program, those who book three months ahead in cabin categories 3–8 can save up to $400 for a family of five—$125 each for the first two passengers, $50 each additional passenger.

The family reunion package for a minimum group of ten people in three staterooms (with six full-fare passengers) gives the first two passengers in each room a 10 percent discount off the one-week cruise/ Orlando package. Premier's senior plan offers a passenger 60 and older and one companion a 10–15 percent discount in cabin categories 3–8.

Passengers making their own air arrangements deduct $200 off the air-inclusive rate for each passenger. Passengers driving their own car on the seven-night package save $250 each for the first two passengers and $200 each for the third, fourth, and fifth passenger.

- Children's Fare: None. Kids Vacation Free is a promotion that allows two children, ages 2–17, to sail free when accompanied by two full-fare adults. The package also includes a free hotel stay and admission into the Orlando theme parks.
- Single Parents: In cabin categories 3–8, single parents pay 125 percent of the full fare and kids 2–11 cruise at low third, fourth, and fifth person rates.
- Single Supplement: 200 percent (for sole occupancy of a cabin).

Packages
- Air/Sea: Yes.
- Others: Honeymoon.
- Pre/Post: Various packages combine cruise with Walt Disney World Resort with airfare, admission to Magic Kingdom Park, EPCOT Center, and Disney-MGM Studios Theme Park; River Country and Pleasure Island; guided tour of Kennedy Space Center's Spaceport USA, Astronaut Hall of Fame, or admission to Splendid China theme park; rental car with unlimited mileage; discounts at Disney Village hotels and Marketplace; choice of Disney Character Breakfast or dinner at King Henry's Feast or Arabian Nights.

Premier has five separate land packages which can be combined with cruises: Central Florida, Disney, Orlando Theme Park, Universal Theme Park, and Beach Bonus. All include hotel accommodations, theme park admissions, rental car, round-trip air transportation, and admission to Kennedy Space Center's Spaceport USA or Wet 'n Wild. A new option is bus transportation for those who do not care to drive. Introduced in 1997 is a package with up to five consecutive days of unlimited admission to Universal Studios, Sea World of Florida, and Wet 'n Wild, with a choice of six different hotels.

Past Passengers   The Captain's Club keeps in mail contact with past passengers and offers them special on-board amenities, but it does not publish a newsletter.

THE LAST WORD   A Big Red Boat cruise, combined with a visit to Walt Disney World, may very well be the perfect family vacation package. The shipboard children's programs keep the kids entertained while giving mom and dad a chance to relax and/or take part in adult activities. The schedule also lets parents spend some quality time with their children on both land and sea. On the other hand, plenty of people who do not have children take these cruises and seem to enjoy them thoroughly.

The Big Red Boat lacks the elegant touches of a deluxe ship and the flashy architectural flourishes of a brand new superliner, but it's a comfortable, first-class operation that provides a great introduction to the world of cruising. The ship is showing its age and the food is no better than average, but as one recent passenger said, "My kids were having such a great time, it hardly mattered."

PREMIER SHIP STANDARD FEATURES

Officers Greek.

Staff Dining, Cabin/International; Cruise/American and British.

Dining Facilities Two seatings in main dining room with different theme every night; adults-only options; outdoor buffet for breakfast and lunch. Children's menu; make-your-own sundae parties; pizza, and insomnia service for night owls.

Special Diets Low-fat, low-cholesterol entrees always available; kosher, low salt, vegetarian available upon request.

Room Service 24-hour menu with limited selection for in-cabin meals.

Dress Code Casual; no shorts in dining room at dinnertime.

Cabin Amenities Radio; television; direct-dial phone; connecting and five-berth family cabins. Welcome-aboard basket; Chocolate Ship cookies.

Electrical Outlets 110 AC.

Wheelchair Access Limited; ramp access, cabins with wheelchair access and wide bathroom doors, bathtubs with grab bar.

Recreation and Entertainment Main showroom with lavish revues; piano bar; lounge with dancing; disco; casino.

Sports and Other Activities Two outdoor pools with retractable glass dome; shuffleboard; skeet shooting; Ping-Pong; snorkeling program.

Beauty and Fitness SeaSport fitness program offers aerobics and fitness equipment; beauty salon; massage.

Other Facilities Conference rooms; laundry; medical facilities.

Children's Facilities Year-round youth counselors and age-specific programs for five levels. See text. Looney Tunes tuck-in; children's pool.

Theme Cruises Yes.

Smoking No smoking in dining room at early seating; late seating has smoking/nonsmoking sections, as do all lounges.

Premier Suggested Tipping Per person per cruise, steward and waiter, $10 (3-day), $12 (4-day); busboy, $5 (3-day), $6 (4-day); maître d'hôtel, $2 (3-day), $3 (4-day). Plan extra money for hotel tax, rental car tax and insurance, meals, and parking for land portion of vacation.

Credit Cards For cruise payment, cruise/package and on board, American Express, Mastercard, Discover, Visa.

Star/Ship Oceanic

	Quality Rating	Value Rating
Star/Ship Oceanic	4	B

Registry: Bahamas	Length: 782 feet	Beam: 96 feet
Cabins: 590	Draft: 28 feet	Speed: 26 knots
Maximum Passengers:	Passenger Decks: 8	Elevators: 5
1,609	Crew: 565	Space Ratio: 25

THE SHIP   Popular with passengers of Home Lines during the 1960s and 1970s, the *Star/Ship Oceanic* has the sleek lines of a classic ocean-liner and sports a structural solidity absent from many of today's glitzy, plastic-looking ships. Reminders of the past include traditional round portholes (which have given way to rectangular windows on contemporary ships), mosaic works of art in the stairwells, and teak decks. Doors to the public rest rooms are so heavy that young children need help opening them.

Despite her age, the *Oceanic* looks good, having undergone a $17 million facelift in 1994 that included major renovations in cabins and public rooms. The decor, colorful but not garish, is accented by plenty of mirrors and twinkly lights. The Lounge Deck, the setting for most of the entertainment, often swarms with people en route to a show, the gift shop, tour desk, or casino. Unfortunately, passengers must pass through the noisy, crowded Lucky Star Casino amidships on their way to other public areas. Passengers looking for semiprivacy usually can find a quiet nook in one of the bars and lounges. Public rooms are comfortable, well appointed, and, on most occasions, large enough to handle the crowds. But evening shows in the Broadway Showroom do fill up fast on a full cruise.

The ship, which catered to older, more demanding passengers in its earlier life, clearly has been refitted to accommodate younger travelers concerned more with fun and frivolity than dressy affairs and white-glove service. The fact that Daffy Duck and Pepé Le Pew show up to pose with passengers at the captain's cocktail reception is evidence that Premier doesn't pretend to be highbrow.

The four-night Big Red Boat cruise includes a day at sea, giving passengers a chance to get acquainted with the ship itself. The more hectic three-night itinerary spends a great percentage of time in port.

ITINERARIES   Three- and four-night cruises from Port Canaveral to the Bahamas. All sailings devote a full day each in Port Lucaya on Grand Bahama Island and Nassau. The 2 A.M. departure from Nassau allows time to sample Bahamian nightlife. The four-night trip adds a day at sea.

Home Port   Port Canaveral.

Port Charges $84.50 per person, including federal departure tax, and $42.25 under age 2.

CABINS   Premier boasts the largest cabins of any cruise line sailing on the three- and four-day Bahamas cruises. Because it targets families, the Big Red Boat has an unusual number of cabins that can accommodate four or five passengers. A cabin sleeping five has a double bed, convertible bed, and two upper berths.

Built during an era when cabin space was more generous, the *Oceanic* provides a number of unusually roomy upper-grade cabins. Spacious apartment suites (for up to four people) on the exclusive top deck offer balconies and king-size beds.

All cabins on the *Oceanic* have a television with nine channels, including the Disney Channel and current movies.

Specifications   329 inside cabins, 261 outside; 65 suites, 8 with verandas. Premier has no standard cabin dimensions; they range from 140 square feet at low end to 455 square feet for the largest suite. 337 cabins with two lower beds (59 accommodate third person, 99 take third and fourth); 1 cabin with just double bed; 2 cabins with queen bed accommodate third person; 101 cabins with double take third; 68 cabins with double accommodate third and fourth; 73 cabins with double take third, fourth, and fifth; 8 suites with king accommodate third and fourth persons.

DINING   Except in terms of quantity and show, food is not one of Premier's strong points. It compares, more or less, to a shoreside family restaurant but served with typical cruise ship flair. Menus brim with familiar foods like turkey, chicken, prime rib, and burgers. Though the caliber of cuisine does not rival that of better restaurants, menu choices often leave a gourmet impression.

French Night, for example, offers escargots, lobster bisque, roast duckling in orange sauce, and chateaubriand. Caribbean Night brings out exotic fare like Jamaican jerk pork in tamarind sauce with black beans and plantains, lobster tail served with lime butter, and chilled cream of coconut soup with a dash of Barbados rum. America the

Beautiful and Italian theme nights also lend festive notes to the *Oceanic's* Seven Continents Restaurant.

Kids can order from the main menu or select from the separate children's menu, which lists favorites like peanut butter and jelly, grilled cheese, pizza, hot dogs, and spaghetti. Mighty Healthy Platters include Blackbeard's Broiled Chicken Drumsticks and Mom's Fresh Fruits and Vegetables with cheese sticks, fruit yogurt, and an oat bran muffin. Waiters are especially attentive to the little ones.

Because of all the children aboard a Premier cruise, the dining room is noisy. Late-seating dinner at 8:15 P.M. is quieter than first seating at 6 P.M. Once every cruise, the ship schedules a kids-only dinner with entertainment in the Riviera Pool area, leaving parents free to dine in peace for one night.

Pool Deck buffets at breakfast and lunch provide a casual alternative to the main dining room. Coffee, lemonade, and juice machines are available all day in these self-service areas. You can make your own sundae every afternoon in the Big Dipper Ice Cream Parlor, and should you need to quiet hunger pains at other times, there's afternoon tea with banana bread, brownies, and finger sandwiches; cocktail hour and late-night snacks in certain lounges; and the dining room's lavish midnight buffet.

The Looney Tunes character breakfast, an extra-cost option offered once during each cruise, gives families a chance to mingle with cartoon favorites in a private dining area. The package includes a full breakfast, character placemat, poster, and photo.

SERVICE   The staff is warm, friendly, professional, and geared to helping families enjoy their first vacation at sea. From the American and British youth counselors to the European, Asian, and Caribbean waiters, the Big Red Boat is a smooth-running operation blessed with top-notch personnel.

FACILITIES AND ENTERTAINMENT   The ship has a main show lounge presenting musical revues, comedy, and magic suitable for the whole family. Most electrifying is *Las Vegas Legends in Concert,* a blockbuster tribute to Elvis Presley, Bette Midler, Madonna, Buddy Holly, and other singers whose costumes, mannerisms, and voices are mimicked to perfection. The *Oceanic's* main show lounge is the Broadway Showroom, where sight lines in many sections are interrupted by posts and people's heads.

The ship also has a cabaret with late-night entertainment and disco dancing. Cabaret shows with audience participation include the 1950s and 1960s Big Chill Oldies Hour and a country western party.

The Carlos 'n' Charlie's party, starting at midnight, invites guests to dance the Tequila Conga and Sangria Shooter Limbo.

Performers also appear in such intimate settings as the *Oceanic's* Tropicana Piano Bar, Heroes and Legends Pub, and Lucky Star Lounge. For fun and games, the ship offers a Star Fighter Arcade video room and the Lucky Star Casino with blackjack, roulette, and slot machines. (Children under 18 are not allowed to gamble in the casino.) Next to the casino are the Milky Way Shops, stocked with beachwear, sundries, Looney Tunes souvenirs, and duty-free luxury goods.

The *Oceanic's* two-level Hollywood Theater features first-run movies and the Big Red Boat's innovative Voyages of Discovery. These live educational presentations employ music, films, special effects, and audience participation to shed light on underwater life, astronomy, Caribbean history, and the great ships of the world.

ACTIVITIES AND DIVERSIONS   Although the ship is known for its ambitious children's program, the daily printed agenda is filled with activities of interest to adults. Choices might include a wine-tasting seminar, trivia quiz, art auction, nutrition lecture, poker lessons, bingo, horse racing, trapshooting, a Family Feud tune-guessing game, or the Newlywed Game. Singles, including single parents, are invited to a party just for them.

Passengers can take center stage during karaoke sessions and at the passenger talent show. Those with cameras and camcorders flock to scheduled photo opportunities with the Looney Tunes characters.

SPORTS, FITNESS, AND BEAUTY   On the Sun Deck, a sliding glass roof shelters the pool area on overcast days and at night. (On some days, the enclosure can be too hot and stuffy for comfort.) The transparent dome covers the *Oceanic's* twin Riviera pools. The ship offers an outdoor whirlpool, a supervised children's pool, and a jogging track overlooking the Pool Deck.

The SeaSport fitness program offers aerobics classes, water aerobics, and a gym with state-of-the-art exercise equipment from Nautilus, Universal, and Lifecycle—all can be used without charge. Steiner Beauty and Fitness Salon offers hair styling, facials, massages, and slimming and toning treatments—all services are extra and pricey.

In conjunction with Premier's popular Splashdown scuba diving outings in the Bahamas, passengers can sign up for on-board scuba classes with professionally trained instructors. Included are a video presentation, introduction to scuba gear, discussion of safety procedures, and pool sessions.

CHILDREN'S FACILITIES   The Big Red Boat goes all out to keep junior cruisers busy from morning to bedtime. With games, crafts, scavenger hunts, karaoke sessions, and Beach Olympics in the pool, there's never a dull moment. Upon embarkation, children in each age group receive a detailed printed agenda of what lies ahead for the next three or four days. The full-time youth staff of about 15 counselors is augmented by five interns during the summer months. All full-time counselors have degrees in education, nursing, or related fields; a few are certified British nannies.

The young sailors spend much of their time in Pluto's Playhouse, a supervised recreational center set up for organized activities and free play time; a kids-only pool is just outside the door. Children from 2–4 years old are enrolled in the First Mates program, which often meets in the Astra Room, a play area two decks below Pluto's. Those from 5–7 are in Kids Call, where activities include stories, sing-alongs, treasure hunts, cartoons, and magic shows. Parents must sign their children in and out of the center.

Activities for the three older groups take place in various lounges and the Space Station Teen Center, where one wall is lined with video games—Nintendo, Super Nintendo, Sega, and more. Starcruisers (ages 8–10) and Navigators (11–13) participate in Ping-Pong tournaments, pool games, autograph hunts, and games like Pictionary and Outburst. Teen Cruisers (14–17) enjoy dances, karaoke, a Midnight Madness party, and the Dating Game. A party featuring a juggler, magician, and Looney Tunes characters is arranged for all but the teen group.

For parents who want to dance the night away without worrying about the kids, child care for ages 2–12 is available for an additional cost after supervised activities end. Between 11 P.M. and 9 A.M. the cost is $3 per hour for one child and $5 per hour for two or more children in the same family. Thus, on the Premier ship, you can get 24-hour child care.

SHORE EXCURSIONS   Premier's cruise brochure describes the shore excursions and the prices. It is one of the few cruise lines that enable passengers to purchase excursions through their travel agents in advance of their cruise.

A favorite from Port Lucaya is the two-hour Dolphin Experience excursion. After a 20-minute boat ride to the world's largest dolphin observation and training facility at Sanctuary Bay, participants can step into the 30-inch-deep wading platform and interact with the Atlantic bottle-nosed dolphins while a guide/researcher answers questions. The $45 fee includes a souvenir T-shirt. These sessions sell fast, so book early.

Note: You should understand that this excursion is handled in large groups; you will have to wait your turn to go into the wading platform and your stay with the dolphins is very brief. Also, contrary to the impression left by some articles and promotional literature, participants do not swim with the dolphins; at best, they get to pat and stroke them a few times.

During the call in Nassau, a similar Dolphin Encounter ($50) is available on sandswept Salt Cay, an uninhabited tropical island where the Big Red Boat provides a buffet lunch and a full day (up to five hours) for water sports, beachcombing, and snoozing in the many hammocks strung between the coconut palms. Youth counselors organize games on Salt Cay. Per cabin, the crowd-pleasing Salt Cay Beach Experience costs $20 for the first passenger, $10 each additional passenger, age 13 and up; under age 13, free. The Splashdown snorkeling program on Salt Cay is a pricey $39 for adults, $31 for kids, ages 8–15.

Another Nassau option, Atlantic Submarine, showcases marine life at depths of 100 feet. Cost is $69 for adults, $40 for children ages 4–16. Glass-bottom boat tours ($21 to $26, adults, $14 for children) are available in both Nassau and Port Lucaya. A two-hour stargazing moonlight cruise in Nassau Harbor ($30 per person) ties in with the on-board Voyages of Discovery enrichment program.

POSTSCRIPT   If ever there were an example of how people's experience on a cruise differs, this is one. On a recent cruise, a couple who did not have children commented, "I went with just my husband and we enjoyed it. We never saw the kids on board; they're well taken care of." But another couple who spent a lot of time with their two children and other kids, commented that the noise level was high and there "sure were a lot of kids." And while one group found the cuisine ordinary, another called it great. Yet another said, "Food and dining were better than I expected, and the childrens' program never seemed to override or interfere with the adults' enjoyment."

PRINCESS CRUISES

10100 Santa Monica Boulevard, Los Angeles, CA 90067
(310) 553-1770; (800) PRINCESS (774-6237); fax (310) 277-6175
http://www.princesscruises.com

TYPE OF SHIPS   Large and midsize traditional ships, superliners, and new megaliners.

TYPE OF CRUISES   Modern, mainstream, worldwide, moderately upscale.

CRUISE LINE'S STRENGTHS
- worldwide itineraries
- extensive shore excursions
- Caribbean "private" island
- "The Love Boat" name recognition
- spacious cabins (large number with verandas on most ships)
- 24-hour restaurant on some ships

CRUISE LINE'S SHORTCOMINGS
- dissimilar ships
- uneven cuisine
- weak production shows on some ships

FELLOW PASSENGERS   With its diverse fleet and wide variety of itineraries and duration of cruises, Princess passengers are difficult to characterize since their age and income vary with the ships, seasons, and destinations. Essentially passengers are 45 years and older with annual incomes of $40,000 and over.

They tend to be experienced travelers who cruise frequently and are looking for Princess's mainstream type of vacation, but they can range widely from a California school teacher on vacation or a midwestern computer-system analyst on their first cruise to an affluent retired couple on their twentieth cruise.

On one-week cruises in the Caribbean, the average age drops to about 35, but on longer cruises and those in Princess's "exotic" destinations group, the average age rises to 55 years or higher. The largest numbers come from Florida and California, followed by Texas, Illinois, and New York. The line also attracts British travelers (the owners are British and half of the ships have British officers).

Recommended For   Modestly affluent first-timers, frequent cruisers who want easy-paced travel, are not demanding, prefer an even balance between sea and land time, and who understand that *The Love Boat* was only a television show.

Not Recommended For   Swingers or first-time cruisers in search of "The Love Boat;" sophisticated or demanding travelers.

CRUISE AREAS AND SEASONS   7–64 days, Caribbean, Panama Canal, Mexico, Amazon, Orient, Australia/South Pacific, Hawaii/ Tahiti, Southeast Asia, Africa, winter; Alaska, Europe, Mediterranean, Baltic, Canada/New England, summer.

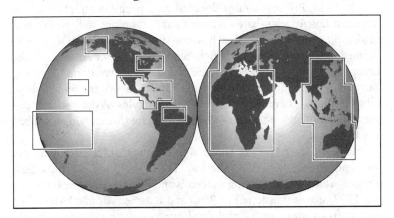

THE LINE   From its inception three decades ago as a West Coast pioneer, Princess Cruises has helped to create the relaxed and casual atmosphere that typifies life on board today's cruises. The line continues to utilize and benefit from its involvement in *The Love Boat* television series, which has had an incalculable impact on modern cruising, popularizing the idea for an entire generation of television viewers—those who make up the bulk of cruise passengers today. By helping to dispel the elitist image of cruising in the past, the show allowed people who might never have considered a cruise holiday to identify with it.

Princess Cruises is a division of P&O (Peninsular and Orient Steam Navigation Company), a British firm and one of the world's oldest and largest steamship companies that marks August 1844 as its entry into the cruise business, when it offered a six-week voyage from Southampton to Constantinople.

In 1974, P&O bought Princess Cruises, which had been a separate American company, acquired the *Island Princess* (formerly *Island Venture*), which had been chartered, and added the first *Sun Princess*. The following year, P&O bought *Island Princess's* sister, *Sea Venture*, and renamed her *Pacific Princess*, better known to one and all as "The Love Boat" (she was the set for the television series). In the early 1980s Princess became a trendsetter for modern mainstream cruising when it launched the *Royal Princess*. Still the flagship and pride of the Princess fleet, she was hailed as the most stylish, elegant ship of the day, setting new standards in passenger comfort and amenities and introducing many cruise ship "firsts." Today, P&O supplies the ships and officers and provides maintenance while Princess handles all other aspects of its operation.

In 1988, Princess almost doubled its capacity overnight when it acquired Los Angeles–based Sitmar Cruises, another well-established cruise pioneer—a move that has not been as wonderful as it first seemed. In essence, Princess bought out its competition. Instead of creating two separate brands as some cruise lines have done following buyouts, Princess immediately changed the names of the Sitmar ships and integrated them into its fleet. Yet, the styles of the two companies—one British, one Italian—were so different that merging them has not been easy.

In the merger Princess acquired three Sitmar ships already in service and three new ones on the way. The first of the new ships, *Star Princess*, came with cascading waterfalls and other dazzling features. (In fall 1997, it was transferred to P&O and renamed *Arcadia*.) The other two ships—*Crown Princess* and *Regal Princess*—with radically different profiles and interiors—were a major break with tradition. No one has rushed to copy them.

Princess's latest ventures—$2.2 billion worth of megaships—are the most dazzling yet. *Sun Princess*, dubbed the "Super Love Boat," was the first of the "Grand Class" series and the line's largest vessel when it came on line in December 1995. She was followed by her twin, *Dawn Princess*, in spring 1997. The duo have the same architect, Njal Eide, as the *Royal Princess*, and like her, have significant new features—cruising's first 24-hour restaurant, two atrium lobbies, two show lounges, and more. Two more sisters, *Sea Princess* and *Ocean Princess*, will debut in 1998 and 1999.

In early 1998, Princess will unveil the 109,000 ton, $400 million *Grand Princess*, the first of its fleet too large to transit the Panama Canal. This expansion will represent a tripling of the line's capacity and the potential to more than double her current half-million passengers annually by the year 2000.

Already a major player in Alaska with six ships and in the Panama Canal with seven ships, Princess has increased its presence in the Caribbean, added new itineraries throughout Asia and the Pacific, and expanded in Europe with an extensive roster of cruises. Indeed, the 1998 season will be the longest in the company's history, beginning on March 23, and concluding on January 3, 1999, after a Christmas cruise in the Holy Land.

Among Princess's newest itineraries are a 23-day West Africa cruise between Cape Town and Rome, visiting eight countries, and an 11-day cruise between Kenya and South Africa, both combined with a 3–7-day safari. In all, Princess calls at over 200 ports on six continents.

Princess's Alaska role was enhanced with the opening in 1997 of the $20 million Mt. McKinley Princess Lodge, featured in many of Princess's Alaska cruise tours. Situated on 146 acres of land owned by Princess inside of Denali State Park, the lodge has a spectacular view of 20,320-foot Mt. McKinley and the Alaska Range.

Throughout the world Princess has one of the best and most extensive selections of shore excursions of any cruise line, and she leads the pack when it comes to aggressive pricing with seasonal savings, deeply discounted advance-purchase fares, and two-for-one promotions.

The Fleet	Built/Renovated	Tonnage	Passengers
Crown Princess	1990/1997	70,000	1,590
Dawn Princess	1997	77,000	1,950
Grand Princess	1998	109,000	2,600
Island Princess	1971/85/92	20,000	640
Ocean Princess	1999	77,000	1,950
Pacific Princess	1972/85/93	20,000	640
Regal Princess	1991/1997	70,000	1,590
Royal Princess	1984/1994	45,000	1,200
Sea Princess	1999	77,000	1,950
Sky Princess	1984/1992	46,000	1,200
Sun Princess	1995	77,000	1,950

STYLE California modern in the mainstream, never on the edge, sedate but not staid, a Princess cruise is the very essence of today's typical, mass-market cruises—warm, inviting, and comfortable, suitable for a broad spectrum of people from all walks of life sailing primarily on seven-day to three-week itineraries.

The fleet has British officers, with their long steamship tradition; Italian officers, with their natural charm; and dining and hotel staffs that are a mini–United Nations at sea. Often trendsetters in passenger facilities and amenities, the ships have the look, atmosphere, and reassurance of a well-bred, middle- to upper-middle-class environment—nothing flashy or exaggerated—where almost anyone could feel at home. Compared to some of today's glitzy ships that assault the senses, a Princess ship is a welcome relief.

In the past year or so, Princess has worked hard to improve its food and entertainment, and it shows. Redesigned breakfast, lunch, and dinner menus have been introduced fleetwide and the new menus feature fresh, contemporary selections—the elements which had been missing. Shipboard activities are varied and many. The line has developed many programs and themes to appeal to special interests such as classical music, big bands, wine, gourmet cooking, photography, and more. There's a great deal of opportunity for fitness folks to keep up their exercise regimes or for others to be pampered. All ships in the fleet have gyms, saunas, and offers massages along with fitness and sports programs on board and in port.

New Waves, Princess's scuba diving program introduced in 1991, is particularly noteworthy and recently was enhanced by the lines' association with PADI (Professional Association of Diving Instructors), offering an on-board program for snorkel and scuba certification. Princess remains the only major, mainstream cruise line to offer passengers the opportunity to become fully-certified divers on a cruise.

Princess cruises are big on passenger participation with karaoke, game shows, and a full roster of diversions and distractions. Much of the entertainment is also designed to get passengers involved. The best example is "Love Boat Legends," a lighthearted, new twist on passenger talent shows. It features passengers selected from first-day tryouts, who, after attending rehearsals along with the regular cast of the show, emerge as one of seven Love Boat Legends.

DISTINCTIVE FEATURES 24-hour restaurants; scuba certification program; bathroom amenities package with terry cloth robes in every cabin; fresh fruit daily in cabins; fresh flowers in all suites. CNN, ESPN,

Discovery and Learning Channels fleetwide. Shore excursions literature; environmentally friendly products; self-service laundromats; seven ships with pizzerias; a high percentage of cabins with verandas and refrigerators. Valentine's Day–Love Boat promotion.

RATES

Highest Per Diem	Lowest Per Diem	Average Per Diem
$456	$150	$274

The above per diems are calculated from the cruise line's nondiscounted *cruise-only* fares on standard accommodations. What you will actually pay *should* be *substantially* less (see Part One, How to Get the Best Deal on a Cruise). Per diems vary by season, by cabin location, and by cruise areas.

Special Fares and Discounts Love Boat Savers are advance-purchase discounts providing 10–25 percent or more (or 50 percent for second person) reduction of brochure prices. Frequent promotional two-for-one fares; savings and upgrades on combination of two consecutive cruises.

- Third/Fourth Berth: 50 percent of fare.
- Children's Fare: Same as Third/Fourth Berth.
- Single Supplement: 150–200 percent, Love Boat Savers discounts of up to 25 percent apply.

Packages
- Air/Sea: Yes.
- Others: Yes.
- Pre/Post: Yes.

Past Passengers Princess does a great deal to maintain the loyalty of past passengers. Members of the Captain's Circle, Princess's past passenger club, are invited to a members-only cocktail party hosted by the captain and to participate in a club photo contest with cruise prizes, among other activities. They receive a membership card with their personal club number, which their travel agents use when booking their cruises, as well as on any correspondence with Princess, to ensure they receive club benefits. Upon booking a second cruise, a member receives a Captain's Circle logbook and pin. Other recognition pins range from

First Officer's pin for third and fourth cruises to a Commodore pin for ten cruises or more. Quality gifts, such as Tiffany crystal, are presented at on-board parties to passengers who have sailed the most days with Princess. Four times a year members get a newsletter with information on new itineraries, new ship plans, Princess staff profiles, chef's recipes, and special cruise offers and discounts. They are also sent coupon savings for specific sailings as well as members-only discount sailings.

THE LAST WORD For millions of Americans, the popular image of cruising is a Princess cruise—perhaps not as luxurious or glamorous as the television image, but apparently close enough to attract over half a million passengers a year. At the same time, Princess is something of a mixed bag. In its fleet there are three sets of twins; while the others are different in size, layout, and caliber. With the new megaliners, additional levels have been added to the Princess family. Some see this diversity as a good thing, with each ship being a new Princess for prospective passengers to meet. Others find the dissimilarity bewildering.

Yet others say the fleet's variety is unimportant; you are buying a cruise not a ship. Princess's strength is in its itineraries and its exceptionally well executed shore excursions, and you should select a Princess cruise on that basis. True. However, in the case of Princess, some of the ships, such as the *Royal Princess* and the *Crown Princess*, are so different it's hard to think of them as belonging to the same cruise line.

So, here's what we can tell you: Despite the dissimilar fleet, very little changes with Princess from ship to ship. The product is fairly consistent with few surprises. Your ship will be comfortable, your cruise enjoyable, and you can get a lot for your money if you have realistic expectations, are not demanding, and plan ahead to take advantage of the line's heavily discounted fares.

PRINCESS CRUISES STANDARD FEATURES

Officers *Crown Princess*, *Regal Princess*, *Sun Princess*/Italian; *Dawn Princess*, *Island Princess*, *Pacific Princess*, *Royal Princess*, *Sky Princess*/British.

Staffs Dining/Italian, European; cabin/British, Italian, Filipino; cruise/ American, British, Filipino.

Dining Facilities One main dining room, two seatings for three meals (*Sky*, *Dawn,* and *Sun* with two dining rooms); informal buffet breakfast and lunch on Lido Deck; pizzeria; patisserie. *Sun*, *Dawn*, *Crown*, *Royal* have 24-hour dining.

Special Diets Diabetic, low calorie/cholesterol/salt, vegetarian.

Room Service 24-hour room service with light menu.

Dress Code Casual during day; evenings vary, usually there are two casual, three informal, and two formal in week's cruise.

Cabin Amenities Television with CNN, ESPN, Discovery/Learning channels and movies; fresh fruit daily in cabins; terry robes; direct-dial phone; mini-fridges on *Royal*, *Crown*, *Regal*, *Dawn*, *Sun*; in suites and deluxe cabins on *Island*, *Pacific*, *Sky*. Hair dryers on *Sun* and *Dawn*.

Electrical Outlets 220/110 AC.

Wheelchair Access 19 cabins on *Dawn*, *Sun*; 10 on *Crown*, *Regal*, *Royal*; 6 on *Sky*; 4 on *Island*, *Pacific*.

Recreation and Entertainment Las Vegas– and Broadway-style revues; music and dancing; casino; disco; wine and caviar bar; karaoke, theatre (except *Island/Pacific*); dance classes; bingo; bridge.

Sports and Other Activities Two or three outdoor pools on all ships; paddle tennis (except *Island/Pacific*); jogging; scuba program; golf practice.

Beauty and Fitness Saunas; beauty/barber salon, spa, fitness program.

Other Facilities Library, hospital, boutiques; self-service laundry (except *Island/Pacific*); meeting facilities; religious services.

Children's Facilities Love Boat Kids is Princess's youth program on all ships, but primarily those with special facilities and full-time youth coodi-nators: *Sun*, *Dawn*, *Sky*, *Crown* and *Regal*. See text.

Theme Cruises Love Boat National Holiday, Valentine's-themed cruises (February).

Smoking No smoking in dining rooms and main showrooms; other pub-lic rooms have designated areas.

Princess Suggested Tipping Per person, per day: cabin steward and waiter, $3 each; busboy, $1.75; 15 percent of bar bill.

Credit Cards For cruise payment and on-board charges, American Express/Optima, Carte Blanche, Diners Club, Mastercard, Visa.

Royal Princess

	Quality Rating	**Value Rating**
Royal Princess	8	B

Registry: Great Britain	Length: 757 feet	Beam: 106 feet
Cabins: 600	Draft: 26 feet	Speed: 20 knots
Maximum Passengers: 1,200	Passenger Decks: 9	Elevators: 6
	Crew: 520	Space Ratio: 38

THE SHIP The ship was so beautiful, people couldn't stop talking about her—or her godmother, the Princess of Wales, who christened her. In their own way, both were destined to make an indelible mark on the 1980s.

Launched in 1984, at a cost of $200 million, the *Royal Princess* was, at the time, the most expensive passenger ship that had ever been constructed. From the outside her sleek lines and long tapered bow looked traditional, but inside, this celebrated beauty had so many innovations she was called revolutionary and set new standards in passenger comfort for the generation of cruise ships that followed.

Among them, the *Royal Princess* was the first large modern cruise ship to have all outside cabins (she still holds the distinction for her size); the first to have closed-circuit television with remote control, mini-refrigerators, and full bathrooms with tub and shower in all cabins. She was the first to have verandas in all suites, deluxe cabins, and some lesser categories, and large picture windows instead of portholes in every category.

The biggest Princess ship when she debuted, but hardly a superliner by today's standards, this trendsetter has two acres of open teak decks, three swimming pools, and a fully equipped health spa. She is still the line's flagship and the apex of the Princess style with refined, easy-to-like decor dedicated to passenger comfort.

In the free-flowing interiors, spaces are defined not so much by walls as by art, sculpture, glass with brass railings, and live plants. Along with a decor of muted colors and an abundance of windows with views of the sea, a sense of openness and spaciousness is created throughout the ship.

The layout of the *Royal Princess* is unusual. Most public rooms are on the two lower levels and virtually all cabins are on the upper decks. The Plaza Deck, the lowest of the two, has a large foyer that spans two decks—the first shipboard atrium, perhaps—with the purser's office and information deck to one side and the entrance to the dining room on the other.

The greenery-filled foyer is dominated by a large sculpture, *Spindrift*, by David Norris, composed of a bronze spiral with seagulls in flight rising over rocks and a splashing fountain. A dramatic staircase with a brass-and-wood-trimmed glass balustrade swings wide in two wings and curves up to the Princess Court on Riviera Deck where a portrait of Princess Diana graces the wall.

The Court is, in fact, a balcony with a piano lounge overlooking the foyer and makes a convenient focal point of the ship, helped along by the comfy leather chairs where passengers sit to enjoy pre-lunch or pre-dinner drinks and a pianist/vocalist who entertains with show tunes and old favorites. The Riviera Deck also has the main showroom, the cabaret-style lounge, casino, boutique, card room, and a theatre where current and classic movies are shown daily.

ITINERARIES *September–October:* 10 days from New York to New England/Canada (and reverse).

- *November–March:* South America. Departing from Ft. Lauderdale in November, *Royal Princess* makes her way through the Caribbean and the Panama Canal to the west coast of South America and around the continent in a series of 14–19-day itineraries. The final one departs from Buenos Aires on March 21, 1998, for Barcelona and the start of her spring/summer European itineraries which will take her to Northern Europe on two-week Baltic cruises from Southampton, visiting Baltic capitals plus St. Petersburg, Amsterdam, Le Havre; Norwegian fjords, Mediterranean, Scotland, and Ireland.
- *Spring and late summer:* 13-day positioning cruises, eastbound from New York/Montreal to Southampton; westbound from London to New York.
- *Fall:* 10 days from New York to New England/Canada (and reverse).

Home Ports Varies, depending on itineraries.
Port Charges $165–250.

CABINS   The *Royal Princess* has 20 categories of cabins—all outside and spacious and all with large picture windows, tiled bathrooms with tubs and showers, retractable clothesline, mirrored medicine cabinet door, and a deluxe amenities package, including terry cloth robes. All cabins are equipped with mini-refrigerator, safe, multifunction phone, four-channel music radio, remote-control television with CNN and other cable channels, and coded key cards for your door.

The outstanding quality of the interiors and attention to details are reflected in such amenities as a large dressing table with makeup lights and mirrors and an easy-to-reach plug for the hair dryer, ample drawers, and three large closets. In many cabins, one of the twin beds folds into a wall providing extra sitting room space during the day. Some cabins on Baja, Caribe, and Dolphin decks have obstructed views; these are marked in the deck plan.

Suites and cabins with verandas are very roomy with the outside deck being large enough to accommodate a chaise lounge, a small table, and a chair. If you can afford one, a veranda is worth the additional cost as it adds another thoroughly enjoyable dimension to your cruise experience. It's your private corner to enjoy breakfast, the peace and serenity of days at sea, and the fresh sea air day or night. It's your own front-row seat for watching the world go by.

The two largest suites have separate sitting and dining rooms, a Jacuzzi bathtub, a separate bedroom with queen-size bed, a large veranda; spacious mini-suites are similar but do not have walls between the bedrooms and sitting areas.

English stewards and stewardesses provide cabin service that is correct, usually punctual, but they could learn a thing or two about being gracious and friendly from the Filipino cabin attendants who assist them. There are several self-service laundrettes with free washers, dryers, irons, and ironing boards. You pay 50 cents for soap.

Specifications   600 outside cabins (150 with verandas, including 52 mini-suites, 12 suites, 2 deluxe suites). Standard dimensions, 168 square feet. All cabins and suites with twin (convertible to queen); some cabins accommodate a third person. Ten are wheelchair accessible.

DINING   The Continental Dining Room on Plaza Deck is a warm, pleasant room, decorated in soft pastels, with large windows. A raised level on the perimeter of the room is delineated with brass railings and small islands of round tables that break up the space and provide some privacy. The arrangement also seems to help lower the noise level and allow easy conversation even though the tables are close together.

The dining room serves three meals in two seatings, usually with open seating on the days in port for breakfast and lunch and assigned seats for dinner. Most tables are for four to eight people and a few "twos" are available. The cuisine is consistently of high quality, well prepared, and a cut above that of other Princess ships.

The senior dining staff is Italian and very attentive. In the European tradition—and as on grand oceanliners of yesteryear—you can count on the maître d'hôtel or one of the senior staff to prepare fresh pasta tableside for you every evening. You need not be shy about asking for your favorite pasta if it is not on the menu. They love showing you how well they can make it.

Dinner menus are available for review at all the bars and posted around the ships. Dinner menus offer six courses for lunch and seven for dinner with generous selections for each course. For example, there are four appetizers, three soups, a salad, a daily pasta special, six entrees (at least one or as many as three are marked as low in calories), four desserts, and assortment of cheeses and fresh fruits.

Following the successful introduction of cruising's first 24-hour restaurant on *Sun Princess*, a 24-hour Lido Cafe was introduced on the *Royal Princess* in late 1996 followed by a pizzeria. The indoor/outdoor cafe with blue-and-turquoise tile-topped tables is a cheerful setting any time of the day and offers separate, glass-enclosed sections for smokers and nonsmokers. There are also sheltered outdoor tables on Lido Deck and open deck space at the stern's breezy deck. Afternoon tea is served in the Riviera Club and a late night buffet, often with a different theme, is available in Princess Court.

SERVICE   The dining room staff, which is made up of Italian senior staff with mostly European waiters is the most service-oriented group on the ship, and they do go out of their way for passengers. The British officers are a part of the social scene in the bars and at meals where they host tables.

FACILITIES AND ENTERTAINMENT   The International Lounge on Riviera Deck is a multipurpose room, used during the day for special concerts like the Regimental Band of the Royal Welsh Fusiliers before departure from Southampton on the Baltic cruise and the Troika Dancers when the ship calls in St. Petersburg.

In the evening, the lounge is the venue for Broadway- and Las Vegas–style shows which have the predictable fare of song and dance and are not up to Princess's long-standing reputation for outstanding shows. The lounge has slightly tiered seats that offer good sightlines except from the back.

The Riviera Club and Bar and adjacent Terrace Room are the most elegant of the lounges and offer cabaret-style entertainment with singers and comedians and dancing in the evening.

If your luck doesn't hold out in the Crown Casino, you might head up to the Horizon Lounge on Sun Deck. It's an observation lounge with floor-to-ceiling windows looking out across 280 degrees of panoramic views. It is usually quiet, except when there is an exercise class in the morning or karaoke in the evening. The large room is a popular spot in the afternoon for a wine tasting or during cocktails to try the drink of the day—a daily cocktail at a special price. After-dinner coffees and liqueurs are served here, with a different special nightly, and around midnight, the room turns into a disco.

ACTIVITIES AND DIVERSIONS   You might start your day's activities with the bridge expert who will help you improve your game and organize a tournament in the card room on Bridge Deck; or the dance couple who will teach you to fox-trot or line dance in the Riviera Club. You could stop by a craft demonstration and learn to make pretty gifts or new ways to tie a scarf or have your handwriting analyzed.

In the afternoon you might join a golf contest or a Ping-Pong tournament, take a lesson in the casino, test your word or trivia skills in a game, or watch a culinary demonstration or the horse races. A different movie will be shown three times daily in the comfortable Princess Theatre. And then, there's bingo.

Books are accessible any hour from the well-stocked library next to Princess Court, but you may have trouble reading there. It's an open space between two lounges—an afterthought, perhaps—and comfortable sofas and chairs make it a popular place for passengers to stop for a chat.

SPORTS, FITNESS, AND BEAUTY   Lido Deck is the main outdoor recreation area centered around an unusual cluster of five small pools. On Sun Deck you can sunbathe on a raised platform, play table tennis and shuffleboard, swim in one of the largest lap pools at sea, and work out at the spa, all while you enjoy ocean views.

The fitness complex has a gym with Nautilus and other exercise equipment, sauna and massage rooms, and a large indoor Jacuzzi. A full day of programmed exercise starts with a walk-a-mile, stretch, and aerobics. You can walk and jog most any time on the wraparound teak deck on Dolphin Deck (three and a half times around equals one mile); the wide deck is partly sheltered by lifeboats overhead. The beauty salon offers hair and body treatments, including herbal facials.

SHORE EXCURSIONS   Princess publishes excellent shore excursion brochures, a specific one for each cruise, and has video material available for purchase. For the *Royal Princess*'s Baltic cruise alone, 40 different tours are available, with half day excursions ranging from $20–48 and all-day ones from $105–159, although in St. Petersburg, private van or car tours can range from $329–1,000 for half- and full-day. The tours, although fairly standard, offer variety; they are well organized and the guides are first-rate.

POSTSCRIPT   From her start, this classy lady was admired by competitors as much as its owners. Whether due to her royal send-off or immense comfort, the *Royal Princess* is one ship that passengers request by name, rather than itinerary as with most others. She has her own fan club, and, like fine wine, has mellowed nicely. Her passengers are older, more affluent and less active than those on Princess's newer Caribbean fleet. Most are Americans but she attracts upscale Brits, too. Her itineraries—mostly two to three weeks—appeal to folks with time—and money—for extended cruises. Those who have tired of glitzy megaliners will appreciate her the most.

Crown Princess / Regal Princess

	Quality Rating	Value Rating
Crown Princess	❻	C
Regal Princess	❼	B

Registry: Liberia	Length: 811 feet	Beam: 105 feet
Cabins: 795	Draft: 26 feet	Speed: 19.5 knots
Maximum Passengers: 1,590	Passenger Decks: 11	Elevators: 9
	Crew: 696	Space Ratio: 44

THE SHIPS   The *Crown Princess* was christened in 1990 by actress Sophia Loren in New York during Princess Cruises's 25th anniversary, and the *Regal Princess*, whose godmother is Margaret Thatcher, was added the following year. These identical twins were not only a major break from Princess tradition, they were very different in profiles and interiors from any other ship. Along with the *Star Princess*, they were part of the work-in-progress inventory that Princess got in its purchase of Sitmar Cruises.

Designed by Renzo Piano, the architect of the controversial Pompidou Center in Paris, these Italian-built megaliners have sleek lines that, according to Piano, were inspired by the shape of a dolphin. The unorthodox design raised the eyebrows of a lot of ship buffs when it was revealed, and the old fashioned upright stack (in this day of sleek slanted funnels) had them shaking their heads. But the true test came when passengers tried out the interiors. To this day, they garner mixed reviews.

Let's begin with the good news: space and comfort. Ships the size of the *Crown* and *Regal* are megaliners, yet the Princess twins carry 25–30 percent *fewer* passengers than their counterparts of similar size. The spaciousness is immediately apparent in the wide corridors and lounges with their high ceilings and large cabins. Even standard cabins on these twins are the size of suites on some other ships and all have walk-in closets.

Throughout the ships, their appointments range from truly elegant with stylish, top-quality fabrics and furnishings with superb workmanship and museum quality art by world renowned artists—Frank Stella, Robert Motherwell, David Hockney—to the eclectic with pop art in some bars and eighteenth-century romantic landscapes and etchings in the dining rooms. The result is a variety of environments—interesting, stimulating, and entertaining.

The main drawback of the interiors is that they look and feel like a hotel rather than a ship. There is a dearth of outside decks; promenades and lounges, which run along the center of the ship, are bordered by corridors that make no visual connection with the sea. Unless you have a cabin with a veranda, you must go to the top deck or two small, upper aft areas to see the seascape and feel the sea air. The forward section, particularly, has a closed-off-from-the-sea environment, and the top of the ship, called the Dome (in profile, it's the head of a dolphin), is meant to be an observation lounge, but it has so much going on—the casino's nonstop buzzing slot machines and people, bars and people, hot dance music and people—any notion of a quiet spot to enjoy scenic views and beautiful Caribbean sunsets, as an observation lounge is meant to be, is lost. In addition, the cavernous Dome takes up topside space that might have been better used for outdoor decks.

The Plaza, on the lowest passenger deck at the heart of the ships, is an unusual oval-shaped three-story atrium surrounded by shops on the second and third levels. Striking in appearance with tony modern furnishings in coral and green and lots of live greenery, it is the ships' focal point, similar to a hotel lobby, where passengers gather, with a patisserie to one side, the purser's office on the other.

A wide curving staircase, anchored by a fountain sculpture, leads up to the next level where the balcony's brass-trimmed glass balustrades enhance the airy spaciousness of the atrium. The third level, Promenade Deck, is devoted entirely to public rooms, with a two-tiered showroom forward and the main dining room at the stern. At the center are two large, attractive back-to-back lounges, each with a different ambience.

CROWN PRINCESS ITINERARIES *May–September:* Alaska, seven days, from Vancouver via Inside Passage to Ketchikan, Juneau, Skagway, Glacier Bay, College Fjord, and Seward/Anchorage; or reverse itinerary from Seward to Vancouver.

- *October–April:* Panama Canal, ten days, round trip from Ft. Lauderdale to Cartagena, Puerto Limón, San Blas, Cozumel, and a partial transit of the Panama Canal, with four days at sea.

Home Ports Ft. Lauderdale; Vancouver; Seward.
Port Charges Alaska, $185; Panama, $211–269.

REGAL PRINCESS ITINERARIES *May–September:* Alaska, seven days, round trip from Vancouver via Inside Passage to Juneau, Skagway, Glacier Bay, and Sitka.

- *October–April:* Panama Canal between San Juan and Acapulco on two different itineraries: westbound from San Juan to St. Thomas, Martinique, Grenada, Caracas, Curaçao, Panama Canal, and Acapulco with two days at sea and one overnight in Acapulco; eastbound from Acapulco to Puerto Caldera, Panama Canal, Cartagena, Aruba, St. Thomas, and San Juan, with four days at sea.

Home Ports San Juan; Acapulco; Vancouver; Seward.
Port Charges Alaska, $144; Panama, $195–342.

CABINS The ships' spacious, cabins are one of their best features. The color scheme of peach, taupe, and white adds to their airy, spacious feeling. The cabins come in 26 categories of four basic arrangements: inside or outside standard doubles; outside double with a tiny balcony; outside mini-suites with small veranda; and full suites with veranda. The six top categories plus the largest of the inside group are found on three upper cabin decks; the other 11 categories are spread across the four lower decks which have lounges and other facilities as well.

All cabins have five-channel television with CNN and ESPN and Discovery channel; four-channel radio, direct-dial telephone, refrigerator, safe, walk-in closets and separate dressing area, generous drawer space, and key card for door locks. Regardless of the category, you will find terry cloth robes and fresh fruit in your cabin. Standard outside cabins without balcony have oversized picture windows. Lifeboats are placed about midway down the sides of the ship due to the height of the superstructure; as a result 26 cabins on Dolphin Deck have obstructed views (indicated on the deck plan).

Specifications   171 inside, 430 outside cabins (134 with verandas); 36 mini-suites, 14 suites with verandas. Standard dimensions, 190 square feet. All with two lower beds, convertible to queen; some have third/fourth berths; no singles. Ten cabins are wheelchair accessible.

DINING   The main dining room at the stern on Promenade Deck has two sittings for three meals. The room is attractive, with an open feeling, high ceilings, and an overall ambience of a deluxe hotel restaurant. On the *Regal* this room has many nooks and corners divided by etched glass and fine wood paneling, added to help dampen the noise level, the lighting was dimmed and made softer. However, most of the tables are rectangular for six or eight diners, making table-wide conversation difficult.

As on all Princess ships, dinner menus are available for review at bars and are posted around the ships. They are essentially the same throughout the fleet, offering six courses for lunch and seven for dinner with generous selections for each course. Both the food and the service have been improved and are getting high marks on the *Crown* or *Regal*.

Pizza lovers will be happy with the ships' poolside pizzerias complete with red checkered tablecloths and Chianti bottles. It is open for lunch and again in the evening, turning out made-to-order pizzas at no extra cost. The patisserie has excellent espresso and cappuccino and an assortment of fresh pastries.

Following the successful introduction of cruising's first 24-hour restaurant on *Sun Princess*, the *Crown Princess*'s casual indoor/outdoor Cafe Cabana (Cafe del Sol on the *Regal*) was made into a 24-hour Lido Cafe in 1997.

SERVICE   The service on the *Crown* has improved and recent reports indicate that Princess is making an effort to correct past flaws in this area.

FACILITIES AND ENTERTAINMENT   The best feature of the twin ships is their lounges—greatly varied in size, decor, ambience, and entertainment. The largest is the handsome International Lounge, a bi-level show lounge set around a deep horseshoe-shaped stage. Recently, Princess has made a major commitment to update and upgrade the big production shows for its Caribbean fleet, which are up against stiff competition from some other lines whose shows are as good as anything on Broadway. A new, 55-minute show called *Pirate Island,* featuring spectacular stunts and special effects and a cast of 22, is scheduled to be added to the *Crown Princess* and *Regal Princess* after its premier on *Dawn Princess* in 1997.

Down the corridor, Chianti (Bacchus on *Regal*) is a small wine-by-the-glass and caviar bar. Further aft Kipling's has a stage for a piano, a dance floor, and a mirrored bar with conversational groupings of leather and rattan chairs. The room sparkles with brass and glass, and has ceiling fans suggesting the days of the raj. A brass statue of a Bengal tiger is the showpiece on *Regal* where the lounge is called The Bengal Bar. To complete the fantasy, whiskey and liquor bottles are stacked to the ceiling and require the bartender to use a ladder to retrieve them.

Next door, Intermezzo, offers the more intimate setting of a piano bar with large murals of fashionably dressed revelers from the Twenties, suggesting the golden era of grand oceanliners. The Adagio, as it is called on the *Regal*, also has a large espresso machine. One flight up on Dolphin Deck at midship, The Stage Door with a sunken dance floor is a cabaret and late-night disco. Characters on the Lido Deck is a colorful poolside specialty bar serving fun, innovative drinks.

The huge top deck Dome with 19-foot ceilings is largely given over to the casino's gaming tables and banks of slot machines. It has a dance floor, bar, and 100 trees! The cinema, down the corridor from the Galleria shopping arcade on Emerald Deck, doubles as a conference room. There is a library and card room.

SPORTS, FITNESS, AND BEAUTY   Sun Deck has two outdoor pools, one with a swim-up bar, Flippers—a reminder of the ship's dolphin profile—and the other with waterfalls and whirlpools. There is a paddle tennis court (also used for volleyball) and a one-sixth-of-a-mile jogging track. The ship has no wraparound deck; the outside Promenade Deck is closed off at both ends. Images, a beauty and fitness center, tucked away on the lowest passenger deck, has state-of-the-art exercise equipment, aerobics area, weight machines, exercise bikes, and steam room.

CHILDREN'S FACILITIES   "Love Boat Kids," Princess's youth program on all ships, includes special facilities and full-time youth coordinators running activities for children ages 2–17, and evening activities while the ship is at sea. Activities may also be conducted when the ship is in port, but children may not be left with the youth coordinator while parents are ashore. Children under 18 must be accompanied by an adult and have written consent from both parents or legal guardians to cruise.

POSTSCRIPT   The stylish ships offer luxury-category space at mid-range prices or even bargain prices if you hit one of the frequent promotional discount fares. They have port-intensive itineraries designed mainly for first-time and novices cruisers. The cruises in both the Caribbean and Alaska have only one or two days at sea even on the ten-day itineraries. Those in the Caribbean have an interesting combination of destinations that balance the region's variety with activity. In Alaska, Princess offers an extensive selection of cruise and land combinations.

Island Princess / Pacific Princess

	Quality Rating	**Value Rating**
Island Princess	**6**	C
Pacific Princess	**5**	C

Registry: Great Britain	Length: 550 feet	Beam: 80 feet
Cabins: 305	Draft: 25 feet	Speed: 19 knots
Maximum Passengers:	Passenger Decks: 7	Elevators: 4
724	Crew: 350	Space Ratio: 33

THE SHIPS   A leisurely pace and a friendly ambience are the hallmark of these ships that changed the face of cruising more than two decades ago. Now, after their $40 million facelift, *Pacific Princess* and *Island Princess*, the original Love Boats, are better than ever.

The renovations, which were extensive from stem to stern, were intended to bring the sister ships up to the standards of the newer vessels in the fleet. Interesting enough, the twins were given a similar overhaul in 1985, to meet the standards set by the *Royal Princess*, which was new at the time.

Among the enhancements, the main lounges received new tiered floors for better show viewing, a larger dance floor, and a new sound system. State-of-the-art exercise equipment was added to the gyms, more space was created for the casino and video arcades, and the ships have new air-conditioning systems, radar equipment, and other operational and structural improvements. The ships were given new fabrics and furnishings, but they retain the comfortable style that is typical of the Princess fleet.

The smallest of the fleet—and almost considered small ships compared to the megaliners—the *Island* and *Pacific* launched Princess cruises and set its style. Built in the early 1970s, the sister ships are classic ships with traditional lines and an abundance of wood and brass. Instead of the hotel feel of the megaliners or the nightclub look of some Princess competitors, the atmosphere on these twins is homey, more like your living room. There is no plastic, no neon.

They are appreciated by their loyal fans—of which they have many—for their warm and more intimate ambience. Designed to appeal primarily to American tastes, the ships with their British owners and officers do attract a certain number of British passengers.

The ships are well laid out, and the layout easy to learn—that's part of the advantage of their size. Passengers arrive on board at Purser's Square, a bilevel lobby that is the heart of the ship on Fiesta Deck. A gracious space with a spiral staircase—not quite as broad as the television version—curves up to Aloha Deck. Both Fiesta and Aloha decks are devoted almost entirely to cabins.

Riviera Deck, another flight up, houses most of the public rooms, while the topside Sun, or Lido, Deck is the sports center with what Princess calls the world's most photographed swimming pool.

ITINERARIES

Island Princess   *September–December:* Mediterranean/Atlantic, Eastern Mediterranean, and Holy Land.

- *January–May:* Middle East/India/Asia. In January and February, the ship will sail on two 17-day cruises between Rome and Bombay calling at Rhodes, Haifa (overnight), Egypt, Yemen, and Oman, with four days at sea. From mid-March–mid-May, she sails on a 64-day voyage between Rome and San Francisco which Princess is calling its first-ever world cruise. The ship visits 20 ports on five continents.

Pacific Princess   *September–December:* Grand Mediterranean and Holy Land.

- *January–March:* Africa and Safari/Cruise combinations. For winter 1998, *Pacific Princess* offers some of the most exotic itineraries in Princess's "Exotic Adventures" collection, designed for seasoned travelers looking for more unusual destinations. In mid-January, the ship departs from Athens for Cape Town on the first leg of circumnavigating Africa. The 24-day southbound trip sails east, with calls in Israel, Egypt, Jordan, overnight at Mombasa, Zanzibar, and three ports in South Africa—Durban, Port Elizabeth, and Cape Town. Afterwards, she offers two 14-day cruises between Cape Town and Kenya combined with 4-day safaris plus calls at Mayotte and Madagascar. Longer safaris are available. The 23-day northbound cruise from Capetown sail along Africa's west coast with stops at Luderitz and Walvis Bay, Namibia; Pointe-Noire, Congo; Lome, Togo; Accra, Ghana; Abidjan, Ivory Coast; Dakar, Senegal; and Casablanca, Gibraltar, and Rome.

Home Port   Varies according to itinerary.
Port Charges $250.

CABINS   Accommodations are small by Princess standards and certainly nothing like the television version, but they are adequate and comfortable. In addition to all-new furnishings, carpeting, and draperies, the recent renovations brought satellite television with CNN, ESPN, and a new telephone system.

The ships offer 18 categories with outside cabins outnumbering inside ones by more than three to one. All cabins have twin beds, usually in an L-shape; often one bed folds into the wall to provide more cabin space during the day. Most bathrooms have shower only; suites and mini-suites have refrigerators and bathrooms with tubs. All have four-channel radios. Two deluxe outside singles on Promenade Deck are always the first to go. And unlike other ships in the Princess fleet, none of the cabins or suites have verandas. There are no wheelchair accessible cabins; wheelchair-bound passengers are limited to four per cruise.

Specifications   67 inside, 223 outside; 9 mini-suites; 4 suites; 2 deluxe outside single cabins. Standard dimensions, 126 square feet. All cabins with twins except 2 singles.

DINING   The attractive Coral Dining Room is on a lower deck as is traditional on older ships. It serves three meals in two seatings, offering menus similar to those found on other Princess ships and prepared primarily by Italian chefs. As an example, dinner offers four appetizers, three soups, a salad, a daily pasta special, six entrees (with one or more marked as low in calories), four desserts, and assortment of cheeses and fresh fruits. The pasta dishes seem to draw the most praise.

Buffet breakfast and lunch are served on Lido Deck. One of the main improvements in the renovations provided new buffet stations that offer made-to-order omelets and waffles for breakfast and a salad bar at lunch, as well as all-new outdoor tables and lounge chairs by the Lido pool for al fresco dining. Afternoon tea is served in the dining room.

SERVICE   Other than the senior Italian dining room staff, this duo is a British affair. The officers, purser and front office staff, cabin stewards and stewardesses, cruise director and staff are British—plus there are some Irish women bartenders. The British officers participate in the social life, hosting tables in the dining room and holding up the bar in the disco. By and large, the small twins get the most accolades for service and even higher marks for food than some other ships in the fleet.

FACILITIES AND ENTERTAINMENT   You could start your mornings at the putting green or join others in a walk around the Sun Deck (18 times equals a mile) or the exercise and aerobics classes. (Promenade Deck does not encircle the ship.) You can also start the morning with a Bloody Mary on Sun Deck, a Princess standard, or wait awhile for the relatively inexpensive drink of the day.

The pool on Sun Deck has a sliding roof designed for use on days of inclement weather. There is plenty of deck space for sunbathing, and toward the stern are the sauna and massage facilities. The beauty salon, barber shop, and gym are on different decks.

During days at sea on longer cruises, you will find bridge and backgammon in the large card and game room on Riviera Deck, dance classes, jackpot bingo, horseracing, crafts, cooking demonstrations, and other diversions in the lounges. A library is tucked away in a quiet location on Promenade Deck, not far from the Terrace Room, another quiet corner for reading and watching the wake.

Nightlife on the Love Boats is mainly on Riviera Deck with Las Vegas–style production shows staged nightly in Carousel Lounge, forward, where the latest renovations provide a tiered floor and new seating for better viewing. They carry the usual array of entertainers— singers, comedians, dancers, and magicians. The cruise director and staff are part of the entertainment on some nights and like other Princess ships, there is a high content of passenger participation in most events.

The popular Carib (or Pacific) Lounge and its adjoining bar at the stern is a good people-watching spot. The nicely appointed lounge has a small stage and dance floor, and a spectacular wall of floor-to-ceiling windows spanning two decks and looking out at the Riviera pool and open sea. Bright and cheerful during the day, it becomes an intimate setting with subdued lighting in the evening. Stairs on the starboard side wind up to the Terrace Room, the upper level of the lounge. Another favorite daytime viewing spot, the topside Starlight Lounge on Sun Deck forward is a popular perch for cocktails and after-dinner drinks.

Movies are shown daily on a large screen in the Princess Theatre, which is arranged like a nightclub with comfortable chairs and cocktail tables. The theatre is used as a meeting room and is the venue for an interdenominational Sunday worship service, a long-standing tradition on British ships. Tucked behind the theatre is the Pirate's Cove, a small disco that gets lively after 10 or 11 P.M., when the British officers show up. Next door is a neon-lit casino with blackjack and a wall of slot machines.

POSTSCRIPT *Island Princess* and *Pacific Princess* may have been overtaken in size and elegance by newer Princess ships, but these midsize twins remain the choice of many of Princess's most loyal fans. Seniors and seasoned cruisers particularly delight in their unhurried pace and their well-organized program ashore. And even if it's been two dozen years since *The Love Boat* aired on prime time, its reruns, across the country and around the world, continue to attract audiences and to get people to try their first cruise.

Sky Princess

	Quality Rating	Value Rating
Sky Princess	❺	C

Registry: Great Britain	Length: 789 feet	Beam: 98 feet
Cabins: 600	Draft: 25 feet	Speed: 19 knots
Maximum Passengers: 1,200	Passenger Decks: 11	Elevators: 6
	Crew: 535	Space Ratio: 38

THE SHIP After a multi-million-dollar refurbishment in 1992, the *Sky Princess* was given a new look, yet her new furnishings and fabrics were in keeping with the casually elegant design theme found throughout the Princess fleet. New color schemes along with improved lighting and decorative greenery were introduced in all of the public areas.

Directing the renovations was Italian architect Giacomo Mortola who was responsible for much of the ship's original interior design when she was built in 1984 as Sitmar's *Fairsky*. Mortola also designed some of the lounges on *Crown Princess* and *Regal Princess* as well as the *Sun Princess*. The *Sky Princess* combines the classic luxury of spacious public areas and cabins with comfortable, contemporary decor.

The Promenade and the Riviera Decks house most of the lounges and bars with a tiered showroom offering good visibility for its Broadway- and Las Vegas–style shows. There is a series of small lounges: Promenade Lounge with 24-hour coffee service, a bright, cheerful pizzeria, shops, and the handsome Melody piano bar with deep, soft leather chairs and sofas that invite friends, old and new, to gather.

The well-appointed Veranda Lounge at the stern has floor-to-ceiling windows that look out to the pool area and open sea. In addition to being totally refurbished, the Veranda Lounge got a new lighting system and electrically controlled sliding glass doors for easy access to the pool deck and the remodeled buffet area. In the evening the Veranda Lounge doubles as a nightclub with a cabaret show and dancing.

One flight up on Riviera Deck, the Horizon Lounge is a forward observation lounge with tall viewing windows across the bow and banquette window seats where passengers can enjoy panoramic sea views. The large casino offers blackjack, craps, roulette, and slot machines. There is a small bar, card room, and a paneled library. The Starlight Room at the stern is a disco.

ITINERARIES

- *May–September:* 11 days, round trip from San Francisco to Victoria, Vancouver, Juneau, Skagway, Hubbard Glacier, and Ketchikan.
- *October–May:* Varying 12–35-day itineraries of Hawaii/Tahiti, Orient/China, Southeast Asia between Hong Kong and Singapore, and Australia/New Zealand and the South Pacific.

Home Ports   Varies with itinerary, winter; San Francisco, summer.
Port Charges $175–475.

CABINS   The *Sky Princess* has large cabins with generous closet and drawer space. The cabins are available in 16 categories and, as with all Princess ships, come in 4 styles: inside and outside cabins, mini-suites, and suites with verandas.

Tastefully decorated in colorful pastels with contemporary art on the walls, all cabins have television, phones, and safes. Most cabins have twin beds, and some can accommodate three or four passengers. Suites and mini-suites have separate sitting areas, refrigerators, and bathrooms with bathtub and shower. The suites have private verandas and double beds. The top suites, Malaga and Amalfi, have whirlpool tubs.

Specifications 215 inside, 385 outside cabins, including 28 mini-suites; 10 suites with private balconies. Standard dimensions, 175 square feet; 590 cabins with twins; suite with double and queen-size beds; some cabins with third and fourth berths; no singles. 6 wheelchair-accessible cabins.

DINING The *Sky Princess* has two attractively decorated dining rooms, Regency and Savoy, both on Aloha Deck, and each providing passengers with a somewhat more intimate dining ambience than is found on a ship with only one dining room. Menus are similar to other Princess ships and offer a wide selection of continental cuisine and American favorites, often with a different theme each night. Excellent pastas are prepared at tableside daily. There are two seatings for three meals; breakfast and lunch are often open seating.

Informal breakfast and luncheon buffets are available at the Deck Buffet by the pool area on Promenade Deck. An improvement of the buffet was a major element in the last renovation when a grill for preparing made-to-order eggs at breakfast and hamburgers and hot dogs at lunch was added, along with a new soup and carving station, and a salad and fresh fruit bar. The ice cream sundae center features three different flavors and a variety of toppings each day. There is a midnight buffet, an early-bird coffee and Danish pastry, afternoon tea, made-to-order pizzas, 24-hour room service, and round-the-clock coffee service in the Veranda Lounge.

SERVICE The *Sky Princess* has British and Italian officers and an international crew who get high marks from passengers as a gracious and dedicated staff providing very good service.

FACILITIES AND ENTERTAINMENT The main lounge show room offers Broadway-style entertainment, another lounge has cabaret shows and dancing, and there is a piano lounge and a theatre for movies and meetings.

Shipboard programs range from backgammon, chess, and bridge tournaments to culinary demonstrations, guest lectures, language lessons, karaoke, and, of course, bingo. There is a library, card and game room, and shopping arcade.

The ship has three pools, including one for children, a full-size paddle tennis court that is also used for volleyball, trapshooting, and Ping-Pong. The top deck fitness center has a gym with state-of-the-art exercise equipment, an aerobics area, indoor hot tub, and sauna and massage rooms. An unobstructed jogging track (a one-fifteenth-of-a-mile circuit) has plastic link matting, a covering similar to the surface used for indoor tennis courts. The beauty/barber salon is on a lower deck.

CHILDREN'S FACILITIES The Youth and Teen centers on Aloha deck have a video arcade, arts and crafts center, television, game tables, a kids pool, and more. A youth program called "Love Boat Kids," for children ages 2–17 years, is supervised by a staff of youth counselors who schedule group activities and fun projects, including arts and crafts, pool games, scavenger hunts, ship tours, story time, cartoons, and more. Kids get a daily agenda. No meals are served in the center; the ship wants children to attend meals with their parents as part of their cruise experience. Parents may leave their children on board at the center when the ship is in port, provided they sign a release form that allows the ship to administer medical treatment in the event of an emergency.

Princess Teen Club, a program designed for children ages 13–17, has its own director and activities when 15 or more teenagers are on board (usually during holiday and summer cruises). The activities include a teen-only disco, late-night movies, shipboard Olympics, karaoke contests, talent shows, theme parties, and more.

POSTSCRIPT *Sky Princess* is a spacious, well-maintained ship, well-suited for passengers who prefer a classic style with Broadway-style entertainment, easy pace, and pleasant surroundings. Readers planning a cruise on *Sky Princess* should review the entire Princess Cruises section for a full picture of the cruise experience the line offers.

Sun Princess / Dawn Princess

	Quality Rating	Value Rating
Sun Princess	⑩	B
Dawn Princess	Preview	

Registry: Italy	Length: 856 feet	Beam: 83 feet
Cabins: 1,050	Draft: 26 feet	Speed: 21 knots
Maximum Passengers: 1,950	Passenger Decks: 14	Elevators: 9
	Crew: 900	Space Ratio: 39.5

THE SHIPS Prior to its launching, when Princess boasted that the *Sun Princess*—the largest cruise ship ever built at the time—would have an intimate feeling, the skepticism the claim engendered was understandable.

But guess what? Princess did it. Well, perhaps "intimate" is a stretch, but it certainly managed to diminish the interiors of this big ship to human scale.

Built at Italy's Fincantieri shipyard for $300 million, the eagerly awaited *Sun Princess* made her debut in December 1995, the first of the line's new Grand Class series. Her almost exact twin, *Dawn Princess*, arrived in May 1997.

From the outside, the gleaming white liners look colossal, towering 14 decks above the sea and stretching almost the length of three football fields. But inside, clever design has shrunk the scale to impart a welcoming, accessible ambience. Spacious without being overwhelming, the ships have warm colors and refined decor that enhances the inviting atmosphere.

All told, *Sun Princess* is even more magnificent than her advance billing. Designer Njal Eide, the Scandinavian architect who created the interiors of the *Royal Princess*, which set the standards for a generation of new ships in the 1980s, did it again. Together with Italian designer Giacomo Mortola, he has set new criteria for megaliners.

The ships' layout is a departure from standard deck plans and is innovative in many ways. The goal was to use small spaces to capture the intimate atmosphere of a small ship, and at the same time, use them to create options. Rather than one cavernous atrium, these ships offer two. Instead of one enormous show lounge, there are two main show lounges, both staging nightly entertainment. There are also two dining rooms, on different decks, and their layout, decor, and table arrangements convey an intimate ambience.

The main deck of public rooms has a variety of small lounges to offer an array of entertainment. Five dining outlets, including cruising's first 24-hour restaurant, provide dining options. Although multiple lounges and dining alternatives are found on other ships, none have developed the concept of options to the extent as the *Sun* and *Dawn*. Princess has made it so whatever you choose to do, you can do, and whatever you miss one night, you can catch the next night.

The four-deck Grand Plaza is the ships' main atrium and social hub. Impressive but not overwhelming, it is a showcase of the exquisite Italian craftsmanship throughout the vessels and sets the tone for the entire ship. The elegant and inviting space uses warm, golden marble reminiscent of the sun and beige, bronze, and brown accents suggesting shade. Sunburst patterns are set in the marble floors at every level of the atrium, and overhead, a back-lit, stained glass dome in shades of aqua and turquoise conveys an abstract, underwater scene. Glass elevators and a circular, floating staircase connect the decks and provide backdrops for people-watching and a stunning setting for the captain's parties.

Among the ships' other amenities are five swimming pools, a huge health center and spa, children's and teen rooms; a multistory shopping arcade; a computerized golf simulator; a library and reading room with "audio chairs," each with its own bay window view of the sea; and a business and conference center for up to 300 people. These grand ladies each have $2.5 million art collections made up of paintings, sculptures, ceramic tiles, and Murano glass, including pieces by the famous designer Seguso, all commissioned specifically for them.

Another significant feature of the ships is their connection to the sea. A wraparound teak promenade deck lined with traditional canopied steamer chairs provides a peaceful setting where passengers can curl up with a book, daydream, or snooze.

ITINERARIES

Sun Princess   Western Caribbean and Panama Canal, winter; Alaska, summer.

- *October–April:* The ship sails weekly round trip from Ft. Lauderdale on Saturday to Princess Cays, the line's private beach at the tip of Eleuthera (Bahamas), Ocho Rios, Grand Cayman, and Playa del Carmen/Cozumel, with two days at sea. To accommodate the *Sun Princess*, Port Everglades rebuilt a pier to ease boarding and baggage handling. At her ports of call, she operates two gangways and at ports where she must tender, she speeds the operation by launching a flotilla of boats.
- *April and September:* 11-day transcanal positioning cruises between Ft. Lauderdale and Acapulco, and 7-day cruises between Acapulco and Los Angeles.
- *May–September:* Seven days, Alaska, from Vancouver to Ketchikan, Juneau, Skagway, Glacier Bay, College Fjord, and Seward/Anchorage.

Home Ports   Ft. Lauderdale; Vancouver; Seward.
Port Charges $115, Caribbean; $185, Alaska.

Dawn Princess   After her debut in May 1997, *Dawn Princess* sailed on an inaugural Panama Canal cruise, and spent the summer in

Alaska, sailing from Vancouver on seven-day cruises. Like her sister ships, the *Dawn* offers a wide variety of shore excursions, many focusing on nature and wildlife, which are among the best-executed excursions this writer has ever experienced.

- *October–April:* She sails on two new seven-day Eastern/ Southern Caribbean itineraries from San Juan, calling at Aruba, Caracas, Grenada, Dominica, and St. Thomas; or Barbados, St. Lucia, Martinique, St. Maarten, and St. Thomas. The two itineraries can be combined into one 14-day cruise, with a two-category upgrade.
- *The February 21* cruise will be geared to the Solar Eclipse, which is expected to take place near Aruba on February 26, 1998. An astronomy expert will be aboard during the cruise.
- *In May and September* en route to/from Alaska, *Dawn Princess* offers 11-day positioning cruises of the Panama Canal between San Juan and Acapulco and seven-day cruises between Acapulco and Los Angeles.

Home Ports   San Juan; Vancouver.
Port Charges $112, Caribbean; $185, Alaska.

CABINS   About two-thirds of the ships' cabins are outside and of those, 70 percent have private balconies. There are 20 cabin categories. Nineteen cabins—among the most on any cruise ship—were designed to Americans with Disabilities Act specifications. Lifeboats obstruct views from 28 outside cabins on Promenade Deck. All standard cabins come with a queen-size bed that converts to two singles, a refrigerator, safe, a roomy closet, and bath with shower, terry bathrobes, and hair dryers. All are well appointed and decorated in light, eye-pleasing colors.

Category A, a mini-suite with private balcony, is lavish in comfort, decor and size—almost 400 square feet, plus the balcony. A small marble-floored foyer with a mirror gives the illusion of a large apartment. Tastefully decorated in beige and soft butter tones accented by light woods and fine fabrics, it has a separate sitting area with comfortable leather chairs and a sofa that converts to a queen-size bed—not to mention mirrors on the ceiling!—plus an entertainment console with television and music channels and a bar with refrigerator.

The bedroom, separated by a curtained archway, has a queen-size bed, a vanity/desk, and a second television. There's ample drawer space and a walk-in closet with a safe. Sliding glass doors in both the sitting area and the bedroom lead to a large balcony extending the length of the suite. Two lounge chairs and a table make it an ideal spot for breakfast or afternoon naps. An unusual feature of this mini-suite is the two-room bath, where etched glass divides the whirlpool tub from a separate shower stall, and a door separates the toilet and wash basin.

Specifications 372 inside, 603 outside cabins (411 with verandas); 32 mini-suites and 6 suites with verandas. Standard dimensions, 135–173 square feet. All with two lower beds, convertible to queen; 300 with third berths; no singles. 19 cabins are wheelchair accessible.

DINING The ships incorporate choice into dining: there are two dining rooms, a 24-hour food court—cruising's first 24-hour restaurant; a pizzeria, a grill, a patisserie, an ice cream bar (there is a charge), and 24-hour room service.

Two main dining rooms, the Regency (Venetian) on Emerald Deck and the Marquis (Florentine) on Plaza Deck on *Sun Princess* (*Dawn Princess*), are laid out with asymmetrical seating arrangements and small groupings of tables in various sizes separated by dividers trimmed with etched glass. The result of this design is to give diners a sense of privacy. The dining rooms are decorated with murals of ancient Pompeii which add to the gracious surroundings. Separate galleys on each level and service stations in every corner reduce traffic and help to ensure that food gets to the tables at the proper temperature.

Menus offer a selection of appetizers, soups, salads, entrees, and desserts at lunch and dinner. A special pasta dish is offered every evening, although it is no longer prepared tableside as in the past. Healthy Choice selections, included on the regular menu, provide low cholesterol, fat, and sodium alternatives. The wine list offers reasonably priced choices, some under $20; wines are also available by the glass.

The Horizon Court forward on Lido Deck above the bridge is an innovative 24-hour cafe with 270-degree ocean views through floor-to-ceiling windows, with seating on a trio of terraces. By day, the Court offers buffets at two separate stations; at night, the center part of the room is transformed into a restaurant with table service and a band that plays for dancing. No reservations are necessary and there's no extra charge.

Breakfast offers an array of choices from fresh fruit to hot dishes, with a different special offering each day. At noon there's a range of entrees such as ravioli and roast beef, as well as a salad bar, but neither the selection nor the preparation match the quality or variety found in the dining room. At night the Court offers a limited menu which has been expanded and improved since it was first introduced on the *Sun*. The Court's 24-hour concept is great but still has room for improvement.

Verdi's pizzeria (La Scala on *Dawn*) in a winter garden setting with marble-top tables and wrought-iron chairs along the balcony overlooking the atrium, has the *ambiente* of a sidewalk cafe. Open for lunch and from 6 P.M.–2 A.M., it serves pizza hot from the ovens which are in plain view. Waiters take orders for drinks and for pizzas. There's no charge for the pizza, but diners tip the waiters.

The outdoor Terrace Grill (Balcony Grill on *Dawn*) offers cooked-to-order hamburgers and hot dogs, and the patisserie on Plaza Deck offers espresso, cappuccino, and pastries. Sundaes, the poolside ice cream parlor, is a Haagen Daz concession and costs $1.90 a scoop, $2.80 for a double dip.

SERVICE   The ships are staffed by Italian officers, European dining and bar staff, Filipino cabin stewards, and American and British reception and cruise staff. For the most part, the crew is friendly and well trained, especially in the dining room. Service at the reception desk was uneven on the *Sun* and cabin stewards have gotten mixed reviews, depending mostly on the individual. On the *Dawn*, the friendly, smiling cabin stewards, who are almost all Filipinos, consistently garner high praise, as do the European dining staff.

FACILITIES AND ENTERTAINMENT   The Grand Plaza, the heart and hub of the ship from which all other spaces flow, is a good place to get your bearings. Promenade Deck contains only public rooms and is anchored by the two showrooms. On the forward end is the Princess Theatre with an enormous proscenium stage for big, Broadway-style productions. Graduated theatre seating and an absence of pillars ensure fine views from almost every seat.

Passengers on *Sun Princess* are dazzled by *Odyssea*, an original production in the fashion of *Cirque du Soleil*, simulating an underwater circus with amazing feats by a balancing act and a troupe of Chinese acrobats. Another show, *Let's Go to the Movies*, is staged on alternate nights. There's no drink service during performances. Those who sail on the *Dawn Princess* are treated to a new stunt show called *Pirate Island*, with spectacular stunts and special effects. The 55-minute show features a cast of 22. After premiering on *Dawn Princess*, it was scheduled to be added to the *Sun Princess*, *Crown Princess*, and *Regal Princess*.

At the aft end, the marble-walled Vista Lounge with tiered seating and floor-to-ceiling ocean views is a venue for dancing and cabaret-style entertainment. As in the Princess Theatre, there are no columns to mar views. To one side, a large, free-form bar encourages mingling. Shows in both lounges are repeated—four performances each for early and late seating over consecutive days. The ship's program suggests passengers attend according to their dining room seating but some passengers prefer to go back to one show for an encore. Apparently, it has created no seating problem as seldom do all passengers attend all of the performances.

The Grand Casino offers slot machines, video poker, blackjack, roulette, and craps tables. The stained glass ceiling, lit to simulate a spinning roulette wheel, is visible on the deck below from where passengers can reach the casino via a staircase in the second atrium. A bronze tubular sculpture by Arizona artist Lyle London decorates the lower level of the space.

Further along, the ship's second atrium is flanked by the Shooting Stars Disco (Jammers on *Dawn*) and the romantic Rendezvous Lounge (Magnums on *Dawn*). You enter the disco, glittering with fiber-optic lights, via revolving doors that give the effect of entering another world. The disc jockey plays a range of music and, from time to time, dons crazy costumes to get the crowd going. The disco has a video dance floor, rather than a video wall as is typical of most, and it's packed with passengers of all ages, all night long. The elegant Rendezvous Lounge, a quiet refuge across from the action-packed disco, serves caviar and imported wines and champagnes by the glass, as well as other drinks.

The Atrium Lounge embracing the Grand Plaza has a white baby grand and dance floor, providing another venue for drinks and music. It is particularly popular for pre-dinner cocktails and late-night sing-alongs. Afternoon tea is served here, too.

The Wheelhouse Bar near the Princess Theatre is one of the ship's most attractive, inviting rooms. Resembling a British men's club, it is furnished in rosewood and dark burgundy with sumptuous spruce-green leather chairs, brass lamps, and bay windows. The decor creates an ideal setting for the ship models and memorabilia from the historic P&O collection which adorn the walls. The band plays lively dance music which seems a jarring note in a room that would be ideal for quiet conversation over after-dinner drinks. Yet, passengers seem to take to the lively, pub-like atmosphere, packing the dance floor before dinner and late into the night. (Shows how much we know!) A gallery outside the bar has a display of opera costumes worn by Dame Joan Sutherland.

ACTIVITIES AND DIVERSIONS   The wood-paneled Bay View Reading Room (Passages Library, *Dawn Princess*) has a large choice of books plus plush leather "audio chairs" with built-in headsets. You pop in a cassette, recline and listen to music or books on tapes while watching the ocean through the large bay windows. Trumps Card Room (Deck to Deck on *Dawn*) is also used as a meeting room or venue for private cocktail parties. As with all Princess ships, *Sun Princess* offers a full schedule of daytime diversions from art auctions and dance lessons to bridge tournaments and bingo. A computer-equipped Business Center is located on Riviera deck, next to the Beauty Parlor.

SPORTS, FITNESS, AND BEAUTY Some of the most innovative architectural designs are found on the top decks for sports and fitness. One of the ship's three pools, with two whirlpools, is open to the sky and set between two decks with its surface between the health club and the Sun Deck above. The Riviera Deck has the main pools and the ocean-view Riviera Spa (Oasis Spa, *Dawn*). Half of this large area is a gym full of high-tech exercise equipment; the other half is a mirrored aerobics room where classes are held. The spa has 11 massage and beauty treatment rooms, saunas, showers and changing facilities, and an ocean-view beauty salon. Next door, Princess Links, a computerized golf center, simulates play on half a dozen of the world's top courses ($20 per half hour).

Sea-view sunning areas are spread across a trio of top decks with a pool and bar which a live band plays during the day on one and another pool, whirlpool, bar and grill on another. The third has a splash pool and bar along with a paddle tennis/volleyball/basketball court sheltered from the wind. A one-sixth-mile jogging track circles the top deck; a broad teak promenade deck encircles the ship.

CHILDREN'S FACILITIES Love Boat Kids, Princess's fleet-wide youth program, is in full-swing on the new megaliners. *Sun Princess*'s colorful Fun Zone is one of the most enchanting children's playrooms at sea. Here, toddlers and youngsters, ages 2–12, romp in a splash pool and ball jump, play in a fun room with a castle and big-as-life doll's house, and put on performances in a little theatre. Trained counselors supervise the activity for various age groups. Next door, Cyberspace is the teens' own gathering place with organized activities, video games, a disco, and refreshment bar.

POSTSCRIPT Of all the megaliners launched between 1995 and 1997, *Sun Princess* and her twin have met the challenge of reducing behemoth interiors to human scale better than any. *Sun Princess* also proves that big can be beautiful—she's the most beautiful megaliner of all those that have made their debut to date, due in large part to the outstanding Italian workmanship seen in details throughout the vessel. With choices 24 hours a day—in dining, activities, entertainment, and even where to curl up with a good book—anyone who thinks that cruising is too regimented should find happiness on the *Sun Princess*.

Grand Princess (Preview)

Registry: Liberia	Length: 935 feet	Beam: 118 feet
Cabins: 1,300	Draft: 26 feet	Speed: 21 knots
Maximum Passengers: 2,600	Passenger Decks: 16	Elevators: 12
	Crew: 1,150	Space Ratio: 40

THE SHIP   In the ongoing contest for the world's largest cruise ship, the 109,000-ton *Grand Princess* will lay claim to the title when she is launched in spring 1998—at least until a bigger one comes along. She will also be the first Princess ship too large to transit the Panama Canal. But the *Grand Princess* will be much more than just another big ship; she will come with many innovations even more exciting than those of the *Sun Princess* group.

On the *Grand Princess*, 710 outside cabins, or 70 percent, have verandas—the largest number of private balconies on any cruise ship, and the standard size of these cabins is 254 square feet, a spaciousness that is generally available only in deluxe suites.

The *Grand Princess* has three main dining rooms along with nine other venues serving various types of food, ranging from a pizzeria and an ice cream parlor to the bistro-style Horizon Court, the innovative 24-hour alternative dining facility which Princess introduced on the *Sun Princess*.

Grand Princess will offer shows nightly in three different locations, along with a sports bar, a golf club with putting green and full-scale golf simulator, as well as a virtual reality arcade featuring a motion-based ride simulator accommodating 18 people at a time.

The ship will have Princess's new "Grand Class Gold" butler service for suites and mini-suites, provided by a specially trained staff. This will include special services and amenities normally found in five-star hotels and on the most luxurious ships. Among them are polishing golf clubs, in-suite afternoon tea service, developing film, posting mail, booking shore excursions, and valet services, as well as personalized stationery and luxury bath amenities.

Two unusual design features will make her profile distinctive: the wraparound Promenade Deck extends all the way forward to the tip of the bow, giving the ship sleek, flowing lines. Suspended high over the stern like the skybox of a stadium is a glass-sheathed observation lounge which becomes the disco in the evening, It will have spectacular, unobstructed views to all sides.

The *Grand Princess* is spending her inaugural season in Europe, cruising the Mediterranean on 12-day itineraries between Barcelona and Istanbul with overnights in both cities and calls at Monte Carlo, Florence, Naples/Capri, Venice, Athens, and Kusadasi (Turkey). She will have a London-to-Istanbul sailing, make a Barcelona-to-New York voyage, and then make her American debut in New York on September 24.

RADISSON SEVEN SEAS CRUISES

600 Corporate Drive, No. 410, Ft. Lauderdale, FL 33334
(305) 776-6123; (800) 477-7500; (800) 333-3333; fax (305) 772-3763
http://www.asource.com/radisson/

TYPE OF SHIPS   Unusual small ships with big-ship facilities.

TYPE OF CRUISES   Quiet, ultradeluxe, destination-oriented, atypical cruises combining personal service and intimate ambience with sophisticated amenities; classic cruises on traditional routes and light adventure to far-flung corners of the world.

CRUISE LINE'S STRENGTHS

- service
- itineraries
- superb cuisine
- single, flextime/open-seating dining
- all-inclusive prices with bar/fine wines on *Diamond* and *Song of Flower*
- *Diamond*'s alternative dining
- all-outside luxurious accommodations and amenities
- low-key ambience

CRUISE LINE'S SHORTCOMINGS

- lack of promenade or outdoor wraparound deck
- limited lounges and public rooms
- limited entertainment and shipboard activities
- *Diamond*'s hotel—rather than ship—interior ambience
- cuisine on *Hanseatic*

FELLOW PASSENGERS   Three distinct ships were brought together under one umbrella in January 1995, joined by a fourth in 1996. Among their similarities is the type of passengers to whom they appeal: affluent, well educated, well traveled, 45 years and older, with $100,000+ income who travel as individuals, cherishing their individuality and shunning group or mass travel. And there are subtle differences, too.

Radisson Diamond's passengers might be slightly more affluent, senior executives, professionals, and high-end resort vacationers. Typical age is 50+; over 75 percent are Americans, others are an upscale international mix. They usually have cruised before on luxury liners, have sophisticated tastes, and care about an elegant ambience and service. Some are likely to be winners of incentive travel awards.

Song of Flower's passengers are active, CEOs and other successful types, retired or semiretired. Average age is 62 and most come from California, Florida, New York, Illinois, and Texas. Passengers during the Asia season tend to be even more seasoned travelers than those cruising Europe. They travel extensively, several times a year, on cruises as well as on other trips, and are interested in foreign cultures. They share a certain ageless quality in that they are involved with the world and are quite active, interesting individuals. They have refined tastes and care about service but may prefer slightly homier surroundings than *Diamond* passengers. Some have not cruised before. Many are repeaters.

Bremen and *Hanseatic*'s passengers are in the affluent 50+ age group and are more adventurous than *Diamond* or *Song of Flower* passengers. They are particularly interested in natural history and committed to preserving the environment. Among the American contingent, passengers are likely to be from California and the Northeast corridor; 50 percent and more are German or other Europeans, although not necessarily on all cruises. They are motivated by the destination, but they like and have the means to get there in luxury and comfort.

Recommended For   Upscale, independent, active, seasoned travelers accustomed to luxury and quality. Small-ship devotees who appreciate the advantages and willingly accept the limitations of small ships, seeing them as assets rather than shortcomings. Pacesetters, trendmakers, and those who dare to be different for *Diamond*; intellectually curious, culturally inclined for *Song of Flower*; ecology attuned for *Hanseatic*.

Not Recommended For   Joiners, people who need to be entertained or want a full day of shipboard activity or those who seek social action of a large, mainstream ship. Those who thrive in a Las Vegas atmosphere.

CRUISE AREAS AND SEASONS   Asia, Caribbean, Transcanal, Galápagos, South America, Tahiti, and Antarctic in winter; Mediterranean, Northern Europe, Norwegian Fjords, Arctic, Iceland, Greenland in summer.

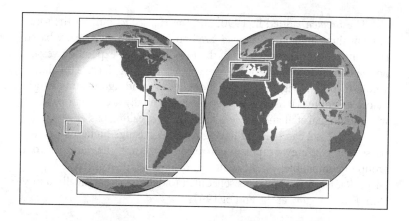

THE LINE In 1995, Radisson Diamond Cruises and Seven Seas Cruise Line merged operations to form Radisson Seven Seas Cruises. The merger represented an expansion in the cruise industry by Radisson Hotels International, while the new cruise line brought three distinct niches—contemporary, traditional, and light adventure—in the luxury cruise market under one umbrella.

The unique *Radisson Diamond*, with its futuristic appearance, was planned primarily for the corporate meeting and incentive market. It combines the amenities of a larger ship with the intimacy of a small one in a contemporary, elegant setting, and offers innovative short cruises in the Caribbean, Panama Canal, and Mediterranean.

The unusual ship was designed and built by Diamond Cruises, which teamed up with Radisson Hotels International to manage and market it. When the corporate market failed to materialize sufficiently, the line changed course and sought affluent, seasoned travelers who care about and are accustomed to luxury and fine cuisine and like to travel in a quiet, sophisticated environment.

The highly acclaimed *Song of Flower*, recognized as one of the best values among luxury cruises, offers traditional, personalized cruises in a refined setting to some of the world's most interesting ports in Europe and Asia. Begun in 1990 by a wealthy Japanese businesswoman who established its high standards, Seven Seas Cruise Line quickly made its mark offering ultradeluxe cruises at rates considerably lower than its competitors and winning accolades and awards after only its first year. Now owned by K Line (one of Japan's largest shipping companies) and its only passenger ship, *Song of Flower* cruises are designed entirely for American and European travelers; Japanese passengers are few.

The *Bremen*, added in 1996, and the *Hanseatic*, built at the same Finnish shipyard as the *Diamond*, are both operated by Germany-based Hanseatic Tours. They are two of the most luxurious expedition vessels on the high seas, offering adventure cruises to remote locales on almost a pole-to-pole navigation of the globe and including far-flung exotic places en route. Hanseatic's cruises are essentially a German product with a bilingual staff and services for English-speaking passengers.

Each vessel can boast of having among cruising's highest space-to-passenger and crew-to-passenger ratios. Together, they add up to a group of compatible, yet different and distinctive, deluxe cruise experiences. Radisson Seven Seas is scheduled to debut another small, luxury ship, *Paul Gauguin*, at the end of 1997.

The Fleet	Built/Renovated	Tonnage	Passengers
Bremen	1990	6,752	184
Hanseatic	1993	9,000	188
Paul Gauguin	1997	18,800	320
Radisson Diamond	1992	20,295	354
Song of Flower	1986/1990	8,282	170

STYLE   The size and small number of passengers sailing on the ships, as well as the price, ensure a certain atmosphere of exclusivity. They also help to define the high level of service and personal attention passengers expect and receive.

Shipboard life on the *Diamond* is elegant but relaxed, informal during the day, formal in style (although not necessarily in dress) in the evening. The exceedingly spacious surroundings are luxurious, the service pampered, the ambience sophisticated. The ship has developed a band of loyal fans and consistently gets rave reviews for its cuisine.

Classy and elegant but unpretentious, *Song of Flower* has been described as having the air of confidence and calm of "old money" at an exclusive club. Its small size, shallow draft, and maneuverability enable it to go where large ships cannot. The *Bremen* and *Hanseatic*'s style is decidedly more European. Daytime has everyone in an adventure mode and dress; nighttime brings out conservative fineries. The *Paul Gauguin* is expected to fit well with the group, combining the luxury of the *Diamond* and *Song of Flower* with the spirit of adventure of *Bremen* and *Hanseatic*, yet have its own distinct character.

DISTINCTIVE FEATURES   No-tipping policy. Extensive book and video libraries. Open bridge policy. *Diamond*'s revolutionary design and its marina; *Song of Flower*'s inclusive prices cover even cigarettes and postage stamps. *Hanseatic*'s 14 Zodiacs. *Diamond, Paul Gauguin, Song of Flower* watersports platform/marina.

RATES

Highest Per Diem	Lowest Per Diem	Average Per Diem
$751	$316	$474

The above per diems are calculated from the cruise line's nondiscounted *cruise-only* fares on standard accommodations. What you will actually pay *should* be *substantially* less (see Part One, How to Get the Best Deal on a Cruise). Per diems vary by season, by cabin location, and by cruise areas.

Special Note: All tips and beverages (including alcoholic drinks) are included in the cruise fare on the *Song of Flower* and the *Radisson Diamond*. Tips and most shore excursions are included on the *Hanseatic*.

Diamond *Special Fares and Discounts*

- Early-booking discounts, 120 days in advance, offer deeper discounts for higher cabin categories, and range from $500–$1,300 per person.
- Single Supplement: Specific amounts per cruise listed in brochure.

Packages

- Air/Sea: Yes.
- Pre/Post: Two-night hotel packages in main gateways.

Song of Flower *Special Fares and Discounts*

- Early booking savings of $500 per person and on combined cruises.
- Third Person: 50 percent of fare.
- Single Supplement: 25 percent surcharge on published per person fare on all but two top categories.

Packages

- Air/Sea: Yes.
- Pre/Post: Yes.

Bremen *and* Hanseatic *Special Fares and Discounts*
- Early booking saves from $350–750 per person. Two or more cruises combined has additional savings.
- Third Person: 50 percent of per person fare.
- Single Cruise Fares: published for each cruise.

Packages
- Air/Sea: All cruise fares include round-trip airfare from 79 North American cities, one precruise hotel night, transfers. Most cruises include Zodiac excursions.
- Pre/Post: Yes.

Past Passengers Radisson Seven Seas Society, the club for repeat passengers, publishes a newsletter, and throughout the year members are offered special sailings with value-added incentives and special prices. Some of these sailings are hosted by the line's president. They also receive quality gifts based on the number of days they cruise.

THE LAST WORD The *Diamond* is so different it is hard to compare it to other cruise ships. Does the design provide advantages over conventional cruise ships? On balance, no. However, the ship exceeds expectations in spaciousness, comfort, and cuisine. Single, open-seating dining, wine with dinner, and a gracious setting are further attractions. The choice of *Diamond* becomes one of selecting something really different or sticking to the tried and true, such as *Song of Flower*, which offers a traditional cruise experience and value. The *Bremen* and *Hanseatic*, on the other hand, are almost totally destination-driven and even then, they are for people whose goal is to visit the most remote, hardest-to-get-to places around the world in complete comfort.

Radisson Seven Seas Standard Features

Officers *Bremen, Hanseatic*/European; *Diamond*/Finnish; *Song of Flower*/Norwegian; *Paul Gauguin*/French.

Staffs Dining & Cabin/European. *Bremen, Hanseatic*: Cruise/European. *Diamond*: Cruise/American. *Paul Gauguin*: Cabin/International; *Song of Flower*: Dining/European and Filipino; Cruise/American and British.

Dining Facilities One dining room (*Paul Gauguin* two dining rooms) with open seating for three meals; informal indoor/outdoor cafe for buffet breakfast and lunch. Reservations-only alternative dining on *Diamond*.

Special Diets Can be accommodated with advance notice.

Room Service 24-hour service with full-meal, in-cabin dining.

Dress Code Casual by day; most evenings jacket required for men. Formal/semiformal for captain's parties. Visits in some ports of call may require women to cover heads, legs, and arms.

Cabin Amenities Direct-dial phone, hair dryer, television, VCR, radio, stocked minibar (*Bremen, Hanseatic, Paul Gauguin* with nonalcoholic); marble bathroom with tub and shower, except *Song of Flower* lowest category with showers. *Diamond*, CNN, safe. *Song of Flower*, flowers & fruit; bathrobes. *Diamond, Hanseatic*, all suites; *Hanseatic*, butler on Bridge Deck. *Paul Gauguin*, verandas, terry robes, safe.

Electrical Outlets 110 AC; *Hanseatic*, 220 AC (converters available).

Wheelchair Access One cabin, *Bremen*; all other, two cabins, except *Song of Flower* limited facilities.

Recreation and Entertainment Nightclub, cabaret and piano entertainment in two lounges, small casino except *Hanseatic*, dancing, card games, backgammon, book/video library, lecture program.

Sports and Other Activities One outside pool. See text.

Beauty and Fitness Beauty salon. Small gym. See text.

Other Facilities Business center on *Diamond*; boutique; hospital.

Children's Facilities None.

Theme Cruises None.

Smoking Sections designated in public areas; no cigar or pipe smoking in dining room; nonsmoking cabins on *Song of Flower*.

Radisson Seven Seas Suggested Tipping No-tipping policy; tips for special service on *Diamond*; none accepted on *Song of Flower* and *Hanseatic*.

Credit Cards For cruise payment and on-board charges, American Express, Diners Club, Mastercard, Visa, plus Discover Card on *Diamond*.

Radisson Diamond

	Quality Rating	Value Rating
Radisson Diamond	❾	D

Registry: Finland	Length: 420 feet	Beam: 103 feet
Cabins: 177	Draft: 26 feet	Speed: 12.5 knots
Maximum Passengers:	Passenger Decks: 3	Elevators: 4
350	Crew: 192	Space Ratio: 58

THE SHIP   If you were the first to fly the Concorde or are on a list for a trip to the moon, you may want to try the *Diamond*, which has the most revolutionary design of any cruise ship built in this century. Sitting high above the water on twin hulls, this ship looks so unusual, people seeing it for the first time stop dead in their tracks in puzzlement.

Diamond's design uses swath (Small Waterplane Area Twin Hull) technology intended to provide less motion, engine noise, and propeller vibration, and greater stability than conventional cruise ships. Does it? Well, maybe. The design has trade-offs. The top cruising speed is slightly over 12 knots per hour, about 40 percent slower than that of most cruise ships. The slow pace puts constraints on the ship's itineraries, limiting its range and flexibility. Moreover, the ship's machinery is located in both hulls but there is no underwater connection between the two. To get from one hull to the other, the operations staff must climb the stairs to the main structure, cross over, and go down into the other side.

The good news is that the ship is unusually spacious, its cuisine superb, and its cabins are among the largest, most elegant on the high seas. Indeed, the interior of the *Diamond* looks and feels almost more like a luxury hotel, complete with a meeting center and boardroom, than a cruise ship. The striking interiors combine contemporary and art deco styles with the finest fabrics, such as Thai silk, throughout the ship. A five-story atrium at the heart of the ship at the entrance contains the reception desk, two glass-enclosed elevators, and a winding staircase of ebony and brass handrails that lead to all decks, including the spa and jogging track at the top.

ITINERARIES   Caribbean, Panama Canal, Costa Rica, transatlantic, Mediterranean.

- *Mid-November–December and February–March:* The *Diamond* sails round trip from San Juan on various itineraries of four- to seven-nights in the Eastern Caribbean. In mid-December, she adds a series of seven- to nine-day transcanal and Costa Rica cruises, round trip from Ft. Lauderdale or San Juan.
- *April:* Transatlantic positioning cruises, eastbound, San Juan/Las Palmas to Cannes; November, westbound, Rome to Las Palmas/San Juan.
- *May–October:* Europe. *Diamond* sails on a series of 4–15-day segments in the Mediterranean from Cannes and Barcelona, followed by wine cruises in Bordeau and Channel Isles, Baltic, Scandinavia, and Russia; and the Eastern Mediterranean between Athens, Istanbul, and Rome. Most itineraries are successive and can be combined into longer cruises.

Home Ports   San Juan and other ports, depending on itinerary.
Port Charges   Caribbean, $66–300; Panama, $240–360; transatlantic, $225–475; Europe, $100–295.

CABINS   The *Diamond* has six categories of cabins; five categories are designated according to their location (Deck 7, 8, or 9). All are large outside suites, either with a veranda or with a larger sitting area instead of veranda, and fitted with twin beds that can be converted to queen size. The lounging area has a sofa, chairs, and large bay windows that look out on panoramic views.

Quietly elegant in decor of fine, high quality fabrics, the suites are very comfortable and have the amenities of a luxury hotel, including a refrigerator stocked with beverages and complimentary initial minibar. Storage space is generous, but given the posh level of the suites—and compared to other new ships in this price range—the bathrooms are something of a letdown, even though they have marble vanity, hair dryer, retractable clothesline, bathtub, and shower.

All suites have entertainment systems with closed-circuit, remote-controlled, five-channel television with CNN and VCR, stereo/radio, CD player, dressing table, international direct-dial telephone, and safe. Two executive suites have king-size bed, whirlpool tub, balcony, and bay window.

Room service, available 24 hours daily, is prompt and efficient. It offers an extensive menu of hot and cold items, including freshly baked pizza, and full course meals from the dining room menu during regular meal hours.

Specifications 177 outside cabins (123 with verandas); 2 executive suites. Standard dimensions are 245 square feet including veranda or separate sitting area. All with twin beds, most convertible to queens. None accommodate third/fourth person; no singles. Two are designated for disabled.

DINING The spacious Grand Dining Room, with high ceilings and an expanse of floor-to-ceiling windows embracing the sea at the stern, is one of the most elegant rooms afloat. Decorated in soft colors and fine silk appointments, the superb service, gracious ambience, and generous space between tables adds to the luxury and feeling of exclusivity, as in a grand European hotel. Seating is open; neither times nor tables are assigned. That adds to the luxury, too.

Superb gourmet cuisine, on par with top restaurants in New York or Paris, is the ship's most outstanding feature. Selections are changed daily and include the finest fresh seafood and prime meats. The preparation is as varied and sophisticated as the presentation; fresh pasta dishes are prepared daily at lunch and dinner. Wine with dinner is included in the price.

The Grill on the top deck has an informal atmosphere and offers indoor/outdoor dining from full menus and elaborate buffets for breakfast and lunch. In the evening, the Grill becomes an Italian specialty restaurant, complete with red tablecloths and singing waiters, as a dining alternative, reservations-only at no extra charge. Heading the Grill team is Nino, the ship's former maître d'hôtel, who has his own fan club from his days with the former, prestigious Home Lines, and exuberant Don Vito, the original Italian showman chef. The Grill is very good and very popular and lots of fun. You must reserve by noon on the day you wish to dine; only 50 people can be accommodated. The menu changes daily and features many different pastas, each one better than the next.

SERVICE The ship's senior hotel and dining staffs, who are mostly Italian, come from years of service on some of the best-known luxury ships. The wine steward and barmen are European and Filipino.

Most cabin and dining room attendants are women—from Austria, Germany, and Sweden; most are working on a ship for the first time. They are courteous, smiling, and eager to please but lack the polish of the senior staff. Given the size of the ship, the cruise director must be an omnipresent one-man show, serving as master of ceremony, DJ, and father-confessor—and he is.

FACILITIES AND ENTERTAINMENT   In the initial planning for conference groups, the space that might have accommodated more public lounges was sacrificed for meeting rooms. Nonetheless, there are ample bars and lounges for a ship of this size.

Windows, at the forward end of the ship, is the largest lounge and takes its name from a wall of windows—something of a waste since the room is used mostly in the evening. The split-level lounge has a bar on the upper level "U" that overlooks a small dance floor and orchestra a few steps below. It is a popular gathering spot for cocktails when a small combo plays dance music, and for after-dinner cabaret entertainment. It becomes the late-night disco, as well.

One deck up, The Club, a piano bar and lounge, features a singer/pianist most nights and makes a comfortable rendezvous for relaxation and conversation most any time. Passengers can also try their luck at roulette, blackjack, and slots in the small Chips Casino.

ACTIVITIES AND DIVERSIONS   Some people find the lack of daily, organized recreation an asset; others could be bored when the ship is not in port. Depending on the itinerary, there are educational and cultural lectures by guest experts—James Michener, for example—in the Constellation Center (the meeting facility), a bridge instructor, card games, and backgammon.

The library has a good selection of books and videotapes, available 24 hours a day with no checking in/out required, for viewing on the VCR and television in your suite. There is also an underwater viewing room. International art works are on exhibit in the Art Gallery.

The ship has a full-service meeting/business center with state-of-the-art audiovisual equipment, publishing facilities, facsimile and communications services, satellite communication facilities, personal computer hookups, desk facilities, and staff support.

SPORTS, FITNESS, AND BEAUTY   At sea, passengers can enjoy a European-style spa with herbal wraps, body massages, and other beauty treatments and pampering at additional fees. The spa has a sauna and steam room and offers daily aerobics, yoga, and other exercise at no charge. The gym has exercise equipment, an outdoor jogging track, a swimming pool, and Jacuzzi.

The *Diamond* has a retractable, hydraulically operated, free-floating marina platform, used for water sports in calm waters, weather permitting. The watersports include waterskiing, sailing, and windsurfing. Other sport facilities include a golf driving range with nets and putting green, shuffleboard, and table tennis. In some locations, passengers with dive certification can enjoy scuba diving.

SHORE EXCURSIONS   Depending on the itinerary, *Diamond* offers a wide selection of sightseeing and sports options.

POSTSCRIPT   By putting the emphasis on superb cuisine and polished service, *Diamond* has found a steadily growing market niche among a certain sophisticated, seasoned traveler at the top end of the income bracket. They are accustomed to the best, have cruised previously on other luxury lines, like their space, savor fine cuisine, prefer to operate on their own juices, and do not want or need an action-packed agenda or large-scale entertainment. Young singles, first-time cruisers, and those who want a full day of shipboard activity should look elsewhere.

Song of Flower

	Quality Rating	Value Rating
Song of Flower	9	B

Registry: Norway	Length: 409 feet	Beam: 52.5 feet
Cabins: 100	Draft: 15 feet	Speed: 17 knots
Maximum Passengers: 172	Passenger Decks: 6	Elevators: 2
	Crew: 144	Space Ratio: 48

THE SHIP   Judging by passenger response, *Song of Flower* has found the key to cruise heaven: exceed passengers' expectations and prove that good things do, indeed, come in small packages. Low key, elegant but unpretentious, the small ship offers superb service that is never ostentatious and outstanding cuisine. It sails on diverse itineraries that combine popular with less-traveled routes—and puts it all together in one package that includes everything down to tips, brand-choice liquors, fine wine, and even postage stamps, at reasonable prices well below any of its high-priced competitors.

Formerly the *Explorer Starship* of the now defunct Exploration Cruise Line, which launched her in 1986, *Song of Flower* was refurbished from stem to stern when she was acquired in 1989 for the new cruise line, Seven Seas. Now owned by K Line America, Inc., a subsidiary of the Japanese worldwide freight and container giant, she is the company's only cruise ship. In 1994, Seven Seas took on the North American marketing of the *Hanseatic*, a small ship offering adventure-in-luxury cruises. At the start of 1995, the two ships joined *Radisson Diamond* to form a new cruise line.

Large enough to offer a variety of public rooms and activities, the *Song of Flower* is still small enough to convey the genuine feeling of a small ship with a friendly, easy-to-approach ambience, which passengers feel from the moment they board the ship. Perhaps that—and the high staff-to-passenger ratio—accounts for passengers' astonishment when the ship delivers the kind of pampering they dream about and at prices, while not cheap, that make people feel they have gotten their money's worth.

Handsome but understated, the *Song of Flower* has tasteful, pleasing appointments enhanced by beautiful arrangements of fresh flowers everywhere. The decor was created by the well-known Norwegian designer, Petter Yran of Yran and Storbraaten, who was also responsible for the *Seabourn* and *Sea Goddess* twins. Public rooms and cabins are distributed on five of the ship's six decks. The attractive Main Lounge on Promenade Deck is the largest room and is used for most functions and evening entertainment.

The ship has designed a cornucopia of interesting cruises that have just the right mix of familiar and exotic ports to attract a wide audience and to keep happy passengers coming back. With its size and shallow draft, it can move into areas where large ships cannot go. The ship also carries a large tender, which expedites conveying passengers to shore when tendering is necessary.

ITINERARIES   7–14 days, Europe, May–October; Middle East to Asia, November–December; Southeast Asia, December–March; India to Arabia, March–April. *Song of Flower* has diverse itineraries calling at more than 130 ports, sailing in almost a contiguous series between Europe and Asia, from London and Stockholm to Singapore and Hong Kong with segments in Indonesia, Thailand, Burma, China, Vietnam, India, the Red Sea, and Suez Canal to the Mediterranean and Black Sea, around Europe to Scandinavia, the Baltic, the Norwegian fjords and Russia, to name a few. Most itineraries are successive and can be combined into longer cruises.

Home Ports   Varies, depending on itinerary.
Port Charges $175–295.

CABINS *Song of Flower* offers six categories of cabins and price levels—a feature that distinguishes it from its all-suite competitors and is seen as an asset, because it enables the ship to attract a wider audience than those with only one type of accommodation at one price.

Song of Flower's choices range from twins with shower, to veranda suites, to some with two baths. Yet, all are outside and amidships or forward, away from engine noise and all have the same amenities: television with CNN and other cable access, VCR, direct-dial phone, hair dryer, and bar-refrigerator replenished daily with passenger's brand choice of beverages at no additional charge. There is ample drawer and closet space, good lighting, mirrors, and such thoughtful additions as umbrellas, slippers, robes, hats and sun visors, along with fine toiletries, fresh fruit, and flowers, also replenished daily.

The spacious cabins are dressed in muted pastels and fitted with blonde furniture giving them a light, airy look. The ten two-room suites on the main deck have a sitting room and two baths, one with a bathtub and the other, a half-bath with shower. The ten veranda suites are topside on the Observation Deck and have bathrooms with full bathtub and shower. Sliding-glass doors open onto their private terraces.

Standard cabins on main and two upper decks have picture windows and bathtubs; those in the lower category have showers and portholes and are located on Galaxy Deck along with the dining room.

Specifications 100 outside cabins (including 10 suites with private veranda; 10 suites with sitting area and 2 baths). Standard dimensions, 200 square feet. 80 with twin beds (30 convertible to doubles); some cabins with convertible sofa bed for third person. No singles.

DINING Like the rest of the ship, the Galaxy Dining Room has a quiet, inviting ambience and accommodates all passengers in a single, open seating with flexible hours, enabling them to dine whenever and with whomever they please, as in a restaurant. Piano background music accompanies lunch and dinner. Tables are set with fine china and silver on well-starched white linen and brightened with fresh flowers. There are tables for two; most accommodate four or six.

The cuisine is excellent with widely varied menus that feature fresh local products bought daily, when practical; the presentation is as splendid as the taste. The emphasis is on quality rather than quantity, although one would hardly say there was any lack of choices when a typical dinner menu has three appetizers, three soups, two salads, a sorbet, four main entrees, three or four desserts, plus ice creams and petit fours. Special requests can be handled but you should make them in advance.

The wines (included in the cruise price) served at lunch and dinner are of good quality and the sommelier, who takes the time to explain the choices for each meal, is diligent about serving and replenishing your glass. The dining room has a cappuccino/espresso machine.

Breakfast and lunch (with the same selections as in the dining room) are served in a casual outdoor cafe on Sun Deck, weather permitting. Lunch offers additional items, such as pasta and a main course, changed daily. An elegant tea is served in the afternoon and the midnight buffets may feature a variety of specialties, such as pizza or sushi. Room service has an extensive menu, available 24 hours.

SERVICE Most passengers rank service, which is superb throughout the ship, as the *Song of Flower's* most outstanding feature. The staff is primarily European and Filipino in the dining room and bar and Scandinavian stewardesses care for the cabins.

From the captain, who maintains an open deck, to the dining room and cabins, the staff members are polished and professional—most having come from other prestigious ships or private yachts. Yet, it's their friendly, caring manner that endears them so much to passengers. They are consistently attentive but never intrusive, anticipating needs and handling requests quickly. Nothing, it seems, is impossible.

Since all gratuities are included in the cruise fare, the staff neither expects or accepts tips. That tells you they are not being gracious and attentive for tips, but rather, because they take pride in their work, like their job, and want to put their best foot forward. It makes you wonder why more cruise lines don't adopt the same policy.

The only fly in the ointment can be the precruise arrangements. The trials and tribulations which one passenger related to us could have been enough to make some people cancel their cruise. However, the passenger said she was glad she did not cancel because once on board the cruise went like clockwork.

FACILITIES AND ENTERTAINMENT The Main Lounge, the showroom, is large enough to accommodate all passengers at one time. It has expansive windows, which make it a pleasant, quiet place to sit by day. It is used for early evening receptions, as well.

Cabaret shows are staged nightly and feature amiable performers—dancers, vocalist, magician, puppeteer, comedian, and other entertainers (some of whom double as shore excursion hosts). The entertainment is not brilliant but enough for the small ship and its audience. The Night Club, on main deck, is a piano bar and lounge, popular for cocktails and after-dinner drinks with lively entertainment;

it doubles as the late-night disco. The casino offers roulette, blackjack, and slot machines.

By day the Observation Lounge, which is topside forward, is the most popular perch for viewing the passing scenery through an expanse of windows on three sides. It is especially pleasant for tea when the soft afternoon light bathes the room.

ACTIVITIES AND DIVERSIONS   Planned daytime activities are modest as the ship is in port on most days. Also, passengers on small ships tend to socialize with one another more than on larger ships and don't seem to need much organized activity to keep busy. Depending on the cruise, the ship has guests lecturers who are experts on the area being visited.

The library, aft on Promenade Deck, is well stocked with books and videos and is open around the clock. There is a small card and reading room and a boutique.

SPORTS, FITNESS, AND BEAUTY   The ship has a heated swimming pool and a large whirlpool tub on Sun Deck. To one side is a bar, to the other, a small but adequate health club with exercise equipment including Lifecycles, Stairmaster, weights, and a sauna. The ship also has a golf driving range.

In warmer climates, a watersports platform—equipped with four jet skis, windsurfing boards, snorkeling equipment, and a Zodiac—is lowered into the sea from the rear of the ship. There is no walkaround promenade.

The beauty salon, operated by the London-based Steiner group, offers hair and beauty care, and Shiatsu, Swedish, and deep tissue massage by experienced, licensed therapists—all at additional cost.

SHORE EXCURSIONS   On all Asia and Northern Australia cruises, airfare, all shore excursions, and pre- and postcruise hotel stays are included in the cruise price, making them exceptional values. In Europe, shore excursions are extra and appear to be more moderately priced than those of other cruise lines in the luxury category; guides are uniformly good. The ship's shore excursions cannot be booked in advance. The concierge will arrange tours for passengers to take on their own.

POSTSCRIPT   If you thought you could not afford to cruise on an ultradeluxe boutique ship, *Song of Flower* could change your mind. When you add up all that is included—drinks, tips, and other on-board expenses, the level of service and cuisine, quality of wines and in some areas, such as the Far East, shore excursions, pre- and postcruise hotel, and airfare—you will see its extraordinary value and understand why it has helped to squelch the notion that small, ultradeluxe ships must be very expensive in order to deliver high quality.

The ship is less formal than some of its rivals, but that's good. It's an easier atmosphere in which to relax. If you like small ships, or if you would like to try a small ship to find out if you like them, you would not go wrong starting with the *Song of Flower*. It offers an extraordinary cruise experience for the price, it is likely to exceed your expectations, you'll get your money's worth, and, if it's the right ship for you, you will probably say what most of its fans say—you don't need to look elsewhere. They got this one right.

Hanseatic

	Quality Rating	Value Rating
Hanseatic	⑧	D

Registry: Bahamas	Length: 403 feet	Beam: 59 feet
Cabins: 94	Draft: 15.4 feet	Speed: 17 knots
Maximum Passengers: 170	Passenger Decks: 7	Elevators: 2
	Crew: 125	Space Ratio: 56

THE SHIP   The *Hanseatic*, which made its debut in 1993, is one of the most luxurious, technologically advanced adventure cruise vessels afloat. Marketed in North America by Radisson Seven Seas Cruises, it is operated by Hanseatic Tours of Hamburg, Germany.

The sleek, state-of-the-art vessel is designated "1A1 Super Ice–class," the highest possible rating for a passenger vessel, enabling it to carry passengers into the far reaches of the Arctic and Antarctica, while its shallow draft, small size, and maneuverability allow it to penetrate deep into the Amazon and other rivers inaccessible to most cruise ships. The ship is also said to be one of the most environmentally friendly cruise ships ever built, with a nonpolluting water disposal system, a pollution-filtered incinerator, and full biological treatment plant.

Like the *Song of Flower*, the *Hanseatic* is a small ship offering a high crew-to-passenger ratio and amenities that are typical of small luxury ships. Its rich wood and brass interiors and fine appointments create the atmosphere of a private yacht.

The ship sails on an unusual pattern, traveling north to south from above the Arctic Circle to Antarctica, visiting locales unknown to most cruise passengers and certainly at a new level of luxury for adventure cruises.

The *Hanseatic* has seven passenger decks with public rooms on all of them. The reception and all-purpose Explorer's Lounge is on Explorer Deck, the dining room is one flight below on Marco Polo Deck, and the Columbus Lounge for casual dining is one flight up on Bridge Deck.

Topside, the Observation Deck is a combination sports and sun deck with a small pool and health club. Forward, the Observation Lounge with a 180° span of windows is the ship's most popular room where passengers socialize and relax while viewing the passing scene. The lounge has a library, ocean charts, maps, and a radar monitor to follow the progress of the ship. However, those with a keen interest in the ship's operation can visit the personable captain who maintains an open bridge.

Darwin Hall, a state-of-the-art lecture hall, is located on the lowest deck. The ship also has a small boutique for gifts and clothing.

ITINERARIES   8–24 days, north-to-south circumnavigation of the globe, from the Spitspergen Archipelago and Greenland to Patagonia and the Antarctic. Two or more cruises can be combined.

- *Summer–fall,* Europe and Far North: British Isles, Scandinavia and Baltic Republics, Norwegian fjords, Iceland and Greenland, the Northwest Passage, Alaska and the Russian Far East.
- *Winter*, the Americas: Central America, Costa Rica, Panama, Belize, South America, Chilean fjords, Antarctica and the Falkland Islands, and Cape to Cape.

Home Ports   Various ports, depending on the itinerary.
Port Charges   n.a.

CABINS   The *Hanseatic* has six categories of cabins found on four of the ship's seven decks. All are large, outside cabins with separate sitting areas and large windows. They are furnished with twin or queen beds, writing desk, spacious closets, color television with VCR, and radio. A refrigerator is stocked with complimentary nonalcoholic beverages; the marble bathroom has a full-size bathtub, shower, and hair dryer.

In addition to these features, four deluxe suites have a separate sleeping area, walk-in closets, and a large entertaining area. Butler service is available for suites and for the eight A category cabins on Bridge Deck.

Specifications   90 outside cabins. Standard dimensions, 236 square feet. Some cabins accommodate third/fourth persons; no singles.

DINING   The Marco Polo Dining Room, an attractive setting with large windows on three sides, is at the stern. It accommodates all passengers at a single, open seating with flexible times for three meals. Passengers who have cruised on deluxe ships in the past will find *Hanseatic's* cuisine bland and boring. A self-service salad buffet is available in addition to the regular menu. There is a good wine list, but unlike the other ships in the group, wine on the *Hanseatic* is not included in the price.

Dress in the evening is more formal than is the norm on adventure ships, with men attired in dark suits or jackets and ties and women in cocktail dresses or chic pantsuits.

A casual breakfast and lunch buffet is served in the light and airy Columbus Lounge with an indoor/outdoor seating—when weather permits. It offers the same menu as in the dining room. An English tea with scones is served on fine china with piano background music daily in the Explorer's Lounge; a light, late-night buffet is also offered. Room service offers dining en suite, served course by course.

ACTIVITIES AND DIVERSIONS   Life aboard is casual, unregimented, and leisurely paced with none of the organized fun and games or nightlife that typify mainstream cruise ships. Each cruise is accompanied by a team of lecturers who are part of an extensive lecture program.

They might include naturalists, marine biologists, geologists, zoologists, research scientists, or anthropologists, who make daily presentations with films and slides in Darwin Hall. Documentary and educational films are also shown on cabin video.

Unfortunately, the lecturers are less scholarly than one is accustomed to finding on educational expedition cruises of this nature. On a recent Antarctica trip, some passengers expressed disappointment with the caliber of the speakers. They did note, however, that they were fully briefed on what to expect when they went ashore.

Four tenders and 14 Zodiac landing craft take passengers on excursions ashore from the Far North and the Galápagos to Antarctica. The naturalists serve as guides accompanying shore excursions. In the late afternoon, when passengers return from their excursions, the naturalists and other lecturers recap the day's visit and answer questions.

After dinner, passengers gather in the piano bar or another lounge for chats over drinks or dance to the ship's small band in the Explorer's Lounge. There are usually a guest vocalist and classical pianist who give one or two performances during the week. Current films are shown in the cinema and over closed-circuit television.

SPORTS, FITNESS, AND BEAUTY   Passengers can enjoy a small swimming pool, and a glass-enclosed whirlpool is on Sun Deck. A beauty salon provides hair and beauty treatments for an extra charge. The ship has a small health club with exercise equipment, sauna, whirlpool, and massage therapy.

SHORE EXCURSIONS   A wide variety of shore excursions are provided, taking passengers ashore in the ship's 14 Zodiac landing craft that provide access to remote areas around the world. Parkas and rubberized boots are issued gratis to all passengers on Arctic and Antarctic voyages; snorkel equipment is provided in the tropics.

POSTSCRIPT   *Hanseatic* cruises are designed for passengers seeking new, off-the-beaten-path voyages in comfort. The food is unremarkable, but then, people do not come on unusual adventure cruises for gourmet feasts. Given the remote areas where the ship travels, it normally must carry provisions for two weeks or longer, with a limited amount of fresh products. The ship's staff is bilingual in English and German; menus, announcements, printed material, and daily agendas are made in both languages, when necessary.

Although most cruises are light adventures, many do entail walking, wet landings, and climbing in and out of Zodiacs in remote areas. Anyone with physical limitations or health problems should not underestimate the difficulties they could encounter. The Antarctica itineraries involve traversing the Drake Channel, a notoriously rough stretch of water.

The *Hanseatic's* small size enables passengers to have a more personalized cruise experience than large ships can offer. The congenial atmosphere and shore excursions taken as a group, make it easy to meet everyone aboard, so a certain camaraderie develops effortlessly.

Its maneuverability enables the captain to explore places that are inaccessible to larger ships, giving passengers yet another dimension to their cruise that a large ship cannot provide.

Paul Gauguin (Preview)

Registry: France	Length: 513 feet	Beam: 71 feet
Cabins: 160	Draft: 16.9 feet	Speed: 19 knots
Maximum Passengers:	Passenger Decks: 7	Elevators: 4
320	Crew: 197	Space Ratio: 59

THE SHIP   Named for the French artist whose life and work embodied the romantic spirit of French Polynesia, *Paul Gauguin* is meant to be the most deluxe cruise ship ever to sail the South Sea waters year-round. Its space ratio of 59 is one of the highest of any cruise ship. Her shallow draft will allow access to small, rarely frequented ports in French Polynesia.

Constructed at France's Chartiers de L'Atlantique, the 18,000-ton vessel is owned by a group of French investors and operated by Radisson Seven Seas.

ITINERARY   Seven days, French Polynesia from Tahiti to Bora Bora, Raiatea, and Moorea in the Society Islands, with an overnight visit to Rangiroa. Special inaugural fares start from $2,795 per person, with low cost air add-ons of $195–395 from 79 U.S. gateways.

CABINS   The cabins, measuring 200–249 square feet, are all outside and 50 percent have verandas. Seven suites range from 300–475 square feet, plus private verandas.

Each cabin and suite has queen- or twin-size beds (convertible to queen), marble bath with full-size bathtub and shower, plus terry cloth robes, hair dryer, closed circuit television and VCR, safe, direct-dial telephone, and refrigerator stocked with soft drinks and mineral water.

Stateroom interiors are enriched by classic crown moldings and wood accents, and fitted with finely crafted furnishings, including a love seat, wardrobe, and a vanity/desk.

Specifications   160 outside cabins and suites; 80 with balconies. 1 wheelchair accessible.

DINING   The ship offers single, open seating and dining at leisure, in two restaurants featuring Continental and French cuisine. Both restaurants offer ocean views on three sides, and one boasts floor-to-ceiling windows. In addition, an outdoor bistro provides dining in a casual, open-air cafe atmosphere. There is an espresso bar and 24-hour room service.

FACILITIES AND ENTERTAINMENT   The ship has a main lounge, a semienclosed observation lounge/nightclub with an intimate piano bar, and a casino with roulette, blackjack, and slot machines.

One of the ship's special features is designed for French Polynesia. In tribute to Paul Gauguin and French Polynesia, the Fare (pronounced faray) Tahiti Gallery will be stocked with books, videos, and other materials on the natural wonders and culture of the islands and on the artist.

The ship's enrichment program will include naturalists, artists, and a variety of experts on French Polynesia. Polynesian culture will be featured in shows and on-board performances of Tahitian dancing, music, and traditional arts. The boutique will feature South Sea jewelry and high quality Polynesian gifts.

SPORTS, FITNESS, AND BEAUTY   The ships has a fully equipped fitness center and a separate Carita of Paris salon and spa facility with steam room that will offer massage, facials, and other beauty treatments such as aromatherapy.

In addition to an outdoor pool and splash bar on one of the upper decks, the *Paul Gauguin* has a state-of-the-art retractable marina at sea level where passengers board the vessel's watersports crafts or don dive or snorkeling gear when they participate in the ship's snorkeling and diving program.

Bremen

	Quality Rating	**Value Rating**
Bremen	❼	C

Registry: Bahamas	Length: 366 feet	Beam: 56 feet
Cabins: 82	Draft: 16 feet	Speed: 14 knots
Maximum Passengers: 164	Passenger Decks: 5	Elevators: n.a.
	Crew: 94	Space Ratio: n.a.

The *Bremen* has been described as a world-class private club aboard a first-class exploration cruise ship. Constructed at the Kobe Shipyard in Japan by Mitsubishi Heavy Industries in 1990, the *Bremen* was formerly the popular *Frontier Spirit,* a ship with special exploration capability and luxurious accommodations, built to go where others cannot.

She is rated a Super Ice–class ship (the highest rating possible) which means she can sail in places such as Antarctica. Her 16-foot draft gives her access to the Amazon and Orinoco Rivers and other remote areas, and her on-board Zodiac landing craft allows for spontaneous exploration of the surrounding areas—outings that are accompanied by regional experts.

The ship has a library, lounge, sauna, gym, swimming pool, observation lounge, and one-seating dining room featuring fine cuisine by European chefs. In its 1995 renovations, a pool bar was added and 60 percent of the deck was covered by awnings. Most of the public areas were refurbished.

For an expedition cruise ship her all-outside cabins, measuring 149 square feet, are spacious. All have a sitting and bedroom area with large panoramic windows and private bath which were renovated during the ship's 1995 facelift. Eighteen cabins have private verandas.

All cabins are fitted with closed-circuit television, refrigerator, satellite telephone, writing desk, spacious closets, and a minibar stocked with sodas, and have hair dryer and bathrobe. In addition to the cabin amenities, suites have a large, comfortable entertaining area and separate sleeping area with twin beds convertible to queen.

ROYAL CARIBBEAN INTERNATIONAL

1050 Caribbean Way, Miami, FL 33132
(305) 539-6000; (800) 659-7225; fax (305) 371-7354
http://www.royalcaribbean.com

TYPE OF SHIPS   Superliners and megaliners.

TYPE OF CRUISES   Mainstream, mass market, modestly upscale, wholesome ambience.

CRUISE LINE'S STRENGTHS
- outstanding facilities and activities
- entertainment
- service
- product consistency

CRUISE LINE'S SHORTCOMINGS
- small cabins on older fleet
- limited storage in cabins on older fleet
- impersonal nature of big ships

FELLOW PASSENGERS   Moderately upscale couples and singles from mid-30s–mid-50s and family vacationers with household income of $40,000+. They are active fun-seekers looking for a wide variety of shipboard activities and destinations. Average age is early 40s, but slightly lower on three- and four-night cruises and slightly higher on ten-night or longer trips. In summer, the median age also drops due to the large number of families traveling with children. Less than 25 percent are 60 or older and they are likely to be on cruises of longer than nine nights.

About half of the passengers have taken at least one cruise and a quarter have sailed with RCCL. They are almost evenly divided between men and women and nine out of ten come from North America. Up to 73 percent of the men and 65 percent of the women are married; 16 percent are retired, 36 percent are professional, managerial, or proprietors; 9

percent say they are homemakers. About 50 percent are taking their first cruise, but vacation twice or more annually.

Passengers have changed slightly over the years, with an increase in the frequency of vacations, and a drop in educational level and age when three- and four-night cruisers are factored in. The less expensive, short cruises appeal to a younger crowd, not only because they are more affordable but first-timers take them as samplers before committing to a longer cruise vacation. Occupations also have changed somewhat with the lower costs of short cruises and Breakthrough Fares.

Recommended For Almost anyone taking a first cruise. Those who like large ships or want an array of options with a touch of class. Those who want to be active, sociable, and don't mind large crowds and lines. It's also ideal for families with several generations traveling together, as the diversity of shipboard activities and programs provides something for every age.

Not Recommended For Small-ship devotees; those who seek a quiet or intellectual milieu, hate crowds, and do not have the patience for long lines; those who expect a luxury cruise with five-star amenities.

CRUISE AREAS AND SEASONS Year-round, Caribbean and Bahamas; Mexico; Far East. Summer, Bermuda; Europe; Alaska from Vancouver. Spring and fall, Hawaii; winter, May, and fall, Panama Canal.

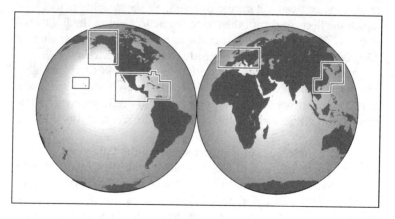

THE LINE Founded in 1969 as a partnership of three prominent Norwegian shipping companies, Royal Caribbean Cruise Line was the first to launch a fleet of ships designed specifically for year-round Caribbean cruising. The ships proved to be so popular that within five years RCCL needed more capacity and got it by "stretching" two vessels. That meant cutting them in half and inserting prefabricated midsections—a method used on cargo vessels, but a first for cruise ships.

For the 1980s RCCL added superliners with unique designs and got a headstart on the 1990s when in 1988 it introduced the *Sovereign of the Seas*, the first of a new generation of megaliners and the largest cruise ship ever built at the time. Few ships in history have received so much attention. Upon her arrival in Miami, the majestic lady stopped traffic for miles with people trying to catch a glimpse of her and honking their horns in welcome.

In the same year, RCCL merged with Admiral Cruises and for the first time began offering short cruises, which had been Admiral's forte. In the bargain, RCCL acquired *Viking Serenade*, which it rebuilt from the hull up, and a brand new ship built specifically for short Bahama cruises. Slightly smaller than its megaliners, *Nordic Empress* came with an eye-popping nine-deck atrium, triple-tiered casino, and a bilevel dining room with floor-to-ceiling windows at the stern.

To get a jump on the twenty-first century, RCCL launched Project Vision for a next generation of six megaliners. Coinciding with the line's twenty-fifth anniversary, *Legend of the Seas*, the first of the group, debuted in May 1995 and quickly became a legend in her own time with acres of glass and cruising's first 18-hole miniature golf course, complete with sand traps and water hazards. By 1998, all six megaliners will have joined the fleet. And with the recent announcement of the Eagle class ships, RCCL becomes the first cruise line ever to build cruise ships of 130,000 tons. The first Eagle is scheduled to enter service in 1999.

Yet, for all its firsts and innovative ship design, RCCL is basically a conservative company that has built its success on having a solid, consistent product with meticulous attention to detail, receiving about every award given, such as Ship or Ships of the Year and Cruise Line of the Year.

After two decades of focusing solely on the Caribbean, the line branched out, first to Bermuda and then to the West Coast, Mexico, Alaska, and Europe. Then, in 1995, it sent a ship to be permanently based in the Far East, and added Panama Canal cruises and seasonal Hawaii ones. To reflect its growth, the line recently changed its marketing name to Royal Caribbean International (the corporate name remains Royal Caribbean Cruises Ltd.) and created a new logo that retains the crown (of its Norwegian origins) and anchor, but in a different presentation. Recently, too, it created a new product, Cruise Hyatt, with Hyatt Hotels in Puerto Rico enabling passengers to combine a three- or four-night hotel stay with a cruise departing from Puerto Rico.

But the biggest surprise came in June of 1997 when the cruise line announced its intention to buy and merge with Celebrity Cruise Lines—a deal worth $1.3 billion that will result in a fleet of 20 ships when all the ships of the two lines, now under construction or on order, enter service by the year 2000. Now and for the forseeable future, Celebrity Cruise Lines will operate as a separate brand, although its ships are likely to sail on new itineraries next year.

Royal Caribbean is a public company, traded on the New York Stock Exchange; however, the majority ownership is still held by one of the original founders, Anders Wilhelmsen and Company, and the Pritzker family of Chicago, who also have controlling interest in Hyatt Hotels.

The Fleet	Built/Renovated	Tonnage	Passengers
Enchantment of the Seas	1997	74,000	1,950
Grandeur of the Seas	1996	74,000	1,950
Legend of the Seas	1995	69,130	1,808
Majesty of the Seas	1992	73,941	2,354
Monarch of the Seas	1991	73,941	2,354
Nordic Empress	1990	48,563	1,606
Rhapsody of the Seas	1997	75,000	2,000
Song of America	1982	37,584	1,414
Sovereign of the Seas	1988/96	73,192	2,276
Splendor of the Seas	1996	69,130	1,800
Sun Viking	1972	18,559	714
Viking Serenade	1982	40,132	1,512
Vision of the Seas	1998	75,000	2,000

STYLE　　RCCL ships are specifically designed for the high-volume, year-round warm weather cruises of the Caribbean, the Bahamas, and Mexico. More recently, the line has taken up seasonal residence in such popular summer areas as Alaska, Bermuda, and Europe.

Now with its new global vision, Royal Caribbean says the "Caribbean" in its name represents a style of cruising, not just a place to cruise. And the "C" could just as well stand for consistency—whether you take a Royal Caribbean cruise in Europe, Asia, or the Caribbean. The atmosphere is friendly and relaxed, and the activities are many and varied with something for everyone.

But make no mistake about it, except for the *Sun Viking*, these are big ships that hum with activities almost around the clock. They have acres of open sun decks, large pools, and lots of outdoor activity—for fun with games and competitions, for fitness as part of the line's Ship-Shape program, and for sports that are often combined with sports in port. For example, through Golf Ahoy! passengers can play golf at courses throughout the cruise line's network. RCCL is the official cruise line of the Professional Golfer's Association of America.

The ships have cheerful, contemporary decor with themes related to Broadway hits, operas, and the circus and enhanced by quality multi-million-dollar art. Cabins are small, but functional, on all but the new Vision group, and all are spotless. All ships have programs for children, which the line seeks in the belief that a happy kid on a cruise now will still be a customer in 2020.

DISTINCTIVE FEATURES   RCCL's signature Viking Crown Lounges; Golf Ahoy! program; *Legend* and *Splendour*'s miniature golf courses; Labadee, RCCL's private beach on the north coast of Haiti. *Crown & Anchor;* lounges in San Juan and St. Thomas. Alternative dining; room service from dining room menus during lunch and dinner; kids program.

RATES

Highest Per Diem	Lowest Per Diem	Average Per Diem
$400	$150	$218

The above per diems are calculated from the cruise line's nondiscounted *cruise-only* fares on standard accommodations. What you will actually pay *should* be *substantially* less (see Part One, How to Get the Best Deal on a Cruise). Per diems vary by season, by cabin location, and by cruise areas.

All prices include port charges.

Special Fares and Discounts

• Breakthrough Fares are capacity-controlled discount rates which change daily and are available through travel agents; they offer up to 40 percent reduction. The earlier you buy a cruise, the better the discount.

- Third/Fourth Person: Yes.
- Children's Fare: Third/fourth person rates, and promotional fares for free travel or as low as $49 or $99 for a child 11 and under.
- Single Supplement: 150 percent when specific cabin requested.
- Single Guarantee: Category and cabin assigned by RCCL.
- Share Fare: RCCL matches persons of same sex and smoking preference.

Packages

- Air/Sea: Yes.
- Cruise-only/Air Add-ons with transfers: Yes.
- Others: Honeymoon, golf, family, wedding. Crowning Touches and Royal Occasions are amenities packages at an extra charge designed for honeymooners or those celebrating a special occasion.
- Pre/Post: In departure port cities and some nearby vacation spots. Cruise Hyatt combines three/four night hotel with cruise.

Past Passengers   Crown and Anchor Society, RCCL's club for repeat passengers, was recently revamped. It has four membership levels based on the number of eligible RCCL cruises you take: Silver membership, after one cruise; Gold after two cruises; Platinum after five cruises; and Diamond after ten or more cruises. There is no cost to join. The biggest benefit is personalized attention by shipboard personnel, *Crown & Anchor* (a quarterly magazine with information on new programs, new itineraries, and new ships) periodic mailings with special offers and coupons, a color-coded landing card sticker, and on seven-night or longer cruises, a special cocktail party during your cruise. In addition to these benefits, Gold members receive other special offers on future cruises; Platinum get terry robes for their use during the cruise; and Diamond receive exclusive coupons, special boarding privileges, and a welcome-aboard bottle of champagne in their cabin.

THE LAST WORD   Royal Caribbean, conservative as it may be in some regards, is a pace-setter among cruise lines, respected by its competitors as much as its friends for its weight and its wisdom. For example, after years of frustration over the discounting games being played, RCCL designed Breakthrough Fares, a capacity-controlled advance booking discount system, which the entire cruise industry adopted instantly—and almost thankfully—because it helped to put some rationality into a chaotic situation. A smaller or less respected line could not have had the same impact.

RCCL is a cruise line of megaliners, and when its new fleet comes on stream in 1999, it will be all the more so. It can no longer sell specific ships, but like all large cruise lines, sells a brand, promising product consistency aimed at appealing to 80 percent of the people buying cruises. Only the two ends of the market are excluded—budget and luxury. But that vision may not be shared by all, particularly its more affluent loyal fans of the past who have seen the product change in terms of service and quality.

There's no denying it, big ships are big and impersonal and they have caused the edge of quality that once separated RCCL from the pack to narrow and blur. If you do not like big ships, this is not the line for you. But, if you want a vacation at sea on ships that have everything, RCCL offers value that's hard to beat.

ROYAL CARIBBEAN INTERNATIONAL STANDARD FEATURES

Officers Norwegian, International.

Staffs Dining, Cabin/International; Cruise/American and British.

Dining Facilities Two seatings for three meals plus midnight buffet; indoor/outdoor cafe with breakfast and lunch buffet. Alternative dining for dinner with table service on all ships except *Son of America* and *Sun Viking*.

Special Diets Low-fat, low-cholesterol, lean cuisine. Full vegetarian menus. Kosher should be requested at time of booking.

Room Service 24 hours with light menu and dining room menus for lunch and dinner.

Dress Code Casual but neat by day; informal in evening with one or two nights formal/semiformal. Tuxedo rental, $75 for week.

Cabin Amenities Direct-dial phone; radio; television (except *Sun Viking*); daily world news update; bathtubs in suites, suites with marble baths on *Majesty, Monarch*.

Electrical Outlets 110 AC.

Wheelchair Access Ramp on all ships; 4 cabins on *Majesty, Monarch, Nordic Empress, Viking Serenade*; 10 on *Sovereign*; 17 on *Legend/Splendour*; 14 on *Grandeur/Enchantment* and *Rhapsody/Vision*.

Recreation and Entertainment Show lounge with entertainment nightly; disco, bingo, horse racing, movies, wine tastings, dance lessons. Viking Crown Lounge, bars/lounges, card room, library.

Sports and Other Activities Two outdoor pools (except *Sun Viking*), *Viking Serenade*, indoor/outdoor pool. Sports deck with basketball, Ping-Pong, shuffleboard, skeet shooting. Miniature golf course on *Legend* and *Splendour*.

Beauty and Fitness Beauty/barbershop; massage; sauna; ShipShape fitness program; jogging track; health club/gym (except *Sun Viking*). Solarium and elaborate Beauty Spa on *Legend* class.

Other Facilities Boutiques; medical facilities; laundry/dry cleaning services; meeting rooms; cinema/theatre on *Majesty, Monarch, Sovereign*.

Children's Facilities Youth programs year-round on all but *Song of America* and *Sun Viking*. Playroom and teen center on *Sovereign* and Legend groups, *Nordic Empress, Viking Serenade*; teen nightclub on *Majesty, Monarch, Viking Serenade* and all Vision Class ships.

Theme Cruises Jazz.

Smoking Public rooms are nonsmoking except in designated areas.

RCCL Suggested Tipping Per person per day, cabin steward, $3; dining room waiter, $3; busboy, $1.50; 15 percent to bar waiters.

Credit Cards For cruise payment and on-board charges, American Express, Carte Blanche, Diners Club, Discover, Mastercard, Visa.

Sovereign of the Seas / Majesty of the Seas
Monarch of the Seas

	Quality Rating	Value Rating
Sovereign	❻	C
Majesty, Monarch	❻	B

Registry: Norway	Length: 880 feet	Beam: 106 feet
Cabins: 1,138/1,177	Draft: 25 feet	Speed: 19 knots
Maximum Passengers:	Passenger Decks: 14	Elevators: 11
2,852/2,744	Crew: 840/822	Space Ratio: 30.8/32.3

THE SHIPS   First, try to grasp the dimensions: three football fields laid end to end and one across. From a lounge 14 decks above the sea, you could look Miss Liberty square in the eyes. At the pier she needs a double berth to park and dwarfs almost every ship in sight. When the *Sovereign of the Seas* was introduced in 1988, she was the largest cruise ship ever built and stirred unprecedented excitement and publicity. More important, the *Sovereign* came with major innovations that have influenced the design of all superliners and megaliners that followed in her wake.

The most exciting feature, a dramatic atrium called the Centrum, was a cruise ship first and the one most quickly copied in new ship design. Located amidships and spanning five decks, the atrium opens the space to create a light and inviting environment. Through the use of glass and muted colors, the stairs and balconies around the atrium and its glass-enclosed elevators seem to be suspended in air. Soft music from a white piano in a garden of tropical foliage at the base of the atrium floats up the stairway to the upper decks and sets the casually elegant, harmonious tone found throughout the ship.

By making the atrium a lobby similar to that of a hotel, it provides the huge ship with a friendly focal point. Passengers are dazzled but not intimidated and the notion of entering a behemoth all but disappears. The atrium also separates the forward section of the ship, which contains the cabins, from the aft section where all the public rooms and dining, sports, entertainment, and recreation facilities reside—an innovative design first used on *Song of America*. The arrangement has several advantages: cabins set away from the action create quieter sleeping areas; in the public areas, walking distances from one location to another are shorter, and, once again, passengers need not confront the ship's enormous size.

Another element: the ship looks outward; very few areas lack natural light or a view to the outdoors. The openness and easy access to open decks lightens the space while it helps passengers relate to the sea—a feature absent on many of today's new ships.

Superb design features that miraculously dispel the *Sovereign's* gigantic size are found throughout the ship. They, together with the incredible array of facilities, explain passengers' immediate acceptance of the new megaliner. Instead of being overwhelmed, they are thrilled.

Sovereign's duplicates, *Monarch of the Seas* and *Majesty of the Seas*, arrived with few changes—a few more cabins, a family suite, and a redesigned Windjammer Cafe—but essentially they are identical, and many of the public rooms even have the same names on all three ships. Following a long-standing RCCL tradition, they are named after Broadway shows and operas. Throughout, the understated decor reflects a timeless yet contemporary elegance with a warm, inviting ambience that has become the trademark of Norwegian designers Njal Eide, Robert Tillberg, and Petter Yran, who were among the seven teams creating the interior decor.

The trio are floating resorts in every sense of the word. They offer so many facilities and activities, it would be impossible for the most frantically active person to participate in all the options offered daily, even if they could keep running on a 24-hour schedule.

The ships make the most of their size by providing spaces for varying tastes. These range from the RCCL signature Viking Crown Lounge perched high on the stack, to the wide, outdoor promenades that encircle the vessels, to the sunny and shaded areas on three decks. So passengers can find their niche, choosing to be at the center of the action or away from it in relative peace and privacy.

The *Sovereign* sisters have similar decor in soothing pastels, but whichever ship or itinerary you chose, the real experience is on board where you can live the good life in megadoses, as one friend put it. In one day, you could start with breakfast in bed; work out in the gym with state-of-the-art equipment; have a massage, facial, and manicure; buy diamonds or duty-free perfume for the folks back home; relax on deck while at the lift of a finger, a smiling waiter brings you another Bloody Mary; take in a movie; and sip champagne and dip caviar in the wine bar before dinner. After a seven-course meal in the dining room, you can two-step or line dance, disco, limbo, or watch the big production number in the show lounge, listen to late-night comedy, or try your luck in the casino, until it's time for the midnight buffet. Robin Leach, eat your heart out.

ITINERARIES

Sovereign   Three and four days, year-round, from Miami on Friday to Nassau and CocoCay; Monday departure (four days), adds Key West.

Home Port   Miami.
Port Charges   Included in cruise price.

Majesty   Seven days, Western Caribbean, year-round from Miami on Sunday to Labadee (Haiti), Ocho Rios, Grand Cayman, and Playa del Carmen/Cozumel (Mexico).

Home Port   Miami.
Port Charges   Included in cruise price.

Monarch   Seven days, Southern Caribbean, year-round from San Juan on Sunday to Martinique, Barbados, Antigua, St. Maarten, and St. Thomas.

Home Port   San Juan.
Port Charges   Included in cruise price.

CABINS   Each of the trio has 16 categories of cabins. *Monarch* and *Majesty* cabins are similar to those on the *Sovereign* in size and decor, but with major enhancements. Verandas were added to 50 deluxe outside cabins on Bridge Deck and suites and family suites sleeping up to six people were created. The latter have two bedrooms and a sitting room, two complete bathrooms, plus a veranda with sliding glass doors. The *Majesty* has 146 cabins in the larger outside category which are considerably more comfortable than those on the *Sovereign*, and all of Bridge Deck contains only suites and deluxe staterooms with private verandas.

Bathrooms, while not large, are well designed with fixtures that provide excellent water pressure and a shower curtain that works. They have plenty of shelves for toiletries, thick towels, and a hair dryer.

Light, airy decor helps to compensate for the small size of the standard cabins, which are designed to make the most out of every inch of space. They are fitted with a vanity table and chair and twin beds with sliding pillowbacks that convert them to couches during the day. Good use of wall space also creates additional storage area.

Sovereign *Specifications*   418 inside cabins, 710 outside; 12 suites. Standard dimensions, inside cabins 119 square feet, outside 122. 945 with twin beds (convertible to doubles); 196 third/fourth persons; no singles.

Majesty *and* **Monarch** *Specifications*   444 inside cabins, 721 outside; 12 suites; 62 deluxe cabins and suites with verandas. Standard dimensions, 120 square feet. 917 with twin beds (convertible to queen); 260 third/fourth persons; no singles.

DINING   RCCL ships do not serve gourmet cuisine and make no boasts that they do; nor is it their aim. Rather, their kitchens turn out tasty food that is plentiful but not excessive with ample variety and choice on menus. All ships have the same menus, regardless of where they cruise (that's consistency at work), although longer European cruises are likely to feature some dishes of the locale and the Far East cruises have oriental selections.

A typical menu has seven juices and appetizers, three soups, two salads, five entrees with a choice of pasta, fish, chicken, veal and beef, three desserts, and a selection of cheese and ice cream. In keeping with its ShipShape program, all menus have light selections annotated with nutritional information regarding calories, fat content, and other such data. One can also choose vegetarian selections, or to have the full vegetarian menu for an entire cruise. The wine list is balanced between California favorites, French and other European wines, and some South American wines. Prices are moderate.

Each of the trio has two dining rooms serving three meals, all with assigned seating. The *Sovereign's* Kismet Dining Room, dressed in rich purple, is adorned with elaborate columns and lighting fixtures; its twin, Gigi Dining Room, in quiet green and white, has columns styled after palm trees. The *Majesty's* Mikado Dining Room takes a Japanese theme while its twin, Maytime, has a springtime theme with a mural of apple trees in blossom and spring colors. The *Monarch's* two dining rooms, by architect Robert Tillberg, offer greater contrast. The Brigadoon Dining Room has a Scottish tartan design and uses frosted glass dividers and gothic arches to break up the space. The Flower Drum Song Dining Room in light yellow, blue, and gray has a mural of Chinese fans that enhances the room's sophisticated, oriental decor. Backlight panels between fluted ornate columns divide the room into more intimate sections.

One of the most noticeable differences between *Sovereign* and her sisters is the two-deck Windjammer Cafe, the scene for casual breakfasts and lunches and for the recently added alternative dinner venue, serving between 6:30 and 10:30 P.M. The indoor/outdoor cafe offers self-service buffets for breakfast and lunch with a variety of hot and cold dishes. The quality of the food is equal to that in the dining room, but selections are more limited and, of course, the ambience is totally different. Dinner, however, has full table service and menus are changed daily.

The Windjammer Cafe, wrapped on three sides by windows and spanning the full width of the ship, was redesigned, expanded, and lightened on the *Monarch* and *Majesty*. In place of *Sovereign's* center-piece—a two-story, mahogany-framed bubble tree (with crystal bubbles and fabric sails suspended above it), the new room on *Monarch* and *Majesty* has a mini-atrium with a winter garden, glass-enclosed water-falls, and a skylight. It is decorated in light aqua and green, giving the room a pleasing and airy appearance.

RCCL has also upgraded room service; now lunch and dinner can be ordered from the full dining room menu.

SERVICE   RCCL's crews, from the Norwegian captains to the front desk to the mini–United Nations that make up the cabin and dining room staff, are courteous and eager to please. A largely Caribbean bunch make up the affable stewards of the *Sovereign* group. They tidy rooms twice a day, and with the evening turn-down service, leave a chocolate on your pillow. They will also bring you continental breakfast, but the 24-hour room service menu is limited mostly to sandwiches and refreshments.

The dining staff has a large number of Europeans and provides friendly, efficient service. Your waiter will know your name after the first dinner, and probably that you prefer the sauce on the side by the sec-ond. The maître d'hôtel is as attentive as your waiter, hovering nearby to grant your every wish. Indeed, the staff is so conscious of the ship's con-stant evaluation of their work, as reflected in passengers' comment cards, that they sometimes overdo their attention. And it is not unlikely that your waiter, when none of his supervisors are around, will all but beg you to fill in your comment cards—with glowing praise, of course.

FACILITIES AND ENTERTAINMENT   Somewhere, almost 24 hours a day, there's music designed to suit every mood from big band, steel band, latin, country, rock, or strolling violins to classical concerts.

The Follies Lounge, *Sovereign's* richly decorated bilevel showroom stages two shows nightly. The week starts with a Welcome Aboard Revue, followed by two big stage Las Vegas and Broadway-type shows, plus a variety of other entertainment, including one show by a headliner such as Diahann Carroll or Phyllis Diller.

Called Sound of Music on the *Monarch*, and A Chorus Line on the *Majesty*, the rooms have video walls with 50 television monitors on two motorized movable banks of 25 screens each. Seating is comfortable with excellent views from all seats except for a few blocked by some columns. Smoking is not permitted in these lounges. Other large lounges, Finian's Rainbow amidships and the Music Man Lounge at the stern, have late-night entertainers and music from blues to country. The Anything Goes nightclub is the late-into-the night disco. The *Monarch's* disco, Ain't Misbehavin', has a glass sculpture of Fats Waller at the piano.

The ships also have small lounges—by the same name and in the same location. The Schooner Bar, with nautical motif and views of the water, is a favorite casual bar by day and a lively piano bar in the evening. It is next to the Casino Royale, which offers blackjack, 170 slot machines, and American roulette. On the *Monarch*, the casino has the action, with neon decor and even carpeting with fiber-optic lights.

For those who like a sophisticated ambience, Touch of Class is a chic little champagne bar where 50 people can clink flutes and scoop caviar. The decor lives up to its name with marble, leather, and two bronze statues of 1920s flappers, so exact they look real.

But the ships' crowning glory is their Viking Crown Lounge, RCCL's unique lounge cantilevered from the funnel stack. Perched 12 stories above the sea, the lounge completely encircles the stack and provides a fabulous 360° view of the sea and sunset. There're also a teen nightclub called Flashes, karaoke, a shopping boulevard, and a theatre where feature films are shown daily.

ACTIVITIES AND DIVERSIONS   Daily activities run the gamut from napkin folding to wine tasting and any number of parlor games, along with bingo, ballroom and line dance classes, bridge, ice carving, singles' parties, kids' parties, teen parties, a costume party, and a passenger talent show. There is a card room and a library resembling a sedate English club with its wood paneling and leather chairs; it can also be used as a meeting room. There are religious services as well.

And for those who want neither activity nor diversion, two levels of sun decks at the bow provide peace, privacy, and a place to catch up on reading or simply watch the world go by.

SPORTS, FITNESS, AND BEAUTY   Fitness folks have a one-third-mile outside deck encircling the vessel, a second jogging track, and one of the best-equipped health clubs at sea, with a large exercise room complete with ballet bars, computerized exercise equipment including stair steppers, bicycles, rowing machines, and an assortment of weight training equipment, plus a high-energy staff to put them through their paces. The sports deck has twin swimming pools, two whirlpools, and a basketball court at the stern. Saunas and locker rooms for men and women are available for use without cost.

ShipShape Fitness activities start with a sunrise stretch class or water exercises, and low-impact aerobics and other programs during the day are timed not to interfere with shore visits. Morning walka-thons, basketball free-throws, and Ping-Pong tournaments round out the program. Participants earn ShipShape "dollars" for each activity, redeemable for T-shirts and visors, as an incentive for those who want to stay fit and have fun doing it. Vitality Unlimited is a class specially designed for senior citizens.

All exercise classes are led by experienced fitness personnel, and all menus offer two low-fat, low-calorie entrees, prepared within the guide-lines of the American Heart Association. The beauty salon/barbershop offers massage and a full line of spa beauty treatments at additional cost.

CHILDREN'S FACILITIES   RCCL was one of the first lines to create a children's program with youth centers, playrooms, and counselors to supervise activities. The *Sovereign* group has the program and coun-selors year-round. They also have video arcades and teen centers, and the *Majesty* and *Monarch* have teen nightclubs.

Kids have their own daily agenda, which is slipped under their cabin door each night. It is packed with activities such as ice cream and pizza parties, dance classes, hat making; golf putting, face painting, Dat-ing Game, midnight basketball, shuffleboard, Ping-Pong, autograph hunts, talent shows, beach parties, and special shore tours. Baby-sitters (at extra cost), cribs, and highchairs are available.

Captain Sealy's Kids' Gallery, a menu for children ages 4–12, offers such favorites as peanut butter and jelly sandwiches, hamburgers, hot-dogs, grilled cheese sandwiches, and pizzas, along with salads, fruit, and alphabet soup. The menu also has word games, puzzles, and crayons.

SHORE EXCURSIONS   Shore excursion booklets are included with the documents mailed to the passenger. The variety of excursions caters to a wide range of interests, but essentially, they are standard, off-the-shelf programs. Except for its golf programs and the cruises that include Labadee in their itinerary, little in RCCL's shore excursions differentiates them from other Caribbean cruise lines. The selection offers island tours, beach trips, snorkeling and diving excursions, among others.

Created in 1987, RCCL's private resort Labadee, on the north coast of Haiti, offers by far the best day at the beach of any line and is very popular with passengers. Its setting is particularly beautiful—an amphitheatre of lush green mountains rises immediately behind a lovely cove with a series of crescent-shaped beaches, providing seclusion and protecting the crystal clear waters of the bay. Here, RCCL built several pavilions for dining, entertainment, and water sports equipment, as well as a marketplace with shops of good quality Haitian art and crafts, which are the best in the Caribbean. Music, dancing, and performances by a local folklore group are provided.

CocoCay is a small island in the Bahamas inherited from Admiral Cruises, where the *Sovereign* spends a day. It has water sports—snorkeling, pedal boats, tubes, floats, and rocket rafts—and a wide range of activities for all ages. There are beach games, shops with native crafts, music by a steel band, visits to an underwater shipwreck with professional snorkeling instructors, a barbecue on a stretch of white sand beach, palm-shaded trails for exploring, six sandy beaches for swimming, and hammocks and beach chairs for lounging. The island is large enough to accommodate those who want to find a secluded spot of their own. Children's programs are provided on the island.

POSTSCRIPT   Royal Caribbean's reputation for delivering a consistent, predictable level of service and quality holds up on all three ships. There are no surprises. But these are megaliners and you will need a certain patience for crowds and long lines, no matter how smoothly RCCL ships operate. At the same time, their sheer size and the array of facilities and activities they offer are treats in themselves.

Nordic Empress

	Quality Rating	**Value Rating**
Nordic Empress	⑥	C

Registry: Liberia	Length: 692 feet	Beam: 100 feet
Cabins: 800	Draft: 25 feet	Speed: 19.5 knots
Maximum Passengers: 2,020	Passenger Decks: 12	Elevators: 7
	Crew: 671	Space Ratio: 30.4

THE SHIP   Created specifically for the short cruise market, the *Nordic Empress* dazzles with its design—from the light that streams in by day to the glitter that turns it on at night. The passengers' first look at the ship focuses on its nine-deck-high atrium, called the Centrum, with four elevators, two of which are glass and overlook a waterfall surrounded by flowers and greenery.

Most of the ship's public rooms flow from here on two center decks that house a bilevel dining room, a bilevel showroom, a trilevel casino, and a series of lounges. Topside, the Sun Deck is designed as a center of activities—day and night—from sunning and swimming and outdoor games to music, entertainment, and dancing under the stars. It also has the fitness center and the kids' center.

ITINERARIES   Three or four days, Bahamas. January–May and mid-September–December, departing from San Juan on Friday for three-day cruises to St. Thomas and St. Maarten. Four-day cruises, departing on Monday, add St. Croix. May–August, three-day cruises depart from Port Canaveral every Sunday to Nassau and CocoCay; four-day cruises depart Thursday and adds a day at sea.

   Home Ports   San Juan; Port Canaveral.
   Port Charges   Included in cruise price.

CABINS   There are a dozen cabin categories with a very high number of inside and lower-priced outside cabins. All are designed to be light and colorful with a tropical feeling. All have two lower beds, color television, three-channel radio, telephone, and private bath. Sixty percent are outside cabins with large picture windows and all suites and deluxe cabins have balconies.

   Specifications   329 inside cabins, 471 outside; 6 suites; 69 deluxe cabins with verandas. Standard dimensions, 194 square feet. 495 with twin beds (all convertible to double); 358 with upper/lower berths accommodating third and fourth persons; no singles; 4 wheelchair accessible.

DINING   The two-tiered Carmen Dining Room, located at the stern, has walls of floor-to-ceiling windows that span two decks and provide 180° of panoramic views. A winding staircase connects the main and mezzanine levels. There are two seatings for the three meals and the same menus as other RCCL ships, including theme dinners and national or regional cuisines.

   Meals and snacks are served around the clock, starting with an early riser's breakfast at 6:30 A.M. and ending with the midnight buffet. A typical seven-course menu has a wide choice of juices and appetizers, soups, salads, pasta, entrees with fish, chicken, veal, and beef, desserts, cheese, and ice cream. All menus have health-conscious selections marked with the ShipShape logo and annotated with nutritional information.

The Windjammer Cafe, where casual breakfast and lunch buffet are available, is located on the top deck at the bow, providing passengers with a view of the port and the ship's arrival while they are enjoying breakfast. The indoor/outdoor cafe is topped with a glass dome. The café is the setting for the recently added alternative dinner restaurant with full table service, serving between 6:30 and 10:30 P.M., and for the midnight buffets. A Sun Worshiper's lunch and afternoon tea are served poolside. RCCL has also upgraded room service; now you can order lunch and dinner from the full dining room menu.

SERVICE   As on the *Sovereign*-class vessels, *Nordic Empress*'s crew is eager to please. Stewards, primarily from the Caribbean, make up rooms twice a day, place a chocolate on your pillow during evening turn-down service, and will also bring you continental breakfast, sandwiches, and refreshments 24 hours a day. The friendly dining staff will make it a point to become familiar with your preferences. Here, as on all other RCCL ships, they are likely to give you a pep talk about the importance of filling in your passenger comment cards, particularly the "excellent" column.

FACILITIES AND ENTERTAINMENT   The nighttime entertainment is some of RCCL's best, with good shows, music, and dancing for every taste from big band and country to disco. Even on a three-day cruise, the ship gets in the captain's cocktail party, a passenger Talent Show, and maybe a 1950s and 1960s hop, along with big Broadway-style productions in the impressive Strike Up The Band show lounge. Sight lines are good from almost any seat in the tiered section and mezzanine, as there is little obstruction. The lounge has a dance floor and retractable stage, which is large enough to accommodate full-scale theatrical and musical productions, and variety shows with magicians, singers, and comedians.

The most dazzling feature of the ship is the trilevel Casino Royal; you can't miss it as you pass through the upper or lower level en route to the dining room or the show lounge. You can try your luck at one of the 220 slot machines or nine blackjack, and there are roulette, craps, and a big wheel of fortune.

Between the casino and the Centrum is the Carousel Pub, designed with a merry-go-round theme under a four-color sailcloth-tented ceiling. A mural with carousel paraphernalia, including real saddles, greets you upon entering this festive lounge and so, too, will music with a

Latin beat. The larger, art deco High Society lounge features entertainment and dance music from the 1950s to the 1990s.

The Viking Crown Lounge on the *Nordic Empress* is at the stern on Sun Deck, rather than cantilevered from the stack as on other RCCL ships. Nonetheless, with its three walls of windows, it makes a dandy perch for viewing the scenery during the day and sipping sunset cocktails. It becomes a state-of-the-art disco for late-nighters.

ACTIVITIES AND DIVERSIONS   Passengers on short cruises usually want to pack in as many activities as possible, and the *Nordic Empress* gives them more than enough choices. The ship's top decks are designed for more than daytime sun and are a center of activity, day and night. By day there are outdoor games and entertainment and by night there're music and dancing under the stars. On several decks sail pavilions instead of umbrellas provide shade. Elsewhere are dance classes, cards, crafts, bingo, and karaoke.

SPORTS, FITNESS, AND BEAUTY   The large Shipshape Fitness Center is also located on the top decks. It has a glass-enclosed exercise area and an array of the latest equipment, along with saunas, showers, and massage rooms. On deck are three whirlpools and two fountains that create waterways that cascade into two pools (one specially for children). The beauty salon offers hair, facial, and spa beauty treatments at additional charge.

The Golf Ahoy! Center provides golfers with computerized video golf, which enables you to try your skill at world famous courses projected on the screen. A computer analyzes the stroke and scores your game.

ShipShape activities range from aquadynamics to basketball free-throws, and as on other RCCL ships, ShipShape "dollars" earned for participation can be redeemed for T-shirts and visors.

CHILDREN'S FACILITIES   Kids' Konnection is a multipurpose, 95-square-foot playroom for children ages of 5–12. Designed in the theme of a space station, the room has an 11-foot-high ceiling, which allows for the Tubular Time network, a labyrinth of huge suspended tubes of brushed aluminum that are lighted and carpeted inside. Children can crawl through the tubes as they would in a real space station to a slide and raised clubhouse platform.

The youth program is similar to those on other RCCL ships and provides its own daily agenda, which kids receive nightly under their cabin door. It is packed with activities from ice cream and pizza parties to face painting, midnight basketball, talent shows, and special shore tours. Menus designed for children ages 4–12 have such favorites as peanut butter and jelly sandwiches, hot dogs, and pizzas, along with salads and fruit. The menu has word games, puzzles, and crayons. Baby-sitters (at extra cost), cribs, and highchairs are available.

SHORE EXCURSIONS Shore excursion booklets are included with the documents mailed to the passenger. The variety of excursions caters to a wide range of interests, but essentially, they are standard, off-the-shelf programs offering island tours, beach trips, snorkeling, and diving excursions, among others.

POSTSCRIPT The *Nordic Empress* continues RCCL's tradition of consistency. There are no surprises except perhaps the ship itself, which has a very different look from the other members of the fleet and is unusual in having flexible open spaces that lend themselves to nighttime as well as daytime activities. The ship is particularly suited to short cruises with lots of dazzle and lots to do. It's a good cruise sampler for those who want to preview a high-energy, nonstop—activity type of cruise and for busy people who take several weekend breaks a year for pure escape.

Song of America

	Quality Rating	Value Rating
Song of America	❺	C

Registry: Norway	Length: 705 feet	Beam: 93 feet
Cabins: 701	Draft: 22 feet	Speed: 19 knots
Maximum Passengers: 1,552	Passenger Decks: 11	Elevators: 7
	Crew: 535	Space Ratio: 27

THE SHIP When *Song of America* was launched, it was the line's first new ship in ten years. Although it is a midsize ship compared to today's megaliners, it was looked upon as big in those days. The ship's layout is unusual and particularly noteworthy for having been the model for RCCL's *Sovereign* group. Most of the public rooms are on three decks aft, rather than running the length of the ship; and the cabins are forward. The main purpose is to isolate the noise of the public areas from the cabin and sleeping areas. The ship's signature Viking Crown Lounge was the first to surround the ship's funnel completely, offering a 360° unobstructed view; it was also the first lounge that could be reached by elevator from inside the ship.

Since its debut, however, *Song of America* has been altered several times and in 1991 was extensively renovated. On Cabaret Deck, the modest gaming area was replaced by a much larger casino; Schooner Bar, the ever-popular piano bar on the *Sovereign* group, was added along with a small conference center and photo gallery in place of the movie theater and the America's Cup bar.

ITINERARIES   Seven days, Mexican Riviera, Winter; Bermuda, summer. January–April and November–December, the ship departs from Los Angeles on Sunday for Cabo San Lucas, Mazatlán, and Puerto Vallarta. From May–October, she sails from New York on Sunday for Bermuda, where she spends two nights each in Hamilton and St. Georges, with two days at sea.

- *In mid-April and November* the ship offers Panama Canal repositioning cruises and San Juan–Bermuda cruises.

Home Ports   Los Angeles; New York.
Port Charges   Included in cruise price.

CABINS   There are 14 cabin categories with the majority located on the two lowest passenger decks. They are typical of RCCL ships—compact, well designed, and immaculate. Cabins have televisions, radios, sofa beds, built-in desks, and vanities; outside cabins have large windows. The suites—all on Promenade Deck—are elegantly decorated and have a small sitting area with sofa, two chairs, and coffee table, dressing table and chair, curtained-off bedroom with two lower beds, and bathrooms with tub and shower, and ample storage.

Specifications   295 inside cabins, 406 outside, including 21 suites. Standard dimensions, 123 square feet. 590 with twin beds (275 convertible to double); 118 third/fourth persons; no singles.

DINING   From the Welcome Aboard dinner to the Captain's Farewell, dining gets higher marks on the *Song of America* than on the line's larger ships, although the menus are the same. There are theme dinners with decorations and dining staff in costumes to suggest the theme and create a festive atmosphere.

The Madame Butterfly Dining Room with its Japanese decor has two additional sections—the Oriental Terrace on the starboard side, Ambassador Room, portside—that are long, narrow extensions of the main room. This arrangement has the advantage of creating a more intimate dining ambience in each of the three areas. Either of the smaller sections can be used as almost a private dining room for a large group. The dining room offers two seatings with assigned tables for the meals.

The Verandah Cafe on Sun Deck is the informal alternative for breakfast and lunch buffet. Although the area is smaller than on the newer ships, it has been improved in recent years and has the merit of being near the swimming pools.

SERVICE   The friendly and efficient dining staff has a large number of Europeans who have a higher degree of professionalism than on most mass-market Caribbean cruise ships. But as we have noted elsewhere, the maître d'hôtel and waiter are likely to hover about with attention that some people can find to be too much.

FACILITIES AND ENTERTAINMENT   Daytime activities run the gamut from dance lessons to ice carving demonstrations and any number of parlor games along the way. There are bingo, bridge, wine tasting, singles' parties, kids' parties, teen parties, a passenger talent show, and a costume party.

In the evening, *Song of America's* lounges and bars offer a variety of entertainment. Can-Can, the main show room, and Oklahoma, another large lounge, are located on the same deck and feature Broadway-style shows, cabaret, comics, and other specialty acts. One deck up, the Guys and Dolls Lounge serves up contemporary dance music till 3 A.M.

The Can Can Lounge, unlike those on the newer ships, is on one level but it is well designed with comfortable seating and good sight lines. The bar at the rear spans the width of the lounge and is particularly popular because patrons can have an excellent view of the stage, yet at the same time can carry on a conversation without disturbing those in the show lounge.

The Schooner Bar, an informal piano bar, is a popular spot to relax with friends and to mingle with new ones, almost any time of day. The hallmark Viking Crown Lounge with its expansive views from high above the sea is especially nice for cocktails at sunset and late in the evening when you want a quiet place away from the nightlife. Between the two lounges and around the bend from the Schooner Bar is the sleek Casino Royale with blackjack, craps, roulette, and slot machines.

SPORTS, FITNESS, AND BEAUTY   *Song of America* was one of the first cruise ships to have twin outdoor swimming pools on the Lido Deck. It also has a second-level walk-around promenade extending to a large sunning deck, which provides spacious areas with deck chairs for sunning, lounging, and watching the world go by.

Those in search of more active pursuits have a golf driving range on Promenade, aft, as well as a basketball court and Ping-Pong tables on sports deck, and a gym with separate saunas for men and women on Bridge Deck. The beauty salon, however, is on one of the lower cabin decks, the more traditional oceanliner location.

SHORE EXCURSIONS   Shore excursion booklets with prices are sent to passengers along with their tickets and documents. The variety of excursions caters to a wide range of interests, but essentially, they are standard, off-the-shelf programs offering island tours, beach trips, snorkeling and diving excursions, among others.

The Bermuda cruise in summer should be of special interest to golfers as RCCL's Golf Ahoy! program arranges play at six of the island's courses.

POSTSCRIPT   *Song of America* packs the variety of activities and options of the megaships within a slightly smaller package, making it a good choice for those wanting choices without as many people as on the larger ships.

Sun Viking

	Quality Rating	**Value Rating**
Sun Viking	❺	A

Registry: Norway	Length: 563 feet	Beam: 80 feet
Cabins: 357	Draft: 22 feet	Speed: 18 knots
Maximum Passengers:	Passenger Decks: 8	Elevators: 4
818	Crew: 71	Space Ratio: 26

THE SHIP   The smallest of Royal Caribbean's fleet, the *Sun Viking* is an easy-to-like ship with many fans among RCCL's most loyal patrons. They like her particularly for the characteristics that are attributable to her size—a cozy, congenial ambience with warm personal service and fine cuisine—all the elements they miss on the megaliners. Not only is a smaller ship like *Sun Viking* less crowded and easier to get around, but, more importantly, it provides a better atmosphere for making friends and for greater interaction between passengers and staff. Undoubtedly, the ship's amiable staff helps ensure the high rate of return passengers.

With her home in the Far East, loyal fans have been trying out her itineraries, sampling the menus now featuring local dishes, the entertainment showcasing native folklore groups, and the enrichment programs highlighting the culture of the Far East. However, RCCL's credo of consistency has not been compromised, and there are enough of its cruise staples to make passengers feel right at home.

ITINERARIES *Sun Viking* sails year-round between Hong Kong and Singapore and between Hong Kong and Japan on seven different itineraries; all are 14 nights, except one, which is 13 nights. The Southeast Asia cruise is round trip from Singapore and includes Bali, Malaysia, and Thailand; others are Singapore to Thailand; China between Hong Kong and Beijing, and between Beijing and Tokyo.

Home Ports Hong Kong; Singapore; other Asian ports, depending on itineraries.

Port Charges Included in cruise price.

CABINS Almost all of *Sun Viking's* cabins are on the lower three decks and come in 14 categories. Only one suite and eight deluxe cabins have bathrooms with tub and shower. All others have shower only. Standard cabins are small but light and airy and about 65 percent offer ocean views. They are fitted with either twins or a double bed. No television.

Specifications 117 inside cabins, 246 outside; 1 suite. Standard dimensions are 120–137 square feet. 303 with twin beds; 39 double; 114 third/fourth persons; no singles.

FACILITIES AND ENTERTAINMENT The Merry Widow Lounge is the main room where most of the shows are staged. It is a sparkling room, with a large dance floor, where several orchestras rotate, playing from before dinner through late evening. The decor takes its theme from a display of black-and-white photos of the actresses who have starred in the famous operetta.

A second lounge, Annie Get Your Gun Lounge, has something of a Western look and doubles as the movie theatre. On the walls are photos of scenes from the 1950s movie. The Lounge of the Northern Lights is the late-night gathering spot. Videos projected on the wall are used to alter the room's mood.

The ship has a salt water pool and an elevated walk-around deck above the pool area. The sports deck has Ping-Pong, shuffleboard, golf driving, skeet shooting, and basketball. The ShipShape exercise program is available but the ship does not have a gym.

The L-shaped HMS Pinafore Dining Room with windows on both sides is bright during the day and has a quiet, relaxing ambience with soft lighting in the evening. The Verandah Cafe on Promenade Deck, one deck down from the swimming pool, serves casual breakfast and lunch buffet. Afternoon tea and the midnight buffet are also served.

POSTSCRIPT The *Sun Viking's* lack of megaliner facilities is the trade-off for the cozier, friendly atmosphere of a smaller ship—and it's a very different cruise experience. Its low-key atmosphere would be a welcome respite for anyone who has tired of big ships. The lack of gym or exercise equipment is its biggest drawback for active passengers.

Readers who are considering a cruise on this ship should review all the RCCL section to have a better understanding of the line's cruise experience.

Viking Serenade

	Quality Rating	Value Rating
Viking Serenade	❹	C

Registry: Liberia	Length: 623 feet	Beam: 89 feet
Cabins: 756	Draft: 24 feet	Speed: 18 knots
Maximum Passengers: 1,863	Passenger Decks: 11	Elevators: 5
	Crew: 610	Space Ratio: 26.5

THE SHIP Atypical of Royal Caribbean's fleet in design, the *Viking Serenade* was formerly the *Stardancer* of Admiral Cruises and was rebuilt completely in 1991, after RCCL acquired Admiral. In her past life, she had been a car ferry, built in 1982, which explains her boxy appearance. In the $75 million conversion, cabins, the line's trademark Viking Crown Lounge, a second dining room, a conference center with audiovisual facilities, and a children's playroom were added, and the existing cabins and public rooms renovated. More recently in 1994, the ship's public rooms were again refurbished and the Teen Center completely redone.

Of its 11 passenger decks, all but the lower 2 have public rooms and all but the top 2 have cabins. The entertainment options include Hello Dolly, the main lounge with Las Vegas revues, Bali Hai for entertainment and dancing, and the trademark Schooner Bar, the popular piano bar next to the Casino Royale. Three meals in two seatings are served in the Magic Flute Dining Room and the smaller Aida Dining Room with Egyptian-inspired decor. And consistent with the RCCL fleet, there are theme dinners and buffets.

Decorated in a blend of California casual and contemporary Scandinavian design, the ship has an upbeat personality with constant activity. Very much identified with the California scene, its casual atmosphere attracts an eclectic mix of passengers.

Action centers on the topside Sun Deck, which has a fitness center with state-of-the-art exercise equipment and the ShipShape program, sauna and massage rooms, the pool with its retractable dome, an open jogging track, teen center, and the glass-walled Windjammer Cafe, another feature added in the RCCL reconstruction. The indoor/outdoor facility is the setting for the informal breakfast and lunch buffets as well as afternoon ice cream, and the recently added alternative dining area, serving between 6:30 and 10:30 P.M. with full table service and daily menus. RCCL has also upgraded room service; now lunch and dinner can be ordered from the full dining room menu.

Directly above is the Viking Crown Lounge with floor-to-ceiling windows on three sides, providing daytime panoramic views and a late-night disco. The ship has a shopping arcade, a beauty salon, and barbershop.

ITINERARIES   Three and four days, West Coast, Mexico. *Viking Serenade* departs from Los Angeles on Friday to Ensenada, and on Monday to Catalina Island, San Diego, and Ensenada (four nights).

Home Port   Los Angeles.
Port Charges   Included in cruise price.

CABINS   The ship has 16 categories of cabins, generally larger than is typical on RCCL's older ships. They are fitted with television, radios, curtained closets, large dressing tables, and two sofa-style beds, convertible to a queen. Five deluxe suites at the stern on Star Deck have private balconies. The Royal Suite has a sitting area, wet bar, whirlpool tub, and walk-in closet.

Specifications   278 inside cabins, 478 outside; 8 suites. Standard dimensions, 162 square feet. 511 with twin beds (499 convertible to double); 358 third/fourth persons; no singles.

POSTSCRIPT   *Viking Serenade* has a different look and feel from the rest of the RCCL fleet, in part for its West Coast location, but it's still part of the family delivering on the line's consistency.

Readers who are considering a cruise on this ship should review all the RCCL section to have a better understanding of the line's cruise experience.

Legend / Splendour of the Seas
Grandeur / Enchantment of the Seas
Rhapsody / Vision of the Seas

	Quality Rating	Value Rating
Legend	❼	B
Splendour, Grandeur	❽	A
Enchantment, Rhapsody	Preview	
Vision	Preview	

Registry (*Legend, Grandeur*): Liberia
Registry (*Splendour, Enchantment, Rhapsody*): Norwegian

Length: 867/916/915 feet	Beam: 105/105.6 feet	Cabins: 902/975/1,000
Draft: 25/24 feet	Speed: 24/22 knots	Maximum Passengers:
Passenger Decks: 11	Elevators: 11/9	2,076/2,446/2,435
Crew: 720/760/765	Space Ratio: 38.32	

THE SHIPS   Already a legend when she arrived in May 1995, the *Legend of the Seas* was the first of six in a new class of megaliners dubbed Project Vision. Her twin, *Splendour of the Seas,* followed in April 1996, and her sister, *Grandeur of the Seas*, in December.

A twin of *Grandeur of the Seas, Enchantment of the Seas* was launched in Europe in July 1997. *Rhapsody of the Seas*, which made her debut in April 1997, will be followed a year later by her twin, *Vision of the Seas.* These twins, also, are sisters of the *Legend*—similar but different—and have their own distinguishing features.

Constructed in France at Chantiers de l'Atlantique shipyard in St. Nazaire and created by renowned designers Njal Eide and Petter Yran, who were responsible for previous Royal Caribbean vessels, the megaliners were quickly labeled "the ships of glass." Each ship has two acres of windows, glass windbreaks, skylights, and walls of windows throughout the public spaces. The Centrum, or atrium, the focal point, rises seven decks—two more than on the *Sovereign*-class vessels—and, for the *pièce de résistance*, it is crowned by the Viking Crown Lounge, the line's signature glass-sheathed observation room. From the Centrum, bubble elevators whisk passengers directly into the lounge. The design tied together two RCCL hallmarks for the first time.

At the base of the Centrum is the Champagne Terrace and Bar, a lobby bar where caviar and fine wines and champagne are served by the glass. The elegant setting sets the tone for the ship. The *Grandeur*'s handsomely appointed Champagne Bar covers the entire lower level of the Centrum, a white baby grand piano at the center stands next to a grand staircase leading to the second level. Space in the lobby bar is broken up with decorative screens inlaid with wood and frosted glass, creating cozy conversation corners. The purser's office and excursion desk are up one level.

Works of art on *Splendour of the Seas* were created by over 50 artists and studios. The ship's atrium art is the most dramatic in the fleet. The work is comprised of three elements which symbolize the solar system. The dominant component, an 18-foot suspended gilded aluminum disc representing the sun, hangs on a diagonal through the center of the Centrum, silhouetted by light coming through the Centrum's skylight. Dichroic glass bulbs (an iridescent-type bulb) around the perimeter of the disc transmit and reflect colored light throughout the atrium, and hundreds of stainless steel cords attached to the upper, outer rim of the disc gather at the top of the Centrum. There are also hundreds of cords attached to the bottom of the disc which gather at the floor of the Centrum in a 54-inch metal globe. Both the globe and the top gathering point are illuminated, creating a glow surrounding the piece.

Throughout, the ships embrace the sea and ever-changing vistas with their windows and glass, allowing all the natural light to give passengers a feeling of space and openness. And they offer an extraordinary amount of open space.

Aft of the pool and funnel on Sun Deck is another new feature, the Solarium, a landscaped indoor/outdoor area with a second swimming pool, whirlpools, and a cafe. It can be covered during inclement weather by a huge glass roof called the Crystal Canopy. Unlike glass roofs on other cruise ships, the Solarium's roof does not retract and stack upon itself; instead it moves as a unit, entirely intact, over the pool area when needed. The design allowed the Crystal Canopy to be built of less heavy load-bearing aluminum and much more glass, permitting the maximum amount of light into the Solarium when the roof is in the closed position.

The most celebrated new feature on the *Legend* and *Splendour* is the Legend of the Links (Splendour of the Greens on *Splendour*), the world's first floating 18-hole miniature golf course. A control station, where golf clubs and tee times can be obtained, is designed like a miniature clubhouse.

LEGEND ITINERARIES

- *January–April and October–November,* 11 and 12 nights, Panama Canal between Miami and Acapulco or San Diego.
- *May–mid-September*, seven-day Alaska cruises, departing on Sunday from Vancouver for the Inside Passage, Hubbard Glacier or Glacier Bay, Skagway, Haines, Juneau, Ketchikan, and Misty Fjords. In between her winter and summer schedules, in April and September/October, she offers Hawaiian Islands cruises.

Home Ports   Miami; Vancouver.
Port Charges   Included in cruise price.

GRANDEUR ITINERARIES   Seven days, Northern/Eastern Caribbean, round-trip from Miami on Saturday to Labadee, San Juan, St. Thomas, And CocoCay.

Home Port   Miami.
Port Charges   Included in cruise price.

SPLENDOUR ITINERARIES   January–April, seven days, Southern Caribbean from San Juan to Aruba, Curaçao, St. Maarten, and St. Thomas; November–December, ten nights, Circle the Caribbean from Miami to Playa del Carmen/Cozumel, Grand Cayman, Ocho Rios, St. Thomas, San Juan, and Labadee; or 11 nights, Key West, Curaçao, Aruba, Ocho Rios, Grand Cayman, and Playa del Carmen/Cozumel.

- *In April and October*, she sails to/from Europe. May–October, she offers six different itineraries in Europe, first from Barcelona to the Mediterranean, then from Harwich, England to the Baltic, the Norwegian Fjords, and British Isles.

Home Ports   San Juan; Barcelona; Harwich.
Port Charges   Included in cruise price.

ENCHANTMENT ITINERARIES After her July 13 inaugural cruise from Southampton to Barcelona, the ship was scheduled to sail on a series of seven-night Mediterranean cruises, followed by a transatlantic voyage in September and two fall foliage cruises from Boston to Newfoundland and Quebec. In October, she begins alternating weekly Eastern and Western Caribbean cruises, year-round, from Miami, calling at Key West, Playa del Carmen/Cozumel, Ocho Rios, and Grand Cayman, with two days at sea; or St. Maarten, St. Thomas/St. John, and CocoCay, and three days at sea.

> ***Home Port*** Miami.
> ***Port Charges*** Included in cruise price.

RHAPSODY ITINERARIES After a New York debut in May, the ship made a 13-night inaugural transcanal cruise from Miami to Los Angeles, followed by seven-day Alaska cruises from June–September round trip from Vancouver, departing on Saturday to the Inside Passage, Juneau, Skagway, Sitka, Ketchikan, and Misty Fjords. On return she has two Hawaiian Islands cruises and a transcanal one before starting weekly Southern Caribbean cruises.

> • Her winter cruises depart from San Juan on Saturday for Aruba, Curaçao, St. Maarten, and St. Thomas, with two days at sea.
>
> ***Home Ports*** San Juan; Vancouver.
> ***Port Charges*** Included in cruise price.

CABINS One of the major improvements of the *Legend* class is the size of standard cabins—153 square feet compared to 122 square feet in comparable cabins on the *Sovereign* group—which allows space for a sitting area. The cabins are handsomely appointed in soft, inviting pastels and light woods. Many more have bathrooms with tubs and showers and one out of four cabins has a private veranda. The large Royal Suite has a baby grand piano, whirlpool tub, and veranda.

Legend/Splendour *Specifications* 327 inside cabins, 575 outside; 83 suites; 4 family suites; 231 with balconies; 388 third/fourth persons; no singles. 17 wheelchair accessible.

Grandeur/Enchantment *Specifications* 399 inside cabins, 576 outside, 18 suites; 4 family suites; 72 deluxe outside; 212 with balconies; 403 third/fourth persons; no singles. 14 wheelchair accessible.

Rhapsody/Vision *Specifications* 407 inside cabins, 593 outside; 18 suites; 72 deluxe; 4 family suites; 229 with balconies; 287 third/fourth persons; no singles. 14 wheelchair accessible.

DINING The *Legend*'s Romeo and Juliet Dining Room (the King and I on *Splendour* and Great Gatsby on *Grandeur*) spans two decks (reminiscent of the restaurant on the *Nordic Empress*) and has 20-foot-high glass walls on each side—perhaps more glass than in any other dining room afloat—offering spectacular sea views from every table. Because the dining room is in the ship's superstructure rather than the hull as on a traditional cruise ship, the room's walls can be virtually all glass, with the load-bearing function handled by interior columns rather than the dining room walls. Inside on the first level, a raised, revolving platform with a grand piano is framed by elegant stairways, which curve up to the balcony.

The decor of the *Splendor*'s King and I is particularly noteworthy. Here, authentic Thai architecture has been replicated in a temple facade at the front of the dining room, and 16 epic historical paintings plus two epic murals were created by the artists of Thailand's royal family. Each painting tells a story from the land once called Siam.

At the forward end of the Sun Deck is the Windjammer Cafe, the casual indoor/outdoor buffet area for breakfast or lunch and the recently added alternative dining option for dinner. The cafe has floor-to-ceiling glass walls on three sides and a sloping glass skylight giving the room an airy appearance. Each day, lunch has a theme—Chinese, Greek, etc.—when ethnic food, along with the regular array of hot dishes, salads and sandwiches, is featured. Dinner, served between 6:30 and 10:30 P.M., offers full table service and daily menus. The nautical-theme cafe, a standard feature on Royal Caribbean ships, is also a popular spot to read a book or play cards while enjoying expansive sea views.

SERVICE The dining room service on these new ships seems to measure up to RCCL's high standards—friendly and efficient; but room stewards are getting mixed reviews. Language is often a problem as many have only a rudimentary knowledge of English; and their lack of training can probably be explained by the line's adding so many large new ships in so short a time.

FACILITIES AND ENTERTAINMENT The *Vision* ships are state-of-the-art at every turn. Most of the entertainment facilities are found on Promenade Deck. The That's Entertainment Theatre on *Legend* (Palladium Theater on *Grandeur* and 42nd Street Theatre on *Splendour*), where full-scale Broadway productions are presented nightly, spans two decks and was designed using computers to ensure good sight lines from every seat. It has a computerized set rigging system to move scenery on and off stage, a device commonly used on Broadway, and an orchestra pit which can be raised and lowered.

The Schooner Bar, another RCCL hallmark, is a piano bar, always popular with passengers, particularly for its sing-along sessions. Located next to the Casino Royale, the bar has authentic rigging as part of the decor and an aroma of tar. The casino on the *Grandeur* has an amusing touch—at the entrance, passengers walk across a glass floor strewn with "sunken treasure" of jewels and gold coins. The casino offers blackjack, Caribbean poker, roulette, craps, and 178 slot machines.

The spacious Anchor's Away Lounge on the *Legend* (South Pacific Lounge on *Grandeur* and Top Hat Lounge on *Splendour*) anchors the aft end of Main Deck and spans the entire width of the ship. It is a second showroom, used for parlor games, art auctions, and dance activities by day and for dancing and late-night entertainment shows in the evening.

Topside, the Viking Crown Lounge, the hallmark of every Royal Caribbean ship, is an observation lounge during the day and a nightclub and disco at night. The room's design allows passengers to enjoy the nightclub action forward or carry on a quiet conversation in the piano bar area aft. Sometimes the lounge is used for karaoke. On all the ships, the lounge is accessible directly from the atrium via glass elevators.

Aft of the show lounge (to entice you coming and going!) is the shopping mall with a variety of shops in attractive settings. For example, the Harbour Shop, a liquor and sundries shop, resembles an old English vintner's with aged timber, antique wine barrels, beer kegs, and stone floors.

There is a conference center which can be divided into four separate rooms, each with a full range of audio/visual support equipment. Adjoined to the center is an attractive lounge, which also can be divided into separate sections. There is a card room that divides into two sections and a 2,000 volume library which on the *Grandeur* has an amusing life-like sculpture titled *Snoozin;* nearby, a statue of a perplexed tourist is called *Where the Heck.*

Explorers Court, off the Centrum on the port side of Deck 8, is the place to relax, read a book, or have quiet conversations. On the starboard side, the Crown & Anchor Study, named after the Royal Caribbean logo, is a gathering place with a more formal atmosphere with its traditional decor.

SPORTS, FITNESS, AND BEAUTY The Sun Deck is an open and airy space with the outdoor pool at the center and a contrast to the quiet Solarium, a second pool area. The Solarium has its own cafe which serves snacks, including pizza, alcoholic beverages, sodas, and juices when the Windjammer and the main dining room are closed. The entire area can be covered by a glass canopy, the largest glass roof afloat.

Beyond the Solarium is the expansive ShipShape fitness center and spa with a beauty salon, an aerobics area, a large gym with a large array of exercise equipment, changing rooms, saunas, and steam baths. There are seven massage rooms where passengers can enjoy pricey treatments such as thalassotherapy and hydrotherapy massage, and a sports deck at the stern. Each ship also has a padded promenade deck which encircles all but the forward end of the ship.

The much-publicized golf course on the *Legend*, Legend of the Links (Splendour of the Greens on *Splendour*), is situated directly above the spa. (There is no course on *Grandeur*.) It was designed by Adventure Golf Services, whose other miniature courses include the indoor course at the Mall of America in Bloomington, Minnesota. RCCL, which is the official cruise line of the Professional Golfer's Association (PGA), the PGA Tour, the Senior PGA Tour, and LPGA Tour (Ladies PGA), also is a member of the Miniature Golf Association of America (MGAA).

The 6,000-square-foot Links consists of high-quality artificial greens with each hole surrounded by rough to duplicate a shore-side golf layout. The 18 holes range in size from 155–230 square feet, tees are five feet wide, and the longest hole is 32 feet in length. Each game costs $5; a $30 membership offers unlimited play. The glass dome over the aft swimming pool and entertainment area can slide from there to the golf course, where it can be mechanically raised to provide almost ten feet of vertical clearance for golfers.

A walkway along one edge of the course has lampposts and park benches, and a sitting area designed to encourage spectators. Halogen lights illuminate nighttime play and glass wind baffles protect the greens from the wind generated by the ship's forward motion. The entire course is surrounded by a jogging track. The ship has tournaments and even exclusive children's tee times.

CHILDREN'S FACILITIES   The *Vision* group has outstanding facilities for kids, along with the RCCL's extensive, year-round supervised youth program, Adventure Ocean, which is available fleetwide. The program provides activities for ages 3–17, and was expanded in 1996, to include special diversions for 3–5-year-olds; it operates throughout the day and evening in port and at sea. An activities schedule is delivered to cabins daily and includes games, fun fitness, educational activities, and special entertainment. Among the most original activities is Mad Science, a Royal Caribbean exclusive, directed by specially trained teachers, to make science entertaining and amusing for kids. There is no charge to participate in the program.

Group baby-sitting in the youth center or other designated public areas is available in the afternoon when the ship is in port and during late evening hours; the cost is $4 per hour per child. Family suites with separate bedrooms for children are found on Deck 8.

Club Ocean on Deck 10 is the children's center. On *Grandeur*, its theme is an underwater submarine and includes a tunnel, slide, pool of colored bubble balls, and a large writing wall for kids' artistic expression. Across the way, Fanta-SEAS (Optix on the *Legend*) is the teen center with a disc jockey, and is designed in a futuristic space odyssey theme with large-screen TVs. The ships also have a video arcade.

Note: If you or your kids are likely to drink a lot of soft drinks, you might want to buy the "Coke Deal" that allows you to get all the fountain soft drinks (but not canned ones) you want for $1 per person per day plus $1. A sticker is placed on your cruise card for identification.

POSTSCRIPT For two decades Royal Caribbean has maintained that cabin size was not important since passengers spend so little time in them, preferring to have the space available for activities instead. Well, maybe. Given the line's track record of success it's hard to argue with them, but it's worth noting that on the new *Vision* series, the cabins are larger and offer greater comfort, with sitting areas and, for the first time, a large number of private balconies. The megaships have an exciting action-packed, high-energy atmosphere about them, but make no mistake, each is one whale of a big ship.

ROYAL OLYMPIC CRUISES
(SUN LINE CRUISES AND EPIROTIKI LINE)

One Rockefeller Plaza, No. 315, New York, NY 10020
(212) 397-6400; (800) 468-6400 (U.S.); (800) 368-3888 (Canada);
fax (212) 765-9685
http://www.royalolympiccruises.com

TYPE OF SHIPS   Small and midsize oceanliners.

TYPE OF CRUISES   Quality, low-key, destination-oriented; short cruises in Greek Isles and Eastern Mediterranean; long cruises on less-traveled paths in a homey ambience.

CRUISE LINE'S STRENGTHS
- friendliness and personal warmth of the crew
- relaxed ambience
- Greek hospitality
- innovative itineraries
- lecture program and quality guides
- host program on white ships

CRUISE LINE'S SHORTCOMINGS
- aging fleet
- small cabins and limited facilities on smaller ships
- dissimilarity in combined fleets
- cuisine on white ships

FELLOW PASSENGERS   In winter, when the white ships* sail on Western Hemisphere itineraries, 80 percent of the passengers are age 55 and older and have the time, means, and inclination for long cruises. They are mature, modestly affluent, seasoned travelers, many retired and semiretired, with some sense of adventure who put destinations,

---

* See information under The Line, below for explanation of blue and white ships under the recent merger.

quality experiences, and value at the top of their priorities. Most are college educated and enjoy the shipboard enrichment programs and shore excursions. Over 50 percent come from Florida, California, New York, and Texas and have a household income of $75,000+; most are frequent cruisers and often 50 percent are repeaters.

In summer, when the white ships are in the Mediterranean, along with the blue ones,* the passenger mix is similar but international, with half the passengers from Australia, Mexico, South America, France, and Italy, and half from the United States. They have a household income of $50,000+. The average age is 40+, but age ranges more widely than in winter and passengers run from newlyweds to retirees, plus families with children. The American contingent has usually been to Europe and has cruised before, but not as frequently as the winter passengers. The attractions of the Mediterranean appeal equally to honeymooners seeking a romantic destination, religious groups tracing the "footsteps of St. Paul," and amateur historians who want to see the places they studied in school.

Recommended For   The blue ships appeal to upscale, adventurous travelers who seek a different kind of travel experience in a refined, conservative ambience and expect the high level of service and amenities found in fine hotels; value-conscious travelers who prefer to stay in cozy local hotels but also want an English-speaking environment; people interested in Greek life, culture, and cuisine; experienced cruisers who enjoy the style of a traditional oceanliner; and those looking for a comfortable way to visit interesting destinations. The white ships are similar in their appeal, but at a lower quality level, particularly of food and accommodations, and with a more casual atmosphere.

Not Recommended For   Party seekers, night owls, those who want big-ship action; unsophisticated travelers; people who want to be entertained and have only marginal interest in history; those who like to dress up in flashy finery.

CRUISE AREAS AND SEASONS   South America, Cape Horn and Falkland Islands, Amazon, Caribbean, and Panama Canal, in winter; Greek Isles, Eastern Mediterranean, and Black Sea, spring–fall; transatlantic, April and November.

---

* See information under The Line, below for explanation of blue and white ships under the recent merger.

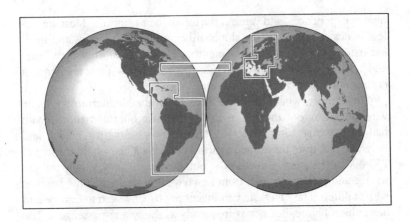

THE LINE   In August 1995, Sun Line Cruises, one of the best known and most respected Greek-owned cruise lines, and Epirotiki Line, one of Greece's oldest and largest lines and long-time Sun Line rival, merged to form a new company, Royal Olympic Cruises. The new line operates ten cruise ships under two brands distinguished by the colors of the Greek flag: Sun Line's "blue" ships—*Stella Solaris*, *Stella Oceanis* and *Odysseus*—are traditional and upscale; and Epirotiki's "white" ships—*Triton*, *Orpheus* and *Olympic*—offer casual cruises. The others, Epirotiki's *Argonaut*, *Jason*, and *Neptune*, and Sun Line's *Stella Maris* are mostly on charter.

Sun Line Cruises was started in the mid-1950s by a well-respected Greek family whose patriarch, the late Ch. A. Keusseoglou, had already made his mark as head of Home Lines. Sun Line was a pioneer from the start—introducing some of the first ships designed specifically for cruising that eliminated class distinction on board and provided large, sunny public rooms and outdoor areas for relaxation and deck sports; developing new itineraries in the lesser-known islands of the Eastern Caribbean a decade before the rest of the cruise world discovered them; combining the small Eastern Caribbean islands with a cruise up the Orinoco River in Venezuela or the Amazon in Brazil; and combining the Amazon and Panama Canal in one cruise.

In 1985, Sun Line was the first to develop Halley's Comet cruises (which were copied by almost everyone with a ship) and to offer a cruise timed for the spring equinox at Chichen Itza in the Yucatan. On February 26, 1998, the *Stella Solaris* will be off the coast of Curaçao to witness the eclipse during her scheduled "Solar Eclipse" cruise, and in 1999, three Royal Olympic ships will be in position in Europe to watch the last eclipse of the twentieth century.

While many cruise lines have added bigger and bigger ships, Royal Olympic's ships remain small and intimate. On the blue ships, the size of the staff in relation to the number of passengers is high. The ships and their staffs are Greek; many have had 20 years or more of uninterrupted service. The combination of unusual itineraries, private yacht-like atmosphere, and stable members-of-the-family crew gives the ships special appeal to seasoned travelers, which is reflected in the line's high number of repeat passengers.

White-shipped Epirotiki generally sells its cruises in the United States through about 60 North American tour companies, which include them as part of a tour program for Greece, the Holy Land, and the Eastern Mediterranean. About 35 percent of the line's passengers are from the United States, most on two-week vacations that combine hotel stays with a cruise. And like Sun Line's blue ships, wherever the white fleet sails, it carries the flavor of Greece with Greek crews and special Greek nights with native food, wine, and music.

The Fleet	Built/Renovated	Tonnage	Passengers
Odysseus(b)	1962/1988	12,000	400
Olympic(w)	1962/76/91/93	27,250	906
Orpheus(w)	1952/69/88	5,092	304
Stella Oceanis(b)	1965/1993	5,500	300
Stella Solaris(b)	1973/1994	17,832	620
Triton(w)	1971/76/91	14,155	704

*b—blue fleet; w—white fleet

STYLE To sail on the ships of Royal Olympic is to live a little while in a small Greek town on the sea. The staff and crew serve their guests with the natural ease of people at home, and passengers are treated as valued friends from far away rather than as tourists passing through.

The involvement in the families in the company is one of its biggest assets, reflecting in the case of the blue ships, Keusseoglou's personal commitment to quality. The ships' size also contributes to the special shipboard atmosphere, offering space on a comfortable scale. And the ships are still traditional enough that you get a passenger list slipped under your cabin door by the second day of your cruise.

The spirit of Greek life and culture is everywhere on these ships and the desire to experience it firsthand is delightfully contagious. Fortunately, the ship offers plenty of ways to satisfy that desire, from feasts of authentic Greek dishes to lessons in traditional Greek dances.

Kalos orisate means welcome aboard. It's the first of a daily sampling of Greek phrases that head the daily agenda. Each day passengers can be heard practicing the latest of these tidbits of conversational Greek, and the crew and staff indulge their efforts with cheerful encouragement.

Entertainment is small cabaret-style, and the highlight of each cruise is Greek Night with traditional Greek music and dancing by members of the crew. In keeping with fitness trends, the blue ships offer spa cuisine, and for its high number of single women passengers, it has a host program. Although the blue ships specialize in long cruises in winter, most itineraries are designed so they can be taken in short segments.

DISTINCTIVE FEATURES   Greek Night; Host program. *Stella Solaris's* Maya Equinox cruise. One of few cruise lines still family-owned. Estate wines from the Keusseoglou family's vineyards in Italy.

RATES

Highest Per Diem	Lowest Per Diem	Average Per Diem
$409	$185	$247

The above per diems are calculated from the cruise line's nondiscounted *cruise-only* fares on standard accommodations. What you will actually pay *should* be *substantially* less (see Part One, How to Get the Best Deal on a Cruise). Per diems vary by season, by cabin location, and by cruise areas.

Special Fares and Discounts   Early bird discounts. Very competitive cruise-only per diems of $115–385, depending upon the cruise itinerary and cabin category.

- Third/Fourth Persons: Yes, free on some sailings.
- Children's Fare: Yes, on certain sailings.
- Single Supplement: 150 percent; guaranteed share available.

Packages
- Air/Sea: Yes.

- Pre/Post: Yes. Summer Greek Islands/Mediterranean cruises can be combined with land tour packages for complete land/sea vacations of one week or longer.

Past Passengers The ROC Circle is a newly created club for past passengers, to extend special recognition to them with special mailings and discounts and upgrades on selected sailings. Passengers are registered as circle members after their first ROC cruise.

THE LAST WORD For those who are turned off by big, glitzy ships and their impersonal nature, Royal Olympic Cruises offers a refreshing change. The cruise line provides the quality of traditional cruising in the easy comfort and warmth of Greek hospitality. Repeaters say it's like coming home; many return to the same ship year after year. The merger of Sun Line and Epirotiki seems to have strengthened both, but it remains to be seen if Royal Olympic can withstand the onslaught of competition from the vastly increased number of cruise lines, many with new ships, now sailing in the Mediterranean.

ROYAL OLYMPIC CRUISES SHIPS STANDARD FEATURES

Officers Greek.

Staffs Dining, Cabin, Cruise/Greek.

Dining Facilities One main dining room (*Odysseus* has two) for all meals and informal buffet breakfast and lunch served poolside. *Solaris* has indoor/outdoor Lido Cafe with breakfast, lunch, late-night buffets.

Special Diets Low-salt, low-fat diets available. Kosher diets are accommodated by request in writing two weeks before departure date.

Room Service 24 hours.

Dress Code Comfortable, casual clothing during day; evening after 6 P.M. varies. *Solaris* cruises of 10–12 days call for three formal evenings, two informal, and remaining evenings casual.

Cabin Amenities Telephone, television, dual-channel radio, private bathroom, and a locking drawer for valuables.

Electrical Outlets 220 AC (110 AC for razors only).

Wheelchair Access None.

Recreation and Entertainment Lounge with nightly dancing to orchestra, cabaret acts, passengers' talent show, Greek Night, Masquerade Night. Bridge, backgammon, bingo, dance classes.

Sports and Other Activities Swimming pool (two-section pool on *Solaris*), exercise classes, shuffleboard, Ping-Pong.

Beauty and Fitness Beauty salon and barbershop.

Other Facilities Boutique; laundry service, no dry cleaning; medical services; religious service; ship-to-shore telephone service.

Children's Facilities None.

Theme Cruises Intermittently.

Smoking No pipes and cigars in the dining room and lounge during show time. Smoking and nonsmoking areas assigned in the dining room.

ROC Suggested Tipping Per person per day, $9. Tips are pooled and divided among ship employees. On the *Solaris*, tips can be paid by credit card when passenger settles final bills.

Credit Cards For cruise payment and on-board charges, American Express, Mastercard, and Visa.

Stella Solaris (b)*

	Quality Rating	Value Rating
Stella Solaris (b) *	7	B

Registry: Greece	Length: 544 feet	Beam: 72 feet
Cabins: 310	Draft: 25.8 feet	Speed: 22 knots
Maximum Passengers:	Passenger Decks: 8	Elevators: 3
620	Crew: 71	Space Ratio: 29

*b—blue fleet; w—white fleet

THE SHIP   The *Stella Solaris* combines the facilities and amenities of a large ship with the atmosphere of a small, classic oceanliner. She epitomizes traditional cruising with her gracious personal service, quality, and warm Greek hospitality.

Built in 1973 from the hull of the French liner *Cambodge*, the ship has trim, flowing lines outside and an abundance of the mellow wood of a traditional liner inside. Fine tuned for North Americans, the *Solaris* nonetheless feels European, reflecting a kind of Old World charm. You get a strong sense of this as soon as you step into the dignified, dark-wood-paneled Main Foyer on Solaris Deck. No soaring atriums or lavish showrooms here; rather, refined continental surroundings are evident in furnishings and decor throughout the ship.

The cruise line has done a remarkable job of keeping the original character of the *Solaris* intact, preserving its style for more than three decades, replacing fabrics and fixtures as needed but retaining the original colors and patterns. The result is a comfortably sophisticated environment that gives passengers a sense of shipboard life in its transatlantic heyday.

By late 1995, the last phase of a major renovation of the *Solaris* was completed, resulting in an enhanced and redecorated main show lounge, an enlarged casino relocated to a larger area, a relocated and upgraded boutique, an enlarged and upgraded spa and gym, new carpets in the public areas, all redecorated cabins, and televisions in every category.

The aim of the renovations was to upgrade the facilities and enhance passenger comfort while preserving the ship's distinctive personality. In keeping with the cruise line's tradition, the $5 million project was supervised by family members—Isabella Keusseoglou, widow of the Sun Line's founder who was the ship's original decorator; daughter Daniela Keusseoglou Cameli, who is an established interior designer and antiques dealer in London; and other family members.

Passengers can orient themselves quickly since the main public rooms and dining room are on Solaris Deck, which runs the full length of the ship. Most of the rooms are open and airy. Extra-high ceilings add a feeling of spaciousness and large windows connect passengers with the sea.

The large Mediterranean-style main lounge is decorated in autumn tones of deep red and brown and hung with scenes from Greek mythology worked in bronze. The Grill Bar, richly paneled in wood, has a stunning decoration of the Minoan double axe pattern from Crete. The piano bar at the stern is a popular cocktail hour gathering spot as well as being suitable for private parties.

One flight up on Boat Deck, a card and reading room provides a quiet refuge; down on Sapphire Deck, the lowest cabin deck, concerts are given occasionally in the large, comfortable movie theater.

ITINERARIES   Caribbean, Amazon, Panama Canal, Western Caribbean in winter; transatlantic; Greek Isles, Mediterranean spring–fall.

- *December–February,* 10–28 days, Caribbean Holiday; Amazon River series between Ft. Lauderdale and Manaus, Brazil; March, 10–12 days, Panama Canal and Western Caribbean. In March, a special cruise to the Maya ruins of Guatemala, Honduras, Belize, and Mexico—timed to coincide with the vernal equinox celebrations at Chichen Itza—is a spring highlight and includes an extensive on-board lecture program.
- *On February 23, 1998,* the ship departs from Ft. Lauderdale on a ten-day Solar Eclipse cruise to Curaçao, Aruba, Ocho Rios, Grand Cayman, Cozumel, and Galveston, with four days at sea. The cruise will be accompanied by a team of experts. The cruise can be combined with an Amazon River or Panama Canal cruise with up to 50 percent savings.
- The *Stella Solaris,* along with two other Royal Olympic ships, will also offer a solar eclipse cruise in 1999 to witness the last total solar eclipse of the millennium which will occur on August 11, 1999 over central Europe, the Middle East, and South Asia. Many of the same experts on the 1998 eclipse cruises are expected to join the 1999 ones. *Stella Solaris* will sail from Athens on August 9 and rendezvous in the Black Sea with the

Triton, which departs from Athens on April 6. Meanwhile, the *Odysseus* will take up a position in the English Channel, sailing from London on August 3.

- *November and April,* transatlantic between Piraeus and Ft. Lauderdale, 21 days, westbound; 20 days, eastbound, Galveston/Ft. Lauderdale to Piraeus.
- *May–September,* 7 and 14 days, Greek Islands, Turkey, Cyprus, Egypt, and Israel.

Home Ports   Ft. Lauderdale; Galveston; Manaus; Piraeus.

Port Charges $135–190 for most cruises; $325–340 on longer cruises.

CABINS   Accommodations are offered in 11 different price categories distributed throughout the ship. Most cabins are large and decorated in coordinated pastel colors, with comfortable furnishings that usually include twin beds, a dresser with lock drawers, a large mirror, and a coffee table setting. The three top categories consist of large deluxe suites with separate sitting areas and bathrooms with tub and shower. All cabins and suites have telephones, multichannel music systems, and newly added television; nearly two-thirds have bathrooms with tub and shower. Closets and drawer space are ample.

Room service is available 24 hours and offers a limited menu.

Specifications   79 inside cabins, 184 outside; 66 suites (6 with double beds). Standard dimensions, 189 square feet. 225 with twin beds (none convertible to double); 79 with upper and lower berths; no singles; no wheelchair accessible.

DINING   The spacious dining room is first class in decor, service, and cuisine. By day the room is cheerful with daylight streaming through banks of windows on both sides of the long room. In the evening, subdued lighting provides just the right atmosphere to capture the spirit of the evening, be it the swank captain's welcome party or the festive Greek Night.

Tablecloth colors change with the theme of the evening, but the tables are always set with Royal Doulton china, Italian silverware, fine French crystal stemware, and fresh flowers. Breakfast and lunch are open seatings; dinner has two assigned seatings. Most tables are for four or six persons, in smoking and nonsmoking sections, and there are tables for two.

Food and service are continental in style but, at the same time, designed to cater to American tastes. Unlike most cruise ships which use an outside catering service, the *Solaris* does its own provisioning. Everything is prepared from scratch on board ship.

Lunch and dinner offer a wide range of choices and include low-fat and low-calorie items. Greek specialties, such as moussaka, are on the menu frequently and genuine Greek salad is almost always available. The wine list includes estate wines from the Keusseoglou family's two vineyards—Sylla Sebaste and Colle Manora—in Italy's Piedmont region.

Topside, the indoor/outdoor Lido Cafe was redesigned in the renovation to offer better food and beverage service for the adjacent pool area and to provide more recreational and entertainment options. It's the place for breakfast, lunch, and late-night buffets, midmorning bouillon, and afternoon tea. Those with a fondness for Greek cuisine will delight at the lunch buffet when it is highlighted.

Passengers who prefer informality often eat outside at umbrella-shaded tables by the ship's dual pools, or they take their trays one flight down to Boat Deck to relax on the old-fashioned wooden deck chairs (now with new cushions) and enjoy views of the sea. The deck is a wraparound promenade, popular for jogging and strolling, particularly on the days at sea.

SERVICE   One factor contributing immensely to the character of all the ships, and in particular to the *Stella Solaris*, is the remarkably large number of the Greek staff and crew who have been with the line for 20 years or more. They deliver gracious, top-notch professional service with a warm, personal touch, exemplifying the tradition of Greek hospitality, and help to create the refined, restful atmosphere that characterizes the line.

Best of all are the pride and pleasure that the crew take in their jobs—particularly in discovering and catering to the small, but important, preferences that passengers have. A case in point: On a recent cruise a passenger asked for a double cappuccino with breakfast the first morning, and the waiter seemed to delight in bringing one each day without prompting.

Solaris's large number of repeat cruisers most often attribute their attraction and loyalty to the ship, to its staff and crew, and the warm ambience they create. Many often request the same dining room and cabin attendants from cruise to cruise.

FACILITIES AND ENTERTAINMENT   Entertainment is small cabaret-style, featuring vocalists, magicians, dancers, and comedians from around the world. There's music for dancing in the main lounge after the show and in the disco, which is located on the ship's lowest deck.

A highlight of each cruise is Greek Night, when dinner features classic Greek specialities, and officers and crew don provincial costumes for an evening of Greek song and dance—passengers get into it, too. The music features the distinctive sounds of George Bouritas's bouzouki and the ship's excellent dance orchestra.

ACTIVITIES AND DIVERSIONS   The daily agenda, delivered under the cabin door, runs the gamut of the usual shipboard activities—fitness classes, bridge tournaments, arts and crafts, dance lessons, backgammon, bingo, and current films shown in the theatre several times a day, depending on the itinerary.

Enrichment programs include lectures by experts in the area of the cruise, particularly on Amazon cruises, which are accompanied by Loren McIntyre, who is credited with discovering the most remote source of the Amazon River. In March, the Mayan cruise coinciding with the equinox celebrations at Chichen Itza also has an extensive on-board lecture program.

SPORTS, FITNESS, AND BEAUTY   On Lido Deck, the ship's two-section swimming pool is surrounded by a large lounging area and there're shuffleboard and table tennis. Aerobic classes are offered throughout the cruise for passengers of all ages and levels of fitness. The newly enlarged gym on one of the cabin decks has exercise bicycles, a step machine, slant boards, and free weights. The outside promenade deck is frequented by walkers and joggers (seven times around is slightly more than a mile). The beauty salon and barbershop are on the same deck but not adjacent to the sauna and massage facilities.

SHORE EXCURSIONS   The line's comprehensive shore excursions are described in a flyer accompanying the cruise documents. Some can be reserved in advance. Tour companies working with the *Solaris* are well organized and use comfortable buses with large windows for easy viewing. Generally, tours allow sufficient time to see the sights as well as to explore on one's own. Most cruises highlight local culture and history with special features. For example, on the Amazon River cruises, a folkloric performance is staged for passengers at the Manaus Opera House; on the Maya cruise, passengers have a full-day excursion to Chichen Itza to see the mystical Feathered Serpent's Descent during the equinox.

In the Aegean, Black Sea, and the Mediterranean, where the ship spends more than half the year, the *Solaris*, with one and sometimes even two port calls almost daily, provides in effect a tour of antiquity by sea. The line's guide describing some of the history, attractions, and significance of the places visited is well written and illustrated, and makes a fine memento of your cruise.

Cruises in the Eastern Mediterranean have very full touring schedules and can be quite tiring. There is little time for lingering over meals or lounging on board the ship, unless you are content to pass up some of the sightseeing and shopping. Two special guides accompany each cruise to prepare passengers for ports and to escort them ashore.

Royal Olympic has also combined its cruise itineraries with land tours to create a catalog of 7–21 days of land and sea holidays.

POSTSCRIPT   The *Stella Solaris* gets high marks for service, food, and its balanced entertainment. Virtually every aspect of the ship reflects the personal involvement of the Keusseoglou family. Their personalities and taste coupled with the experience and attitude of the staff prove a happy combination. The Mediterranean cruises are suitable for all ages, but they are especially recommended for history buffs and travelers who want a cruise to be a culturally enriching experience.

---

*Stella Oceanis (b)**

	Quality Rating	**Value Rating**
Stella Oceanis	❸	C

Registry: Greece	Length: 350 feet	Beam: 53 feet
Cabins: 159	Draft: 15 feet	Speed: 16 knots
Maximum Passengers:	Passenger Decks: 6	Elevators: 1
369	Crew: 140	Space Ratio: 12

---

*b—blue fleet; w—white fleet

THE SHIP   Built in 1965, the *Stella Oceanis* is a smaller version of the *Stella Solaris*. Comfortable, functional, and well run, the small ship is well suited for Greek Isles and Eastern Mediterranean cruises and offers excellent shore excursions and guides.

Most public rooms are on Oceanis Deck, including the Minos Lounge (which is similar to the main lounge on the *Solaris*, but a third its size) used for dancing and entertainment, the Club, a small writing room at the stern, a small casino and shop amidship, and the Aphrodite Dining Room, forward.

At sea, the center of activity is poolside on Sun Deck, where a daily hot and cold lunch buffet with Greek specialties is set up near the bar.

One flight down on Lido Deck, the popular Plaka Taverna serves as a bar, movie theatre, room for predinner lectures and special functions, and a home for the midnight buffet and late-night disco. The deck also houses a beauty salon and barbershop; an outside promenade wraps around all but the forward section. The cuisine and service are outstanding and combine the line's Greek heritage with continental selections catering to American as well as European tastes.

ITINERARIES   Greek Isles, Eastern Mediterranean.

- *April–October:* Three-, four-, and seven-day port-intensive cruises through Greek Islands and Turkey. A comprehensive selection of shore excursions (described in a flyer accompanying the cruise documents) are available for sale on-board the ship. Three-day itinerary departs from Piraeus for Mykonos, Rhodes, Patmos, and Kusadasi (the port for Ephesus in Turkey). The four-day itinerary departs from Piraeus for Mykonos, Crete, Santorini, Rhodes, Kusadasi, and Patmos. Either itinerary can be combined with a hotel package for 7-, 10-, and 11-day land/sea programs.
- *The seven-day cruise* departs on Friday from Piraeus to Santorini, Crete, Port Said, Ashdod, Patmos, and Kusadasi.

Home Port   Piraeus.
Port Charges $50–135.

CABINS   The majority of the cabins are outside and rather simply furnished. They have a private bathroom with shower, telephone, and dual-channel radio. The 38 deluxe cabins have private baths with tubs, and the 6 suites are aft on Sun Deck.

Specifications   46 inside cabins, 107 outside; 6 suites. Standard dimensions, 130 square feet. 127 with twin beds (none convertible to double); 17 upper/lower berths; no singles; none wheelchair accessible.

POSTSCRIPT   The *Stella Oceanis* is a comfortable, well-run ship suitable for short, destination-oriented itineraries. Most days are spent in port with one or two half-days of daylight cruising between ports. The atmosphere and crew are Greek, while the passengers are from North

America and Europe. Cruises are very port-intensive, some with two ports of call in one day. They should not be thought of as a cruise in the usual sense as much as a tour of the Greek and Mediterranean islands by sea. Greek tour guides are among the best in the world, having to be university graduates and to meet very high standards to qualify. They are extremely proud of their country and of being Greek and are very eager for those on tour to benefit from their extensive knowledge. Hence, shore excursions are comprehensive tours of the famous sites of antiquity and can be tiring. You should pace yourself.

In the busy summer months, the line endeavors to get its passengers to popular historic sites before the competition, even if it means an early morning call. Most travelers will be grateful for it. The port-intensive nature of the itinerary will be most appreciated by those interested in Greek history and antiquity. Readers planning to take a cruise on the Oceanis should review all the section on Royal Olympic Cruises.

Odysseus (b)*

	Quality Rating	**Value Rating**
Odysseus	❷	C

Registry: Greece	Length: 483 feet	Beam: 61 feet
Cabins: 226	Draft: 21 feet	Speed: 17 knots
Maximum Passengers: 486	Passenger Decks: 7	Elevators: 1
	Crew: 200	Space Ratio: 19

*b—blue fleet; w—white fleet

THE SHIP The former *Aquamarine,* built in 1962, was virtually rebuilt by Epirotiki before she reappeared as the *Odysseus* in 1989. She was refurbished again in 1995 when she became part of Royal Olympic's blue fleet. The ship combines the cozy qualities of a small ship with the amenities of a large one. Her stability and deep draft make her well suited for the new South American winter and north European summer itineraries she was recently assigned.

Most of the public rooms are on Jupiter Deck with a main lounge forward; a casino, bar/lounge, nightclub, and card room amidships; and an outdoor swimming pool and large deck area aft. Topside there is an observation deck forward and a large solarium aft, along with the beauty salon and spa which offer massage, sauna, and beauty treatments; and a fitness center with an exercise room. The ship also has a sheltered teak-decked promenade. Other facilities include four Jacuzzis, four bars/lounges, shops, library, and 24-hour room service.

ITINERARIES   South America, winter; Europe, summer.

- *December–March:* 7–14 days, South America between Buenos Aires, Argentina and Puerto Montt, Chile through the Straits of Magellan. There are also two cruises from Rio de Janeiro.
- *November and April:* 21 day-transatlantic positioning cruises, westbound from Piraeus; eastbound from Rio de Janeiro to Lisbon.
- *April–October:* 10–14 days, Mediterranean between Lisbon and Piraeus; North Europe from Lisbon to London, the Baltic, and to the Eastern Mediterranean.
- The *Odysseus* will be one of three ROC ships offering a solar eclipse cruise in 1999 to witness the last total eclipse of the millennium on August 11, 1999, over central Europe, the Middle East, and South Asia. She will be in the English Channel, sailing from London on August 3.

Home Ports   Buenos Aires and other ports, depending on itinerary.
Port Charges   n.a.

CABINS   The attractive, spacious cabins are located on five of the seven passenger decks and about 80 percent are outside. Most are furnished with convertible sofa-beds but a few have double beds. All have bathrooms with shower and limited hanging space.

Specifications   43 inside cabins, 183 outside; 2 deluxe; 143 with twin beds; 10 with double; 12 triples; 31 with upper and lower berths; no singles; no wheelchair accessible.

DINING   The attractive dining room has two seatings for three meals and serves European cuisine with Greek specialties. The ship's most popular spot is the Taverna where passengers gather around the bar in lively camaraderie throughout the cruise.

The atmosphere and the service are warm, friendly, and attentive in true Greek style. Greek Night is the highlight of the entertainment when the ship's public rooms virtually become a taverna. The evening is a cultural immersion with the joyful participation by the Greek staff and passengers enjoying Greek music, dance, and cuisine.

POSTSCRIPT *Odysseus* is well suited for those who prefer a small, comfortable ship, friendly environment at a modest price, and neither want nor need the flash and dazzle of the megaliners. The *Odysseus,* the *Stella Solaris,* and the *Triton* will all offer solar eclipse cruises in 1999 to witness the last total solar eclipse of the millennium. The *Odysseus* will take up a position in the English Channel sailing from London on August 3. The other ships will rendezvous in the Black Sea.

---

*Olympic (w)**

	Quality Rating	*Value Rating*
Olympic	❷	C

Registry: Greece	Length: 650 feet	Beam: 86 feet
Cabins: 457	Draft: 29 feet	Speed: 17 knots
Maximum Passengers: 1,240	Passenger Decks: 9	Elevators: 2
	Crew: 550	Space Ratio: 30

*b—blue fleet; w—white fleet

THE SHIP Built in Scotland as the *Empress of Britain* in 1956, the *Olympic* sailed as the *Queen Anna Maria* for ten years and became the *Carnivale* in 1976, when she was renovated extensively as a member of the two-vessel fleet of the then-fledgling Carnival Cruise Lines. In 1993, she had a short life as the *FiestaMarina,* for Carnival's aborted cruise venture to cater to the Latin market.

Over the years and all the reincarnations, she has retained some of the essential qualities of her traditional interiors such as the wood paneling and polished brass, but lightened and brightened by more recent renovations. Such embellishments from the past as Wedgewood etched glass doors have been carefully preserved. Yet, any way you look at it, the lady is showing her age.

The ship has generous open space on its upper decks, but is crowded when the ship is full of passengers. Its facilities include one indoor and two outdoor swimming pools, a Jacuzzi, show lounge, piano bar, casino, disco, theatre, gift shop, library, and self-service laundry. The dining room with its new marble entrance and contemporary decor is located on a lower deck and has two-seatings for three meals.

The gym, also located on a lower deck, offers exercise classes and equipment and there is a beauty salon/barbershop. Deck sports include shuffleboard, table tennis, and trapshooting. The ship has enclosed promenade decks.

ITINERARIES The *Olympic*, the largest ship on three- and four-day Greek Isles itineraries, sails round trip from Piraeus from March through October. The three-day cruises depart on Friday to Mykonos, Rhodes, Kusadasi, and Patmos. The four-day cruises depart on Monday and visit Mykonos, Kusadasi, Patmos, Rhodes, Crete, and Santorini.

CABINS The cabins are located on four of the eight passenger decks and range in size from very small to very large. Those in the upper categories, particularly, are quite spacious; some cabins even have king-size beds.

Specifications 265 inside cabins, 216 outside; 5 deluxe; 13 singles; 318 with twin beds; 58 with double beds; 87 with upper and lower berths; none wheelchair accessible.

Orpheus (w)*

Orpheus	Quality Rating ❷	Value Rating C
Registry: Greece	Length: 375 feet	Beam: 50 feet
Cabins: 152	Draft: 16 feet	Speed: 17 knots
Maximum Passengers: 318	Passenger Decks: 4	Elevators: n.a.
	Crew: 140	Space Ratio: 30

*b—blue fleet; w—white fleet

THE SHIP Chartered by Swan Hellenic Cruises for years until 1995, the *Orpheus* was lovingly cared for by her devoted patrons. The charming ship has comfortable public rooms with pleasant decor and ample open deck space for her small size. The pretty dining room has an open seating policy and offers attentive, friendly service from its Greek crew.

Facilities include an outdoor pool, Jacuzzis, beauty shop, showroom, three bars/lounges, casino, shops, and library. The cabins, which were refurbished recently, are nicely appointed but small, although adequate for the kind of cruises the ship offers. With port-intensive itineraries you are likely to spend more time sightseeing than sleeping. The ship has 35 inside cabins, 116 outside; 7 singles.

ITINERARIES The *Orpheus* sails on an unusual seven-day itinerary that combines the Greek Isles and Crete with Albania. She departs weekly from Piraeus every Saturday between May and October, sailing west to the Corinth Canal with calls at Delphi, Ithaca, Saranda (Albania), Corfu, Zante, Katakolon, Crete, Santorini, Mykonos, and Nauplion.

Triton (w)*

	Quality Rating	*Value Rating*
Triton	❸	C

Registry: Greece	Length: 491 feet	Beam: 70 feet
Cabins: 352	Draft: 21 feet	Speed: 17 knots
Maximum Passengers:	Passenger Decks: 7	Elevators: 2
898	Crew: 265	Space Ratio: 20

*b—blue fleet; w—white fleet

THE SHIP Built in 1971 as the *Cunard Adventurer*, the ship was bought by Norwegian Cruise Line in 1976, which refurbished and renamed her *Sunward II*. In 1991, she was acquired by Epirotiki Lines which renovated her prior to introducing her as the *Triton* in 1992.

The public rooms, including the dining room, and recreational facilities are on the top four of the seven passenger decks while most of the cabins are on the bottom three decks. Her facilities include a showroom, nightclub, four bars/lounges, a casino, beauty/barbershop, boutique, and a theatre with daily movies.

Triton has wide teak decks and a large outdoor swimming pool with an expansive open deck area; next to the pool is the fitness center.

A light and bright dining room dressed in contemporary colors offers two seatings for three meals and serves Continental cuisine and Greek specialties. The service is cheerful and attentive; the ambience is friendly.

CABINS   Cabins are fairly small and narrow but attractively furnished. Standard outside cabins have two lower beds that in most cases can be combined into a queen-size bed. All are furnished with desk/dresser and chair and have bathroom with shower.

Specifications   112 inside cabins, 223 outside; 32 deluxe. 299 with twin beds, convertible to double; 4 with upper and lower berths; no singles; none wheelchair accessible.

ITINERARIES   The *Triton* sails on seven-day cruises of the Greek Isles, Crete, and Turkey from March–November, departing round trip from Piraeus on Friday for Santorini, Heraklion (Crete), Rhodes, Patmos, Kusadasi, Istanbul (overnight), Delos, and Mykonos.

- As one of the larger ships with weekly Greece/Turkey itineraries, the *Triton* offers more facilities than smaller ships and good value. She is popular with budget-minded Europeans.
- The *Triton*, along with *Stella Solaris* and the *Odysseus* will offer solar eclipse cruises in 1999 to witness the last total solar eclipse of the millennium on August 11, 1999 over central Europe, the Middle East, and South Asia. The *Triton* will depart from Athens on April 6 and rendezvous with *Stella Solaris* in the Black Sea. Meanwhile, the *Odysseus* will take up a position in the English Channel, sailing from London on August 3.

SEABOURN CRUISE LINE

55 Francisco Street, San Francisco, CA 94133
(415) 391-7444; (800) 929-9595; (800) 527-0999 (Canada);
fax (415) 391-8518
email: seabourn@aol.com

TYPE OF SHIPS   Small, modern, ultraluxurious oceanliners.

TYPE OF CRUISES   Top-of-the-line luxury cruises on worldwide itineraries.

CRUISE LINE'S STRENGTHS
- impeccable service
- luxurious accommodations
- exclusivity
- ship size/maneuverability
- single, open-seating dining
- cuisine
- worldwide itineraries

CRUISE LINE'S SHORTCOMINGS
- limited activities
- limitations on use of water sports facilities
- poor positioning of outdoor pool
- room service breakfast

FELLOW PASSENGERS   Sophisticated, discriminating, well-heeled, experienced travelers; 80 percent are from North America; others are wealthy, seasoned, international travelers from the United Kingdom, Switzerland, Germany, and around the world. Age can vary widely, depending on season and destinations. Most are 50 and older, but some are young professionals—doctors, lawyers, entrepreneurs—and honeymooners. They come mainly from the Northeastern Seaboard, Florida, California, and the Chicago area but might come from anywhere. A high number, sometimes as many as 50 percent, will be repeaters.

Passengers on shorter cruises, such as those in the Caribbean, are likely to be active business owners and professionals, some semiretired, age 55 and above; but the mix could include a childless couple in their upper 30s, a honeymoon couple in their 40s, and a family of three generations, ranging from 4–70 years in age. Passengers, however diverse, have very similar backgrounds. They are likely to have sailed on other luxury vessels and stayed in five-star hotels. They know and understand quality; their expectations are high and their judgment tough.

Recommended For   Sophisticated, seasoned travelers accustomed to the best; affluent passengers whose first priority is service; those who seek exclusivity; people looking for a good trip rather than a good time; yacht owners who want to leave the driving to others; those who shun cruises due to their big ship, glitzy image; first-timers who can afford it and seek small ship ambience; honeymooners with rich daddys; anyone who has won the lottery.

Not Recommended For   Those unaccustomed to luxury or a posh, sophisticated environment; anyone uncomfortable in a fancy restaurant or five-star or grand-luxe European hotel; flashy dressers, late-night revelers, inexperienced travelers, children.

CRUISE AREAS AND SEASONS   Winter: Caribbean, transcanal, South America, Asia, Australia, South Pacific. Spring: Mediterranean, South Asia. Summer/Fall: Canada, Alaska, Europe, Norwegian fjords, Baltic, British Isles.

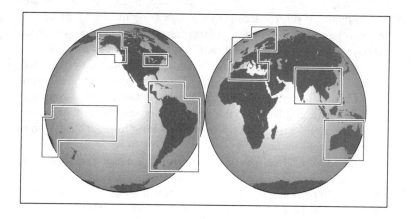

THE LINE   Founded in 1987 by a young Norwegian industrialist, Atle Brynestad, Seabourn Cruise Line's goal from the outset was to create the world's most luxurious cruises on the most elegant ships afloat, setting new standards and appealing to the world's most discriminating travelers.

To guide its debut, the line selected Warren Titus, whose stewardship of Royal Viking Lines from its inception in the 1970s had helped to set top-quality standards for the entire cruise industry for two decades. Despite very high per diem rates, Seabourn quickly won enough fans with its first ship, *Seabourn Pride*, to add a second one.

Seabourn's posh ships with their sleek profiles resembling modern yachts fall into a category all their own: small enough to have the exclusivity of *Sea Goddess* (although more than twice the size), yet large enough to have the spaciousness and most facilities of a large vessel like *Crystal Harmony* (but at a quarter its size)—and with an ambience that touches on the carefree elegance of *Wind Star*.

In designing the ship, Seabourn had a certain person in mind—one who normally stays in the best room at a luxury hotel and books a deluxe suite on a luxury liner. The assumption was that such people like the space and facilities of a large ship but want the exclusivity and personalized service of a yacht. The result: Seabourn ships have six decks with lounges, bars, boutique, casino, swimming pool, and spa but carry a maximum of 212 passengers—and all in suites.

The cruises follow the sun on worldwide itineraries that, in effect, circle the globe in a year's time. They range from 3–23 days but most are 10–14 days and run consecutively through a specific area, such as the Mediterranean or the Far East, so that passengers might cruise for up to 60 days without repeating ports and can benefit from substantial savings on the second, third, or fourth segment. The shortest cruises are meant as samplers to broaden the line's base. Also to that end, Seabourn often features celebrities, such as Victor Borge, David McCulloch, and celebrity chefs, and has special interest cruises, such as golf. Most Far East cruises and many Eastern Mediterranean cruises include some shore excursions in the price.

Dubbed the "Rolls Royce of the cruise industry" and winner of every top prize that's offered to cruise lines, Seabourn is a privately held company, 75 percent owned by its founder and 25 percent by Carnival Cruise Line. In 1996, with the demise of Royal Viking and Royal Cruise lines, Seabourn acquired the *Royal Viking Queen* (aka *Queen Odyssey*) which had originally been intended as the third member of the Seabourn group.

The Fleet	Built/Renovated	Tonnage	Passengers
Seabourn Legend	1991	10,000	204
Seabourn Pride	1988	10,000	204
Seabourn Spirit	1989	10,000	204

STYLE   Elegant but not stuffy, glamorous without glitz, the *Seabourn Pride* and *Seabourn Spirit* are in the style of a toney international resort. Quality is the keynote, starting with an embarkation that is made almost effortless and a smiling, white-gloved attendant who will escort you to your suite—a suite that's every inch as luxurious as the brochure shows it to be—where fruit and a bottle of champagne are awaiting your arrival.

The decor is one of understated elegance. The service is as polished as the silver with which you dine—always attentive but never intrusive. You will be addressed by name by the staff after your first appearance.

A favorite among savvy travelers from several continents, Seabourn attracts both the old-monied who disdain today's mainstream cruise ships and the newly rich who appreciate its status symbolism. It also caters to stressed-out professionals and others seeking privacy and exclusivity. Whatever their background—whether to the manner born or acquired—they are affluent enough to be accustomed to a high level of service and style without a lot of fuss. There's very little pretension.

Days at sea are meant to relax, with dress and atmosphere informal and time unstructured. There is none of the usual atmosphere of a cruise ship with announcements, pool games, and contests. In fact, a Seabourn cruise is so low-key, you may need to read your daily agenda even to know where you are and what's happening.

Each cruise has one or two special events meant to be highlights. It might be a special concert in an unusual location held only for Seabourn passengers, a visit to a private island, marina, or estate, a sporting event, or some other unusual activity. Evenings aboard ship are somewhat more formal, with fine dining the highlight of the day. On the evenings you prefer to relax, a full-course dinner will be served in your suite.

Adding to the luxury, in 1997 Seabourn introduced "As You Like It," which it calls the ultimate in vacation flexibility, giving passengers the freedom to choose from a variety of options. Passengers can custom-tailor their cruise with separate and independently priced cruise fares, air-travel options, pre- and postcruise tours, hotel and transfers. For the air portions, passengers have three choices: Seabourn's air program with preselected carriers, economy, business, first class, or the Concorde; the cruise line's independent air program, booked through Seabourn; or third, transport by a chartered Gulfstream to and from their Seabourn cruise and anywhere in the world.

DISTINCTIVE FEATURES   No tipping allowed. Very low single supplements; unusual care for solo passengers' welfare. Worldfare. Underwater viewing room; foldout water sports marina. Personalized stationery. Complimentary self-service laundry/dryer. The "As You Like It" booking options; golf program with the Wide World of Golf.

RATES

Highest Per Diem	Lowest Per Diem	Average Per Diem
$1,629	$539	$675

The above per diems are calculated from the cruise line's nondiscounted *cruise-only* fares on standard accommodations. What you will actually pay *should* be *substantially* less (see Part One, How to Get the Best Deal on a Cruise). Per diems vary by season, by cabin location, and by cruise areas.

Special Note: All tips are included in the cruise fare on the Seabourn fleet.

Special Fares and Discounts   Advance purchase discounts of 10 percent for 12 months and 5 percent for 6 months on cruise only. Second cabin purchase by family or friends and combination cruises for certain two or more successive cruises also garner additional savings.

- Worldfare: Advance purchase of 45 cruising days for $29,500 to 120 days for $66,500.
- Third Person: 25 percent of per person published tariff.
- Children's Fare: Same as third person rate.
- Single Supplement: 110 percent, 125 percent, 150 percent of per person double occupancy basic suite, depending on cruise.

Packages
- Air/Sea: All cruises packaged with economy class air; first and business class upgrades available for an additional charge.
- Others: Yes.

- Pre/Post: Yes. Many of the basic air/sea packages include one hotel night in the departure city; extensions are available in all major gateways.

Past Passengers   Past passengers become members of the Seabourn Club; they receive a members-only quarterly magazine with articles by established writers and information on member-designated cruises with discounts, sometimes up to 50 percent; other benefits include shipboard events hosted by the captain. Members can get fare reductions for accumulated days of sailing on Seabourn ships, ranging from a 25 percent saving after 28 days to a free 14-day cruise after 140 days. For a second Seabourn cruise, members get free trip cancellation/interruption insurance plus other insurance and medical coverage.

THE LAST WORD   Seabourn says it may be expensive but not overpriced. If you can afford the price tag, you are not likely to find anything finer, even if you own your own yacht. And not to be overlooked regarding prices, tipping is absolutely forbidden, a fact that does not influence the exceptionally high quality of service.

Seabourn offers one of cruising's lowest single supplement fares of 110 percent on over half of its cruises and 125 percent on others, rather than the cruise industry's standard 150 percent, which Seabourn applies to only a few of its offerings. Its Worldfare is an innovative advance purchase plan that is something like a time-share or buying season tickets to the opera or a sporting event and is intended for seasoned cruisers who take several voyages each year.

Seabourn's aim is to exceed expectations. And, judging from the awards and accolades it has received since its inception and its high number of repeaters—they seem to do just that.

Seabourn Standard Features

Officers Norwegian.

Staffs Dining/European; Cabin/Scandinavian; Cruise/British and American.

Dining Facilities All meals served at one seating in restaurant; indoor/outdoor cafe for casual breakfast and lunch and one evening specialty dinner. En suite dining.

Special Diets Available upon request.

Room Service 24 hours, cabin menu and full-service dining room menu.

Dress Code Casual, informal, or formal. By day, casual but conservative, comfortable. Dinner is a dressy affair, informal (jacket and tie for men) or formal (two black-tie evenings on one-week cruise; four formal dinners on two-week cruise).

Cabin Amenities Stocked bar, mini-refrigerator; television with CNN, VCR, direct-dial phone; marble bathroom with twin sinks, tub and shower, toiletries, hair dryer, bathrobes, walk-in closet, safe.

Electrical Outlets 110/220 AC.

Wheelchair Access Limited.

Recreation and Entertainment Three lounges with entertainment/dance music nightly; cabaret, classical music concerts, folkloric performances in ports of call; weekly dinner-dance; casino; cruise-related lectures.

Sports and Other Activities Water sports marina, outdoor pool, deck sports; bridge instructor/lessons; enrichment programs.

Beauty and Fitness Two saunas, two outdoor whirlpools, small gym, exercise classes, beauty salon, spa with massage, beauty treatments.

Other Facilities Self-service laundry, laundry/dry cleaning; library; boutique; hospital; nondenominational religious services.

Children's Facilities None; children under 18 years of age must be accompanied by parent or adult with written permission.

Theme Cruises Golf, classical music, food and wine.

Smoking Public rooms are designated as nonsmoking. One lounge is a smoker for after dinner.

Seabourn Suggested Tipping Strict no-tipping policy.

Credit Cards For cruise payment and on-board charges, American Express, Diners Club, Mastercard, Visa.

Seabourn Legend /Seabourn Pride Seabourn Spirit

	Quality Rating	Value Rating
Seabourn Legend	Preview	
Seabourn Pride	⑨	D
Seabourn Spirit	⑨	D

Registry: Norway	Length: 439 feet	Beam: 63 feet
Cabins: 106	Draft: 16 feet	Speed: 18 knots
Maximum Passengers: 212	Passenger Decks: 6	Elevators: 4
	Crew: 145	Space Ratio: 49

THE SHIPS   In this age of glitzy ships and awesome atriums, the Seabourn triplets, which are almost identical, are masters in understatement. Clean lines, soft pastels, fine fabrics, all subtle and styled, are meant to soothe the senses.

The lobby where passengers enter the ship is both a focal point and an instant revelation of its character. Quietly elegant, it has a small atrium that spans five decks with a double circular stairway accented by brass railings and etched glass balustrades. Diffused natural light from a glass dome at the top on the Sky Deck illuminates the stairway and adjacent hallways and orchestrates a harmony of the soft apricot and mauve carpeting with the matching blush tone marble and wood used throughout the vessel. The sense of space and serenity is immediate and one of the ships' most appealing features.

The public rooms occupy all of the two top levels and are aft on the two center decks; the accommodations are forward on three decks; and the dining room is amidships on the lowest passenger level.

On Magellan Deck, aft of the lobby, is the Magellan Lounge (King Olav on *Legend*; Amundsen Lounge on *Spirit*), the main showroom with a stage and dance floor, used for both daytime lectures and evening entertainment. In the immediate area of the lobby is the tour desk, cruise director's office, a card and writing room, and a small business services center with a computer.

One flight up on Marco Polo Deck (Monte Carlo on *Spirit*/Oslo on *Legend*), the Club is a second entertainment lounge, cleverly divided into three glass-partitioned sections: to starboard, a small casino with roulette, blackjack, and slot machines; to port, a bar with seats that invite an informal atmosphere; and in the center, an all-purpose lounge with a piano, which is used for activities, socializing, and parties during the day and predinner cocktails with music. It doubles as the nightclub for after-dinner drinks and dancing in the evening. There is also a small book and video library.

The first of the two top levels, the Leif Eriksson Deck (Spa Deck on *Legend* and *Spirit*) is the sports and spa deck with the indoor/outdoor Veranda Cafe at the stern. Another flight up on the top deck, forward above the bridge, is the Constellation Lounge (Midnight Sun on *Legend*; Horizon Lounge on *Spirit*), a beautiful observation center with sloping floor-to-ceiling windows looking out over panoramic views of the sea. The nicest of the public rooms but surprisingly underutilized, it has a radar screen linked to the bridge, a huge globe, and a computerized nautical wall display that reads out weather conditions, itineraries, maps, and charts.

Early bird continental breakfast and afternoon tea are served here—both stellar times for enjoying scenic views. Reference material on shore excursions, board games, and puzzles are available to enjoy at leisure. Outside, there's a bar with outdoor seating—a place for morning boullion and a popular socializing nook on fair weather days. The bar is connected to a sunning deck at the stern by a promenade used by walkers and joggers for their daily rounds.

ITINERARIES   The Seabourn triplets roam the globe seasonally on cruises usually in contiguous segments of 3–22 days that can be combined into long voyages of 27–87 days. Essentially, each series is focused on a particular area of the world:

Seabourn Legend: Through 1997, China, South Asia, South Pacific, Australia/New Zealand. For 1998, Australia/New Zealand, South Pacific, Philippines/Hong Kong, China, Japan/Russian, Far East/Alaska, and return to China, Asia, and Australia/New Zealand.

Seabourn Pride: Through 1997, New England/Canada; Caribbean; Panama Canal. For 1998, January–March, South America; summer, Europe, Norwegian fjords, Baltic, British Islands; September–October, New York/New England/Canada; November/December, Eastern and Western Caribbean.

Seabourn Spirit: Through 1997, Eastern Mediterranean, Middle East, Africa/Seychelles, Southeast Asia to Hong Kong. For 1998, Southeast Asia, India to Eastern Mediterranean via the Suez Canal.

April–October, Eastern and Western Mediterranean; November and December, Africa/Indian Ocean, Southeast Asia to Hong Kong.

The ships often visit little-frequented ports, such as Mayreau in the Grenadines, and exotic destinations such as Nosy Komba, Madagascar; Ho Chi Minh City, Vietnam; Vladivostok, Russia; and Salalah, Oman. Extensive pre- and postcruise add-ons and optional shore excursions, such the Galápagos on the South America itineraries, allow for in-depth inland travel.

Because of their size and turn-on-a-dime maneuverability, the Seabourn ships are often able to reach places inaccessible to large ships. For example, on the Norwegian fjords cruises, the ship sails into the beautiful Trollfjord, with walls almost straight up and so narrow at the end that even a small ship barely has space to turn around.

The ships' small size also gives their captains the option to surprise passengers occasionally by turning a day at sea into a surprise beach party in a remote location, or, in the case of the fjords, a salmon bake on the private island of Seabourn's owner.

Home Ports Ft. Lauderdale and worldwide ports, depending on cruise.

Port Charges Vary, depending on itinerary, but average about $175 for 7 days in Mediterranean to $245 for 14 days in Asia.

CABINS The elegant accommodations—all spacious, outside suites—are one of the ships' finest features. Even the standard ones, called Seabourn Suites, are among the largest accommodations on any ship. They are brilliantly designed to maximize space—and oh, so practical. The exquisite appointments—wall coverings, carpets, draperies, bed-covers of fine, lightly textured fabrics—are coordinated in either muted light blue, teal or apricot monotones and trimmed with light wood, giving the rooms a sense of harmony and enhancing their spaciousness.

Superbly designed to maximize space, they have two well-defined sections: a roomy sitting area with a sofa, two chairs, and a coffee table that can be raised and transformed into a dining table for en suite dining. Tucked under the table are two round, cushioned stools that provide extra seats for guests or comfortable leg rests for reading or watching television or a movie on your VCR.

The sitting area is next to a five-foot-wide picture window placed low enough on the wall for you to lie in bed or enjoy breakfast and watch the passing panorama. The adjacent, mirrored wall reflects the view of what lies ahead, bringing the outdoors inside, and enhances the feeling of spaciousness. The window has an electrically operated shade that can be raised or lowered by a switch conveniently located by the desk, and an automatic mechanism to clean the windows on the outside.

The sitting area can be separated by a curtain from the sleeping area for total darkness and the beds can be configured either as twins or a queen. The bedroom section has a long built-in dresser/desk with drawers and a large mirror with makeup lights.

On one wall between the bedroom and sitting area is a mini-refrigerator and bar stocked with four full bottles of spirits, which you select at the time of booking. These, along with the welcome champagne, are provided without charge; replenishments are charged. There is no charge for mineral water and soft drinks. The bar is also supplied with fine crystal glassware provided by Seabourn's owner, who also owns a well-known crystal factory in Norway.

On the opposite wall is another built-in cabinet with a pull-out writing desk, which contains a supply of your personalized stationery and a small sewing kit with an assortment of already threaded needles. The cabinet conceals a remote-controlled color television, with channels for CNN and other satellite stations as well as on-board programs, and a VCR. There is a radio with four music channels and a phone. The walk-in closet, with heavy wooden suit and pants hangers and soft dress ones, has additional small drawer and shelf space and a combination safe.

The marble bathroom is almost as elegant as the bedroom. It has twin sinks (*Legend*, one sink) and mirrored storage shelves as well as open shelves, a large tub, and a shower. Thick terry cloth bathrobes, a hair dryer, and a selection of toiletries are supplied.

Even the cabin doors have a thoughtful touch—an attractive brass clamp that holds such items as the daily agenda, messages, and menus for lunch and dinner, which are delivered daily. A hall-side door can be used to convert adjacent standard suites into double ones.

In addition to the standard staterooms, there are 16 larger suites in four different configurations. Classic suites have queen beds only, a larger sitting area, and a small veranda. Regal suites have a separate bedroom and living room, two bathrooms (one with a shower and one with a tub), a table with four chairs, two walk-in closets, and two sofas. The two owner's suites are the largest and have small private verandas and a large sitting area.

Specifications All suites: 88 standard suites *Seabourn* (90 *Legend/Spirit*), 2 classic with verandas, 10 regal (12 *Legend/Spirit*), 4 owner's with verandas. Standard dimensions, 277 square feet. 102 with twins (convertible to queen); no singles.

DINING   Fine dining is central to a Seabourn cruise and the choices are more diverse than you might think for a ship of this size. For any of the three meals, you can dine when and with whom you like in the Restaurant, the elegant dining room that operates like a restaurant with open seating; the casual Veranda Cafe, an indoor/outdoor venue for buffet breakfast and lunch and an occasional specialty dinner; or in your suite where a 24-hour cabin menu is available or a full-course meal from the dining room menu will be served course by course. There is also morning bouillon in the Sky Bar and afternoon tea with real cucumber sandwiches in the Constellation Lounge.

Seabourn claims it spends the highest amount for food of any cruise line and, given its very high quality, there is little reason to doubt the assertion. The emphasis at all times is on fresh, local ingredients, such as seafood, fruits, and vegetables, from ports of call. Breads, pastries, and ice cream are prepared on board.

Menus, changed daily and repeated on a 60-day cycle, offer a great variety with three appetizers, two soups, two salads, four entrees, four desserts, and selections of cheese and ice cream. Generally, the cuisine is light, creative, and sophisticated. While you will find a familiar fettuccine alfredo or poached halibut, you are just as likely to be tempted with exotic choices, such as seared reindeer or grilled marlin with strawberry and cilantro sauce. There are vegetarian specialties and lean and light ones, too.

Menu entrees are cooked to order and the presentation is as outstanding as the cuisine. Menus have at least two suggested wines, usually moderate in price; there is also an elaborate wine list. Wine is available by the glass.

The Restaurant is a pretty room where the same muted pastels used throughout the ship continue but in different designs and textures. Tables in the dining room are set with Wedgewood china, fine crystal and silverware, and fresh flowers on starched linens. Most tables are for four or six, but twos and eights or tens will be accommodated.

Breakfast and lunch here appeal most to those who prefer a quiet environment and full table service. Dinner is a lavish, somewhat formal affair to be savored leisurely with good wine and good company. Two evenings in the week call for formal attire, and for all but the one or two casual nights, you will want to be fashionably dressed, as when attending the theatre or dining in a fine restaurant in New York or Paris.

The service is unfailingly superb. Indeed, the service in the Restaurant is the best, most professional service we have had on any cruise ship and equals that in the most swank restaurant in London or Paris.

The food does not always match it. When the chef creates his signature dishes at dinner, the results are fabulous and comparable to the finest restaurants anywhere. At other times, particularly at breakfast and lunch, it can be simply good and sometimes, very good. But cold croissants for breakfast are a disappointment.

At least once during a cruise there is a dinner dance with live music in the Restaurant. Unlike other cruise ships, where singles are usually left to their own devices, passengers traveling solo on Seabourn are invited to join an officer's table or one hosted by management or a social staff member. An invitation to join one of them will be slipped under your door almost daily unless you indicate, of course, that you prefer to dine alone.

The informal, convivial atmosphere of the Veranda Cafe makes it the most popular choice for breakfast and lunch. The lively cafe bustles with people and conversation indoors, and outside, a wide deck that wraps around the stern has tables under protective awnings. In fair weather, with the open sea or beautiful scenery all around you, the outside deck is simply one of the most delightful, agreeable dining places anyone could devise.

For breakfast, the buffet has selections of fresh fruit, freshly made breads and pastries, smoked fish, cheeses, and eggs, pancakes, and waffles made to order. For lunch, the buffet includes an array of salads, made-to-order pasta with a different sauce each day, hot and cold seafood, chicken and meats, or grilled fish or meat on request. There are daily surprises—guacamole or an oriental buffet—and a cheese and dessert bar with too many hard-to-resist specialties, including homemade ice cream—a passenger favorite.

But do understand, these repasts are not your ordinary cruise ship self-service buffets. An army of dining stewards take drink orders and almost never let you carry a plate to your table. They return frequently to ask if you need a refill or second helpings, which they rush off to get for you before you can get up from your chair.

Normally on one evening of a cruise, the Veranda Cafe becomes a trattoria with a special menu and lively music as an informal alternative to the Restaurant. The meal and the evening are wonderful and very popular. You should reserve early as space is limited.

A 24-hour room service menu has standard fare of sandwiches, soups, salad, and cheese plates. A full five-course dinner will be served in your suite, one or two courses at a time, as you prefer. But unless you want or need privacy or a respite from the dress code (particularly after a long shore excursion day), room service dining at its best is never as good as the Restaurant.

SERVICE   Most passengers rate service as the single best feature—and with good reason: it's impeccable. Throughout the ship, the staff is gracious, highly attentive but never intrusive, congenial but never obtrusive, and thoroughly professional in the most exquisite European manner. The Norwegian captain and officers, the European hotel staff, the Swedish stewardesses (all from Gothenberg, I am told), and the British and American cruise and social staff—all seem to work in harmony and are visibly proud of their ship. A concierge is available for special services, as well. Needless to say, the small size of a Seabourn ship lends itself to a higher, more personalized level of service than is possible on a larger ship. Then too, there's more opportunity to provide good service in a luxury setting, and the high crew-to-passenger ratio enables them to deliver it. There is no tipping. Period. When ships with the most laudable service have a no-tipping policy, it makes you wonder why other ships don't get the message.

FACILITIES AND ENTERTAINMENT   In the evening, entertainment, like everything else aboard, is toney and designed for people with sophisticated tastes. The ship's small orchestra plays easy listening and dancing music in the Club, or a pianist/vocalist offers light tunes for cocktails a la Bobby Short. Evening cabaret and variety shows in the Magellan Lounge are equally as stylish and urbane and usually very good. They feature the cruise director and three or four of the social staff who are talented, professional entertainers doing double duty. The seats in the lounge are slightly tiered in theatre style, providing excellent sight lines.

Some evenings, or perhaps in the late afternoon, there will be a concert of classical music or a musical program by a young artist; another evening, the Restaurant becomes a supper club with dancing. And the casino offers roulette, blackjack, slot machines, and lessons, if you need them.

ACTIVITIES AND DIVERSIONS   Time aboard Seabourn is yours to do as you please. You receive a daily agenda, just as on other cruise ships, but it will not be taxing and might include a cooking demonstration by the guest chef, particularly if you have chosen a gourmet cruise, or an afternoon talk session if there is an ambassador, best-selling author, or well-known person from the arts, academia, politics, or show business aboard. Experts on the area of the cruise give several lectures, and depending on the port, a folkloric show by a local group might be staged.

There will be a morning port talk and likely a movie on one of Seabourn's other cruises—a not-too-subtle sales pitch for future bookings. There will likely be a session with a golf pro, an art class, and certainly, talks about bridge on a day at sea or a lesson or tournament set up by the American Contract Bridge League instructor on board. The agenda will call for a galley tour one day, a cheese and wine party or an ice cream social on another. What it will not have is bingo or horse racing and no pool games or costume parties.

Those fascinated by the sea might spend time in the Nautilus Room, the underwater viewing room with a glass window in the hull for watching the ocean below. But the view from the upper-deck observatory might prove more interesting. The library is stocked with books and first-run and classic movie videos, but supplies could stand some beefing up. And occasionally, you will want to check out the boutique.

And then, you can simply do nothing at all. If the weather is fair, you'll likely be out on deck, relaxing or snoozing in a lounge chair or soaking in the Jacuzzi. There are places to lounge with some protection in hot weather or on cool days. If the weather turns foul, it might be time for a movie on your cabin television or some reading in your beautiful suite while you listen to one of the daily concerts on your cabin radio.

SPORTS, FITNESS, AND BEAUTY   Topside has ample space for sunning and the two upper decks have a full promenade teak deck for walking or jogging. The whirlpools and a small deep swimming pool are aft, just before the Veranda Cafe, but it's a peculiar location because the pool is often shaded by the ship's own structure, thus inhibiting its use. With a ship so well designed otherwise, this element is a mystery.

The ships have a water sports platform at the stern with a 30-by-30-foot steel-meshed cage that drops directly into the sea, creating a protected saltwater pool, bordered by a broad teak sunning deck. The deck also makes an instant dock to launch paddleboats, windsurfing boards, and sailboats. Two high-speed boats are used for waterskiing or to take snorkelers and divers to choice locations. These marinas have their limitations as they can only be used in a calm sea with the ships at anchor. The ships try to use them at least once a week, but obviously it depends on local conditions. On some cruises, they are never used.

Fitness facilities include a small exercise room with weights, walkers, and bicycles. There will be one and sometimes two daily stretch and exercise classes for various workout levels; individual training is available. The beauty salon offers spa beauty treatments including toning, body wrap, and herbal massage, and there are sauna and steam rooms.

CHILDREN'S FACILITIES   While Seabourn is not the ideal family vacation, it's a testimony to the staff that on a recent cruise three kids under age nine reported having the time of their lives.

SHORE EXCURSIONS   In port, excursions are well organized and orchestrated by an experienced, very knowledgeable staff. On a recent Norwegian fjord cruise, passengers were given the most thorough briefing we have had on any but expedition-type cruises accompanied by specialists. There's no push to sell shore excursions, and the tours, including the usual, off-the-shelf motorcoach tours, tend to be pricey. Information on shore excursions is sent to passengers in advance of their cruise.

Also during each cruise, one or two special events are designated as Signature Series shore excursions, which are often a highlight of the cruise and may be limited in the number of guests they can handle. As an example, on a recent Norwegian fjord cruise, passengers attended a concert of Edvard Grieg's music at his lakeside home near Bergen, held only for them and given by Norway's foremost pianist and interpreter of Grieg's music.

THEME CRUISES   In conjunction with the Wide World of Golf, Seabourn offers a collection of Golf Cruises at prestigious private golf clubs around the world. Each trip includes up to six rounds of golf and costs $610–1,555 per golfer. Each includes green fees, carts, caddies, and transfers; a Seabourn golf bag travel cover; golf bag handling and storage; tournament awards and prizes; Wide World of Golf tour escort, and more. In addition, an instructional program, "Seabourn School at Sea," is available on selected sailings. The program, designed for beginners to advanced golfers, includes seminars and private lessons from a Teaching Professional using high-tech video equipment with electronic swing analyzer and other devices.

POSTSCRIPT   Although the ships travel on some of cruising's most interesting itineraries, the main focus of a Seabourn cruise is the ship. For those who can afford it, a Seabourn cruise delivers quality and exclusivity along with the best service on the high seas.

SEAWIND CRUISE LINE

Bay Point Office Tower, 4770 Biscayne Boulevard, No. 700, Miami, FL 33137
(305) 573-3222; (800) 258-8006; fax (305) 576-1060
http://www.seawindcruises.com

TYPE OF SHIP   Renovated midsize classic oceanliner.

TYPE OF CRUISE   Mainstream, budget, less-traveled ports.

CRUISE LINE'S STRENGTHS

- itineraries
- lively international passenger mix
- full day in each port
- European service
- spacious ship and large cabins with ample storage space

CRUISE LINE'S SHORTCOMINGS

- cuisine
- gym facilities
- loud music on deck
- aging vessel

FELLOW PASSENGERS   An international group made up roughly of 25 percent South American, 25 percent European, and 50 percent North American. Their average age is 50–55; the average income is $45,000–50,000. Eighty percent of the North American passengers have cruised before—primarily on large ships departing from Miami and San Juan—and they are looking for a different itinerary and like the less-traveled part of the Caribbean. On a recent cruise, the crowd on board was fairly young, ranging from the late 20s–mid-50s; some were honeymooners; about one-third of the passengers came from Brazil.

Recommended For   Repeat Caribbean cruisers who have tired of glitzy ships and crowded Caribbean ports and are seeking more off-the-beaten-path trips in a traditional cruise setting at reasonable prices; travelers who enjoy meeting people from other parts of the world.

Not Recommended For Passengers looking for nonstop activities and a modern resort-style cruise experience with high-tech entertainment; sophisticates in search of luxury and exclusivity; Joe Six-pack sporting a "Buy America" button.

CRUISE AREAS AND SEASONS Year-round, Southern Caribbean from Aruba.

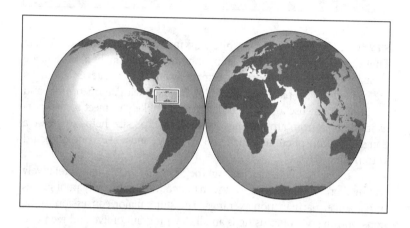

THE LINE Launched in 1991, Seawind Cruise Line was the first to use Aruba as its Home Port to cruise to the uncrowded ports of the Southern Caribbean on a weekly basis—a refreshing alternative to the more traveled Caribbean routes. The cruises are designed for seasoned passengers who prefer to travel at an unhurried pace. They have been called a second-timer's cruise because of the nature of the ship and its itineraries.

Seawind Cruise Lines was originally owned by First Ocean Steamship Company, a complex partnership between Nordisk, a large Swedish travel conglomerate, and Waybell, a firm owned by George Potamianos, whose family owns Epirotiki Line. Together the two own Panama-based Trans World Cruises, which in turn owned the *Seawind Crown*.

In early 1997, Cruise Holdings, a private investment group which had been an investor in Seawind, obtained majority control of the cruise line at the same time that it acquired Dolphin Cruise Line. The move is part of a long range plan to buy vintage ships which are becoming available as large cruise lines replace them with new megaliners.

The *Seawind Crown* (the former *Vasco da Gama*), is a spacious ship mellowed by the fine wood paneling and trim found on older ships, and combining old-world grace with contemporary features. It was given a $40 million overhaul in 1988, and in 1994, more cabins were added.

The Fleet	Built/Renovated	Tonnage	Passengers
Seawind Crown	1961/89/94	24,000	720

STYLE   The *Seawind Crown* offers an international ambience. While English is the language of the ship, announcements might also be made in Spanish, Dutch, Portuguese, German, Swedish, or whatever languages are needed for the passenger makeup. Travelers with an open mind and a willingness to use a bit of sign language are likely to meet some interesting people from around the world. The ship's size helps to create a congenial atmosphere in which you recognize most everyone on board within a few days.

In the spirit of classic cruising, the *Seawind Crown* offers a relatively subdued cruise experience; you won't encounter many silly pool games or passenger participation evenings. The ship's major concession to the nonstop-fun style of cruising is an all-day program of live and recorded Caribbean and reggae music on deck.

But passengers on the *Seawind Crown* don't need spectacular lounges and round-the-clock activities; they create fun wherever they go, whether dancing to the poolside band or cheering on a fellow passenger in the talent show. Their youngish age and Latin American influence creates a delightful energy that comes from the passengers, rather than from the neon decor and pumped-up cruise staff found on mass-market cruise ships in the Caribbean.

And don't confuse merriment with lack of sophistication. This is not a beer-guzzling crowd. They dress for dinner, and their dress is stylish and tasteful. The international passengers tend to dress more formally than North Americans; you would feel out of place wearing jeans in the evening. Men wear tailored sport jackets or suits and women don cocktail dresses or stylish pant outfits. Bikinis—some quite tiny—are *de rigueur* at poolside.

DISTINCTIVE FEATURES   Free pre- or postcruise stays of up to a week in Aruba for certain cabin categories. Renewal of marriage vows in ship's chapel.

RATES

Highest Per Diem	Lowest Per Diem	Average Per Diem
$237	$139	$149

The above per diems are calculated from the cruise line's nondiscounted *cruise-only* fares on standard accommodations. What you will actually pay *should* be *substantially* less (see Part One, How to Get the Best Deal on a Cruise). Per diems vary by season, by cabin location, and by cruise areas.

Special Fares and Discounts   Advance purchase program provides for up to $520 discount with a deposit 60 days prior to sailing. Special add-on rates ranging from $600–900 per person for second week on 14-night program.

- Children's Fare: (2–11 years) $100 less than third and fourth passenger rate.
- Single Supplement: 100 percent for category M, 150 percent for categories E–L, and 200 percent for categories A–D.

Packages

- Honeymooners and anniversary couples sailing within seven days of wedding dates are given a commemorative gift plus a $20 gift certificate and complimentary fruit and champagne in cabin.
- Pre/Post: On a one-week cruise, for passengers in cabin categories A–G, "Free-Aruba" program provides three- to seven-night free stays at La Cabana Beach Resort and Casino, an all-suite resort in Aruba with headliner entertainment.

Past Passengers   Past passengers receive four savings certificates, each offering savings of $400 per cabin. They are only redeemable at the original booking agent and can be used any time within a year of issuance.

THE LAST WORD   Seawind offers classic cruising with an international flair in the Southern Caribbean. The *Seawind Crown* is in fairly good shape for her age; public areas and cabins are pleasant and spacious, though not always as spiffy as they should be. Her European staff delivers traditional service with a smile. The ship appeals to cruisers looking for an excellent value on more distant Caribbean paths. These cruises are for people who like to spend time on shore exploring a locale beyond the shopping streets, although each itinerary has at least one port of call with a large selection of duty-free and other stores.

SEAWIND SHIPS STANDARD FEATURES

Officers Greek and Portuguese.

Staffs Dining/European and International; Cabin/European; Cruise/International.

Dining Facilities Two dining rooms. Main dining room for three meals with open seating for breakfast and lunch, assigned tables for dinner. Breakfast, lunch buffets, afternoon tea in smaller dining room. During days at sea, lunch buffet served in small indoor/outdoor dining facility near pool.

Special Diets Requests must be made two weeks in advance of sailing.

Room Service 7 A.M.–midnight; no charge.

Dress Code Casual, two formal nights, one Caribbean night. Most passengers dress well-women in dresses or stylish slacks outfits, men in sports coats.

Cabin Amenities Television, hair dryers, small refrigerators, radio with music, telephone; robes in suites.

Electrical Outlets 220 AC; passengers must bring their own adapters for 220 volts in order to use hair curlers and curling irons.

Wheelchair Access Two designated cabins. Passengers confined to wheelchairs must notify Seawind at time of booking. Seawind requires wheelchair passengers travel with companion able to assist them.

Recreation and Entertainment Five bars/lounges; showroom with nightly entertainment. Bingo, casino, disco, cinema, card room, library.

Sports and Other Activities Two outdoor pools, snorkel/scuba program.

Beauty and Fitness Hairdresser; exercise room with treadmills and other equipment, exercise class daily, massage, sauna.

Other Facilities Small meeting room; chapel.

Children's Facilities None. Youth counselors added in summer.

Theme Cruises None.

Smoking Dining room has smoking and nonsmoking sections.

Seawind Suggested Tipping Per person per day, cabin steward, $3; waiter, $3; busboy, $2; 15 percent of check added to wine and bar bill.

Credit Cards For cruise reservations and on-board charges, American Express, Discover, Mastercard, and Visa.

Seawind Crown

	Quality Rating	**Value Rating**
Seawind Crown	3	B

Registry: Panama	Length: 641 feet	Beam: 81 feet
Cabins: 300	Draft: 27 feet	Speed: 17 knots
Maximum Passengers:	Passenger Decks: 10	Elevators: 4
756	Crew: 71	Space Ratio: 38.5

THE SHIP   The *Seawind Crown*, built in 1962 as the *Infante Dom Enrique*, originally accommodated 1,100 passengers on voyages to Portugal's former colonies in Africa. It later became the *Vasco da Gama* and continued to make long cruises for European passengers.

The spacious ship combines an old-world ambience with contemporary features, such as refrigerators and hair dryers in the cabins and twin beds that can be converted to doubles. In addition to being a low-density ship, she provides a inviting, friendly atmosphere and a high level of personal attention.

The *Seawind Crown* underwent a $40 million renovation in 1988 and an additional $4-million overhaul in 1994, when 52 new cabins and an exercise room were added and other major improvements were made. The new cabins increased the vessel's passenger capacity by 15 percent, but the expansion did not compromise the ship's traditional lines as unoccupied space was utilized.

The *Seawind Crown* has a much more subdued ambience than today's typical Caribbean superliner or megaliners. Its decor is understated, with a consistent color scheme of mauves and grays. There's no neon, no vaulted atrium. It's a classic oceanliner with fine wood paneling and trim that enhances the ship's attractive decor and creates a warm feeling. It is, however, showing signs of wear and tear.

The ship has a variety of small lounges and bars, a casino, and shops. Most public rooms are found on the Promenade Deck, higher placed than is typical of older ships. The evening atmosphere here is one of a lively main street—you might catch some of the show, walk through the casino where passengers socialize in small groups while their spouses play the slot machines, and continue on to join the dancing in the Panorama Lounge.

ITINERARIES   Seven-day cruises depart weekly from Aruba, on Sundays to Curaçao, Caracas, Barbados, and St. Lucia, making full-day stops at each port; two full days at sea.

Home Port   Aruba.

Port Charges $138 per person; Canadian departures require additional $33 departure tax.

CABINS   The *Seawind Crown* has 13 categories of cabins, most located on Ocean and Baltic decks, the midlevel decks. Generally spacious and well lighted, the midrange outside cabins have big double closets with full-length mirrors. There's lots of storage space, and the wood trim adds a homey touch. The few outside cabins on the Atlantic Deck (restaurant deck) are larger than the higher-category ones on Pacific Deck above, but their bathrooms are much smaller.

The 52 newest cabins were added in unused cargo and cabin space and did not take up the ship's public spaces. Most are large, outside cabins, similar to the older ones. All cabins have mini-fridges, hair dryers, radio, telephone (no international direct dial), and television.

Specifications   121 inside cabins, 246 outside; 16 suites. Standard dimensions, 160 square feet. 149 cabins with two lower beds; 8 with king-size, 26 with queen-size, 29 with double, 32 with upper/lower, 52 with three beds, 26 with four beds, 6 with single beds. 2 wheelchair accessible.

DINING   The Vasco da Gama Restaurant, which offers a quiet, pleasant atmosphere, has open seating for breakfast and lunch and two assigned seatings at dinner. Cuisine on board is good for this price range, but not memorable and it's inconsistent. Pastry-wrapped appetizers such as *empanadas* are delicious; chilled soups and ice cream also get high marks. But fish and beef entrees can be good one night, mediocre the next. The mostly European waiters cheerfully switch entrees or bring sauce on the side when passengers request them.

A typical dinner menu offers three appetizers, three soups, two salads, a pasta, three entrees, and three desserts. Health- and weight-conscious travelers may find it rather difficult to watch calories. Although one entree on each menu is highlighted as lighter, no nutritional information is offered. The salad bar at lunch has nicely prepared salads but few raw vegetables. On a recent sailing, skimmed milk was only available two days at breakfast.

Unlike the indoor/outdoor lido cafe on newer ships, the Madeira Restaurant, also on Atlantic Deck, where breakfast and lunch buffets and afternoon tea are served, is a carpeted dining room with cloth-covered tables. Buffets are set up on tables in the middle of the room. It's a plus for those passengers who prefer dining in air-conditioned comfort but a minus for those who like an outdoor setting.

On days at sea a lunch buffet is offered in the Taverna, a wonderfully cheery Portuguese-style room with wooden tables inlaid with decorative tiles. As it is quite small, many people bring plates to poolside. Ample table space is lacking outside as well, and so, most people end up balancing their plates on their laps.

SERVICE   Service receives high marks from passengers. The ship has Greek and Portuguese officers and a European hotel staff, mostly Portuguese and other Europeans who were with the *Vasco da Gama* and who are accustomed to delivering traditional European cruise-style service. The dining room staff is friendly while retaining a strong sense of professionalism. Bar staff are more chatty yet industrious, often remembering passengers' names and beverage preferences. Poolside drink service, in particular, is excellent—waiters circulate constantly with both alcoholic and nonalcoholic drinks and large bottles of cold Evian water. Drinks are reasonably priced.

FACILITIES AND ENTERTAINMENT   Evening shows feature singers, jugglers, dance trios, and a revue by the *Seawind Crown* dancers, who are also part of the cruise staff. Performances take place in the show lounge on the Promenade Deck, which is full to capacity on most evenings. If not the cruise highlight, entertainment is quite acceptable for this price range. The casino offers slot machines and blackjack.

Also on the Promenade is the Panorama Lounge, a quiet, pleasant corner during the day to get away from the activity. In the evening it has dancing to the sounds of a trio or perhaps a singer with a computer keyboard as his backup. The disco, on Pacific Deck, is thankfully low-tech for those who get turned off rather than turned on by too much neon. *Seawind Crown* passengers like to dance. The disco starts bopping around midnight and goes until the wee hours.

ACTIVITIES AND DIVERSIONS   While the *Seawind Crown* is in port, activities are limited to volleyball, Ping-Pong, and board games. During days at sea, passengers are kept busy with activities, such as hair and beauty demonstrations presented by salon staff, a wine and cheese party, a visit to the bridge, cooking demonstrations, casino lessons, an afternoon dance class, steel drum lessons, and bingo. A different movie is shown throughout each day on cabin television, as well as in the ship's cinema, and there's a card room and a library.

SPORTS, FITNESS, AND BEAUTY For fitness enthusiasts, *Seawind Crown* recently converted what was a squash court into an exercise room with treadmills and other exercise equipment. However, it is situated on the lowest deck and can be warm. An early morning exercise class is offered each day in the show lounge. A volleyball court on the top deck is a popular diversion, and the wraparound Promenade Deck attracts joggers in the morning and walkers at sunset. Certified scuba divers will appreciate the Reef Roamers program, which offers diving and snorkeling trips at most ports of call. For novices, a dive resort course starting with lessons in the ship's pool is also available.

The hair and beauty salon and massage operated by Steiner of London are also available. At designated periods throughout each day the ship's sauna is open for men only, women only, and mixed.

SHORE EXCURSIONS The *Seawind Crown* spends at least eight hours at each port, so you have time to tour, check out the beach, and go shopping at a leisurely pace. Passengers never need to board tenders, and the ship docks almost always in front of the main town or a short walk away.

In most ports, *Seawind Crown's* Reef Roamers snorkel/scuba program offers a dive trip for about $65 and a snorkeling excursion for about $42. Among the other excursions are a Jolly Roger party ship in Barbados and island tours in St. Lucia—all cost between $28–35.

POSTSCRIPT Seawind offers excellent value and good itineraries. Its "Free-Aruba" program is one of travel's biggest bargains and has been enormously successful—over 40 percent of its passengers take advantage of the program.

SILVERSEA CRUISES

110 East Broward Boulevard, Ft. Lauderdale, FL 33301
Reservations: (954) 522-4477; (800) 722-6655; fax (305) 522-4499

TYPE OF SHIP   Ultraluxury, all-suite, small ships.

TYPE OF CRUISE   Luxurious cruises on worldwide itineraries.

CRUISE LINE'S STRENGTHS
- luxurious accommodations
- ship size/maneuverability
- single, open-seating dining
- cuisine
- impeccable service
- worldwide itineraries
- congenial atmosphere

CRUISE LINE'S SHORTCOMINGS
- somewhat staid evening activities and entertainment
- coordination problems with pre-/postcruise hotels and tour operators

FELLOW PASSENGERS   A fairly diverse group demographically, Silversea passengers are experienced cruisers, many of whom have made the rounds of the luxury ships. Convivial, well traveled, and typically outgoing, passengers range in age from young professionals in their 30s to lively 80-year-olds. The majority of the passengers are over 50 and most passengers are American. Couples are the rule, singles the exception. Geographically, Silversea passengers come from throughout the United States, with a higher than average concentration from the northeast. Silversea also has a loyal European following, particularly among the British and Germans. For a cruise line as young as Silversea, an astounding number of passengers are repeaters.

Recommended For   Silversea cruises are ideal for sophisticated, knowledgeable travelers who prefer a finely crafted ship and low-key atmosphere to glitz and fun and games, who appreciate fine details, and who expect exacting service. Silversea provides value and luxury in an atmosphere of casual elegance.

Not Recommended For   Those for whom subtle luxury and infinite attention to detail is unimportant; anyone who feels uncomfortable among non-Americans. Nor is this ship for late-night revelers or children.

CRUISE AREAS AND SEASONS   Africa, the Seychelles, Madagascar, the Mediterranean, the Baltic, Canada and New England, the Far East and China, Australia, New Zealand and the South Pacific, South America, and the Caribbean.

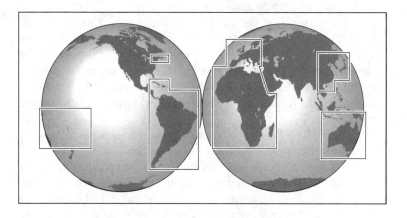

THE LINE   Silversea Cruises was conceived and organized in the early 1990s by the Lefebvre family of Rome and the Vlasov Group of Monaco. The line targets the ultraluxury segment of the market. The name "Silversea" was chosen to suggest quality and luxury as well as to capture the romance of the sea. Having been involved in commercial and passenger shipping for several generations, the Vlasov and Lefebvre families were previously the owners of Sitmar Cruises.

The *Silver Wind* and the *Silver Cloud*, identical twin ships, were built in Italy in 1994 and designed by the well-known Norwegian team of Petter Yran and Bjorn Storbraaten. Launched in 1995, Silversea took the luxury cruise market by storm with reasonable pricing, uncompromising service, and possibly the nicest accommodations afloat. The six-deck ships are ultradeluxe and very spacious with a space ratio of 55.74, which is one of the highest of any cruise ship. Intended to be all-inclusive, luxury cruises at lower per diems than their competitors, they offer big-ship facilities and comfort in a small-ship atmosphere and all-suite accommodations. Although the ships are substantially larger than their direct ultradeluxe competitors, the biggest advantage the ships have over their competitors is the high number of cabins with verandas.

Silversea's inclusive prices are meant to be the most comprehensive in the world of luxury cruises and cover airfare, transfers, port taxes, travel insurance, beverage service (liquors and nonalcoholic drinks) and selected wines at lunch and dinner, in-suite service of hors d'oeuvres and full meals, a special shoreside event, baggage handling, gratuities, and precruise accommodations in a deluxe hotel.

Although much of the competition has modified its product to emulate Silversea, few can rival Silversea's combination of deluxe accommodations and seamless hospitality. The service, provided by European crews, is flawless, with special requests of any nature handled cheerfully and expeditiously. The ratio of crew to passengers is .66 to 1. *Travel* magazine reader polls routinely accord Silversea their highest rankings.

The ships have Italian officers and a European service staff, many of whom worked previously for the line's competitors.

The cruises follow the sun with the *Silver Wind* operating in the Far East, South Pacific, Mediterranean, India, and Africa, and the *Silver Cloud* cruising South America, Europe and the Baltic, and Canada and New England. Most cruises are 7–21 days in length and move from area to area on itineraries that allow passengers to cruise for several months without repeating a port.

The line offers cruises with two of the world's most famous names: Le Cordon Bleu and the National Geographic Traveler. The first features menu selections created for the ships by the famed school in conjunction with the line's Chef de Cuisine, as well as select cruises throughout the year when specialties of a particular region on the ships' itineraries are highlighted, along with cooking demonstrations and lessons in table settings and floral arrangements. Photographers and journalists of *National Geographic* join noted experts to lecture on selected cruises and a special library with *National Geographic* articles, CD-ROMs, maps, and other information is available for passengers.

The Fleet	Built/Renovated	Tonnage	Passengers
Silver Cloud	1994	16,500	296
Silver Wind	1994	16,500	296

STYLE Sparkling clean, impeccably maintained, and luxurious in an understated way consistent with the nautical aesthetics of the finest yachts, the *Silver Wind* and the *Silver Cloud* offer elegance undisturbed by pretense or formality. From the time you board until the minute you disembark, you are attended by a crew that genuinely makes an effort to get to know you, and more, to anticipate your every need. Miraculously this is accomplished in a direct and friendly manner without being suffocating or obsequious.

The suites exceed their representation in the line's brochure, and while exceptionally comfortable, only account for a fraction of what these well-designed ships have to offer. The ship's public areas are inviting as well as elegant, and provide plenty of incentive to get out of your suite. If you enjoy structured activities, they are available, but tend toward the relaxing and the cerebral. Announcements, games, and contests are the exception rather than the rule.

Both at sea and in port, days are laid-back and casual. Evenings likewise are low-key, but dressier. On many cruises a "Silversea Experience," one of the line's signature events, is scheduled. Silversea Experience is usually an excursion coupled with dining and drinks in an incredibly beautiful setting, sometimes a private island, private club, or deserted coast.

Silversea seems to attract a gregarious and adventuresome clientele. And while the atmosphere is social and decidedly conducive to meeting new friends, there are dozens of delightful nooks and spaces to enjoy solitary time.

DISTINCTIVE FEATURES All suite accommodations, comprehensive air/sea travel with personalized service at intermediate travel stops, all beverages, gratuities, and port charges are included in the cruise price. The Silversea Experience is available on most sailings. Single supplements start at 125 percent.

RATES

Highest Per Diem	Lowest Per Diem	Average Per Diem
$894	$424	$652

The above per diems are calculated from the cruise line's nondiscounted *cruise-only* fares on standard accommodations. What you will actually pay *should* be *substantially* less (see Part One, How to Get the Best Deal on a Cruise). Per diems vary by season, by cabin location, and by cruise areas.

Special Note: All tips, on-board beverages, and port charges are included in the cruise fare on the *Silver Wind* and the *Silver Cloud*.

Special Fares and Discounts   Advance payment bonus of 15 percent when final payment is made six months prior to sailing. Substantial savings available by combining consecutive voyages. Advance purchase discount of 10 percent for booking four months in advance of sailing, 5 percent for booking three months prior to sailing. Advance purchase discounts cannot be combined with the advance payment bonus.

- Third Person: Approximately 50 percent of the Vista or Veranda Suite per person published rate.
- Single Supplement: 125 percent, 150 percent, 175 percent of per person double occupancy basic suite, depending on cruise.

Packages
- Air/Sea: All cruises packaged with economy class air; first and business class air upgrades available for an additional charge.
- Others: Yes, including extensive pre- and postcruise tours.
- Pre/Post: Yes. Many of the basic air/sea packages include one or more nights in the departure or termination city; extensions are available in all major gateways.

Past Passengers   Past passengers automatically become members of the Venetian Society, the name for which was chosen to reflect the line's Italian ownership and heritage. Members on their second voyage receive a silver pin in the society's emblem of a winged lion, the emblem of Venice. After they have sailed for 100-, 200-, 500-plus days, they receive sapphire, emerald and diamond pins, respectively. Additionally, past passengers receive a members-only newsletter three times a year with information on member-designated cruises with discounts. Other benefits include shipboard events hosted by the captain. Members are eligible for fare reductions of 5 percent that are combinable with early booking incentives, advance payment bonus, and combination cruise savings.

THE LAST WORD   On the water, Silversea is about as good as its gets. It's impossible to fault the accommodations, service, or food, and not having to pay extra for beverages or worry about tipping is a big plus. Itineraries are creative, nonrepetitive, and pretty much cover the globe, calling on many ports seldom seen by cruise ships. The officers and crew are totally professional, yet accessible and friendly, and most importantly, are actively involved in providing a very personalized service that is genuinely caring. The ships are new and intelligently designed. Public areas are inviting and warm, and there is never a sense of crowding. Daily programs and activities are adequate but do not break any new ground. Evening entertainment is competent though somewhat staid, and there's not much to do on a Silversea cruise after about 10:30 P.M.

Off the water, Silversea is still sorting out its vendor relations with tour operators and hotels and trying to fine-tune its pre- and postcruise transitional programs. It's not easy, especially for a new cruise line, to integrate third party suppliers into a seamless, all-inclusive package. Continually adding new, exotic, and often remote ports of call makes finding dependable tour operators and hospitality partners all the more difficult. The last word is that Silversea, on the sea, is as close to perfection as you are likely to find. Off the ship, Silversea is still experiencing growing pains, and you may experience a few rough edges.

SILVERSEA STANDARD FEATURES

Officers Italian.

Staffs Dining/European; Cabin/European; Cruise/British and American.

Dining Facilities All meals served at one seating in restaurant; indoor/outdoor cafe for casual breakfast and lunch. Alternative dining specialty dinner on two or more evenings per cruise. En suite dining.

Special Diets Available upon request.

Room Service 24 hours, cabin menu and full-service dining room menu.

Dress Code Casual, informal, or formal. By day, casual but conservative, comfortable. Dinner is a dressy affair, informal (jacket and tie for men) or formal (two black-tie evenings on one-week cruise; four formal dinners on two-week cruise).

Cabin Amenities Stocked bar, mini-refrigerator; television with CNN, VCR, direct-dial phone; Italian marble bathroom with sink, tub and shower, toiletries, hair dryer, bathrobes, walk-in closet, safe.

Electrical Outlets 110/220 AC.

Wheelchair Access Limited.

Recreation and Entertainment Three lounges with entertainment/dance music nightly; cabaret, classical music concerts, folkloric performances in ports of call; nightly dancing; casino; cruise-related lectures.

Sports and Other Activities Outdoor pool, deck sports; bridge instructor/lessons; enrichment programs.

Beauty and Fitness Two saunas, two outdoor whirlpools, small gym, exercise classes, beauty salon, spa with massage, beauty treatments.

Other Facilities Self-service laundry, laundry/dry cleaning; library with books and video; boutique; hospital; nondenominational religious services.

Children's Facilities None; children under 18 years of age must be accompanied by parent or adult with written permission.

Theme Cruises Le Cordon Bleu food and wine specialty cruises.

Smoking Public rooms are designated as nonsmoking except for lounges.

Silversea Suggested Tipping Strict no-tipping policy.

Credit Cards For cruise payment and on-board charges, American Express, Diners Club, Mastercard, Visa.

Silver Cloud / Silver Wind

	Quality Rating	Value Rating
Silver Cloud/Silver Wind	❿	A

Registry: Bahamas
Cabins: 148
Maximum Passengers: 314

Length: 514 feet
Draft: 18 feet
Passenger Decks: 6
Crew: 196

Beam: 70.62 feet
Speed: 20.5 knots
Elevators: 4
Space Ratio: 56.8

THE SHIP Understated, with an emphasis on nautical tradition, the Silversea twins are the antithesis of the glitzy floating hotels that dominate the travel press. Elegance anchored in simplicity with clean lines, earth tone fabrics, polished wood and brass, are the signature decor of Silversea ships. Far from an assault on the senses, Silversea ships are styled to soothe.

The entry lobby surprises with its modest and very human-sized proportions. No six-story atrium or rotunda here; the feeling is that of boarding a yacht. The ship is remarkably simple in its layout. There are nine decks. On Deck 9, the top deck, are a forward observation lounge and a jogging/walking track that runs the circumference of the ship (overlooking the pool on Deck 8). Surprisingly underutilized, the observation lounge has a radar screen linked to the bridge and a computerized nautical display that provides information on weather conditions, ship speed, projected arrival times, and the like. One deck down on Deck 8, the bridge is forward with the swimming pool, twin whirlpools, and pool bar amidships. Aft on Deck 8 is the Panorama Lounge with indoor and outdoor seating surveying the stern. The Panorama Lounge offers live music and dancing and serves as the ship's late-night venue. Next to the lounge is the library, well supplied with books, magazines, periodicals, and movies on video. Unlike the library on many ships, this one stays open all the time.

Below the pool deck on Decks 4–7, all of the suites are forward, and all of the public areas are aft. Elevators and a circular stairwell are situated just aft of amidships.

In the center of the ship on Deck 7 are the fitness center, spa, and beauty salon. The fitness center is modest but well equipped with

Lifecycles, a Stairmaster, and a good selection of free weights. Adjacent to the fitness center is the spa offering both sauna and massage. All the way aft is a the Terrace Cafe for informal dining and buffets at breakfast and lunch. Like the Panorama Lounge on the deck above, the Terrace Cafe provides seating both indoors and out with a view over the stern.

Down one deck, on Deck 6 are the main lobby flanked by the travel desk and the reception desk. Moving aft there are a card and conference room, and at the stern, the Parisian Lounge, the main showroom with plush bench and stuffed chair seating rising in tiers above the stage. The showroom is large enough to accommodate small production shows but small enough to encourage a level of intimacy between audience and performers. The Parisian Lounge is also the ship's primary venue for dancing and special events such as the captain's reception.

Deck 5 houses a modest shopping boutique as well as the casino and The Bar. The Bar serves as a gathering area for the showroom. The casino offers roulette, blackjack, and slots. On Deck 4 is the restaurant serving breakfast, lunch, and dinner in a plush setting with Schott Crystal and Christofle silverware on fine linens.

Public areas aboard are extensive for a ship of *Silver Wind*'s size. For those with cabin fever, there are dozens of quiet places throughout the ship to curl up with a book or to watch the sea.

ITINERARIES As a newer cruise line, Silversea continues to change and refine its itineraries. In general, however, the Silversea ships circle the globe seasonally in contiguous segments of 7–21 days that can be combined into longer voyages of 28–90 days.

- *Silver Cloud* spends November–April cruising South America before repositioning to Europe and the Baltic for the warmer months of May–September. During the crisp fall colors season, the *Silver Cloud* cruises eastern Canada and New England.
- *Silver Wind* begins its calendar year in the South Pacific, Indian Ocean, and South China Sea calling at Singapore, Bangkok, Sydney, Hong Kong, and Bombay. During the summer and early fall, the *Silver Wind* cruises the Mediterranean, shifting to East Africa in November and returning to the Far East in December.

Home Ports Ft. Lauderdale and worldwide ports, depending on the cruise.

Port Charges Included in price of the cruise.

CABINS The spacious, all-outside suites are among the ships' signature features. Suites provide convertible twin-to-queen beds, walk-in closet, sitting area with loveseat, coffee table and side chairs, writing desk, dressing table with hair dryer, Italian marble bathroom with full-size tub and shower, stocked refrigerator and cocktail bar, entertainment center with remote-controlled satellite television and videocassette player, and direct dial telephone. A curtain allows the sleeping area to be partitioned from the living area. Seventy-five percent of the liner's 148 suites have private teak verandas, with the remainder providing large picture windows. All the suites are decorated in light earth tones or pastel blues with traditional nautical trim of polished wood and brass. The overall effect is warm and just a tiny bit masculine.

Suites with verandas offer an unobstructed view of the sea through floor-to-ceiling glass. Large picture windows provide panoramic views in suites without verandas. In addition to the standard veranda suites (with verandas) at 295 square feet and the standard 240-square-foot vista suites (without verandas), the ships offer deluxe suites ranging in size from 541–1,314 square feet.

Many extras boost the accommodations into the ultradeluxe categories: pure cotton Frette bed linens (with the Silversea logo) and robes, down pillows, personalized stationery, a bowl of fresh fruit, large umbrellas in the closets, complimentary shoe-shine service, and 24-hour room service.

Specifications   All suites: 102 veranda suites, 34 vista suites, 3 silver suites (541 square feet), 2 royal suites (1,031 square feet in the two-bedroom configuration), 2 grand suites (1,314 square feet with two bedrooms), and 1 owner's suite (827 square feet). All larger suites have verandas. No singles.

DINING   The Silversea ships have a distinct advantage in the area of food service and dining. The relatively small number of passengers allows for dishes cooked to order as in a restaurant.

Silversea Cruises has an affiliation with Le Cordon Bleu, the world-renowned culinary academy for French master chefs. Le Cordon Bleu participates in Silversea menu planning and culinary-focused cruises. Interestingly, Silversea also provides for the picky eater, the health conscious diner, and the meat and potatoes set. Menus are designed to inform rather than to impress, and only the finest of ingredients are used regardless of how simple or complex the dish. Meat eaters in search of a cruise ship that can prepare a good steak, chop, or slab of prime rib will be in nirvana on Silversea. Menus offer three appetizers, a pasta, two soups, two salads, sherbet, three main courses, and usually a grilled selection. In addition, there is always a "Light and Healthy" and a vegetarian entree. A separate dessert menu is presented after each meal. Several wines are chosen to accompany each evening meal, all included in the price of the cruise.

We rate the food on the *Silver Wind* as excellent in both quality and presentation, with our only complaint relating to variety. On some cruises, menu selections, though extensive, are unremittingly Western and primarily Eurocentric. For those not accustomed to a diet rich in sauces, creams, and oils, it's a little overwhelming. (Admittedly, none of our readers write complaining about being fed gourmet French or Italian dishes everyday.) In any event, if ethnic diversity is somewhat of a problem, freshness of ingredients is not. One day, riding the ship's tender back to the ship from shore, we were assaulted by an unexpected but familiar smell. Peering around the bulkhead, we discovered a grinning chef with a huge string of fresh fish just purchased from local fishermen.

The dining room is open at published times for breakfast, lunch, and dinner. Passengers are free to dine at their leisure as at a restaurant without the regimentation of assigned seating times or tables. Lunch and breakfast buffets in the Terrace Cafe provide an option for more informal dining. Departing from the custom of most ships, no late-night buffet is offered. Room service is available 24 hours a day and is delivered with the same elegance and attention to detail characteristic of the dining room. Service at all of the ships' dining venues is outstanding. Even at breakfast and lunch buffets, the wait staff will serve you and the chefs will prepare dishes to order on request.

Aesthetically, the main dining room, known on both ships as The Restaurant, is reminiscent of an exclusive private club with Villeroy & Boch china, Christofle silver, linen, Schott Crystal, silver table settings, and patterned upholstered chairs. Draped picture windows line each side of this elegant room, and a domed center section adds to the feeling of spaciousness. In addition, a small marble dance floor allows for occasional dinner dances. Though formal in the tradition of most cruise ship dining rooms, The Restaurant is also comfortable, relaxed, and nonpretentious.

The Terrace Cafe, a casual dining venue, sits high on the stern and draws a clean, breezy ambience from its commanding view of the sea. A lush planter and a wall of windows faces aft to the sea and the sheltered outside dining area. Furnished with dark wood-framed chairs upholstered in pale green fabrics, tables are always set with china, crystal, and silver. Buffet waiters take orders for drinks and for hot entrees, cooked to order. Special dinners are occasionally held here.

Several times each cruise, a specially prepared multicourse meal is offered on a first-come, first-served reservations basis in an alternative, smaller, more intimate dining room. These meals, in addition to providing a change of scenery, give the chefs an opportunity to recreate the traditional European fine dining experience.

SERVICE Most passengers rate service in a dead heat with accommodations as Silversea's best feature. If service could be better, we're not sure how. Without exception, the staff is professional, highly attentive but never intrusive, congenial without being familiar, and thoroughly gracious in the most exquisite European manner. Working in total harmony, the officers and crew form a highly effective and immensely responsive team. A concierge is available for special services, as well. As you would expect, the small size of a Silversea ship lends itself to a higher, more personalized level of service than is possible on a larger ship. Then too, there's more opportunity in a luxurious setting to provide good service. Extensive training and a high .66 to 1 crew-to-passenger ratio combine to make Silversea service an industry standard setter. There is no tipping. Period.

FACILITIES AND ENTERTAINMENT In the evening, the ship's small orchestra plays easy listening and dancing music in The Bar and a pianist or vocalist duo offer light tunes for cocktails in the Panorama Lounge. The casino offers roulette, blackjack, slot machines, and lessons, if you need them. Evening entertainment focuses on individual entertainers and production shows by six-member group in the Parisian Lounge. The room is furnished in dark red and blues with metallic threads adding a bit of glitter to the upholstery. Murals of sinuous ladies along the side of the stage add a definite Art Deco touch. The Parisian Lounge accommodates all passengers in a steeply tiered, two-level room. Most sight lines are good.

Productions in the ship's showroom, though entirely professional, lack vitality and imagination. Late-night entertainment consists of audience participation games, dancing, and piano music in the Panorama Lounge. OK, but not inspiring: most folks retire early.

ACTIVITIES AND DIVERSIONS Time aboard Silversea is yours to do as you please. A daily program for the next day is dutifully delivered to your suite each night. The program and included activities are more mainstream than you might expect on an ultraluxury cruise, but obviously the pampered and the sophisticated like to play bingo too! A typical day aboard a Silversea ship will look something like this:

8:00	Power Walk-a-Mile with fitness instructor Jennifer
9:30	The captain invites guests to visit the Navigational Bridge
9:30	CD-ROM class with Jessica: learn the basics of multimedia
10:00	High and Low Aerobics with Jennifer
10:15	Cross Stitch Club, with Jessica
11:00	BLT Time!! Buns, Legs, and Tums exercises with Jennifer
11:00	Wine Tasting with Head Sommelier Wolfgang Zehnter
11:30	Lecture on "Blocking and Unblocking Bridge Play" with Bill Howland
12:05	Navigation and weather information from the Bridge
2:15	$Bingo, Bingo$$! Join Nigel for cash prizes
2:30	Shuffleboard Competition with Kyle
3:00	Backgammon Tournament with Kyle
3:00	Water Volleyball with Jessica and Bruce as your team mates
3:30	Golf Putting Competition with Nigel
4:00	Afternoon Tea with Rosario playing for you at the piano
4:30	Team Trivia with Nigel and Jessica
5:00	Macarena Line Dance lessons with Tanya
7:00	Dance to the music of The *Silver Wind* Quartet
10:15	Evening Showtime: *Visions* Direct from Las Vegas, the award-winning comedy and magic of Rory and Catherine Johnston also featuring the wonderful talent of "The Styleliners"
11:15	"Name That Tune!!" Roasario plays as Nigel provides clues to the music
11:30	Late-Night Dancing to the fabulous music of The *Silver Wind* Quartet

Experts on the area of the cruise give several lectures, and depending on the port, a folkloric show by a local group might be staged. There will be a morning port talk and a sales pitch for port tours.

Of course, if you wish, you can simply do nothing at all. Sleeping in is a great option on ships with complete room service. If the weather is fair, you'll likely be out on deck, relaxing or snoozing in a lounge chair or soaking in the Jacuzzi. There are plenty of places to lounge in the shade on hot days or out of the wind on cool days. If the weather turns foul, it might be time for a video movie on your cabin television or some reading in your beautiful suite.

SPORTS, FITNESS, AND BEAUTY The pool deck has ample space for sunning as well as shady space for reading and snoozing while you monitor the doneness of your spouse in the sun. Blue-and-white striped lounge and chair cushions give the spacious, teak-deck pool area a crisp, nautical atmosphere. Two whirlpools and a surprisingly large swimming pool are supported by a well-supplied pool bar. The upper-most deck has a full promenade AstroTurf carpeted deck for walking or jogging. Fitness facilities include an exercise room with weights, walkers, Stairmaster, and LifeCycles. There will be one and sometimes two daily stretch and exercise classes for various workout levels; individual training is available. The beauty salon offers spa beauty treatments including toning, body wrap, and herbal massage, and there are sauna and steam rooms.

CHILDREN'S FACILITIES Because children are rare on Silversea cruises, the occasional child receives a lot of extra attention. Although there are no children's facilities or programs per se, children generally enjoy the experience. The nice pool and the privilege of obtaining drinks and snacks under the all-inclusive pricing policy help.

SHORE EXCURSIONS Shore excursions are administered efficiently onboard, and the staff does more than its part to deliver passengers to the landside tour operators. In its fourth year of operation, however, Silversea is still sorting out its shore excursion providers and refining its tour offerings. So as not to overstate the case, Silversea has quite a good batting average with its shore excursions. Silversea passengers, however, have very high expectations, expectations that the excursion operator will provide the same level of service that they are accustomed to on the ship. Silversea is having to look hard to find excursion partners that can approximate that standard.

Shore excursion sales are low-key and the cruise director does an excellent job differentiating the options and matching passengers with the best tour relative to their tastes. Not unexpectedly, shore excursions, including the usual, off-the-shelf motorcoach tours, tend to be pricey. Information on shore excursions is sent to passengers in advance of their cruise.

Each cruise includes one "Silversea Experience," a special shore excursion designed to showcase the culture of an area. This may be a private tour or dinner in an extraordinary location, which may not be open to the public. For example, the line has hosted wine tastings at private chateaux and dinner at a palace in St. Petersburg.

THEME CRUISES In conjunction with Le Cordon Bleu Cooking Academy, Silversea offers a number of L'Art Culinaire cruises where there is an emphasis on food, wine, and new culinary creations. Silversea also offers a small number of opera-themed cruises. While theme cruises are offered, they are not aggressively promoted by the cruise line. In fact, you have to look pretty hard to find any mention of them in the comprehensive, 90+ page Silversea promotional brochure. But exist they do, and they are well worth your attention if you a gourmand or opera lover. Be sure to inquire before booking.

POSTSCRIPT   Elegant but not stuffy, expensive yet a bargain in the ultraluxury cruise market sums up the Silversea product. *Silver Wind* and *Silver Cloud* are the ideal size—large enough to be more stable at sea, to have good size swimming pools, lots of deck space, and a variety of public rooms, but small enough to sail up rivers, to allow passengers to get to know each other, and enjoy the single-seating, open dinner.

After a rocky start that got Silversea mixed reviews and three presidents in one year, it took awhile to develop a smooth-running operation. When the cruise line did get its act together (with some of the top professionals in the cruise industry in charge), Silversea quickly went to the head of the class, becoming the crème de la crème of all the cruise lines. The ships are beautiful, the service impeccable, and the itineraries, a cruise-lover's dream.

STAR CLIPPERS, INC.

4101 Salzedo Avenue, Corl Gables, FL 33146
(800) 442-0551; fax (305) 442-1611
http://www.globalint.com/mart/star.html

TYPE OF SHIPS   Replicas of nineteenth-century clipper sailing ships.

TYPE OF CRUISE   Casual, active, sports-oriented, for those who relish the experience of sailing under canvas to out-of-the-way places.

CRUISE LINE'S STRENGTHS
- traditional sailing with some cruise ship comforts
- camaraderie
- ship size/maneuverability
- itineraries

CRUISE LINE'S SHORTCOMINGS
- meager port information
- potential language/cultural collisions among passengers
- small cabins
- cuisine

FELLOW PASSENGERS   An international mix with about half being Americans, Canadians, and Latin Americans, and the other half Europeans, particularly Germans, including non-English speakers. The average age of passengers is 45, but some cruises have 20- and 30-year-olds. The majority are couples, including a dozen newlyweds.

As many as 50 percent may be repeaters, attracted by sailing on a true square-rigger. Many too are travelers who appreciate the beauty and authenticity of the clipper ships, have no interest whatever in nightclubs, casinos, and the glitter of mainstream cruise ships, and have probably shunned such cruises in the past.

Recommended For   Independent, active travelers who seek light adventure and off-the-beaten-track itineraries; small-ship devotees; stressed-out city dwellers, honeymooners, and other romantics captivated by the notion of sailing on a tall ship; avid sailors eager to be on a real sailing ship; water sports enthusiasts; experienced cruisers who have tired of large, crowded ships; conservationists who can feel good about environment-friendly travel on ships that use their engines only when they must. It's a great experience for children seven years and older who mix well with adults.

Not Recommended For Those who prefer gourmet cuisine, sophisticated ambience; others who want round-the-clock activity and the floating resort facilities of a superliner. Physically impaired travelers.

CRUISE AREAS AND SEASONS Caribbean, South Asia, winter; Mediterranean, summer; transatlantic and trans-Indian Ocean, April and October.

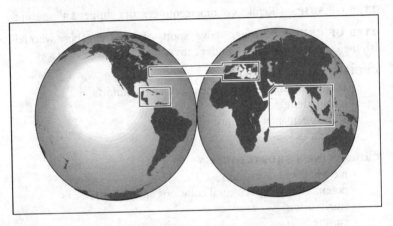

THE LINE Launched in 1991, Star Clippers is a dream-come-true of Swedish shipping entrepreneur Mikael Krafft, whose passion for sailing and building yachts and love of the clipper ship (which he says is one of America's greatest inventions) led him to create an unusual cruise line with replicas of the sleek trading ships that ruled the seas during the mid-nineteenth century. Called the greyhounds of the sea, they were the fastest ships on the high seas until the coming of the steam age in the late 1860s.

About 100 feet longer than the original clippers and equipped with the latest marine technology, today's clippers combine the romance of yesteryear's sailing with some modern cruising amenities; they offer the excitement of manning an authentic square rigger and cruising the out-of-the-way waters of the Caribbean, Mediterranean, or South Asia.

The Fleet	Built/Renovated	Tonnage	Passengers
Star Clipper	1991	3,025	172
Star Flyer	1992	3,025	172

STYLE   Star Clippers' cruises have the freewheeling spirit of a private yacht and are intended to fit between budget-priced Windjammer Barefoot Cruises and pricey Windstar Cruises. They are designed for active, sporty, healthy folks who want their travel to be interesting and educational as well as fun, with kindred souls who want none of the crowds or glitz of big ships. Dress is very casual with shorts and deck shoes the uniform of the day but a bit dressier in the evening. Cabins are average size; public rooms are few, but the teak decks are roomy.

The cruises offer island-hopping in a comfortable, laid-back atmosphere with a variety of options at each port of call. The clippers can anchor in bays where large cruise ships cannot go; launches take passengers to isolated beaches and to spots to enjoy scuba, snorkeling, and other water sports.

After a week's cruise, you will know on a first-name basis many passengers and most of the crew, who double in their duties as deck hands and sports instructors. If you are so inclined, you can help the crew hoist the sails or simply laze about the deck doing little more than watching the sails and the sea. Itineraries are scheduled to ensure daylight time for cruising under sail. The cruises are a great environment for families with children from ages 7–17, as well.

DISTINCTIVE FEATURES   The ship itself and being able to participate in sailing it. Daily briefings by the captain. PADI certification.

RATES

Highest Per Diem	Lowest Per Diem	Average Per Diem
$242	$70	$119

The above per diems are calculated from the cruise line's nondiscounted *cruise-only* fares on standard accommodations. Per diems vary by season, by cabin location, and by cruise areas.

Special Fares and Discounts Early booking program offers 10 percent discount on published rates for 120-day advance booking on selected cruises.

- Single Fare: Guaranteed at a specific rate, depending on season, with cabin assigned two weeks prior to departure.
- Single Supplement: 150 percent of published fare.

Packages
- Air/Sea: Yes.
- Others: Honeymoon.
- Pre/Post: Yes.

Past Passengers Membership cards for the Past Passengers Club are sent after your first voyage and special discounts are routinely offered to members. All club members also receive a bottle of champagne in their cabins on their boarding, and are placed on the ship's VIP list.

THE LAST WORD Star Clippers provides an unusual cruise experience on unique ships that are modern and comfortable yet steeped in tradition. More affordable than the *Sea Cloud* and more upscale than the *Sir Francis Drake*, the Star Clippers are more authentic as sailing ships than either the Club Med twins or the Windstar trio. Yet, for all their romance, they are definitely not for everyone.

The ships cannot readily accommodate handicapped passengers and are definitely not for people who want the comforts and options of mainstream cruises. English is the language of the ship, but there are likely to be announcements in German and other languages, depending on the makeup of the passengers.

Language can get to be a problem when English speakers are outnumbered by those who do not speak English and communicating is difficult, or some feel they are being left out of activities. Obviously, the language problem can vary with the staff, some being more careful to translate than others.

STAR CLIPPERS STANDARD FEATURES

Officers European.

Staffs Dining, Cabin/International; Cruise/Swedish, Australian, and Hungarian.

Dining Facilities One dining room for three meals with open unassigned seating. Light breakfast, occasional buffet lunch, hors d'oeuvres at 5 P.M. served on deck.

Special Diets Accommodated with advance notice.

Room Service None.

Dress Code Relaxed and casual. Walking shorts, bathing attire with cover up, skirts, slacks for daytime; slacks with polo or casual shirts, no jackets required for men in evening.

Cabin Amenities Radio, hair dryer, safe, cellular-satellite phone; movies, ports of call videos, and music; bathrooms with showers; upper category with whirlpool bath and mini-refrigerator.

Electrical Outlets 110 AC.

Wheelchair Access None.

Recreation and Entertainment Piano bar with entertainer; outdoor deck bar for dancing and local entertainment; library/writing room; backgammon and bridge.

Sports and Other Activities Two outdoor pools; water sports and equipment; sailing dinghies, windsurfers, water skiing, underwater viewing craft, waterjet launches and inflatables carried on board. Learn-to-Sail and dive certification programs.

Beauty and Fitness No beauty/barber service. Daily exercise sessions.

Other Facilities Dining room doubles as conference room; audiovisual equipment. Nurse on seven-day cruises; doctor and nurse on transatlantic. Ship's officers trained in emergency medicine.

Children's Facilities None; under 18 must be accompanied by adult.

Theme Cruises None.

Smoking No smoking in cabins. At first briefing, captain emphasizes that smoking is allowed on deck or in rear of dining room.

Star Clippers Suggested Tipping Per person per day, cabin steward, $3; waiter and busboy, $5; 12.5 percent added to bar bills.

Credit Cards For cruise payment and on-board charges, American Express, Mastercard, and Visa.

Star Clipper / Star Flyer

	Quality Rating	Value Rating
Star Clipper/Star Flyer	7	A

Registry: Luxembourg	Length: 360 feet	Beam: 50 feet
Cabins: 84	Draft: 18.5 feet	Speed: 17 knots
Maximum Passengers: 180	Passenger Decks: 4	Elevators: none
	Crew: 60	Space Ratio: 15

THE SHIPS   The *Star Clipper* and *Star Flyer* are identical twins, with four masts and square-rigged sails on the forward mast—a Barquentine configuration—with a total of 16 sails (36,000 square feet of dacron). They are manned, not computerized, and are capable of attaining speeds of up to 19 knots. A diesel engine is in reserve for calms and maneuvering in harbors.

At 226 feet tall, they are among the tallest of the Tall Ships and the first true sailing ships to be classified by Lloyd's Register of Shipping since 1911. Built in Belgium, the twin vessels comply with the latest safety regulations for passenger vessels on worldwide service, including those of the U.S. Coast Guard.

The ships have four passenger decks with all but eight cabins on the two lower decks and the public space on the two top ones. There, amidst the sails and rigging and the open bridge, every secret Walter Mitty begins to salivate with anticipation. They can help hoist the sails or watch in wonder.

STAR CLIPPER ITINERARIES   Not all ports are always included on every cruise, as itineraries are subject to weather conditions and alterations by the captain in search of the calmest sailing and best anchorages.

- *November–April,* Caribbean, seven days, departing from Barbados on Saturdays to Carriacou, Grenada, Union Island, St. Vincent, and St. Lucia; or Martinique, Dominica, St. Lucia, Tobago Cays, and Bequia. Alternating itineraries can be combined into a 14-day cruise. In 1998, the ship is scheduled to change its home port to Antigua.
- *May–October,* Mediterranean, seven days, departing from Cannes each Saturday on two alternating itineraries to Calvi (Corsica),

beach stop at Bonifacio, Costa Smeralda (Sardinia), Portoferraio (Elba), Portofino, and St. Tropez; or, to Ille Rousse or St. Florent (Corsica), beach stop at Ajaccio (Corsica), Porto Rotondo or Porto Cervo (Sardinia), Island of Giglio, Portovenere, and Monte Carlo.

- *Repositioning cruises:* Transatlantic between Caribbean and Mediterranean are well suited for those who enjoy being under sail at sea more than visiting ports. Those for *Star Clipper* are scheduled twice a year: Eastbound in April, 27 days from Barbados to the Azores (14 days), followed (in two 7-day segments) by calls at Malaga, Cabo de Gata, Ibiza, Palma de Mallorca, St. Tropez and Cannes. Westbound in October from Cannes, the ship calls at Palma de Mallorca, Ibiza, Malaga, Funchal, Madeira, Canary Islands, and Barbados and usually includes some ports on the coast of Spain and the Canary Islands.

Home Ports Barbados; Cannes.

Port Charges $118. Transatlantic: $75–$320 (eastbound); $100–285 (westbound).

STAR FLYER ITINERARIES Seven days, South Asia from November–March, departs from Singapore on Saturday to Pangkor, Batong Group (Malaysia), Phi Phi Island (Thailand), sailing via Pang, Khai Nok Island, Phuket (Patong Beach). Or, from Phuket to Surin Island, Similan Island, Rok Nok Island, Langkawi (Malaysia), Malacca, and Singapore.

- *May–September,* seven days, Greek Isles and Turkey, on four different itineraries: Athen to Kusadasi via Kea, Mykonos, Santorini, Astipalaia, Symi, and Bodrum; Kusadasi round trip via Bodrum, Marmaris, Kekova, Lindos, Kos, and Samos; Mykonos, Santorini, Iraklion, Karpathos, Rhodes, and Patmos; or to Patmos, Datchka, Santorini, Naxos, Tinos, Milos, and Rhodes.
- The *Star Flyer* has two Indian Ocean crossings, west from Phuket to Athens via Colombo, Goa, Sharm el-Sheik (Egypt); east from Rhodes to Phuket via Aqaba, Bombay, Colombo.

Home Ports Singapore; Phuket; Athens; Kusadasi.

Port Charges $145. Indian Ocean: $95–185.

CABINS The small but comfortable, carpeted, air-conditioned cabins are tastefully furnished with a small counter/desk and a built-in upholstered seat, a large mirror, wood paneling, brass lamps and trim, and prints of sailing scenes on the walls. Two portholes let in light. There is storage space under the bed for luggage or scuba gear, and adequate closet and drawer space for the informal nature of these cruises.

Most cabins are outside and fitted with twin beds that can be converted to a double bed. They have multichannel radio, phone, hair dryer, safe, ceiling-mounted television/video monitor for viewing movie videos (videotapes are available from the ship's library in English and German) and 24-hour news, which is prepared in English English, American English, Canadian English, and German, each version written separately and localized to include news of particular interest to that group.

The bathrooms with marble-trimmed fixtures are very small and all have showers, except for eight top category cabins on the main and sun decks, which have whirlpool bathtubs plus hair dryers and mini-refrigerators, which are stocked at the outset of the cruise; occupants pay only for the restocks. These larger cabins open directly onto the open deck, which some people prefer but others may not, for their lack of privacy. Cabin service is limited to cleaning. The ships' inside cabins are sold only when the ship is fully booked.

Specifications   6 inside cabins, 78 outside; no suites. Standard dimensions, 120 square feet. 66 cabins with two lower beds (convertible to queen-size); 18 cabins with fixed double beds; 8 cabins accommodate third passenger; 4 inside cabins have uppers and lowers; no singles.

DINING   The Clipper Dining Room, resplendent with shining brass and etched glass, is a rather formal room for such an informal ship. Situated amidships on Clipper Deck, it has seating at large tables for six, between or around a forest of columns, and banquettes on the sides along the walls where portholes let in light. All passengers and ship's officers are accommodated at one time in an open-seating arrangement that encourages both to mingle. When the ship is full the room is very crowded.

The buffet breakfast has made-to-order omelets and lunch has a different pasta daily and a self-service salad bar. A light, early morning breakfast and an occasional lunch buffet are also served on deck.

Dinner offers selections of beef, chicken, and fish, vegetables, cheeses, and desserts. The food is plentiful but ordinary, appealing to those with a minimal interest in epicurean delights. In the course of a week the food can range from adequate to good, but never gourmet. The menu does, however, emphasize fresh ingredients, fruit, salads, vegetables, and seafood. A variety of wines are available at reasonable prices. Wine prices are reasonable. Some samples are Robert Mondavi Cabernet Sauvignon, $26; Kendall-Jackson Chardonnay, $18; and house wine, Cuvee Lupe Cholet, France, red or white, $14, or $3.50 per glass.

SERVICE   The captain, officers, and deck crew are a friendly, energetic, easygoing lot who mix freely and easily with the passengers, helping to create the ship's relaxed social atmosphere. The dining and hotel staff is low key and congenial, also in keeping with the casual ambience of the cruise.

FACILITIES AND ENTERTAINMENT   A small U-shaped piano lounge wraps around the landing of the stairway between main deck and the dining room. It has brass-framed panoramic windows, carved paneling, and small tables with cushioned banquettes that seat about two dozen people. Overhead, a skylight is actually the transparent bottom of a pool on the sun deck. The resident pianist, and on some cruises a vocalist, entertain before and after dinner.

From the piano lounge, you pass between swinging doors to the Tropical Bar, an outdoor bar with a broad canvas awning on the main deck. Depending on the hour of the day, it serves as a social center, meeting area, or stage—the place where the captain holds his daily talks, the scene for local entertainment, a spot for light breakfast and an occasional lunch buffet, and dance floor for disco dancing to taped music or an electronic keyboard. There is no casino or gambling on board.

ACTIVITIES AND DIVERSIONS   Passengers might be found playing backgammon or bridge. The library/writing room on the main deck is a cozy teak-paneled room, resembling an English club with large brass-framed windows, oil paintings of nautical scenes and famous sailing ships, and a fireplace (which is not allowed by the U.S. Coast Guard to function although it is designed to do so).

The room is furnished with card tables and comfortable chairs and doubles as a reception desk at the time of boarding. It is also used for small meetings and is stocked with a good selection of popular fiction, travel, and coffee-table books. A tiny shop sells film and ship souvenirs. The dining room converts into a meeting room with screen projectors and video monitors and is used for port lecturers and others.

The captain and cruise director hold "story time," an informal briefing session for passengers on deck in the late afternoon or the morning before arriving in port. Passengers tend to congregate around the open bridge where they can hear the captain and his mates at work and watch the sails being raised and lowered. They can also lend a hand—and many try—but only a few hang in for the full cruise.

SPORTS, FITNESS, AND BEAUTY   Two tiny outdoor pools found on the sun deck can be filled with either fresh water or seawater; both normally are filled with seawater. The pools are filled when the ship is at anchor and are kept filled at sea, if the wind is moderate. The forward pool is used at sea for scuba classes for beginners.

You can do your morning constitutional in the open air by walking from the stern to the bow around the open parts of main and sun decks. Every morning at 8 A.M. sharp, one of the water sports team leads passengers in a half-hour aerobic session on the main deck using deck mats brought down from the swimming pools.

In the Caribbean, waters sports are a more important part of the cruise than in the Mediterranean. The ships carry sailing dinghies, windsurfers, underwater viewing craft, boats for waterskiing and skis, snorkel gear, scuba equipment for certified divers, volleyballs, and kadima paddles (oversized, solid-surface paddles) used for beach sports. The ship might drop anchor in a remote cove or off a deserted beach, and launches shuttle passengers to and from the shore for snorkeling, sailing, windsurfing, and swimming.

The ship's sports and recreational staff include multilingual instructors who are on hand to provide assistance and equipment for beach activities. Snorkel gear, issued to passengers at no cost, is retained by them for the duration of the cruise; the ship organizes snorkeling almost every day in the Caribbean. For a charge of $40 per dive, certified divers (with their C cards) can sign up for trips to reefs and underwater wrecks. The charge covers air tank refill, personal supervision by a water sports team member, and use of a Zodiac to take the diver to dive sites from the ship.

Star Clippers offers three dive programs: a resort course for $79; a PADI certification completion course for $195 for those who bring documentation of having completed classroom requirements; and a full PADI certification course for $295. For the latter, however, the cruise line recommends that divers spread the course over a two-week cruise. Another program, Learn-to-Sail, is a basic course for wannabe sailors. Lessons are daily and the textbook used is *How to Sail a Square Rigger*, a 114-page manual that includes information on clipper-ship history and describes all 16 sails, rigging, etc.

SHORE EXCURSIONS   Guided tours, usually costing $30–40, focus on a destination's architectural, historical, and environmental points of interest and are likely to be more interesting than those offered by mainstream cruise ships. Also, the small number of passengers and the ships' off-the-beaten-track itineraries help ensure more stimulating, personalized tours for participants.

The ships tie up in port as few times as possible. Huge stabilizing tanks (which are patented) keep the ship steady at anchor. As soon as the ship is cleared on arrival by local authorities, tender service is offered every half hour until the posted sailing time, usually around 6 P.M.

POSTSCRIPT The ships are generally under sail from late evening to the following midmorning, and under normal conditions can make their next port entirely under sail, using the engine only to maneuver in and out of the port. For true salts and romantics, the setting with the balmy tropical air filling the giant, white sails against a star-filled night sky is the picture of heaven and bliss. Many stay up half the night just to savor it.

WINDSTAR CRUISES

300 Elliott Avenue West, Seattle, Washington 98119
(206) 281-3535; (800)967-8103; fax (206) 286-3229
http://www.windstarcruises.com

TYPE OF SHIPS   Deluxe sailing yacht/cruise ship.

TYPE OF CRUISES   Low-key, laid-back, yet luxurious, for active, affluent travelers with cosmopolitan tastes for off-beat corners in sunny climes and warm waters.

CRUISE LINE'S STRENGTHS
- appealing lifestyle
- value for money
- itineraries
- private yacht exclusivity
- cabins
- romantic escape and totally different experience
- water sports

CRUISE LINE'S SHORTCOMINGS
- uneven cuisine level
- evening activity
- port-intensive itineraries with minimal time under canvas

FELLOW PASSENGERS   The mix is actually broader than the perception of a Windstar passenger, which has them driving BMWs and Porsches. Actually, about 25 percent have Mercedes or BMWs, but 40 percent have Jeeps and Fords, and more telling, 77 percent buy the family version rather than sports models. They range from 20–80 in age, but the majority are 35–55 years; their incomes range, too, and they might be first-time or experienced cruisers. Despite many differences, they share one aspect in common—lifestyle, or at least a lifestyle preference, even if not all can enjoy it 365 days of the year.

Passengers are likely to be an international collection of well-traveled, multilingual Europeans and Latin Americans as well as those from across the United States. For many passengers, that's part of the appeal.

About 75 percent are professionals—lawyers, doctors, business executives—and probably work in high-pressure jobs; the balance are likely to be retirees from similar pressure cookers, and, surely, there will be a few honeymooners. Fifty percent read business and professional magazines more than lifestyle or fashion magazines; their occupations are mentally demanding, requiring them to keep abreast of their specific fields of expertise constantly.

Windstar has been described as the sports car of the cruise industry, but the metaphor might not be correct because 80 percent of the passengers describe a perfect evening as dining out with their significant other, and, as a second choice, attending the theatre. Although they are active people, more than half enjoy individual and low-energy sports, such as golfing, walking, and swimming rather than heavy-duty athletic activities. Many participate in the on-board watersports program, but just as many might go off to swim or snorkel on their own.

Recommended For   Active, affluent, A-type, individualists, 25–65 years old, who really mean it when they say they want to chill out; those who wouldn't be caught dead on a mainstream cruise ship; divers and others who enjoy water sports in moderation; experienced cruisers looking for something different; those attracted by the romance of sailing ships but want upscale cruise ship luxury; self-starters, those with an active lifestyle and a taste for the finer things in life who can relax long enough to enjoy them.

Not Recommended For   Anyone who prefers large ships, thrives on being in the center of the action, or enjoys dressing up in fancy clothes; those who need to be entertained, don't relate to or are uncomfortable in a sophisticated ambience; shy first- or second-time cruisers; those who prefer a burger to brûlée.

CRUISE AREAS AND SEASONS   Eastern and Southern Caribbean, Costa Rica, winter; Mediterranean, spring–fall; transcanal and transatlantic, April and October.

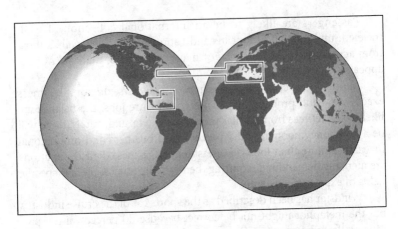

THE LINE   Four masts in a row, each as high as a 20-story building and with enormous triangular sails, stand above a deck one and a half times the length of a football field and half its width. The great sails are manned by computers, not deck hands; the computers controlling the sails are designed to monitor the direction and velocity of the wind to keep the ship from heeling more than six degrees. The sails can be furled in less than two minutes.

This is the ship which, when it was introduced in 1985, was called the most revolutionary vessel since the introduction of the steamship in the last century. The windcruiser, as the ship is known, marries the romance and tradition of sailing with the comfort and amenities of a cruise ship. Its all-outside cabins are larger, better designed, and better appointed than most standard cabins on modern mainstream cruise ships, and they have some amenities found only in suites of the most luxurious ships.

Built by Société Nouvelle des Ateliers et Chantiers du Havre et La Rochelle-Pallice, France, the vessels were the prototype for the larger Club Med ships, but the Windstar's small size makes its cruise experience very different. The ships have shallow drafts that enable them to call at less-visited ports, private marinas, and secluded beaches. They are fitted with a water sports platform at the stern that folds out to give passengers direct access to the sea. The windcruisers use wind power alone up to 50 percent of the time at sea, depending on the itinerary; electrical power and backup propulsion are provided by three diesel-electric engines.

Windstar Cruises was acquired by Holland America Line in 1987, and the following year both companies were purchased by Carnival

Cruise Lines. Windstar, however, continues to operate as a separate entity with its own special type of cruises.

In April 1997, Windstar Cruises bought *Club Med 1*, one of two identical ships in the Club Med fleet and that are larger versions of Windstar's ships, and at press time, was negotiating for the second ship, *Club Med 2*, which is owned by a group of independent investors. *Club Med 1*, to be renamed *Wind Surf*, will enter service for Windstar Cruises in May 1998.

The Fleet	Built/Renovated	Tonnage	Passengers
Wind Song	1987	5,350	148
Wind Spirit	1988	5,350	148
Wind Star	1986	5,350	148
Wind Surf	1990/98	14,745	312

STYLE   Windstar's tagline—"180° from the Ordinary"—describes it well. Laid-back, romantic, informal, the cruises are meant to combine the casual atmosphere of a private yacht with the amenities and services of a cruise ship.

From the outset, the ships have had an appeal of exclusivity, not only because of price and their off-the-beaten-track itineraries but because of their size, ambience, and the people they attract—upscale working professionals who can afford to take a cruise and like the luxury of a cruise ship or upscale resort but who want a less-structured environment and a more unusual vacation than that associated with traditional cruises. Often, too, they are people who have shunned conventional cruise ships in the past.

The ships are wonderfully quiet under sail; you can hear the ocean wash against the hull and the sails snap as the wind fills them. The bridge is open for passengers to see for themselves how everything works. The captains—their sure hands never far from the wheel—usually give passengers who yearn to try a few minutes at the helm.

There's a casual elegance, an easygoing informality about the ship and the people who fit into it comfortably. Regardless of age, passengers seem to blend easily and by the end of the week are good friends. There's never any pressure to do anything in particular at any time. You decide how to spend your day. Even the most ardent Type A personalities can unwind on this ship in spite of themselves.

DISTINCTIVE FEATURES The ship. Water sports platform; use of most gear without additional charge. Any passenger lucky enough to hook a fish on a deep-sea outing can have it cooked to order by the chef.

RATES

Highest Per Diem	Lowest Per Diem	Average Per Diem
$599	$207	$410

The above per diems are calculated from the cruise line's nondiscounted *cruise-only* fares on standard accommodations. What you will actually pay *should* be *substantially* less (see Part One, How to Get the Best Deal on a Cruise). Per diems vary by season, by cabin location, and by cruise areas.

Tipping included in price.

Special Fares and Discounts Advance Savings Program provides up to 50 percent for booking six months in advance. Windstar publishes a monthly brochure containing listings for each ship, its departure dates, and the percentage of price reduction for each sailing. It also offers two-for-one promotions from time to time.

- Single Supplement: 150 percent of the published per person rate.

Packages
- Air/Sea: Yes.
- Others: Yes.
- Pre/Post: Yes.

Past Passengers Foremast Club. All who have taken a Windstar cruise are sent a newsletter and other literature on a regular basis, highlighting new itineraries and special discounts.

THE LAST WORD On my first Windstar cruise, having expected Princess Di or, at the least, Cheryl Tiegs, the ones who seemed to be enjoying themselves the most were a blue-collar couple from Massachusetts on their second honeymoon—and their first cruise.

A Windstar cruise is a relaxing, romantic escape, but as noted earlier, the perception more than the reality seems to put it out of reach in price and ambience of most people. Although it's definitely a way to impress your friends back in the office, deciding whether or not this cruise is for you should not be based on price (although you get a lot for your money) but rather, on the type of cruise it offers—a small ship with a sophisticated ambience and with little to do that isn't of your own making, except for water sports and sailing to out-of-the-way places. Those who relate to it think it's heaven; those who do not would probably be bored to tears.

Our only complaint with Windstar is that the itineraries are so port intensive that they do not leave time for passengers to enjoy the ships, particularly to enjoy the ships under sail. For the summer of 1997, Windstar added a day at sea to the Mediterranean cruises. That's a step in the right direction, but we would like to see another sea day, at least.

WINDSTAR SHIPS STANDARD FEATURES

Officers British, some Norwegians.

Staffs Dining, Cabin/Indonesian and Filipino; Cruise/American, British, and some Scandinavian hostesses.

Dining Facilities One open-seating restaurant; outdoor cafe for breakfast and lunch buffet featuring traditional and tropical specialties; occasional barbecues on the beach.

Special Diets Advance notice requested.

Room Service 24 hour.

Dress Code Casual and elegantly casual.

Cabin Amenities Color television, VCR, CD player, three-channel radio; international direct-dial telephone; safe; minibar and refrigerator; hair dryer and terry-cloth robe.

Electrical Outlets 110 AC.

Wheelchair Access None. Seeing-eye dogs have been permitted.

Recreation and Entertainment Piano bar, casino, lounge with local musicians or ship's band, library, videocassette library.

Sports and Other Activities Watersports platform for sailboats, windsurfers, motorized inflatables, waterskiing, scuba diving; snorkeling equipment carried on board; saltwater pool.

Beauty and Fitness Beauty salon; hot tub/Jacuzzi, sauna, masseuse, fitness room with weight-training equipment.

Other Facilities Laundry; doctor, infirmary.

Children's Facilities None.

Theme Cruises None.

Smoking Smoking allowed throughout ship but no cigars or pipes permitted in dining room.

Windstar Suggested Tipping None. Tipping included in price.

Credit Cards For cruise payment and on-board charges, American Express, Mastercard, Visa. No cash system on board.

Wind Song / Wind Spirit / Wind Star

	Quality Rating	Value Rating
Wind Song, Wind Spirit	8	C
Wind Star	9	C

Registry: Bahamas	Length: 440 feet	Beam: 64 feet
Cabins: 74	Draft: 13.5 feet	Speed: 8–12 knots
Maximum Passengers:	Passenger Decks: 4	Elevators: none
159/168	Crew: 81/91	Space Ratio: 36

THE SHIPS   The three Windstar ships are identical, inside and out, and except for their itineraries, it would be difficult to tell them apart. Throughout, the tasteful appointments—well designed and inviting—are the last word in understatement. They have the feel of a sailing ship with wood and leather, portholes, and nautical blue and white decor, yet they are consciously modern with expanses of picture windows that create a spacious, open-to-the-sea feeling and space-station-white walls adorned with contemporary art.

Because the number of passengers is small, boarding formalities are speedy. Upon boarding, you're greeted with a glass of champagne or a chilled fruit drink and escorted into the main lounge to complete paperwork in comfort. Then, you are taken to your cabin where your luggage should already be stowed.

The cabins, gym, and sauna are located on the bottom two of four passenger decks. The third deck has a main lounge and dining salon—both handsome rooms that have the ambience of a private yacht. Through the overhead sunlight of the lounge, passengers get dramatic views of the majestic sails overhead—one of the ships' most delightful features. There are a tiny casino, boutique, and beauty salon. The top deck has a swimming pool, bar, and a veranda lounge used for lunch by day and a disco by night.

ITINERARIES

- *Wind Spirit* and *Wind Star*, 7–16 days, Caribbean in winter, Mediterranean in summer.
- *Wind Song*, seven days, Costa Rico, winter; Italy, summer.

- All three ships offer transatlantic voyages in April and October.
- Although the itineraries are more port intensive then we think necessary—often calling at a different locale each day—their main feature has less to do with where they sail than with the types of places they visit—small harbors, remote beaches, interesting, out-of-the-way places where large cruise ships cannot go.

WIND SPIRIT ITINERARIES

- *From January–early April, Wind Spirit* departs on Sunday on seven-day cruises of the United States and British Virgin Islands round trip from St. Thomas with calls at St. John, Tortola, Virgin Gorda (overnight), Jost Van Dyke, St. Maarten, and St. Barts.
- *From mid-May–early November,* she offers seven-day cruises in the Greek Islands and the coast of Turkey, between Athens and Istanbul. The ship calls at Mykonos, Santorini, and Rhodes in Greece, and Bodrum and Kusadasi in Turkey (or the reverse itinerary).
- *In spring and fall,* she sails on 8- and 14-day positioning and transatlantic cruises between Athens and St. Thomas via Rome, calling at a delightful group of small ports in Spain, France, and Italy en route to Rome and in Italy and Greece en route to Athens.

Home Ports   St. Thomas, winter; Athens, Istanbul, summer.
Port Charges $145–225, depending on itinerary.

WIND STAR ITINERARIES

- *From January–March, Wind Star* sails on two seven-day itineraries in the Windward and Leeward Islands from Barbados: Southbound, she departs every Sunday for Tobago Cays and Bequia in the Grenadines, Martinique (Grande Anse), St. Lucia (Pigeon Island), and Carriacou. Northbound from Barbados, she sails to St. Lucia (Pigeon Island), Iles des Saintes (Guadeloupe), St. Maarten, St. Barts, and St. Kitts. There is an overnight in St. Maarten and the last day is at sea.
- *For the Christmas and New Year holidays,* there are two 7-day cruises, with additional calls in Nevis, Bequia, and Tintamarre (St. Maarten).
- *From late May–early October, Wind Star* cruises the Mediterranean, departing on Saturday from her new home in Nice on seven-day cruises of the Italian Riviera to Gaeta, Portoferraio,

Portovenere, and Portofino, Italy, and Monte Carlo. In spring and fall, she has 13-, 14- and 15-day positioning and transatlantic cruises between Barbados via Lisbon and Nice.

Home Ports   Barbados, winter; Nice, summer.
Port Charges $145–225, depending on itinerary.

WIND SONG ITINERARIES

- *From mid-December–March, Wind Song* is charting a new course with a series of seven-day cruises along the coast of Costa Rica, from Puerto Caldera to Coiba Island, Drake Bay, Cano Island, Quepos, Flamingo, and Tortuga Island.
- *In May and October,* she offers 8- to 14-day Panama Canal positioning and transatlantic cruises from Puerto Caldera via Aruba to Barbados and then to Portugal.
- *In summer, from May–late September, Wind Song* sails on seven-day cruises along Italy's coast from Rome (Civitavecchia) to Livorno, Ajaccio, Amalfi, Capri, and Ischia, with one day at sea.

Home Ports   Puerto Caldera; Rome (Civitavecchia).
Port Charges $160 Costa Rica; $145–225, other itineraries.

CABINS   With the exception of the owner's suite, all of the cabins are identical—outside and large. Indeed, they are larger than those on regular cruise ships. These well-designed, nicely appointed cabins make optimum use of space and are fitted with queen-size or twin beds.

The marriage of tradition and technology is nowhere more apparent than in the cabins, each with twin portholes with brass fittings and real wood cabinetwork, including a foldout vanity with a makeup mirror. Modern amenities include a remote control television, VCR, international direct-dial phone, CD player, safe, and a minibar stocked daily with a selection of beer, wine, spirits, and soft drinks. (Note, however, that drinks are fairly pricey: a cold beer, for example, costs $4.00). The efficient bathrooms have showers, teak decking, well-lighted mirrors, hair dryers, terry robes, and adequate storage.

Specifications   74 outside cabins; 1 suite with queen-size bed. Standard dimensions, 182 square feet. 73 with twin beds (all convertible to double); 11 (20 on *Wind Star*) with third berths; no singles; none wheelchair accessible.

DINING   The teak-lined dining room—in nautical design with pillars wrapped in rope—has low ceilings and subdued lighting, giving it a warm, intimate feeling. There is open seating, as in a restaurant. Overall, there is less emphasis on food aboard the Windstar ships than on mainstream vessels, but given the upscale nature of the cruise, you expect the kitchen to live up to the decor and ambience. Over the years, the food has been uneven, ranging from super to ordinary. The cruise line diligently perseveres at improving it but continues to get mixed reviews.

In 1996, Windstar introduced new menus by celebrity chef Joachim Splichal of Patrina in Los Angeles. Splichal received the Best California Chef award in 1991 from the prestigious James Beard Society. Translated that means his French cooking has the light touch of California style, and it matches Windstar's casual and relaxed style of cruising. The line also debuted a new wine list of California vintages to complement the cuisine. Wine tastings are held to familiarize passengers with them. Later in 1996, "Lighter Fare" menus by Jeanne Jones, noted author and columnist who developed the spa menus for Canyon Ranch and the Pritiken Center, among others, were also added.

Coffee, tea, juices, and breakfast rolls are served around the pool area for early risers. Breakfast in the glass-enclosed veranda offers an abundance of fresh tropical fruit and fresh-baked breads. Afternoon tea on the pool deck with finger sandwiches and pastries is a popular repast.

In the Caribbean, the galley shines at the pool deck barbecue when grilled lobster tails, shrimp, and other seafood are the highlight and music by a local band puts everyone in a festive mood.

Room service is available 24 hours a day.

SERVICE   The captain and his European officers are affable, accessible, and always visible, inviting passengers to watch the ship in operation, visiting with passengers to ensure their comfort, and participating in activities when possible. They seem happy to talk about the ship and to answer passengers' questions.

The cabin staff and most of the restaurant personnel are Indonesian; deck stewards, bar personnel, and section captains are Filipino. And all get very high marks.

FACILITIES AND ENTERTAINMENT   Night life on board is low-key and minimal. The tiny casino has blackjack tables, a Caribbean stud poker table, and slot machines. Nightly, a trio plays easy listening and dancing music in the lounge; those more energetic go topside for rock by video in the veranda-converted disco. You can also pass the evening watching a movie on your cabin television from the large selection of videos available on loan at the reception desk. A Caribbean night has a reggae band from the islands and passengers young and old dancing on the pool deck.

ACTIVITIES AND DIVERSIONS   The Windstar ships do not have a schedule of daily activities, as is typical of most cruise ships. You set your own schedule, make your own activity—on your own or with newfound friends. That's what this cruise is really all about. Days are passed sunbathing, reading, deep-sea fishing, swimming, and watching the ship being maneuvered. Avid readers should bring their own books as the ship's selection is limited. The ship's television features two current movies daily plus satellite news updates around the clock.

SPORTS, FITNESS, AND BEAUTY   The absence of on-board sports is more than made up for by the water sports available directly from the ships' foldout platform, particularly in the Caribbean. What's more, the ships' shallow drafts enable them to stop in less-visited ports and at secluded beaches and coves that passengers can enjoy away from the crowd. On Caribbean cruises, more than Mediterranean ones, water sports are one of the main attractions.

Sailboats, windsurf boards, snorkeling and diving equipment, including tanks, are carried on board, as are Zodiacs (inflatable boats) to take passengers snorkeling, scuba diving, waterskiing, and deep-sea fishing. All the gear is available for use without additional charge, except for scuba, which costs $65; divers must have their certifications with them. Lessons for beginners are available. Dive masters and water sports directors are well qualified, personable, and eager to help you have a good time.

Snorkeling and scuba trips as well as lessons for novices are organized daily. Often when the ships anchor off deserted islands, beach-bound passengers need to make wet landings from the Zodiacs.

Each ship has a fitness room with some exercise equipment, sauna, and a masseuse; Jacuzzis are on the pool deck. Aromatherapy, in the method developed by pioneer Judith Jackson, is available in the beauty salon.

SHORE EXCURSIONS   Daily island excursions are mostly half-day tours with an emphasis on tropical gardens, national parks, and other natural attractions, and are slightly on the high side, ranging from $17–89. On a Caribbean itinerary during the call in St. Kitts, for example, the shore excursions include a rainforest hike and horseback riding. The new Costa Rica cruises are expected to be sports and nature oriented, as well. But in the Mediterranean, the emphasis is on sightseeing.

POSTSCRIPT   A Windstar cruise is the closest you can get to being on someone's private yacht, short of having your own. For the right people, the cruise is bliss. When you ask them why they like the cruise, they give you several reasons but topping the list is: value for money. "You get more than your money's worth" is a frequently heard comment, and most are ready to sign up for another cruise tomorrow. On the other hand, if you want to disco until dawn, Windstar is not for you.

If you need more convincing, Windstar has a new CD-ROM that's yours for $14.95 by calling Vacations on Video (602-483-1551).

Wind Surf (Preview)

Registry: Bahamas	Length: 617 feet	Beam: 66 feet
Cabins: 156	Draft: 16 feet	Speed: 12 knots
Maximum Passengers:	Passenger Decks: 6	Elevators: 2
312	Crew: n.a.	Space Ratio: 34

THE SHIP   *Wind Surf,* which was acquired by Windstar Cruises in April 1997, from Club Med, is the former *Club Med 1,* one of two identical ships in the Club Med fleet and a larger version of the Windstar ships and built at the same shipyard in France.

Windstar expects to take delivery of the ship in March 1998. After extensive remodeling of the interiors, she will be rechristened *Wind Surf* and will begin her inaugural season on May 4, 1998. During the renovations, one deck of the ship will be remodeled to create 30 suites and the ship's capacity will be reduced from 386 to 312 passengers. The suites will measure approximately 400 square feet or about double the size of the present cabins which are already spacious. The suites will have a dining/living area and two bathrooms. With the debut of the ship, Windstar is planning to launch a new spa program with a full arrange of treatments.

ITINERARIES   For her inaugural summer/fall season, *Wind Surf* will be based in Nice and sail on seven-day Mediterranean cruises from May–October 1998 calling at Cannes, St. Tropez, Portofino, Portovenere, Portoferraio, and Monte Carlo. In November, she will cross the Atlantic to her winter home in Barbados from where she will sail on

Caribbean cruises through March of 1999, sailing on two alternating itineraries to Nevis, St. Maarten, St. Barts, Iles des Saintes, Bequia; or, Tobago Cays, Tobago, Grenada, Martinique, and St. Lucia.

At press time, Windstar Cruises was negotiating for the second ship, *Club Med 2*, which is owned by a group of independent investors.

For additional information on the ships, see the Club Med profile in Part II, pages 266–278.

WORLD EXPLORER CRUISES

555 Montgomery Street, San Francisco, CA 94111-2544
(415) 393-1565; (800) 854-3835; fax (415) 391-1145

TYPE OF SHIP Classic oceanliner.

TYPE OF CRUISES Educational, port intensive, light adventure to Alaska in summer; Caribbean and Central America in January; Semester at Sea for college students and adults spring and fall.

CRUISE LINE'S STRENGTHS
- the destinations
- exceptional lectures on Alaska
- cultural presentations
- shore excursions
- warm, informal atmosphere
- friendly, efficient staff and crew
- 15,000-volume library
- value

CRUISE LINE'S SHORTCOMINGS
- aging ship
- so-so cuisine

FELLOW PASSENGERS From May–September, mature, experienced travelers over 50, retired couples, seniors, and some families with school-aged children embark on Alaska cruises. They are friendly, unpretentious types of varied means who don't miss casinos or glitzy revues. They would rather watch whales and glaciers and attend cultural shows and mind-enriching seminars. They come from all over the United States and Canada.

Most are well-educated, well-read, curious good sports who participate enthusiastically in activities and shore excursions. They are interested in nature, culture, and learning, but know how to have fun, too. They play bridge, games and quizzes, and attend functions. They are highly active, physically and mentally, regardless of their age. Spring and fall Semester at Sea programs now accept a limited number of adult participants who may study for credit or audit courses as they choose. Most are veteran travelers who fit the profile of Alaska passengers.

Recommended For Travelers seeking a cultural travel experience focused on learning about the areas visited; those who prefer Bach to rock and enjoy the informal, friendly milieu of a small ship.

Not Recommended For Gamblers, snobs, flashy types, those who like to dress up, foodies, the fastidious; first-time or other cruisers who perceive a lack of value in the absence of luxury.

CRUISE AREAS AND SEASONS Alaska in summer; South America, Africa, and Asia during spring and fall Semester at Sea voyages, and Caribbean/Central America for a ten-day period in January.

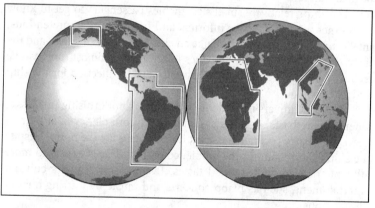

THE LINE Since 1978, World Explorer has been offering the most in-depth cruises of Alaska when its ship sails to Alaska in the summer months. During the remainder of the year, she is a floating campus for two 100-day voyages with the Semester at Sea program, sponsored by the nonprofit Institute for Shipboard Education in cooperation with the University of Pittsburgh. More recently, a ten-day Caribbean cruise has been fitted between the two programs in early January. The institute provides top lecturers for the Alaska and Caribbean cruises and a fully qualified faculty and curriculum for about 600 students each semester when the ship is their classroom. The company belongs to a Chinese owner, C. Y. Tung—and his Seawise Foundation—who is committed to learning. The ship is on charter from Commodore Cruises and went by the name *Enchanted Seas* when it was in that line's service.

The Fleet	Built/Renovated	Tonnage	Passengers
Universe Explorer	1957/1995	23,500	739

STYLE   World Explorer's advertising theme, "Come for the Wildlife, not the Nightlife," pretty much sums up a cruise on *Universe Explorer*. It's Alaska-by-immersion with the emphasis on the art, history, flora, fauna, culture, and geography so passengers can get a real feel for the region. Through the in-depth educational program with on-board lecturers, visits to off-the-beaten-path ports, adventurous shore excursions, and a leisurely pace, passengers have an intimate interaction with Alaska. Along with the serious study there's plenty of time for light-hearted fun, too.

The ship's relatively small size enables passengers to get to know each other without fanfare. Informal and friendly, the unpretentious, intellectual atmosphere is more like an elderhostel than a cruise, and the many cultural and creative activities foster a close, almost campus-like feeling. Passengers also seem to have an unusual affection for the ship and its crew.

Home to university students when she is not cruising in Alaska, amenities are basic. Dress is casual and comfortable, even at dinner. Leave your fancy cocktail dresses at home—jeans are the norm. Despite the ship's shortcomings, the ambience on board does appeal to more affluent travelers with refined tastes. Every cruise features cultural entertainment, such as piano concerts and music by a string quartet during dinner.

DISTINCTIVE FEATURES   Exceptional educational program, the world's largest library-at-sea.

RATES

Highest Per Diem	Lowest Per Diem	Average Per Diem
$264	$103	$148

The above per diems are calculated from the cruise line's nondiscounted *cruise-only* fares on standard accommodations. Per diems vary by season, by cabin location, and by cruise areas.

Special Fares and Discounts   In lieu of discounts, World Explorer Cruises offers an early booking incentive to passengers who book five months in advance on selected sailings, namely, a free two- to three-day hotel stay in Vancouver or Seattle, either before or after the cruise. The Vancouver package includes two nights in a hotel, transfer between hotel/pier, and a deluxe city tour. The Seattle package offers one night in a deluxe hotel, transfers, and motorcoach transfers to or from Seattle and Vancouver.

- Third Passenger: $795. Some cruises offer free third and fourth passengers in cabins with two full-fare passengers.
- Single Supplement: Specific rate for single cabins, $2,695–3,695.

Packages
- Air/Sea: None.
- Others: None.
- Pre/Post: See above.

Past Passengers   No club or special deals.

THE LAST WORD   This is a budget cruise ship and not recommended for everyone. But for those who want a learning vacation and friendship in an informal atmosphere on a small ship, this can be an absolutely delightful Alaska experience. Passengers say they would cruise with her again. Even for those who prefer a more deluxe setting, it could still turn out to be a good experience if they take advantage of the outstanding lectures, excursions, and unusually sophisticated entertainment. Many well-educated, well-traveled passengers who have been on luxury liners give the experience high marks. The opportunity for nonmatriculating adults to join the 100-day Semester at Sea voyages represents the ultimate educational travel experience.

WORLD EXPLORER CRUISES STANDARD FEATURES

Officers International.

Staff Dining, Cabin/Filipino, and Chinese; Cruise/American.

Dining Facilities Breakfast is open seating; lunch and dinner have two assigned seatings in the dining room. Breakfast and lunch, open seating in the Harbor Grill. The dining room is nonsmoking. Classical music often accompanies dinner in the dining room.

Special Diets Basic requests can be handled with advance notice.

Room Service None.

Dress Code Casual. Warm clothing and walking shoes for excursions and glacier watching. Rain gear and rubber-sole shoes are useful, as are binoculars. Gentlemen may want a jacket for dinner but the only dress-up times are captain's parties, when ties and jackets for men and dresses or pantsuits for women are appropriate.

Cabin Amenities Private bath with showers; top category with bathtub.

Electrical Outlets 110 AC. Hair dryers may be used in cabins.

Wheelchair Access Some doorways have raised thresholds; elevator does not reach main deck cabins.

Recreation and Entertainment Four bars in six lounges; including one for lectures, presentations on art, history, geology, botany, biology, and culture of Alaska. Nightly entertainment, including classical and folk music, opera performers, movies, talent shows and dances. There is also a movie theatre on the Aloha deck.

Sports and Other Activities Swimming pool, basketball, volleyball, Ping-Pong, walking on upper promenade decks, animal and bird-watching on deck at any time. Impromptu viewings of the northern lights. Bingo, horse racing, and games.

Beauty and Fitness Beauty salon and barbershop, massage, fitness center featuring a variety of weight and exercise equipment.

Other Facilities 15,000-volume library; self-serve washing machines and dryers; gift shop; medical unit.

Children's Facilities Youth center, youth counselors who plan special activities, children's prices for shore excursions.

Theme Cruises None.

Smoking No smoking in dining room; other areas, designated.

World Explorer Suggested Tipping Per person per day, cabin steward, $2.50; dining room stewards, $2.50; 15 percent added to bar bill.

Credit Cards For cruise and on-board ship account payments, American Express, Discover, Mastercard and Visa.

Universe Explorer

	Quality Rating	Value Rating
Universe Explorer	③	B

Registry: Panama	Length: 617 feet	Beam: 88 feet
Cabins: 373	Draft: 28 feet	Speed: 20 knots
Maximum Passengers: 840	Passenger Decks: 7	Elevators: 3
	Crew: 330	Space Ratio: 33

THE SHIP The *Universe Explorer* has had more lives than a cat. First as the *Brasil,* it sailed to South America for the old Moore-McCormack Lines; then it passed to Holland America as the *Liberté*, and to other lines as the *Queen of Bermuda* and *Volendam*. More recently, she was the Commodore Cruises' *Enchanted Seas*.

The ship has a variety of public rooms and lounges and ample deck space. The public rooms are in good shape, and the air conditioning functions well, considering the age of the ship.

Most of the public rooms are on the Promenade Deck which runs the full length of the ship from the library at the fore to pool at the stern. The side decks are teak and spacious, but they do not encircle the ship completely. The ships' limited number of elevators requires long walks from some cabins, which can be hard for less-than-hearty passengers.

Unique to a ship of this category is the ship's celebrated library, housing over 15,000 volumes.

The ship has large cabins that serve it well on the long cruises for which it was built, but some cabins have seen better days. On the other hand, passengers seem to have a good time and are not too concerned about the decor.

The *Universe Explorer* has a fitness center, youth center, self-service laundry room, a theatre, beauty shop, and medical clinic.

ITINERARIES The *Universe Explorer* sails from May–September on 14-day cruises of Alaska, round trip from Vancouver along British Columbia's Inside Passage to Ketchikan, Juneau, Skagway, to Glacier Bay/Yakutat Bay/Hubbard Glacier, Valdez, Seward, Gulf of Alaska, Sitka,

Wrangell, and Victoria, B.C. There are optional excursions to Haines (from Skagway) and Anchorage (from Seward). *Explorer* calls at more ports for longer periods of time (an average of nine hours) than most other Alaska cruises and has four days at sea.

• During the balance of the year she makes two 100-day Semester at Sea voyages to South America, Africa, and Asia during the spring and fall and one Caribbean/Central America voyage for a 10-day period in January.

Home Port   Vancouver.
Port Charges $149.

CABINS   Most cabins are spacious and comfortable with ample closets and storage space for two, perhaps three persons, but are cramped for four. More than 75 percent are outside; most top-priced cabins have bathrooms with tubs; others have showers only. Some bathrooms have a bidet. The water is steaming hot and the bathrooms spotless.

The usual bathroom amenities, such as shampoo, are not provided. The number of electrical outlets is limited; one accommodates a hair dryer. Reading lights set into the wall beside the bed provide plenty of light.

The noise through the walls appears to be more of a problem on the lower levels, where passengers are bothered by cleaning noises by the crew and the humming of the engines. Some cabins on the Boat and Sun Decks have views partially obstructed by the lifeboats, but they are not indicated on the deck plan. Cabins on the lowest deck do not have elevator access.

The ship has nine categories of cabins, but since the ship spends more time as a campus than a cruise, the accommodations could be more aptly described as collegiate-looking, like student quarters rather than cruise ship ones. Some cabins are small and plain with twin beds, and collapsible upper berths. All recently got new mattresses, bed coverings, and pillows. All cabins are equipped with color television and direct-dial telephones. Baby cribs are available.

Specifications   80 inside cabins, 293 outside; 32 with double bed, 4 with kings; 1 single. Standard dimensions, inside or outside, 152 square feet; deluxe and superior, 191–293 square feet. Large variety of configurations: some twins with upper and lower berths; 169 with twin beds convertible to doubles; some connecting cabins. 70 cabins have bathtubs.

DINING   The Dining Room, located on the main deck, has open seating for breakfast but there are two seatings for lunch and dinner, with assigned seats. In the evening passengers dine to classical music by guest string quartets. Tables for two are available upon request.

The menu's catch of the day—probably halibut or salmon—does not taste fresh, even if the cruise line claims otherwise. Some oriental and Italian selections and all-American favorites from prime rib to Baked Alaska are also on the menu. Asian specialties, including a festive Chinese dinner, are popular, as are the lunchtime salad bar and pasta. Some passengers find the menu selection is limited; others say it is quite good.

Early birds can enjoy a continental breakfast buffet on the glass-enclosed promenade of the Promenade Deck. A full buffet breakfast and lunch is served in the Harbor Grill on the same deck. Afternoon tea with finger sandwiches and the late-night snack (usually at about 10:45 to 11:45 P.M.) with hot dishes and desserts are served in the same place.

SERVICE   The captain and crew are excellent and help create a wonderfully warm, informal atmosphere that enables passengers to become one big family very quickly. The Filipino staff, in particular, is genuinely nice and accommodating.

FACILITIES AND ENTERTAINMENT   Enchanting entertainment in harmony with Alaska's natural beauty is scheduled nightly and might include a classical guitarist, flutist, light opera singer, cabaret and pop vocalists, classical pianist, or string quartet. The ship's five-piece orchestra plays dance music in the evenings. A recognized entertainer is featured on each cruise and first-run films are shown daily in the theatre. There may be a passenger talent show in the lounge, but no flashy revues and no casino.

ACTIVITIES AND DIVERSIONS   The most distinctive feature of a World Explorer cruise and the one that sets it apart from others is the enrichment of the passengers' Alaska experience through lively lectures by guest experts, most with doctorate degrees.

Each day, lectures cover some aspect of Alaska—history, wildlife, geology, anthropology, art, botany, biology, or culture, depending on the presenter's field of expertise, often accompanied by videos, films, and slide presentations. One lecturer might speak on Native American arts; another speaker might be a biologist describing the bald eagle's typical habitat and lifestyle to help passengers spot them along the way. (For a closer view, you can visit the Alaska State Museum in Juneau, where a two-story eagle nesting tree is on display.)

Geologists, along with park rangers from Glacier Bay National Park and Preserve who board all cruise ships that sail into the bay, give running commentary to help passengers understand this awesome sight. Artist Sue Coleman, known to Pacific Northwest audiences for her Alaska-inspired works, or another artist, is on board to give art classes, normally three sessions in a two-week voyage.

At most any time, narrated animal and bird-watching on deck might take place (remember to bring binoculars) or impromptu viewings of the northern lights, along with bingo, games, and even horse racing. The days at sea are a welcome respite to browse in the library and enjoy the camaraderie of interesting fellow passengers.

SPORTS, FITNESS, AND BEAUTY   Facilities and activities include a swimming pool, basketball, Ping-Pong, volleyball, and a fitness center. There is a beauty/barber shop and massage.

CHILDREN'S FACILITIES   A youth center (actually one of the classrooms) is found on Sun Deck. Youth counselors are on every cruise in summer to provide activities for children. There are children's prices for shore excursions.

SHORE EXCURSIONS   Forty-four innovative and varied shore excursions are summarized (with prices) in a 36-page, well-written booklet which is sent to passengers with their documents about a month in advance of their cruise. Excursions range from adventurous rafting through moderate rapids to heart-stopping helicopter flights that land at the top of glaciers where you step out in traction boots.

More sedate options visit local museums and galleries and pan for gold, but all are intended to give passengers memorable experiences that add to an in-depth understanding of Alaska.

Sometimes, the expert lecturers accompany a group on an excursion—for example, the botanist might lead a botanical walk to find flora for the herbarium. At Sitka, where passengers are tendered ashore, be sure to visit the Alaska Raptor Rehabilitation Center, where sick and injured birds of prey are rehabilitated for release back into the wild. With an average of nine hours in each port, there is time to make more than one outing in some ports. Passengers should become familiar with the shore excursions in advance. The choices are not easy and many require an all-day commitment.

POSTSCRIPT   The combination of experience, expert lectures, cultural entertainment, and shore excursions makes the World Explorer

Alaska cruise an unusual, well-rounded experience at affordable prices that, for the right persons, offsets the shortcomings of the ship.

For information on the Semester at Sea program, write to: Institute for Shipboard Education, 811 William Pitt Union, University of Pittsburgh, Pittsburgh, PA 15260, or phone (800) 854-0195 or (412) 648-7490; fax (412) 648-2298.

OTHER CRUISE LINES AND THEIR SHIPS

In addition to the 32 cruise lines with their 131 cruise ships in the American mainstream of cruising, which have already been profiled in this section, another group of cruise lines with 34 ships, mostly based in Europe, may be of interest to readers. Space does not allow us to give them the same in-depth treatment as the others.

But in general, they are small to midsize ships operated in the European tradition for Europeans, with very interesting itineraries, which visit places many Americans would need an atlas to find. The ships have English-speaking staff and although the majority of passengers are Europeans speaking a babble of languages, many speak English, too.

The degree of luxury these ships offer covers a broad range, some being brand new luxury vessels launched in only the last year or so. They will appeal particularly to those who have traveled the main routes often and are looking for new places to visit or a new environment in which to return to places they might have visited in the past. They will also appeal to those who might never consider stepping into the mainstream on a typical cruise ship, preferring rather to explore less-traveled byways.

Included here, too, are a few cruise lines and ships that might have been part of the mainstream group, in that they cater mainly to the U.S. market. However, they were not listed there for a variety of reasons: they are sold mainly through tour companies in combination with larger tour programs; they are under charter a large part of the year; we had difficulty obtaining information; or some similar reasons.

In parentheses following the ship's name is information pertaining to cabins, number of passengers, officers and crew, and the ship's length and tonnage.

(Key: Cabins/Passengers; Officers/Crew; Ship Length/Tonnage)

Cape Canaveral Cruise Line

501 N. Wymore Road, Winter Park, FL 32789
(409) 975-5000; (800) 910-SHIP

Dolphin IV   (294/692; Greek/International; 501 ft./13,007 tons). This new cruise line was launched in 1996 after acquiring the *Dolphin IV* from Dolphin Cruise Line. The smallest ship in Bahamas service, the *Dolphin IV* has a coziness and friendly atmosphere that passengers seem to love and is well suited for short cruises. The ship departs from Port Canaveral on informal, two- to four-day cruises from Port Canaveral to the Bahamas and Key West, catering to budget-minded, first-time cruisers.

Originally built in 1956 as a combination passenger-cargo ship for Israeli Zim Lines, *Dolphin IV* has had as many lives as a cat. She was sold to the Portuguese in 1966, renamed *Amelia Del Mello*, and sailed between Lisbon and the Canary Islands. In 1972, she was bought by her Greek owners, gutted and rebuilt as a cruise ship, and cruised the Mediterranean as the *Ithaca* for Ulysses Lines and later as the *Dolphin IV* of Paquet Cruises. In 1984, she became Dolphin Cruise Line's first ship and in 1991, was given a major renovation with reflective metal ceilings and mirrored walls, bold and pastel colors in public areas, and enlarged facilities.

Passenger facilities and cabins are on six decks. The Promenade Deck has the main public rooms: a lounge, showroom, library/video room, casino, disco, boutique, hair salon, video game room, children's playroom, pool, and lido dining area. Topside, the Sun Deck has large lounging areas aft.

The ship offers 12 cabin categories from inside cabins with upper and lower berths to junior suites with sitting rooms and full baths. More than half of the cabins are outside and most are furnished with twin beds, radio, phone, but no television. Tastefully furnished in earth tones and pastels, the cabins are small but adequate for two persons for short cruises. Inside cabins are often more spacious than outside ones. Most have minimal storage space; bathrooms have a small shower unit and small shelf for toiletries.

The dining room, situated on a lower deck, as is typical of older ships, is cozy and nicely decorated in pinks and other soft colors. There are two seatings. Live dinner music by a pianist at the grand piano adds a pleasant touch. Self-service breakfast and lunch buffets are available in the Miramar Cafe and the outside lido area has a barbecue grill close to the swimming pool.

Classical Cruises

132 East 70th Street, New York, NY 10021
(212) 794-3200; (800) 252-7745; fax (212) 518-0077

The retail marketing arm of Travel Dynamics, an incentive travel company, Classical Cruises specializes in educational and culturally oriented cruises, using a wide variety of well-known deluxe and luxury ships. The programs are designed for well-traveled, destination-oriented individuals accustomed to independent travel, who are looking for a learning experience but don't want to forego their comfort. The itineraries span the world and include exotic as well as more typical destinations. Lecturers and academics with destination-specific knowledge accompany the cruises. Rates are high.

The company also markets the *Panorama,* a 45-passenger, three-masted, sailing/motor yacht, offering a seven-day cruise of the Turkish coast in a 14-day package. Another series uses the 275-passenger *Arcadia* for a 10-day Greece and Turkey combination.

Croatia Cruise Lines (See OdessAmerica)

The newly formed Croatia Cruise Lines launched its first cruises in summer 1997, with the 137-cabin *Adriana*, offering six itineraries of 7–15 days, beginning and ending in Venice. The ships calls at Dubrovnik and at the Croatian ports of Split and Korcula. Stay-over packages for escorted tours of Croatia and cruises through Croatia's Dalmatian islands are also available.

Cruise Holdings, Ltd.

4770 Biscayne Boulevard, No. 700, Miami, FL 33137
(305) 573-5640

Cruise Holdings, Ltd., a privately held investment group and cruise ship operator and the parent company of Seawind Cruise Line and Dolphin Cruise Line, recently purchased Premier Cruise Lines and its ship, the *Oceanic*. Promoted as the "Big Red Boat" in combination with Orlando based theme parks, the *Oceanic* sails from Port Canaveral to Nassau and Port Lucaya on three- and four-day cruises.

The *Seawind Crown* follows Southern Caribbean itinerary from Aruba and Barbados on one-week cruises. Dolphin's fleet consists of the *SeaBreeze, OceanBreeze,* and *IslandBreeze.*

CTC Lines (See OdessAmerica)

Dolphin Hellas Shipping c/o Aegean Travelvision

Ridgeway Center, 26 Sixth Street, No. 505, Stamford, CT 06905
(800) 473-3239; (203) 973-0111; fax (203) 969-0799

Aegean Travelvision handles individual bookings as well as travel companies specializing in the Eastern Mediterranean. The *Aegean Dolphin*, which belongs to Dolphin Hellas Shipping, is under charter by Renaissance Cruises.

Epirotiki Lines (See Royal Olympic Cruises)

EuroCruises

303 West 13th Street, New York, NY 10014
(212) 691-2099; (800) 688-EURO; fax (212) 366-4747

EuroCruises is a U.S. tour company that specializes in European cruises, particularly of an unusual, off-the-beaten-track nature. It is the U.S. representative for over 60 different ocean-going ships and riverboats—all of which are European owned and managed. The cruises cover all corners of the continent from Portugal to Russia and from the Mediterranean to the edge of the North Pole. While the majority sail between early spring and late fall, there are some cruises in the winter season for the Mediterranean and Canary Islands.

Included here are the cruise lines and their ships for which EuroCruises is the representative and which offer ocean cruises, mainly of the Baltic, North Cape, Norwegian fjords, and the Mediterranean. EuroCruises' portfolio of river cruises are covered in Part Three, River and Barge Cruises. In all cases, EuroCruises can provide greater details on the ships and their itineraries with brochures that show deck plans and further describe the ships' features.

Azur-Bolero Cruises (Medov Cruises/EuroCruises)

Azur (750 passengers; 15,000 tons). The *Azur* has one dining room, several bars, two swimming pools, a cinema, casino, sports center, disco, karaoke bar, and activities. It departs on 4–11-night cruises from April–November from Venice and Genoa on various eastern Mediterranean and Greek Islands cruises and from Savona on western Mediterranean itineraries that are combined with North African ports.

Bolero (900 passengers; Greek/Greek; 525 ft./16,000 tons) Built in Germany in 1968, the *Bolero* (formerly the *Starward* of Norwegian Cruise Line) was completely renovated in 1995. Her facilities include large public areas and comfortable lounges, a piano bar, casino, two outdoor pools, fully equipped gym, sauna, beauty salon, library, disco, and a restaurant with great views. She is fully air conditioned and has four elevators and stabilizers. All cabins (most measuring 125 square feet) have private baths with showers; six suites have bathtubs; and eight categories have third and fourth berths. The *Bolero* cruises the Mediterranean year-round on 4–15-night itineraries from Genoa to the Western and Eastern Mediterranean and the Canary Islands, and from Savona around Europe.

Flamenco (750 passengers; Ukrainian; 535 ft./17,270 tons) The former *Southern Cross* of CTC Cruise lines, after being acquired by its new owners, will be renamed *Flamenco* and sail on Baltic Sea and Norwegian fjords cruises in the summer of 1998.

Fred Olsen Lines (EuroCruises)

Black Prince (450 passengers; Norwegian/Filipino; 465 ft./11,500 tons). Built in 1966 and renovated in 1987, the seven-deck ship caters primarily to a British audience and sails on 14–32-night cruises from Dover, England, year-round, for the African coast, Canary Islands, Norwegian coast, Caribbean, and the Mediterranean. Some cruises in May to July depart from Harwich, England, for the Baltic, Norwegian fjords, and North Cape. The ship has a gym, pool, sauna, beauty salon, disco, and casino, and provides international entertainment and sports. It is a good choice for gregarious 50+ travelers. She starts 1998 with a 37-night South American voyage that includes a cruise up the Amazon to Manaus, departing from Dover on January 17, and calling at Madeira, Barbados, and Trinidad en route. This is a cruise for those who love to cruise as 23 days are spent at sea.

Black Watch (438/832; Norwegian/International; 674 ft./28,492 tons) The latest ship to join the EuroCruises team, *Black Watch,* was formerly Royal Cruise Line's *Star Odyssey,* and before that, the *Royal Viking Star,* a much-beloved ship. Her history is typical of many medium-size ships in that she was ultimately judged too small and too old to compete effectively in the U.S. market, and was sold to a cruise line that operates in specialized markets. Her acquisition by Fred Olsen Lines makes her the largest vessel in a fleet consisting of one small cruise ship, the *Black Prince*, and a number of island-hopping ferries. Following her acquisition, the *Black Watch* underwent a $6 million dollar refurbishment.

Black Watch will start 1998 with a 28-night cruise departing on January 6 from Dover to Singapore and Hong Kong via Malta, Suez Canal, Yemen, India, Goa, and Thailand. Between Singapore and Hong Kong she will cruise via Indonesia and the Philippines and on the return voyage will visit Vietnam. After her return to Dover in March, she will head to the Caribbean for a 35-day cruise that takes in Antigua, San Juan, Santo Domingo, Ocho Rios, Belize, Playa del Carmen/Cozumel, Cuba, Nassau, and Bermuda. Her summer will be spent on 13-night cruises of the Western Mediterranean and Canary Islands, North Cape and Greenland, and the Baltic to St. Petersburg via Estonia and Germany.

Cabins on the *Black Watch* come in a bewildering number of configurations. Though most are small by today's standards, all are nicely appointed, and 90 percent are outside cabins with portholes, a picture window, or in the case of several suites, a private veranda. Baths are very plain but well designed, as are closets and other storage areas. All cabins have televisions and phones, and many have refrigerators.

Though cabins aboard the *Black Watch* are more than adequate, the ship's real strength lies in its exceptional public areas. The *Black Watch* boasts one of the largest and most splendidly appointed libraries afloat, but unfortunately, it is open only a couple of hours each day. Contiguous with the library is an equally impressive card and game room. Both rooms feature nautical artifacts from previous incarnations of ships bearing the name *Black Watch*. A large observation lounge on Deck 9 overlooks the bow, while a similar lounge aft surveys the stern. Both lounges provide live music well into the night. A third, pub-like watering hole adjoining the main showroom draws on the history of the Scottish Black Watch Regiment for its theme and decor. On the same deck, adjacent to the dining room, is an immense lounge packed with brightly colored stuffed chairs. This room, with its clubby atmosphere and maritime accents, is given over entirely to the British passion for drinking tea, which is available 24 hours a day. Though properly known as the Braemar Room, Americans often refer to it as the British Dialysis Center. Well-designed public areas continue outside with a promenade on the Lido Deck that encircles the ship. The stern is the out-of-doors activity center with pools, Jacuzzis, bars, and cafes on both Decks 6 and 9. On intervening Decks 7 and 8, spacious outdoor areas, some open, some covered, provide a cheerful venue for sunning, reading, and relaxing.

Another strength of the *Black Watch* is her entertainment. Professional, varied, and appealing to a wide range of ages and backgrounds, the entertainment aboard the *Black Watch* puts that of many of her superliner competitors to shame. During a recent voyage, we enjoyed Las Vegas–style production shows, an incredibly talented opera company (who succeeded in making opera accessible to the uninitiated), an illusionist, a stand-up comic, a celebrity vocalist, and several classical music concerts. The evening entertainment is usually so stimulating that most passengers seek to prolong the evening. Lounges, along with the casino and the Star Night Club, a dance venue, bustle with activity into the wee hours.

For an American, the greatest pleasure of cruising on the *Black Watch* is the opportunity to meet and mix with her delightful British passengers. After four centuries, the British curiosity about Yanks remains virtually irrepressible, and the same, of course, can be said of many Americans concerning things British. On the *Black Watch*, long hours are spent with new English, Scot, and Irish friends exploring and laughing about the subtleties that make our cultures so similar yet at the same time so different. Misunderstandings of idiom and accent, of course, are legion and commonly uproarious (an announcement of a "Folkloric Presentation" was heard by the Americans as a "Full Colonic Presentation" . . . We couldn't wait!). Because the British are so unfailingly gracious and friendly, sailing aboard the *Black Watch* makes being a minority a very special pleasure.

Fritidskryss (EuroCruises)

Funchal   (217/424; Portuguese/Swedish; 500 ft./10,000 tons). Streamlined and compact, the Danish-built ship was extensively refurbished in 1987, 1991 and again in 1996. She has two dining rooms, several lounges and bars, a library, card room, beauty salon, tax-free shop, pool, and sauna. All cabins have a shower and toilet. Her cruises depart from Oslo/Gothenburg for the North Cape (11 days) in June and July; and for Faroe Islands, Iceland, and Spitsbergen (17 days) in July. Her size enables her to slip through the narrowest fjord effortlessly. She is frequently on charter to a large European tour company.

Grimaldi Cruises (EuroCruises)

Ausonia   (550 passengers; Italian crew; 13,000 tons). The fully air-conditioned *Ausonia* is Italy on the sea with an Italian crew and

Italian cuisine. All cabins have phone and private bath. The ship has a restaurant (two sittings for dinner), two lounges, nightclub, bars, boutique, hairdresser, piano bar, Jacuzzi, pool, cinema, and gym.

She departs on 6–12-day cruises from Genoa, March–October, with a variety of Mediterranean itineraries, west to France and Spain and east to Crete and Greece. Others include Egypt, Israel, and Cyprus or Syria and Turkey. Special savings are available for children up to 18 years who may travel free when with two adults and occupy the third/fourth berths in certain cabin categories; seniors (60 years or older), who receive a 15 percent discount on fares in most categories; and honeymooners.

Kristina Cruises (EuroCruises)

Kristina Regina (143/220; Finnish/Finnish; 328 ft./3,878 tons). The ship, which has found a receptive audience among experienced American travelers, sails on three- to ten-night cruises from May–August in Scandinavia and Russia between Helsinki and Bergen, calling at ports in Poland, Latvia, Estonia, and Russia. Other itineraries sail between Helsinki and St. Petersburg and the Norwegian fjords and Russia. Her small size enables her to slip into ports of call so that docking is within walking distance of the town center. Although she has a capacity for 381 passengers, the ship normally does not carry more than 189 passengers.

Kristina Brahe (80 passengers; Finnish/Finish; 190 ft./1,105 tons) An expedition-style ship with two restaurants, Sun Deck, and shop, the four-deck ship is the largest operating on the Saimaa Canal. Christened the *HMS Kilcheman*, the ship was built in Chicago in 1943 and served as a submarine destroyer on the west coast of Africa. After the war, she was renamed and sailed under the Norwegian flag; later in 1974, she was renovated, named the *Kristina Brahe* and came under Finish registry. Since being acquired by her new Finnish owners in 1985, she has been extensively renovated and her engines rebuilt.

Outside cabins in the top Category A have private bath; those in other categories have wash basins in cabins but share other bath facilities. The ship sails on six-night cruises in July from Helsinki for St. Petersburg and other ports. An eight-day package includes round-trip airfare from New York.

Hebridean Island Cruises

Acorn Park, Skipton, North Yorkshire BD23 2UE;
(01756) 701338; fax (01756) 701455

MV *Hebridean Princess* (50 passengers; British/Scottish; 235 ft./1,420 tons). Originally built in 1964 to carry 600 passengers, the ship was remodeled and redesigned in 1994 to carry only 50 passengers in the style of a deluxe country inn. Accommodations vary from singles with shared facilities to suites. The ship has a lounge, restaurant, library of books and videos, and a shop. She visits lochs, estuaries, and islands of the Inner and Outer Hebrides on Scotland's west coast, such as Iona, Rhum, Muck and Eigg, Lewis, Skye, Staffa, and the Orkney Islands.

Mediterranean Shipping Cruises

420 Fifth Avenue, New York, NY 10018-2702;
(800-666-9333); (212) 764-4800; fax (212) 764-8592

Part of a large Swiss group that operates a global fleet of 87 container ships, Mediterranean Shipping Cruises (known as StarLauro Cruises until a name change in 1995) has made a major commitment to the cruise business, having acquired three of its four ships in less than four years. The second largest cruise line in the Mediterranean with a cruise-ferry operation as well, the firm recently expanded its cruise offerings to South Africa and South America. With their Italian staffs and Italian ambience, the ships offer classic European cruises with good food and service.

Melody (549/1,500; Italian; 672 ft./36,000 tons). Formerly the *Star/Ship Atlantic* of Premier Cruise Lines, the *Melody* was acquired in early 1997 by MSC for $70 million. The ship began life in 1982 as Home Lines' *Atlantic*. She has several lounges, showroom, piano bar, disco, casino, two outdoor swimming pools, and beauty salon. Cabins are moderate size and have radio, direct-dial phone, and private bathrooms. MSC's largest cruise ship, the *Melody* began cruising for MSC in June from Genoa to Capri, Sicily, Tunisia, and Spain. She will cruise in the Caribbean in winter.

Monterey (300/550; Italian; 563 ft./21,051 tons). Built in 1952 and refurbished in 1991, the *Monterey* once belonged to Matson Line and sailed for Aloha Pacific Cruises. The steam-operated vessel has been well maintained and is a pleasant older ship with fine style and a friendly crew. The classic ship, gleaming with the brass rails and polished mirrors of her art-deco style, has two swimming pools, a fitness center with two whirlpools, sauna and massage, a hospital, library, beauty salon, boutiques, casino, disco, cinema, and two elevators. The attractive dining room offers two seatings.

The cabins on the top three decks are large with generous storage space and have private bathrooms. There are cabins for the disabled. The passengers are mainly Italian and British, 55 and older and middle income. The ship sails on 5–31-day cruises of the Mediterranean in summer; Caribbean, Brazil, Argentina, and Africa in winter.

Rhapsody (425/850; Italian; 537 ft./17,495 tons). Built in 1977 as the *Cunard Princess*, the *Rhapsody* was refurbished in 1995 after she was purchased by MSC. The ship's facilities include a swimming pool, whirlpool, sauna and massage, fitness center, two elevators, conference room, library, a cafe, bars, casino, video arcade, cinema, disco, beauty and barber shops, laundry and dry-cleaning services, and a medical center.

A pleasant, comfortable ship enhanced by a friendly Italian atmosphere, she has nice lounges and bars and ample deck space for sunning. International cuisine with an Italian emphasis is served in the window-lined Meridian Dining Room at two seatings. The cabins are small with limited storage space and thin walls; all have private bathrooms. The passengers are European, over 50, middle income, and tend to be smokers. In summer, the ship sails on 7–14-day Eastern Mediterranean cruises, departing from Genoa; and on South America itineraries in winter.

Symphony (322/644; Italian; 579 ft./16,500 tons). Formerly the *EnricoCosta* of Costa Cruises, the ship was built in 1950 and was given a multimillion-dollar facelift by MSG in 1994. The *Symphony* has a classic art-deco style highlighted by traditional wood and brass features as well as modern amenities. Renovations included new furnishings throughout and the addition of a casino.

The *Symphony* has three outside pools, gym with aerobic classes, sauna and massage, two elevators, a main dining room with two seatings, bars, boutique, casino, disco, cinema, beauty and barber shops, library, and a hospital. Higher category cabins are recommended as the lower ones are very small. The ship has a children's playroom and during peak season, provides children's counselors.

The *Symphony* offers comfortable, friendly European cruising with an Italian ambience and good service. The passengers are European, middle income, over 45, and smokers. The ship sails on seven-day Mediterranean cruises, departing from Genoa; and 2–15-day cruises of Africa and the coastal islands, departing from South Africa.

OdessAmerica (Odessa America Cruise Company)

170 Old Country Road, Suite 608, Mineola, NY 11501
(516) 747-8880; (800) 221-3254; fax (516) 747-8367

Formed in 1991 by two long-established companies, one Russian and one American, OdessAmerica is a joint venture between the Black Sea Shipping Company (BLASCO) of Odessa, Ukraine, and International Cruise Center of Mineola, New York, which was BLASCO's marketing arm in the United States for many years. BLASCO, the largest shipping company in the former Soviet Union and one of the largest in the world with 15 passenger ships and over 300 cargo vessels, was established in 1833.

OdessAmerica represents CTC Cruise Lines of London, with a wide variety of cruises leaving from English ports, and Marine Expeditions, one of the largest ship-based expedition companies in the world. OdessAmerica offers cruises of the Indian Ocean, the Galápagos, the Adriatic, and the Chilean Archipelago, as well as the rivers of Europe and Russia and remote destinations throughout the world, such as Antarctica. See further listings in Part Three, River and Barge Cruises and Adventure and Cultural Cruises.

Adriana   (300; Croatia; 340 ft./4,600 tons). The ship of the newly formed Croatia Cruise Line, *Adriana* offers 7–15-day cruises in the Adriatic and Aegean, beginning and ending in Venice and calling at ports in Italy, Croatia, Greece, Turkey, France, Tunisia, and Malta. The cruises can be combined with tours that have motorcoach, schooner, ferry, and private yacht options. The ship has six decks, serves regional cuisine, and offers nightly entertainment.

Royal Star   (220; 396 ft./6,179 tons). Formerly the *Ocean Islander* of the defunct Ocean Cruise Lines, she sails from Mombassa on 17–25-day Indian Ocean, East African coast cruise/land tours in conjunction with the African Safari Club. Five decks offer air-conditioned staterooms, pool, entertainment, casino and health club. Destinations include Kenya and South Africa, with stops at Zanzibar, Mayotte, and Nosy Bé.

Southern Cross   (750; Ukrainian; 270 ft./17,535 tons). A part of CTC Cruise Lines until she goes to her new owners (see Azur-Bolero Cruises), the ship sails around the world from English ports, catering mainly to British passengers. The informal ship sports seven decks with a pool, casino, cinema, library, and nightclub. Cabins are compact, but most have sea views; suites are available, and two cabins have wheelchair access. Sixteen itineraries focus on Europe; others sail to Australia, Tahiti, and the Caribbean from April–December.

Paquet French Cruises

5 Boulevard Malesherbes, 75008 Paris, France
331-1-49-24.42.00; fax 331-1-49-24.42.01

Paquet, which is part of Accor, one of Europe's largest hotel groups, no longer has a sales office in the United States. For information, contact the line directly.

Mermoz (275/530; French/European, Indonesian; 532 ft./13,691 tons). Built in 1957 and refurbished in 1985, the ship is a favorite of sophisticated travelers, offering old-world charm with paneling and fresh flowers everywhere and a full line of activities from aerobics classes to yoga. She has two outdoor swimming pools, a health club with sauna, massage, hydrotherapy, and whirlpool, a driving range, and a jogging area. There are a beauty salon, boutique, library, and cinema.

The show lounge has nightly evening entertainment and there's a disco and piano bar. Two dining rooms serve classic French cuisine with complimentary wine at lunch and dinner. Breakfast and luncheon buffets are available on the lido, and a midnight buffet is laid out in the grill room.

All cabins are small and functional with two single beds; some can accommodate three or four persons in upper and lower berths, and are equipped with phones and full baths. Most are outside cabins. Higher-priced cabins have double beds and windows instead of portholes; two suites provide separate sitting rooms and bedroom.

The *Mermoz* usually cruises the Caribbean and South America during the winter season on unusual itineraries. In Europe, she makes the rounds of Baltic capitals, Norwegian fjords, and the Mediterranean; she also sails to Asia. The ship caters mainly to French passengers and Francophiles from North America and is best known for her annual classical music cruise.

Peter Deilmann EuropAmerica River Cruises

1800 Diagonal Road, Suite 170, Alexandria, VA 22314
(703) 549-1741; (800) 348-8287; fax (703) 549-7924
http://www.deilmann-cruise.com

Peter Deilmann Cruises is currently building a new traditional luxury oceanliner in the grand European style with three restaurants and a promenade deck. The ship will accommodate 650 passengers in a wide variety of mostly outside staterooms. Delivery of the ship is expected in May 1998.

Regal Cruises

4199 34th Street, Suite B103, St. Petersburg, FL 33711
(813) 867-1300; (800) 270-SAIL
http://www.regalcruises.com

Regal Empress (451/902; European/International; 612 ft./23,000 tons). Built in 1953 as the *Olympia* of Greek Line and later the *Caribe I* of Commodore Cruises, the handsome ship was refurbished in 1993, when it was taken over by the owner of Liberty Travel. She offers short, budget-priced cruises from New York in summer, and from Port Manatee at the mouth of Tampa Bay to Playa del Carmen/Cancún and Cozumel during the remainder of the year. The latter is also available in six-night cruises that add Grand Cayman and Key West; or as seven-night cruises that call at Montego Bay and Ocho Rios. More recently, the line has added ten-night voyages from Port Manatee that include a partial transit of the Panama Canal, San Blas Islands, Puerto Limón, Costa Rica, and San Andres, as well as Grand Cayman and Playa del Carmen/Cozumel or Montego Bay and Key West.

A 53-night "Cruise of the Americas" from late October–December is Regal Cruises' 1997 highlight—a rather spectacular undertaking considering that most of the line's normal cruises are less than week. The cruise is available in six segments ranging from a 26-night cruise from Port Manatee to Buenos Aires to an 11-night voyage from Buenos Aires to Valparaiso, Chile through the Straits of Magellan.

The *Regal Empress*' two- and three-night cruises are party cruises attracting young city dwellers; longer trips of up to one week along the New England coast to Canada appeal to couples and families. The atmosphere of the ship changes remarkably between the two types of cruises. The same is true of the longer cruises in the Caribbean and South America.

The ship's interior is quite cut up, reflecting the changes made by her various owners over the years. Some of her public rooms, however, show the ship's high quality when she was built. The most outstanding is the dining room, which has fine decorative woods, etched glass, and some of the original murals. The dining room serves steaks, lobster, and similar choices sure to appeal to its budget audience, and they're quite good for the budget price. The main showroom offers nightly entertainment, but viewing is difficult when the ship sails full. There are other lounges, including the Mermaid on Sun Deck, which has a bar and dance floor, a casino, and a rather unusual disco created in the former theatre.

The ship has an enclosed promenade deck (typical of older ships), an outdoor swimming pool, two whirlpools, a Jacuzzi, skeet shooting, shuffleboard, gym, beauty salon, boutique, small playroom, and a paneled library with glass-front bookcases and comfortable reading chairs.

There are as many inside cabins—453 in total—as outside ones, and they come in a very wide range of configurations. Most cabins have one upper berth. Bathrooms are small with shower only. Only suites have television. You'll get your money's worth, but make no mistake, the lady has seen better days.

Renaissance Cruises

1800 Eller Drive, Suite 300, P. O. Box 350307,
   Ft. Lauderdale, FL 33335
(305) 463-0982; (800) 525-5350
http://www.rencruises.com

Renaissance V–VIII   (50–57/100–114; Italian/European; 290–297 ft.).

Aegean I (285/550; Greek/Greek; 461 ft./11,500 tons).

R1, R2, R3, R4 (316/690; t.b.a.; 594 ft./30,200 tons).

In 1989, Renaissance Cruises launched the first ship of eight small, deluxe ships intended to blanket the world. But the plan didn't quite work out and only four of the ships are now in service. Meanwhile, it has chartered the *Aegean I* (the *Aegean Dolphin* of Dolphin Hellas Cruises); has taken space on Orient Lines' *Marco Polo* for its Eastern Mediterranean cruises from time to time; and now has four, 690-passenger ships under construction. The first is scheduled to debut in August 1998, followed by the second in February 1999.

The cruise line combines round-trip airfare from the United States and a hotel package with a cruise at surprisingly low prices and promotes them almost exclusively by direct mail. The aggressive promotions obviously work as Renaissance has increased its 1997–98 departures by 50 percent over the previous year.

Renaissance IV–VIII are small, luxurious Italian-built ships finished in fine woods, with lovely appointments and all-suite cabins. Facilities include a restaurant, lounge, piano bar, pool, casino, Jacuzzi, and beauty salon. The ships are fitted with a sports platform at the stern and carry water sports equipment.

Aegean I is a small, attractive ship, well suited for Greek Island cruises. The eight-deck ship, rebuilt in 1988, has a large lounge, bar, gym, sauna, theatre, casino, disco, and dining room with two seatings. Cabins range from small to moderate; all have private bathrooms. The ship sails from its base in Piraeus from spring through fall.

The new, spacious R quartet has eight passenger decks and will offer single, open-seating dining in a choice of four different restaurants: a steak house; an Italian specialty restaurant; a club-like restaurant with a pizzeria and barbecue grill; and one formal restaurant, although the cruise line will continue to offer a casual on-board atmosphere by not scheduling formal nights. Other facilities include a cabaret and main lounge, several bars, casino, sports club with live ESPN, pool and bar, shops, card room, library, beauty salon and full spa, gym with Nautilus and other equipment, jogging track, and self-service launderette.

Approximately 66 percent of all cabins have private verandas. They range in size from the 30 inside cabins with 159 square feet and 67 standard outside cabins with 162 square feet to 10 deluxe suites with 325 square feet plus balcony. The majority of the accommodations are the 170 veranda-cabins with 172 square feet. All have television with CNN, minisafe, phone, breakfast table, vanity with mirror, full-length mirror, and bath with shower.

In response to demand, Renaissance has for the first time moved its smallest ships from Southeast Asia to the Mediterranean for the fall and winter seasons and has introduced a new 14-day combination cruise and land tour of the Greek Isles, Israel, Turkey, and Egypt, adding also for the first time, Port Said. The package includes round-trip air, one night each at the Inter-Continental Hotel in Athens and the Bosphorus Hotel in Istanbul.

Now in their fifth season, *Renaissance VII* and *VIII* offer a 16-day Seychelles/African Safari/Ancient Egypt cruise-tour from November through March. The program includes a six-day cruise of the Seychelles; a four-day safari in Kenya's Maasai Mara game reserve; and a three-night Egypt package in Luxor. Passengers travel to Africa and return in the comfort of Renaissance's own plane. Originally designed to carry over 200 passengers, the plane was reconfigured to accommodate only 114 persons; business and first class upgrades are available. Prices start from $4,499, including round-trip air from the United States, the cruise, safari, and Egypt package. Passengers who pay in full within five days of booking get a $500 per person "early bird" discount.

The *Aegean I*, which Renaissance has chartered through April 1998, has scheduled 15 cruise/tours beginning in December 1997. They combine the Greek Isles, Cyprus, Israel, and Turkey and include a ten-day cruise, round-trip airfare from New York, transfers, and pre- and postcruise hotel stays.

For her inaugural season, *R1* is scheduled to sail on ten-day Greek Island/Turkey cruises, beginning August 1998. Rates for the cruise, including round-trip airfare, and pre- and postcruise hotel stays, begin at $2,499 per person, double occupancy. *R2*'s itineraries are likely to be similar.

R3 and *R4*, scheduled for delivery in April and October 1999, will be based in Tahiti and will be the largest cruise ships sailing in French Polynesia year-round.

Special Expeditions
(See Part Three, Adventure and Cultural Cruises)

Star Cruises

> 391B Orchard Road, No. 13-01, Ngee Ann City, Tower B
> Singapore 0923; (65) 733-6988

Malaysian-based Star Cruises is something of a phenomenon in Far Eastern cruising. Launched in late 1993 with two ships, it quickly grew into a five-ship cruise line sailing from Hong Kong and Singapore and already is the world's eighth largest cruise line by number of berths. And that's not the end.

By the turn of the century, Star Cruise plans to double its fleet and expand beyond Asia. The company already has a foothold in Europe and Australia, and when it takes delivery in 1998 of two new, 2,000-berth, 75,000-ton ships being built at Germany's Meyer Werft, Star Cruise plans to move into the North America market.

The Star fleet consists of three distinct brands: Star, SuperStar and MegaStar.

Star Aquarius (713/1,900; Scandinavian/International) and *Star Pisces* (700/1,700; Scandinavian/International; 574 ft./40,000 tons) are the two ships of the Star group. Both are former Baltic ferries, *Athena* and *Kalypso*, and designed for the regional Asian market. The ships sail on short voyages from Hong Kong and Singapore, catering largely to families and first-time cruisers.

The Star ships, which have been extensively refurbished, are exceedingly well maintained; each has no fewer than ten food and beverages options. Child-care facilities are extensive, with everything from a playroom to an overnight baby-sitting room to an area for computer classes. Activities and entertainment are geared to the whole family, with karaoke, Ping-Pong and other sports, a library, spa, a range of boutiques, and shows by big-name stars. The line gets high marks for its food and incredibly friendly crew. On all Star Cruise ships, there is no tipping.

SuperStar Gemini (400/900; International/International; 532 ft./ 19,089 tons) is the SuperStar brand's single ship. The former *Crown Jewel* of the short-lived Crown Cruise Line and later of Cunard, it offers deluxe, traditional cruises with five-night itineraries from Singapore to Kuala Lumpur, Medan, Indonesia, and Phuket, Thailand. Most guests are European and Australian, with the balance from Japan, Taiwan, and Hong Kong. Now, Americans are catching on.

The brand's two new ships, *SuperStar Leo* and *SuperStar Virgo*, to be added in 1998, will offer a high crew-to-passenger ratio of one to two. Besides a standard dining room, the ships will offer Chinese and Japanese cuisine in two restaurants and Southeast Asian specialties will be among the choices in the Lido Cafe. Karaoke lounges and a public observation area of the bridge, with videos detailing bridge and engine operations, are among the more unusual features. The ships' cruising speed will be a zippy 24 knots, enabling them to offer four to six ports of call on a seven-night itinerary. Destinations will include Malaysia, Thailand, Indonesia, Burma, and India's Andaman Islands. During summer, one ship may sail on seven-night cruises to China, Hong Kong, Taiwan, Korea, and Japan.

MegaStar Taurus and *MegaStar Aries* (35/72; International/International; 267 ft./3,264 tons) comprise the third brand. The MegaStar group is the most deluxe of Star's three brands. Its ships, formerly the *Aurora I* and *II*, built in 1991, are among the most luxurious small ships of the 1990s. Each carries only 72 passengers and is usually chartered to corporations, wedding parties, and other groups.

Star Cruises is owned by Malaysia's Genting International, a cash-rich, publicly traded investment group whose holdings include hotels and casinos. The cruise line is headed by a savvy travel executive who came to cruising after a career with Sheraton Hotels and other leading hotel companies.

Swan Hellenic Cruises

77 New Oxford Street, London WC1A 1PP
0171 800 2200; fax 0171 800 2723

2815 Second Avenue, Suite 400, Seattle, WA 98121
(888) 6-MINERVA (888-664-6378) or (800) 340-7674
(P&O Cruises)

Minerva (194/392; British/Filipino and Ukrainian; 432 ft./12,500 tons). Named for the Roman goddess of wisdom, arts, and literature, the *Minerva*, the new ship of Swan Hellenic replacing the *Orpheus*, does credit to her namesake in design and decor as well as in the type of cruises she offers, dedicated as they are to education, culture and the arts, and exploration.

Decorated to resemble an English country house, the small ship's lounges and public rooms are comfortably furnished with patterned upholstery and leather couches and chairs. The artwork throughout the ship is authentic and was purchased especially for the ship at country house auctions.

The main deck has the restaurant, the Wheeler bar, and the beauty center. On the Bridge Deck, you will find an auditorium, smoking room, card room, swimming pool, the Orpheus Room and Bridge Cafe, along with the extensive library, which has several thousands of books on a wide variety of subjects. The Promenade Deck is unobstructed and encircles the ship completely.

The *Minerva* offers open seating in the main dining room and buffet-style dining in the informal cafe; both provide indoor or outdoor seating. The staff seats passengers at different tables each evening. The menu selections are well prepared and presented, and based on fresh produce and meats purchased locally when possible. A full English breakfast and afternoon tea are served. Service is courteous, unobtrusive, and eager to please.

The two lowest of five decks have cabins only. They include standard singles and doubles, deluxe and superior singles and doubles, and suites. The latter have separate sitting areas and bathrooms with tubs as well as showers. Four of the cabins are equipped for disabled passengers. All cabins have televisions, phones, terry-cloth robes, mirrored closets, and private bathrooms stocked with amenities.

The *Minerva* sails on a wide variety of itineraries from the Mediterranean to the Gulf of Arabia, India, and the Far East. Guest lectures, tailored to each cruise, provide background and history about each port of call. Lectures are given in English. The fares include most excursions and gratuities.

Swan Hellenic, which is owned by P&O Cruises, the parent company of Princess Cruises, and has a large following in the United Kingdom, Australia, and Canada, as well as among Americans, caters to an older clientele, mostly over age 50, who are intellectually curious and are interested in the art and culture of the destinations they visit, as well as in enjoying a cruise vacation.

Part Three

CRUISING ALTERNATIVES

River and Barge Cruises

A river cruise is not only a different way to see a country; it is a different country you will see. Whether you sail down the Danube or the Yangtze, up the Hudson or the Nile, or float through the byways of Europe or the Erie Canal, the adventure by water will be a new travel experience, even for those who may have visited the same area by land.

Steamboating on the Mississippi is probably the most familiar of the river cruises to those in the United States, but there are many different kinds of river cruises, their character having been shaped by the locale and the nature of the waterway. For example, an adventure cruise on the upper Amazon is as different from a barge in Burgundy as a steamer on the Nile. Nonetheless, river cruises do share certain characteristics, and all are light years away from a cruise on an oceanliner or mainstream cruise ship.

For starters, boats (a vessel is a ship on the ocean but a boat on a river) on river cruises are generally small and certainly much smaller than oceangoing cruise ships. Most carry 100–200 passengers, although some of the new riverboats hold 250 or more and Delta Queen's *American Queen* takes 400 passengers. The barges that glide along small canals and waterways are much, much smaller, usually taking about 12 and never more than 24 passengers.

The small size of the vessels as well as the nature of the waterways enable you to get an up-close, intimate look at the locale where you are cruising, heightening the sense of place and of history in a way an oceanliner can never do. The destination, rather than the ship, is the main attraction on a river cruise.

Riverboat cabins are small, but comfortable. The ambience is informal, the dress casual. Except for some of the newest large riverboats, you will not find nightly entertainment. Rather, you are left to your own devices and you will rediscover the pleasure of conversation and friendship.

RIVER AND BARGE CRUISES IN EUROPE

River cruises are available on the major rivers of the world but the largest selection by far is in Europe—Rhine, Rhone, Seine, Danube, Volga—where rivers have been thoroughfares of commerce and culture down through the centuries.

Operated mostly from April–November, European cruises take you to the great cities of the continent through beautiful scenery interlaced with ancient forts, mighty cathedrals, and storybook castles. They dock in the heart of town in a different locale each day. Tours are available for additional cost, but in most places passengers can easily sightsee on their own.

River cruises allow you to see Europe the way it was meant to be seen. Almost all the historic buildings were built facing the river, so when the boat docks in front of the Pillnitz Palace on the Elbe, for example, passengers enter the same way that guests of Augustus the Strong would have, hundreds of years ago.

Some itineraries stay overnight in port, allowing passengers to attend a local show or dine on shore. Others sail at night, so that after a night's sleep passengers can wake up refreshed and ready for the next day of sightseeing.

More than a dozen companies offer these cruises; KD River Cruises of Europe, one of the oldest companies, is typical. Its fleet of ten ships sails the length of the Rhine, as well as the Elbe, Moselle, Seine, Saone, and Rhone. More recently, the line added the Danube and the newly completed Rhine-Main-Danube Canal, which in 1994 linked the North Sea to the Black Sea for the first time in history. In 1995, it introduced cruises on the Volga between St. Petersburg and Moscow. It should also be noted that often several different U.S. travel companies will have the same boats in their portfolios; not all have exclusive agreements.

River boats and barges offer a unique cruise experience, but they do so in completely different styles. Canals and the smaller rivers of Europe deep in the countryside are traversed by barges that glide gently over the waters through some of the most beautiful and historic areas of England and the Continent. They flow silently under ancient bridges and pass under avenues of trees along medieval villages, vineyards, and grand chateaux.

The pace is so leisurely—three or four miles per hour—passengers can get off to walk in the woods or bike in the village and move faster than their boat. The tortoise's pace, the utter peace and relaxation unmatched by any other mode of travel, are for some the best vacation they ever had; for others, it's watching grass grow.

By day, passengers lounge on deck, play cards, and read as the boat navigates the locks. You can walk or bike on your own, discovering places and friendly local people, and reboard at the next lock. Usually included in the price is a choice of tours by minibus or bicycle to nearby castles, wineries, and towns with medieval architecture. Your guide might be your chef or another crew member.

Hotel barges, as they are known, are like floating country inns and vary in size, carrying from 6–24 passengers on cruises of 3, 6, and 13 days. Cabins are small and bathrooms are tiny, but often the barges, like those of French Country Waterways, are luxurious. Many, also, like Country Waterways, serve outstanding gourmet cuisine prepared by Cordon Bleu chefs who use fresh products purchased in villages and markets along the way. Wines of the region, normally included in the cruise price, flow generously. The atmosphere is very informal—and very romantic.

Dozens of boats and barges cruise the rivers and canals of Europe. Usually the season begins in April and continues through October. The following are a sample of those with offices or representatives in the United States. It should be noted that several U.S. travel companies often have the same boats in their portfolios; not all have exclusive agreements.

(Key: Cabins/Passengers; Officers/Crew; Vessel Length)

Abercrombie & Kent International, Inc.

1520 Kensington Road, Suite 212, Oak Brook, IL 60521
(708) 954-2944; (800) 323-7308; fax (708) 954-3324
http://www.abercrombiekent.com

Actief (6/12; British; 100 ft.). Three to six days, upper Thames River.

Alouette (3/6; French/British; 98 ft.). Six nights in Burgundy and Franche Comte.

Anacoluthe (26/51; French; 210 ft.). Six nights, Seine and Yonne Rivers from Paris.

Chanterelle (14/24; British/French; 128 ft.). Six nights in the Upper Loire.

Fleur de Lys (5/7; French/British; 129 ft.). Six nights in Burgundy.

Hirondelle (4/8; French/British; 128 ft.). Six nights in Burgandy and Franche Comte.

L'Abercrombie (10/20; French/British; 128 ft.). Three to six nights in Northern Burgundy.

Lafayette (12/22; British/French; 128 ft.). Three to six nights in Lower Burgundy.

Libellule (10/20; British/French; 128 ft.). Six nights in Champagne.

Litote (10/20; British/French; 128 ft.). Six nights in Central Burgundy.

Marjorie (4/8; Flemish; 129 ft.). Six nights on the Seine and Yonne in France.

Napoleon (6/12; French; 129 ft.). Six nights on the Rhone in Provence.

Rembrandt (10/20; Dutch/Flemish; 133 ft.). Six nights, inland waterways of Belgium.

Vincent Van Gogh (16/32; Dutch/Flemish; 217 ft.). Six nights in Holland and Belgium.

(Also see Abercrombie & Kent International: Amazon River Cruises, page 749; Nile River Cruises, page 741; and *River Cloud*, page 733.)

The Barge Lady

No. 325, 225 North Michigan Avenue, Chicago, IL 60601
(800) 880-0071; fax (312) 540-5503

Variety of barges on the canals of France and Britain, including six designed for golfers.

Cruise Company of Greenwich

31 Brookside Drive, Greenwich, CT 06830
(203) 622-0203; (800) 825-0826; fax (203) 622-4036

Represents a medley of barges and riverboats for 6–14 passengers on the Shannon River in Ireland, the Thames and other waterways of Britain, and the Burgundy and other canals of France. The seven-day cruises on the *Shannon Princess* can be geared to special interests such as golf, sport fishing, equestrian, culinary, cycling, wildlife, and poetry, among others. Cruise Company also represents the luxury sailing ship, *Sea Cloud* (see Part Three, Sailing Ships) and Temptress Cruises, which offers cruises of Belize and Costa Rica (see Part Three, Adventure and Cultural Cruises).

Etoile de Champagne

89 Broad Street, Boston, MA 02110
(617) 426-1776; (800) 280-1492

Etoile de Champagne   (7/12; International/Dutch; 300 ft.). 12 days,
Holland, Belgium, and France, spring–fall.

EuroCruises

303 West 13th Street, New York, NY 10014
(212) 691-2099; (800) 688-EURO; fax (212) 366-4747

EuroCruises is a U.S. tour company that specializes in European
cruises, particularly of an unusual, off-the-beaten-track nature. It is the
U.S. representative for over 60 different riverboats and oceangoing
ships—all European owned and managed. The river cruises cover all
corners of the European continent from Portugal to Russia and operate
mainly between early spring and late fall.

Included here are the river cruise lines and boats for which Euro-
Cruises is the representative. For EuroCruises's portfolio of oceangoing
cruises see Part Two, Other Cruise Lines and Their Ships. In all cases,
EuroCruises can provide greater details on the vessels and their itineraries
with brochures that show deck plans and describe the ships' features.

Europe Cruise Line (EuroCruises)

Rhine Princess   (60/148 passengers; Dutch/European; 273 ft.). The
modern, deluxe boat, completely reconstructed in 1992, is in effect
a new vessel. All cabins have private bath; half with shower, half
with bathtub. The restaurant has two seatings with Dutch and German theme dinners. The boat sails on five- to seven-day cruises on
the Rhine and Moselle rivers between Basel and Amsterdam every
other Sunday, May–September. It also offers a special six-day Tulip
Time cruise in April.

Blue Danube I & II   (148/144 passengers). Built in 1995 and in 1997,
the deluxe riverboats have large cabins with direct-dial telephone,
television, full-size beds, and bath with choice of tub or shower. The
ships have swimming pools, whirlpools, sauna, large salons, and all-
glass nonsmoking lounge. The *Blue Danube I* sails on 5–14-night
cruises between Budapest and Amsterdam, Vienna, and other ports
from May–September. The *Blue Danube II*, scheduled to enter service
in 1997, is almost identical to her sister ship, except that the new
ship has a golf simulator.

Gota Canal (EuroCruises)

Diana (60 passengers). Six days, Stockholm/Gothenburg, June–August.

Wilhelm Tham (60 passengers), *Juno* (60 passengers). Four days, Gothenburg/Stockholm, May–August.

One of northern Europe's truly unique experiences is cruising down the Gota Canal aboard a converted vintage steamer in a part of Sweden from times gone by. You also enjoy fine smorgasbords with fresh gravlax (salmon), sherried herring, caviar-stuffed eggs, reindeer meat, and cloudberry jam as part of the lavish daily luncheon.

Northwestern River Shipping Company (EuroCruises)

Sergei Kirov (136/280 passengers; Swiss/Finnish; 424 ft.). The German-built ship sails on Russian inland waters in comfort. All cabins are outside; the cruise staff speaks English. The ship has two itineraries sailing from mid-May–mid-October between St. Petersburg and Moscow on 12- and 13-night cruises. In addition to the cruise, the price includes all shore excursions and one night's hotel with breakfast.

Peter Deilmann EuropAmerica Cruises

1800 Diagonal Road, Suite 170, Alexandria, VA 22314
(703) 549-1741; (800) 348-8287; fax (703) 549-7924
http://www.deilmann-cruise.com

This European cruise line markets five riverboats and *Lili Marleen*, a barquentine launched in September 1994. It has a luxury oceanliner under construction, scheduled to debut in May 1998. Designed in the grand European style, the ship to be named the *Deutschland*, will accommodate 650 passengers in mostly outside cabins.

Danube Princess (95/200; Austrian/German; 364 ft.). Seven days, Danube. The *Danube Princess*'s facilities include an outdoor swimming pool, single-seating dining room, two bars, conference room, library, a gift shop, beauty salon, and more. Cabins have private bathrooms, telephone, radio, and color television. The ship sails on seven-day cruises from Munich to Austria, Hungary, and Slovakia; and on 10- and 11-day cruises of the Black Sea.

Dresden (54/110; European/German; 304 ft.). Seven days, Elbe River. The *Dresden*'s facilities include single-seating dining room, bar, gift shop, beauty salon, fitness equipment, sauna, library, infirmary, and laundry room. All cabins have private shower and toilet, telephone, radio, and color television. It departs on seven-day cruises from Hamburg or Dresden to Meissen, Prague, and Wittenberg.

Mozart (100/204; International; 396 ft.). Seven days, Danube. The deluxe boat has large, all-outside cabins with spacious private bathrooms, television, minibar, hair dryer, and telephone. Facilities include an indoor swimming pool, whirlpool, sauna, and fitness center. From March–October the boat sails on seven-day cruises on the Danube, departing on Sunday from Passau and calling at Bratislava, Budapest, Kalocza, Esztergom, Duernstein, and Melk. Several classical music cruises are scheduled in the summer.

Princesse de Provence (71/148; German/European; 363 ft.). Seven days, Rhone and Saone. The *Princess de Provence* offers large cabins with private bathrooms, hair dryer, telephone, and radio. Facilities include fitness equipment, single-seating dining room, two bars, conference room, library, laundry services, infirmary, and gift shop. The boat sails on seven-day cruises round-trip from Lyon up the Saone River and down the Rhone to Vienne, Macon, Arles, and Avignon.

Prussian Princess (69/142 passengers; Austrian/German; 363 ft.). Seven days, Rhine and Moselle rivers and Main-Danube canal. The deluxe boat offers spacious outside cabins with full-length French doors on upper deck and large picture windows on the lower deck. All cabins have private bathrooms, telephone, radio, and hair dryer. The facilities include single-seating dining room, lounge and two bars, library, dance floor, fitness equipment, conference room, boutique, and beauty salon. The boat offers seven-day cruises on the Rhine and Moselle rivers and Main-Danube Canal, between Amsterdam and Basel; round trip from Frankfurt or Amsterdam through German, Belgian, and Dutch canals.

Reiseburo Mittelthurgau (EuroCruises)

Anton Tchekhov (Swiss managed). The Austrian-built ship, renovated in 1993, has all outside cabins with refrigerator and bath. There is a sun deck, sauna, and swimming pool. She cruises from May–August on the Yenisey River through the heart of Russia from Dudinka (240 miles north of the Arctic Circle) to Krasnoyarsk in the south (on the same latitude as Sitka, Alaska) on 10- or 11-night voyages. The cruises are sold as packages with roundtrip air fare from Zurich, Switzerland, to St. Petersburg or Moscow and a connecting flight with either Krasnoyarsk or Dudinka.

European Waterways/Barge France

140 E. 56th Street, New York, NY 10022
(212) 688-9538; (800) 217-4447; fax (800) 296-4554

Anjodi, La Joie de Vivre, La Reine Pedauque (5–6/10–12; French/French and English; 98–128 ft.). Six nights, rivers and canals of France.

Stella (4/8; French/French, English; 102 ft.). Six nights, between Amsterdam and Brussels during spring tulip season; canals of Alsace-Lorraine in France.

French Country Waterways

P.O. Box 2195, Duxbury, MA 02331
(617) 934-2354; (800) 222-1236; fax (617) 934-9048

Esprit, Horizon II, Nenuphar (6–9/12–18; French/English; 128 ft.). Six nights, Marne River from Meaux to Reims (*Esprit*); Saone and Canal du Centre from Dijon to St. Leger-sur-Dheune (*Horizon II*); and northern section of the Canal de Bourgogne from Venarey-les-Laumes to Tonnerre (*Nenuphar*).

Liberté (4/8; French/English; 100 ft.). Six nights, Canal du Nivernais (Burgundy) and Yonne River from Joigny to Clamecy.

GT Corporate Cruises

1239 39th Street, Brooklyn, NY 11218
(718) 934-4100; (800) 828-7970; fax 718-934-9419

Russ (332 passengers; Russian; 425 ft.). 14 days, Russian waterways connecting Moscow and St. Petersburg; 14 days, Moscow to Rostov on Moscow Canal, Volga, Svir, and Neva Rivers.

Inland Voyages

c/o McGregor Travel, 112 Prospect Street, Stamford, CT 06901
(203) 978-5010; (800) 786-5311

Luciole (8/14; Belgian, French/British, French; 100 ft.). Six nights, Canal de Bourgogne or the Nivernais from Montbard.

KD River Cruises of Europe

2500 Westchester Avenue, Purchase, NY 10577
(914) 696-3600; (800) 346-6525 (East); (800) 858-8587 (West)
http://www.rivercruises.com

As noted earlier, the cruise line sails the length of the Rhine, Elbe, Moselle, Seine, Saone, Danube, and the newly completed Rhine-Main-Danube Canal that links the North Sea to the Black Sea. In 1995, it introduced cruises on the Volga between St. Petersburg and Moscow.

Arlene and *Normandie*   (104 passengers; French/International; 300 ft.). Inland waterways of France; Rhone and Saone Rivers (*Arlene*), and the Seine (*Normandie*).

Austria, Britannia, Deutschland, Heinrich Heine, Italia   (50–92/104–184; German/German, International; 290–361 ft.). 2–12 nights, Rhine, Moselle, and Main Rivers; eight days, Rhine, Main, and Danube Canal (*Heinrich Heine*).

Clara Schumann and *Theodor Fontane*   (62/128; German/German, International; 312 ft.). Five to seven days, Elbe River, including regions of Saxony and Prussia.

Helvetia   (72/140) Seven nights on the Rhine and Moselle between Basel and Amsterdam; and *William Tell* (50/100), seven nights on the Danube between Regensburg and Budapest. Both boats are operated by Triton Reisen, a KD subsidiary.

Le Boat

215 Union Street, Hackensack, NJ 07601
(201) 342-1838; (800) 922-0291; fax (201) 342-7498

Le Boat specializes in barge charters and self-drive boats on canals in Britain, Scotland, France, Holland, Ireland, and Germany; and yacht charters worldwide.

OdessAmerica Cruise Company

170 Old Country Road, Suite 608, Mineola, NY 11501
(516) 747-8880; (800) 221-3254; fax (516) 747-8367

Andropov, Lenin, Litvinov   (270 passengers; Russian; 424 ft.). All vessels offer outside cabins. On these 14-day voyages, passengers arrive in a different port each morning and normally have most of the day for sightseeing, with optional guided tours. Russian entertainers and guest lecturers add to cruisers' knowledge of history and culture in an informal atmosphere. The ships sail from May–September, on the rivers, lakes, and canals connecting Moscow and St. Petersburg, plus three nights each in Moscow and St. Petersburg, where passengers stay aboard the boat and can take guided shore excursions.

Lev Tolstoy (210 passengers; Russian; 380 ft.). This newest and more upscale addition to the Russian waterways fleet has a staff of 100. The 11- or 12-day itinerary is similar to that of the other vessels, with shorter, two-night stays in Moscow and St. Petersburg. The ship sails from June–September.

Rousse, Volga, Deltastar (180–236 passengers; European; 347–370 ft.). A variety of cruises on the Danube River link central and south-eastern Europe, the Balkans, and Black Sea, with cruise/tour options from Amsterdam to Prague for many of the nine countries which share the waters. Itineraries include entertainment, guest lecturers, and shore excursions. Ships have all outside cabins, informal atmosphere, and regional cuisine. The *Rousse* offers four-to 12-day cruises, including one with a classical music theme; the *Volga* offers four- to eight-day cruises, and the *Deltastar*, eight-day cruises. Ports include Passau, Budapest, Vienna, Bratislava, Tulcea, and Weissenkirchen.

Viktor Glushkov (270 passengers; Ukrainian; 424 ft.). The 11- and 12-day cruises connect three countries on the Black Sea and Danube Delta: Ukraine, Romania, and Bulgaria, with an optional extension to Turkey. Ports of call with guided tours include Kiev, Sevastopol, Yalta, Odessa, Rousse, Braila, and Tulcea. The ship has all outside cabins and an informal atmosphere, with local entertainment and lecturers. It sails from April–September.

River Cloud c/o Networld

300 Landex Plaza, Parsippany, NJ 07054
(201) 884-7474; (800) 992-3411; fax (201) 884-1711

River Cloud (49/98; European; 360 ft.) Launched in 1996, the splendidly appointed *River Cloud* is one of the finest boats on the European waterways and reflects the impeccable service and fine cuisine for which her famous sister ship, *Sea Cloud*, is known.

The *River Cloud* was designed by premier German architects and interior decorators, Seigfried Schindler and Kai Bunge, and constructed in the Netherlands. Its interiors are rich with decorative teakwood, rosewood furniture, and brass fittings and convey a 1930s luxury reminiscent of the "Orient Express."

The elegant dining room, enhanced by large viewing windows, serves meals in a single seating with unassigned tables in a relaxed and friendly atmosphere. Breakfast and lunch are buffet, while dinner is served at tables. Menus feature continental specialties accompanied by fine wines.

The handsome lounge encircled by windows at the bow has as its centerpiece a specially built, seven-foot Steinway grand piano which is very much in use during afternoon tea and during the boat's music cruises when renowned Steinway pianists and opera stars sail with the boat or join her en route for an evening's entertainment. The Promenade Deck has a library, boutique, and hair salon. Other amenities include an exercise room and sauna, an on-board putting green, and a large-scale chessboard on the aft Sun Deck. All cabins have telephone, radio, television, VCR, and marble bathrooms with showers and gold-plated fittings.

The *River Cloud* sails on the Rhine, Main, Moselle, and Danube from April–October. The cruises are also sold through Dailey-Thorp Travel of New York, (212) 307-1555; Abercrombie & Kent, (800) 323-7308; and other U.S. travel companies.

Swan Hellenic Cruises

77 New Oxford Street, London WC1A 1PP
0171 800 2200; fax 0171 800 2723

2815 Second Avenue, Suite 400, Seattle, WA 98121
(888) 6-MINERVA (888-664-6378) or (800) 340-7674
(P&O Cruises)

Rembrandt Van Rijn   (90 passengers; European; 390 ft.). Eight and ten days of Holland from Amsterdam; 13–18 days, Rhine, Moselle, Main, and Danube Rivers; 16 days, Danube between Budapest and Nuremberg; 16–18 days, Main to Danube including Rhine, Main, and Danube Canal.

YANGTZE RIVER CRUISES IN CHINA*

The Chinese call it prosaically Changjiang, "long river," which the Yangtze (a local name) certainly is. Rising from the Tibetan plateau, it plunges through mountain passes into Sichuan to form a border between Hubei and Hunan before reaching the fertile flood plains of Jiangsu and Shanghai, a journey of almost 4,000 miles.

The Yangtze is more than a great scenic wonder for the Chinese. It was the site of some epic battles during the Wars of the Three Kingdoms,

---

*This section, Yangtze River Cruises in China, was written by Shann Davies.

in the second century B.C., and archeological excavations suggest the area was a cradle of Chinese civilization.

Equally important, the river was and remains the great highway of central China for passenger ferries, patrol boats, barges piled with coal, limestone, timber, and cement, plus small freighters that deliver supplies to the towns built into the cliffsides and collect the oranges and other fruit that is grown in terraced orchards.

The river is always busy, especially as it narrows into the gorges. Here traffic control is essential, and cruise ship captains are in telephone contact with the shore pilot stations, while they steer the shallow-hulled vessels between gravel shoals.

The Three Gorges: Qutang, Wu, Xiling

The Qutang Gorge, also known for good reason as the Wind Box Gorge, is only five miles long but nowhere is it more than 490 feet wide; limestone cliffs seem to erupt on either side in sheer walls up to 4,000 feet high. The cliff face is pitted with caves, where 2,000-year-old coffins have been found. There is also a strangely shaped rock that the Chinese call Rhinoceros Looking at the Moon, although it's hard to discern. More dramatic is the remains of an old towpath, which was the only way through the gorge for travelers before the river was cleared of its biggest boulders.

Less than an hour after leaving the Qutang, cruise ship passengers enter the Wu Gorge. It stretches 25 miles and takes an hour and a half to navigate. Its cliffs are so high and steep that the sun rarely touches the water. Twelve peaks dominate the skyline. According to myth they are a goddess and her handmaidens, who chose to be turned to stone and stand sentinel over the river.

Midway through the gorge is the border between Sichuan and Hubei provinces, indicated with an inscription on the cliff and a small market town of whitewashed houses and terraced orchards producing apples, persimmons, and peaches. The exit from the gorge is only 164 feet across, the narrowest part of the river.

It takes another day for the cruise ships to reach the Xiling Gorge, the longest of the canyons, which winds for 47 miles through a series of small gorges amid fierce rapids. On either side are magnificent examples of the mountains beyond mountains of classic Chinese scenery. The cliffs have been stratified, scarred, and sculpted over the millennia into strange shapes, which have earned such names as Ox Liver and Horse Lungs, Iron Coffin Rock, and Yellow Cat.

Three Gorges Dam

The Three Gorges Dam is now under construction at Sandouping, at the eastern mouth of the gorges. Its scope is undeniable. It will feature a dam wall almost two miles long and 607 feet high. Behind it a lake will stretch 373 miles and cover an area of 418 square miles, inundating most of the Xiling and half the Wu Gorges as well as forcing the evacuation of a million or more people.

Its cost has soared to $34 billion and could be a lot more before the scheduled completion in 2009. Its supporters say it will control flooding and generate 84.7 billion kilowatt hours a year for Shanghai and the Lower Yangtze Basin. Opponents say it will destroy the environment and build up a reservoir of toxic silt in an earthquake-prone region. Either way it adds a deep poignancy to a Yangtze cruise.

Before the new dam was proposed, the 230-foot-high Gezouba Dam was the modern attraction of the Yangtze cruises. It was completed in 1988 and cuts across a third of the river close to Yichang. It has three locks in which the water level rises and falls 66 feet. It takes two hours for cruise ships and other vessels to pass through. (When the big dam is built it will have a staircase of eight such locks!) After September 1997, all boats on the river will take a specially created detour around the new dam wall. This does not affect the cruises, contrary to some news reports that make it sound as though the river will then be completely dammed.

The first westerners who sailed up the Yangtze River were British colonial administrators, who in the 1840s established the inland port of Hankow (now part of Wuhan). The most adventurous continued upstream and found the Three Gorges, which were famous in Chinese history as one of the battlegrounds in the epic, second century B.C. Wars of the Three Kingdoms. The area was a mountainous wilderness, sparsely populated by minority tribes whose only communication and trading links were the river and its many tributaries.

Transport was by sailing ships, which had to be hauled by teams of trackers through raging rapids and over great boulders, until English trader Archibald Little pioneered steamship service from Wuhan, finally reaching Chongqing in 1898. Nevertheless, the voyage remained extremely hazardous and time-consuming until the 1950s when the Chinese government blasted out the largest of the boulders.

In the early 1980s the first regular cruises were introduced through the gorges, with increasingly more comfortable and better-equipped vessels being built for the purpose. As a result a Yangtze cruise became an established part of many all-China itineraries. The Gorges are located on the 120-mile (192-km.) stretch of river between Baidicheng and

Yichang. There are some itineraries between Chongqing (formerly written Chungking) and Yichang, which reduce the trip by a day and night. However, it has often proved difficult to arrange air or land transfers to or from Yichang, and therefore most cruises now cover the full 850-mile (1,370-km.) section between Chongqing and Wuhan.

Shore Excursions *(Either upstream or downstream)*

Shennong Stream/Daning River Gorges   All cruises offer a side trip up one of the Yangtze's many tributaries, to give passengers a closer look at the natural grandeur—and some of the excitement that used to be part of a journey on the river.

The excursions feature fast-flowing, crystal-clear streams with shifting, pebbled shoals and sheer cliffs pocked with caves (some containing coffins), clad in waterfalls, and encrusted with ancient ferns.

The Shennong Stream is the better option, partly because the journey is taken in wooden longboats, which are steered, pushed, and sometimes hauled by husky young men of the Tujia minority (which once provided the trackers who pulled boats upstream through the gorges in the old days). Also included on the half-day excursion is a visit to a Tujia-style house, where a local dance is performed and some worthwhile souvenirs are sold. (Local people also offer transfers by bamboo sedan chairs down the narrow steps leading to the boats.)

Zigui   This historic town, poised like an eyrie on the cliffs at the entrance to the Xiling Gorge, retains an air of ancient certainty, but in fact it will be swallowed up along with the gorge by the dam. Only one building will be preserved and moved downstream along with the population, and that is the traditional temple dedicated to Chu Yuan, the scholar statesman who in 278 B.C. drowned himself in protest of his government's policy. His friends tried to save his body by beating gongs and throwing dumplings into the water—giving rise to the famous Dragon Boat Festival that is now celebrated in many parts of Asia. What will be lost will be the scattering of vest-pocket farms—some worked by ox-drawn ploughs—and the town, where tourists today delight in a main street packed with sidewalk kitchens, vegetable stalls, alfresco hairdressers, one-room tailors, an alley of pool tables, and a storefront video game center.

Shashi/Jingzhou   Located a little upstream from Wuhan, this bustling port city contains the remains of a royal capitol from the seventh century B.C. Some of the original walls are maintained and the museum contains an incredibly well-preserved 2,000-year-old mummy.

Yueyang Tower   On the Hunan banks of the River, upstream from Wuhan, this gold-tiled pavilion was built in 716 as a military lookout, but it was later expanded and beautified to provide a belvedere over scenic Dongting Lake.

Fengdu   Situated close to the western entrance of Qutang Gorge, this ancient town, perched on the cliff, is famous as the place where all people's spirits go after death. To placate these unhappy and potentially dangerous phantoms there is a temple to the God of Hades, where visitors can buy a "passport to hell" and other souvenirs. There is also a Ghost City park, with displays of Life in Hell.

Shibaozhai   Located between Chongqing and the first gorge, the town is built into the riverside cliff with a 12-story red pagoda and a hilltop temple.

Cruise Lines and Ships

There are now about 40 ships offering cruises though the Yangtze Gorges. The majority are owned by local tourist and government authorities and marketed internationally by the China Merchants Changjiang Cruise Company, a Sino-Hong Kong joint venture with offices in Hong Kong (1607 Wing On Centre, 111 Connaught Road, Hong Kong). Among them is the *Bashan*, which was chartered regularly for almost a decade by U.S. tour companies—Lindblad Tours and later Abercrombie & Kent—for deluxe adventure cruises.

Today a new generation of vessels has been introduced, basically to cater to the market of international travelers whose interest has been fueled by news that the days of the gorges are numbered. All these ships are operated on regular itineraries that have to be designed to allow passage through the different gorges during daylight hours. From this has evolved a series of shore excursions that are conveniently located as well as interesting, varied, and in keeping with the history of the area.

The season lasts from late February to early December, with the summer months being extremely hot. (During winter the water level is low and temperatures are well below freezing.) There are almost weekly departures for the four-day, three-night downstream cruise from Chongqing and the five-day, four-night upstream trip from Wuhan.

Abercrombie & Kent International, Inc.

1520 Kensington Road, Suite 212, Oak Brook, IL 60521
(708) 954-2944; (800) 323-7308; fax (708) 954-3324
http://www.abercrombiekent.com

27/F Tai Sang Commercial Bldg., 24-34 Hennessy Road,
    Wanchai, Hong Kong
2865-7818; fax 2866-0556

East King, East Queen   (78/156; Chinese/Chinese; 300 ft.)

The twin boats, *East King* and *East Queen*, were built in the Shanghai shipyards for $10 million each. The boats, the fastest on the route, are the most modern, being equipped with state-of-the-art engineering from Europe and navigation systems from Japan. All cabins are a spacious 183 square feet and have picture windows, minibars, satellite television, international direct-dial telephones, safes, terry robes, hair dryers, and well-designed bathrooms. There are also two suites, which can be combined conveniently with a tea lounge for seminars, groups, or small meetings.

The public facilities consist of a main dining room-serving western and Chinese meals—a nightclub, five karaoke rooms, an enclosed observation deck with a cafe, and an open sun deck with a swimming pool. The boat also has a fully equipped business center and a 100-seat function room. The recreational facilities include card rooms, a gym, and sauna; massage service is available.

Regal China Cruises

57 W. 38th St., New York, NY 10018
(212) 768-3388; (800) 808-3388

Princess Sheena, Princess Jeannie, Princess Elaine   (135 cabins, 10 suites/ 289 passengers; Chinese/Chinese; 424 ft.).

These boats were designed and built in Germany and are managed by Regal China Cruises, a Sino-American joint venture headquartered in Nanjing. They are the longest on the river and are like minicruise ships with five decks containing Continental and Chinese restaurants, a ballroom, bar, sun deck, and a full-service business center. Cabins are small.

The health club, complete with sauna and gym, has a resident practitioner in acupuncture and qigong. In addition, the ships feature t'ai chi lessons, displays of folk art, and performances of Chinese opera, acrobatics, and martial arts. It does not have lecture programs or provide the kind of background information that U.S. visitors may feel they need. However, such material is likely to be provided by the U.S. tour companies, such as Abercrombie & Kent, which uses these boats in its programs.

Victoria Cruises

57-08 Thirty-Ninth Avenue, Woodside, NY 11377
(212) 818-1680; (800) 348-8084

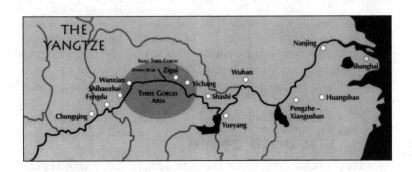

Victoria I, II, III, IV (77/154; Chinese/Chinese). Victoria Cruises, a
Chongqing-based Sino-American joint venture, was the first of the
new operators to begin cruises. It has four identical boats with the
wedding-cake look and character of Mississippi riverboats rather
than cruise ships. Each boat has Chinese and western dining rooms,
a health club, an outdoor Jacuzzi, a karaoke cafe, a nightclub, and a
business center with international phone and fax system.

Each boat has four decks and offers single-seating dining, three
bars, library, observation deck, and an outdoor jogging track.

The cabins are small and bathrooms have hand-held showers.
What they lack in amenities however, is made up for by the cruise directors, who have in-depth knowledge of China and offer outstanding lectures and cultural programs.

Victoria Cruises has also recently begun operation of another group
of boats that are more in the style of deluxe cruise ships. *Victoria 21st
Century*, the first, sails on three-day cruises between Chongqing and
Shashi. Two more, *Victoria Three Kingdoms*, and *Victoria Dragon*, offer
six-day cruises between Wuhan and Chongqing.

Other U.S.-based tour companies with Yangtze River cruises, in
addition to Abercombie & Kent, include Japan & Orient Tours (800)
377-1080; Maupintour (800) 255-4266; Orient Flexi-pax (800) 545-
5540; Pacific Bestour (800) 688-3288; Pacific Delight (800) 221-7179;
Uniworld (800) 733-7820; and Visits Plus (800) 321-3235. All include
the cruises as part of a longer China itinerary ranging from 12–24 days.

For example, Pacific Delight has nine different programs of 15–24 days from April–November, each with a four- or five-day Yangtze cruise primarily on the Victoria or Regal boats.

OTHER ASIAN RIVERS

Orient Express Cruises

c/o Orient Express Hotels
1155 Avenue of the Americas, New York, NY 10036
(212) 302-5055; fax (212) 302-5073

Road to Mandalay (71/138; European/Burmese; 305 ft.) Perhaps the most unusual cruises are the series of river cruises in Myanmar (formerly Burma) being offered by the Eastern & Oriental Express (the Asia counterpart of Venice-Simplon-Orient Express, which is the owning company that operates the famous Orient Express). Myanmar, long closed to visitors, only recently opened its door to tourists.

Road to Mandalay sails on five- and six-night itineraries on the Ayeyarwady River between Mandalay and Pagan. The cruises are part of a package that departs from Bangkok, Thailand, with round-trip flights to Yangon. It is the only scheduled cruise vessel on the river.

The *Road to Mandalay*, a deluxe river cruiser, was built in Germany in 1964 and sailed on the Rhine and later on the Elbe. Prior to starting these cruises in 1996, the boat was renovated and has a swimming pool, a large sun deck, observation lounge, several bars, and a dining room that accommodates all passengers in a single seating, serving international and Asian cuisine.

The vessel offers three types of cabins, including some singles. All have private bath and air conditioning. The doubles are fitted with twin beds; larger cabins have a sitting area.

NILE RIVER CRUISES

No trip to Egypt is complete without a cruise on the Nile. It is the perfect way to enjoy the Egyptian countryside as well as ancient temples and monuments, because most of the famous sites of antiquity are clustered along this great river.

Your first view of the Nile River snaking through the desert will illustrate dramatically why it has been so important throughout Egypt's history. Quite literally, Egypt without the Nile would not exist. Beyond the ribbon of green—the land irrigated by the Nile—the desert begins and stretches endlessly into the horizon on both sides of the river.

The Nile flows so gently that ships glide along as though not moving. The banks of the river are never more than a short distance away, enabling passengers to enjoy a close-up view of rural life in Upper Egypt. Along the river banks and in the fields of the green valley, Egyptians live today much as they have lived for thousands of years. Life and land have a continuity bridging the centuries, as cruise visitors will see from the ancient drawings on the walls of the temples and tombs and the present scenes of the countryside.

This panorama is a scene from the beginning of time, and the sense of endless tranquility is overwhelming sensation throughout the Nile cruise. It is also a complete contrast from the roar and clamor of Cairo; the juxtaposition seems to make the pastoral setting of the Nile Valley all the more remote.

Itineraries

Those who begin their cruise in Upper Egypt travel to Luxor or Aswan by plane or train. You can either begin your trip in Aswan and cruise to Luxor or do the reverse. We recommend the former, then your trip can climax with a sightseeing journey through Karnak and the Valley of the Kings at Luxor, saving the best for last.

Aswan was the capital of Nubia in ancient times and an important trading place. Today, it is primarily a winter resort and the administrative center for the High Dam and the surrounding region.

Aswan is dotted with antiquities, but the most important is the Temple of Philae—one of the many temples saved from the High Dam waters—located on an island in the middle of the river. The botanical gardens, also on an island in the Nile, and the Mausoleum of the Agha Khan, which commands a spectacular view of the valley, are the usual stops on a popular afternoon excursion made by felucca, the graceful sailboat of the Nile.

From Aswan, ships sail downstream (north) to Luxor, stopping at Kom Ombo, Edfu, and Esna—all sites of temples dating from the Ptolemaic or Greek period. One temple bears the only known likeness of Queen Cleopatra in a wall carving. Another has the remains of mummified crocodiles that were worshiped as gods by the ancients.

Luxor is the modern town next to the ancient city of Thebes, capital of ancient Egypt for much of its most illustrious history. The ship docks on the east bank of the river near the Etap and Winter Palace hotels, both within walking distance of Luxor Temple and a short carriage ride to Karnak Temple, the most colossal ancient monument in the world.

The full-day excursion covers the West Bank to visit the Valley of the Kings, where the tombs of Tutankhamen and other pharaohs were found; the Valley of the Queens; the Tombs of the Nobles, which contain some of the most important art from ancient Egypt; and other great temples and monuments.

Many cruises also sail north to visit the Temples of Dendera and Abydos, one of the oldest sites of worship in the world and considered the most important temple in Egypt for its artwork.

A limited number of cruises beyond Abydos are available on longer cruises that stop at Tel al Amarna, the capital of the revolutionary pharaoh, Akhenaton, and his beautiful wife, Nefertiti; Minya, the largest town of central Egypt; and Beni Hassan, site of twelfth-century tombs with some very unusual drawings that show the ancient Egyptians practicing judo and playing ball games we enjoy today.

Lake Nasser Cruise

The building of the Aswan High Dam created Lake Nasser, a vast body of water stretching over 300 miles south from Aswan to the Sudanese border. Its rising waters were the cause for the colossal international effort undertaking in the 1950s to save the famous Temple of Abu Simbel from inundation by moving it to higher ground. The temple complex now rests near the shores of the lake. During the construction of the Aswan Dam and for the decades that followed, visitors flew or drove to Abu Simbel, but now for the first time since its completion, they can take a Nile steamer, departing from the south side of the dam. (See Misr Travel.)

Nile Steamers

A cruise on the Nile differs from ocean cruising in several ways. Nile steamers are small and cozy, giving them a friendly club or yachtlike atmosphere. Some boats accommodate as few as 20, while the largest takes 152 passengers.

Cabins, smaller than those on standard cruise ships, are comparable in size to those on Greek Islands cruise ships. They are well appointed and comfortable. Most are fitted with twin lower beds (some have wall pull-down bunks for a third person), dressing table or nightstand, closet, and private bath with shower. Suites, on those boats that have them, often have a full bath with tub.

The small size of the ship limits its recreational and entertainment facilities, but these are not important considerations on a Nile cruise, where the attractions are the antiquities and the scenic countryside. The amount of "roaming" room is surprisingly ample. There are deck chairs for lounging and watching the history lessons of the day float by.

Boats holding 80 or more passengers have lounges for reading and relaxing, a bar, sun deck, pleasant dining room with full table service, and light evening entertainment. Laundry service is also available. Some have Ping-Pong or swimming in a (tiny) pool on deck.

Newer vessels are in the four- and five-star categories and offer three- to five-night cruises between Luxor and Aswan. Some add Abydos and Dendera, and feature longer cruises of six or seven nights as well as optional tours by land. Occasionally, some boats sail during the winter season on long cruises between Cairo and Aswan.

Nile cruises are now divided into three seasons and prices. Prices include all meals, service, taxes, and sightseeing in the company of a trained guide or Egyptologist.

High season (October–April): five-star boats range from $130–200 per person per night; four-star boats range from $75–140 per person per night. Shoulder season (May and September): reduction of 15 percent off the high-season rates. Low season (June–August): reduction of 50 percent off the high season rates.

Although the price is lower in summer and many of the boats are air-conditioned, the heat in sightseeing areas such as the Valley of the Kings can be intense. Don't go if you can't handle the heat. A dust mask (or a handkerchief held over the mouth) can be a good precaution when sightseeing in some areas. When you walk with a large group, clouds of dust can make it difficult to breath. The boat food is usually quite good, but you should be very careful and eat only fruits and vegetables that can be peeled.

There are more than 200 boats or Nile steamers offering cruises, many chartered on a long-term basis by European and other tour companies as well as U.S. ones. Unless you have the opportunity to inspect the ship yourself, you would be well advised to deal only with companies that have established reputations in the hotel and cruise businesses. The five-star ships operated by Hilton International, Mena House Oberoi, Meridian, Movenpick, Sheraton, Sonesta, and Swan Hellenic Cruises are the main ones used by major U.S. tour companies.

If you arrive in Egypt without reservations and decide to take a cruise, it is wise to make inquiries and reservations through the managing company's offices in Cairo where cabin space is controlled. If you wait until you arrive in Luxor or Aswan to find space, you must walk from ship to ship, inquiring from the boat manager if space is available.

However, the latter method does have merit if you have ample time. First, it enables you to see the ship and its cabins before booking it and, perhaps, take a quick reading of its cleanliness (an important indication of how the ship is run, particularly of boats less than five-star). And, if you are good at bargaining, you can probably negotiate a better price for an empty cabin on the day of sailing than if you were to book in advance in Cairo.

A partial list of companies and Nile steamers follows.

(Key: Cabins/Passengers; Officers/Crew; Vessel Length)

Abercrombie & Kent International, Inc.

1420 Kensington Road, Oak Brook, IL 60521
(800) 323-7308

Sun Boat I (24 cabins); *Sunboat II* (32 cabins); *Sun Boat III* (20 cabins); *Sunboat IV* (42 cabins). Cruises of four to seven days between Luxor and Aswan are part of an Egypt tour or an Egypt and Kenya safari package of 10–14 days.

Esplanade Tours

581 Boylton Street, Boston, MA 02116
(617) 266-7465; (800) 426-5492; fax (617) 262-9829

Monarch, Regency, Regina, and *Royale* (51/102; Egyptian; 238 ft.). The luxury quartet, owned and operated by Travcotels of Egypt, are fully air-conditioned. There are 49 double cabins and two singles and suites. Each boat has lounges, bars, panoramic windows, a single-seating dining room, two sun decks, swimming pool, gift shop, beauty salon, and laundry facilities. Cabins measure 230 square feet; and the two suites have 380 square feet. All cabins have television, video, mini-fridge, and bathrooms with shower, toilet, bidet, and hair dryer. The boats sail on seven-night cruises as part of a two-week Egypt program.

Mena House Oberoi Hotel/Misr Travel

Pyramids Road, Giza, Cairo, Egypt
20-2-383-3222; fax 20-2-383-7777

Sheherayar (74 cabins) and *Shehrazah* (74 cabins) are owned and operated by Oberoi Hotels, an international chain which has hotels in Cairo and Aswan. Their newest boat, the *Oberoi Philae* (58/105 cabins), resembles a paddlewheeler. Each cabin has floor-to-ceiling sliding glass doors that lead to private balconies. On the *Oberoi Philae*, a jacket and tie are required for men at dinner.

Misr Travel

605 Rockefeller Center, New York, NY 10158
(212) 582-9210; (800) 223-4978

Eugenie (55/100) and *Nubian Sea* (60/120). Three and four nights on Lake Nasser. Both boats have outside cabins with private baths. The four-night program sails south from Aswan on Mondays and ends at Abu Simbel on Friday; the three-night cruises sails north on Friday from Abu Simbel to Aswan. The highlight of the cruise is Abu Simbel which is visited during the daytime. A special feature is a candlelight dinner on deck in front of the floodlit temple of Ramses II. The price, which includes all meals and shore excursions, is about $150 per person double, in the winter season; lower in the off season. The 120-passenger *Kasr Ibrim* was expected to be commissioned at the end of May 1997. The boats, which are owned by Belle Epoque Travel Company, are represented by Misr Travel in the United States.

Misr Travel, a quasi-governmental travel agency of Egypt, owns the boats operated by Hilton International, Sheraton, and other companies with hotels in Egypt. These also include Movenpick's *Radamis* (67 cabins) and Meridian's *Champillon* (67 cabins).

Hilton International Nile Cruises/Misr Travel

605 Third Avenue, New York, NY 10158
(212) 973-2200; (800) HILTONS (reservations); (800) 223-4978

Isis, Osiris (48/124; Egyptian; 232 ft.); *Nephtis* (60/144; Egyptian). Three and six nights, the Nile between Luxor and Aswan.

Sheraton Nile Cruises/Misr Travel

630 Fifth Avenue, New York, NY 10111
(212) 582-9210; (800) 22-EGYPT; fax (212) 247-8142

Anni, Aton, Hotep, Tut (76/152; Egyptian/Egyptian; 72 ft.). Three, four, and seven nights, the Nile River between Luxor and Aswan.

Nabila Nile Cruises

Naggar Tours of Egypt, 605 Market Street, Suite 1310,
San Francisco, CA 94105
(800) 443-NILE; fax (415) 979-0163

Ramses of Egypt, Queen Nabila I & III, Ramses King of the Nile, Queen of Sheeba (40–83/78–154; Egyptian; 172–234 ft.). Four and six nights, the Nile from Luxor to Aswan.

Sonesta International Hotels Corporation

200 Clarendon Street, Boston, MA 02116
(617) 421-5400; (800) SONESTA (766-3782)
Or, 4 El Tayaran Street, Nasr City, Cairo, Egypt
001-20 262-8111; fax 262-5731

Nile Goddess (68/136; Egyptian); *Sun Goddess* (61 suites; Egyptian). Four to six nights, the Nile between Luxor and Aswan.

Swan Hellenic Cruises

77 New Oxford Street, London WC1A 1PP
0171 800 2200; fax 0171 800 2723

2815 Second Avenue, Suite 400, Seattle, WA 98121
(888) 6-MINERVA (888-664-6378) or (800) 340-7674 (P&O Cruises)

London-based Swan Hellenic is one of the oldest tour companies offering Nile cruises. The company has introduced a new program that includes a four-day cruise on Lake Nasser to Abu Simbel.

Nile Monarch (40/74; Egyptian; 235 ft.). 17 days between Cairo and Aswan, except December–January, when low water levels make cruising uncertain. 15 days between Luxor and Aswan and as far as Nag Hamadi. Special excursion to Lake Qaran in the Fayoum for birding cruise.

U.S. AND CANADIAN RIVER CRUISES

The Mississippi River has the best-known river cruises, but there are others and the attraction is growing with new companies and new cruises being added every year. Spectacular scenery is the main attraction but the opportunity to see areas difficult to see by other means is another. In the Northeast, the favorite season is autumn, with its brilliant foliage.

(Key: Cabins/Passengers; Officers/Crew; Vessel Length)

Alaska Sightseeing/Cruise West

Fourth and Battery Building, Suite 700, Seattle, WA 98121
(206) 441-8687; (800) 426-7702; fax (206) 441-4757

Round trip from Portland through the locks and dams of the Columbia and Snake rivers. (See Part Two, Cruise Lines and Their Ships.)

American Canadian Caribbean Line

461 Water Street, Warren, RI 02885
(401) 247-0955; (800) 556-7450; fax (401) 245-8303

Four boats sail on various cruises of 6–15 days, from Warren, Rhode Island, via Hudson River, Erie Canal to Lake Ontario and St. Lawrence Seaway to Montreal and Quebec City; through Erie Canal to Buffalo and Mississippi. (See Part Two, Cruise Lines and Their Ships.)

American West Steamboat Company

Two Union Square, 601 Union Street, Suite 4343,
    Seattle, WA 98101
(206) 621-0913; (800) 434-1232; fax (206) 340-0975

Queen of the West   (73/165; American/American; 230 ft.). A newly built, deluxe paddle wheeler is the first vessel of a new company created by the owners of Alaska's Glacier Bay Tours and Cruises and YachtShip CruiseLine. Inaugurated in July 1995, the boat offers three- to seven-night cruises from March–December from her home base in Portland on the Columbia, Snake, and Willamette rivers, with nightly entertainment in turn-of-the-century decor. All shore excursions are included in the cruise price.

Delta Queen Steamboat Company

30 Robin Street Wharf, New Orleans, LA 70130
(504) 586-0631; (800) 543-1949; fax (504) 585-0630

Three steamboats sail on 3–14-day cruises, year-round from New Orleans on America's heartland rivers, the Mississippi, Ohio, Cumberland, Tennessee, Atchafalaya, and Arkansas. (See Part Two, Cruise Lines and Their Ships.)

St. Lawrence Cruise Lines

253 Ontario Street, Kingston, Ontario, Canada K7L 2Z4
(613) 549-8091; (800) 267-7868; fax (613) 549-8410

Canadian Empress   (32/64; Canadian; 108 ft.). Four and five nights of St. Lawrence, Ottawa, and Saguenay Rivers. Boarding ports include Kingston, Ottawa, Montreal, and Quebec City.

AMAZON RIVER CRUISES

Many of the mainstream cruise ships that have South American itineraries include a cruise on the Amazon River as part of their itinerary, entering from the lower delta on the Atlantic and sailing up the river as far as Manaus. The river is very wide and any intimate view needs to be made into tributaries in small craft. The more exotic regions of the upper Amazon are reached mainly from Iquitos, Peru. Many of the companies that operate tours from the United States use the same boats on the Amazon; descriptive information on the vessels generally appears the first time it is named.

(Key: Cabins/Passengers; Officers/Crew; Vessel Length)

Abercrombie & Kent International, Inc.

1520 Kensington Road, Suite 212, Oak Brook, IL 60521
(708) 954-2944; (800) 323-7308; fax (708) 954-3324

Explorer   The ship sails on new Amazon cruises in March and April, beginning from Belem, Brazil, on an 18-day cruise of the Lower Amazon and its tributaries to Manaus and a second leg in the Upper Amazon from Manaus to Iquitos, Peru. The Upper Amazon leg is also available as a 10-day trip starting from Peru. (See Part Two, Cruise Lines and Their Ships.)

Amazon Explorers/African Explorers

197 Wall Street, West Long Branch, NJ 07764
(800) 631-5650

The tour company offers a variety of Amazon adventures using the *Amazon Clipper, Amazon Explorer, Arca, Delfin,* and *Rio Amazonas*—all riverboats (see below for descriptions) which depart from Iquitos, except the Amazon Clipper which leaves from Manaus, and offer two- to seven-night cruises on the Upper Amazon.

Amazon Tours & Cruises

8700 West Flagler Street, Miami, FL 33174
(305) 227-2266; (800) 423-2791

Amazon Explorer   (8/16; Peruvian; 85 ft.). Three- or six-night round-trip cruises, upriver from Iquitos. The steel-constructed boat has three decks and was refurbished in 1994. She has a small air-conditioned lounge, dining room/bar, and sun deck. The cabins are outside; all are air-conditioned and have private bath and shower.

Arca   (29/37; Peruvian; 98 ft.). Three to six nights, upper Amazon River. The air-conditioned, steel-hulled riverboat operates between Iquitos and the twin cities of Tabatinga, Brazil and Leticia, Colombia. She was refurbished in 1995 and offers ten twin-bedded cabins with upper/lower berths; and three triples with lower beds. All cabins have private bath and shower. The boat has a lounge/bar and covered and uncovered sun deck areas.

Delfin   (10/20; 65 ft.) Three- and six-night adventure expeditions to the remote backwaters of the Upper Amazon. A three-deck, steel hull riverboat, the *Delfin* was built in 1982 and has been refurbished. All cabins are outside and furnished with lower beds; bathroom facilities are communal. There is an enclosed lounge, dining area and bar, and an upper deck with covered and uncovered areas. She has a bilingual naturalist guide and carries motor launches for excursions into remote tributaries. The *Amazon Discoverer*, similar to the *Delfin*, offers the same excursions.

Rio Amazonas   (21/44; Peruvian; 146 ft.). Three- to six-night exploration cruises of the upper Amazon River, sailing down the river on Sunday from Iquitos to the twin cities of Tabatinga, Brazil and Leticia, Colombia; up the river on Wednesday from Leticia; itineraries can be combined. Built in 1981 and refurbished in 1994, *Rio Amazonas* has an air-conditioned dining room and library, covered and uncovered deck areas, and Jacuzzi/hot tub. The upper deck cabins were recently renovated and have private bath with shower and picture windows. Sun Deck cabins are larger and offer three twin beds, closet, and chair.

Ecotour Expeditions

P.O. Box 381066, Cambridge, MA 02238-1066
39 Mt. Pleasant St., Suite 2, Cambridge, MA 02140
(617) 876-5817; (800) 688-1822; fax (617) 876-3638

Tucano   (8 cabins; 80 ft.) has wood-paneled walls, a large observation deck, living room, and balcony in the middle deck. There are 76 windows throughout the boat for views of the forest. All cabins have private bathrooms, with a shower, toilet, and sink.

The company offers 10–12-day trips, year-round, from Miami, along the Amazon River and its tributaries. The nature-oriented trips are accompanied by naturalists.

Fourth Dimension Tours

71-01 South West, 99th Ave., Suite 106, Miami, FL 33173
(305) 279-0014; (800) 343-0020; fax (305) 273-9777

Desafio (12/24; Brazilian; 109 ft.), one of the newest, most advanced yachts sailing the Amazon River, has sophisticated navigation and safety equipment, central air conditioning, television, video, dining room, bar, sun deck, and two excursion boats. Cabins have double or twin beds and private bathroom with shower. The boat has two- to three-night cruises from Manaus along the Amazon River and its tributaries as part of a land expedition.

Flotel Orellana (22/48) has cabins with upper and lower beds, private bathrooms, including hot water showers, electric fans, and large windows for viewing the passing jungle. The sun deck has a cocktail lounge and a conference room where naturalist guides conduct slide presentations. The boat sails on four-day cruises from Quito to Tarapoa or Lago Agrio. An extra day adds a hike along Terra Firma forest and the Aguarico River. The company also has seven-day safaris to La Selva, heart of the Ecuadorian Amazon Basin.

International Expeditions

1 Environs Park, Kenneth Helena, AL 35080
(800) 633-4734

La Esmeralda (16 passengers/91 ft.). A Brazilian-built exploratory vessel, she sails from Iquitos into the Amazon, taking the Ucayali branch of the river. All cabins have private facilities. The trips are accompanied by Amazonian naturalist guides.

IST Cultural Tours

225 West 34th Street, Suite 913, New York, NY 10022
(212) 563-1202; (800) 833-2111; fax (212) 594-6953

Amazon Clipper (8/16; Peruvian; 65 ft.). All cabins have private bathrooms, bunk berths, and nighttime air conditioning. Facilities include covered saloon, bar, dining area, video and library, and fully equipped kitchen. Meals consist of local cuisine, mainly fresh fish; mineral water is always served. Two-night cruises on the *Amazon Clipper* exploring the tributaries for bird watching, piranha fishing, and a visit to Ecopark, a wildlife rehabilitation sanctuary, are part of the tour operator's nine-day Amazon expeditions, which also include three nights in Manaus and three days at the treetop Ariau Jungle Tower Hotel, in the middle of the rain forest.

Ladatco Tours

2220 Coral Way, Miami, FL 33145
(305) 854-8422; (800) 327-6162; fax (305) 285-0504

Amazon Clipper   (See above). Three- to four-day cruises, departing on Monday and Wednesday, to the Amazon and Negro Rivers; or, a six-day cruise which combines the two cruises. The trips are accompanied by a multilingual local guide.

Rio Amazonas   (See above). Six-day cruises, round trip, departing on Sunday from Iquitos along the Amazon. Three-night cruises are available. The itinerary includes bird watching, an early morning jungle walk, fishing in the Ataquari river, and more.

Marco Polo Vacation and Galápagos Cruises

16776 Bernando Center Drive, No. 106A, San Diego, CA 92128
(800) 421-5276

Desafio   (See above). Two- and three-night cruises year round, departing from Manaus on Monday or Thursday to the Amazon River and its tributaries. The trips are accompanied by a multilingual naturalist guide. Continental and Brazilian cuisine is served buffet style. The three-day Tucano program includes a walking trip into the jungle to explore the region's flora. The four-day Maguari program adds a visit to the Samauma village in the Anavilhanas Islands and a sail to the "wedding of the waters," where the Negro and Solimoes rivers meet to form the Amazon River.

Tara Tours

7595 North West 36th St., Suite 306A, Miami, FL 33166
(305) 871-1246; (800) 327-0080

Dolphin or *Rio Amazonas*   (See above). Seven-night Amazon packages, year-round from Miami to Iquitos, include boat trips and two to three nights at the Amazon Camp and Hotel Safari, with jungle walks, visits to native villages, and English-speaking guides. The company also offers six-night round trips to Tabatinga, Brazil, with one night in Iquitos.

Norwegian Coastal Cruises and Other Cruise Ferries

The craggy coast of Norway is deeply indented like the fingers on your hand, created eons ago by, as one person has written, "some seriously large glaciers." These crevices, which we know as fjords, can be up to ten miles deep. From their dark mirror-still waters rise almost vertical rocky cliffs, and awesome mountains climb to several thousand feet on both sides.

Often at the head of the fjords are snow-capped peaks, and in some places glaciers or ice fields inch along to their end in the North Sea. Along the shores of the fjords, where in summer the climate is very mild, are lilliputian fishing villages and isolated farmhouses. Farther up on the mountain sides will be an occasional lodge where hearty hikers bed down in summer and Olympian hopefuls fine-tune their skiing skills in winter.

The setting is beautiful and from late May through early autumn the weather is considered ideal for cruising. Most of the major cruise lines that have ships in Europe have a series of Norwegian fjord cruises. Each has a slightly different itinerary perhaps but essentially the same program: departing from Copenhagen or Oslo or Bergen and going as far north as Trondheim, Norway's original capital and third largest city, or Tromso, the largest town north of the Arctic Circle. Others sail farther north to the North Cape, the northernmost point in Europe and 1,300 miles from the North Pole, and to Spitzbergen, a group of islands where massive glaciers inch their way to the sea at Magdalena Bay.

Another way to cruise the coast—the way the Norwegians do—is on the Norwegian Coastal Express.

NORWEGIAN COASTAL VOYAGES*

Eleven working passenger-cargo ships, known as the *Hurtigruten* (which means "fast route" in Norwegian), operate a daily mail service from Bergen to 35 ports up and down Norway's coast, well beyond the North Cape to Kirkenes, near the Russian border.

A Norwegian institution begun in 1893, the ships operate year-round like clockwork through all weather and are a lifeline for the people living in small, often isolated communities along the way. They serve as transportation for local people and the mail as well as haul cargo ranging from automobiles and farm equipment to frozen fish and other produce.

The ships also carry tourists who, like the local residents, may board and disembark at any port. Many visitors, however, take the 2,500-mile round-trip voyage as an 11-day cruise. Others sail one way and return by road, rail, or air.

Time in port, geared to a strict schedule, varies from as little as 15 minutes to several hours. There are shore excursions ranging from about $20–40 at a few ports plus more costly trips that leave the ship in one port, travel inland, and join it in another. (Note that some open water passages can be rough so passengers should come prepared.)

The best time to make the trip is during the period with 24 hours of daylight from mid-May to July—hence the name, Land of the Midnight Sun. Some people, however, prefer the quieter months of spring and fall. Summer sailings are as popular with Europeans as with Americans and book up quickly, although space is often available at short notice. During the off-season, there are normally plenty of cabins available.

In the height of summer, some stretches are crowded with deck passengers, especially between the mainland and islands. Generally, about half of the passengers will be made up of local commuters and the balance will be an international mix, with Germans often in the majority. There are usually many English-speaking people and other Europeans so announcements are made in the languages required by the passenger makeup. However, in the height of the summer season, the camera-toting tourists are likely to outnumber local folks.

Meals are served at two seatings when the traffic warrants. Breakfast and lunch are buffet style, while dinner is from a set menu and served by waitresses at reserved tables. Special dietary requests should be made

---

*The remainder of this chapter was written by Theodore W. Scull.

at the time of booking. The cooking is straightforward, continental style with Norwegian specialties, and lunch offers the widest selection of hot and cold foods.

Because of hefty taxes, domestic rum, beer, wine, and spirits are very expensive—$6 for a bottle of beer is not unusual.

Entertainment is limited to the gorgeous scenery, enlivened by commentary on the passing scene, good conversation, cargo handling, and the festive occasion of crossing the Arctic Circle. The line provides an excellent guidebook. In the summer months, the newest ships might have a band for listening and dancing.

Bergen Line, the Norwegian shipping company that operates the service, has 11 ships, which it groups in three classifications: new ships, newer generation ships, and traditional ships.

New Ships

In the new ships group, the *Kong Harald, Nordkapp, Nordlys, Nordnorge, Polarlys* and *Richard With,* all completed since 1993, add the concept of the cruise ferry with its greater comfort and luxury (already well established and very popular in Baltic waters) to the *Hurtigruten.* Large and boxy on their exteriors, the 11,204-ton ships (390 feet long and 63 feet wide) take up to 490 passengers in relatively roomy accommodations. Their cargo is handled via ramps.

The modern cabins are mostly outside with spare decor and have foldaway beds and upper berths, audio channels, automated wake-up calls, tiled baths with showers, and hair dryers.

The public rooms, on the other hand, have the fashionable look of a modern cruise ship with rich matching fabrics, thick carpets, and ample use of brass, glass, veneers, and creative decorative touches. On the highest deck is a wraparound observation lounge with comfortable seats that is divided into three sections, one being a cocktail lounge/bar.

Another middle deck has a forward cocktail lounge, library/card room, conference rooms for meetings, small souvenir shop, playroom, video arcade, 24-hour cafeteria, and a long side gallery lounge leading to the 240-seat restaurant and a private dining room. Each of the new trio also offers a sauna, small gym, and passenger laundry.

Newer Generation Ships

The so-called newer generation ships are the 6,617-ton *Midnatsol, Narvik*, and *Vesteraalen,* built in 1982–83 and enlarged in 1988–89 with berths to carry up to 325 passengers. The cabins are smaller and plainer, but most are outside and all have private bathrooms with showers. The ships' attractive features include a forward-facing observation lounge and a glass-enclosed top deck lounge, similar to an enlarged version of one of the full-length dome cars operating in Alaska. Freight and vehicles are handled via roll-on ramps that adjust to tidal levels.

Traditional Ships

The two remaining traditional ships—*Harald Jarl* and *Lofoten*—were built in 1960 and 1964 respectively and have 169 and 223 berths in very small outside and inside cabins, some without private facilities. The best cabins sell out fast.

On these 2,600-ton ships, cargo, mail, and vehicles are handled in a traditional and now almost extinct way by crane loading onto the deck and into the holds. These ships possess rich maritime character with paneled lounges, lovely decorative features, teak decks, and battered hulls from thousands of dockings.

They both have two forward-facing lounges with smoking forbidden in the upper one. The restaurant spans the full width of the ship and an aft cafeteria and lounge are used mainly by short-run passengers.

One other traditional ship, the 179-passenger *Nordstjernen* built in 1956, is currently undertaking a series of eight-day summer cruises from Tromso to Spitsbergen and the North Cape. In the first season, these cruises sold out quickly. At other times of the year, this ship may substitute for a Coastal Express vessel while another is being overhauled. Advance information was unavailable regarding the vessel's role in 1998.

On the Coastal Express

Billed as the World's Most Beautiful Voyage, especially when the weather cooperates, the Coastal Express offers a relaxed and informal adventure that sees many repeaters. The service is presently subsidized by the Norwegian government, and while the future remains bright, the now unique traditional ships are likely to be withdrawn within the next several years as new ships are completed.

Aboard the *Harald Jarl*, one of the traditional ships, the feeling is like that of a small country hotel, with the rhythmic throb of the diesel engine pounding softly in the background. Outside, on the first morning at sea, a sheer mountain wall plunges straight into the narrow channel, and, to port, Norwegian Sea breakers pile up against a string of low-lying islands.

At a briefing in the dining room, the courier reminds everyone that they are traveling on a working ship, not a cruise ship, and that local passengers will be boarding and leaving at each port.

At Bodo, a medium-size city located at the northern end of Norway's main rail line, about 100 new passengers board for the six-hour crossing to the Lofoten Islands. From the dock, a crane swings aboard an automobile, whole fish, bundles of tiny evergreen saplings, building materials, and canvas sacks of mail for safe stowage on the open deck or in the forward hold.

During brief port calls, you can walk briskly to the main shopping street to look for souvenirs and newspapers. Longer excursions leave the ship in one port and meet it in another. On a recent trip, during the stop at Harstad, passengers attended a short Lutheran worship service in a former Catholic fortress church predating the Reformation.

On a drive inland along the shore of the Godfjord, red farmhouses dot sloping fields that end abruptly at the base of snowcapped mountain peaks. The bus winds down to a small white ferry for a 20-minute crossing to the start of a gravel road that parallels a second, deeper fjord with scant room for cultivation.

There are visits to the promontory at the North Cape, an excursion from Kirkenes (the turnaround port) to the Russian border, and a cruise into the narrow Trollfjord, a one-mile passage between vertical rock cliffs bubbling with rivulets of falling water. The turning basin catches the reflection of the new moon as the captain deftly revolves his ship in a tight half circle. (The *Seabourn Pride* is one of the few regular cruise ships small enough to make this maneuver as well.)

By the end of the voyage, the round-trip passengers have shared a wonderful 2,500-mile feast of dramatic mountain scenery, varied visits ashore, good fresh food, and constantly changing weather that might range from bright sunshine to blinding snow squalls.

EUROPEAN CRUISE FERRIES

Cruise ferry is an inadequate term for a highly sophisticated breed of ship that takes passengers on overnight sea voyages but provides most of the comforts and amenities of a deluxe cruise liner. Below decks, out of sight, the ships take cars, recreational vehicles, and large trucks.

Operating throughout northern Europe, they crisscross the Baltic and North Seas, linking cities such as Copenhagen and Oslo, Stockholm and Helsinki, Newcastle and Bergen. When matched with connecting trains, creative rail-sea itineraries can be designed that are often part of the Eurail pass network.

Most passengers are Scandinavians (Danish, Finnish, Norwegian, Swedish) or have a Scandinavian connection and are traveling to visit friends and relations or simply cruising. Germans are the second most numerous nationality; North Sea sailings carry many British as well.

The shipboard attractions are numerous with the larger, newer ships offering a variety of restaurants, from a la carte dining of a very high standard to an elaborate 60-item smorgasbord to simpler (and cheaper) cafeteria-style dining. The *Silja Europa* even offers a seagoing McDonald's.

After-dinner entertainment includes cabarets, dancing, gambling, and films. There are playrooms for children, video arcades for teenagers, saunas, and shopping for a wide range of duty-free goods with supermarket carts to wheel purchases to the checkout counter. English is widely spoken aboard all ships.

Cabins vary from well-appointed rooms with windows and cruise ship amenities to large family cabins with more basic facilities and private showers. Most ship designs have the cabin accommodations located away from the activity and noise of the public rooms. For example, the arrangement might have the cabins forward and the public rooms aft.

The following lines are represented in North America, and they offer the most extensive routes and some of the newest and most sophisticated ships. However, they are only a sampling of a much wider network that spans all the seas of Europe, including the Mediterranean. Most major intercity services are year-round. It should also be noted that ships occasionally may be shifted from one route to another or sold to another line and renamed.

In addition to operating the Norwegian Coastal Express, Bergen Line is the U.S. general sales agent for all the lines described below except Viking Line, but including DFDS, which has its own offices as well. See Information and Reservations on page 762 for details.

Color Line

Norwegian-based, the Color Line offers North Sea sailings between Bergen and Stavanger, Norway, and Newcastle, England; between Oslo, Norway, and Kiel, Germany; and between Oslo or Kristiansand, Norway, and Hirtshals in northern Denmark. In 1997, several new fast, short sea routes opened up between the northern Danish port of Skagen and southern Norwegian ports of Larvik and Moss.

The largest and most impressive of its ships are the *Kronprins Harald* and the *Princesse Ragnhild* on the Oslo-Kiel Flagship route, which leaves daily from either port for the 20-hour overnight run. The ships enter and leave Oslo via the scenic Oslofjord (a two-hour stretch). Most passengers will be German or Norwegian.

The sailings from Newcastle connect two to three times a week in Bergen with Norwegian Coastal Express evening northbound departures, a popular combination for British passengers.

The Fleet	Built/Renovated	Tonnage	Passengers
Christian IV	1982	15,064	2,000
Color Festival	1986/1992	34,314	1,937
Color Viking	1975/1989	20,581	1,250
Kronprins Harald	1987	31,914	1,432
Pegasus II	1997	3,500	600
Peter Wessel	1981/1988	29,704	2,180
Princesse Ragnhild	1981/1992	38,500	1,875
Silvia Ana	1996	7,505	1,200
Skagen	1975/1982	12,333	1,238

Scandinavian Seaways (DFDS)

Danish-owned Scandinavian Seaways, often better known as DFDS, operates an extensive route of cruise ferries between England and Denmark; England and Sweden; England and Germany; England and Netherlands; Denmark and Sweden; and Denmark and Norway.

The largest ships operate the flagship route between Copenhagen and Oslo with scenic departures from both cities at 5 P.M. and arrival the next morning at about 9 A.M. The northbound route from Copenhagen passes Hamlet's Castle at Helsingor during the narrow passage between Denmark and Sweden, calls at Helsingborg (Sweden) and enters the Oslofjord at dawn.

Two-night round-trip cruises are popular outings from both Oslo and Copenhagen, giving passengers time for a day ashore between the morning arrival and late-afternoon departure. The Copenhagen pier is adjacent to the central business district, and the Oslo pier is a short bus ride away from the city's center.

The English port of Harwich from where DFDS departs year-round is reached by connecting boat train from London. It has three year-round overnight services to Esbjerg on the west coast of Denmark, with connecting boat train service to Copenhagen, to Gothenburg, Sweden, and to Hamburg from where there are train connections to all of Germany.

Seasonal sailings operate from Newcastle to Gothenburg, Hamburg, and Amsterdam.

The Fleet	Built/Renovated	Tonnage	Passengers
Crown of Scandinavia	1994	35,498	2,026
Dana Anglia	1978	14,000	1,235
Hamburg	1976	13,141	1,085
King of Scandinavia	1975/1988	15,800	1,175
Prince of Scandinavia	1975	15,794	1,525
Princess of Scandinavia	1975	15,794	1,525
Queen of Scandinavia	1981	25,941	1,535

Silja Line

Now operating the largest cruise ferries in the world, the Silja Line is the best known of all the Scandinavian ferry companies. The ships are virtual cities at sea with some carrying up to 3,000 passengers and grossing almost 60,000 tons.

Everything is on a vast scale, and, while busy, they are designed to avoid crowding and long queues. Cruise-ship-style atriums form the centerpiece, off of which are numerous eateries, lounges, and bars catering to all ages and incomes.

The prestige route is Stockholm to Helsinki where a ship leaves each port at 6 P.M. every night of the year (this being the Land of the Midnight Sun, there is sunlight throughout the summer months until 10 P.M. or later) and arrives the next day at 8:30 A.M. The two-hour passage through the Stockholm archipelago is a highlight. You need to be up by about 6:30 A.M. to enjoy the full voyage through the islands. The ships dock conveniently next to the city center in Helsinki, with a day ashore for those making the very popular two-night round voyage. Extended stopovers are easily arranged. The arrival dock in Stockholm is equally convenient.

The Stockholm to Turku, Finland, overnight route is also daily with a companion daylight service taking about 11 hours.

The fastest single-hull ship in northern Europe is the 25,908-ton gas turbine *Finnjet,* whose 23-hour summer schedule between Helsinki and

Travemunde, Germany, calls for speeds of 30 knots. In the off-season, the ship operates at a more economical speed on a more relaxed schedule.

The Fleet	Built/Renovated	Tonnage	Passengers
Fennia	1966/1986	10,515	1,200
Finnjet	1977	25,908	1,602
Silja Europa	1993	59,914	3,000
Silja Festival	1986/1992	34,414	1,740
Silja Scandinavia	1992	35,285	2,400
Silja Serenade	1990	58,376	2,700
Silja Symphony	1991	58,376	2,700
Wasa Queen	1975/1992	16,546	1,400

Viking Line

Viking Line, Silja Line's main competitor, has red-hulled ships that offer much the same routes and has ships almost as large. The Stockholm to Turku daylight route also calls at Mariehamn, in the beautiful, wooded Aland Islands, located about halfway between Sweden and Finland. The Stockholm-Helsinki route may be taken as two-night round-trip cruises with packages including cabin, two dinners, and two breakfasts.

The Fleet	Built/Renovated	Tonnage	Passengers
Amorella	1988	34,384	2,112
Cinderella	1989	46,398	2,500
Isabella	1989	34,384	2,112
Kalypso	1990	40,012	2,165
Mariella	1985	37,799	2,500
Rosella	1986	10,757	750

INFORMATION AND RESERVATIONS

Bergen Line
    405 Park Avenue, New York, NY 10022
    (212) 319-1300; (800) 323-7435; fax (212) 319-1390

DFDS Seaways (USA) Inc.
    Cypress Creek Business Park, 6555 N.W. 9th Avenue,
    No. 207, Ft. Lauderdale, FL 33309
    (800) 533-3755; fax (305) 491-7958

EuroCruises
    303 West 13th Street, New York, NY 10014
    (212) 691-2099; (800) 688-EURO; fax (212) 366-4747

EuroCruises is a wholesaler that packages all these lines in its tour/cruise programs but is not entitled to sell point-to-point ferry services.

Adventure and Cultural Cruises

Whether it is called an adventure or expedition cruise or an educational or cultural cruise is a matter of definition on which few people agree. And while there are differences there are also similarities, particularly in the type of person to whom they appeal, namely, experienced travelers who prefer an intellectually stimulating or educational environment when they travel and do not need—or want—the activities and entertainment typical of mainstream cruises. They prefer the close-up, hands-on learning experience that adventure and educational cruises provide and the companionship of like-minded travelers.

Ships offering adventures or expeditions normally are small, accommodating fewer than 150 passengers, and have an informal atmosphere. Their small size enables them to sail into places where large ships cannot go. Those providing educational or cultural cruises might be larger and have a somewhat more formal atmosphere. In all cases, the destination of the cruise and the opportunity to learn in the company of experts are the motivation and main attraction. The itineraries tend to be two weeks or perhaps longer.

A few adventure ships are deluxe, but most are comfortable workhorses that go safely through icy waters or jungle rivers. They have cozy functional cabins, friendly, congenial service, and good cuisine, served at one open seating, often family style, and dress is casual. Most have an open bridge policy.

The cruises are almost always seasonal to take advantage of optimum weather and wildlife conditions. On board, cruise passengers attend lectures by naturalists and other specialists and have time to read about the places they are visiting and to enjoy the company of shipmates with whom they share common interests. The destinations are likely to be remote and passengers travel by Zodiac boats to reach the most inaccessible areas, often making wet landings to go ashore where no docks are available.

On shore, participants often spend their time viewing wildlife and spectacular scenery, hiking into coastal forests, or encountering remote cultures. Not all, of course, require heavy duty exertion—many are light adventure, nothing more more than a short walk. In the evening, the staff's naturalists and guest lecturers usually recap the day's excursion. These sessions are always well attended.

On educational or cultural cruises, the lecturers are more likely to be historians, anthropologists, museum authorities, and area specialists. Indeed, many are organized and sponsored by universities and museum groups. They are a particularly popular alumni fund-raising vehicle.

The ports of call might be world-renowned sites visited by general tours; the difference is that participants on cultural cruises get an in-depth review on board ship from specialists and shoreside sightseeing guided by experts rather than commercial tour guides, which regular cruise lines use. Members are also likely to attend cultural and folklore events.

It is not unusual for an adventure cruise and a cultural one to overlap in their interests or activities, particular those offering light adventure (or "soft" adventure, the most unappealing term that the travel trade uses). Not only do these cruises appeal to the same type of people, as we noted earlier, they also appeal to the same people.

Expedition cruises don't require physical training to join but participants need to be in good physical condition, able to endure a certain amount of exertion. More important, they need to be flexible in temperament as well as body. They should be good sports, always keeping a sense of humor, and be ready to forgo some creature comforts momentarily. Those who are meant for these cruises will feel they are being so richly rewarded by the experience that any temporary discomfort matters little.

Adventure or expedition cruises take you off-the-beaten-path near home or to the far reaches of the earth from the Arctic to Antarctica and around the globe. The cruises tend to be more expensive than mainstream tours not only because of the limited number of people to spread the cost but because of the added costs for a ship to operate in remote areas and offer many different itineraries. Also, keep in mind that shore excursions are included in the fare. Then, too, there is the cost to the cruise line of guest lecturers who must be accommodated in cabins that would otherwise draw revenue.

The people you are likely to find on these cruises tend to be strong environmentalists and will expect their fellow travelers to be of like mind. They like to be outdoors, are active, well traveled, well educated, intellectually curious, affluent, perhaps semiretired professionals 50 years or older. They belong to a museum or natural history group. They probably read *Audubon, National Geographic,* or *Smithsonian* magazine, watch public television, are members of a nature club, and support the local zoo.

The following is a representative list of companies offering adventure or expedition/educational/cultural cruises. They have brochures, usually with deck plans of the vessels they use and descriptions of their itineraries and other literature. Being specialists in their area, they usually can answer questions with more firsthand authority than a general travel agent or cruise line.

Note: As part of an overall effort to prevent overcrowding at certain visitor sites, the Galápagos National Park Service has revised the itineraries of many tour boats. You will need to check with the tour company for the latest information.

(Key: Cabins/Passengers; Officers/Crew; Ship Length/Tonnage)

Abercrombie & Kent International, Inc.
(See Part Two, Cruise Lines and Their Ships)

Explorer   Sails to Antarctica, the Falklands, South Georgia, and the Chilean fjords in astral summer and a series of Amazon cruises in March and April. Expeditions at other times of the year might go to the South Pacific, Borneo, Indonesia, and Papua New Guinea.

A variety of small boats are chartered, mostly in the winter months, for 7–12-day Galápagos cruises.

Alaska's Glacier Bay Tours and Cruises
520 Pike Street, No. 1400, Seattle, WA 98101
(206) 623-7110; (800) 451-5952; fax (206) 623-7809

Wilderness Explorer   (18/36; American; 112 ft.). Two- to five-night cruises of Alaska's Glacier Bay National Park, Admiralty Island National Monument, Juneau and Tracy Arm.

Amazon Tours & Cruises (See Part Three, River and Barge Cruises)

Arca, Amazon Clipper, Delfin, Rio Amazonas   Two- to six-night adventure cruises of the upper Amazon River.

Classical Cruises (See Part Two, Other Cruise Lines and Their Ships)

Classical Cruises specializes in educational and culturally oriented cruises, using a wide variety of well-known deluxe and luxury ships.

Clipper Cruises (See Part II: Cruise Lines and Their Ships)

The cruise line offers light adventure cruises on the Orinoco River, in Costa Rica, and the Sea of Cortez, among others.

Cruceros Australis (See OdessAmerica)

Ecoventura S.A. (See Galápagos Network)

Esplanade Tours

(See Spice Island Cruises below; and Part III, River and Barge Cruises, Nile River Cruises)

Esplanade Tours also offers Russian river cruises and represents Noble Caledonia, a British company with worldwide cruises and tours.

Fourth Dimension Tours

71-01 South West 99th Ave., Suite 106, Miami, FL 33173
(305) 279-0014; (800) 343-0020; fax (305) 273-9777

Santa Cruz   (See Galápagos Cruises) 7–12-night programs from Miami to Ecuador, including four nights in Quito; and three- to seven-day Galápagos cruises on the *Santa Cruz, Delphin II, Diamante,* and *Rachel III.*

Galápagos Cruises

c/o Adventure Associates
13150 Coit Road, Suite 110, Dallas, Texas 75240
(972) 907-0414; (800) 527-2500; fax (972) 783-1286

Adventure Associates is the U.S. representative of Quito-based Metropolitan Touring, the leading tour company in Ecuador and the oldest of the companies offering cruises of the Galápagos. The ships are well run and have excellent naturalist guides.

Flotel Orellana   (22/48; Ecuadorian; 154 ft.). The ship sails on tributaries in Ecuador's northwestern corner of Amazonia and on the lower Aguarico in the Cuyabeo Wildlife Reserve to communities of Cofan and Quichua Indians. (See Part III, River and Barge Cruises, Amazon River.)

Isabela II   (20/40; Ecuadorian; 166 ft.). Seven-night cruise of the Galápagos Islands.

Santa Cruz   (40/90; Ecuadorian; 230 ft.). Three-, four-, and seven-night cruises of the Galápagos Islands. The ship is the largest and most comfortable of the vessels sailing in Galápagos waters. Cabins are comparable to the ships on Greek Islands cruises. The food and service are good and the ship is well run. The three-day cruises visit the southern group of islands; the four-day tours go to the central and north groups. The two can be combined into one week. Naturalist guides trained and licensed by the National Park of the Galápagos give nightly briefings on the next day's visit and accompany passengers on all visits to the islands and hikes in groups of 20 people maximum.

The ship carries 90 passengers on three decks. All cabins have private facilities and twin beds. The 1,500-ton ship is fully carpeted and air conditioned, with a large dining room, cocktail lounge, bar, and spacious decks.

The company has added the *Rachel III* (4/8; Ecuadorian; 85 ft.) and the *Diamante* (12 passengers; 97 ft.).

Galápagos Network

7200 Corporate Center Drive, Suite 309, Miami, FL 33126
(305) 592-2294; (800) 633-7972; fax (305) 592-6394

The tour company, affiliated with a group of privately owned companies in Ecuador, offers year-round, three- to seven-night cruises in the Galápagos Islands in its fleet of small vessels. The cruises are designed for the well educated, well traveled, and those eager to learn about nature, ecology, and environmental issues. The small boats provide the opportunity to sail into isolated waters to visit remote islands. Naturalist guides accompany all sailings and give on-board lectures as well as lead walks. Passengers are ferried to the islands by launches.

The three-night cruises visit the Southern Islands of Española (Hood), Floreana, and Santa Cruz. The four-night trips visit the Central and Northern Islands of Bartolome, Plazas, Santiago (James), Tower, and Santa Cruz. All vessels depart from the Island of San Cristóbal and can be chartered. Passengers can snorkel throughout the year and scuba dive on designated cruises. Pre- and postcruise packages are available in mainland Ecuador.

Corinthian (24/48; Ecuadorian; 195 ft.). Built in the United States and recently renovated, the motor vessel has a spacious dining room, three bars, a large television, library, Jacuzzi, and outside sun deck. Cabins are air conditioned and have private bathrooms. The ship sails every Monday and Thursday.

Eric, Flamingo, Letty (10/20; Ecuadorian; 83 ft.). Built in 1993, *Letty* is the newest of three luxury motor yachts. All three yachts are air conditioned. Cabins have private bathrooms, a VCR, and stereo equipment. Letty departs on Monday and Thursday; the others on Tuesdays and Fridays. At least four hours per day are spent on each island. The boats are well suited for families or groups of friends. The three yachts have new seven-night itineraries, which now include the western islands of Fernandina and Isabela as well as Española, Tower, Santa Cruz, Bartolome, South Plaza, Floreana, Santa Fe, and Santiago. In addition, passengers will have lunch at a ranch when visiting the highlands of Santa Cruz.

Sea Cloud (4/10; Ecuadorian; 85 ft.).The motor sailor has four double cabins with private bath and sails on seven-night cruises.

Galápagos Yacht Cruises

c/o Galápagos, Inc.,
7800 Red Road, Suite 112, South Miami, FL 33143
(305) 665-0841; (800) 327-9854; fax (305) 661-1457

Cruz del Sur, Dorado, Estrella del Mar (6–8/12–16; Ecuadorian; 75–80 ft.). Small boats sail from San Cristóbal with stops at the main islands of the Galápagos and others where larger ships do not go.

Yolita (6/12; Ecuadorian; 17 ft.). From San Cristóbal to Islas Lobos, Española, Punta Suarez, Gardener, Darwin Station, North Seymour, Baltra, Bachas, Rabida, Puerto Egas, Bartholome, Sullivan, Islas Plazas, Santa Fe, and Santa Cruz.

Marine Expeditions

30 Hazelton Avenue, Toronto, Ontario, Canada M5R 2E2
(416) 964-9069; (800) 263-9147; fax (416) 964-2366

The company, which was founded in 1992, has a fleet of five Russian expedition vessels with "ice capability" which, for marketing purposes, were given names easier for North Americans to remember. The moderately priced expeditions are designed for well-traveled passengers with a sense of adventure. From November–March, all the ships, which are also sold in the U.S. through OdessAmerica, offer the following: eight-night Antarctic expedition cruises; ten-night, extended Antarctica; 14-night, Antarctica and Falklands; and 18-night, adding South Georgia. The ships' small size enable them to traverse waters inaccessible to large vessels and they carry Zodiacs to transport passengers close to wildlife and natural wonders where the ships cannot go. All expeditions are accompanied by experts in the region visited who give lectures and often act as guides. In addition to Antarctica, the ships sail in various out-of-the-way locations at other times of the year as follows:

Marine Adventurer (Akademik Ioffe) and *Marine Voyager (Akademik Sergey Vavilov)* (37/80; Russian/North American; 384 ft./6,231 tons). Expedition cruises aboard the icebreaker visit Antarctica during November through February; South America's Patagonia region March/April and October/November; and Norway's North Cape from May–July.

Marine Intrepid (Professor Multanousky) and *Marine Spirit (Akademik Shuleykin)* (20/44; Russian/North American; 235 ft./1,754 tons). From March 13–May 1, 1998, the *Marine Intrepid* cruises the islands of the South Atlantic; and from March 28–April 26, 1998, the *Marine Spirit* sails to the islands of the South Pacific. In summer, the ship has a new, comprehensive Russian Far East program with three different itineraries.

Marine Discovery (Alla Tarasova) (60/120; Russian/North American; 328 ft./4,364 tons). From March–May 1998, the *Marine Discovery* will have a new series of 12-night Amazon River cruises, between Belem and Iquitos, and seven-night cruises between Manaus and Iquitos. New also are cruises around Greenland.

Melanesian Tourist Services/Niugini Exploration Cruises

302 West Grand Avenue, Suite 10-B, El Segundo, CA 90245
(310) 785-0370; fax (310) 785-0314

Coral Princess (27/54; Australian; 116 ft.). Three-night cruises of the Great Barrier Reef of Australia and the islands and coastline between Cairns and Townsville, with stops at Dunk Island and Orpheus Island.

Melanesian Discoverer (21/35–54; New Guinean; 117 ft.). Four-, five-, and seven-night cruises of the Melanesian islands along the north coast of Papua New Guinea.

Metropolitan Touring (See Galápagos Cruises)

OdessAmerica

170 Old Country Road, Suite 608, Mineola, NY 11501
(516) 747-8880; (800) 221-3254; fax (516) 747-8367

Ambassador I   (86; Ecuadorian; 296 ft.) is air conditioned and has a pool, lido bar, and single-seating dining room.

Three- and four-night cruises of the Galápagos start and end in Baltra and visit Española, Santa Cruz, Bartolome, Isabela, Santiago, and Floreana islands. Visitors go ashore in 20-foot fiberglass boats holding 20 people, including two crew members and a guide. Landings may be by wading. Twelve-day cruises include stayovers in Quito, Equador.

Skorpios II   (160; Chilean; 230 ft.) Built in 1988 to American standards, the ship has all outside cabins with television, a daily filming of activities and sights, and an open bar. From September–May, she sails on six-day cruises that are combined with five days on land between Puerto Montt south of Santiago to the San Rafael Lagoon—a total of 800 miles, through channels, fjords and archipelagos. Remote fishing villages, ice-age glaciers, and the historic city of Castro are highlights. A four-day, postcruise extension covers the Lake Region.

OdessAmerica/Cruceros Australis

170 Old Country Road, Suite 608, Mineola, NY 11501
(516) 747-8880; (800) 221-3254; fax (516) 747-8367

Terra Australis   (62/108; Chilean; 213 ft.) Built in the United States in 1984 as the *Savannah,* this ship is classified under the strict safety rules of the American Bureau of Shipping and features large cabins and good food washed down with Chilean wines. The ship sails from September to April from Punta Arenas through the Strait of Magellan and Chile's inland waterways, visiting Beagle Channel and its famous glaciers, Puerto Williams, the southernmost town in the world, Ushuaia, Harberton/Tierra del Fuego, and Magdalena Island with its huge penguin colony.

Orient Lines (See Part Two, Cruise Lines and Their Ships)

Marco Polo   Expedition cruises to Antarctica; cultural trips in Asia.

Quark Expeditions

980 Post Road, Darien, CT 06820
(203) 656-0499; (800) 356-5699; fax (203) 655-6623

The tour company, a pioneer in Arctic and Antarctic expedition cruises, handles a group of Russian-built ships, all with Russian officers and crew, which sail on adventure cruises. They are accompanied by a cruise staff, which consists of an expedition leader, an assistant expedition leader, lecturers, and Zodiac drivers. They may be from the United States or Europe or South America, depending on the destinations and their knowledge of specific areas.

The Antarctica departures include some combination of the following: Antarctic Peninsula, Weddell Sea, South Georgia, Falkland Islands, Chilean fjords, Ross Sea, New Zealand, and Australian subantarctic islands. Some depart from Cape Town, as well. Some of the ships also sail around the Arctic Circle or up the Amazon River. The itineraries vary depending on the ship. Quark Expeditions publishes excellent brochures describing the itineraries and displaying deck plans of their ships.

Akademik Golitsyn   (24/50) and *Professor Khromov* (38 passengers). The ship has a lounge, bar, library, two dining rooms (with one doubling as the lecture and video room), sauna, gift shop, and infirmary. It carries scuba equipment. The *Khromov* is to be replaced by the *Golitsyn*. Mid-December–mid-February, Antarctic Peninsula and South Shetland Islands round trip from Ushuaia.

Akademik Shokalskiy   (21/36; European; 386 ft.). The ship has a lounge, bar, library, two dining rooms, with one doubling as the lecture and video room, gift shop, infirmary, and sauna. It also carries scuba equipment. The ship cruises from the Falkland Islands to the Antarctic.

Bremen   (82/164). Antarctic Peninsula and South Shetland Islands, January 15, 1998, round trip from Ushuaia. For more information on the ship, see Part II, Cruise Lines and Their Ships, Radisson Seven Seas Cruises.

Clipper Adventurer   (50/100). The ship has a lounge, bar, library, dining room, lecture room, gift shop, infirmary, and gym. She departs from Lonyearbyen on July 15, 1998, for Spitsbergen and Norway to Bergen. From December to February 1998–99, she will sail on Antarctic, South Georgia, and Falkland cruises with a series of different itineraries departing from Cape Town, Hobart, Ushuaia, or Port Stanley. In October, she sails the Amazon. (See Clipper Cruises, Part II, Cruise Lines and Their Ships. Clipper purchased the ship in 1997, and now Quark charters it for its cruises.)

Kapitan Dranitysn   (96; Russian/Russian and European; 437 ft.). The ship has a lounge, bar, library, dining room, lecture room, gift shop, infirmary, gym, sauna, pool, and helicopter. From July 2–September 1, 1998, the ship is circumnavigating the Arctic, starting and ending in Murmansk. The voyage can be taken in one of four segments:

Greenland, from Lonyearbyen, Norway, to Sondre Stromfjord; High Arctic, Sondre Stromfjord to Resolute; Northwest Passage, Resolute to Provideniya; Northeast Passage, Provideniya to Lonyearbyen.

Kapitan Khlebnikov   (56/106; Russian; 437 ft.). The ship has a lounge, bar, library, dining room, lecture room, gift shop, infirmary, gym, sauna, pool, and helicopter. She sails round trip from Hobart, January 22, 1998, on a semi-circumnavigation of Antarctica, including Peter Island and the Ross Ice Shelf and visits to the subantarctic islands of New Zealand and Australia. In late July and August, she sails on Canadian Arctic expeditions.

Professor Molchanov   (19/48). The ship has a lounge, bar, library, two dining rooms, with one doubling as the lecture and video room, gift shop, infirmary, and sauna. Early November–late February, Falkland Islands, South Georgia and Antarctic Pennisula from Puerto Madryn or round trip from Ushuaia. Mid-March–mid-May, South Atlantic from Ushuaia to Vlissingen; voyage can also be booked to Ascension Island, Cape Verde, Tenerife, or Folkestone. She sails to Spitsbergen from Longyearbyen in June and July.

Yamal and *Sovetsky Soyuz*   (56/106; Russian; 500 ft.). Each ship has a lounge, bar, library, gift shop, infirmary, dining room, lecture room, gym, sauna, pool, and helicopter. *Yamal* departs on July 4, 1998, on a 14-day expedition round trip from Murmansk to the geographic North Pole. The *Soyuz* will replace the *Yamal*.

Radisson Seven Seas (See Part Two, Cruise Lines and Their Ships)

Bremen   (Also see Quark Expeditions)

Hanseatic   The ship is a hybrid—part expedition, part cruise—with the shipboard amenities of a deluxe cruise ship. She sails from the Arctic to Antarctica with a great variety of itineraries.

Society Expeditions

2001 Western Avenue, No. 300, Seattle, WA 98121
(800) 548-8669; fax (206) 728-2301

World Discoverer   (71/138; European/International; 285 ft.). Adventure in comfort on a specially built expedition ship that sails on exotic, worldwide, nature-oriented itineraries accompanied by experts who give daily shipboard lectures and act as guides. 11–21-day cruises of Alaska and British Columbia; Bering Strait, Russian Far East, and above the Arctic Circle; Antarctica, the Falklands, and Chilean fjords; western coast of South America; French Polynesia, Pitcairn and Easter islands.

Southern Heritage Expeditions

6033 West Century Boulevard, No. 1270, Los Angeles, CA 90045
(310) 338-1538; (800) 351-2323; fax (310) 215-9705

Professor Shokalski   (19/38; Russian/Russian; 236 ft.). Built in Finland in the 1980s as a research vessel, she is a steel-built, ice-strengthened vessel suited for cruising the Subantarctic Islands of New Zealand and Australia and the Antarctic. The dining room serves international cuisine and doubles as a lecture room with television and VCR. There is also a library/card room, bar, sauna, and doctor. The ship carries Zodiac-type landing craft. Cruises depart from New Zealand's southernmost town, Invercargill, on six different itineraries from November–February.

Special Expeditions

720 Fifth Avenue, New York, NY 10019
(212) 765-7740; (800) 762-0003; fax (212) 265-3770

The globe-roaming company, which operates four ships, was founded by Sven-Olaf Lindblad, son of the late adventure travel pioneer Lars-Eric Lindblad, who pioneered modern expedition cruising when in 1969 he launched the *Lindblad Explorer*, designed to take regular travelers to remote corners of the world in comfort and safety. Special Expeditions has set as its mission, "providing travelers with a more thoughtful way to see the world avoiding crowded destinations and seeking out natural ones" and offers a wide selection of light adventure cruises in various parts of the world.

Caledonian Star   (68/110; Scandinavian/International; 293 ft.). After using this ship for several years, Special Expeditions bought her in October 1996 and will offer a series of off-the-beaten-track cruises through Europe and Asia. In late October–November she sails from Turkey to Aqaba; from December–March, she will offer different itineraries in the Seychelles; and in April and May, she sails in the Red Sea and Mediterranean. From May–August, she will make her way from Lisbon to Dartmouth, England, around the British Isles, along the Norwegian Fjords to Spitsbergen. Afterwards, the ship offers a combination of Scotland and the Baltic to St. Petersburg, returning to Amsterdam.

Polaris   (41/80; Swedish/Filipino, Swedish; 238 ft.). The ship has a new mission that will keep her on Galápagos cruises almost year-round. The program is a joint venture with Metropolitan Touring, Ecuador's oldest and largest travel company which operates the well-regarded *Santa Cruz* and *Isabella II*. Since May 1997, with an inaugural cruise that marked the thirtieth anniversary of Lars-Eric Lindblad's first Galápagos cruise, the *Polaris* has been sailing on 11-day land and sea itineraries, accompanied by outstanding naturalists, such as Dr. Lynn Fowler, who has lived and conducted wildlife research in the area for 20 years. Intermittently, the *Polaris* offers several Panama and Costa Rica cruises.

Sea Bird and *Sea Lion*   (36/70; American; 152 ft.). 4–12-day cruises of Alaska's Inside Passage; Columbia and Snake Rivers to Hells Canyon, Idaho; San Juan islands; and an annual cruise to Baja California and the Sea of Cortez timed for optimum whale watching.

From time to time, the company also charters the *Sea Cloud* and other ships and operates cruises for universities and other groups.

Spice Island Cruises

c/o Esplanade Tours, 581 Boylton Street, Boston, MA 02116
(617) 266-7465; (800) 426-5492; fax (617) 262-9829

Bali Sea Dancer   (140 passengers; formerly, the *Illira*) is well known to U.S. cultural groups, who charter her often. The ship has spacious outside cabins with private bathroom and shower; single-seating dining room; and pool. Facilities include a library, lido bar, exercise room, and beauty salon. There are Zodiacs for shore excursions. The ship sails through the Indonesian archipelago to Bali, West Sumbawa, Komodo, and Lombok.

Oceanic Odyssey   (60/120; Bahamas; 336 ft./5,050 tons). Designed in Holland and built in Japan in 1989, the deluxe ship, formerly the *Oceanic Grace,* was acquired by Spice Island Cruises in the summer of 1997. It offers three- and four-night cruises of Indonesia. The ship has a restaurant serving Asian and International cuisine. Other features are a main lounge, health spa, sauna, massage, pool, Jacuzzi, and beauty salon. All cabins have a marble bath with tub and shower, twin or queen-size bed, VCR, phone, refrigerator, minibar, safe, and hair dryer.

Sunmakers Travel Group

100 West Harrison St., South Tower, Suite 350, Seattle, WA 98119
(206) 216-2905; (800) 255-7380

The tour company offers a series of 10–14-day South Pacific Cruise Tours on the *World Discoverer*, the expedition ship of Society Expeditions, which take in Tahiti and the Cook Islands and are accompanied by naturalist guides. Passengers also have the option of diving, deepsea fishing, biking, golf, and other sports.

Sunnyland Tours, Inc.

166 Main Street, Hackensack, NJ 07601
(201) 487-2150; (800) 783-7839; fax (201) 487-1546

The tour company offers six-, seven-, or ten-day packages which include cruises of the Galápagos on a selection of small yachts or on the well-regarded *Santa Cruz* (see Galápagos Cruises above). Sunnyland also offers Amazon cruises as options to the Galápagos programs.

Svalbard Polar Travel (EuroCruises)

303 West 13th Street, New York, NY 10014
(212) 691-2099; (800) 688-EURO; fax (212) 366-4747

Nordbrise   (19/38; Norwegian/Norwegian; 148 ft./491 tons). The small, three-deck icebreaker *Nordbrise* sails to Svalbard, a group of Norwegian islands at the rim of the North Pole, and cruises the fjords, icebergs, and glaciers. Built in 1951, the ship was renovated about 1990. She departs from Tromso, Norway, from mid-June–late August on four-day, Monday–Thursday voyages. Using Zodiacs, passengers make landings to visit interesting places; in the locales of Barentsburg and Ny-Alesund the ship berths dockside.

Polarstar   (10/25; Norwegian/Norwegian; 152 ft.). Built in 1948, the small icebreaker offers an unusual eight-day expedition to the wild and remote areas of northernmost parts of Norway's North Pole archipelago, which can only be reached by an expedition ship such as the *Polarstar*. Cabins for two and three people; each cabin has a wash basin; showers and bath facilities are communal. She departs on Saturdays from Tromso, Norway, from late June–mid-August. Route and landing sites depend on weather and ice conditions.

Swan Hellenic/Classical Cruises
(See Part II, Other Cruise Lines and Their Ships)

Temptress Cruises

1600 Northwest LeJuene Road, Suite 301, Miami, FL 33126
(305) 871-2663; (800) 336-8423; fax (305) 871-2657

The cruise line's adventure cruises of Costa Rica have been expanded and new programs for Belize added. The cruises combine natural history and light adventure and offer snorkeling, diving, kayaking, sportfishing, and waterskiing. The line has also added children's programs with trained counselors in charge.

Temptress Voyager (62 passengers; 173 ft.). Formerly the line's only ship making cruises in Costa Rica, the ship has all outside cabins with private bath and air conditioning. She sails on a series of Belize and Guatemala cruises, departing from Belize City. They can be taken as three-, four-, or seven-day cruises.

Temptress Explorer (99 passengers; 185 ft.). Built in 1995, the ship cruises in Costa Rica on new three- and four-day itineraries that can be combined into one week. It was built in Seattle, Washington, specifically to meet the requirements of the Costa Rica route, allowing for easier navigation of the rivers and shallow bays while maintaining the stability of a heavier ship. All cabins are outside and have private bath and air conditioning.

Spirit of Endeavour (100 passengers), the newly-renovated flagship of Alaska Sightseeing/Cruise West, is chartered from its owners during the winter season for Costa Rica cruises. (See Part II, Cruise Lines and Their Ships, for ship description.)

Wilderness Travel

801 Allston Way, Berkeley, CA 94710
(510) 548-0420; (800) 368-2794; fax (510) 548-0347

The adventure tour company has several programs to the Galápagos almost year-round, some with up to three departures monthly. They combine cruises on small yachts with hiking in some areas not usually covered by the more conventional excursions. The company also has a combination of the Galápagos and the Upper Amazon River. On February 19 and 23, 1998, it will offer Solar Eclipse Cruises in either the Caribbean, where Wilderness Travel marks its twentieth anniversary, or the Galápagos.

World Explorer Cruises (See Part Two: Cruise Lines and Their Ships)

Universe Explorer The ship specializes in culture-oriented, two-week cruises of Alaska from May–August and makes two Caribbean cruises in January. For almost six winter months she sails around the world via Central and South America and South Africa on a Semester-at-Sea program organized by the University of Pittsburgh. (See Part II, Cruise Lines and Their Ships.)

FREIGHTERS

The following information was adapted, with permission, from "Setting Sail by Freighter," by Dave G. Houser and Rankin Harvey, published as a special issue of *Cruises & Tours* magazine.

INTRODUCTION TO FREIGHTER TRAVEL

Freighter travel may be the least-understood segment of the cruise industry. You don't read or hear much about it, and cargo lines that offer passenger service rarely advertise in the mainstream media. Many travel agents, too, lack experience and expertise in booking freighter cruises.

Freighters roam the globe, visiting ports both famous and exotic. They offer a carefree, informal environment conducive to total relaxation, and they cost much less than conventional cruise ships.

Prior to the post–World War II boom in air travel and cruises, freighters were a significant mode of international travel. Expanding air routes, lower fares, and the growth of the cruise industry gradually relegated freighter travel to a minor niche in the cruise market. But now freighter travel is making a comeback, as veteran cruisers in growing numbers turn to freighters for a change of pace and place in a desire to recapture a type of travel missing today.

Cargo lines, too, are recognizing this revival of interest. Some have introduced new, combined container and passenger vessels that can accommodate larger numbers of passengers. About 100 traditional freighters, which carry from 4–12 passengers, are presently in service. Most are enjoying brisk bookings and operate at maximum capacity during peak seasons.

Freighters: Defining the Breed

What exactly is a freighter? First, let's say what it is not. A modern-day freighter certainly isn't a rust bucket of a tramp steamer sailing off on a mission of intrigue or romance as popularized in movies and novels. The vast majority of cargo vessels today are less than 20 years old. Trim and handsome in design, they are loaded with sophisticated navigation and communication equipment. Most are fully containerized, that is, their freight is carried in large metal containers resembling box cars systematically stacked below and above decks.

The International Conventions and Conferences on Marine Safety defines the *passenger-carrying freighter* as a vessel principally engaged in transporting goods that is licensed to carry a maximum of 12 passengers. Those licensed to carry more than 12 are defined as *combination cargo-passenger ships*. The latter must meet stricter safety standards and carry more staff, including a doctor, and they have the advantage of gaining preferred docking privileges over ordinary freighters.

Nowadays, nearly all cargo ships run on fixed schedules along established routes, except for those in so-called tramp service. Tramps do not sail on regular routes or schedules and can be hired to haul almost anything, anywhere, anytime. A few take passengers.

Why People Choose Freighters

Traveling by freighter offers a rare opportunity in today's steadily shrinking world truly to get away from it all. There are no crowds, no planned activities, no waiting in line, no dress code, and no hoopla. In short, the atmosphere aboard a freighter is relaxed and unstructured. You can be as active or as lazy as you wish, but the choice is yours.

Freighters are for travelers—not tourists—who want to see the world on their own terms and at their own pace. Most people who turn to freighters are veteran travelers who have become bored or disillusioned with conventional tours, cruises, and popular vacation destinations. They are folks whose sense of adventure and yearning for discovery demand something different. Even a cursory glance at freighter itineraries will reveal many ports of call that would be impractical or prohibitively expensive to visit any other way.

Freighter travelers recognize good value when they see it, and, on a per diem basis, there is no better travel value available than freighters. With careful research and planning, you can still roam the world for months on end aboard a freighter for about $100 per day.

Some people are attracted by the camaraderie they enjoy with fellow passengers. Sailing with a group of usually no more than a dozen like-minded, well-informed veteran travelers in a low-key, relaxing atmosphere is their ideal travel environment and often leads to lasting friendships.

Is Freighter Travel for You?

Judging from the high rate of repeat bookings, once a freighter traveler, always a freighter traveler. If you haven't tried it but you've read this far, you may be a good candidate.

You must have plenty of time. Most folks just can't get away for a 30-, 60-, or 90-day voyage. For that reason alone, the majority of freighter travelers are retirees, teachers and professors, self-employed professionals, and occasionally an artist or writer. Characteristics common to the breed include an extensive travel background, a love of the sea, a preference for traveling independently, and an abhorrence of hoopla.

Wherever on this planet your imagination might roam, chances are you can go there on a freighter. Some of the more exotic and popular routes (round trip from the United States) include: East Africa from the Gulf Coast (60–70 days), East or West Coast to New Zealand/Australia (45–75 days), around the world from Los Angeles (84 days), Marquesas Islands from Tahiti (16 days), Mediterranean from East or Gulf Coast (33–70 days) and South America from East or Gulf Coast (44–52 days).

Accommodations and Facilities

The majority of cargoliners have spacious, comfortable accommodations equal to, and often better than, those found on cruise ships. Normally they are located in a multistory superstructure at the stern. Cabins have showers and sometimes bathtubs. In most cases they are air conditioned and tastefully furnished. Often, they have taped music, service phones, VCRs, mini-fridges, and picture windows rather than portholes.

Comfy, smartly decorated lounges invite card games, conversation, and an evening round of cocktails. Most vessels have large-screen televisions with an extensive library of videotapes. Many cargoliners, too, have small swimming or plunge pools, exercise rooms, and saunas for officer and passenger use, and plenty of deck space for walking.

An open bridge policy seems to prevail among the freighter fleet, meaning you're welcome on the bridge to watch officers and crew in action except during critical maneuvers such as docking. On most freighters, in fact, passengers are free to go almost anywhere they please.

Pampering is not part of the program aboard freighters. Basic services are handled by a small contingent of stewards who usually double as cabin boys and waiters. These personable, hard-working lads keep your cabin made up and linen changed, assist the galley staff, and are on hand to satisfy special needs. A washer and dryer are generally available for passenger use. Phone and fax services are always available in emergencies, but policies on routine or casual use varies from line to line.

Ships carrying more than 12 passengers will have a doctor on board and will generally have a small hospital or treatment center. But medical services aboard freighters carrying 12 or fewer passengers are limited. All, however, carry basic medical supplies and someone aboard will be trained in first aid. In case of serious illness, the freighter captain will contact the nearest ship or shore station with a doctor available for advice. In a grave emergency, the victim will be transferred to a ship with appropriate medical facilities or else be put ashore at the nearest port. Costs incurred in medical evacuation and treatment are, of course, the passenger's responsibility.

In view of this, you are advised to take out a travel health insurance policy with medical evacuation coverage and carry more than enough of any prescription medications you require. Don't count on being able to refill prescriptions in foreign countries.

Dining and Food

Every freighter has a comfortable dining room shared by officers and passengers, and dining is the day's special event and a regular opportunity to socialize. Most officers are congenial, anxious to please, and happy to share their knowledge of the ship, the sea, and the world as few others probably have seen it.

Tasty, nutritious food is essential to officer and crew morale as well as to passenger satisfaction. So you'll find most freighter fare to be of good restaurant quality, well prepared, and plentiful. Menus are varied, often featuring the national cuisine of the ship's and/or officers' origin.

Breakfast and lunch are usually presented buffet-style while dinners are served at your table, often in four or five courses. Coffee and tea are available anytime and stewards routinely set out trays of snacks for between-meal munching. Beer, wine, and liquor is available on most, but not all, ships. Check ahead to know if it's necessary for you to BYOB.

PLANNING YOUR FREIGHTER VOYAGE

The majority of freighters, with space for only a few passengers, tend to book up early, especially during peak summer months. You, too, must start early—six months or more—to get your choice of ship and routing, and a year ahead is not unusual on the most popular voyages.

Planning can take much longer than you ever imagined to book and confirm the voyage of your choice. Depending upon the itinerary, you may have to secure travel documents, such as visas; you'll have arrangements to make concerning your home or business; you'll have to have a physical checkup; and you'll need to decide on trip and travel health insurance options.

As a first step, consult a current issue of *Ford's Freighter Travel Guide* (19448 Londelius Street, Northridge, CA 91324; (818) 701-7414), a comprehensive twice-a-year guide that lists almost all passenger-carrying freighter itineraries. Your local university library may have a copy. A subscription costs $24 (plus $3 for first-class postage and $1.98 sales tax for California residents).

As a smart second step, join TravLtips Cruise and Freighter Association (P.O. Box 580188, Flushing, NY 11358; (800) 872-8584; $20 membership fee for one year or $35 for two) to connect with this loose-knit group of 28,000 freighter and offbeat cruising buffs and get bimonthly issues of *TravLtips*, the association magazine; periodic issues of *Roam the World by Freighter,* which includes member-written reports of freighter voyages; access to the association's travel planning and reservation services; and member-only invitations on special and unusual cruises. TravLtips in Flushing, New York, as well as California-based Freighter World Cruises (180 S. Lake Avenue, No. 335, Pasadena, CA 91101; (818) 449-3106) can also aid you in your selection of a vessel or voyage and in actually booking it, plus handling air and other travel arrangements.

Many cargo lines are represented by similar specialized agents. These services can prove a real blessing, particularly to first-timers, because booking passage on a freighter is not the quick and easy process that it is to sign up for a cruise.

You need lead time. Since freighter schedules are prone to change, some lines require waitlisting prospective passengers until firm schedules are released. Only then will waiting passengers be given an option on a cabin. There is no charge for waitlisting. A deposit—usually 10–20 percent—is required only after accepting a cabin option. Final payment is usually due 45–60 days prior to sailing.

During the months before sailing, the departure date you select may shift a few days either way; the routing may be altered a bit, for example, you may be going to Wellington rather than Auckland. You get the picture. And it should illustrate at least two things: first, the value of having an experienced agent to keep you informed of changes and to help deal with them, and second, the need for flexibility on your part in terms of both schedule and attitude.

Every freighter company has its own terms and policies affecting passengers. Most have brochures, information sheets, and/or contracts outlining these policies and describing their ships and itineraries. Make sure you obtain all such literature through your travel agent or directly, and read it thoroughly—including the fine print. Pay particular attention to the company's cancellation policy and take it into account when you consider trip cancellation insurance.

Solo travelers should note that a number of cargo lines offer single cabins, while others charge the dreaded single supplement, though it is usually less than 50 percent.

Because freighters are working vessels, most lines won't accept young (preteen) children for passage. Those that do take kids usually levy the same fare for them as adults. Pets are not permitted on freighters.

Owing to the fact that less than 40 nations still require visiting U.S. citizens to carry visas, you may not need any. But there are some surprises on the list, such as Australia and Brazil—countries that are frequented by passenger-carrying freighters and do require visas.

Your Health

Cargo lines require passengers 65 or older to present a certificate of good health from their doctor before booking can be completed. Review your itinerary with your physician regarding potential risk of disease or infection and concerning any immunizations or protective medicines needed. For most tropical destinations, you'll need a prescription for antimalarial medication and a yellow fever vaccination, possibly other immunizations, and medication for the treatment of diarrheal illness. You can get up-to-the-minute immunization recommendations from the Centers for Disease Control's (CDC) 24-hour hotline in Atlanta: (404) 332-4559. You'll need a touchtone phone to receive recorded messages.

Clothing and Essentials

Packing for a 90-day freighter voyage shouldn't be different from selecting your gear and garments for a 10-day trip. Nor should it be any more in terms of gross tonnage either. You may only have to tote your bags on and off the vessel once, but remember, cargo lines, unlike cruise lines, aren't obligated to provide baggage service. There may be someone around to help, but don't bank on it. So, don't bring more than you can handle.

Casual attire is the rule aboard freighters. It is possible that there might be a special occasion on-board ship calling for dressier-than-usual attire, or that restaurants ashore may require a coat and tie and similarly appropriate dress for women. Bring low-heeled, nonskid, rubber-soled shoes. They are essential for safe maneuvering aboard ship in rough seas. Be prepared for just about any kind of climate. Light wraps (even in the tropics) and rain gear are essential.

Foul weather is almost a certainty at some point during any long voyage and many freighter veterans take along a lightweight, two-piece rain suit (parka and pants), and rubber boots. They also come in handy for wading through the dust and residue that frequently cakes bulk loading docks. You should also bring a pair of binoculars, some reading material (but don't overdo it as most ships have extensive libraries), washcloths, and facial tissue—most vessels don't provide these.

Electrical current on most foreign flagged freighters is 220/250 AC, whereas your appliances are 110/120 AC. You'll need a voltage converter and plug adapter to use them. Funds for any shipboard expenses should be in U.S. currency. Traveler's checks are generally accepted, but very few lines take credit cards or personal checks.

Tipping policies seem something of an enigma among freighter companies. Most lines claim they have no official policy. A few say that their stewards who serve passengers get extra pay and suggest that tipping be reserved for exceptional or special service. The norm seems to be $1.50 per person per day to the room steward and an equal amount to the dining steward.

Smoking is allowed on nearly all freighters because many officers and crew members smoke. A few lines have adopted no-smoking policies in the dining rooms. The majority of officers and crew who do smoke are extremely courteous around their nonsmoking guests, and most passengers say that smoking is not a big problem on freighters.

FREIGHTER TRAVEL DIRECTORY

The following directory is in two parts: the first part provides information on nine cargo lines, their vessels departing from North American ports, and their booking contacts (addresses/phone are listed at the end of the section). The asterisk indicates the agent can arrange ancillary requirements, including air transportation (in some cases, air/sea package), hotel, transfers, hiring a car, sightseeing, and travel insurance. The second part, Freighter Routing Directory, is organized by ports of departure and gives a line's voyage duration and price range. Itineraries are available from cargo lines and sources cited previously in this chapter. The data are subject to change.

Bank Line

Two ships (registry: Isle of Man; officers and crew: British/Bangladeshi), one ship (registry: Panama; officers and crew: British/Filipino), on tramp itineraries from Norfolk, VA or Philadelphia, PA between various ports in Southeast Asia, Thailand, Indonesia, and Australia and in regular service from Savannah, Georgia, to South Africa and Brazil.

Agent: Freighter World Cruises.*

Ivybank (built 1974, 15,460 tons) and *Moraybank* (built 1973, 15,469 tons) each carry nine passengers; one owner's cabin, three double cabins, and one single cabin.

Olivebank (built 1977, 25,270 tons) carries eight passengers; one suite, two double cabins, two singles. All three ships have cabins with private bath and shower, refrigerator, TV/VCR, and short-wave radio. Each vessel has a lounge and swimming pool. The *Olivebank* also has a library and self-service laundry. Age limit: 82 (older passengers with additional insurance).

Blue Star Line

Five ships (registry: Bahamas; officers and crew: British/Filipino), regular service from U.S. ports to Australia and New Zealand.

Agent: TravLtips.*

American Star, Melbourne Star, Queensland Star, and *Sidney Star* (built 1972, 24,907 tons) each carry ten passengers in four double and two single cabins. *Columbia Star* (built 1980, 19,613 tons) carries 12 passengers in ten cabins (sold double or single occupancy). All five ships have cabins with bath and shower; passenger laundry, pantry, bar/lounge, game room with TV/VCR, and library. *Columbia Star* also has an exercise room. Age limit: 79 (medical certificate required).

Chilean Line

Two ships (registry: Liberia; officers and crew: Indian/Chilean) cruising between the U.S. East Coast and the East Coast of South America.

Agent: Freighter World Cruises.*

Lircay and *Laja* (built 1978, 14,689 tons) each carry twelve passengers in four double cabins and four single cabins. All cabins have private bath and shower. Both ships have a lounge with TV/VCR. Age limit: 82.

Columbus Line

Five ships (registry: Germany; officers and crew: German) offer regular service from U.S. ports to Australia and New Zealand.

Agent: Freighter World Cruises.*

Columbus Queensland (built 1979, 21,872 tons) carries eight passengers in four double cabins. *Columbus America, Columbus Australia,* and *Columbus New Zealand* (built 1971, 19,145 tons) each carry 12 passengers in three double cabins and six singles.

Columbus Victoria (built 1978, 24,081 tons) carries eight passengers in four double cabins. All five vessels have larger than ordinary cabins with view windows, private bath/shower, and refrigerator. Large, nicely furnished lounge, library, bar, swimming pool, deck chairs. Age limit: 79.

DSR (Deutsche Seereederei Rostock)

Six ships (registry: Germany; officers and crew: German) in regular service from New York to the Orient.

Agent: Freighter World Cruises.*

Pacific Senator, Patmos Senator, DSR Atlantic, Palermo Senator, Choyang Elite, and *DSR America* (built 1992, 45,000 tons) each carry four passengers in two double cabins. Cabins have bath, shower, refrigerator. Lounge with radio, TV and VCR, tape deck, sauna, swimming pool. Age limit: 79.

Egon Oldendorff Lines

Two ships (registry: Liberia; officers and crew: International), service from U.S. Gulf Coast to the West Coast of South America.

Agent: Freighter World Cruises.*

FMG Santiago and *FMG Mexico* (built 1992, 21,763 tons) carry ten passengers in double and single cabins. Cabins have private bath and shower. Both ships have a lounge/bar and swimming pool. Age limit: 79.

Ivaran Lines

Two container ships (registry: Norway; officers and crew: Norwegian/International), regular service from U.S. East and Gulf coasts to South America.

Agent: Ivaran Agencies.*

Americana (built 1988, 19,203 tons) carries 80 passengers in 2 suites, 20 double cabins, 8 outside and 10 inside singles. All cabins have

bath and shower, TV and VCR, minibar, refrigerator, telephone,
and personal safe. Ship has lounge with dance floor, cocktail bars,
minicasino, library, hairdresser, sauna/Jacuzzi, swimming pool,
health club, and hospital. There is also regular cruise ship-style
entertainment. No age limit.

San Antonio (built 1994, 20,000 tons) carries 12 passengers in three
double cabins and six singles. All cabins have bath and shower,
TV/VCR, and refrigerator. Ship has lounge, sun deck, and swimming pool. Age limit: 79.

Leonhardt & Blumberg

Two ships (registry: Germany; officers and crew: German/South
Sea Islanders from the Kiribati Islands), service between the U.S. East
Coast and U.S. West Coast via the Far East and Suez Canal.

Agent: Freighter World Cruises.*

Dagmar Maersk and *Doerthe Maersk* (built 1996, 50,644 tons) carry
three passengers in one double and one single cabin. Cabins have
private bath and shower. Each vessel has a lounge and a swimming
pool. Age Limit: 79.

Mineral Shipping

Three ships (registry: Singapore; officers and crew: Croatian), one
ship (registry: Bahamas; officers and crew: Croatian), in regular service
from U.S. East Coast to Holland and on tramp itineraries in Mediterranean. German owners.

Agent: Freighter World Cruises.*

Julia (built 1978, 12,165 tons) and *Clary* (built 1979, 12,165 tons) each
carry 12 passengers in four double cabins and some single cabins.
Patty (built 1976, 11,293 tons) carries seven passengers in one
double cabin and five singles. *Christiane* (built 1982, 14,647 tons)
carries seven passengers in two double cabins and three singles. All
cabins have bath and shower. On the *Patty,* four single cabins
adjoin in pairs with a shared bathroom. Each vessel has a lounge
with TV/VCR; all but *Patty* have swimming pools. Age limit: 82.

Martime Reederei

One ship (registry: Germany; officers and crew: German) in regular
service from U.S. West Coast to the Mediterranean.

Agent: Freighter World Cruises.*

Cielo di Los Angeles (built 1994, 23,500 tons) carries six passengers in
three double cabins. Cabins have refrigerators and private bath and

shower. The ship is fully air conditioned and offers a self-serve laundry, lounge/bar, exercise room, sauna, and swimming pool. Age limit: 79.

Niederelbe Schiffahrtsgesellschaft Buxtehude

Sixteen ships (registry: Germany; officers and crew: German/Filipino), four of which are in round-the-world service from Long Beach, CA; seven in round-the-world service from Charleston, SC; four in service between the U.S. East Coast and U.S. West Coast via the Far East and the Suez Canal; and one in service from Los Angeles, CA, to New Zealand and Australia.

Agent: Freighter World Cruises.*

Washington Senator, California Senator, London Senator, and *Hong Kong Senator* (built 1994, 45,470 tons) carry eight passengers in three double suites and two single cabins, all with private bath and shower. Each vessel offers a lounge, laundry, sauna, fitness room, indoor pool, and outdoor pool. Age limit: 80.

Contship Germany (built 1992), *Contship France* (built 1993), *Contship Singapore, Contship Ticino, Contship Lavagna, Contship Italy* (all built 1994), and the *Contship Europe* (built 1995). All seven are 22,500 tons and carry ten passengers in one owner's suite and four double cabins. All cabins have private bath and shower. Each ship features a lounge, laundry, exercise room, sauna, and indoor swimming pool. Age limit: 80.

Sea-Land Endeavour, Sea-Land Initiative, Sea-Land Victory, and *Sea-Land Mistral* (built 1996, 37,549 tons) carry eight passengers in four suites, each with refrigerator and private bath and shower. All four vessels offer a lounge, laundry, exercise room, and sauna. Age limit: 80.

Direct Currawong (built 1990, 23,500 tons) carries ten passengers in one owner's cabin and four double cabins. Each cabin has private bath and shower. The ship features a lounge, laundry, exercise room, sauna, and indoor swimming pool. Age limit: 80.

Projex Line

One ship (registry: Germany; officers and crew: German and Polish/Filipino) in service from the U.S. West Coast to the Mediterranean via the Panama Canal.

Agent: Freighter World Cruises.*

Pacifico (built 1996, 30,000 tons) carries eight passengers in four double cabins with sitting area, refrigerator, and private bath and shower. The vessel has a lounge, laundry, game room, exercise room, and outdoor pool. Age limit: 79.

Schepers Line

One ship (registry: Elsfleth, Germany, Antigua, and Barbuda; officers and crew: German/Filipino) in service from Miami, FL, to the Caribbean.
Agent: Freighter World Cruises.*

Santa Paula (built 1995, 11,800 tons) carries four passengers in one owner's cabin and two single cabins. Cabins have private bath and shower. The ship has a pool, sauna, and exercise room. Age limit: 79.

Schluter Line

Three ships (registry: Germany; officers and crew: German/Filipino) in service from Long Beach, CA, to the Far East.
Agent: Freighter World Cruises.*

Hyundai Majesty, Hyundai Fidelity, and *Hyundai Trusty* (built 1996, 40,000 tons) carry four passengers in two double cabins. Cabins have separate sitting areas, TV/VCR, refrigerator, and private bath and shower. Each vessel has a lounge, exercise room, and indoor swimming pool. Age limit: 70.

Transeste Shipping

Two ships (registry: Germany; officers and crew: German/Filipino) in service from Port Everglades, FL, to the Caribbean.
Agent: Freighter World Cruises.*

Widukind and *Ulf Ritscher* (built 1990, 15,174 tons) carry eight passengers in three double cabins and two single cabins. All cabins have private bath and shower. Both ships have a lounge, laundry, and outdoor swimming pool. The *Ulf Ritscher* has a covered table tennis area. Age limit: 79.

Freighter Travel Agents

Freighter World Cruises
180 South Lake Avenue, Suite 335, Pasadena, CA 91101
(818) 449-3106; fax (818) 449-9573

Ivaran Agencies, Inc., Newport Financial Centre
111 Pavonia Avenue, Jersey City, NJ 07310
(201) 798-5656; (800) 451-1639

TravLtips,
163-07 Depot Road, P.O. Box 580188, Flushing, NY 11358
(718) 939-2400; (800) 872-8584; fax (718) 939-2047

FREIGHTER ROUTING DIRECTORY
(by destination from North American ports)

Atlantic and Gulf Coasts

Around the World

Niederelbe Schiffahrtsgesellschaft Buxtehude: Seven ships departing from Charleston, SC. Duration is about 101–104 days. Rates: owner's cabin $11,413–11,700 per person (pp), sole occupancy of owner's cabin $13,938–$14,300; double cabin $9,090–10,400 pp, sole occupancy of a double $11,847–12,675; single cabin $11,700. Plus $292.50 pp port taxes, deviation insurance, and U.S. Customs/INS fees.

Australia and New Zealand

Blue Star Line: Three ships departing from Jacksonville, FL, or Houston, TX. Duration is about 65–70 days. Shorter segments available. Rates: fall/winter, pp/double $6,800–7,700; single $7,600–8,500. Spring/summer, pp/double $5,400–6,150; single $6100–6,800.

Columbus Line: Boomerang Service with about two departures per month from Jacksonville, FL. Duration about 68–70 days. Rates: high season (October 1–February 28), pp/double $7,650; single $8,700. Low season, pp/double $5,450; single $6,070.

Caribbean

Schepers Line: One ship departing from Miami, FL. Duration is about 10–12 days. Rates: owner's cabin $1,125 pp, sole occupancy of owner's cabin $1,400, single cabin $1,275. Plus $212.50 pp port taxes, deviation insurance, and U.S. Customs/INS fees.

Transeste Shipping: Two ships departing from Port Everglades, FL. Duration is 12–28 days. Rates: double cabin $1,130–2,620 pp, sole occupancy of a double $1,260–2,950; single cabin $1,130–2,620.

Mediterranean/South America

Mineral Shipping: Two ships running tramp itineraries usually calling to Italy, Sardinia, Greece, Netherlands, and sometimes Amazon

River ports, Brazil. Depart from Savannah, GA, and return to another U.S. East Coast port. Duration is about 70 days; beyond 70 days, passengers may fly back to the United States from a European port. Rates: pp/double $5,775; single $6,300.

Netherlands

Mineral Shipping: Two ships departing from Savannah, GA. Duration is about 32–40 days. One-way segments of about 12 days are available. Rates: round trip $2,520–2,775; one way $1,160–1,290.

South America

Chilean Line: Two ships departing from Port Elizabeth, NJ, or Miami, FL. Duration is about 46 days. Rates: double cabins $4,600 pp, single cabins $5,060 pp. Plus $12.50 pp U.S. Customs/INS fees.

Egon Oldendorff: Two ships departing from New Orleans, LA. Duration is about 40 days with 8–24 hours at each port. Rates: pp/double $3,130–3,740; owner's cabin and singles $3,610–4,220. Port taxes and deviation insurance of $212.50 added to all fares. Air/Sea packages are available through Freighter World Cruises.

Ivaran Lines: Two itineraries—luxury and standard cargo, both departing from New Orleans, LA. Duration of luxury itinerary is about 47–48 days. Rates: $7,840–13,965. Standard cargo duration is about 47 days. Rates: $5,525–6,500. One-way sail/fly packages are available.

South America and South Africa

Bank Line: One ship regularly departs from Savannah, GA. Duration is about 70–75 days. Rates: pp/double $7,770; suites and singles $8,450. Rates include travel insurance; additional prepaid insurance of $150 is required of passengers 80 years and over.

Southeast Asia

Bank Line: Two ships on tramp service from Norfolk, VA, or Philadelphia, PA. Duration is about 120 days round trip and 70 days one way. Round-trip rates: double or single cabin $11,400 pp; owner's cabin or sole occupancy of a double cabin $13,200 pp. Rates one way: double or single cabin $6,650 pp; owner's cabin or sole occupancy of a double cabin $7,700 pp. A $200 insurance premium is added for passengers 80 and under, and a $400 premium is added for passengers over 80.

DSR (Deutsche Seereederei Rostock):   Six ships departing from New York, NY. Duration is about 91 days. Rates: double cabins

$9,555 pp, sole occupancy $10,647. Plus $212.50 pp U.S. Customs/INS fees and deviation insurance. Freighter World Cruises will customize air/sea packages to/from various ports en route. Call for fares.

Pacific Coast

Around the World

Niederelbe Schiffahrtsgesellschaft Buxtehude: Four ships departing from Long Beach, CA. Duration is about 77 days. Rates: owner's cabin $9,240 pp, sole occupancy of owner's cabin $11,319, double cabin $8,239 pp, sole occupancy of a double $10,010; single cabin $8,239. Plus $292.50 pp port taxes, deviation insurance, and U.S. Customs/INS fees.

Australia and New Zealand

Blue Star Line: Two ships departing from Los Angeles, CA. Duration is about 49 days. One-way segments available. Rates: pp/double, $3,975–4,550; single $4,775–$5,300.

Columbus Line: Kiwi Service with departures every other month from Los Angeles, CA. Duration about 42–45 days. Rates: high season (October 1–February 28), pp/double $5,400; single $7,370. Low season, pp/double $4,798; single $7,100.

Niederelbe Schiffahrtsgesellschaft Buxtehude: One ship departing from Long Beach, CA. Duration is about 46 days. Rates: owner's cabin $4,600 pp, sole occupancy of owner's cabin $5,520; double cabin $3,910–4140 pp, sole occupancy of a double $4,600–4,968. Plus $292.50 pp port taxes, deviation insurance, and U.S. Customs/INS fees.

Mediterranean

Martime Reederei: One ship departing from Los Angeles, CA. Duration is about 50–59 days. Rates: double cabin $5,000–5,900 pp, owner's cabin or sole occupancy of a double $5,500–6,490. Plus $262.50 pp port taxes, deviation insurance and U.S. Customs/INS fees. One-way air/sea packages are available through Freighter World Cruises.

Projex Line: One ship departing from Los Angeles, CA. Duration is about 50 days. Rates: double cabin $5,000 pp, sole occupancy of a double $5,500. Plus $262.50 pp port taxes, deviation insurance, and U.S. Customs/INS fees. One-way air/sea packages are available through Freighter World Cruises.

Pendulum Route

Between U.S. East Coast and U.S. West Coast via the Far East and Suez Canal.

Leonhardt & Blumberg: Two ships departing from Long Beach, CA, or Newark, NJ. Duration is about 45–50 days. Rates: double cabin $4,500–5,000 pp, sole occupancy of a double $5,265–5,850; single cabin $4,725–5,250. Plus $305.50 pp port taxes, deviation insurance, and U.S. customs/INS fees.

Niederelbe Schiffahrtsgesellschaft Buxtehude: Four ships departing from Long Beach, CA, or Newark, NJ. Duration is about 45–50 days. Rates: owner's cabin $5,400–6,000 pp, sole occupancy of owner's cabin $6,525–7,250; double cabin $4,725–5,250 pp, sole occupancy of a double $5,670–6,300. Plus $292.50 pp port taxes, deviation insurance, and U.S. Customs fees.

Southeast Asia

Schluter Line: Three ships departing from Long Beach, CA. Duration is about 42 days. Rates: double cabin $4,410 pp, sole occupancy of a double $5,070. Plus $262.50 pp port taxes, deviation insurance, and U.S. Customs/INS fees.

Note to Readers

For reasons of space limitations, we have included only the freighters departing from U.S. ports. However, many others depart from ports in other countries. For more listings and information, consult the source upon which this chapter was based: "Setting Sail by Freighter" by Dave G. Houser and Rankin Harvey, available from Vacation Publications, 1502 Augusta Drive, No. 415, Houston, TX 77057; (713) 974-6903. To purchase, send $3.95 plus $2.25 shipping and handling. Texas residents add 8.25 percent sales tax.

SAILING SHIPS

Another group of ships are a totally different cruise experience, offering a casual atmosphere and congenial company in the most romantic of sea adventures—sailing under canvas. They are as varied as an eight-passenger catamaran to the magnificent *Sea Cloud* to windjammers that sail the coast of Maine and through the Caribbean, where it's more like a beach party sailing to small islands, inland waterways, and other places where larger ships cannot go.

Although it may seem puzzling, three of the cruise lines with sailing vessels—Club Med, Star Clippers, and Windstar—have been included in Part Two, Cruise Lines and Their Ships along with the mainstream cruise lines. In two cases the product is something of a hybrid, and with all three of them their product is more sophisticated than the more traditional sailing vessels listed below.

(Key: Cabins/Passengers; Officers/Crew; Vessel Length)

Club Med (See Part Two, Cruise Lines and Their Ships)

Coastal Cruises

P. O. Box 798, Camden, ME 04843
(207) 236-2750; (800) 992-2218

SV Mary Day (15/28; American/American; 90 ft.). A two-masted schooner, she sails on six-day cruises along the coast of Maine from June–October.

Compagnie des Isles du Ponant

c/o Tauck Tours, 276 Post Road, Westport, CT 06880
(203) 226-6911; (800) 468-2825; fax (203) 454-3081

Le Ponant   (34/64; French/European; 289 ft.). A luxury yacht in the fashion of *Windstar*, the ship is under charter by Tauck Tours, which offers a wide range of cruises in Caribbean in winter and the Mediterranean in summer, usually sold as part of a land/sea package. The size of the four-deck, four-masted vessel allows entry into less-visited scenic ports and bays.

Dirigo Cruises

39 Waterside Lane, Clinton, CT 06413
Tel./fax (203) 669-7068

The company has 16 sailing ships, which can be found in Europe, the British Isles, the Maritimes of Newfoundland, Caribbean, Galápagos, New Zealand, Tongo, and other islands of the South Seas.

Cuan Law, Lammer Law   (9/18; American/American, Chilean; 105 ft.). Two of the world's largest trimarans sail on six-night cruises of the British Virgin Islands from Tortola (*Cuan Law*), and seven-night tours of the Galápagos Islands from San Cristóbal (*Lammer Law*).

Harvey Gamage   (12/27; American/American; 95 ft.). In winter, the ship has seven-day cruises from St. Thomas to the United States and British Virgin Islands. In summer, she moves to New England with three-night cruises between Bath, Maine, and Boston.

Soren Larson   (9/18; British; 105 ft.). This two-masted brigadine sails on 10–17-day cruises in New Zealand waters from November to April, and from Auckland to Tonga, Western Samoa, Fiji, and other islands of the South Pacific the remainder of the year.

Mackay International, Ltd.

3190 Airport Way, Boise, ID 83705
(800) 635-5336

Mackay   (Privilege catamaran; 8 passengers; 48 ft.). *Mackay* offers week-long adventures in the British Virgin Islands from Soper's Hole on Tortola each Saturday with a three-person crew (captain, chef, steward), dropping anchor in bays and coves on such out-of-the-way islands as Green Cay, Norman, Peter, Virgin Gorda, Anegada, Guana, as well as Tortola, during the winter season from January–April. State-of-the-art scuba and snorkeling equipment, sea kayaks, and windsurfers are available for use. Dining is gourmet. Cabins have deluxe appointments with private bathroom, sink, and shower. The cruises are well suited as charters for families or groups of friends.

Maine Windjammers

Box 482, Rockland, ME 04841
(207) 594-8007; (800) 648-4544; fax (207) 374-2417

American Eagle (11/22–28; United States; 92 ft.). Three- to seven-day sails from Rockland, ME, to Penobscot Bay and various coastal islands and small towns, such as Mt. Desert Island, Pemaquid, Monhegan, and Boothbay, and sometimes to Boston.

Heritage (16/33; American; 94 ft.). Seven-day cruises from Rockland, ME, to various islands, including Mt. Desert Island.

Isaac H. Evens (11/22; American; 94 ft.). Three- to seven-day sails from Rockland, ME, to various coastal islands and small towns, such as Stonington, Frenchboro, and Burnt Coat Harbor. No set schedule.

Nathaniel Bowditch

Box 459, Warren, ME 04864
(207) 273-4062; (800) 288-4098

Nathaniel Bowditch (11/24; American; 82 ft.). Three-, four-, and six-day sails from Rockland, ME, through the bay waters of midcoast Maine, including Frenchman, Blue Hill, and Penobscot.

Pan Orama Cruises (See Zeus Tours and Cruises)

Peter Deilmann EuropAmerica Cruises

1800 Diagonal Road, Suite 170, Alexandria, VA 22314
(703) 549-1741; fax (703) 549-7924

Lili Marleen (25/50; German/European; 249 ft.) A new yacht, launched in September 1994, the *Lili Marleen* is a re-creation of a 19th century three-masted barquentine, a sailing vessel with one square-rigged mast and two gaff- or schooner-rigged masts.

Operated by Peter Deilmann EuropAmerica Cruises, the sailing vessel has a lounge decorated with polished hardwoods and paintings of historic maritime scenes. There are three bars—two on Main Deck, indoors and out, and Lili's Bar, with a small library on the Promenade Deck. The restaurant, also on Main Deck, accommodates all passengers at one seating; cuisine is international with local specialties.

The *Lili Marleen* has 25 twin outside cabins (2 standard, 20 superior and 3 deluxe, which measure 108 square feet). The cabins are decorated with burled wall finishes and pastel upholstery and carpeting.

They are furnished with a sofa bed that converts into a double bed plus an upper pullman berth, a large wardrobe, safe, table and chair, sideboard, radio, and international dial phone. The tiled bathroom has brass fittings and a shower, hair dryer, and bathrobes. The ship offers laundry service and fax and telex.

Lili *Marleen* sails on a series of varied cruises in Europe, Western Mediterranean and Baltic in spring and summer and Canary Islands in the fall. New for winter 1997–98 are Red Sea cruises beginning December 1997.

Sea Cloud Cruises

c/o Networld, 300 Lanidex Plaza, Parsippany, NJ 07054
(201) 884-7474; (800) 992-3411; fax (201) 884-1711

Sea Cloud (34/69; International; 316 ft.). One of the world's most luxurious sailing ships, *Sea Cloud* was built as a wedding present by E. F. Hutton for his bride, Majorie Merriweather Post. The ship has 34 air-conditioned cabins with phone, safe, hair dryer, and bathrobes. The elegant dining room accommodates all passengers at one seating; complementary wines are served at lunch and dinner. The ship also has a library and boutique. The four-masted barque sails on different itineraries throughout the year.

Normally, she sails in the Eastern Caribbean in the winter and the Mediterranean during the remainder of the year and is marketed by several U.S. tour companies. *Sea Cloud* is owned by the same company as the deluxe *River Cloud*, which sails on European river cruises (see River and Barge Cruises in Europe).

Star Clipper (See Part Two, Cruise Lines and Their Ships)

Tall Ship Adventures

1389 South Havana Street, Aurora, CO 80012
(303) 755-7983; (800) 662-0090; fax (303) 755-9007
http://www.tallshipadventures.com

Sir Francis Drake (14/28; International; 165 ft.). Built in 1917 in Weser, Germany, and registered in Honduras, the authentic three-masted ship was reconditioned in 1981 and refurbished in 1988 and 1992. She has somewhat more upgraded cabins with private facilities and more comforts and amenities then the usual tall ship. The Drake is air conditioned and has a lounge with full bar, stereo, video, television, and library, and a large, wide-open sun deck. She carries windsurfing and snorkeling equipment.

The *Drake* sails from Tortola, British Virgin Islands; itineraries vary slightly depending on sailing dates and include such locations as The Baths at Virgin Gorda, Cooper Island, Jost Van Dyke, Norman Island, Peter Island, and Marina Cay, among others. Rates are from $995 per person, double, and there is a 10 percent discount for cruises between April and May. An additional third adult over 12 in a double is $100 per day. Children 12 and under sharing with two adults pay 50 percent of the adult fare.

In autumn the ship has a new seven-day cruise in the Grenadines between Grenada and St. Vincent, calling at Bequia, Canouan, Tobago Cays, Petit Martinique, Petit St. Vincent, Carriacou, Ronde, Palm Island, and Mayreau. The itinerary in each direction is different so passengers cruising for two weeks will visit different locations in each one-week segment. Rates are from $995 for seven days; a 10 percent discount is available for two weeks. The ship is available for charter.

Victory Chimes

P.O. Box 1401, Rockland, ME 04841
(207) 594-0755; (800) 745-5651

Victoria Chimes   (44 passengers; American/American; 170 ft.).

This three-masted schooner is the largest windjammer under the U.S. flag. In summer she sails the 3,478-mile coast of Maine. In the early part of the century, this ship hauled cargo up the Atlantic Coast; she began taking passengers in 1945. Although she has been refurbished with modern amenities, she looks the same as she did almost a century ago. She has all outside cabins, some for two and others for four, with opening portholes, bunk beds, hot and cold water.

Windjammer Barefoot Cruises

1759 Bay Road, P.O. Box 190120, Miami Beach, FL 33119
(305) 672-6453; (800) 327-2601; fax (305) 674-1219
http://www.windjammer.com

For sailors of age 7–70, with good sea legs and something of a Captain Mitty spirit, Windjammer Barefoot Cruises—shorts and beachwear worn full-time—offers a chance to stand watch at the wheel or climb the mast and live the barefoot adventure of their fantasies. The line has a fleet of famous tall ships including those once owned by Onassis, the Duke of Westminister, and financier E. F. Hutton. Most cabins have bunk beds, private facilities, and steward service. The ships have super itineraries, sailing in the Grenadines (often called by yachtsmen the most beautiful sailing waters in the world) and in the Eastern and Southern Caribbean, visiting offbeat destinations, such as Saba and St. Eustatius. Most cruises are six days in length; some have different southbound and northbound legs that can be combined into a two-week cruise.

Amazing Grace (96 passengers; British/West Indian; 234 ft.). A supply ship and the only freighter in the cruise line's fleet, she offers 13-day cruises between Freeport, Bahamas, and Grenada along the routes of the tall ships.

Fantome (128 passengers; British/West Indian; 282 ft.). The *Fantome* was extensively renovated in 1992, adding an upper teak deck and a new dining salon. New cabins were also added. The *Fantome* is the flagship of the fleet and one of the largest four-masted staysail schooners in the world. Her keel was laid during World War I in Leghorn, Italy, for the Italian navy, and was intended to be a destroyer. After the war she was bought by the Duke of Westminster and converted to a private floating palace. This work was completed in 1927 and she was named *Flying Cloud*. She was later sold to a wealthy American who sailed her around the Mediterranean— with two seasick cows aboard to keep him in fresh milk. When acquired by the Guinness brewery family, she was renamed *Fantome* and spent most of World War II anchored in Puget Sound to avoid foreign submarines. Over the years, she had many owners but the most famous was Aristotle Onassis, who purchased her to be presented to the late Princess Grace and Prince Rainier on the occasion of their marriage. Onassis felt snubbed by not receiving a wedding invitation, however, and she was never delivered. In 1969, she joined the Windjammer fleet and was refurbished. In 1992, she had a $6 million refurbishing.

From late April–October, *Fantome* sails weekly round trip from Belize City on alternating itineraries: *Bay Island Cruise* to Goff's Cay, Lighthouse Reef/Half Moon Cay, Roatan, Cayos Cochinos, and Glovers Reef/Northern Cay; or, *Spanish Main Cruise* to Placencia, Puerto Cortes, Roatan, and Utila/Half Moon Cay. The itineraries are ideal for snorkelers and divers as the Bay Islands are completely surrounded by a coral reef. Rates range from $875–1,075.

Flying Cloud (18/78; British/West Indian; 208 ft.). Built in Nantes, France, in 1935 for the French navy as a cadet training ship, Oisseau des Isles (Bird of the Islands), the ship originally had her home port in Papeete, Tahiti.

She joined the Windjammer fleet in 1968 after extensive remodeling in Miami. A special honeymoon suite, handsomely paneled with stained glass windows, was added in her large stern. Teak decks, rosewood-paneled benches, and a charthouse give the look of an old privateer. In Windjammer's continuing efforts to preserve the romance of the sea, couples can tie the knot at sea aboard the *Flying Cloud*. This package includes cabin, champagne, floral arrangements, wedding certificate, souvenir photograph, and a 50 percent anniversary discount.

Six-day cruises of the Caribbean depart from Tortola to some of the following: Salt Island, Virgin Gorda, Beef Island, Green Cay, Sandy Cay, Norman Island, Deadman's Bay, Cooper Island, Jost Van Dyke, Peter Island, depending on the wind, weather, and island events.

Mandalay (72 passengers; British/West Indian; 236 ft.). The queen of the fleet, *Mandalay* was once the luxury yacht of financier E. F. Hutton and an oceanographic research vessel of Columbia University.

She has three tall masts and 22,000 feet of sail. She was Hutton's personal yacht for ten years and was considered the most luxurious private yacht in the world. At the time of her retirement from Columbia University in March 1981, nearly half the existing knowledge of the ocean floor had been gathered by this single ship. She was added to the Windjammer fleet in 1982, following two years of extensive renovation. If you look closely, you might recognize her as the ship in a number of television commercials.

The *Mandalay* sails on six-day cruises from Antigua or Grenada to a selection of Palm Island, Mayreau, Tobago, Bequia, St. Vincent, St. Lucia, Martinique, Dominica, Isle des Saintes, Nevis, Montserrat, and Carriacou, depending on the wind.

Polynesia (52/126; British/West Indian; 248 ft.). Built in Holland, this legendary fishing schooner has been featured in articles in *National Geographic* magazine and television productions.

She was added to the Windjammer fleet in 1975 after extensive remodeling as a passenger yacht. Following months of stripping out old crew and officer accommodations, two new decks of cabins were added, all with private bathrooms and showers. Twelve deck cabins, 40 regular cabins, and 2 admiral suites, all double occupancy, were constructed, all with private bathrooms and showers. Exotic wood paneling and tile floors were used to enhance the appearance. Three bachelor quarters accommodating six each were built for people traveling alone or with their families. In addition to the new plumbing, air conditioning and a

110 AC electrical system were installed. An entire new teak deck was built, complete with turned-wood spindles, benches, and tables. A specially designed dining salon, built in the curved stern area, has large tables, each depicting one of the islands on *Polynesia*'s itinerary, and panoramic windows. The mascot parrot keeps watch over the ship's slot machine.

Probably the most popular of the Windjammer fleet, *Polynesia* plays hostess to Windjammer's monthly singles' cruises, as well as other theme cruises throughout the year. She sails on six-day cruises of the Caribbean from St. Maarten to St. Barts, St. Kitts, Saba, Nevis, Prickly Pear, Anguilla, and Montserrat, depending on the wind.

Yankee Clipper   (65 passengers; British/West Indian; 197 ft.). In 1927, Alfred Krupp, German industrialist and manufacturer of armaments, built as the *Cressida* in Kiel, Germany, probably the only armor-plated private yacht in the world.

Adolf Hitler was aboard during World War II to award the Iron Cross to one of his U-boat commanders. She was later confiscated as a war prize and commandeered by the U.S. Coast Guard. After the war, she was acquired by the Vanderbilts, renamed *Pioneer*, and became a regular sight off Newport Beach, California. She was considered the fastest two-masted sailing ship on the West Coast, at one point doing 22 knots under sail. In 1965, she joined the Windjammer fleet and was rechristened *Yankee Clipper* following extensive remodeling. In 1984, *Yankee Clipper* was renovated from stem to stern. Though she was built with two masts, the new design included modifications for three, a continuous upper deck, cabins redesigned for double occupancy with private bathrooms and showers. She is still considered one of the fastest tall ships still sailing.

Yankee Clipper makes six-day cruises of the Caribbean, leaving from Grenada to Petit St. Vincent, Bequia, Mayreau, Palm Island, Union Island, Young Island, or Carriacou.

Windstar Cruises (See Part Two, Cruise Lines and Their Ships)

Zeus Tours and Cruises

566 Seventh Avenue, New York, NY 10018
(800) 447-5667; fax (212) 764-7912

The Zeus Group, which will mark its fiftieth year in operation in 1998, operates programs in the eastern Mediterranean and wears other hats as well. In addition to chartering other vessels, it has some of its own, *Zeus I–III, Lady Caterina,* and *Pan Orama* (24/48; Greek/European, American; 174 ft.), which sail on seven-day cruises in the Mediterranean in summer and are often chartered for other cruises.

Galileo Cruises, another member of the group, offers seven day Greek Isles cruises aboard the sail-cruiser *Galileo Sun.* Built in 1994, the yacht has a bar-lounge and 18 air-conditioned cabins with private bath and telephone. It carries windsurfers and snorkeling and fishing equipment.

APPENDIX

CRUISE SHIPS INDEX

Ship	Cruise Line	Type	Page
California Senator	Niederelbe Schiffahrtsgesell-schaft Buxtehude	F	787
Canadian Empress	St. Lawrence Cruise Lines	R	748
Caribbean Prince	American Canadian Caribbean Line	M	186
Carnival Destiny	Carnival Cruise Lines	M	227
Celebration	Carnival Cruise Lines	M	223
Century	Celebrity Cruises	M	247
Champillon	Misr Travel	R	746
Chanterelle	Abercrombie & Kent	R	726
Choyang Elite	DSR	F	785
Christian IV	Color Line	EC	759
Christiane	Mineral Shipping	F	786
Cielo di Los Angeles	Martime Reederei	F	786
Cinderella	Viking Line	EC	761
Clara Shumann	KD River Cruises of Europe	R	732
Clary	Mineral Shipping	F	786
Clipper Adventurer	Clipper Cruise Line/ Quark Expeditions	M	264, 771
Club Med 1	Club Med	SS	273
Club Med 2	Club Med	SS	273
Color Festival	Color Line	EC	759
Color Viking	Color Line	EC	759
Columbia Star	Blue Star Line	F	784
Columbus America	Columbus Line	F	785
Columbus Australia	Columbus Line	F	785
Columbus New Zealand	Columbus Line	F	785
Columbus Queensland	Columbus Line	F	785
Columbus Victoria	Columbus Line	F	785
Contship Europe	Niederelbe Schiffahrtsgesell-schaft Buxtehude	F	787
Contship France	Niederelbe Schiffahrtsgesell-schaft Buxtehude	F	787

Ship	Cruise Line	Type	Page
Deltastar	OdessAmerica	R	733
Desafio	Fourth Dimension Tours/ Marco Polo	R	751, 752
Deutschland	KD River Cruises of Europe	R	732
Diamante	Fourth Dimension Tours/ Galápagos Cruises	A	766, 767
Diana	Gota Canal (EuroCruises)	R	729
Direct Currawong	Niederelbe Schiffahrtsgesell- schaft Buxtehude	F	787
Disney Magic	Disney Cruise Line	M	382
Disney Wonder	Disney Cruise Line	M	382
Doerthe Maersk	Leonhardt & Blumberg	F	786
Dolphin	Tara Tours	R	752
Dolphin IV	Cape Canaveral Cruise Line	M	705
Dorado	Galápagos Yacht Cruises	A/G	768
Dreamward	(see *Norwegian Dream*)		
Dresden	Peter Deilmann EuropAmerica	R	729
DSR America	DSR	F	785
DSR Atlantic	DSR	F	785
East King	Abercrombie & Kent	R	739
East Queen	Abercrombie & Kent	R	739
Ecstasy	Carnival Cruise Lines	M	214
Elation	Carnival Cruise Lines	M	214
Enchanted Isle	Commodore Cruise Line	M	284
Enchantment of the Seas	Royal Caribbean International	M	600
Eric	Galápagos Network	A/G	768
Esprit	French Country Waterways	R	731
Estrella del Mar	Galápagos Yacht Cruises	A/G	768
Etoile de Champagne	Etoile de Champagne	R	728
Eugenie	Misr Travel	R	746
Explorer	Abercrombie & Kent	M/A/R	157, 749, 765

Ship	Cruise Line	Type	Page
Horizon II	French Country Waterways	R	731
Hotep	Sheraton Nile Cruises/ Misr Travel	R	746
Hyundai Fidelity	Schluter Line	F	788
Hyundai Majesty	Schluter Line	F	788
Hyundai Trusty	Schluter Line	F	788
Imagination	Carnival Cruise Lines	M	214
Independence	American Hawaii Cruises	M	200
Inspiration	Carnival Cruise Lines	M	214
Isaac H. Evens	Maine Windjammers	SS	795
Isabela II	Galápagos Cruises	A/G	766
Isabella	Viking Line	EC	761
Isis	Hilton International Nile Cruises/Misr Travel	R	746
IslandBreeze	Dolphin Cruise Line	M	392, 706
Island Princess	Princess Cruises	M	534
Italia	KD River Cruises of Europe	R	732
Ivybank	Bank Line	F	784
Jubilee	Carnival Cruise Lines	M	223
Julia	Mineral Shipping	F	786
Juno	Gota Canal (EuroCruises)	R	729
Kalypso	Viking Line	EC	761
Kapitan Dranitsyn	Quark Expeditions	A	771
Kapitan Khlebnikov	Quark Expeditions	A	772
Kasr Ibrim	Misr Travel	R	746
King of Scandinavia	Scandinavian Seaways (DFDS)	EC	760
Kong Harald	Bergen Line	NC	755
Kristina Brahe	Kristina Cruises (EuroCruises)	E	711
Kristina Regina	Kristina Cruises (EuroCruises)	E	711
Kronprins Harald	Color Line	EC	758, 759
L'Abercrombie	Abercrombie & Kent	R	727
Lady Caterina	Zeus Tours and Cruises	SS	801
La Esmeralda	International Expeditions	R	751

Ship	*Cruise Line*	*Type*	*Page*
Marine Spirit	Marine Expeditions	A	769
Marine Voyager	Marine Expeditions	A	769
Marjorie	Abercrombie & Kent	R	727
Mary Day	Coastal Cruises	SS	793
Mayan Prince	American Canadian Caribbean Line	M	186
MegaStar Aries	Star Cruises	M	720
MegaStar Taurus	Star Cruises	M	720
Melanesian Discoverer	Melanesian Tourist Services/ Niugini Exploration Cruises	A	769
Melbourne Star	Blue Star Line	F	784
Melody	Mediterranean Shipping Cruises	M	712
Mercury	Celebrity Cruises	M	247
Mermoz	Paquet French Cruises	M	715
Midnatsol	Bergen Line	NC	755
Minerva	Swan Hellenic Cruises	O	721
Mississippi Queen	Delta Queen Steamboat Company	M	370
Monarch	Esplanade Tours	R	745
Monarch of the Seas	Royal Caribbean International	M	582
Monterey	Mediterranean Shipping Cruises	M	712
Moraybank	Bank Line	F	784
Mozart	Peter Deilmann EuropAmerica	R	730
Nantucket Clipper	Clipper Cruise Line	M	260
Napoleon	Abercrombie & Kent	R	727
Narvik	Bergen Line	NC	755
Nathaniel Bowditch	Nathaniel Bowditch	SS	795
Nenuphar	French Country Waterways	R	731
Nephtis	Hilton International Nile Cruises/Misr Travel	R	746
Niagara Prince	American Canadian Caribbean Line	M	191
Nieuw Amsterdam	Holland America Line	M	420

Ship	Cruise Line	Type	Page
Nile Goddess	Sonesta International Hotels	R	747
Nile Monarch	Swan Hellenic Cruises	R	747
Noordam	Holland America Line	M	420
Nordbrise	Svalbard Polar Travel (EuroCruises)	A	775
Nordic Empress	Royal Caribbean International	M	589
Nordkapp	Bergen Line	NC	755
Nordlys	Bergen Line	NC	755
Nordnorge	Bergen Line	NC	755
Nordstjernen	Bergen Line	NC	756
Normandie	KD River Cruises of Europe	R	732
Norway	Norwegian Cruise Line	M	441
Norwegian Crown	Norwegian Cruise Line	M	460
Norwegian Dream	Norwegian Cruise Line	M	448
Norwegian Dynasty	Norwegian Cruise Line	M	464
Norwegian Majesty	Norwegian Cruise Line	M	467
Norwegian Sea	Norwegian Cruise Line	M	454
Norwegian Star	Norwegian Cruise Line	M	472
Norwegian Wind	Norwegian Cruise Line	M	448
Nubian Sea	Misr Travel	R	746
Oberoi Philae	Mena House Oberoi Hotel	R	745
OceanBreeze	Dolphin Cruise Line	M	394
Oceanic	Premier Cruise Lines	M	706
Oceanic Odyssey	Spice Island Cruises	A	774
Odysseus	Royal Olympic Cruises	M	622
Olivebank	Bank Line	F	784
Olympic	Royal Olympic Cruises	M	624
Oriana	P&O Cruises	M	493
Orpheus	Royal Olympic Cruises	M	625
Osiris	Hilton International Nile Cruises/Misr Travel	R	746
Pacifico	Projex Line	F	787
Pacific Princess	Princess Cruises	M	534

Ship	Cruise Line	Type	Page
Pacific Senator	DSR	F	785
Palermo Senator	DSR	F	785
Panorama	Classical Cruises	O	706
Pan Orama	Zeus Tours and Cruises	SS	801
Paradise	Carnival Cruise Line	M	214
Patmos Senator	DSR	F	785
Patty	Mineral Shipping	F	786
Paul Gauguin	Radisson Seven Seas Cruises	M	570
Pegasus II	Color Line	EC	759
Peter Wessel	Color Line	EC	759
Polaris	Special Expeditions	A	774
Polarlys	Bergen Line	NC	755
Polarstar	Svalbard Polar Travel (EuroCruises)	A	775
Polynesia	Windjammer Barefoot Cruises	SS	799
Prince of Scandinavia	Scandinavian Seaways (DFDS)	EC	760
Princesse de Provence	Peter Deilmann EuropAmerica	R	730
Princess Elaine	Regal China Cruises	R	739
Princesse Ragnhild	Color Line	EC	758, 759
Princess Jeannie	Regal China Cruises	R	739
Princess of Scandinavia	Scandinavian Seaways (DFDS)	EC	760
Princess Sheena	Regal China Cruises	R	739
Professor Khromov	Quark Expeditions	A	771
Professor Molchanov	Quark Expeditions	A	772
Professor Multanousky	(see Marine Intrepid)		
Professor Shokalski	Southern Heritage Expeditions	A	773
Prussian Princess	Peter Deilmann EuropAmerica	R	730
QE2	Cunard	M	336
Queen Nabila I & II	Nabila Nile Cruises	R	747
Queen of Scandinavia	Scandinavian Seaways (DFDS)	E	760
Queen of Sheeba	Nabila Nile Cruises	R	747
Queen of the West	American West Steamboat Company	R	748

Ship	Cruise Line	Type	Page
San Antonio	Ivaran Lines	F	786
Santa Cruz	Galápagos Cruises	A/G	766, 775
Santa Paula	Schepers Line	F	788
Sea Bird	Special Expeditions	A	774
Seabourn Legend	Seabourn Cruise Line	M	635
Seabourn Pride	Seabourn Cruise Line	M	635
Seabourn Spirit	Seabourn Cruise Line	M	635
SeaBreeze	Dolphin Cruise Line	M	394, 706
Sea Cloud	Sea Cloud Cruises/ Galápagos Network	A/G/SS	768, 796
Sea Goddess I	Cunard	M	353
Sea Goddess II	Cunard	M	353
Sea-Land Endeavour	Niederelbe Schiffahrtsgesell- schaft Buxtehude	F	787
Sea-Land Initiative	Niederelbe Schiffahrtsgesell- schaft Buxtehude	F	787
Sea-Land Mistral	Niederelbe Schiffahrtsgesell- schaft Buxtehude	F	787
Sea-Land Victory	Niederelbe Schiffahrtsgesell- schaft Buxtehude	F	787
Sea Lion	Special Expeditions	A	774
Seaward	(see *Norwegian Sea*)		
Seawind Crown	Seawind Cruise Line	M	650, 706
Sensation	Carnival Cruise Lines	M	214
Sergei Kirov	Northwestern River Shipping (EuroCruises)	R	729
Shannon Princess	Cruise Company of Greenwich	R	727
Sheherayar	Mena House Oberoi Hotel	R	745
Shehrazah	Mena House Oberoi Hotel	R	745
Sheltered Seas	Alaska Sightseeing/Cruise West	O	179
Sidney Star	Blue Star Line	F	784
Silja Europa	Silja Line	EC	761
Silja Festival	Silja Line	EC	761

Ship	Cruise Line	Type	Page
Sun Boat I–IV	Abercrombie & Kent	R	745
Sun Goddess	Sonesta International Hotels	R	747
Sun Princess	Princess Cruises	M	541
Sun Viking	Royal Caribbean International	M	596
SuperStar Gemini	Star Cruises	M	720
SuperStar Leo	Star Cruises	M	720
SuperStar Virgo	Star Cruises	M	720
Symphony	Mediterranean Shipping Cruises	M	713
Temptress Explorer	Temptress Cruises	A	776
Temptress Voyager	Temptress Cruises	A	776
Terra Australis	OdessAmerica/ Cruceros Australis	A	770
Theodor Fontane	KD River Cruises of Europe	R	732
Triton	Royal Olympic Cruises	M	626
Tropicale	Carnival Cruise Lines	M	231
Tucano	Ecotour Expeditions	R	750
Tut	Sheraton Nile Cruises/ Misr Travel	R	746
Ulf Ritscher	Transete Shipping	F	788
Universe Explorer	World Explorer Cruises	M/A	699, 776
Veendam	Holland America Line	M	406
Vesteraalen	Bergen Line	NC	755
Victoria	P&O Cruises	M	496
Victoria I–IV	Victoria Cruises	R	740
Victoria 21st Century	Victoria Cruises	R	740
Victoria Chimes	Victory Chimes	SS	797
Victoria Dragon	Victoria Cruises	R	740
Victoria Three Kingdoms	Victoria Cruises	R	740
Viking Serenade	Royal Caribbean International	M	598
Viktor Glushkov	OdessAmerica	R	733
Vincent Van Gogh	Abercrombie & Kent	R	727
Vision of the Seas	Royal Caribbean International	M	600

Ship	Cruise Line	Type	Page
Vistafjord	Cunard	M	349
Volga	OdessAmerica	R	733
Wasa Queen	Silja Line	EC	761
Washington Senator	Niederelbe Schiffahrtsgesell-schaft Buxtehude	F	787
Westerdam	Holland America Line	M	417
Widukind	Transete Shipping	F	788
Wilderness Explorer	Alaska's Glacier Bay Tours and Cruises	A	765
Wilhelm Tham	Gota Canal (EuroCruises)	R	729
William Tell	KD River Cruises of Europe	R	732
Wind Song	Windstar Cruises	M	687
Wind Spirit	Windstar Cruises	M	687
Wind Star	Windstar Cruises	M	687
Wind Surf	Windstar Cruises	M	692
Windward	(see *Norwegian Sea*)		
World Discoverer	Society Expeditions	A	772, 775
Yamal	Quark Expeditions	A	772
Yankee Clipper	Windjammer Barefoot Cruises	SS	800
Yolita	Galápagos Yacht Cruises	A/G	768
Yorktown Clipper	Clipper Cruise Line	M	260
Zenith	Celebrity Cruises	M	241
Zeus I–III	Zeus Tours and Cruises	SS	801

1998 Unofficial Guide Reader Survey

If you would like to express an opinion about your cruise or this guide-book, complete the following survey and return to:

Unofficial Guide Reader Survey
P.O. Box 43059
Birmingham, AL 35243

Name of ship:

Date, duration, and destination of cruise:

Please circle one of the following:

—*Was this your*   1st   2nd   3rd   4th   5th   6th or more cruise?

—*Would you take another cruise on this ship?*   Yes   No

—*Recommend it to a friend?*   Yes   No

—*Do you plan to cruise*   within a year   within next 3 years   longer?

—*Your age:*   teens   20s   30s   40s   50s   60s   70s   over 80

—*You are:*   employed   self-employed   retired

—*Line of work:*

Please score items below from 1 to 10 with 10 being the highest or best.
Feel free to add your comments.

Value for money:

Total cruise experience:

Your overall impression of the ship *(appearance, appeal, furnishings and decor, cleanliness, sports and recreation facilities, consistency, comfort, boarding/disembarking procedures):*

Cruise director *(available, helpful, friendly):*

Cruise staff:

Dining room food *(choices, quality, taste, presentation):*

Breakfast and lunch buffet:

Dining room service:

Bar service:

Cabin *(size, layout, soundproofing, cleanliness, appearance, condition):*

Bathroom:

Cabin attendant *(service, attitude):*

Enrichment programs, lectures, games *(variety and quality):*

Entertainment in the main lounge:

Entertainment in other lounges:

Children's programs:

Youth counselors:

Shore excursions *(guides, variety, advanced information, value)*:

Some more questions:

—Was the food quality better, worse, or about what you expected?

—Were wine and bar prices low, moderate, or high?

—Was the music level tolerable or too loud, especially by the pool?

—Were you bothered by announcements over the public address system?

—Was the promotion of shipboard shops low key, moderate, or hard sell?

—Was the fire drill well executed?

—Did you choose your cruise for its itinerary?

—Which ports of call did you like best?

—Were port talks poor or helpful?

—Did the speakers plug specific shops?

—Was passenger information available prior to the cruise? in your cabin? during the cruise?

Your hometown:

How did you learn about your cruise?
How did you learn about this book?
Where did you buy your cruise?
When and where did you buy this book?

(Optional) If you are available for a telephone interview, please give us your name, address, telephone number, and a convenient time to call.

THANK YOU!